μC/OS-III™

The Real-Time Kernel

Jean J. Labrosse

Micrium
Press

Weston, FL 33326

Micriµm Press
1290 Weston Road, Suite 306
Weston, FL 33326
USA
www.micrium.com

Library of Congress Control Number: 2011931642

Library of Congress subject headings:

1. Embedded computer systems
2. Real-time data processing
3. Computer software - Development

For bulk orders, please contact Micrium Press at: +1 954 217 2036

978-0-9823375-2-3
100-uCOS-III-Freescale-Kinetis-002

To my loving and caring wife, Manon,
and our two children James and Sabrina.

Table of Contents

Part I: µC/OS-III – The Real-Time Kernel

Foreword to µC/OS-III — by Jack Ganssle... 19
Preface 21

Chapter 1	Introduction	31
1-1	Foreground/Background Systems	32
1-2	Real-Time Kernels	33
1-3	RTOS (Real-Time Operating System)	35
1-4	µC/OS-III	35
1-5	µC/OS, µC/OS-II and µC/OS-III Features Comparison	40
1-6	How the Book is Organized	42
1-7	µC/Probe	42
1-8	Conventions	43
1-9	Chapter Contents	44
Chapter 2	Directories and Files	49
2-1	Application Code	52
2-2	CPU	53
2-3	Board Support Package (BSP)	54
2-4	µC/OS-III, CPU Independent Source Code	55
2-5	µC/OS-III, CPU Specific Source Code	59
2-6	µC/CPU, CPU Specific Source Code	60
2-7	µC/LIB, Portable Library Functions	62
2-8	Summary	64
Chapter 3	Getting Started with µC/OS-III	67
3-1	Single Task Application	68
3-2	Multiple Tasks Application with Kernel Objects	76

Chapter 4	Critical Sections 85
4-1	Disabling Interrupts 86
4-1-1	Measuring Interrupt Disable Time 86
4-2	Locking the Scheduler 87
4-2-1	Measuring Scheduler Lock Time 88
4-3	µC/OS-III Features with Longer Critical Sections 89
4-4	Summary 90

Chapter 5	Task Management 91
5-1	Assigning Task Priorities 100
5-2	Determining the Size of a Stack 102
5-3	Detecting Task Stack Overflows 103
5-4	Task Management Services 107
5-5	Task Management Internals 108
5-5-1	Task States 108
5-5-2	Task Control Blocks (TCBs) 113
5-6	Internal Tasks 125
5-6-1	The Idle Task (OS_IdleTask(), os_core.c) 125
5-6-2	The Tick Task (OS_TickTask(), os_tick.c) 127
5-6-3	The Statistic Task (OS_StatTask(), os_stat.c) 134
5-6-4	The Timer Task (OS_TmrTask(), os_tmr.c) 137
5-6-5	The ISR Handler Task (OS_IntQTask(), os_int.c) 138
5-7	Summary 139

Chapter 6	The Ready List 141
6-1	Priority Levels 142
6-2	The Ready List 146
6-3	Adding Tasks to the Ready List 149
6-4	Summary 150

Chapter 7	Scheduling 151
7-1	Preemptive Scheduling 152
7-2	Scheduling Points 154
7-3	Round-Robin Scheduling 156
7-4	Scheduling Internals 158
7-4-1	OSSched() 159

7-4-2	OSIntExit()	160
7-4-3	OS_SchedRoundRobin()	161
7-5	Summary	163

Chapter 8	Context Switching	165
8-1	OSCtxSw()	168
8-2	OSIntCtxSw()	170
8-3	Summary	173

Chapter 9	Interrupt Management	175
9-1	Handling CPU Interrupts	176
9-2	Typical µC/OS-III Interrupt Service Routine (ISR)	177
9-3	Non Kernel-Aware Interrupt Service Routine (ISR)	180
9-4	Processors with Multiple Interrupt Priorities	181
9-5	All Interrupts Vector to a Common Location	183
9-6	Every Interrupt Vectors to a Unique Location	185
9-7	Direct and Deferred Post Methods	186
9-7-1	Direct Post Method	186
9-7-2	Deferred Post Method	189
9-8	Direct vs. Deferred Post Method	192
9-9	The Clock Tick (or System Tick)	193
9-10	Summary	195

Chapter 10	Pend Lists (or Wait Lists)	197
10-1	Summary	202

Chapter 11	Time Management	203
11-1	OSTimeDly()	204
11-2	OSTimeDlyHMSM()	209
11-3	OSTimeDlyResume()	211
11-4	OSTimeSet() and OSTimeGet()	212
11-5	OSTimeTick()	212
11-6	Summary	212

Chapter 12	Timer Management	213
12-1	One-Shot Timers	215
12-2	Periodic (no initial delay)	216
12-3	Periodic (with initial delay)	217
12-4	Timer Management Internals	217
12-4-1	Timer Management Internals - Timers States	217
12-4-2	Timer Management Internals - OS_TMR	219
12-4-3	Timer Management Internals - Timer Task	221
12-4-4	Timer Management Internals - Timer List	223
12-5	Summary	229
Chapter 13	Resource Management	231
13-1	Disable/Enable Interrupts	234
13-2	Lock/Unlock	236
13-3	Semaphores	237
13-3-1	Binary Semaphores	239
13-3-2	Counting Semaphores	246
13-3-3	Notes on Semaphores	248
13-3-4	Semaphore Internals (for resource sharing)	249
13-3-5	Priority Inversions	254
13-4	Mutual Exclusion Semaphores (Mutex)	256
13-4-1	Mutual Exclusion Semaphore Internals	261
13-5	Should You Use a Semaphore Instead of a Mutex?	267
13-6	Deadlocks (or Deadly Embrace)	267
13-7	Summary	271
Chapter 14	Synchronization	273
14-1	Semaphores	274
14-1-1	Unilateral Rendez-vous	276
14-1-2	Credit Tracking	279
14-1-3	Multiple Tasks Waiting on a Semaphore	281
14-1-4	Semaphore Internals (for synchronization)	282
14-2	Task Semaphore	289
14-2-1	Pending (i.e., Waiting) on a Task Semaphore	290
14-2-2	Posting (i.e., Signaling) a Task Semaphore	291
14-2-3	Bilateral Rendez-vous	292
14-3	Event Flags	294
14-3-1	Using Event Flags	296

14-3-2	Event Flags Internals	300
14-4	Synchronizing Multiple Tasks	306
14-5	Summary	308
Chapter 15	Message Passing	309
15-1	Messages	310
15-2	Message Queues	310
15-3	Task Message Queue	312
15-4	Bilateral Rendez-vous	313
15-5	Flow Control	314
15-6	Keeping the Data in Scope	316
15-7	Using Message Queues	319
15-8	Clients and Servers	327
15-9	Message Queues Internals	328
15-10	Summary	331
Chapter 16	Pending On Multiple Objects	333
16-1	Summary	341
Chapter 17	Memory Management	343
17-1	Creating a Memory Partition	344
17-2	Getting a Memory Block from a Partition	348
17-3	Returning a Memory Block to a Partition	349
17-4	Using Memory Partitions	350
17-5	Summary	354
Chapter 18	Porting µC/OS-III	355
18-1	Conventions	359
18-2	µC/CPU	360
18-2-1	cpu_bsp.h	361
18-2-2	cpu_def.h	361
18-2-3	cpu_cfg.h	361
18-2-4	cpu_core.c	363
18-2-5	cpu_core.h	364
18-2-6	cpu.h	364
18-2-7	cpu_c.c	368
18-2-8	cpu_a.asm	368

18-3	µC/OS-III Port	369
18-3-1	os_cpu.h	371
18-3-2	os_cpu_c.c	372
18-3-3	os_cpu_a.asm	381
18-3-4	os_cpu_a.inc	388
18-4	Board Support Package (BSP)	392
18-4-1	bsp.c and bsp.h	392
18-4-2	bsp_int.c and bsp_int.h	393
18-5	Testing a Port	395
18-5-1	Creating a Simple Test Project	395
18-5-2	Verifying Task Context Switches	400
18-5-3	Verifying Interrupt Context Switches	407
18-6	Summary	411
Chapter 19	Run-Time Statistics	413
19-1	General Statistics – Run-Time	414
19-2	Per-Task Statistics – Run-Time	419
19-3	Kernel Object – Run-Time	422
19-4	os_dbg.c – Static	425
19-5	os_cfg_app.c – Static	438
19-6	Summary	441
Appendix A	µC/OS-III API Reference	443
A-1	Task Management	444
A-2	Time Management	446
A-3	Mutual Exclusion Semaphores – Resource Management	447
A-4	Event Flags – Synchronization	448
A-5	Semaphores – Synchronization	449
A-6	Task Semaphores – Synchronization	450
A-7	Message Queues – Message Passing	451
A-8	Task Message Queues – Message Passing	452
A-9	Pending on Multiple Objects	453
A-10	Timers	454
A-11	Fixed-Size Memory Partitions – Memory Management	455
A-12	OSCtxSw()	456
A-13	OSFlagCreate()	458
A-14	OSFlagDel()	460

A-15	OSFlagPend()	462
A-16	OSFlagPendAbort()	466
A-17	OSFlagPendGetFlagsRdy()	469
A-18	OSFlagPost()	471
A-19	OSIdleTaskHook()	474
A-20	OSInit()	476
A-21	OSInitHook()	479
A-22	OSIntCtxSw()	480
A-23	OSIntEnter()	482
A-24	OSIntExit()	484
A-25	OSMemCreate()	485
A-26	OSMemGet()	488
A-27	OSMemPut()	490
A-28	OSMutexCreate()	492
A-29	OSMutexDel()	494
A-30	OSMutexPend()	496
A-31	OSMutexPendAbort()	500
A-32	OSMutexPost()	503
A-33	OSPendMulti()	506
A-34	OSQCreate()	511
A-35	OSQDel()	514
A-36	OSQFlush()	516
A-37	OSQPend()	519
A-38	OSQPendAbort()	523
A-39	OSQPost()	526
A-40	OSSafetyCriticalStart()	530
A-41	OSSched()	531
A-42	OSSchedLock()	533
A-43	OSSchedRoundRobinCfg()	535
A-44	OSSchedRoundRobinYield()	537
A-45	OSSchedUnlock()	539
A-46	OSSemCreate()	541
A-47	OSSemDel()	544
A-48	OSSemPend()	547
A-49	OSSemPendAbort()	551
A-50	OSSemPost()	554
A-51	OSSemSet()	557
A-52	OSStart()	559

A-53	OSStartHighRdy()	561
A-54	OSStatReset()	563
A-55	OSStatTaskCPUUsageInit()	565
A-56	OSStatTaskHook()	567
A-57	OSTaskChangePrio()	569
A-58	OSTaskCreate()	571
A-59	OSTaskCreateHook()	581
A-60	OSTaskDel()	583
A-61	OSTaskDelHook()	586
A-62	OSTaskQFlush()	588
A-63	OSTaskQPend()	590
A-64	OSTaskQPendAbort()	593
A-65	OSTaskQPost()	595
A-66	OSTaskRegGet()	598
A-67	OSTaskRegSet()	601
A-68	OSTaskReturnHook()	604
A-69	OSTaskResume()	606
A-70	OSTaskSemPend()	608
A-71	OSTaskSemPendAbort()	611
A-72	OSTaskSemPost()	613
A-73	OSTaskSemSet()	615
A-74	OSStatTaskHook()	617
A-75	OSTaskStkChk()	619
A-76	OSTaskStkInit()	622
A-77	OSTaskSuspend()	627
A-78	OSTaskSwHook()	629
A-79	OSTaskTimeQuantaSet()	632
A-80	OSTickISR()	634
A-81	OSTimeDly()	636
A-82	OSTimeDlyHMSM()	639
A-83	OSTimeDlyResume()	642
A-84	OSTimeGet()	644
A-85	OSTimeSet()	646
A-86	OSTimeTick()	648
A-87	OSTimeTickHook()	649
A-88	OSTmrCreate()	651
A-89	OSTmrDel()	656
A-90	OSTmrRemainGet()	658

A-91	OSTmrStart()	660
A-92	OSTmrStateGet()	662
A-93	OSTmrStop()	664
A-94	OSVersion()	667
Appendix B	µC/OS-III Configuration Manual	669
B-1	µC/OS-III Features (os_cfg.h)	672
B-2	Data Types (os_type.h)	683
B-3	µC/OS-III Stacks, Pools and other (os_cfg_app.h)	683
Appendix C	Migrating from µC/OS-II to µC/OS-III	689
C-1	Differences in Source File Names and Contents	692
C-2	Convention Changes	695
C-3	Variable Name Changes	701
C-4	API Changes	702
C-4-1	Event Flags	703
C-4-2	Message Mailboxes	705
C-4-3	Memory Management	707
C-4-4	Mutual Exclusion Semaphores	708
C-4-5	Message Queues	710
C-4-6	Semaphores	712
C-4-7	Task Management	714
C-4-8	Time Management	718
C-4-9	Timer Management	719
C-4-10	Miscellaneous	721
C-4-11	Hooks and Port	723
Appendix D	MISRA-C:2004 and µC/OS-III	725
D-1	MISRA-C:2004, Rule 8.5 (Required)	726
D-2	MISRA-C:2004, Rule 8.12 (Required)	727
D-3	MISRA-C:2004, Rule 14.7 (Required)	728
D-4	MISRA-C:2004, Rule 15.2 (Required)	729
D-5	MISRA-C:2004, Rule 17.4 (Required)	730

Appendix E   Bibliography 731

Appendix F   Licensing Policy 733

Part II: µC/OS-III and the Freescale Kinetis ARM® Cortex™-M4

                  Foreword 737

Chapter 1   Introduction 739
1-1   Part II Chapter Contents 744
1-2   Acknowledgements 746

Chapter 2   Freescale's Tower System Controller TWR-K53N512 749
2-1   TWR-K53N512 Pin Usage 752
2-2   TWR-K53N512 Jumper Settings 755
2-3   The Freescale TWR-K53N512 758
2-4   Expanding the Capabilities 762

Chapter 3   The ARM® Cortex™-M4 and the Kinetis K53 765
3-1   Nested Vector Interrupt Controller (NVIC) 766
3-2   Asynchronous Wake-Up Interrupt Controller (AWIC) 767
3-3   Debug Interfaces 767
3-4   System Modules 768
3-5   Memories 770
3-6   Clocks 770
3-7   Security and Integrity Modules 771
3-8   Analog Modules 772
3-9   Timer Modules 775
3-10   Communication Interfaces 776
3-11   Human-Machine Interfaces 777

Chapter 4   Setup 779
4-1   Downloading µC/OS-III Projects for this Book 780
4-1-1   \EvalBoards 782

4-1-2	\uC-CPU	784
4-1-3	\uC-LIB	784
4-1-4	\uCOS-III	785
4-2	Downloading µC/Probe	786
4-3	Downloading the IAR Embedded Workbench for ARM	787
4-4	Setting up the Hardware	788
4-5	Downloading the TWR-K53N512 documentation	790

Chapter 5	**ECG / Heart Rate Monitor**	791
5-1	The Heart	791
5-2	Biological Electrical Potentials	798
5-3	ECG Leads	801
5-4	Cardiovascular Diseases (CVD)	806
5-5	ECG Design	808
5-6	Running the Example Project	814
5-7	How the Code Works	821
5-7-1	Biomedical Signal Analysis	825
5-8	Summary	827

Chapter 6	**Blood Glucose Meter**	829
6-1	Glucose	829
6-2	Diabetes Mellitus	835
6-3	Blood Glucose Sensor	837
6-4	Blood Glucose Meter Design	842
6-5	Running the Example Project	846
6-6	How the Code Works	851
6-7	Summary	857

Chapter 7	**Pulse Oximeter**	859
7-1	Respiration	860
7-2	Pulse Oximetry	865
7-3	Pulse Oximeter Design	870
7-4	Running the Example Project	875
7-5	How the Code Works	880
7-5-1	Biomedical Signal Analysis	885
7-5-2	Data Processing State Machine	887
7-6	Summary	891

Chapter 8	Blood Pressure Monitor 893	
8-1	Blood Pressure 894	
8-2	The Baroreceptor Reflex 896	
8-3	Renin-Angiotensin-Aldosterone System (RAAS) 898	
8-4	Hypertension 902	
8-5	Indirect Measurement of Arterial Blood Pressure 904	
8-6	Design of a Blood Pressure Monitor 906	
8-7	Running the Example Project 917	
8-8	How the Code Works 922	
8-8-1	Biomedical Signal Analysis 926	
8-8-2	Data Processing State Machine 929	
8-9	Summary 932	
Appendix A	Certification of Medical Systems 933	
A-1	"Off-the-Shelf" Software 934	
A-2	Medical Device Software – Recalls 935	
A-3	Safety Critical 936	
A-4	Traceability 938	
A-5	Cost of Safety Critical Software 939	
A-6	Medical Device Market Regulatory Environment 941	
A-6-1	The Regulators 941	
A-6-2	Industry and Standards Bodies 941	
A-6-3	The Regulatory Environment in the United States 942	
A-6-4	FDA 510(k) 943	
A-6-5	FDA Premarket Approval 943	
A-6-6	FDA Development Guidance 943	
A-6-7	Device Class 944	
A-6-8	Level of Concern (FDA/CDRH) 945	
A-7	Regulatory Environment in the European Union 947	
A-7-1	EU Device Classes 947	
A-8	Medical Standards 948	
A-8-1	IEC 62304 948	
A-8-2	ISO 14971 950	
A-8-3	ISO 13485 950	
A-9	Medical Software in the Future 950	
A-10	Common Safety-Critical Development Standards 951	

A-11	Standards Bodies and Worldwide Standards Organizations	952
A-12	FDA Guidance and Documents	954
A-13	References	956

Appendix B	µC/OS-III Port for the Cortex-M4	959
B-1	os_cpu.h	960
B-2	os_cpu_c.c	961
B-2-1	os_cpu_c.c – OSIdleTaskHook()	962
B-2-2	os_cpu_c.c – OSInitHook()	963
B-2-3	os_cpu_c.c – OSStatTaskHook()	963
B-2-4	os_cpu_c.c – OSTaskCreateHook()	964
B-2-5	os_cpu_c.c – OSTaskDelHook()	965
B-2-6	os_cpu_c.c – OSTaskReturnHook()	966
B-2-7	os_cpu_c.c – OSTaskStkInit()	967
B-2-8	os_cpu_c.c – OSTaskSwHook()	971
B-2-9	os_cpu_c.c – OSTimeTickHook()	973
B-2-10	os_cpu_c.c – OS_CPU_SysTickHandler()	974
B-2-11	os_cpu_c.c – OS_CPU_SysTickInit()	975
B-3	os_cpu_a.asm	976
B-3-1	os_cpu_a.asm – OSStartHighRdy()	976
B-3-2	os_cpu_a.asm – OSCtxSw() and OSIntCtxSw()	977
B-3-3	os_cpu_a.asm – OS_CPU_PendSVHandler()	978

Appendix C	µC/CPU Port for the Cortex-M4	981
C-1	cpu_core.c	982
C-2	cpu_core.h	982
C-3	cpu_def.h	982
C-4	cpu_cfg.h	982
C-5	µC/CPU Functions in bsp.c	984
C-5-1	µC/CPU Functions in bsp.c, CPU_TS_TmrInit()	984
C-5-2	µC/CPU Functions in bsp.c, CPU_TS_TmrRd()	985
C-6	cpu.h	986
C-6-1	cpu.h – #defines	986
C-6-2	cpu.h – Data Types	987
C-6-3	cpu.h – Function Prototypes	990
C-7	cpu_a.asm	990

Appendix D	Micriµm's µC/Probe	993
D-1	Downloading µC/Probe	995
D-2	µC/Probe is a Windows™-Based Application	996
D-3	Assigning a Variable to an Object	998
Appendix E	IAR Systems IAR Embedded Workbench for ARM	1001
E-1	IAR Embedded Workbench for ARM – Highlights	1002
E-2	Modular and Extensible IDE	1004
E-3	Highly Optimizing C/C++ Compiler	1006
E-4	Device Support	1007
E-5	State-of-the-Art C-SPY® Debugger	1008
E-6	C-SPY Debugger and Target System Support	1009
E-7	IAR Assembler	1009
E-8	IAR J-LINK Linker	1009
E-9	IAR Library and Library Tools	1010
E-10	Comprehensive Documentation	1010
E-11	First Class Technical Support	1010
Appendix F	Freescale Semiconductor's CodeWarrior for MCUs	1011
Appendix G	Bibliography	1017
Appendix H	Licensing Policy	1019
Index		1021

Foreword to µC/OS-III — by Jack Ganssle

Your system has to read a keyboard and update the display. That's pretty easy to handle in a simple loop.

Oh, wait, then there's the A/D converter which needs service once a millisecond. The data is noisy so ten samples must be averaged and the result fed into a computation which is sent to the display. But you can't do the math till the results of the encoder become available, and that can only be read on 20 msec intervals.

But don't forget to monitor the radiation source; if it goes out of limits a safety protocol has to be invoked to avoid harming users. That has to be monitored every 250 milliseconds.

How would one write this code? Sure, it's possible to write an interrupt handler that takes clock ticks and then, via a number of tortured loops, sequences off the proper activities. It'll be tough to debug and harder to maintain. You can be sure the boss will come in, red-faced, wondering why the heck the system only looks at safety parameters every quarter second when any idiot knows the rate should be 0.230 sec, no matter how he wrote the spec. The loops grow more complex and the program ever more convoluted.

This is a very old problem, one solved by the use of a Real-Time Operating System (RTOS). Write each activity as a separate task. The code is simple, crystal clear, and easy to change.

An old problem, yes. But there's surprisingly little written about the use of an RTOS. Jean Labrosse wrote one of the first and best books on the subject: the first edition of this volume. I'm told the first edition, and the subsequent second edition, are the best selling books ever published about embedded systems, and I'm not surprised. Extremely-well written, they covered the subject in depth and with finesse. He wrote using the µC/OS and µC/OS-II RTOSes as examples.

Now Jean and the crew at Micrium have a new and hugely improved version of that RTOS: µC/OS-III. Where µC/OS-II is a commercial quality product, one that even meets the highest safety-critical requirements, µC/OS-III takes that quality and reliability level to even the most demanding applications.

Jean has supplemented the new RTOS with this book. It's much weightier than his previous RTOS books as this volume goes in depth into the nuances of using an operating system in real applications. µC/OS-III lays out the rationale behind an RTOS, and then in a very logical fashion presents each of the resources provided by an RTOS and how one goes about using those features in a product. Though µC/OS-III is used as an example, it is not presented as the canonical RTOS, and users of any real-time operating system will find this material immensely usable.

I have long counted Jean a friend, and have great respect for his perfectionism. That is clear when reading the µC/OS source code, which is probably the most beautiful code I have read, and, since it has been used in products certified to DO-178B level A, also works!

That perfectionism also manifests itself in this book, in which it's clear he has taken pains to get every fact right, every drawing clear, all while maintaining a very consistent style.

This is a book by an engineer, for engineers (including engineering students). Devoid of fluff, it's packed with information about using an RTOS in a real system... today. What do I need to do to get started? What are all those files? Where is the information I need located?

Are you using an RTOS? If so, read this book. If you're not using one, read this book; not every embedded system needs an operating system, but there are too many that have been cobbled together through the painful use of ad hoc loops that an RTOS would vastly improve.

Preface

WHAT IS μC/OS-III?

μC/OS-III (pronounced "Micro C O S Three) is a scalable, ROMable, preemptive real-time kernel that manages an unlimited number of tasks. μC/OS-III is a third-generation kernel and offers all of the services expected from a modern real-time kernel, such as resource management, synchronization, inter-task communications, and more. However, μC/OS-III offers many unique features not found in other real-time kernels, such as the ability to complete performance measurements at run-time, to directly signal or send messages to tasks, achieve pending on multiple kernel objects, and more.

WHY A NEW μC/OS VERSION?

The μC/OS series, first introduced in 1992, has undergone a number of changes over the years based on feedback from thousands of people using and deploying its evolving versions.

μC/OS-III is the sum of this feedback and experience. Rarely used μC/OS-II features were eliminated and newer, more efficient features and services, were added. Probably the most common request was to add round robin scheduling, which was not possible for μC/OS-II, but is now a feature of μC/OS-III.

μC/OS-III also provides additional features that better exploit the capabilities of today's newer processors. Specifically, μC/OS-III was designed with 32-bit processors in mind, although it certainly works well with 16- and even several 8-bit processors.

WHAT'S NEW ABOUT THIS BOOK?

The MicroC/OS-II book focused primarily on documenting the µC/OS-II product with a great, yet brief, RTOS introduction. This book changes that focus. This time, the spotlight is on real-time kernels and Real-Time Operating Systems (RTOS), with µC/OS-III used as a reference. In-depth product documentation is now provided in the appendices.

By taking this approach, the intent is to reach a larger target audience, especially those from industry and academia alike that are completely new to the topic of RTOS, This book is also suitable for use as the foundation of a generic RTOS class.

From a didactic perspective, every person has four different learning styles:

- Activist (A)
- Observational (O)
- Theoretical (T)
- Pragmatic (P)

The style that is more dominant differs from person to person. Based on these learning styles, there are strong improvements over the previous book, MicroC/OS-II, The Real-Time Kernel, which primarily focused on theoretical and, thanks to the good illustrations, also the observational learning styles. However, activist and pragmatic styles were somewhat missing. This book answers more questions for the pragmatist concerning: Why would I be interested in this? What could I use this for? What does this mean for my project? How does this help me get the job done?

Typically, books completely lack an activist learning style. This is a tricky one for a book because the question then becomes, how do you get readers to become active and do something with the material? That's where the companion evaluation board and tools come in. This two-part text, combined with tools and evaluation board, enable readers to receive the material, and begin to have a hands-on experience right away.

This book is split into two parts. The first part describes real-time kernels in generic terms, using µC/OS-III as a real-life example. The second part, which actually looks like a completely different book, provides examples using a popular microprocessor or microcontroller. As mentioned, the book is accompanied by a matching evaluation board and such tools as a compiler, assembler, linker, and debugger, which enable the reader to experiment with µC/OS-III and become proficient with its use.

In summary, the general topic of RTOS is now the prevailing topic of this book. Explaining the concept of RTOS in combination with µC/OS-III, an evaluation board and tools simply makes sense.

µC/OS-III GOALS

The main goal of µC/OS-III is to provide a best-in-class real-time kernel that literally shaves months of development time from an embedded-product schedule. Using a commercial real-time kernel such as µC/OS-III provides a solid foundation and framework to the design engineer dealing with the growing complexity of embedded designs.

Another goal for µC/OS-III, and therefore this book, is to explain inner workings of a commercial-grade kernel. This understanding will assist the reader in making logical design decisions and informed tradeoffs between hardware and software that make sense.

INTENDED AUDIENCE

This book is written for embedded systems programmers, consultants, hobbyists and students interested in understanding the inner workings of a real-time kernel. µC/OS-III is not just a great learning platform, but also a commercial-grade software package ready to be part of a range of products.

To get the most from this book, it is assumed that the reader has a good working knowledge of microprocessors, microcontrollers, and/or Digital Signal Processors (DSPs). That knowledge should extend to CPU instructions, interrupts, I/O devices, RAM and ROM or Flash, memory addresses, and stack pointers.

It is also expected that the reader will have a good working knowledge of the C programming language and assembly language.

THE µC/OS STORY

The µC/OS story started when, in 1989, I joined Dynalco Controls in Fort Lauderdale, Florida, and began working on the design of a new microprocessor-based ignition control system for a large industrial reciprocating engine.

Given that I had experience using a kernel, I was convinced that an operating system would substantially benefit this project and other planned projects at Dynalco. Time to market was of paramount importance for this ignition control system, and I knew that a kernel would help meet scheduling requirement. I also knew that new features would be added to this product in the future, and a preemptive operating system would allow for such updates without negatively impacting system responsiveness.

The kernel that I initially considered was one that had served me well in the past. However, it carried a hefty price tag, and my budget was somewhat meager. The alternative was a kernel that I had not used before, but it was five-times cheaper than my original choice. Ultimately, I decided that the financial benefits of using the unfamiliar operating system outweighed the potential advantages that its higher-priced counterpart could offer.

I quickly realized, however, that I would pay for the seemingly cheaper operating system with my time. During the two months after receiving the kernel, I was in constant contact with technical support, trying fruitlessly to determine why even the simplest applications would not run. The operating system, said to be written in C, required me to initialize all of the kernel's internal variables in assembly language, a task laden with problems. I eventually discovered that I was one of the first customers to purchase this operating system and was essentially an unknowing beta tester.

Frustrated with the software's many shortcomings, I turned to the relatively expensive operating system that I originally rejected. It seems that if a project is late, money is no object. Within two days, I was running simple applications that the cheap operating system seemed unable to support. My kernel-related problems seemed to be over.

Before long, however, I would find myself at another impasse. My second set of problems began when one of my engineers reported that the new operating system seemed to contain a bug. I promptly relayed the engineer's findings to the software vendor, assuming that the company would be interested. Instead of receiving assurance that the bug would be fixed, I was notified that the 90-day warranty expired. Unless I purchased a maintenance contract, the bug would not be eliminated, which was absurd to me. The software provider thought otherwise, and I forked over the maintenance fee.

Incredibly, the vendor took six months to actually remove the bug. All told, I completed my ignition system, incorporating the second operating system, a year after receiving the software. Clearly, I needed a better solution.

Twice disappointed, I began to develop my own kernel. In my naive opinion, all a kernel really did was to save and restore CPU registers; writing one should not be especially challenging.

The project kept me busy at night and on weekends, and proved to be much more difficult than anticipated. Approximately a year after I starting the project, my first operating system was complete.

With a new kernel in hand, there was finally a handy means of developing multitasking applications. The operating system, consisted of little more than a single C file and allowed up to 64 tasks to be created in a single application. Each task was required to be have a unique priority. The highest priority task that was ready to run when the operating system's scheduler was invoked was given control of the CPU. µC/OS was preemptive, so scheduling could occur at practically any time.

Efficient task scheduling was actually one of many services offered by µC/OS. The operating system also facilitated inter-task communication (via message queues and mailboxes) and task synchronization (through semaphores). All elements of µC/OS were designed to be both highly dependable and easy to use.

Presumably, most kernel developers have similar goals in mind when they write new software. I was especially well equipped to meet these goals, in part because of my punctilious coding style. Throughout my career, I focused on consistency and documentation. I began using formal coding standards in 1984, and the consistency of the µC/OS code is a testimony to this process.

µC/OS was designed according to the stringent standards that I created and promulgated at Dynalco. The operating system's source code featured liberal spacing, carefully worded comments, and consistent naming. Offering further evidence of the prudent coding techniques, the kernel was also highly portable. Although µC/OS, like its kernel peers, featured a small number of processor-specific functions, these routines were clearly separated from other portions of the operating system. Engineers could easily adapt µC/OS to new CPU architectures.

Unfortunately, I was the only one to know about the virtues of µC/OS. Eager to describe my new software to others, I wrote an in-depth paper explaining the inner workings of µC/OS. There was plenty to say, and my final paper was approximately 70 pages in length.

I offered my paper to C User's Journal, and they rejected it on the grounds that it was too long and that its subject matter wasn't fresh. The magazine had already published several kernel articles, and this was just one more. Convinced that my article was unique, I offered it to Embedded Systems Programming. The editor of this periodical likewise expressed misgivings, but I convinced him that µC/OS was attention-worthy. I explained that the operating system was comparable in quality to products that major embedded software companies offered (and better than at least two). I also explained that the source code for µC/OS could actually be placed on the publication's bulletin board service (BBS).

Embedded Systems Programming published a trimmed-down version of the paper as a two-part series. Both issues generated strong responses. Engineers were grateful that the inner workings of a high-quality kernel were revealed, and they downloaded the µC/OS source code in droves. kernel vendors, on the other hand, were less than thrilled with the article. In fact, the vendor of the low cost kernel was especially upset claiming that I had copied his work. Imagine that I would base µC/OS on software that didn't work!

There would soon be even more reason for the kernel vendors to be upset. Shortly after my article appeared in Embedded Systems Programming, R & D Publications, publisher of C User's Journal contacted me, and they were interested in printing an entire µC/OS book.

Originally, the plan for the book simply involved printing all of the material that I had originally submitted to C User's Journal. Had I taken that route, the resulting book would have been approximately 80 pages or so in length. To make the most of this opportunity, I prepared a comprehensive text. With the consent of R & D, I spent the next several months writing. In late 1992, my first book, aptly titled µC/OS, The Real-Time Kernel, was released. The book had 250 pages, and was available in paperback form.

Although initial sales of the book were somewhat disappointing, R & D advertised µC/OS, The Real-Time Kernel each month in C User's Journal. At the same time, I was beginning to gain attention as a kernel expert. In the spring of 1993, I was invited to speak at the Embedded Systems Conference (ESC) in Atlanta, Georgia, where I described operating system fundamentals to a highly receptive audience of more than 70 embedded enthusiasts. Within a few years, I was an ESC fixture, delivering my kernel lectures to hundreds of engineers at each conference.

While my popularity as a speaker rose, interest in my book also picked up steam. After its slow start, μC/OS, The Real-Time Kernel, went on to sell more than 15,000 copies.

Thanks to the success of my book, the number of engineers using μC/OS increased substantially throughout the 1990s. Developers easily adapted the operating system to new hardware platforms, and were designing a myriad of μC/OS-based applications. Although several μC/OS users simply tinkered with the operating system in their spare time, many engineers used the software commercially in complex and demanding projects. Comments and suggestions from μC/OS users helped me to continue to refine and evolve the operating system.

For several years, only minor changes were made to μC/OS. However, when R & D asked me to write a second edition, I decided that a substantial update of both the operating system and the book was warranted. The updated operating system became μC/OS-II.

A quick glance at the μC/OS-II files revealed that this operating system was different from μC/OS. Whereas all of the processor-independent code incorporated by μC/OS was contained in a single C file, μC/OS-II spanned multiple files, each corresponding to one of the operating system's services. μC/OS-II also offered many features that its predecessor lacked, including stack-checking capabilities, hook functions, and a safe means to dynamically allocate memory.

To fully describe all of the new operating system's features, I nearly doubled the size of the book. Just as the latest version of the software received a new name, the new edition became MicroC/OS-II, The Real-Time Kernel. ("Micro" was used in place of "μ" because titles incorporating Greek letters posed problems for many book retailers.) Unlike my first text, the new book would be a hardcover.

MicroC/OS-II, The Real-Time Kernel was released in 1998. This new text was accompanied by the source code that it described and I would again have thousands of developers testing the kernel and providing valuable feedback.

Among the thousands of readers of my books using the software, there were many kernel rookies. For them, the book provided thorough and accessible coverage of operating system fundamentals. Many university professors recognized the book's appeal to new kernel users and started designing entire courses around μC/OS-II. Soon college graduates whose kernel training focused on the operating system made their way into the workforce, where they continued to use μC/OS-II.

While students gravitated to µC/OS-II because of my book and readily available source code, a substantial number of engineers using µC/OS-II commercially selected the software for its reliability. Definitive proof of the operating system's reliability was provided in July 2000, when DO-178B Level A certification was conferred on an avionics product incorporating µC/OS-II. This certification, recognized by the Federal Avionics Administration (FAA), is awarded to software deemed safe enough to be used in aircraft. To this day, there are few operating systems that have successfully completed the rigorous testing that certified software must undergo.

DO-178B certification is only one of µC/OS-II's credentials. Additional certifications include Food and Drug Administration (FDA) pre-market notification (510(k)), pre-market approval (PMA) for medical devices, and IEC-61508 for industrial controls. Compliance with such standards is critical within industry segments; however, the certifications also have value for engineers in other industries as they evidence reliability, documentation, and time-to-market advantages beneficial to any design.

As the decade came to a close, I still worked full time at Dynalco, and experienced difficulty keeping up with the demand for the operating system. I felt obligated to respond to each µC/OS-II user that contacted me, and the flow of messages into my inbox was unrelenting. Since I could no longer treat the operating system as a side project, I made the decision to found my own software company. In September 1999, Micriµm, officially came into being. Micriµm comes from the word 'Micro' (for microprocessors or microcontrollers) and 'ium' (which means the Universe of) and thus, Micriµm means the Universe of Microprocessors (as seen through the eyes of software).

In the months before incorporating Micriµm, I began working on a second edition of the µC/OS-II book, which made its debut in November 1999 and was accompanied by a new version of the kernel. Two major features to the operating system were added: event flags and mutual exclusion semaphores. These new features, fully described in the book, were heartily welcomed by µC/OS-II users. The book itself was similarly embraced; the second edition of MicroC/OS-II, The Real-Time Kernel quickly became common sight on the bookshelves of embedded software developers. In fact, the MicroC/OS-II book is the most popular embedded systems book ever sold.

Micrium expanded. Engineers were hired to adapt µC/OS-II to new hardware platforms and develop a bevy of example projects and application notes. A long-time friend of mine, Christian Legare joined Micrium as Vice President in 2002, and his substantial corporate and technical expertise further accelerated the company's rapid growth. Since Christian joined Micrium, the company expanded from a one-product company to one with a portfolio of 15 products.

Meanwhile, new features were added to satisfy the ever-evolving needs of µC/OS-II users, including a variety of new API functions to the operating system and expanding the maximum number of tasks supported by the kernel from 64 to 255.

As Micrium's president, I remain dedicated to writing world-class kernel code, most recently µC/OS-III. The product of countless hours of meticulous programming and testing, this robust operating system has its roots in µC/OS-II, yet is an entirely new kernel. Addressing input received from customers and all of the lessons learned along the way, several additional important µC/OS-III features were included (see Introduction).

I am highly circumspect of fads and unproven technology as I write new software. Although I like to keep abreast of the latest developments in the high-tech world, the focus is on solving engineers' problems and providing a solid and complete infrastructure, rather than on how to prematurely exploit emerging trends.

This philosophy has yielded considerable success. Micrium, now in its tenth year, is a highly respected embedded software provider. Industry surveys consistently show the operating systems to be among the most popular in the embedded space. My goal has always been, and continues to be to provide effective solutions for the same types of problems that I confronted at Dynalco, and that millions of embedded systems developers continue to face today.

ACKNOWLEDGEMENTS

First and foremost, I'd like to thank my loving and caring wife Manon for her unconditional support, encouragement, understanding and patience. This new book and µC/OS-III software was again a huge undertaking, and I could not have done it without her.

I would also like to thank many fine people at Micriµm who have tested the code and reviewed the book. In alphabetic order:

- Brian Nagel

- Eric Shufro

- Hong Soong

- Freddy Torres

A special thanks to Frank Voorburg from Feaser and to Ian Hall and Robert Mongrain from Renesas for feedback and corrections to the book, to Michael Barr for sharing his real life RTOS experiences, and to Carolyn Mathas for the incredible job of editing this huge project.

A very special thanks to my long-time friend, colleague and partner, Christian Legare, who has provided his advice and support throughout this project and on a day-to-day basis at Micriµm. Thank you also to the dozens of people who provided feedback about the µC/OS-III code, as well as reviewers of the book.

Finally, I listen to music when I write software, and artist Gino Vannelli's awesome music has provided a creative environment for me for over three decades. I would be remiss if I did not acknowledge his contribution here as well.

1

Introduction

Real-time systems are systems whereby the correctness of the computed values and their timeliness are at the forefront. There are two types of real-time systems, hard and soft real time.

What differentiates hard and soft real-time systems is their tolerance to missing deadlines and the consequences associated with those misses. Correctly computed values after a deadline has passed are often useless.

For hard real-time systems, missing deadlines is not an option. In fact, in many cases, missing a deadline often results in catastrophe, which may involve human lives. For soft real-time systems, however, missing deadlines is generally not as critical.

Real-time applications cover a wide range, but many real-time systems are embedded. An embedded system is a computer built into a system and not acknowledged by the user as being a computer. Embedded systems are also typically dedicated systems. In other words, systems that are designed to perform a dedicated function. The following list shows just a few examples of embedded systems:

Aerospace
- Flight management systems
- Jet engine controls
- Weapons systems

Audio
- MP3 players
- Amplifiers and tuners

Automotive
- Antilock braking systems
- Climate control
- Engine controls
- Navigation systems (GPS)

Communications
- Routers
- Switches
- Cell phones

Computer peripherals
- Printers
- Scanners

Domestic
- Air conditioning units
- Thermostats
- White goods

Office automation
- FAX machines / copiers

Process control
- Chemical plants
- Factory automation
- Food processing

Robots

Video
- Broadcasting equipment
- HD Televisions

And many more

Real-time systems are typically more complicated to design, debug, and deploy than non-real-time systems.

1-1 FOREGROUND/BACKGROUND SYSTEMS

Small systems of low complexity are typically designed as foreground/background systems or super-loops. An application consists of an infinite loop (F1-1(1)) that calls modules (i.e., tasks) to perform the desired operations (background). Interrupt Service Routines (ISRs) shown in F1-1(3) handle asynchronous events (foreground). Foreground is also called interrupt level; background is called task level.

Critical operations that should be performed at the task level must unfortunately be handled by the ISRs to ensure that they are dealt with in a timely fashion. This causes ISRs to take longer than they should. Also, information for a background module that an ISR makes available is not processed until the background routine gets its turn to execute, which is called the task-level response. The worst-case task-level response time depends on how long a background loop takes to execute and, since the execution time of typical code is not constant, the time for successive passes through a portion of the loop is nondeterministic. Furthermore, if a code change is made, the timing of the loop is affected.

Most high-volume and low-cost microcontroller-based applications (e.g., microwave ovens, telephones, toys, etc.) are designed as foreground/background systems.

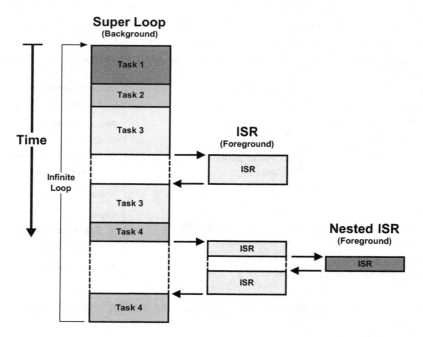

Figure 1-1 **Foreground/Background (SuperLoops) systems**

1-2 REAL-TIME KERNELS

A real-time kernel is software that manages the time and resources of a microprocessor, microcontroller or Digital Signal Processor (DSP).

The design process of a real-time application involves splitting the work into tasks, each responsible for a portion of the job. A task (also called a thread) is a simple program that thinks it has the Central Processing Unit (CPU) completely to itself. On a single CPU, only one task executes at any given time. A task is also typically implemented as an infinite loop.

The kernel is responsible for the management of tasks. This is called multitasking. Multitasking is the process of scheduling and switching the CPU between several tasks. The CPU switches its attention between several sequential tasks. Multitasking provides the illusion of having multiple CPUs and maximizes the use of the CPU. Multitasking also helps in the creation of modular applications. One of the most important aspects of multitasking is that it allows the application programmer to manage the complexity inherent in real-time applications. Application programs are easier to design and maintain when multitasking is used.

μC/OS-III is a preemptive kernel, which means that μC/OS-III always runs the most important task that is ready-to-run as shown in Figure 1-2.

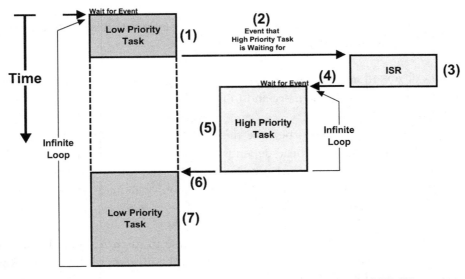

Figure 1-2 μC/OS-III is a preemptive kernel

F1-2(1)   A low-priority task is executing.

F1-2(2)   An interrupt occurs, and the CPU vectors to the ISR responsible for servicing the interrupting device.

F1-2(3)   The ISR services the interrupt device, but actually does very little work. The ISR will typically signal or send a message to a higher-priority task that will be responsible for most of the processing of the interrupting device. For example, if the interrupt comes from an Ethernet controller, the ISR simply signals a task, which will process the received packet.

F1-2(4)   When the ISR finishes, µC/OS-III notices that a more important task has been made ready-to-run by the ISR and will not return to the interrupted task, but instead context switch to the more important task.

F1-2(5)   The higher-priority task executes and performs the necessary processing in response to the interrupt device.

F1-2(6)   When the higher-priority task completes its work, it loops back to the beginning of the task code and makes a µC/OS-III function call to wait for the next interrupt from the device.

F1-2(7)   The low-priority task resumes exactly at the point where it was interrupted, not knowing what happened.

Kernels such as µC/OS-III are also responsible for managing communication between tasks, and managing system resources (memory and I/O devices).

A kernel adds overhead to a system because the services provided by the kernel require time to execute. The amount of overhead depends on how often these services are invoked. In a well-designed application, a kernel uses between 2% and 4% of a CPU's time. And, since µC/OS-III is software that is added to an application, it requires extra ROM (code space) and RAM (data space).

Low-end single-chip microcontrollers are generally not able to run a real-time kernel such as µC/OS-III since they have access to very little RAM. µC/OS-III requires between 1 Kbyte and 4 Kbytes of RAM, plus each task requires its own stack space. It is possible for µC/OS-III to work on processors having as little as 4 Kbytes of RAM.

Finally, μC/OS-III allows for better use of the CPU by providing approximately 70 indispensable services. After designing a system using a real-time kernel such as μC/OS-III, you will not return to designing a foreground/background system.

1-3 RTOS (REAL-TIME OPERATING SYSTEM)

A Real Time Operating System generally contains a real-time kernel and other higher-level services such as file management, protocol stacks, a Graphical User Interface (GUI), and other components. Most additional services revolve around I/O devices.

Micriμm offers a complete suite of RTOS components including: μC/FS (an Embedded File System), μC/TCP-IP (a TCP/IP stack), μC/GUI (a Graphical User Interface), μC/USB (a USB device and host stack), and more. Most of these components are designed to work standalone. Except for μC/TCP-IP, a real-time kernel is not required to use the components in an application. In fact, users can pick and choose only the components required for the application. Contact Micriμm (www.micrium.com) for additional details and pricing.

1-4 μC/OS-III

μC/OS-III is a scalable, ROMable, preemptive real-time kernel that manages an unlimited number of tasks. μC/OS-III is a third-generation kernel, offering all of the services expected from a modern real-time kernel including resource management, synchronization, inter-task communication, and more. However, μC/OS-III also offers many unique features not found in other real-time kernels, such as the ability to perform performance measurements at run time, directly signal or send messages to tasks, and pending (i.e., waiting) on such multiple kernel objects as semaphores and message queues.

Here is a list of features provided by μC/OS-III:

Source Code: μC/OS-III is provided in ANSI-C source form. The source code for μC/OS-III is arguably the cleanest and most consistent kernel code available. Clean source is part of the corporate culture at Micriμm. Although many commercial kernel vendors provide source code for their products, unless the code follows strict coding standards and is accompanied by complete documentation with examples to show how the code works, these products may be cumbersome and difficult to harness. With this book, you will gain a deep understanding of the inner workings of μC/OS-III, which will protect your investment.

Intuitive Application Programming Interface (API): µC/OS-III is highly intuitive. Once familiar with the consistent coding conventions used, it is simple to predict the functions to call for the services required, and even predict which arguments are needed. For example, a pointer to an object is always the first argument, and a pointer to an error code is always the last one.

Preemptive multitasking: µC/OS-III is a preemptive multi-tasking kernel and therefore, µC/OS-III always runs the most important ready-to-run task.

Round robin scheduling of tasks at equal priority: µC/OS-III allows multiple tasks to run at the same priority level. When multiple tasks at the same priority are ready-to-run, and that priority level is the most important level, µC/OS-III runs each task for a user-specified time called a time quanta. Each task can define its own time quanta, and a task can also give up the CPU to another task at the same priority if it does not require the full time quanta.

Low interrupt disable time: µC/OS-III has a number of internal data structures and variables that it needs to access atomically. To ensure this, µC/OS-III is able to protect these critical regions by locking the scheduler instead of disabling interrupts. Interrupts are therefore disabled for very little time. This ensures that µC/OS-III is able to respond to some of the fastest interrupt sources.

Deterministic: Interrupt response with µC/OS-III is deterministic. Also, execution times of most services provided by µC/OS-III are deterministic.

Scalable: The footprint (both code and data) can be adjusted based on the requirements of the application. Adding and removing features (i.e., services) is performed at compile time through approximately 40 **#defines** (see **os_cfg.h**). µC/OS-III also performs a number of run-time checks on arguments passed to µC/OS-III services. Specifically, µC/OS-III verifies that the user is not passing **NULL** pointers, not calling task level services from ISRs, that arguments are within allowable range, and options specified are valid, etc.. These checks can be disabled (at compile time) to further reduce the code footprint and improve performance. The fact that µC/OS-III is scalable allows it to be used in a wide range of applications and projects.

Portable: µC/OS-III can be ported to a large number of CPU architectures. Most µC/OS-II ports are easily converted to work on µC/OS-III with minimal changes in just a matter of minutes and therefore benefit from more than 45 CPU architectures already supported by µC/OS-II.

ROMable: µC/OS-III was designed especially for embedded systems and can be ROMed along with the application code.

Run-time configurable: µC/OS-III allows the user to configure the kernel at run time. Specifically, all kernel objects such as tasks, stacks, semaphores, event-flag groups, message queues, number of messages, mutual exclusion semaphores, memory partitions and timers, are allocated by the user at run time. This prevents over-allocating resources at compile time.

Unlimited number of tasks: µC/OS-III supports an unlimited number of tasks. From a practical standpoint, however, the number of tasks is actually limited by the amount of memory (both code and data space) that the processor has access to. Each task requires its own stack space and, µC/OS-III provides features to allow stack growth of the tasks to be monitored at run-time.

µC/OS-III does not impose any limitations on the size of each task, except that there be a minimum size based on the CPU used.

Unlimited number of priorities: µC/OS-III supports an unlimited number of priority levels. However, configuring µC/OS-III for between 32 and 256 different priority levels is more than adequate for most applications.

Unlimited number of kernel objects: µC/OS-III allows for any number of tasks, semaphores, mutual exclusion semaphores, event flags, message queues, timers, and memory partitions. The user allocates all kernel objects at run-time.

Services: µC/OS-III provides all the services expected from a high-end real-time kernel, such as task management, time management, semaphores, event flags, mutexes, message queues, software timers, fixed-size memory pools, etc.

Mutual Exclusion Semaphores (Mutexes): Mutexes are provided for resource management. Mutexes are special types of semaphores that have built-in priority inheritance, which eliminate unbounded priority inversions. Accesses to a mutex can be nested and therefore, a task can acquire the same mutex up to 250 times. Of course, the mutex owner needs to release the mutex an equal number of times.

Nested task suspension: µC/OS-III allows a task to suspend itself or another task. Suspending a task means that the task will not be allowed to execute until the task is resumed by another task. Suspension can be nested up to 250 levels deep. In other words, a task can suspend another task up to 250 times. Of course, the task must be resumed an equal number of times for it to become eligible to run on the CPU.

Software timers: You can define any number of "one-shot" and/or "periodic" timers. Timers are countdown counters that perform a user-definable action upon counting down to 0. Each timer can have its own action and, if a timer is periodic, the timer is automatically reloaded and the action is executed every time the countdown reaches zero.

Pend on multiple objects: µC/OS-III allows an application to wait (i.e., pend) on multiple events at the same time. Specifically, a task can wait on multiple semaphores and/or message queues to be posted. The waiting task wakes up as soon as one of the events occurs.

Task Signals: µC/OS-III allows an ISR or task to directly signal a task. This avoids having to create an intermediate kernel object such as a semaphore or event flag just to signal a task, and results in better performance.

Task Messages: µC/OS-III allows an ISR or a task to send messages directly to a task. This avoids having to create and use a message queue, and also results in better performance.

Task registers: Each task can have a user-definable number of "task registers." Task registers are different than CPU registers. Task registers can be used to hold "errno" type variable, IDs, interrupt disable time measurement on a per-task basis, and more.

Error checking: µC/OS-III verifies that NULL pointers are not passed, that the user is not calling task-level services from ISRs, that arguments are within allowable range, that options specified are valid, that a pointer to the proper object is passed as part of the arguments to services that manipulate the desired object, and more. Each µC/OS-III API function returns an error code concerning the outcome of the function call.

Built-in performance measurements: µC/OS-III has built-in features to measure the execution time of each task, stack usage of each task, number of times a task executes, CPU usage, ISR-to-task and task-to-task response time, peak number of entries in certain lists, interrupt disable and scheduler lock time on a per-task basis, and more.

Can easily be optimized: µC/OS-III was designed so that it could easily be optimized based on the CPU architecture. Most data types used in µC/OS-III can be changed to make better use of the CPU's natural word size. Also, the priority resolution algorithm can easily be written in assembly language to benefit from special instructions such as bit set and clear, as well as count-leading-zeros (CLZ), or find-first-one (FF1) instructions.

Deadlock prevention: All of the µC/OS-III "pend" services include timeouts, which help avoid deadlocks.

Tick handling at task level: The clock tick manager in µC/OS-III is accomplished by a task that receives a trigger from an ISR. Handling delays and timeouts by a task greatly reduces interrupt latency. Also, µC/OS-III uses a hashed delta list mechanism, which further reduces the amount of overhead in processing delays and timeouts of tasks.

User definable hooks: µC/OS-III allows the port and application programmer to define "hook" functions, which are called by µC/OS-III. A hook is simply a defined function that allows the user to extend the functionality of µC/OS-III. One such hook is called during a context switch, another when a task is created, yet another when a task is deleted, etc.

Timestamps: For time measurements, µC/OS-III requires that a 16-bit or 32-bit free running counter be made available. This counter can be read at run time to make time measurements of certain events. For example, when an ISR posts a message to a task, the timestamp counter is automatically read and saved as part of the message posted. When the recipient receives the message, the timestamp is provided to the recipient, and by reading the current timestamp, the time it took for the message to be received can be determined.

Built-in support for Kernel Awareness debuggers: This feature allows kernel awareness debuggers to examine and display µC/OS-III variables and data structures in a user-friendly way. The kernel awareness support in µC/OS-III can be used by µC/Probe to display this information at run-time.

Object names: Each µC/OS-III kernel object can have a name associated with it. This makes it easy to recognize what the object is assigned to. You can thus assign an ASCII name to a task, a semaphore, a mutex, an event flag group, a message queue, a memory partition, and a timer. The object name can have any length, but must be NUL terminated.

1-5 µC/OS, µC/OS-II AND µC/OS-III FEATURES COMPARISON

Table 1-1 shows the evolution of µC/OS over the years, comparing the features available in each version.

Feature	µC/OS	µC/OS-II	µC/OS-III
Year introduced	1992	1998	2009
Book	Yes	Yes	Yes
Source code available	Yes	Yes	Yes
Preemptive Multitasking	Yes	Yes	Yes
Maximum number of tasks	64	255	Unlimited
Number of tasks at each priority level	1	1	Unlimited
Round Robin Scheduling	No	No	Yes
Semaphores	Yes	Yes	Yes
Mutual Exclusion Semaphores	No	Yes	Yes (Nestable)
Event Flags	No	Yes	Yes
Message Mailboxes	Yes	Yes	No (not needed)
Message Queues	Yes	Yes	Yes
Fixed Sized Memory Management	No	Yes	Yes
Signal a task without requiring a semaphore	No	No	Yes
Option to Post without scheduling	No	No	Yes
Send messages to a task without requiring a message queue	No	No	Yes
Software Timers	No	Yes	Yes
Task suspend/resume	No	Yes	Yes (Nestable)
Deadlock prevention	Yes	Yes	Yes
Scalable	Yes	Yes	Yes
Code Footprint	3K to 8K	6K to 26K	6K to 24K
Data Footprint	1K+	1K+	1K+
ROMable	Yes	Yes	Yes

Feature	µC/OS	µC/OS-II	µC/OS-III
Run-time configurable	No	No	Yes
Compile-time configurable	Yes	Yes	Yes
ASCII names for each kernel object	No	Yes	Yes
Pend on multiple objects	No	Yes	Yes
Task registers	No	Yes	Yes
Built-in performance measurements	No	Limited	Extensive
User definable hook functions	No	Yes	Yes
Time stamps on posts	No	No	Yes
Built-in Kernel Awareness support	No	Yes	Yes
Optimizable Scheduler in assembly language	No	No	Yes
Catch a task that returns	No	No	Yes
Tick handling at task level	No	No	Yes
Source code available	Yes	Yes	Yes
Number of services	~20	~90	~70
MISRA-C:1998	No	Yes (except 10 rules)	N/A
MISRA-C:2004	No	No	Yes (except 7 rules)
DO178B Level A and EUROCAE ED-12B	No	Yes	In progress
Medical FDA pre-market notification (510(k)) and pre-market approval (PMA)	No	Yes	In progress
SIL3/SIL4 IEC for transportation and nuclear systems	No	Yes	In progress
IEC-61508	No	Yes	In progress

Table 1-1 **µC/OS, µC/OS-II and µC/OS-III Features Comparison Chart**

1-6 HOW THE BOOK IS ORGANIZED

This book actually consists of two books in one.

Part I describes µC/OS-III and is not tied to any specific CPU architecture. Here, the reader will learn about real-time kernels through µC/OS-III. Specifically, critical sections, task management, the ready list, scheduling, context switching, interrupt management, wait lists, time management, timers, resource management, synchronization, memory management, how to use µC/OS-III's API, how to configure µC/OS-III, and how to port µC/OS-III to different CPU architectures, are all covered.

Part II describes the port of a popular CPU architecture. Here, you will learn about this CPU architecture and how µC/OS-III gets the most out of the CPU. Examples are provided to actually run code on the evaluation board that is available with this book.

As I just mentioned, this book assumes the presence of an evaluation board that allows the user to experiment with the wonderful world of real-time kernels, and specifically µC/OS-III. The book and board are complemented by a full set of tools that are provided free of charge either in a companion CD/DVD, or downloadable through the Internet. The tools and the use of µC/OS-III are free as long as they are used with the evaluation board, and there is no commercial intent to use them on a project. In other words, there is no additional charge except for the initial cost of the book, evaluation board and tools, as long as they are used for educational purposes.

The book also comes with a trial version of an award-winning tool from Micrium called µC/Probe. The trial version allows the user to monitor and change up to eight (8) variables in a target system.

1-7 µC/PROBE

µC/Probe is a Microsoft Windows™ based application that enables the user to visualize variables in a target at run time. Specifically, you can display or change the value of any variable in a system while the target is running. These variables can be displayed using such graphical elements as gauges, meters, bar graphs, virtual LEDs, numeric indicators, and many more. Sliders, switches, and buttons can be used to change variables. This is accomplished without the user having to write a single line of code!

µC/Probe interfaces to any target (8-, 16-, 32-, 64-bit, or even DSPs) through one of the many interfaces supported (J-Tag, RS-232C, USB, Ethernet, etc.). µC/Probe displays or changes any variable (as long as they are global) in the application, including µC/OS-III's internal variables.

µC/Probe works with any compiler/assembler/linker able to generate an ELF/DWARF or IEEE695 file. This is the exact same file that the user will download to the evaluation board or a final target. From this file, µC/Probe is able to extract symbolic information about variables, and determine where variables are stored in RAM or ROM.

µC/Probe also allows users to log the data displayed into a file for analysis of the collected data at a later time. µC/Probe also provides µC/OS-III kernel awareness as a built-in feature.

The trial version that accompanies the book is limited to the display or change of up to eight (8) variables.

µC/Probe is a tool that serious embedded software engineers should have in their toolbox. The full version of µC/Probe is available from Micriµm, see www.micrium.com for more details.

1-8 CONVENTIONS

There are a number of conventions in this book.

First, you will notice that when a specific element in a figure is referenced, the element has a number next to it in parenthesis. A description of this element follows the figure and in this case, the letter "F" followed by the figure number, and then the number in parenthesis. For example, F3-4(2) indicates that this description refers to Figure 3-4 and the element (2) in that figure. This convention also applies to listings (starts with an "L") and tables (starts with a "T").

Second, you will notice that sections and listings are started where it makes sense. Specifically, do not be surprised to see the bottom half of a page empty. New sections begin on a new page, and listings are found on a single page, instead of breaking listings on two pages.

Third, code quality is something I've been avidly promoting throughout my whole career. At Micriµm, we pride ourselves in having the cleanest code in the industry. Examples of this are seen in this book. I created and published a coding standard in 1992 that was published in the original µC/OS book. This standard has evolved over the years, but the spirit of the standard has been maintained throughout. The Micriµm coding standard is available for download from the Micriµm website, www.micrium.com

One of the conventions used is that all functions, variables, macros and **#define** constants are prefixed by "OS" (which stands for Operating System) followed by the acronym of the module (e.g., **Sem**), and then the operation performed by the function. For example **OSSemPost()** indicates that the function belongs to the OS (µC/OS-III), that it is part of the Semaphore services, and specifically that the function performs a **Post** (i.e., signal) operation. This allows all related functions to be grouped together in the reference manual, and makes those services intuitive to use.

You should notice that signaling or sending a message to a task is called posting, and waiting for a signal or a message is called pending. In other words, an ISR or a task signals or sends a message to another task by using **OS???Post()**, where **???** is the type of service: **Sem, TaskSem, Flag, Mutex, Q**, and **TaskQ**. Similarly, a task can wait for a signal or a message by calling **OS???Pend()**.

1-9 CHAPTER CONTENTS

Figure 1-3 shows the layout and flow of Part I of the book. This diagram should be useful to understand the relationship between chapters. The first column on the left indicates chapters that should be read in order to understand µC/OS-III's structure. The second column shows chapters that are related to additional services provided by µC/OS-III. The third column relates to chapters that will help port µC/OS-III to different CPU architectures. The top of the fourth column explains how to obtain valuable run-time and compile-time statistics from µC/OS-III. This is especially useful if developing a kernel awareness plug-in for a debugger, or using µC/Probe. The middle of column four contains the µC/OS-III API and configuration manuals. You will be referencing these sections regularly when designing a product using µC/OS-III. Finally, the bottom of the last column contains miscellaneous appendices.

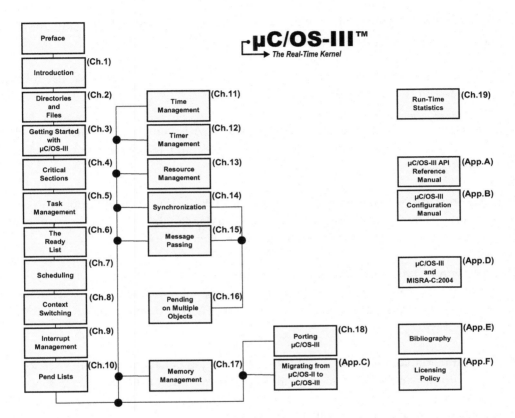

Figure 1-3   µC/OS-III Book Layout

Chapter 1, Introduction. This chapter.

Chapter 2, Directories and Files. This chapter explains the directory structure and files needed to build a µC/OS-III-based application. Here, you will learn about the files that are needed, where they should be placed, which module does what, and more.

Chapter 3, Getting Started with µC/OS-III. In this chapter, you will learn how to properly initialize and start a µC/OS-III-based application.

Chapter 4, Critical Sections. This chapter explains what critical sections are, and how they are protected.

Chapter 5, Task Management. This chapter is an introduction to one of the most important aspects of a real-time kernel, the management of tasks in a multitasking environment.

Chapter 6, The Ready List. In this chapter, you will learn how µC/OS-III efficiently keeps track of all of the tasks that are waiting to execute on the CPU.

Chapter 7, Scheduling. This chapter explains the scheduling algorithms used by µC/OS-III, and how it decides which task will run next.

Chapter 8, Context Switching. This chapter explains what a context switch is, and describes the process of suspending execution of a task and resuming execution of a higher-priority task.

Chapter 9, Interrupt Management. Here is how µC/OS-III deals with interrupts and an overview of services that are available from Interrupt Service Routines (ISRs). Here you will learn how µC/OS-III supports nearly any interrupt controller.

Chapter 10, Pend Lists (or Wait Lists). Tasks that are not able to run are most likely blocked waiting for specific events to occur. Pend Lists (or wait lists), are used to keep track of tasks that are waiting for a resource or event. This chapter describes how µC/OS-III maintains these lists.

Chapter 11, Time Management. In this chapter, you will find out about µC/OS-III's services that allow users to suspend a task until some time expires. With µC/OS-III, you can specify to delay execution of a task for an integral number of clock ticks or until the clock-tick counter reaches a certain value. The chapter will also show how a delayed task can be resumed, and describe how to get the current value of the clock tick counter, or set this counter, if needed.

Chapter 12, Timer Management. µC/OS-III allows users to define any number of software timers. When a timer expires, a function can be called to perform some action. Timers can be configured to be either periodic or one-shot. This chapter also explains how the timer-management module works.

Chapter 13, Resource Management. In this chapter, you will learn different techniques so that tasks share resources. Each of these techniques has advantages and disadvantages that will be discussed. This chapter also explains the internals of semaphores, and mutual exclusion semaphore management.

Chapter 14, Synchronization. µC/OS-III provides two types of services for synchronization: semaphores and event flags and these are explained in this chapter, as well as what happens when calling specific services provided in this module.

Chapter 15, Message Passing. µC/OS-III allows a task or an ISR to send messages to a task. This chapter describes some of the services provided by the message queue management module.

Chapter 16, Pending on multiple objects. In this chapter, see how µC/OS-III allows an application to pend (or wait) on multiple kernel objects (semaphores or message queues) at the same time. This feature makes the waiting task ready-to-run as soon as any one of the objects is posted (i.e., OR condition), or a timeout occurs.

Chapter 17, Memory Management. Here is how µC/OS-III's fixed-size memory partition manager can be used to allocate and deallocate dynamic memory.

Chapter 18, Porting µC/OS-III. This chapter explains, in generic terms, how to port µC/OS-III to any CPU architecture.

Chapter 19, Run-Time Statistics. µC/OS-III provides a wealth of information about the run-time environment, such as number of context switches, CPU usage (as a percentage), stack usage on a per-task basis, µC/OS-III RAM usage, maximum interrupt disable time, maximum scheduler lock time, and more.

Appendix A, µC/OS-III API Reference Manual. This appendix provides a alphabetical reference for all user-available services provided by µC/OS-III.

Appendix B, µC/OS-III Configuration Manual. This appendix describes how to configure a µC/OS-III-based application. os_cfg.h configures the µC/OS-III features (semaphores, queues, event flags, etc.), while os_cfg_app.h configures the run-time characteristics (tick rate, tick wheel size, stack size for the idle task, etc.).

Appendix C, Migrating from µC/OS-II to µC/OS-III. µC/OS-III has its roots in µC/OS-II and, in fact, most of the µC/OS-II ports can be easily converted to µC/OS-III. However, most APIs have changed from µC/OS-II to µC/OS-III, and this appendix describes some of the differences.

Appendix D, MISRA-C:2004 rules and µC/OS-III. µC/OS-III follows most of the MISRA-C:2004, except for a few of these rules.

Appendix E, Bibliography.

Appendix F, Licensing µC/OS-III.

Directories and Files

μC/OS-III is fairly easy to use once it is understood exactly which source files are needed to make up a μC/OS-III-based application. This chapter will discuss the modules available for μC/OS-III and how everything fits together.

Figure 2-1 shows the μC/OS-III architecture and its relationship with hardware. Of course, in addition to the timer and interrupt controller, hardware would most likely contain such other devices as Universal Asynchronous Receiver Transmitters (UARTs), Analog to Digital Converters (ADCs), Ethernet controller(s) and more.

This chapter assumes development on a Windows®-based platform and makes references to typical Windows-type directory structures (also called Folder). However, since μC/OS-III is provided in source form, it can also be used on Unix, Linux or other development platforms.

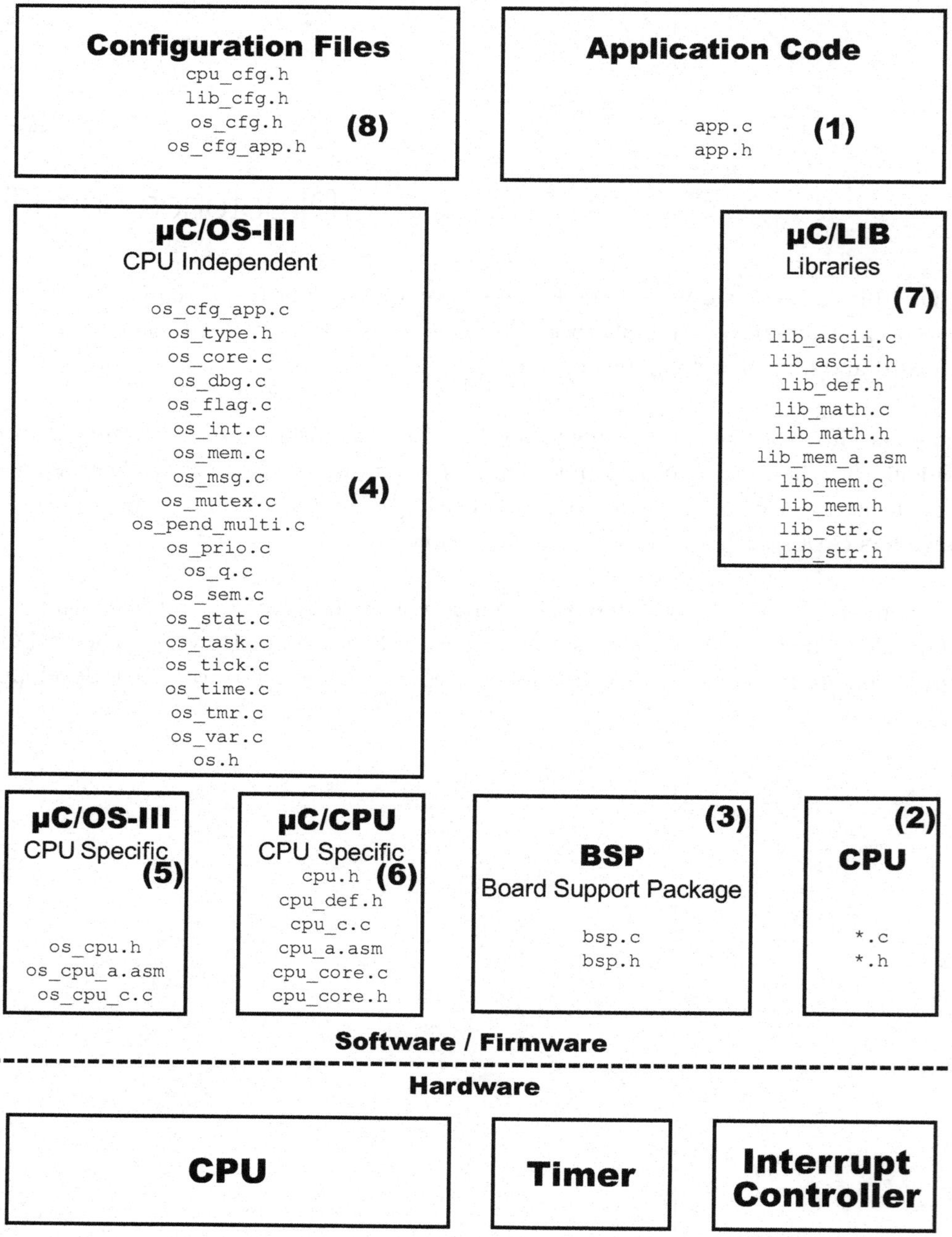

Configuration Files	Application Code
cpu_cfg.h lib_cfg.h os_cfg.h os_cfg_app.h **(8)**	app.c **(1)** app.h

µC/OS-III
CPU Independent

```
os_cfg_app.c
os_type.h
os_core.c
os_dbg.c
os_flag.c
os_int.c
os_mem.c
os_msg.c
os_mutex.c          (4)
os_pend_multi.c
os_prio.c
os_q.c
os_sem.c
os_stat.c
os_task.c
os_tick.c
os_time.c
os_tmr.c
os_var.c
os.h
```

µC/LIB
Libraries
(7)

```
lib_ascii.c
lib_ascii.h
lib_def.h
lib_math.c
lib_math.h
lib_mem_a.asm
lib_mem.c
lib_mem.h
lib_str.c
lib_str.h
```

µC/OS-III
CPU Specific
(5)

```
os_cpu.h
os_cpu_a.asm
os_cpu_c.c
```

µC/CPU
CPU Specific
cpu.h **(6)**
```
cpu_def.h
cpu_c.c
cpu_a.asm
cpu_core.c
cpu_core.h
```

(3)
BSP
Board Support Package

```
bsp.c
bsp.h
```

(2)
CPU

```
*.c
*.h
```

Software / Firmware
- -
Hardware

CPU	Timer	Interrupt Controller

Figure 2-1 µC/OS-III Architecture

F2-1(1)   The application code consists of project or product files. For convenience, these are simply called **app.c** and app.h, however an application can contain any number of files that do not have to be called **app.***. The application code is typically where one would find the **main()**.

F2-1(2)   Semiconductor manufacturers often provide library functions in source form for accessing the peripherals on their CPU or MCU. These libraries are quite useful and often save valuable time. Since there is no naming convention for these files, ***.c** and ***.h** are assumed.

F2-1(3)   The Board Support Package (BSP) is code that is typically written to interface to peripherals on a target board. For example such code can turn on and off LEDs, turn on and off relays, or read switches, temperature sensors, and more.

F2-1(4)   This is the µC/OS-III processor-independent code. This code is written in highly portable ANSI C.

F2-1(5)   This is the µC/OS-III code that is adapted to a specific CPU architecture and is called a port. µC/OS-III has its roots in µC/OS-II and benefits from being able to use most of the 45 or so ports available for µC/OS-II. µC/OS-II ports, however, will require small changes to work with µC/OS-III. These changes are described in Appendix C, "Migrating from µC/OS-II to µC/OS-III" on page 689.

F2-1(6)   At Micrium, we encapsulate CPU functionality. These files define functions to disable and enable interrupts, **CPU_???** data types to be independent of the CPU and compiler used, and many more functions.

F2-1(7)   µC/LIB is of a series of source files that provide common functions such as memory copy, string, and ASCII-related functions. Some are occasionally used to replace **stdlib** functions provided by the compiler. The files are provided to ensure that they are fully portable from application to application and especially, from compiler to compiler. µC/OS-III does not use these files, but µC/CPU does.

F2-1(8)   Configuration files are used to define µC/OS-III features (**os_cfg.h**) to include in the application, specify the size of certain variables and data structures expected by µC/OS-III (**os_cfg_app.h**), such as idle task stack size, tick rate, size of the message pool, configure the µC/CPU features available to the application programmer (**cpu_cfg.h**) and also configure µC/LIB options (**lib_cfg.h**).

2-1 APPLICATION CODE

When Micriµm provides example projects, they are placed in a directory structure shown below. Of course, a directory structure that suits a particular project/product can also be used.

```
\Micrium
    \Software
        \EvalBoards
            \<manufacturer>
                \<board_name>
                    \<compiler>
                        \<project name>
                        \*.*
```

\Micrium

This is where we place all software components and projects provided by Micriµm. This directory generally starts from the root directory of the computer.

\Software

This sub-directory contains all software components and projects.

\EvalBoards

This sub-directory contains all projects related to evaluation boards supported by Micriµm.

\<manufacturer>

This is the name of the manufacturer of the evaluation board. The "<" and ">" are not part of the actual name.

\<board name>

This is the name of the evaluation board. A board from Micriµm will typically be called **uC-Eval-xxxx** where "**xxxx**" represents the CPU or MCU used on the board. The "<" and ">" are not part of the actual name.

\<compiler>

This is the name of the compiler or compiler manufacturer used to build the code for the evaluation board. The "<" and ">" are not part of the actual name.

\<project name>

The name of the project that will be demonstrated. For example, a simple µC/OS-III project might have a project name of "**OS-Ex1**". The "**-Ex1**" represents a project containing only µC/OS-III.

.

These are the project source files. Main files can optionally be called **app*.***. This directory also contains configuration files **os_cfg.h**, **os_cfg_app.h** and other required source files.

2-2 CPU

The directory where you will find semiconductor manufacturer peripheral interface source files is shown below. Any directory structure that suits the project/product may be used.

```
\Micrium
    \Software
        \CPU
            \<manufacturer>
                \<architecture>
                    \*.*
```

\Micrium

The location of all software components and projects provided by Micriµm.

\Software

This sub-directory contains all software components and projects.

\CPU

This sub-directory is always called CPU.

\<manufacturer>

Is the name of the semiconductor manufacturer providing the peripheral library.

\<architecture>

The name of the specific library, generally associated with a CPU name or an architecture.

.

Indicates library source files. The semiconductor manufacturer names the files.

2-3 BOARD SUPPORT PACKAGE (BSP)

The Board Support Package (BSP) is generally found with the evaluation or target board as it is specific to that board. In fact, when well written, the BSP should be used for multiple projects.

```
\Micrium
    \Software
        \EvalBoards
            \<manufacturer>
                \<board name>
                    \<compiler>
                        \BSP
                            \*.*
```

\Micrium
Contains all software components and projects provided by Micriµm.

\Software
This sub-directory contains all software components and projects.

\EvalBoards
This sub-directory contains all projects related to evaluation boards.

\<manufacturer>
The name of the manufacturer of the evaluation board. The "<" and ">" are not part of the actual name.

\<board name>
The name of the evaluation board. A board from Micriµm will typically be called **uC-Eval-xxxx** where "**xxxx**" is the name of the CPU or MCU used on the evaluation board. The "<" and ">" are not part of the actual name.

\<compiler>
The name of the compiler or compiler manufacturer used to build code for the evaluation board. The "<" and ">" are not part of the actual name.

\BSP

This directory is always called BSP.

.

The source files of the BSP. Typically all of the file names start with BSP. It is therefore normal to find **bsp.c** and **bsp.h** in this directory. BSP code should contain such functions as LED control functions, initialization of timers, interface to Ethernet controllers and more.

2-4 μC/OS-III, CPU INDEPENDENT SOURCE CODE

The files in these directories are μC/OS-III processor independent files provided in source form. See Appendix F, "Licensing Policy" on page 733.

```
\Micrium
    \Software
        \uCOS-III
            \Cfg\Template
                \os_app_hooks.c
                \os_cfg.h
                \os_cfg_app.h
            \Source
                \os_cfg_app.c
                \os_core.c
                \os_dbg.c
                \os_flag.c
                \os_int.c
                \os_mem.c
                \os_msg.c
                \os_mutex.c
                \os_pend_multi.c
                \os_prio.c
                \os_q.c
                \os_sem.c
                \os_stat.c
                \os_task.c
                \os_tick.c
                \os_time.c
```

```
\os_tmr.c
\os_var
\os.h
\os_type.h
```

\Micrium

Contains all software components and projects provided by Micriµm.

\Software

This sub-directory contains all software components and projects.

\uCOS-III

This is the main µC/OS-III directory.

\Cfg\Template

This directory contains examples of configuration files to copy to the project directory. You will then modify these files to suit the needs of the application.

os_app_hooks.c shows how to write hook functions that are called by µC/OS-III. Specifically, this file contains eight empty functions.

os_cfg.h specifies which features of µC/OS-III are available for an application. The file is typically copied into an application directory and edited based on which features are required from µC/OS-III. See Appendix B, "µC/OS-III Configuration Manual" on page 669.

os_cfg_app.h is a configuration file that is typically copied into an application directory and edited based on application requirements. This file enables the user to determine the size of the idle task stack, the tick rate, the number of messages available in the message pool and more. See Appendix B, "µC/OS-III Configuration Manual" on page 669.

\Source

The directory containing the CPU-independent source code for μC/OS-III. All files in this directory should be included in the build. Features that are not required will be compiled out based on the value of #define constants in **os_cfg.h** and **os_cfg_app.h**.

os_cfg_app.c declares variables and arrays based on the values in **os_cfg_app.h**.

os_core.c contains core functionality for μC/OS-III such as OSInit() to initialize μC/OS-III, OSSched() for the task level scheduler, OSIntExit() for the interrupt level scheduler, pend list (or wait list) management (see Chapter 10, "Pend Lists (or Wait Lists)" on page 197), ready list management (see Chapter 6, "The Ready List" on page 141), and more.

os_dbg.c contains declarations of constant variables used by a kernel aware debugger or μC/Probe.

os_flag.c contains the code for event flag management. See Chapter 14, "Synchronization" on page 273 for details about event flags.

os_int.c contains code for the interrupt handler task, which is used when **OS_CFG_ISR_POST_DEFERRED_EN** (see **os_cfg.h**) is set to 1. See Chapter 9, "Interrupt Management" on page 175 for details regarding the interrupt handler task.

os_mem.c contains code for the μC/OS-III fixed-size memory manager, see Chapter 17, "Memory Management" on page 343.

os_msg.c contains code to handle messages. μC/OS-III provides message queues and task specific message queues. **os_msg.c** provides common code for these two services. See Chapter 15, "Message Passing" on page 309.

os_mutex.c contains code to manage mutual exclusion semaphores, see Chapter 13, "Resource Management" on page 231.

os_pend_multi.c contains the code to allow code to pend on multiple semaphores or message queues. This is described in Chapter 16, "Pending On Multiple Objects" on page 333.

os_prio.c contains the code to manage the bitmap table used to keep track of which tasks are ready-to-run, see Chapter 6, "The Ready List" on page 141. This file can be replaced by an assembly language equivalent to improve performance if the CPU used provides bit set, clear and test instructions, and a count leading zeros instruction.

os_q.c contains code to manage message queues. See Chapter 15, "Message Passing" on page 309.

os_sem.c contains code to manage semaphores used for resource management and/or synchronization. See Chapter 13, "Resource Management" on page 231 and Chapter 14, "Synchronization" on page 273.

os_stat.c contains code for the statistic task, which is used to compute the global CPU usage and the CPU usage of each task. See Chapter 5, "Task Management" on page 91.

os_task.c contains code for managing tasks using **OSTaskCreate()**, **OSTaskDel()**, **OSTaskChangePrio()**, and many more. See Chapter 5, "Task Management" on page 91.

os_tick.c contains code to manage tasks that have delayed themselves or that are pending on a kernel object with a timeout. See Chapter 5, on page 91.

os_time.c contains code to allow a task to delay itself until some time expires. See Chapter 11, "Time Management" on page 203.

os_tmr.c contains code to manage software timers. See Chapter 12, "Timer Management" on page 213.

os_var.c contains the μC/OS-III global variables. These variables are for μC/OS-III to manage and should not be accessed by application code.

os.h contains the main μC/OS-III header file, which declares constants, macros, μC/OS-III global variables (for use by μC/OS-III only), function prototypes, and more.

os_type.h contains declarations of μC/OS-III data types that can be changed by the port designer to make better use of the CPU architecture. In this case, the file would typically be copied to the port directory and then modified. See Appendix B, "μC/OS-III Configuration Manual" on page 669.

2-5 µC/OS-III, CPU SPECIFIC SOURCE CODE

The µC/OS-III port developer provides these files. See also Chapter 18, "Porting µC/OS-III" on page 355.

```
\Micrium
    \Software
        \uCOS-III
            \Ports
                \<architecture>
                    \<compiler>
                        \os_cpu.h
                        \os_cpu_a.asm
                        \os_cpu_c.c
```

\Micrium
Contains all software components and projects provided by Micriµm.

\Software
This sub-directory contains all software components and projects.

\uCOS-III
The main µC/OS-III directory.

\Ports
The location of port files for the CPU architecture(s) to be used.

\<architecture>
This is the name of the CPU architecture that µC/OS-III was ported to. The "<" and ">" are not part of the actual name.

\<compiler>
The name of the compiler or compiler manufacturer used to build code for the port. The "<" and ">" are not part of the actual name.

The files in this directory contain the µC/OS-III port, see Chapter 18, "Porting µC/OS-III" on page 355 for details on the contents of these files.

os_cpu.h contains a macro declaration for **OS_TASK_SW()**, as well as the function prototypes for at least the following functions: **OSCtxSw()**, **OSIntCtxSw()** and **OSStartHighRdy()**.

os_cpu_a.asm contains the assembly language functions to implement at least the following functions: **OSCtxSw()**, **OSIntCtxSw()** and **OSStartHighRdy()**.

os_cpu_c.c contains the C code for the port specific hook functions and code to initialize the stack frame for a task when the task is created.

2-6 µC/CPU, CPU SPECIFIC SOURCE CODE

µC/CPU consists of files that encapsulate common CPU-specific functionality and CPU and compiler-specific data types. See Chapter 18, "Porting µC/OS-III" on page 355.

```
\Micrium
    \Software
        \uC-CPU
            \cpu_core.c
            \cpu_core.h
            \cpu_def.h
            \Cfg\Template
                \cpu_cfg.h
            \<architecture>
                \<compiler>
                    \cpu.h
                    \cpu_a.asm
                    \cpu_c.c
```

\Micrium
Contains all software components and projects provided by Micrium.

\Software
This sub-directory contains all software components and projects.

\uC-CPU

This is the main µC/CPU directory.

cpu_core.c contains C code that is common to all CPU architectures. Specifically, this file contains functions to measure the interrupt disable time of the **CPU_CRITICAL_ENTER()** and **CPU_CRITICAL_EXIT()** macros, a function that emulates a count leading zeros instruction in case the CPU does not provide such an instruction, and a few other functions.

cpu_core.h contains function prototypes for the functions provided in **cpu_core.c** and allocation of the variables used by the module to measure interrupt disable time.

cpu_def.h contains miscellaneous **#define** constants used by the µC/CPU module.

\Cfg\Template

This directory contains a configuration template file (**cpu_cfg.h**) that must be copied to the application directory to configure the µC/CPU module based on application requirements.

cpu_cfg.h determines whether to enable measurement of the interrupt disable time, whether the CPU implements a count leading zeros instruction in assembly language, or whether it will be emulated in C, and more.

\<architecture>

The name of the CPU architecture that µC/CPU was ported to. The "<" and ">" are not part of the actual name.

\<compiler>

The name of the compiler or compiler manufacturer used to build code for the µC/CPU port. The "<" and ">" are not part of the actual name.

The files in this directory contain the µC/CPU port, see Chapter 18, "Porting µC/OS-III" on page 355 for details on the contents of these files.

cpu.h contains type definitions to make µC/OS-III and other modules independent of the CPU and compiler word sizes. Specifically, one will find the declaration of the **CPU_INT16U**, **CPU_INT32U**, **CPU_FP32** and many other data types. This file also specifies whether the CPU is a big or little endian machine, defines the **CPU_STK** data type used by µC/OS-III, defines the macros **CPU_CRITICAL_ENTER()** and **CPU_CRITICAL_EXIT()**, and contains function prototypes for functions specific to the CPU architecture, and more.

cpu_a.asm contains the assembly language functions to implement code to disable and enable CPU interrupts, count leading zeros (if the CPU supports that instruction), and other CPU specific functions that can only be written in assembly language. This file may also contain code to enable caches, setup MPUs and MMU, and more. The functions provided in this file are accessible from C.

cpu_c.c contains C code of functions that are based on a specific CPU architecture but written in C for portability. As a general rule, if a function can be written in C then it should be, unless there is significant performance benefits available by writing it in assembly language.

2-7 µC/LIB, PORTABLE LIBRARY FUNCTIONS

µC/LIB consists of library functions meant to be highly portable and not tied to any specific compiler. This facilitates third-party certification of Micriµm products. µC/OS-III does not use any µC/LIB functions, however µC/OS-III and µC/CPU assumes the presence of `lib_def.h` for such definitions as: `DEF_YES`, `DEF_NO`, `DEF_TRUE`, `DEF_FALSE`, `DEF_ON`, `DEF_OFF` and more.

```
\Micrium
    \Software
        \uC-LIB
            \lib_ascii.c
            \lib_ascii.h
            \lib_def.h
            \lib_math.c
            \lib_math.h
            \lib_mem.c
            \lib_mem.h
            \lib_str.c
            \lib_str.h
            \Cfg\Template
                \lib_cfg.h
            \Ports
                \<architecture>
                    \<compiler>
                        \lib_mem_a.asm
```

\Micrium
Contains all software components and projects provided by Micriµm.

\Software
This sub-directory contains all software components and projects.

\uC-LIB
This is the main µC/LIB directory.

lib_ascii.c and lib_ascii.h contain source code to replace some standard library functions such as tolower(), toupper(), isalpha(), isdigit(), etc. with µC/LIB equivalent functions ASCII_ToLower(), ASCII_ToUpper(), ASCII_IsAlpha(), and ASCII_IsDig(), respectively.

lib_def.h defines constants for many common values such as TRUE/FALSE, YES/NO, ENABLED/DISABLED; as well as for integer, octet, and bit values. However, all #define in this file starts with DEF_ so those constants are actually called DEF_TRUE/DEF_FALSE, DEF_YES/DEF_NO, DEF_ENABLED/DEF_DISABLED, etc. This file also contains macros for common mathematical operations like min(), max(), abs(), bit_set(), bit_clr(), etc. with DEF_MIN(), DEF_MAX(), DEF_ABS(), DEF_BIT_SET(), DEF_BIT_CLR(), respectively.

lib_math.c and lib_math.h contain source code to replace some standard library functions such as rand(), srand(), etc. with µC/LIB equivalent functions Math_Rand(), Math_SetSeed(), respectively.

lib_mem.c and lib_mem.h contain source code to replace some standard library functions such as memclr(), memset(), memcpy(), memcmp(), etc. with µC/LIB equivalent functions Mem_Clr(), Mem_Set(), Mem_Copy(), Mem_Cmp(), respectively.

lib_str.c and lib_str.h contain source code to replace some standard library functions such as strlen(), strcpy(), strcmp(), memcmp(), etc. with µC/LIB equivalent functions Str_Lenr(), Str_Copy(), Str_Cmp(), respectively.

\Cfg\Template

This directory contains a configuration template file (`lib_cfg.h`) that should be copied to the application directory to configure the µC/LIB module based on application requirements.

> `lib_cfg.h` determines whether to enable assembly language optimization (assuming there is an assembly language file for the processor, i.e., `lib_mem_a.asm`) and a few other `#defines`.

\Ports\Architecture\Compiler

This directory contains optimized assembly language files specific to the CPU architecture to replace C functions with much faster assembly language implementations. The presence of this folder depends on whether such assembly language functions were implemented by the port developer of the µC/LIB module.

> `lib_mem_a.asm` contains optimized versions of the `lib_mem.c` functions.

2-8 SUMMARY

Below is a summary of all directories and files involved in a µC/OS-III-based project. The "**<-Cfg**" on the far right indicates that these files are typically copied into the application (i.e., project) directory and edited based on the project requirements.

```
\Micrium
    \Software
        \EvalBoards
            \<manufacturer>
                \<board name>
                    \<compiler>
                        \<project name>
                            \app.c
                            \app.h
                            \other
        \CPU
            \<manufacturer>
                \<architecture>
                    \*.*
```

```
\uCOS-III
    \Cfg\Template
        \os_app_hooks.c
        \os_cfg.h                       <-Cfg
        \os_cfg_app.h                   <-Cfg
    \Source
        \os_cfg_app.c
        \os_core.c
        \os_dbg.c
        \os_flag.c
        \os_int.c
        \os_mem.c
        \os_msg.c
        \os_mutex.c
        \os_pend_multi.c
        \os_prio.c
        \os_q.c
        \os_sem.c
        \os_stat.c
        \os_task.c
        \os_tick.c
        \os_time.c
        \os_tmr.c
        \os_var.c
        \os.h
        \os_type.h                      <-Cfg
    \Ports
        \<architecture>
            \<compiler>
                \os_cpu.h
                \os_cpu_a.asm
                \os_cpu_c.c
\uC-CPU
    \cpu_core.c
    \cpu_core.h
    \cpu_def.h
    \Cfg\Template
        \cpu_cfg.h                      <-Cfg
```

```
        \<architecture>
            \<compiler>
                \cpu.h
                \cpu_a.asm
                \cpu_c.c
\uC-LIB
    \lib_ascii.c
    \lib_ascii.h
    \lib_def.h
    \lib_math.c
    \lib_math.h
    \lib_mem.c
    \lib_mem.h
    \lib_str.c
    \lib_str.h
    \Cfg\Template
        \lib_cfg.h                      <-Cfg
    \Ports
        \<architecture>
            \<compiler>
                \lib_mem_a.asm
```

Chapter

3

Getting Started with µC/OS-III

µC/OS-III provides services to application code in the form of a set of functions that perform specific operations. µC/OS-III offers services to manage tasks, semaphores, message queues, mutual exclusion semaphores and more. As far as the application is concerned, it calls the µC/OS-III functions as if they were any other functions. In other words, the application now has access to a library of approximately 70 new functions.

In this chapter, the reader will appreciate how easy it is to start using µC/OS-III. Refer to Appendix A, "µC/OS-III API Reference" on page 443, for the full description of several of the µC/OS-III services presented in this chapter.

It is assumed that the project setup (files and directories) is as described in the previous chapter, and that a C compiler exists for the target processor that is in use. However, this chapter makes no assumptions about the tools or the processor that is used.

3-1 SINGLE TASK APPLICATION

Listing 3-1 shows the top portion of a simple application file called **app.c**.

```
/*
****************************************************************************
*                           INCLUDE FILES
****************************************************************************
*/
#include <app_cfg.h>                                                   (1)
#include <bsp.h>
#include <os.h>
/*
****************************************************************************
*                       LOCAL GLOBAL VARIABLES
****************************************************************************
*/
static  OS_TCB          AppTaskStartTCB;                               (2)
static  CPU_STK         AppTaskStartStk[APP_TASK_START_STK_SIZE];      (3)
/*
****************************************************************************
*                         FUNCTION PROTOTYPES
****************************************************************************
*/
static  void  AppTaskStart (void *p_arg);                              (4)
```

Listing 3-1 **app.c (1st Part)**

L3-1(1)   As with any C programs, you need to include the necessary headers to build the application.

app_cfg.h is a header file that configures the application. For our example, **app_cfg.h** contains **#define** constants to establish task priorities, stack sizes, and other application specifics.

bsp.h is the header file for the Board Support Package (BSP), which **defines** **#defines** and function prototypes, such as **BSP_Init()**, **BSP_LED_On()**, **OS_TS_GET()** and more.

os.h is the main header file for μC/OS-III, and includes the following header files:

```
os_cfg.h
cpu.h
cpu_core.h
lib_def.h
os_type.h
os_cpu.h
```

L3-1(2)   We will be creating an application task and it is necessary to allocate a task control block (**OS_TCB**) for this task. The **OS_TCB** data type will be described in Chapter 5, "Task Management" on page 91.

L3-1(3)   Each task created requires its own stack. A stack must be declared using the **CPU_STK** data type as shown. The stack can be allocated statically as shown here, or dynamically from the heap using **malloc()**. It should not be necessary to free the stack space, because the task should never be destroyed, and thus, the stack would always be used.

L3-1(4)   This is the function prototype of the task that we will create.

Most C applications start at **main()** as shown in Listing 3-2.

```
void  main (void)
{
    OS_ERR  err;

    BSP_IntDisAll();                                                      (1)
    OSInit(&err);                                                         (2)
    if (err != OS_ERR_NONE) {
        /* Something didn't get initialized correctly ...        */
        /* ... check os.h for the meaning of the error code, see OS_ERR_xxxx */
    }
    OSTaskCreate((OS_TCB       *)&AppTaskStartTCB,                        (3)
                 (CPU_CHAR     *)"App Task Start",                        (4)
                 (OS_TASK_PTR )AppTaskStart,                             (5)
                 (void         *)0,                                       (6)
                 (OS_PRIO      )APP_TASK_START_PRIO,                      (7)
                 (CPU_STK      *)&AppTaskStartStk[0],                     (8)
                 (CPU_STK_SIZE)APP_TASK_START_STK_SIZE / 10,             (9)
                 (CPU_STK_SIZE)APP_TASK_START_STK_SIZE,                  (10)
                 (OS_MSG_QTY  )0,
                 (OS_TICK     )0,
                 (void         *)0,
                 (OS_OPT       )(OS_OPT_TASK_STK_CHK | OS_OPT_TASK_STK_CLR),  (11)
                 (OS_ERR      *)&err);                                   (12)
    if (err != OS_ERR_NONE) {
        /* The task didn't get created.  Lookup the value of the error code ... */
        /* ... in os.h for the meaning of the error                      */
    }
    OSStart(&err);                                                        (13)
    if (err != OS_ERR_NONE) {
        /* Your code is NEVER supposed to come back to this point.       */
    }
}
```

Listing 3-2 **app.c (2nd Part)**

L3-2(1)   The startup code for the compiler will bring the CPU to **main()**. **main()** then starts by calling a BSP function that disables all interrupts. On most processors, interrupts are disabled at startup until explicitly enabled by application code. However, it is safer to turn off all peripheral interrupts during startup.

L3-2(2)   **OSInit()** is the called to initialize µC/OS-III. **OSInit()** initializes internal variables and data structures, and also creates between two (2) and five (5) internal tasks. At a minimum, µC/OS-III creates the idle task (**OS_IdleTask()**), which executes when no other task is ready-to-run. µC/OS-III also creates the tick task, which is responsible for keeping track of time.

Depending on the value of **#define** constants, µC/OS-III will create the statistic task (**OS_StatTask()**), the timer task (**OS_TmrTask()**), and the interrupt handler queue management task (**OS_IntQTask()**). Those are all discussed in Chapter 5, "Task Management" on page 91.

Most of µC/OS-III's functions return an error code via a pointer to an **OS_ERR** variable, err in this case. If **OSInit()** was successful, err will be set to **OS_ERR_NONE**. If **OSInit()** encounters a problem during initialization, it will return immediately upon detecting the problem and set err accordingly. If this occurs, look up the error code value in **os.h**. Specifically, all error codes start with **OS_ERR_**.

It is important to note that **OSInit()** must be called before any other µC/OS-III function.

L3-2(3)   You create a task by calling **OSTaskCreate()**. **OSTaskCreate()** requires 13 arguments. The first argument is the address of the **OS_TCB** that is declared for this task (see L3-1(2)). Chapter 5, "Task Management" on page 91 provides additional information about tasks.

L3-2(4)   **OSTaskCreate()** allows a name to be assigned to each of the tasks. µC/OS-III stores a pointer to the task name inside the **OS_TCB** of the task. There is no limit on the number of ASCII characters used for the name.

L3-2(5)   The third argument is the address of the task code. A typical µC/OS-III task is implemented as an infinite loop as shown:

```
void  MyTask (void *p_arg)
{
    /* Do something with "p_arg".
    while (1) {
        /* Task body */
    }
}
```

The task receives an argument when it first starts. As far as the task is concerned, it looks like any other C function that can be called by the code. However, your code *must not* call **MyTask()**. The call is actually performed through µC/OS-III.

L3-2(6)   The fourth argument of **OSTaskCreate()** is the actual argument that the task receives when it first begins. In other words, the "**p_arg**" of **MyTask()**. In the example a **NULL** pointer is passed, and thus "**p_arg**" for **AppTaskStart()** will be a **NULL** pointer.

The argument passed to the task can actually be any pointer. For example, the user may pass a pointer to a data structure containing parameters for the task.

L3-2(7)   The next argument to **OSTaskCreate()** is the priority of the task. The priority establishes the relative importance of this task with respect to the other tasks in the application. A low-priority number indicates a high priority (or more important task). You can set the priority of the task to any value between 1 and **OS_CFG_PRIO_MAX-2**, inclusively. Avoid using priority #0, and priority **OS_CFG_PRIO_MAX-1**, because these are reserved for µC/OS-III. **OS_CFG_PRIO_MAX** is a compile time configuration constant, which is declared in **os_cfg.h**.

L3-2(8)   The sixth argument to **OSTaskCreate()** is the base address of the stack assigned to this task. The base address is always the lowest memory location of the stack.

L3-2(9)   The next argument specifies the location of a "watermark" in the task's stack that can be used to determine the allowable stack growth of the task. See Chapter 5, "Task Management" on page 91 for more details on using this feature. In the code above, the value represents the amount of stack space (in **CPU_STK** elements) before the stack is empty. In other words, in the example, the limit is reached when there is 10% of the stack left.

L3-2(10)   The eighth argument to **OSTaskCreate()** specifies the size of the task's stack in number of **CPU_STK** elements (not bytes). For example, if you want to allocate 1 Kbyte of stack space for a task and the **CPU_STK** is a 32-bit word, then you need to pass 256.

L3-2(11)   The next three arguments are skipped as they are not relevant for the current discussion. The 12th argument to **OSTaskCreate()** specifies options. In this example, we specify that the stack will be checked at run time (assuming the statistic task was enabled in **os_cfg.h**), and that the contents of the stack will be cleared when the task is created.

L3-2(12)   The last argument of **OSTaskCreate()** is a pointer to a variable that will receive an error code. If **OSTaskCreate()** is successful, the error code will be **OS_ERR_NONE** otherwise, you can look up the value of the error code in **os.h** (see **OS_ERR_xxxx**) to determine the cause of the error.

L3-2(13)   The final step in **main()** is to call **OSStart()**, which starts the multitasking process. Specifically, µC/OS-III will select the highest-priority task that was created before calling **OSStart()**.

You should note that the highest-priority task is always **OS_IntQTask()** if that task is enabled in **os_cfg.h** (through the **OS_CFG_ISR_POST_DEFERRED_EN** constant). If this is the case, **OS_IntQTask()** will perform some initialization of its own and then µC/OS-III will switch to the next most important task that was created.

A few important points are worth noting. For one thing, you can create as many tasks as you want before calling **OSStart()**. However, it is recommended to only create one task as shown in the example because, having a single application task allows µC/OS-III to determine the relative speed of the CPU. This allows µC/OS-III to determine the percentage of CPU usage at run-time. Also, if the application needs other kernel objects such as semaphores and message queues then it is recommended that these be created prior to calling **OSStart()**. Finally, notice that interrupts are not enabled. This will be discussed next by examining the contents of **AppTaskStart()**, which is shown in Listing 3-3.

```
static   void  AppTaskStart (void *p_arg)                      (1)
{
    OS_ERR  err;


    p_arg = p_arg;
    BSP_Init();                                                (2)
    CPU_Init();                                                (3)
    BSP_Cfg_Tick();                                            (4)
    BSP_LED_Off(0);                                            (5)
    while (1) {                                                (6)
        BSP_LED_Toggle(0);                                     (7)
        OSTimeDlyHMSM((CPU_INT16U)  0,                         (8)
                      (CPU_INT16U)  0,
                      (CPU_INT16U)  0,
                      (CPU_INT32U)100,
                      (OS_OPT      )OS_OPT_TIME_HMSM_STRICT,
                      (OS_ERR    *)&err);
        /* Check for 'err' */
    }
}
```

Listing 3-3 **app.c (3rd Part)**

L3-3(1)   As previously mentioned, a task looks like any other C function. The argument "**p_arg**" is passed to **AppTaskStart()** by **OSTaskCreate()**, as discussed in the previous listing description.

L3-3(2)   **BSP_Init()** is a Board Support Package (BSP) function that is responsible for initializing the hardware on an evaluation or target board. The evaluation board might have General Purpose Input Output (GPIO) lines that might need to be configured, relays, sensors and more. This function is found in a file called **bsp.c**.

L3-3(3)   **CPU_Init()** initializes the µC/CPU services. µC/CPU provides services to measure interrupt latency, obtain time stamps, and provides emulation of the count leading zeros instruction if the processor used does not have that instruction, and more.

L3-3(4)   **BSP_Cfg_Tick()** sets up the µC/OS-III tick interrupt. For this, the function needs to initialize one of the hardware timers to interrupt the CPU at a rate of: **OSCfg_TickRate_Hz**, which is defined in **os_cfg_app.h** (See **OS_CFG_TICK_RATE_HZ**).

L3-3(5)   **BSP_LED_Off()** is a function that will turn off all LEDs. **BSP_LED_Off()** is written such that a zero argument means all the LEDs.

L3-3(6)   Most µC/OS-III tasks will need to be written as an infinite loop.

L3-3(7)   This BSP function toggles the state of the specified LED. Again, a zero indicates that all the LEDs should be toggled on the evaluation board. You simply change the zero to 1 and this will cause LED #1 to toggle. Exactly which LED is LED #1? That depends on the BSP developer. Specifically, access to LEDs are encapsulated through the functions: **BSP_LED_On()**, **BSP_LED_Off()** and **BSP_LED_Toggle()**. Also, for sake of portability, we prefer to assign LEDs logical values (1, 2, 3, etc.) instead of specifying which port and which bit on each port.

L3-3(8)   Finally, each task in the application must call one of the µC/OS-III functions that will cause the task to "wait for an event." The task can wait for time to expire (by calling **OSTimeDly()**, or **OSTimeDlyHMSM()**), or wait for a signal or a message from an ISR or another task. In the code shown, we used **OSTimeDlyHMSM()** which allows a task to be suspended until the specified number of hours, minutes, seconds and milliseconds have expired. In this case, 100 ms. Chapter 11, "Time Management" on page 203 provides additional information about time delays.

3-2 MULTIPLE TASKS APPLICATION WITH KERNEL OBJECTS

The code of Listing 3-4 through Listing 3-8 shows a more complete example and contains three tasks: a mutual exclusion, semaphore, and a message queue.

```
/*
*********************************************************************************
*                                INCLUDE FILES
*********************************************************************************
*/
#include <app_cfg.h>
#include <bsp.h>
#include <os.h>
/*
*********************************************************************************
*                            LOCAL GLOBAL VARIABLES
*********************************************************************************
*/
static  OS_TCB          AppTaskStartTCB;                         (1)
static  OS_TCB          AppTask1_TCB;
static  OS_TCB          AppTask2_TCB;
static  OS_MUTEX        AppMutex;                                (2)
static  OS_Q            AppQ;                                    (3)
static  CPU_STK         AppTaskStartStk[APP_TASK_START_STK_SIZE];(4)
static  CPU_STK         AppTask1_Stk[128];
static  CPU_STK         AppTask2_Stk[128];
/*
*********************************************************************************
*                              FUNCTION PROTOTYPES
*********************************************************************************
*/
static  void  AppTaskStart (void *p_arg);                        (5)
static  void  AppTask1     (void *p_arg);
static  void  AppTask2     (void *p_arg);
```

Listing 3-4 **app.c (1st Part)**

L3-4(1)   Here we allocate storage for the **OS_TCB**s of each task.

L3-4(2)   A mutual exclusion semaphore (a.k.a. a mutex) is a kernel object (a data structure) that is used to protect a shared resource from being accessed by more than one task. A task that wants to access the shared resource must obtain the mutex before it is allowed to proceed. The owner of the resource relinquishes the mutex when it has finished accessing the resource. This process is demonstrated in this example.

L3-4(3)   A message queue is a kernel object through which Interrupt Service Routines (ISRs) and/or tasks send messages to other tasks. The sender "formulates" a message and sends it to the message queue. The task(s) wanting to receive these messages wait on the message queue for messages to arrive. If there are already messages in the message queue, the receiver immediately retrieves those messages. If there are no messages waiting in the message queue, then the receiver will be placed in a wait list associated with the message queue. This process will be demonstrated in this example.

L3-4(4)   A stack is allocated for each task.

L3-4(5)   The prototype of the tasks are declared.

Listing 3-5 shows the C entry point, i.e. **main( )**.

```
void  main (void)
{
    OS_ERR  err;

    BSP_IntDisAll();
    OSInit(&err);
    /* Check for 'err' */

    OSMutexCreate((OS_MUTEX   *)&AppMutex,                                          (1)
                  (CPU_CHAR   *)"My App. Mutex",
                  (OS_ERR     *)&err);
    /* Check for 'err' */

    OSQCreate    ((OS_Q       *)&AppQ,                                             (2)
                  (CPU_CHAR   *)"My App Queue",
                  (OS_MSG_QTY )10,
                  (OS_ERR     *)&err);
    /* Check for 'err' */

    OSTaskCreate((OS_TCB      *)&AppTaskStartTCB,                                  (3)
                 (CPU_CHAR    *)"App Task Start",
                 (OS_TASK_PTR )AppTaskStart,
                 (void        *)0,
                 (OS_PRIO     )APP_TASK_START_PRIO,
                 (CPU_STK     *)&AppTaskStartStk[0],
                 (CPU_STK_SIZE)APP_TASK_START_STK_SIZE / 10,
                 (CPU_STK_SIZE)APP_TASK_START_STK_SIZE,
                 (OS_MSG_QTY  )0,
                 (OS_TICK     )0,
                 (void        *)0,
                 (OS_OPT      )(OS_OPT_TASK_STK_CHK | OS_OPT_TASK_STK_CLR),
                 (OS_ERR      *)&err);
    /* Check for 'err' */

    OSStart(&err);
    /* Check for 'err' */
}
```

Listing 3-5 **app.c (2nd Part)**

L3-5(1)   Creating a mutex is simply a matter of calling **OSMutexCreate()**. You need to specify the address of the **OS_MUTEX** object that will be used for the mutex. Chapter 13, "Resource Management" on page 231 provides additional information about mutual exclusion semaphores.

You can assign an ASCII name to the mutex, which is useful when debugging.

L3-5(2)   You create the message queue by calling **OSQCreate()** and specify the address of the **OS_Q** object. Chapter 15, "Message Passing" on page 309 provides additional information about message queues.

You can assign an ASCII name to the message queue which can also be useful during debugging.

You need to specify how many messages the message queue is allowed to receive. This value must be greater than zero. If the sender sends messages faster than they can be consumed by the receiving task, messages will be lost. This can be corrected by either increasing the size of the message queue, or increasing the priority of the receiving task.

L3-5(3)   The first application task is created.

Listing 3-6 shows how to create other tasks once multitasking as started.

```
static  void  AppTaskStart (void *p_arg)
{
    OS_ERR  err;


    p_arg = p_arg;
    BSP_Init();
    CPU_Init();
    BSP_Cfg_Tick();
    OSTaskCreate((OS_TCB     *)&AppTask1_TCB,                                    (1)
                 (CPU_CHAR   *)"App Task 1",
                 (OS_TASK_PTR )AppTask1,
                 (void       *)0,
                 (OS_PRIO     )5,
                 (CPU_STK    *)&AppTask1_Stk[0],
                 (CPU_STK_SIZE)0,
                 (CPU_STK_SIZE)128,
                 (OS_MSG_QTY  )0,
                 (OS_TICK     )0,
                 (void       *)0,
                 (OS_OPT      )(OS_OPT_TASK_STK_CHK | OS_OPT_TASK_STK_CLR),
                 (OS_ERR     *)&err);

    OSTaskCreate((OS_TCB     *)&AppTask2_TCB,                                    (2)
                 (CPU_CHAR   *)"App Task 2",
                 (OS_TASK_PTR )AppTask2,
                 (void       *)0,
                 (OS_PRIO     )6,
                 (CPU_STK    *)&AppTask2_Stk[0],
                 (CPU_STK_SIZE)0,
                 (CPU_STK_SIZE)128,
                 (OS_MSG_QTY  )0,
                 (OS_TICK     )0,
                 (void       *)0,
                 (OS_OPT      )(OS_OPT_TASK_STK_CHK | OS_OPT_TASK_STK_CLR),
                 (OS_ERR     *)&err);
    BSP_LED_Off(0);
    while (1) {
        BSP_LED_Toggle(0);
        OSTimeDlyHMSM((CPU_INT16U)  0,
                      (CPU_INT16U)  0,
                      (CPU_INT16U)  0,
                      (CPU_INT32U)100,
                      (OS_OPT     )OS_OPT_TIME_HMSM_STRICT,
                      (OS_ERR    *)&err);
    }
}
```

Listing 3-6 **app.c (3rd Part)**

L3-6(1)   Task #1 is created by calling **OSTaskCreate()**. If this task happens to have a higher priority than the task that creates it, µC/OS-III will immediately start Task #1. If the created task has a lower priority, **OSTaskCreate()** will return to **AppTaskStart()** and continue execution.

L3-6(2)   Task #2 is created and if it has a higher priority than **AppTaskStart()**, µC/OS-III will immediately switch to that task.

```
static  void  AppTask1 (void *p_arg)
{
    OS_ERR  err;
    CPU_TS  ts;


    p_arg = p_arg;
    while (1) {
        OSTimeDly ((OS_TICK    )1,                          (1)
                   (OS_OPT     )OS_OPT_TIME_DLY,
                   (OS_ERR     *)&err);
        OSQPost    ((OS_Q      *)&AppQ,                      (2)
                    (void      *)1;
                    (OS_MSG_SIZE)sizeof(void *),
                    (OS_OPT     )OS_OPT_POST_FIFO,
                    (OS_ERR     *)&err);
        OSMutexPend((OS_MUTEX  *)&AppMutex,                  (3)
                    (OS_TICK    )0,
                    (OS_OPT     )OS_OPT_PEND_BLOCKING;
                    (CPU_TS     *)&ts,
                    (OS_ERR     *)&err);
        /* Access shared resource */                        (4)
        OSMutexPost((OS_MUTEX  *)&AppMutex,                  (5)
                    (OS_OPT     )OS_OPT_POST_NONE,
                    (OS_ERR     *)&err);
    }
}
```

Listing 3-7 **app.c (4th Part)**

L3-7(1)   The task starts by waiting for one tick to expire before it does anything useful. If the µC/OS-III tick rate is configured for 1000 Hz, the task will be suspended for 1 millisecond.

L3-7(2) The task then sends a message to another task using the message queue **AppQ**. In this case, the example sends a fixed message of value "1," but the message could have consisted of the address of a buffer, the address of a function, or whatever would need to be sent.

L3-7(3) The task then waits on the mutual exclusion semaphore since it needs to access a shared resource with another task. If the resource is already owned by another task, **AppTask1()** will wait forever for the mutex to be released by its current owner. The forever wait is specified by passing 0 as the second argument of the call.

L3-7(4) When **OSMutexPend()** returns, the task owns the resource and can therefore access the shared resource. The shared resource may be a variable, an array, a data structure, an I/O device, etc. You should note that we didn't actually show the access to the shared resource. This is not relevant at this point.

L3-7(5) When the task is done with the shared resource, it must call **OSMutexPost()** to release the mutex.

```
static  void  AppTask2 (void *p_arg)
{
    OS_ERR        err;
    void          *p_msg;
    OS_MSG_SIZE   msg_size;
    CPU_TS        ts;
    CPU_TS        ts_delta;


    p_arg = p_arg;
    while (1) {
        p_msg = OSQPend((OS_Q          *)&AppQ,                       (1)
                        (OS_MSG_SIZE *)&msg_size,
                        (OS_TICK      )0,
                        (OS_OPT       )OS_OPT_PEND_BLOCKING,
                        (CPU_TS       *)&ts,
                        (OS_ERR       *)&err);
        ts_delta = OS_TS_GET() - ts;                                 (2)
        /* Process message received */                              (3)
    }
}
```

Listing 3-8 **app.c (5th Part)**

L3-8(1)   Task #2 starts by waiting for messages to be sent through the message queue **AppQ**. The task waits forever for a message to be received because the third argument specifies an infinite timeout.

When the message is received **p_msg** will contain the message (i.e., a pointer to "something"). In our case, **AppTask2()** will always receive a message value of '1'. Both the sender and receiver must agree as to the meaning of the message. The size of the message received is saved in "**msg_size**". Note that "**p_msg**" could point to a buffer and "**msg_size**" would indicate the size of this buffer.

Also, when the message is received, "**ts**" will contain the timestamp of when the message was sent. A timestamp is the value read from a fairly fast free-running timer. The timestamp is typically an unsigned 32-bit (or more) value.

L3-8(2)   Knowing when the message was sent allows the user to determine how long it took this task to get the message. This is done by reading the current timestamp and subtracting the timestamp of when the message was sent allows users to know how long it took for the message to be received. Note that the receiving task may not get the message immediately since ISRs or other higher-priority tasks might execute before the receiver gets to run.

L3-8(3)   Here you would add your own code to process the received message.

Chapter

4

Critical Sections

A critical section of code, also called a *critical region*, is code that needs to be treated indivisibly. There are many critical sections of code contained in µC/OS-III. If a critical section is accessible by an Interrupt Service Routine (ISR) and a task, then disabling interrupts is necessary to protect the critical region. If the critical section is only accessible by task level code, the critical section may be protected through the use of a *preemption lock*.

Within µC/OS-III, the critical section access method depends on which ISR post method is used by interrupts (see Chapter 9, "Interrupt Management" on page 175). If **OS_CFG_ISR_POST_DEFERRED_EN** is set to 0 (see **os_cfg.h**) then µC/OS-III will disable interrupts when accessing internal critical sections. If **OS_CFG_ISR_POST_DEFERRED_EN** is set to 1 then µC/OS-III will lock the scheduler when accessing most of its internal critical sections.

Chapter 9, "Interrupt Management" on page 175 discusses how to select the method to use.

µC/OS-III defines one macro for entering a critical section and two macros for leaving:

```
OS_CRITICAL_ENTER(),
OS_CRITICAL_EXIT() and
OS_CRITICAL_EXIT_NO_SCHED()
```

These macros are internal to µC/OS-III and must not be invoked by the application code. However, if you need to access critical sections in your application code, consult Chapter 13, "Resource Management" on page 231.

4-1 DISABLING INTERRUPTS

When setting OS_CFG_ISR_POST_DEFERRED_EN to 0, µC/OS-III will disable interrupts before entering a critical section and re-enable them when leaving the critical section.

OS_CRITICAL_ENTER() invokes the µC/CPU macro CPU_CRITICAL_ENTER() that, in turn, calls CPU_SR_Save(). CPU_SR_Save() is a function typically written in assembly language that saves the current interrupt disable status and then disables interrupts. The saved interrupt disable status is returned to the caller and in fact, it is stored onto the caller's stack in a variable called "cpu_sr".

OS_CRITICAL_EXIT() and OS_CRITICAL_EXIT_NO_SCHED() both invoke the µC/CPU macro CPU_CRITICAL_EXIT(), which maps to CPU_SR_Restore(). CPU_SR_Restore() is passed the value of the saved "cpu_sr" variable to re-establish interrupts the way they were prior to calling OS_CRITICAL_ENTER().

The typical code for the macros is shown in Listing 4-1.

```
#define  OS_CRITICAL_ENTER()          { CPU_CRITICAL_ENTER(); }
#define  OS_CRITICAL_EXIT()           { CPU_CRITICAL_EXIT();  }
#define  OS_CRITICAL_EXIT_NO_SCHED()  { CPU_CRITICAL_EXIT();  }
```

Listing 4-1 **Critical section code – Disabling interrupts**

4-1-1 MEASURING INTERRUPT DISABLE TIME

µC/CPU provides facilities to measure the amount of time interrupts are disabled. This is done by setting the configuration constant CPU_CFG_INT_DIS_MEAS_EN to 1 in cpu_cfg.h.

The measurement is started each time interrupts are disabled and ends when interrupts are re-enabled. The measurement keeps track of two values: a global interrupt disable time, and an interrupt disable time for each task. Therefore, it is possible to know how long a task disables interrupts, enabling the user to better optimize their code.

The per-task interrupt disable time is saved in the task's OS_TCB during a context switch (see OSTaskSwHook() in os_cpu_c.c and described in Chapter 8, "Context Switching" on page 165).

The unit of measure for the measured time is in CPU_TS (timestamp) units. It is necessary to find out the resolution of the timer used to measure these timestamps. For example, if the timer used for the timestamp is incremented at 1 MHz then the resolution of **CPU_TS** is 1 microsecond.

Measuring the interrupt disable time obviously adds measurement artifacts and thus increases the amount of time the interrupts are disabled. However, as far as the measurement is concerned, measurement overhead is accounted for and the measured value represents the actual interrupt disable time as if the measurement was not present.

Interrupt disable time is obviously greatly affected by the speed at which the processor accesses instructions and thus, the memory access speed. In this case, the hardware designer might have introduced wait states to memory accesses, which affects overall performance of the system. This may show up as unusually long interrupt disable times.

4-2 LOCKING THE SCHEDULER

When setting **OS_CFG_ISR_POST_DEFERRED_EN** to 1, µC/OS-III locks the scheduler before entering a critical section and unlocks the scheduler when leaving the critical section.

OS_CRITICAL_ENTER() simply increments **OSSchedLockNestingCtr** to lock the scheduler. This is the variable the scheduler uses to determine whether or not the scheduler is locked. It is locked when the value is non-zero.

OS_CRITICAL_EXIT() decrements **OSSchedLockNestingCtr** and when the value reaches zero, invokes the scheduler.

OS_CRITICAL_EXIT_NO_SCHED() also decrements **OSSchedLockNestingCtr**, but does not invoke the scheduler when the value reaches zero.

The code for the macros is shown in Listing 4-2.

```
#define  OS_CRITICAL_ENTER()              {                                              \
                                            CPU_CRITICAL_ENTER();                        \
                                            OSSchedLockNestingCtr++;                     \
                                            CPU_CRITICAL_EXIT();                         \
                                          }
#define  OS_CRITICAL_EXIT()               {
                                            CPU_CRITICAL_ENTER();                        \
                                            OSSchedLockNestingCtr--;                     \
                                            if (OSSchedLockNestingCtr == (OS_NESTING_CTR)0) {  \
                                                CPU_CRITICAL_EXIT();                     \
                                                OSSched();                               \
                                            } else {                                     \
                                                CPU_CRITICAL_EXIT();                     \
                                            }                                            \
                                          }
#define  OS_CRITICAL_EXIT_NO_SCHED()      {
                                            CPU_CRITICAL_ENTER();                        \
                                            OSSchedLockNestingCtr--;                     \
                                            CPU_CRITICAL_EXIT();                         \
                                          }
```

Listing 4-2 **Critical section code – Locking the Scheduler**

4-2-1 MEASURING SCHEDULER LOCK TIME

µC/OS-III provides facilities to measure the amount of time the scheduler is locked. This is done by setting the configuration constant **OS_CFG_SCHED_LOCK_TIME_MEAS_EN** to 1 in **os_cfg.h**.

The measurement is started each time the scheduler is locked and ends when the scheduler is unlocked. The measurement keeps track of two values: a global scheduler lock time, and a per-task scheduler lock time. It is therefore possible to know how long each task locks the scheduler allowing the user to better optimize code.

The per-task scheduler lock time is saved in the task's **OS_TCB** during a context switch (see **OSTaskSwHook()** in **os_cpu_c.c** and described in Chapter 8, "Context Switching" on page 165).

The unit of measure for the measured time is in **CPU_TS** (timestamp) units so it is necessary to find the resolution of the timer used to measure the timestamps. For example, if the timer used for the timestamp is incremented at 1 MHz then the resolution of **CPU_TS** is 1 microsecond.

Measuring the scheduler lock time adds measurement artifacts and thus increases the amount of time the scheduler is actually locked. However, measurement overhead is accounted for and the measured value represents the actual scheduler lock time as if the measurement was not present.

4-3 µC/OS-III FEATURES WITH LONGER CRITICAL SECTIONS

Table 4-1 shows several µC/OS-III features that have potentially longer critical sections. Knowledge of these will help the user decide whether to direct µC/OS-III to use one critical section over another.

Feature	Reason
Multiple tasks at the same priority	Although this is an important feature of µC/OS-III, multiple tasks at the same priority create longer critical sections. However, if there are only a few tasks at the same priority, interrupt latency would be relatively small. If multiple tasks are not created at the same priority, use the interrupt disable method.
Event Flags Chapter 14, "Synchronization" on page 273	If multiple tasks are waiting on different events, going through all of the tasks waiting for events requires a fair amount of processing time, which means longer critical sections. If only a few tasks (approximately one to five) are waiting on an event flag group, the critical section would be short enough to use the interrupt disable method.
Pend on multiple objects Chapter 16, "Pending On Multiple Objects" on page 333	Pending on multiple objects is probably the most complex feature provided by µC/OS-III, requiring interrupts to be disabled for fairly long periods of time should the interrupt disable method be selected. If pending on multiple objects, it is highly recommended that the user select the scheduler-lock method. If the application does not use this feature, the interrupt disable method is an alternative.
Broadcast on Post calls See OSSemPost() and OSQPost() descriptions in Appendix A, "µC/OS-III API Reference" on page 443.	µC/OS-III disables interrupts while processing a post to multiple tasks in a broadcast. When not using the broadcast option, you can use the interrupt disable method.

Table 4-1 **Disabling interrupts or locking the Scheduler**

4-4 SUMMARY

µC/OS-III needs to access critical sections of code, which it protects by either disabling interrupts (OS_CFG_ISR_POST_DEFERRED_EN set to 0 in **os_cfg.h**), or locking the scheduler (OS_CFG_ISR_POST_DEFERRED_EN set to 1 in **os_cfg.h**).

The application code must not use:

```
OS_CRITICAL_ENTER( )
OS_CRITICAL_EXIT( )
OS_CRITICAL_EXIT_NO_SCHED( )
```

When setting CPU_CFG_INT_DIS_MEAS_EN in **cpu_cfg.h**, µC/CPU measures the maximum interrupt disable time. There are two values available, one for the global maximum and one for each task.

When setting **OS_CFG_SCHED_LOCK_TIME_MEAS_EN** to 1 in **os_cfg.h**, µC/OS-III will measure the maximum scheduler lock time.

Task Management

The design process of a real-time application generally involves splitting the work to be completed into tasks, each responsible for a portion of the problem. µC/OS-III makes it easy for an application programmer to adopt this paradigm. A task (also called a *thread*) is a simple program that thinks it has the Central Processing Unit (CPU) all to itself. On a single CPU, only one task can execute at any given time.

µC/OS-III supports multitasking and allows the application to have any number of tasks. The maximum number of task is actually only limited by the amount of memory (both code and data space) available to the processor. Multitasking is the process of *scheduling* and *switching* the CPU between several tasks (this will be expanded upon later). The CPU switches its attention between several *sequential* tasks. Multitasking provides the illusion of having multiple CPUs and, actually maximizes the use of the CPU. Multitasking also helps in the creation of modular applications. One of the most important aspects of multitasking is that it allows the application programmer to manage the complexity inherent in real-time applications. Application programs are typically easier to design and maintain when multitasking is used.

Tasks are used for such chores as monitoring inputs, updating outputs, performing computations, control loops, update one or more displays, reading buttons and keyboards, communicating with other systems, and more. One application may contain a handful of tasks while another application may require hundreds. The number of tasks does not establish how good or effective a design may be, it really depends on what the application (or product) needs to do. The amount of work a task performs also depends on the application. One task may have a few microseconds worth of work to perform while another task may require tens of milliseconds.

Tasks look like just any other C function except for a few small differences. There are two types of tasks: run-to-completion (Listing 5-1) and infinite loop (Listing 5-2). In most embedded systems, tasks typically take the form of an infinite loop. Also, no task is allowed to return as other C functions can. Given that a task is a regular C function, it can declare local variables.

5

When a µC/OS-III task begins executing, it is passed an argument, **p_arg**. This argument is a pointer to a **void**. The pointer is a universal vehicle used to pass your task the address of a variable, a structure, or even the address of a function, if necessary. With this pointer, it is possible to create many identical tasks, that all use the same code (or task body), but, with different run-time characteristics. For example, you may have four asynchronous serial ports that are each managed by their own task. However, the task code is actually identical. Instead of copying the code four times, you can create the code for a "generic" task that receives a pointer to a data structure, which contains the serial port's parameters (baud rate, I/O port addresses, interrupt vector number, etc.) as an argument. In other words, you can instantiate the same task code four times and pass it different data for each serial port that each instance will manage.

A run-to-completion task must *delete* itself by calling **OSTaskDel()**. The task starts, performs its function, and terminates. There would typically not be too many such tasks in the embedded system because of the overhead associated with "creating" and "deleting" tasks at run-time. In the task body, you can call most of µC/OS-III's functions to help perform the desired operation of the task.

```
void MyTask (void *p_arg)
{
    OS_ERR   err;
    /* Local variables                         */


    /* Do something with 'p_arg'               */
    /* Task initialization                     */
    /* Task body ... do work!                  */
    OSTaskDel((OS_TCB *)0, &err);
}
```

Listing 5-1 **Run-To-Completion task**

With µC/OS-III, you either can call a C or assembly language functions from a task. In fact, it is possible to call the same C function from different tasks as long as the functions are reentrant. A *reentrant* function is a function that does not use static or otherwise global variables unless they are protected (µC/OS-III provides mechanisms for this) from multiple access. If shared C functions only use local variables, they are generally reentrant (assuming that the compiler generates reentrant code). An example of a non-reentrant function is the famous **strtok()** provided by most C compilers as part of the standard library. This function is used to parse an ASCII string for "tokens." The first time you call this function, you specify the ASCII string to parse and a list of token delimiters. As soon as the function finds the first token, it returns. The function "remembers" where it was last so when called again, it can extract additional tokens, which is clearly non-reentrant.

The use of an infinite loop is more common in embedded systems because of the repetitive work needed in such systems (reading inputs, updating displays, performing control operations, etc.). This is one aspect that makes a task different than a regular C function. Note that one could use a "**while (1)**" or "**for (;;)**" to implement the infinite loop, since both behave the same. The one used is simply a matter of personal preference. At Micrium, we like to use "**while (DEF_ON)**". The infinite loop **must** call a μC/OS-III service (i.e., function) that will cause the task to wait for an event to occur. It is important that each task wait for an event to occur, otherwise the task would be a true infinite loop and there would be no easy way for other lower priority tasks to execute. This concept will become clear as more is understood regarding μC/OS-III.

```
void MyTask (void *p_arg)
{
    /* Local variables                                          */


    /* Do something with "p_arg"                                */
    /* Task initialization                                      */
    while (DEF_ON) {        /* Task body, as an infinite loop.  */
        :
        /* Task body ... do work!                               */
        :
        /* Must call one of the following services:             */
        /*    OSFlagPend()                                       */
        /*    OSMutexPend()                                      */
        /*    OSPendMulti()                                      */
        /*    OSQPend()                                          */
        /*    OSSemPend()                                        */
        /*    OSTimeDly()                                        */
        /*    OSTimeDlyHMSM()                                    */
        /*    OSTaskQPend()                                      */
        /*    OSTaskSemPend()                                    */
        /*    OSTaskSuspend()      (Suspend self)               */
        /*    OSTaskDel()          (Delete  self)               */
        :
        /* Task body ... do work!                               */
        :

    }
}
```

Listing 5-2 **Infinite Loop task**

The event the task is waiting for may simply be the passage of time (when **OSTimeDly()** or **OSTimeDlyHMSM()** is called). For example, a design may need to scan a keyboard every 100 milliseconds. In this case, you would simply delay the task for 100 milliseconds then see if a key was pressed on the keyboard and, possibly perform some action based on which key was pressed. Typically, however, a keyboard scanning task should just buffer an "identifier" unique to the key pressed and use another task to decide what to do with the key(s) pressed.

Similarly, the event the task is waiting for could be the arrival of a packet from an Ethernet controller. In this case, the task would call one of the **OS???Pend()** calls (pend is synonymous with wait). The task will have nothing to do until the packet is received. Once the packet is received, the task processes the contents of the packet, and possibly moves the packet along a network stack.

It's important to note that when a task waits for an event, it does not consume CPU time.

Tasks must be created in order for µC/OS-III to know about tasks. You create a task by simply calling **OSTaskCreate()** as we've seen in Chapter 3. The function prototype for **OSTaskCreate()** is shown below:

```
void  OSTaskCreate (OS_TCB         *p_tcb,
                    OS_CHAR        *p_name,
                    OS_TASK_PTR     p_task,
                    void           *p_arg,
                    OS_PRIO         prio,
                    CPU_STK        *p_stk_base,
                    CPU_STK_SIZE    stk_limit,
                    CPU_STK_SIZE    stk_size,
                    OS_MSG_QTY      q_size,
                    OS_TICK         time_slice,
                    void           *p_ext,
                    OS_OPT          opt,
                    OS_ERR         *p_err)
```

A complete description of **OSTaskCreate()** and its arguments is provided in Appendix A, "µC/OS-III API Reference" on page 443. However, it is important to understand that a task needs to be assigned a *Task Control Block* (i.e., TCB), a stack, a priority and a few other parameters which are initialized by **OSTaskCreate()**, as shown in Figure 5-1.

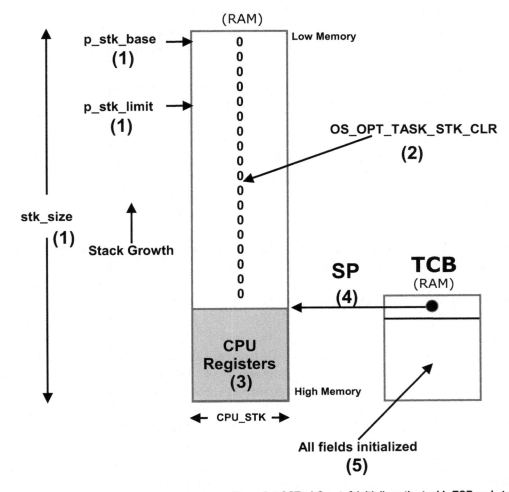

Figure 5-1 **OSTaskCreate() initializes the task's TCB and stack**

F5-1(1)   When calling **OSTaskCreate()**, you pass the base address of the stack (**p_stk_base**) that will be used by the task, the watermark limit for stack growth (**stk_limit**) which is expressed in number of **CPU_STK** entries before the stack is empty, and the size of that stack (**stk_size**), also in number of **CPU_STK** elements.

F5-1(2)   When specifying **OS_OPT_TASK_STK_CHK** + **OS_OPT_TASK_STK_CLR** in the opt argument of **OSTaskCreate()**, µC/OS-III initializes the task's stack with all zeros.

F5-1(3)   µC/OS-III then initializes the top of the task's stack with a copy of the CPU registers in the same stacking order as if they were all saved at the beginning of an ISR. This makes it easy to perform context switches as we will see when discussing the context switching process. For illustration purposes, the assumption is that the stack grows from high memory to low memory, but the same concept applies for CPUs that use the stack in the reverse order.

F5-1(4)   The new value of the stack pointer (SP) is saved in the TCB. Note that this is also called the **top-of-stack**.

F5-1(5)   The remaining fields of the TCB are initialized: task priority, task name, task state, internal message queue, internal semaphore, and many others.

Next, a call is made to a function that is defined in the CPU port, **OSTaskCreateHook()** (see **os_cpu_c.c**). **OSTaskCreateHook()** is passed the pointer to the new TCB and this function allows you (or the port designer) to extend the functionality of **OSTaskCreate()**. For example, one could printout the contents of the fields of the newly created TCB onto a terminal for debugging purposes.

The task is then placed in the ready-list (see Chapter 6, "The Ready List" on page 141) and finally, if multitasking has started, µC/OS-III will invoke the scheduler to see if the created task is now the highest priority task and, if so, will context switch to this new task.

The body of the task can invoke other services provided by µC/OS-III. Specifically, a task can create another task (i.e., call **OSTaskCreate()**), suspend and resume other tasks (i.e., call **OSTaskSuspend()** and **OSTaskResume()** respectively), post signals or messages to other tasks (i.e., call **OS??Post()**), share resources with other tasks, and more. In other words, tasks are not limited to only make "wait for an event" function calls.

Figure 5-2 shows the resources with which a task typically interacts.

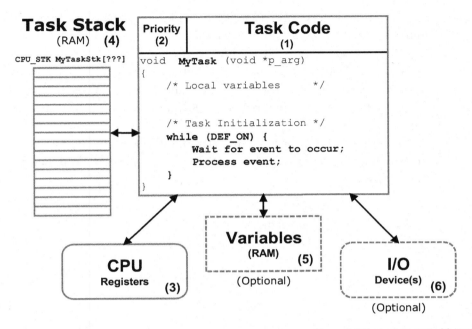

Figure 5-2 **Tasks interact with resources**

F5-2(1)   An important aspect of a task is its code. As previously mentioned, the code looks like any other C function, except that it is typically implemented as an infinite loop and, a task is not allowed to return.

F5-2(2)   Each task is assigned a priority based on its importance in the application. μC/OS-III's job is to decide which task will run on the CPU. The general rule is that μC/OS-III will run the most important *ready-to-run* task (highest priority).

With μC/OS-III, a low priority number indicates a high priority. In other words, a task at priority 1 is more important than a task at priority 10.

μC/OS-III supports a compile-time user configurable number of different priorities (see **OS_PRIO_MAX** in **os_cfg.h**). Thus, μC/OS-III allows the user to determine the number of different priority levels the application is allowed to use. Also, μC/OS-III supports an unlimited number of tasks at the same priority. For example, μC/OS-III can be configured to have 64 different priority levels and one can assign dozens of tasks at each priority level.

See section 5-1 "Assigning Task Priorities" on page 100.

F5-2(3)   A task has its own set of CPU registers. As far as a task is concerned, the task thinks it actually has the CPU all to itself.

F5-2(4)   Because µC/OS-III is a preemptive kernel, each task must have its own stack area. The stack always resides in RAM and is used to keep track of local variables, function calls, and possibly ISR (Interrupt Service Routine) nesting.

Stack space can be allocated either statically (at compile-time) or dynamically (at run-time). A static stack declaration is shown below. This declaration is made outside of a function.

```
static  CPU_STK MyTaskStk[???];
```

or,

```
CPU_STK MyTaskStk[???];
```

Note that "**???**" indicates that the size of the stack (and thus the array) depends on the task stack requirements. Stack space may be allocated dynamically by using the C compiler's heap management function (i.e., **malloc()**) as shown below. However, care must be taken with fragmentation. If creating and deleting tasks, the process of allocating memory might not be able to provide a stack for the task(s) because the heap will eventually become fragmented. For this reason, allocating stack space dynamically in an embedded system is typically allowed but, once allocated, stacks should not be deallocated. Said another way, it's fine to create a task's stack from the heap as long as you don't free the stack space back to the heap.

```
void SomeCode (void)
{
    CPU_STK *p_stk;
    :
    :
    p_stk = (CPU_STK *)malloc(stk_size);
    if (p_stk != (CPU_STK *)0) {
        Create the task and pass it "p_stk" as the base address of the stack;
    }
    :
    :
}
```

See section 5-2 "Determining the Size of a Stack" on page 102.

F5-2(5)   A task can also have access to global variables. However, because µC/OS-III is a preemptive kernel care must be taken with code when accessing such variables as they may be shared between multiple tasks. Fortunately, µC/OS-III provides mechanisms to help with the management of such shared resources (semaphores, mutexes and more).

F5-2(6)   A task may also have access to one or more Input/Output (I/O) devices (also known as *peripherals*). In fact, it is common practice to assign tasks to manage I/O devices.

5

5-1 ASSIGNING TASK PRIORITIES

Sometimes task priorities are both obvious and intuitive. For example, if the most important aspect of the embedded system is to perform some type of control and it is known that the control algorithm must be responsive then it is best to assign the control task(s) a high priority while display and operator interface tasks are assigned low priority. However, most of the time, assigning task priorities is not so cut and dry because of the complex nature of real-time systems. In most systems, not all tasks are considered critical, and non-critical tasks should obviously be given low priorities.

An interesting technique called rate monotonic scheduling (RMS) assigns task priorities based on how often tasks execute. Simply put, tasks with the highest rate of execution are given the highest priority. However, RMS makes a number of assumptions, including:

■ All tasks are periodic (they occur at regular intervals).

■ Tasks do not synchronize with one another, share resources, or exchange data.

■ The CPU must always execute the highest priority task that is ready-to-run. In other words, preemptive scheduling must be used.

Given a set of **n** tasks that are assigned RMS priorities, the basic RMS theorem states that all task hard real-time deadlines are always met if the following inequality holds true:

$$\sum_i \frac{E_i}{T_i} \le n \left(2^{1/n} - 1 \right)$$

Where **Ei** corresponds to the maximum execution time of task **i**, and **Ti** corresponds to the execution period of task **i**. In other words, **Ei/Ti** corresponds to the fraction of CPU time required to execute task **i**.

Table 5-1 shows the value for size $n(2^{1/n} - 1)$ based on the number of tasks. The upper bound for an infinite number of tasks is given by **ln(2)**, or **0.693**, which means that you meet all hard real-time deadlines based on RMS, CPU usage of all time-critical tasks should be less than 70 percent!

Note that you can still have non time-critical tasks in a system and thus use close to 100 percent of the CPU's time. However, using 100 percent of your CPU's time is not a desirable goal as it does not allow for code changes and added features. As a rule of thumb, always design a system to use less than 60 to 70 percent of the CPU.

RMS says that the highest rate task has the highest priority. In some cases, the highest rate task might not be the most important task. The application should dictate how to assign priorities. However, RMS is an interesting starting point.

Number of Tasks	$n(2^{1/n}-1)$
1	1.00
2	0.828
3	0.779
4	0.756
5	0.743
:	:
:	:
:	:
Infinite	0.693

Table 5-1 **Allowable CPU usage based on number of tasks**

5-2 DETERMINING THE SIZE OF A STACK

The size of the stack required by the task is application specific. When sizing the stack, however, one must account for the nesting of all the functions called by the task, the number of local variables to be allocated by all functions called by the task, and the stack requirements for all nested interrupt service routines. In addition, the stack must be able to store all CPU registers and possibly Floating-Point Unit (FPU) registers if the processor has a FPU. In addition, as a general rule in embedded systems, avoid writing recursive code.

It is possible to manually figure out the stack space needed by adding all the memory required by all function call nesting (1 pointer each function call for the return address), plus all the memory required by all the arguments passed in those function calls, plus storage for a full CPU context (depends on the CPU), plus another full CPU context for each nested ISRs (if the CPU doesn't have a separate stack to handle ISRs), plus whatever stack space is needed by those ISRs. Adding all this up is a tedious chore and the resulting number is a minimum requirement. Most likely you would not make the stack size that precise in order to account for "surprises." The number arrived at should probably be multiplied by some safety factor, possibly 1.5 to 2.0. This calculation assumes that the exact path of the code is known at all times, which is not always possible. Specifically, when calling a function such as **printf()** or some other library function, it might be difficult or nearly impossible to even guess just how much stack space **printf()** will require. In this case, start with a fairly large stack space and monitor the stack usage at run-time to see just how much stack space is actually used after the application runs for a while.

There are really cool and clever compilers/linkers that provide this information in a link map. For each function, the link map indicates the worst-case stack usage. This feature clearly enables you to better evaluate stack usage for each task. It is still necessary to add the stack space for a **full CPU** context plus, another **full CPU** context for each nested ISR (if the CPU does not have a separate stack to handle ISRs), plus whatever stack space is needed by those ISRs. Again, allow for a safety net and multiply this value by some factor.

Always monitor stack usage at run-time while developing and testing the product as stack overflows occur often and can lead to some curious behaviors. In fact, whenever someone mentions that his or her application behaves "strangely," insufficient stack size is the first thing that comes to mind.

5-3 DETECTING TASK STACK OVERFLOWS

1) Using an MMU or MPU

Stack overflows are easily detected if the processor has a Memory Management Unit (MMU) or a Memory Protection Unit (MPU). Basically, MMUs and MPUs are special hardware devices integrated alongside the CPU that can be configured to detect when a task attempts to access invalid memory locations, whether code, data, or stack. However, setting up an MMU or MPU is well beyond the scope of this book.

2) Using a CPU with stack overflow detection

Some processors, however, do have simple stack pointer overflow detection registers. When the CPU's stack pointer goes below (or above depending on stack growth) the value set in this register, an exception is generated and the exception handler ensures that the offending code does not do further damage (possibly issue a warning about the faulty code or even terminate it). The **.StkLimitPtr** field in the **OS_TCB** (see Task Control Blocks) is provided for this purpose as shown in Figure 5-3. Note that the position of the stack limit is typically set at a valid location in the task's stack with sufficient room left on the stack to handle the exception itself (assuming the CPU does not have a separate exception stack). In most cases, the position can be fairly close to **&MyTaskStk[0]**.

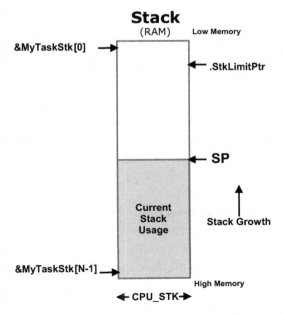

Figure 5-3 **Hardware detection of stack overflows**

As a reminder, the location of the **.StkLimitPtr** is determined by the "**stk_limit**" argument passed to **OSTaskCreate( )**, when the task is created as shown below:

```
OS_TCB  MtTaskTCB;
CPU_STK MyTaskStk[1000];


OSTaskCreate(&MyTaskTCB,
             "MyTaskName",
             MyTask,
             &MyTaskArg,
             MyPrio,
             &MyTaskStk[0],   /* Stack base address                        */
              100,            /* Used to set .StkLimitPtr to trigger exception ... */
                             /* ... at stack usage > 90%                  */
             1000,            /* Total stack size (in CPU_STK elements)    */
             MyTaskQSize,
             MyTaskTimeQuanta,
             (void *)0,
             MY_TASK_OPT,
             &err);
```

Of course, the value of **.StkLimitPtr** used by the CPU's stack overflow detection hardware needs to be changed whenever µC/OS-III performs a context switch. This can be tricky because the value of this register may need to be changed so that it first points to **NULL**, then the CPU's stack pointer is changed, and finally the value of the stack checking register is set to the value saved in the TCB's **.StkLimitPtr**. Why? Because if the sequence is not followed, the exception could be generated as soon as the stack pointer or the stack overflow detection register is changed. You can avoid this problem by first changing the stack overflow detection register to point to a location that ensures the stack pointer is never invalid (thus the **NULL** as described above). Note that I assumed here that the stack grows from high memory to low memory but the concept works in a similar fashion if the stack grows in the opposite direction.

3) Software-based stack overflow detection

Whenever µC/OS-III switches from one task to another, it calls a "hook" function (**OSTaskSwHook( )**), which allows the µC/OS-III port programmer to extend the capabilities of the context switch function. So, if the processor doesn't have hardware stack pointer overflow detection, it's still possible to "simulate" this feature by adding code in the context switch hook function and, perform the overflow detection in software. Specifically, before a task is *switched* in, the code should ensure that the stack pointer to load into the CPU does not exceed the "limit" placed in .StkLimitPtr. Because the software implementation cannot detect the stack overflow "as soon" as the stack pointer exceeds the value of .StkLimitPtr, it is important to position the value of .StkLimitPtr in the stack fairly far from &MyTaskStk[0], as shown in Figure 5-4. A software implementation such as this is not as reliable as a hardware-based detection mechanism but still prevents a possible stack overflow. Of course, the .StkLimitPtr field would be set using OSTaskCreate() as shown above but this time, with a location further away from &MyTaskStk[0].

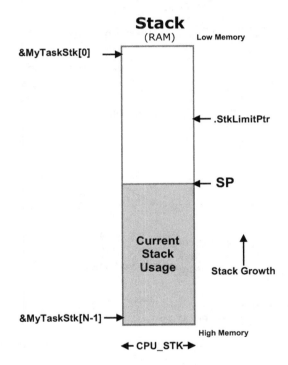

Figure 5-4 **Software detection of stack overflows, monitoring .StkLimitPtr**

4) Counting the amount of free stack space

Another way to check for stack overflows is to allocate more stack space than is anticipated to be used for the stack, then, monitor and possibly display actual maximum stack usage at run-time. This is fairly easy to do. First, the task stack needs to be cleared (i.e., filled with zeros) when the task is created. Next, a low priority task *walks the stack* of each task created, from the bottom (&MyTaskStk[0]) towards the top, counting the number of zero entries. When the task finds a non-zero value, the process is stopped and the usage of the stack can be computed (in number of bytes used or as a percentage). Then, you can adjust the size of the stacks (by recompiling the code) to allocate a more *reasonable* value (either

5

increase or decrease the amount of stack space for each task). For this to be effective, however, you need to run the application long enough for the stack to grow to its highest value. This is illustrated in Figure 5-5. µC/OS-III provides a function that performs this calculation at run-time, `OSTaskStkChk()` and in fact, this function is called by `OS_StatTask()` to compute stack usage for every task created in the application (to be described later).

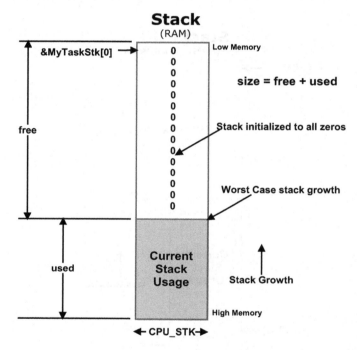

Figure 5-5 **Software detection of stack overflows, walking the stack**

5-4 TASK MANAGEMENT SERVICES

μC/OS-III provides a number of task-related services to call from the application. These services are found in **os_task.c** and they all start with **OSTask???()**. The type of service they perform groups task-related services:

Group	Functions
General	OSTaskCreate() OSTaskDel() OSTaskChangePrio() OSTaskRegSet() OSTaskRegGet() OSTaskSuspend() OSTaskResume() OSTaskTimeQuantaSet()
Signaling a Task (See Chapter 14, "Synchronization" on page 273)	OSTaskSemPend() OSTaskSemPost() OSTaskSemPendAbort()
Sending Messages to a Task (See Chapter 15, "Message Passing" on page 309)	OSTaskQPend() OSTaskQPost() OSTaskQPendAbort() OSTaskQFlush()

Table 5-2 **Task Management Services**

A complete description of all μC/OS-III task related services is provided in Appendix A, "μC/OS-III API Reference" on page 443.

5

5-5 TASK MANAGEMENT INTERNALS

5-5-1 TASK STATES

From a µC/OS-III user point of view, a task can be in any one of five states as shown in Figure 5-6. Internally, µC/OS-III does not need to keep track of the dormant state and the other states are tracked slightly differently. The actual µC/OS-III states will be discussed after a discussion on task states from the user's point of view. Figure 5-6 also shows which µC/OS-III functions are used to move from one state to another. The diagram is actually simplified as state transitions are a bit more complicated than this.

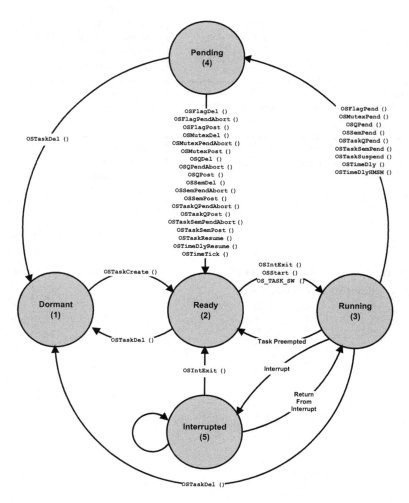

Figure 5-6 **Five basic states of a task**

F5-6(1)   The *Dormant* state corresponds to a task that resides in memory but has not been made available to μC/OS-III.

A task is made available to μC/OS-III by calling a function to create the task, **OSTaskCreate()**. The task code actually resides in code space but μC/OS-III needs to be informed about it.

When it is no longer necessary for μC/OS-III to manage a task, your code can call the task delete function, **OSTaskDel()**. **OSTaskDel()** does not actually delete the code of the task, it is simply not eligible to access the CPU.

F5-6(2)   A task is in the *Ready* state when it is ready-to-run. There can be any number of tasks ready and μC/OS-III keeps track of all ready tasks in a **ready list** (discussed later). This list is sorted by priority.

F5-6(3)   The most important ready-to-run task is placed in the *Running* state. On a single CPU, only one task can be running at any given time.

The task selected to run on the CPU is *switched in* by μC/OS-III when the application code calls **OSStart()**, or when μC/OS-III calls either **OSIntExit()** or **OS_TASK_SW()**.

As previously discussed, tasks must wait for an event to occur. A task waits for an event by calling one of the functions that brings the task to the pending state if the event has not occurred.

F5-6(4)   Tasks in the *Pending* state are placed in a special list called a *pend-list* (or wait list) associated with the event the task is waiting for. When waiting for the event to occur, the task does not consume CPU time. When the event occurs, the task is placed back into the ready list and μC/OS-III decides whether the newly readied task is the most important ready-to-run task. If this is the case, the currently running task will be preempted (placed back in the ready list) and the newly readied task is given control of the CPU. In other words, the newly readied task will run immediately if it is the most important task.

Note that the **OSTaskSuspend()** function unconditionally blocks a task and this task will not actually wait for an event to occur but in fact, waits until another task calls **OSTaskResume()** to make the task ready-to-run.

F5-6(5)   Assuming that CPU interrupts are enabled, an interrupting device will suspend execution of a task and execute an Interrupt Service Routine (ISR). ISRs are typically events that tasks wait for. Generally speaking, an ISR should simply notify a task that an event occurred and let the task process the event. ISRs should be as short as possible and most of the work of handling the interrupting devices should be done at the task level where it can be managed by μC/OS-III. ISRs are only allowed to make "Post" calls (i.e., **OSFlagPost()**, **OSQPost()**, **OSSemPost()**, **OSTaskQPost()** and **OSTaskSemPost()**). The only post call not allowed to be made from an ISR is **OSMutexPost()** since mutexes, as will be addressed later, are assumed to be services that are only accessible at the task level.

As the state diagram indicates, an interrupt can interrupt another interrupt. This is called **interrupt nesting** and most processors allow this. However, interrupt nesting easily leads to stack overflow if not managed properly.

Internally, μC/OS-III keeps track of task states using the state machine shown in Figure 5-7. The task state is actually maintained in a variable that is part of a data structure associated with each task, the task's TCB. The task state diagram was referenced throughout the design of μC/OS-III when implementing most of μC/OS-III's services. The number in parentheses is the state number of the task and thus, a task can be in any one of eight (8) states (see **os.h,** **OS_TASK_STATE_???**).

Note that the diagram does not keep track of a dormant task, as a dormant task is not known to μC/OS-III. Also, interrupts and interrupt nesting is tracked differently as will be explained further in the text.

This state diagram should be quite useful to understand how to use several functions and their impact on the state of tasks. In fact, I'd highly recommend that the reader bookmark the page of the diagram.

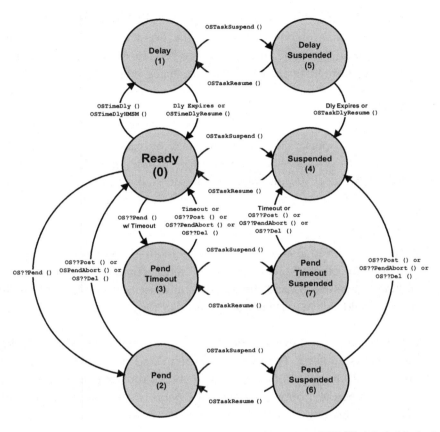

Figure 5-7 **µC/OS-III's internal task state machine**

F5-7(0)   A task is in State 0 when a task is ready-to-run. Every task "wants" to be ready-to-run as that is the only way it gets to perform their duties.

F5-7(1)   A task can decide to wait for time to expire by calling either **OSTimeDly()** or **OSTimeDlyHMSM()**. When the time expires or the delay is cancelled (by calling **OSTimeDlyResume()**), the task returns to the ready state.

F5-7(2)   A task can wait for an event to occur by calling one of the pend (i.e., wait) functions (**OSFlagPend()**, **OSMutexPend()**, **OSQPend()**, **OSSemPend()**, **OSTaskQPend()**, or **OSTaskSemPend()**), and specify to wait forever for the event to occur. The pend terminates when the event occurs (i.e., a task or an ISR performs a "post"), the awaited object is deleted or, another task decides to abort the pend.

F5-7(3)   A task can wait for an event to occur as indicated, but specify that it is willing to wait a certain amount of time for the event to occur. If the event is not posted within that time, the task is readied, then the task is notified that a timeout occurred. Again, the pend terminates when the event occurs (i.e., a task or an ISR performs a "post"), the object awaited is deleted or, another task decides to abort the pend.

F5-7(4)   A task can suspend itself or another task by calling **OSTaskSuspend()**. The only way the task is allowed to resume execution is by calling **OSTaskResume()**. Suspending a task means that a task will not be able to run on the CPU until it is resumed. If a task suspends itself then it must be resumed by another task.

F5-7(5)   A delayed task can also be suspended by another task. In this case, the effect is additive. In other words, the delay must complete (or be resumed by **OSTimeDlyResume()**) and the suspension must be removed (by another task which would call **OSTaskResume()**) in order for the task to be able to run.

F5-7(6)   A task waiting on an event to occur may be suspended by another task. Again, the effect is additive. The event must occur and the suspension removed (by another task) in order for the task to be able to run. Of course, if the object that the task is pending on is deleted or, the pend is aborted by another task, then one of the above two condition is removed. The suspension, however, must be explicitly removed.

F5-7(7)   A task can wait for an event, but only for a certain amount of time, and the task could also be suspended by another task. As one might expect, the suspension must be removed by another task (or the same task that suspended it in the first place), and the event needs to either occur or timeout while waiting for the event.

5-5-2 TASK CONTROL BLOCKS (TCBs)

A task control block (TCB) is a data structure used by kernels to maintain information about a task. Each task requires its own TCB and, for µC/OS-III, the user assigns the TCB in user memory space (RAM). The address of the task's TCB is provided to µC/OS-III when calling task-related services (i.e., **OSTask???()** functions). The task control block data structure is declared in **os.h** as shown in Listing 5-3. Note that the fields are actually commented in **os.h**, and some of the fields are conditionally compiled based on whether or not certain features are desired. Both are not shown here for clarity.

5

Also, it is important to note that even when the user understands what the different fields of the **OS_TCB** do, the application code must never directly access these (especially change them). In other words, **OS_TCB** fields must only be accessed by µC/OS-III and not the code.

```
struct os_tcb {
    CPU_STK          *StkPtr;
    void             *ExtPtr;
    CPU_STK          *StkLimitPtr;
    OS_TCB           *NextPtr;
    OS_TCB           *PrevPtr;
    OS_TCB           *TickNextPtr;
    OS_TCB           *TickPrevPtr;
    OS_TICK_SPOKE    *TickSpokePtr;
    OS_CHAR          *NamePtr;
    CPU_STK          *StkBasePtr;
    OS_TASK_PTR       TaskEntryAddr;
    void             *TaskEntryArg;
    OS_PEND_DATA     *PendDataTblPtr;
    OS_STATE          PendOn;
    OS_STATUS         PendStatus;
    OS_STATE          TaskState;
    OS_PRIO           Prio;
    CPU_STK_SIZE      StkSize;
    OS_OPT            Opt;
    OS_OBJ_QTY        PendDataEntries;
    CPU_TS            TS;
    OS_SEM_CTR        SemCtr;
    OS_TICK           TickCtrPrev;
    OS_TICK           TickCtrMatch;
    OS_TICK           TickRemain;
    OS_TICK           TimeQuanta;
    OS_TICK           TimeQuantaCtr;
    void             *MsgPtr;
    OS_MSG_SIZE       MsgSize;
    OS_MSG_Q          MsgQ;
    CPU_TS            MsgQPendTime;
    CPU_TS            MsgQPendTimeMax;
    OS_REG            RegTbl[OS_TASK_REG_TBL_SIZE];
    OS_FLAGS          FlagsPend;
    OS_FLAGS          FlagsRdy;
    OS_OPT            FlagsOpt;
```

```
          OS_NESTING_CTR      SuspendCtr;
          OS_CPU_USAGE        CPUUsage;
          OS_CTX_SW_CTR       CtxSwCtr;
          CPU_TS              CyclesDelta;
          CPU_TS              CyclesStart;
          OS_CYCLES           CyclesTotal;
          OS_CYCLES           CyclesTotalPrev;
          CPU_TS              SemPendTime;
          CPU_TS              SemPendTimeMax;
          CPU_STK_SIZE        StkUsed;
          CPU_STK_SIZE        StkFree;
          CPU_TS              IntDisTimeMax;
          CPU                 SchedLockTimeMax;
          OS_TCB              DbgNextPtr;
          OS_TCB              DbgPrevPtr;
          CPU_CHAR            DbgNamePtr;
};
```

Listing 5-3 **OS_TCB Data Structure**

.StkPtr

This field contains a pointer to the current top-of-stack for the task. µC/OS-III allows each task to have its own stack and each stack can be any size. .StkPtr should be the only field in the OS_TCB data structure accessed from assembly language code (for the context-switching code). This field is therefore placed as the first entry in the structure making access easier from assembly language code (it will be at offset zero in the data structure).

.ExtPtr

This field contains a pointer to a user-definable data area used to extend the TCB as needed. This pointer is provided as an argument passed in OSTaskCreate(). This pointer is easily accessible from assembly language since it always follows the .StkPtr. .ExtPtr can be used to add storage for saving the context of a FPU (Floating-Point Unit) if the processor you are using has a FPU.

.StkLimitPtr

The field contains a pointer to a location in the task's stack to set a *watermark* limit for stack growth and is determined from the value of the "stk_limit" argument passed to OSTaskCreate(). Some processors have special registers that automatically check the value of the stack pointer at run-time to ensure that the stack does not overflow. .StkLimitPtr may be used to set this register during a context switch. Alternatively, if the processor does not have such a register, this can be "simulated" in software. However, this is not as reliable as a hardware solution. If this feature is not used then you can set the value of "**stk_limit**" can be set to **0** when calling **OSTaskCreate( )**. See also section 5-3 "Detecting Task Stack Overflows" on page 103).

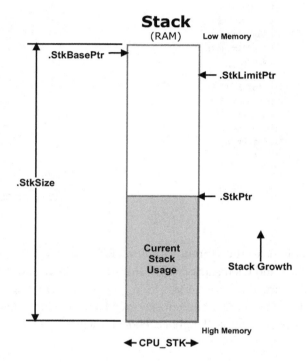

.NextPtr and .PrevPtr

These pointers are used to doubly link **OS_TCBs** in the ready list. A doubly linked list allows **OS_TCBs** to be quickly inserted and removed from the list.

.TickNextPtr and .TickPrevPtr

These pointers are used to doubly link **OS_TCBs** in the list of tasks waiting for time to expire or to timeout from pend calls. Again, a doubly linked list allows **OS_TCBs** to be quickly inserted and removed from the list.

.TickSpokePtr

This pointer is used to know which spoke in the "tick wheel" the task is linked to. The tick wheel will be described in "Chapter 9, "Interrupt Management" on page 175."

.NamePtr

This pointer allows a name (an ASCII string) to be assigned to each task. Having a name is useful when debugging, since it is user friendly compared to displaying the address of the **OS_TCB**. Storage for the ASCII string is assumed to be in user space, either in code memory (ASCII string declared as a const) or in RAM.

.StkBasePtr

This field points to the base address of the task's stack. The stack base is typically the lowest address in memory where the stack for the task resides. A task stack is declared as follows:

```
CPU_STK MyTaskStk[???];
```

CPU_STK is the data type you must use to declare task stacks and **???** is the size of the stack associated with the task. The base address is always **&MyTaskStk[0]**.

.TaskEntryAddr

This field contains the entry address of the task. As previously mentioned, a task is declared as shown below and this field contains the address of **MyTask**.

```
void  MyTask (void *p_arg);
```

.TaskEntryArg

This field contains the value of the argument that is passed to the task when the task starts. As previously mentioned, a task is declared as shown below and this field contains the value of **p_arg**.

```
void  MyTask (void *p_arg);
```

.PendDataTblPtr

µC/OS-III allows the task to pend on any number of semaphores or message queues simultaneously. This pointer points to a table containing information about the pended objects. This is described in Chapter 10, "Pend Lists".

.PendOn

This field indicates what the task is pending on and contains one of the following values declared in **os.h**:

```
OS_TASK_PEND_ON_NOTHING
OS_TASK_PEND_ON_FLAG
OS_TASK_PEND_ON_TASK_Q
OS_TASK_PEND_ON_MULTI
OS_TASK_PEND_ON_MUTEX
OS_TASK_PEND_ON_Q
OS_TASK_PEND_ON_SEM
OS_TASK_PEND_ON_TASK_SEM
```

.PendStatus

This field indicates the outcome of a pend and contains one of the values declared in **os.h**:

```
OS_STATUS_PEND_OK
OS_STATUS_PEND_ABORT
OS_STATUS_PEND_DEL
OS_STATUS_PEND_TIMEOUT
```

.TaskState

This field indicates the current state of a task and contains one of the eight (8) task states that a task can be in. These states are declared in **os.h**:

```
OS_TASK_STATE_RDY
OS_TASK_STATE_DLY
OS_TASK_STATE_PEND
OS_TASK_STATE_PEND_TIMEOUT
OS_TASK_STATE_SUSPENDED
OS_TASK_STATE_DLY_SUSPENDED
OS_TASK_STATE_PEND_SUSPENDED
OS_TASK_STATE_PEND_TIMEOUT_SUSPENDED
```

.Prio

This field contains the current priority of a task. **.Prio** is a value between 0 and **OS_CFG_PRIO_MAX-1**. In fact, the idle task is the only task at priority **OS_CFG_PRIO_MAX-1**.

.StkSize

This field contains the size (in number of **CPU_STK** elements) of the stack associated with the task. Recall that a task stack is declared as follows:

```
CPU_STK MyTaskStk[???];
```

`.StkSize` is the number of elements in the above array.

.Opt

This field saves the "options" passed to `OSTaskCreate()` when the task is created as shown below. Note that task options are additive.

```
OS_OPT_TASK_NONE
OS_OPT_TASK_STK_CHK
OS_OPT_TASK_STK_CLR
OS_OPT_TASK_SAVE_FP
```

.PendDataTblEntries

This field works with the `.PendDataTblPtr` and indicates the number of objects a task is pending on at the same time.

.TS

This field is used to store a "time stamp" of when an event that the task was waiting on occurred. When the task resumes execution, this time stamp is returned to the caller.

.SemCtr

This field contains a semaphore counter associated with the task. Each task has its own semaphore built-in. An ISR or another task can signal a task using this semaphore. `.SemCtr` is therefore used to keep track of how many times the task is signaled. `.SemCtr` is used by `OSTaskSem???()` services.

.TickCtrPrev

This field stores the previous value of `OSTickCtr` when `OSTimeDly()` is called with the `OS_OPT_TIME_PERIODIC` option.

.TickCtrMatch

When a task is waiting for time to expire, or pending on an object with a timeout, the task is placed in a special list of tasks waiting for time to expire. When in this list, the task waits for `.TickCtrMatch` to match the value of the "tick counter" (`OSTickCtr`). When a match occurs, the task is removed from that list.

.TickRemain

This field is computed at run time by OS_TickTask() to compute the amount of time (expressed in "ticks") left before a delay or timeout expires. This field is useful for debuggers or run-time monitors for display purposes.

.TimeQuanta and .TimeQuantaCtr

These fields are used for time slicing. When multiple tasks are ready-to-run at the same priority, .TimeQuanta determines how much time (in ticks) the task will execute until it is preempted by µC/OS-III so that the next task at the same priority gets a chance to execute. .TimeQuantaCtr keeps track of the remaining number of ticks for this to happen and is loaded with .TimeQuanta at the beginning of the task's time slice.

.MsgPtr

When a message is sent to a task, this field contains the message received. This field only exists in a TCB if message queue services (OS_CFG_Q_EN is set to 1 in os_cfg.h), or task message queue services, are enabled (OS_CFG_TASK_Q_EN is set to 1 in os_cfg.h) at compile time.

.MsgSize

When a message is sent to a task, this field contains the size (in number of bytes) of the message received. This field only exists in a TCB if message queue services (OS_CFG_Q_EN is set to 1 in os_cfg.h), or task message queue services, (OS_CFG_TASK_Q_EN is set to 1 in os_cfg.h) are enabled at compile time.

.MsgQ

µC/OS-III allows tasks or ISRs to send messages directly to tasks. Because of this, a message queue is actually built into each TCB. This field only exists in a TCB if task message queue services are enabled at compile time (OS_CFG_TASK_Q_EN is set to 1 in os_cfg.h). .MsgQ is used by the OSTaskQ???() services.

.MsgQPendTime

This field contains the amount of time it took for a message to arrive. When OSTaskQPost() is called, the current time stamp is read and stored in the message. When OSTaskQPend() returns, the current time stamp is read again and the difference between the two times is stored in this variable. A debugger or µC/Probe can be used to indicate the time taken for a message to arrive by displaying this field.

This field is only available if setting OS_CFG_TASK_PROFILE_EN to 1 in os_cfg.h.

.MsgQPendTimeMax

This field contains the maximum amount of time it takes for a message to arrive. It is a peak detector of the value of .MsgQPendTime. The peak can be reset by calling OSStatReset().

This field is only available if setting OS_CFG_TASK_PROFILE_EN to 1 in os_cfg.h.

.RegTbl[]

This field contains a table of "registers" that are task-specific. These registers are different than CPU registers. Task registers allow for the storage of such task-specific information as task ID, "errno" common in some software components, and more. Task registers may also store task-related data that needs to be associated with the task at run time. Note that the data type for elements of this array is OS_REG, which can be declared at compile time to be nearly anything. However, all registers must be of this data type. This field only exists in a TCB if task registers are enabled at compile time (OS_CFG_TASK_REG_TBL_SIZE is greater than 0 in os_cfg.h).

.FlagsPend

When a task pends on event flags, this field contains the event flags (i.e., bits) that the task is pending on. This field only exists in a TCB if event flags services are enabled at compile time (OS_CFG_FLAG_EN is set to 1 in os_cfg.h).

.FlagsRdy

This field contains the event flags that were posted and that the task was waiting on. In other words, it allows a task to know which event flags made the task ready-to-run. This field only exists in a TCB if event flags services are enabled at compile time (OS_CFG_FLAG_EN is set to 1 in os_cfg.h).

.FlagsOpt

When a task pends on event flags, this field contains the type of pend (pend on any event flag bit specified in .FlagsPend or all event flag bits specified in .FlagsPend). This field only exists in a TCB if event flags services are enabled at compile time (OS_CFG_FLAG_EN is set to 1 in os_cfg.h). There can be up to eight main values as shown below plus add-on options. Possible values are:

```
OS_OPT_PEND_FLAG_CLR_ALL
OS_OPT_PEND_FLAG_CLR_ANY
OS_OPT_PEND_FLAG_CLR_AND
OS_OPT_PEND_FLAG_CLR_OR
OS_OPT_PEND_FLAG_SET_ALL
```

```
OS_OPT_PEND_FLAG_SET_ANY
OS_OPT_PEND_FLAG_SET_AND
OS_OPT_PEND_FLAG_SET_OR
```

You can also 'add' OS_OPT_PEND_FLAG_CONSUME and either OS_OPT_PEND_BLOCKING or OS_OPT_PEND_NON_BLOCKING to the above options.

.SuspendCtr

This field is used by OSTaskSuspend() and OSTaskResume() to keep track of how many times a task is suspended. Task suspension can be nested. When .SuspendCtr is 0, all suspensions are removed. This field only exists in a TCB if task suspension is enabled at compile time (OS_CFG_TASK_SUSPEND_EN is set to 1 in os_cfg.h).

.CPUUsage

This field is computed by OS_StatTask() if OS_CFG_TASK_PROFILE_EN is set to 1 in os_cfg.h. .CPUUsage contains the CPU usage of a task in percent (0 to 100%). As of version V3.03.00, .CPUUsage is multiplied by 100. In other words, 10000 represents 100.00%.

.CtxSwCtr

This field keeps track of how often the task has executed (not how long it has executed). This field is generally used by debuggers or run-time monitors to see if a task is executing (the value of this field would be non-zero and would be incrementing). The field is enabled at compile time when OS_CFG_TASK_PROFILE_EN is set to 1 in os_cfg.h.

.CyclesDelta

.CyclesDelta is computed during a context switch and contains the value of the current time stamp (obtained by calling OS_TS_GET()) minus the value of .CyclesStart. This field is generally used by debuggers or a run-time monitor to see how long a task had control of the CPU until it got switched out. The field is enabled at compile time when OS_CFG_TASK_PROFILE_EN is set to 1 in os_cfg.h.

.CyclesStart

This field is used to measure how long a task had control of the CPU. .CyclesStart is updated when μC/OS-III performs a context switch. .CyclesStart contains the value of the current time stamp (it calls OS_TS_GET()) when a task is switched-in. The field is enabled at compile time when OS_CFG_TASK_PROFILE_EN is set to 1 in os_cfg.h.

.CyclesTotal

This field accumulates the value of **.CyclesDelta**, so it contains the total execution time of a task during a set period of time. **.CyclesTotal** is used by **OS_StatTask()** to determine CPU usage on a per-task basis. This is typically a 32-bit value because of the accumulation of cycles over time. On the other hand, using a 64-bit value ensures that we can accumulate CPU cycles for almost 600 years even if the CPU is running at 1 GHz! Of course, it's assumed that the compiler supports 64-bit data types. The field is enabled at compile time when **OS_CFG_TASK_PROFILE_EN** is set to 1 in **os_cfg.h.**. **.CyclesTotal** is used by **OS_StatTask()** to determine CPU usage on a per-task basis.

.SemPendTime

This field contains the amount of time taken for the semaphore to be signaled. When **OSTaskSemPost()** is called, the current time stamp is read and stored in the **OS_TCB** (see **.TS**). When **OSTaskSemPend()** returns, the current time stamp is read again and the difference between the two times is stored in this variable. This field can be displayed by a debugger or µC/Probe to indicate how much time it took for the task to be signaled.

This field is only available when setting **OS_CFG_TASK_PROFILE_EN** to 1 in **os_cfg.h**.

.SemPendTimeMax

This field contains the maximum amount of time it took for the task to be signaled. It is a peak detector of the value of **.SemPendTime**. The peak can be reset by calling **OSStatReset()**.

This field is only available if setting **OS_CFG_TASK_PROFILE_EN** to 1 in **os_cfg.h**.

.StkUsed and .StkFree

µC/OS-III is able to compute (at run time) the amount of stack space a task actually uses and how much stack space remains. This is accomplished by a function called **OSTaskStkChk()**. Stack usage computation assumes that the task's stack is "cleared" when the task is created. In other words, when calling **OSTaskCreate()**, it is expected that the following options be specified: **OS_TASK_OPT_STK_CLR** and **OS_TASK_OPT_STK_CHK**. **OSTaskCreate()** will then clear all the RAM used for the task's stack.

µC/OS-III provides an internal task called **OS_StatTask()** that checks the stack of each of the tasks at run-time. **OS_StatTask()** typically runs at a low priority so that it does not interfere with the application code. **OS_StatTask()** saves the value computed for each task in the TCB of each task in these fields, which represents the maximum number of stack bytes used and the amount of stack space still unused by the task. These fields only exist in a TCB if the statistic task is enabled at compile time (**OS_CFG_STAT_TASK_STK_CHK_EN** is set to 1 in **os_cfg.h**).

.IntDisTimeMax

This field keeps track of the maximum interrupt disable time of the task. The field is updated only if µC/CPU supports interrupt disable time measurements. This field is available only if setting **OS_CFG_TASK_PROFILE_EN** to 1 in **os_cfg.h** and µC/CPU's **CPU_CFG_INT_DIS_MEAS_EN** is defined in **cpu_cfg.h**.

.SchedLockTimeMax

The field keeps track of the maximum scheduler lock time of the task. In other words, the maximum amount of time the task locks the scheduler.

This field is available only if you set **OS_CFG_TASK_PROFILE_EN** to 1 and **OS_CFG_SCHED_LOCK_TIME_MEAS_EN** is set to 1 in **os_cfg.h**.

.DbgNextPtr

This field contains a pointer to the next **OS_TCB** in a doubly linked list of **OS_TCB**s. **OS_TCB**s are placed in this list by **OSTaskCreate()**. This field is only present if **OS_CFG_DBG_EN** is set to 1 in **os_cfg.h**.

.DbgPrevPtr

This field contains a pointer to the previous **OS_TCB** in a doubly linked list of **OS_TCB**s. **OS_TCB**s are placed in this list by **OSTaskCreate()**. This field is only present if **OS_CFG_DBG_EN** is set to 1 in **os_cfg.h**.

.DbgNamePtr

This field contains a pointer to the name of the object that the task is pending on when the task is pending on either an event flag group, a semaphore, a mutual exclusion semaphore or a message queue. This information is quite useful during debugging and thus, this field is only present if **OS_CFG_DBG_EN** is set to 1 in **os_cfg.h**.

5-6 INTERNAL TASKS

During initialization, µC/OS-III creates a minimum of two (2) internal tasks (OS_IdleTask() and OS_TickTask()) and, three (3) optional tasks (OS_StatTask(), OS_TmrTask() and OS_IntQTask()). The optional tasks are created based on the value of compile-time #defines found in os_cfg.h.

OS_CFG_STAT_TASK_EN	enables OS_StatTask()
OS_CFG_TMR_EN	enables OS_TmrTask()
OS_CFG_ISR_POST_DEFERRED_EN	enables OS_IntQTask()

5-6-1 THE IDLE TASK (OS_IdleTask(), os_core.c)

OS_IdleTask() is the very first task created by µC/OS-III and always exists in a µC/OS-III-based application. The priority of the idle task is always set to OS_CFG_PRIO_MAX−1. In fact, OS_IdleTask() is the only task that is ever allowed to be at this priority and, as a safeguard, when other tasks are created, OSTaskCreate() ensures that there are no other tasks created at the same priority as the idle task. The idle task runs whenever there are no other tasks that are ready-to-run. The important portions of the code for the idle task are shown below (refer to **os_core.c** for the complete code).

```
void  OS_IdleTask (void *p_arg)
{
    while (DEF_ON) {                       (1)
        OS_CRITICAL_ENTER();
        OSIdleTaskCtr++;                   (2)
        OSStatTaskCtr++;
        OS_CRITICAL_EXIT();
        OSIdleTaskHook();                  (3)
    }
}
```

Listing 5-4 **Idle Task**

L5-4(1)   The idle task is a "true" infinite loop that never calls functions to "wait for an event". This is because, on most processors, when there is "nothing to do," the processor still executes instructions. When µC/OS-III determines that there is

5

no other higher-priority task to run, µC/OS-III "parks" the CPU in the idle task. However, instead of having an empty "infinite loop" doing nothing, µC/OS-III uses this "idle" time to do something useful.

L5-4(2)   Two counters are incremented whenever the idle task runs.

OSIdleTaskCtr is typically defined as a 32-bit unsigned integer (see **os.h**). **OSIdleTaskCtr** is reset once when µC/OS-III is initialized. **OSIdleTaskCtr** is used to indicate "activity" in the idle task. In other words, if your code monitors and displays **OSIdleTaskCtr**, you should expect to see a value between 0x00000000 and 0xFFFFFFFF. The rate at which **OSIdleTaskCtr** increments depend on how busy the CPU is at running the application code. The faster the increment, the less work the CPU has to do in application tasks.

OSStatTaskCtr is also typically defined as a 32-bit unsigned integer (see **os.h**) and is used by the statistic task (described later) to get a sense of CPU utilization at run time.

L5-4(3)   Every time through the loop, **OS_IdleTask()** calls **OSIdleTaskHook()**, which is a function that is declared in the µC/OS-III port for the processor used. **OSIdleTaskHook()** allows the implementer of the µC/OS-III port to perform additional processing during idle time. It is very important for this code to not make calls that would cause the idle task to "wait for an event". This is generally not a problem as most programmers developing µC/OS-III ports know to follow this simple rule.

OSIdleTaskHook() may be used to place the CPU in low-power mode for battery-powered applications and thus avoid wasting energy. However, doing this means that **OSStatTaskCtr** cannot be used to measure CPU utilization (described later).

```
void  OSIdleTaskHook (void)
{
    /* Place the CPU in low power mode */
}
```

Typically, most processors exit low-power mode when an interrupt occurs. Depending on the processor, however, the Interrupt Service Routine (ISR) may have to write to "special" registers to return the CPU to its full or desired speed. If the ISR wakes up a high-priority task (every task is higher in priority than the idle task) then the ISR will not immediately return to the interrupted idle task, but instead switch to the higher-priority task. When the higher-priority task completes its work and waits for its event to occur, µC/OS-III causes a context switch to return to **OSIdleTaskHook()** just "after" the instruction that caused the CPU to enter low-power mode. In turn, **OSIdleTaskHook()** returns to **OS_IdleTask()** and causes another iteration through the "infinite loop" which places the CPU back in the low power state.

5-6-2 THE TICK TASK (OS_TickTask(), os_tick.c)

Nearly every RTOS requires a periodic time source called a *Clock Tick* or *System Tick* to keep track of time delays and timeouts. µC/OS-III's clock tick handling is encapsulated in the file **os_tick.c**.

OS_TickTask() is a task created by µC/OS-III and its priority is configurable by the user through µC/OS-III's configuration file **os_cfg_app.h** (see **OS_CFG_TICK_TASK_PRIO**). Typically **OS_TickTask()** is set to a relatively high priority. In fact, the priority of this task is set slightly lower than your most important tasks.

OS_TickTask() is used by µC/OS-III to keep track of tasks waiting for time to expire or, for tasks that are pending on kernel objects with a timeout. **OS_TickTask()** is a periodic task and it waits for signals from the tick ISR (described in Chapter 9, "Interrupt Management" on page 175) as shown in Figure 5-8.

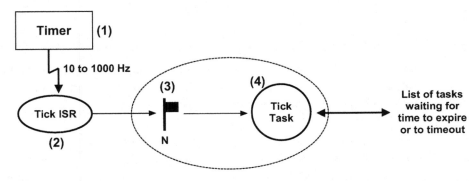

Figure 5-8 **Tick ISR and Tick Task relationship**

5

F5-8(1) A hardware timer is generally used and configured to generate an interrupt at a rate between 10 and 1000 Hz (see **OS_CFG_TICK_RATE** in **os_cfg_app.h**). This timer is generally called the *Tick Timer*. The actual rate to use depends on such factors as: processor speed, desired time resolution, and amount of allowable overhead to handle the tick timer, etc.

The tick interrupt does not have to be generated by a timer and, in fact, it can come from other regular time sources such as the power-line frequency (50 or 60 Hz), which are known to be fairly accurate over long periods of time.

F5-8(2) Assuming CPU interrupts are enabled, the CPU accepts the tick interrupt, preempts the current task, and vectors to the tick ISR. The tick ISR must call **OSTimeTick()** (see **os_time.c**), which accomplishes most of the work needed by µC/OS-III. The tick ISR then clears the timer interrupt (and possibly reloads the timer for the next interrupt). However, some timers may need to be taken care of prior to calling **OSTimeTick()** instead of after as shown below.

```
void  TickISR (void)
{
    OSTimeTick();
    /* Clear tick interrupt source         */
    /* Reload the timer for the next interrupt */
}
```

or,

```
void  TickISR (void)
{
    /* Clear tick interrupt source         */
    /* Reload the timer for the next interrupt */
    OSTimeTick();
}
```

OSTimeTick() calls **OSTimeTickHook()** at the very beginning of **OSTimeTick()** to give the opportunity to the µC/OS-III port developer to react as soon as possible upon servicing the tick interrupt.

F5-8(3) **OSTimeTick()** calls a service provided by µC/OS-III to signal the tick task and make that task ready-to-run. The tick task executes as soon as it becomes the most important task. The reason the tick task might not run immediately is that the tick interrupt could have interrupted a task higher in priority than the tick task and, upon completion of the tick ISR, µC/OS-III will resume the interrupted task.

F5-8(4)   When the tick task executes, it goes through a list of all tasks that are waiting for time to expire or are waiting on a kernel object with a timeout. From this point forward, this will be called the tick list. The tick task will make ready-to-run all of the tasks in the tick list for which time or timeout has expired. The process is explained below.

µC/OS-III may need to place literally hundreds of tasks (if an application has that many tasks) in the tick list. The tick list is implemented in such a way that it does not take much CPU time to determine if time has expired for those tasks placed in the tick list and, possibly makes those tasks ready-to-run. The tick list is implemented as shown in Figure 5-9.

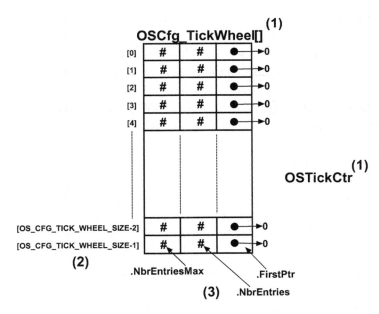

Figure 5-9 **Empty Tick List**

F5-9(1)   The tick list consists of a table (OSCfg_TickWheel[], see **os_cfg_app.c**) and a counter (OSTickCtr).

F5-9(2)   The table contains up to **OS_CFG_TICK_WHEEL_SIZE** entries (see **os_cfg_app.h**), which is a compile time configuration value. The number of entries depends on the amount of memory (RAM) available to the processor and the maximum number of tasks in the application. A good starting point for **OS_CFG_TICK_WHEEL_SIZE** may be: **#Tasks / 4**. It is recommended not to make **OS_CFG_TICK_WHEEL_SIZE** an even multiple of the tick rate. If the tick rate is 1000 Hz and you have 50 tasks in the application, you should avoid setting **OS_CFG_TICK_WHEEL_SIZE** to 10 or 20 (use 11 or 23 instead). Actually, prime numbers are good choices. Although it is not really possible to plan at compile time what will happen at run time, ideally, the number of tasks waiting in each entry of the table will be distributed uniformly.

F5-9(3)   Each entry in the table contains three fields: **.NbrEntriesMax**, **.NbrEntries** and **.FirstPtr**.

.NbrEntries indicates the number of tasks linked to this table entry.

.NbrEntriesMax keeps track of the highest number of entries in the table. This value is reset when the application code calls **OSStatReset()**.

.FirstPtr contains a pointer to a doubly linked list of tasks (through the tasks **OS_TCB**) belonging to the list, at that table position.

OSTickCtr is incremented by **OS_TickTask()** each time the task is signaled by the tick ISR.

Tasks are automatically inserted in the tick list when the application programmer calls a **OSTimeDly???()** function, or when an **OS???Pend()** call is made with a non-zero timeout value.

Example 5-1

Using an example to illustrate the process of inserting a task in the tick list, let's assume that the tick list is completely empty, **OS_CFG_TICK_WHEEL_SIZE** is configured to 12, and the current value of **OSTickCtr** is 10 as shown in Figure 5-10. A task is placed in the tick list when **OSTimeDly()** is called and let's assume **OSTimeDly()** is called as follows:

```
    :
    OSTimeDly(1, OS_OPT_TIME_DLY, &err);
    :
```

Referring to the µC/OS-III reference manual in Appendix A, notice that this action indicates to µC/OS-III to delay the current task for 1 tick. Since **OSTickCtr** has a value of 10, the task will be put to sleep until **OSTickCtr** reaches 11 and thus sleep until the very next clock tick interrupt. Tasks are inserted in the **OSCfg_TickWheel[]** table using the following equation:

```
MatchValue                   = OSTickCtr + dly
Index into OSCfg_TickWheel[] = MatchValue % OS_CFG_TICK_WHEEL_SIZE
```

Where "**dly**" is the value passed in the first argument of **OSTimeDly()** or, 1 in this example. We therefore obtain the following:

```
MatchValue                   =  10 + 1
Index into OSCfg_TickWheel[] = (10 + 1) % 12
```

or,

```
MatchValue                   = 11
Index into OSCfg_TickWheel[] = 11
```

Because of the "circular" nature of the table (a modulo operation using the size of the table), the table is referred to as a *tick wheel* and each entry is a *spoke* in the wheel.

The **OS_TCB** of the task being delayed is entered at index 11 in **OSCfg_TickWheel[]** (i.e., spoke 11 using the wheel analogy). The **OS_TCB** of the task is inserted in the first entry of the list (i.e., pointed to by **OSCfg_TickWheel[11].FirstPtr**), and the number of entries at spoke 11 is incremented (i.e., **OSCfg_TickWheel[11].NbrEntries** will be 1). Notice that the **OS_TCB** also links back to **&OSCfg_TickWheel[11]** and the "MatchValue" is placed in the **OS_TCB** field **.TickCtrMatch**. Since this is the first task inserted in the tick list at spoke 11, the **.TickNextPtr** and **.TickPrevPtr** of the task's **OS_TCB** both point to **NULL**.

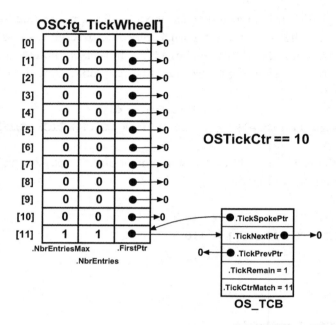

Figure 5-10 **Inserting a task in the tick list**

OSTimeDly() takes care of a few other details. Specifically, the task is removed from μC/OS-III's ready list (described in Chapter 6, "The Ready List" on page 141) since the task is no longer eligible to run (because it is waiting for time to expire). Also, the scheduler is called because μC/OS-III will need to run the next most important ready-to-run task.

If the next task to run also happens to call OSTimeDly() "before" the next tick arrives and calls OSTimeDly() as follows:

```
    :
    OSTimeDly(13, OS_OPT_TIME_DLY, &err);
    :
```

μC/OS-III will calculate the match value and spoke as follows:

```
MatchValue                    = 10 + 13
OSCfg_TickWheel[] spoke number = (10 + 13) % 12
```

or,

```
MatchValue                    = 23
OSCfg_TickWheel[] spoke number = 11
```

The "second task" will be inserted at the same table entry as shown in Figure 5-11. Tasks sharing the same spoke are sorted in ascending order such that the task with the least amount of time remaining is placed at the head of the list.

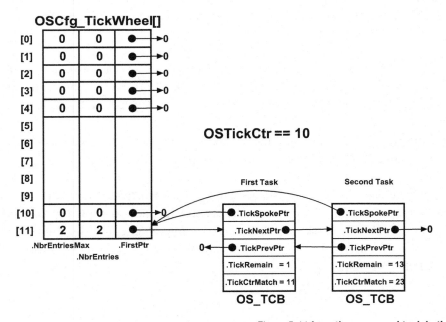

Figure 5-11 **Inserting a second task in the tick list**

When the tick task executes (see `OS_TickTask()` and also `OS_TickListUpdate()` in os_tick.c), it starts by incrementing `OSTickCtr` and determines which table entry (i.e., which spoke) needs to be processed. Then, if there are tasks in the list at this entry (i.e., `.FirstPtr` is not `NULL`), each `OS_TCB` is examined to determine whether the `.TickCtrMatch` value "matches" `OSTickCtr` and, if so, we remove the `OS_TCB` from the list. If the task is only waiting for time to expire, it will be placed in the ready list (described later). If the task is pending on an object, not only will the task be removed from the tick list, but it will also be removed from the list of tasks waiting on that object. The search through the list terminates as soon as `OSTickCtr` does not match the task's `.TickCtrMatch` value; since there is no point in looking any further in the list.

Note that `OS_TickTask()` does most of its work in a critical section when the tick list is updated. However, because the list is sorted, the critical section has a chance to be fairly short.

5-6-3 THE STATISTIC TASK (OS_StatTask(), os_stat.c)

µC/OS-III contains an internal task that provides such run-time statistics as overall CPU utilization (0.00 to 100.00%), per-task CPU utilization (0.00 to 100.00%), and per-task stack usage. As of V3.03.00, CPU utilization is represented as a integer from 0 to 10,000 (0.00% to 100.00%). Prior to V3.03.00, CPU utilization was represented an integer ranging from 0 to 100.

The statistic task is optional in a µC/OS-III application and its presence is controlled by a compile-time configuration constant `OS_CFG_STAT_TASK_EN` defined in `os_cfg.h`. Specifically, the code is included in the build when `OS_CFG_STAT_TASK_EN` is set to 1.

Also, the priority of this task and the location and size of the statistic task's stack is configurable via `OS_CFG_STAT_TASK_PRIO` declared in `os_cfg_app.h` ().

If the application uses the statistic task, it should call `OSStatTaskCPUUsageInit()` from the first, and only application task created in the `main()` function as shown in Listing 5-5. The startup code should create only one task before calling `OSStart()`. The single task created is, of course, allowed to create other tasks, but only after calling `OSStatTaskCPUUsageInit()`.

```
void main (void)                        (1)
{
    OS_ERR  err;
    :
    OSInit(&err);                       (2)
    if (err != OS_ERR_NONE) {
        /* Something wasn't configured properly, µC/OS-III not properly initialized */
    }
    /* (3) Create ONE task (we'll call it AppTaskStart() for sake of discussion)    */
    :
    OSStart(&err);                     (4)
}


void AppTaskStart (void *p_arg)
{
    OS_ERR  err;
    :
    /* (5) Initialize the tick interrupt                                          */
#if OS_CFG_STAT_TASK_EN > 0
    OSStatTaskCPUUsageInit(&err);      (6)
#endif
    :
    /* (7) Create other tasks                                                     */
    while (DEF_ON) {
        /* AppTaskStart() body                                                    */
    }
}
```

Listing 5-5 **Proper startup for computing CPU utilization**

L5-5(1)   The C compiler should start up the CPU and bring it to **main()** as is typical in most C applications.

L5-5(2)   **main()** calls **OSInit()** to initialize µC/OS-III. It is assumed that the statistics task was enabled by setting **OS_CFG_STAT_TASK_EN** to 1 in **os_cfg.h**. You should always examine µC/OS-III's returned error code to make sure the call was done properly. Refer to **os.h** for a list of possible errors, **OS_ERR_???**.

L5-5(3)   As the comment indicates, you should create a single task called **AppTaskStart()** in the example (its name is left to the creator's discretion). When creating this task, give it a fairly high priority (do not use priority 0 since it's reserved for µC/OS-III).

Normally, µC/OS-III allows the user to create as many tasks as are necessary prior to calling **OSStart()**. However, when the statistic task is used to compute overall CPU utilization, it is necessary to create only one task.

L5-5(4) You need to call **OSStart()** to let µC/OS-III start the highest-priority task which, in our case is **AppTaskStart()**. At this point, there should be either four (4) to six (6) tasks created depending on configuration option: **OS_IdleTask()**, **OS_TickTask()**, **OS_StatTask()**, **OS_TmrTask()** (optional), **OS_IntQTask()** (optional) and now **AppTaskStart()**.

L5-5(5) The start task should then configure and enable tick interrupts. This most likely requires that the user initialize the hardware timer used for the clock tick and have it interrupt at the rate specified by **OS_CFG_TICK_RATE_HZ** (see **os_cfg_app.h**). Additionally, Micriµm provides sample projects that include a basic board-support package (BSP). The BSP initializes many aspects of the CPU as well as the periodic time source required by µC/OS-III. If available, the user may utilize BSP services by calling **BSP_Init()** from the startup task. After this point, no further time source initialization is required by the user.

L5-5(6) **OSStatTaskCPUUsageInit()** is called to determine the maximum value that **OSStatTaskCtr** (see **OS_IdleTask()**) can count up to for **1/OS_CFG_STAT_TASK_RATE_HZ** second when there are no other tasks running in the system (apart for the other µC/OS-III tasks). For example, if the system does not contain an application task and **OSStatTaskCtr** counts from 0 to 10,000,000 for **1/OS_CFG_STAT_TASK_RATE_HZ** second, when adding tasks, and the test is redone every **1/OS_CFG_STAT_TASK_RATE_HZ** second, the **OSStatTaskCtr** will not reach 10,000,000 and actual CPU utilization is determined as follows:

$$CPU\_Utilization_{\%} = \left(100 - \frac{100 \times OSStatTaskCtr}{OSStatTaskCtrMax}\right)$$

For example, if when redoing the test, **OSStatTaskCtr** reaches 7,500,000 the CPU is busy 25% of its time running application tasks:

$$25\% = \left(100 - \frac{100 \times 7,500,000}{10,000,000}\right)$$

L5-5(7)   **AppTaskStart()** can then create other application tasks as needed.

As previously described, µC/OS-III stores run-time statistics for each task in each task's **OS_TCB**.

OS_StatTask() also computes stack usage of all created tasks by calling **OSTaskStkChk()** (see **os_task.c**) and stores the return values of this function (free and used stack space) in the **.StkFree** and **.StkUsed** field of the task's **OS_TCB**, respectively.

5-6-4 THE TIMER TASK (OS_TmrTask(), os_tmr.c)

µC/OS-III provides timer services to the application programmer and this code is found in **os_tmr.c**.

The timer task is optional in a µC/OS-III application and its presence is controlled by the compile-time configuration constant **OS_CFG_TMR_EN** defined in **os_cfg.h**. Specifically, the code is included in the build when **OS_CFG_TMR_EN** is set to 1.

Timers are countdown counters that perform an action when the counter reaches zero. The action is provided by the user through a callback function. A callback function is a function that the user declares and that will be called when the timer expires. The callback can thus be used to turn on or off a light, a motor, or perform whatever action needed. It is important to note that the callback function is called from the context of the timer task. The application programmer may create an unlimited number of timers (limited only by the amount of available RAM). Timer management is fully described in Chapter 12, "Timer Management" on page 213 and the timer services available to the application programmer are described in Appendix A, "µC/OS-III API Reference" on page 443.

OS_TmrTask() is a task created by µC/OS-III (this assumes setting **OS_CFG_TMR_EN** to 1 in **os_cfg.h**) and its priority is configurable by the user through µC/OS-III's configuration constant **OS_CFG_TMR_TASK_PRIO** found in **os_cfg_app.h**. **OS_TmrTask()** is typically set to a medium priority.

5

OS_TmrTask() is a periodic task using the same interrupt source that was used to generate clock ticks. However, timers are generally updated at a slower rate (i.e., typically 10 Hz). This is accomplished by dividing down the timer tick rate in software. In other words, if the tick rate is 1000 Hz and the desired timer rate is 10 Hz, the timer task will be signaled every 100th tick interrupt as shown in Figure 5-12.

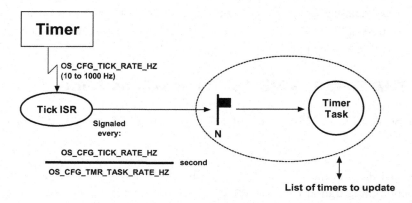

Figure 5-12 **Tick ISR and Timer Task relationship**

5-6-5 THE ISR HANDLER TASK (OS_IntQTask(), os_int.c)

When setting the compile-time configuration constant OS_CFG_ISR_POST_DEFERRED_EN in os_cfg.h to 1, μC/OS-III creates a task (called OS_IntQTask()) responsible for "deferring" the action of OS post service calls from ISRs.

As described in Chapter 4, "Critical Sections" on page 85, μC/OS-III manages critical sections either by disabling/enabling interrupts, or by locking/unlocking the scheduler. If selecting the latter method (i.e., setting OS_CFG_ISR_POST_DEFERRED_EN to 1), μC/OS-III "post" functions called from interrupts are not allowed to manipulate such internal data structures as the ready list, pend lists, and others.

When an ISR calls one of the "post" functions provided by μC/OS-III, a copy of the data posted and the desired destination is placed in a special "holding" queue. When all nested ISRs complete, μC/OS-III context switches to the ISR handler task (OS_IntQTask()), which "re-posts" the information placed in the holding queue to the appropriate task(s). This extra step is performed to reduce the amount of interrupt disable time that would otherwise be necessary to remove tasks from wait lists, insert them in the ready list, and perform other time-consuming operations.

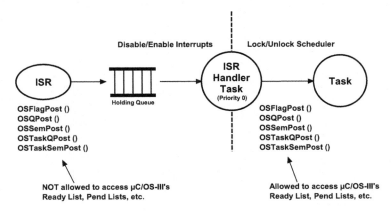

Figure 5-13 **ISR Handler Task**

`OS_IntQTask()` is created by µC/OS-III and always runs at priority 0 (i.e., the highest priority). If `OS_CFG_ISR_POST_DEFERRED_EN` is set to 1, no other task will be allowed to use priority 0.

5-7 SUMMARY

A task is a simple program that thinks it has the CPU all to itself. On a single CPU, only one task executes at any given time. µC/OS-III supports multitasking and allows the application to have any number of tasks. The maximum number of tasks is actually only limited by the amount of memory (both code and data space) available to the processor.

A task can be implemented as a run-to-completion task in which the task deletes itself when it is finished or more typically as an infinite loop, waiting for events to occur and processing those events.

A task needs to be created. When creating a task, it is necessary to specify the address of an `OS_TCB` to be used by the task, the priority of the task, an area in RAM for the task's stack and a few more parameters. A task can perform computations (CPU bound task), or manage one or more I/O (Input/Output) devices.

µC/OS-III creates up to five internal tasks: the idle task, the tick task, the ISR handler task, the statistics task, the ISR handler task and the timer task. The idle and tick tasks are always created while statistics, timer and the ISR handler tasks are optional.

The Ready List

Tasks that are ready to execute are placed in the Ready List. The ready list consists of two parts: a bitmap containing the priority levels that are ready and a table containing pointers to all the tasks ready.

6-1 PRIORITY LEVELS

Figures 5-1 to 5-3 show the bitmap of priorities that are ready. The "width" of the table depends on the data type **CPU_DATA** (see **cpu.h**), which can either be 8-, 16- or 32-bits. The width depends on the processor used.

µC/OS-III allows up to **OS_CFG_PRIO_MAX** different priority levels (see **os_cfg.h**). In µC/OS-III, a low-priority number corresponds to a high-priority level. Priority level zero (0) is thus the highest priority level. Priority **OS_CFG_PRIO_MAX-1** is the lowest priority level. µC/OS-III uniquely assigns the lowest priority to the idle task and thus, no other tasks are allowed at this priority level. If there are tasks that are ready-to-run at a given a priority level, then its corresponding bit is set (i.e., 1) in the bitmap table. Notice in Figures 5-1 to 5-3 that "priority levels" are numbered from left to right and, the priority level increases (moves toward lower priority) with an increase in table index. The order was chosen to be able to use a special instruction called Count Leading Zeros (CLZ), which is found on many modern processors. This instruction greatly accelerates the process of determining the highest priority level.

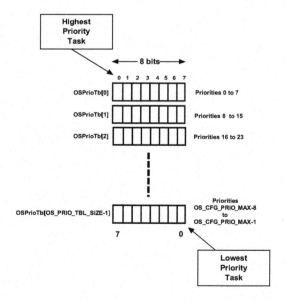

Figure 6-1 **CPU_DATA declared as a CPU_INT08U**

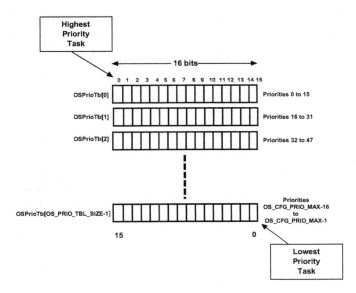

Figure 6-2 **CPU_DATA declared as a CPU_INT16U**

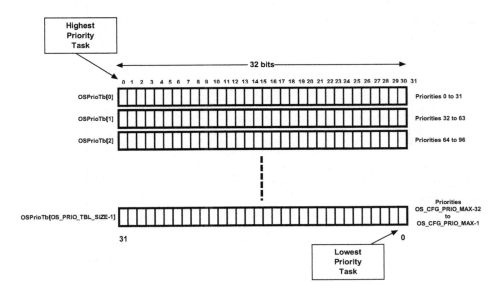

Figure 6-3 **CPU_DATA declared as a CPU_INT32U**

6

os_prio.c contains the code to set, clear, and search the bitmap table. These functions are internal to μC/OS-III and are placed in **os_prio.c** to allow them to be optimized in assembly language by replacing **os_prio.c** with an assembly language equivalent **os_prio.asm**, if necessary.

Function	Description
OS_PrioGetHighest()	Find the highest priority level
OS_PrioInsert()	Set bit corresponding to priority level in the bitmap table
OS_PrioRemove()	Clear bit corresponding to priority level in the bitmap table

Table 6-1 **Priority Level access functions**

To determine the highest priority level that contains ready-to-run tasks, the bitmap table is scanned until the first bit set in the lowest bit position is found using **OS_PrioGetHighest()**. The code for this function is shown in Listing 6-1.

```
OS_PRIO  OS_PrioGetHighest (void)
{
    CPU_DATA   *p_tbl;
    OS_PRIO     prio;


    prio  = (OS_PRIO)0;
    p_tbl = &OSPrioTbl[0];
    while (*p_tbl == (CPU_DATA)0) {            (1)
        prio += DEF_INT_CPU_NBR_BITS;          (2)
        p_tbl++;
    }
    prio += (OS_PRIO)CPU_CntLeadZeros(*p_tbl);  (3)
    return (prio);
}
```

Listing 6-1 **Finding the highest priority level**

L6-1(1) **OS_PrioGetHighest()** scans the table from **OSPrioTbl[0]** until a non-zero entry is found. The loop will always terminate because there will always be a non-zero entry in the table because of the idle task.

L6-1(2)   Each time a zero entry is found, we move to the next table entry and increment "**prio**" by the width (in number of bits) of each entry. If each entry is 32-bits wide, "**prio**" is incremented by 32.

L6-1(3)   Once the first non-zero entry is found, the number of "**leading zeros**" of that entry is simply added and we return the priority level back to the caller. Counting the number of zeros is a CPU-specific function so that if a particular CPU has a built-in CLZ instruction, it is up to the implementer of the CPU port to take advantage of this feature. If the CPU used does not provide that instruction, the functionality must be implemented in C.

The function **CPU_CntLeadZeros()** simply counts how many zeros there are in a **CPU_DATA** entry starting from the left (i.e., most significant bit). For example, assuming 32 bits, **0xF0001234** results in 0 leading zeros and **0x00F01234** results in 8 leading zeros.

At first view, the linear path through the table might seem inefficient. However, if the number of priority levels is kept low, the search is quite fast. In fact, there are several optimizations to streamline the search. For example, if using a 32-bit processor and you are satisfied with limiting the number of different priority levels to 64, the above code can be optimized as shown in Listing 6-2. In fact, some processors have built-in "Count Leading Zeros" instructions and thus, the code can even be written with just a few lines of assembly language instead of C. Remember that with µC/OS-III, 64 priority levels does not mean that the user is limited to 64 tasks since with µC/OS-III, any number of tasks are possible at a given priority level (except 0 and **OS_CFG_PRIO_MAX-1**).

```
OS_PRIO  OS_PrioGetHighest (void)
{
    OS_PRIO  prio;


    if (OSPrioTbl[0] != (OS_PRIO_BITMAP)0) {
        prio = OS_CntLeadZeros(OSPrioTbl[0]);
    } else {
        prio = OS_CntLeadZeros(OSPrioTbl[1]) + 32;
    }
    return (prio);
}
```

Listing 6-2 **Finding the highest priority level within 64 levels**

6

6-2 THE READY LIST

Tasks that are ready-to-run are placed in the Ready List. As shown in Figure 6-4, the ready list is an array (OSRdyList[ ]) containing OS_CFG_PRIO_MAX entries, with each entry defined by the data type OS_RDY_LIST (see os.h). An OS_RDY_LIST entry consists of three fields: .Entries, .TailPtr and .HeadPtr.

.Entries contains the number of ready-to-run tasks at the priority level corresponding to the entry in the ready list. .Entries is set to zero (0) if there are no tasks ready-to-run at a given priority level.

.TailPtr and .HeadPtr are used to create a doubly linked list of all the tasks that are ready at a specific priority. .HeadPtr points to the head of the list and .TailPtr points to its tail.

The "index" into the array is the priority level associated with a task. For example, if a task is created at priority level 5 then it will be inserted in the table at OSRdyList[5] if that task is ready-to-run.

Table 6-2 shows the functions that µC/OS-III uses to manipulate entries in the ready list. These functions are found in **os_core.c** and are internal to µC/OS-III so, the application code must never call them.

Function	Description
OS_RdyListInit()	Initialize the ready list to "empty" (see Figure 6-4)
OS_RdyListInsert()	Insert a TCB into the ready list
OS_RdyListInsertHead()	Insert a TCB at the head of the list
OS_RdyListInsertTail()	Insert a TCB at the tail of the list
OS_RdyListMoveHeadToTail()	Move a TCB from the head to the tail of the list
OS_RdyListRemove()	Remove a TCB from the ready list

Table 6-2 **Ready List access functions**

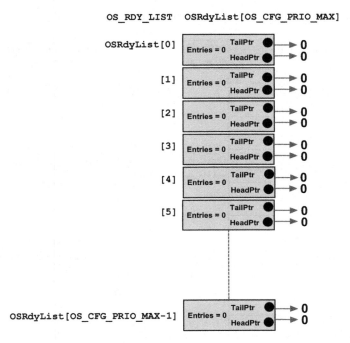

Figure 6-4 **Empty Ready List**

Assuming all internal µC/OS-III's tasks are enabled, Figure 6-5 shows the state of the ready list after calling **OSInit()** (i.e., µC/OS-III's initialization). It is assumed that each µC/OS-III task had a unique priority. With µC/OS-III, this does not have to be the case.

F6-4(1)   There is only one entry in **OSRdyList[OS_CFG_PRIO_MAX-1]**, the idle task.

F6-4(2)   The list points to OS_TCBs. Only relevant fields of the TCB are shown. The **.PrevPtr** and **.NextPtr** are used to form a doubly linked list of **OS_TCBs** associated to tasks at the same priority. For the idle task, these fields always point to **NULL**.

F6-4(3)   **Priority** 0 is reserved to the ISR handler task when **OS_CFG_ISR_DEFERRED_EN** is set to 1 in **os_cfg.h**. In this case, this is the only task that can run at priority 0.

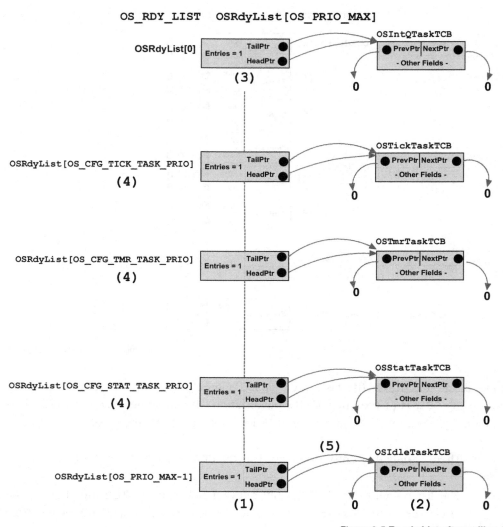

Figure 6-5 **Ready List after calling OSInit()**

F6-5(1)   The tick task and the other three optional tasks have their own priority level, as shown. Typically, you would set the priority of the tick task higher than the timer task and, the timer task higher in priority than the statistic task.

F6-5(2)   Both the tail and head pointers point to the same TCB when there is only one TCB at a given priority level.

6-3 ADDING TASKS TO THE READY LIST

Tasks are added to the ready list by a number of µC/OS-III services. The most obvious service is **OSTaskCreate()**, which always creates a task in the ready-to-run state and adds the task to the ready list. As shown in Figure 6-6, we created a task, and specified a priority level where tasks already existed (two in this example) in the ready list at the desired priority level. **OSTaskCreate()** will then insert the new task at the end of the list of tasks at that priority level.

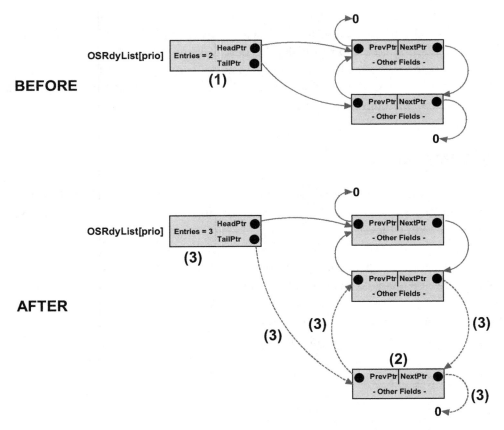

Figure 6-6 **Inserting a newly created task in the ready list**

F6-6(1)   Before calling **OSTaskCreate()** (in this example), two tasks were in the ready list at priority "**prio**".

F6-6(2)   A new TCB is passed to **OSTaskCreate()** and, µC/OS-III initialized the contents of that TCB.

149

6

F6-6(3)   **OSTaskCreate()** calls **OS_RdyListInsertTail()**, which links the new TCB to the ready list by setting up four pointers and also incrementing the **.Entries** field of **OSRdyList[prio]**. Not shown in Figure 6-6 is that **OSTaskCreate()** also calls **OS_PrioInsert()** to set the bit in the bitmap table. Of course, this operation is not necessary as there are already entries in the list at this priority. However, **OS_PrioInsert()** is a very fast call and thus it should not affect performance.

The reason the new TCB is added to the end of the list is that the current head of the list could be the task creator and it could be at the same priority. So, there is no reason to make the new task the next task to run. In fact, a task being made ready will be inserted at the tail of the list if the current task is at the same priority. However, if a task is being made ready at a different priority than the current task, it will be inserted at the head of the list.

6-4 SUMMARY

µC/OS-III supports any number of different priority levels. However, 256 different priority levels should be sufficient for the most complex applications and most systems will not require more than 64 levels.

The ready list consist of two data structures: a bitmap table that keeps track of which priority level is ready, and a table containing a list of all the tasks ready at each priority level.

Processors having "count leading zeros" instructions can accelerate the table lookup process used in determining the highest priority task.

Scheduling

The scheduler, also called the dispatcher, is a part of µC/OS-III responsible for determining which task runs next. µC/OS-III is a *preemptive, priority-based kernel*. As we have seen, each task is assigned a priority based on its importance. The priority for each task depends on the application, and µC/OS-III supports multiple tasks at the same priority level.

The word preemptive means that when an event occurs, and that event makes a more important task ready-to-run, then µC/OS-III will immediately give control of the CPU to that task. Thus, when a task signals or sends a message to a higher-priority task, the current task is suspended and the higher-priority task is given control of the CPU. Similarly, if an Interrupt Service Routine (ISR) signals or sends a message to a higher priority task, when the message has been sent, the interrupted task remains suspended, and the new higher priority task resumes.

7-1 PREEMPTIVE SCHEDULING

μC/OS-III handles event posting from interrupts using two different methods: Direct and Deferred Post. These will be discussed in greater detail in Chapter 9, "Interrupt Management" on page 175. From a scheduling point of view, the end result of the two methods is the same; the highest priority ready task will receive the CPU as shown in Figures 6-1 and 6-2.

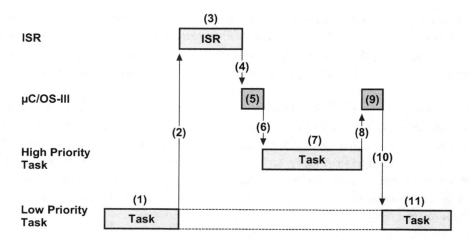

Figure 7-1 **Preemptive scheduling – Direct Method**

F7-1(1)   A low priority task is executing, and an interrupt occurs.

F7-1(2)   If interrupts are enabled, the CPU vectors (i.e., jumps) to the ISR that is responsible for servicing the interrupting device.

F7-1(3)   The ISR services the device and signals or sends a message to a higher-priority task waiting to service this device. This task is thus ready-to-run.

F7-1(4)   When the ISR completes its work it makes a service call to μC/OS-III.

F7-1(5)
F7-1(6)   Since there is a more important ready-to-run task, μC/OS-III decides to not return to the interrupted task but switches to the more important task. See Chapter 8, "Context Switching" on page 165 for details on how this works.

F7-1(7)

F7-1(8)   The higher priority task services the interrupting device and, when finished, calls µC/OS-III asking it to wait for another interrupt from the device.

F7-1(9)

F7-1(10)   µC/OS-III blocks the high-priority task until the next time the device needs servicing. Since the device has not interrupted a second time, µC/OS-III switches back to the original task (the one that was interrupted).

F7-1(11)   The interrupted task resumes execution, exactly at the point where it was interrupted.

Figure 7-2 shows that µC/OS-III performs a few extra steps when it is configured for the Deferred Post method. Notice that the end results is the same; the high-priority task preempts the low-priority one.

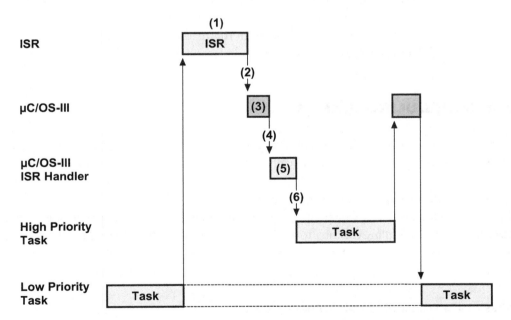

Figure 7-2 **Preemptive scheduling – Deferred Post Method**

7

F7-2(1)   The ISR services the device and, instead of signaling or sending the message to the task, μC/OS-III (through the POST call) places the post call into a special queue and makes a very high-priority task (actually the highest-possible priority) ready-to-run. This task is called the *ISR Handler Task*.

F7-2(2)   When the ISR completes its work, it makes a service call to μC/OS-III.

F7-2(3)
F7-2(4)   Since the ISR made the ISR Handler Task ready-to-run, μC/OS-III switches to that task.

F7-2(5)
F7-2(6)   The ISR Handler Task then removes the post call from the message queue and reissues the post. This time, however, it does it at the task level instead of the ISR level. The reason this extra step is performed is to keep interrupt disable time as small as possible. See Chapter 9, "Interrupt Management" on page 175 to find out more on the subject. When the queue is emptied, μC/OS-III removes the ISR Handler Task from the ready list and switches to the task that was signaled or sent a message.

7-2 SCHEDULING POINTS

Scheduling occurs at scheduling points and nothing special must be done in the application code since scheduling occurs automatically based on the conditions described below.

A task signals or sends a message to another task:
This occurs when the task signaling or sending the message calls one of the post services, OS???Post(). Scheduling occurs towards the end of the OS???Post() call. Note that scheduling does not occur if one specifies (as part of the post call) to not invoke the scheduler (i.e., by setting the option argument to OS_OPT_POST_NO_SCHED).

A task calls OSTimeDly() or OSTimeDlyHMSM():
If the delay is non-zero, scheduling always occurs since the calling task is placed in a list waiting for time to expire. Scheduling occurs as soon as the task is inserted in the wait list and this call will always result in a context switch to the next task that is ready-to-run at the same or lower priority than the task that called OSTimeDly() or OSTimeDlyHMSM().

A task waits for an event to occur and the event has not yet occurred:
This occurs when one of the OS???Pend() functions are called. The task is placed in the wait list for the event and, if a non-zero timeout is specified, the task is also inserted in the list of tasks waiting to timeout. The scheduler is then called to select the next most important task to run.

If a task aborts a pend:
A task is able to abort the wait (i.e., pend) of another task by calling OS???PendAbort(). Scheduling occurs when the task is removed from the wait list for the specified kernel object.

If a task is created:
The newly created task may have a higher priority than the task's creator. In this case, the scheduler is called.

If a task is deleted:
When terminating a task, the scheduler is called if the current task is deleted.

If a kernel object is deleted:
If you delete an event flag group, a semaphore, a message queue, or a mutual exclusion semaphore, if tasks are waiting on the kernel object, those tasks will be made ready-to-run and the scheduler will be called to determine if any of the tasks have a higher priority than the task that deleted the kernel object. Those tasks will be notified that the kernel object was deleted.

A task changes the priority of itself or another task:
The scheduler is called when a task changes the priority of another task (or itself) and the new priority of that task is higher than the task that changed the priority.

A task suspends itself by calling OSTaskSuspend():
The scheduler is called since the task that called OSTaskSuspend() is no longer able to execute. The suspended task must be resumed by another task.

A task resumes another task that was suspended by OSTaskSuspend():
The scheduler is called if the resumed task has a higher priority than the task that calls OSTaskResume().

At the end of all nested ISRs:

The scheduler is called at the end of all nested ISRs to determine whether a more important task is made ready-to-run by one of the ISRs. The scheduling is actually performed by `OSIntExit()` instead of `OSSched()`.

The scheduler is unlocked by calling OSSchedUnlock():

The scheduler is unlocked after being locked. You can lock the scheduler by calling `OSSchedLock()`. Note that locking the scheduler can be nested and the scheduler must be unlocked a number of times equal to the number of locks.

A task gives up its time quanta by calling OSSchedRoundRobinYield():

This assumes that the task is running alongside with other tasks at the same priority and the currently running task decides that it can give up its time quanta and let another task run.

The user calls OSSched():

The application code can call `OSSched()` to run the scheduler. This only makes sense if calling `OS???Post()` functions and specifying `OS_OPT_POST_NO_SCHED` so that multiple posts can be accomplished without running the scheduler on every post. However, in the above situation, the last post can be a post without the `OS_OPT_POST_NO_SCHED` option.

7-3 ROUND-ROBIN SCHEDULING

When two or more tasks have the same priority, µC/OS-III allows one task to run for a predetermined amount of time (called a *Time Quanta*) before selecting another task. This process is called *Round-Robin Scheduling* or *Time Slicing*. If a task does not need to use its full time quanta it can voluntarily give up the CPU so that the next task can execute. This is called *Yielding*. µC/OS-III allows the user to enable or disable round robin scheduling at run time.

Figure 7-3 shows a timing diagram with tasks running at the same priority. There are three tasks that are ready-to-run at priority "X". For sake of illustration, the time quanta occurs every 4th clock tick. This is shown as a darker tick mark.

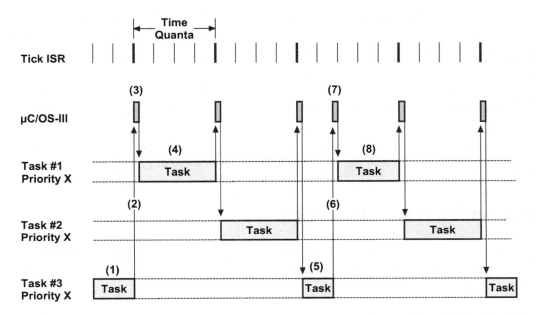

Figure 7-3 **Round Robin Scheduling**

F7-3(1)   Task #3 is executing. During that time, a tick interrupt occurs but the time quanta have not expired yet for Task #3.

F7-3(2)   On the 4th tick interrupt, the time quanta for Task #3 expire.

F7-3(3)   µC/OS-III resumes Task #1 since it was the next task in the list of tasks at priority "X" that was ready-to-run.

F7-3(4)   Task #1 executes until its time quanta expires (i.e., after four ticks).

F7-3(5)
F7-3(6)
F7-3(7)   Here Task #3 executes but decides to give up its time quanta by calling the µC/OS-III function **OSSchedRoundRobinYield()**, which causes the next task in the list of tasks ready at priority "X" to execute. An interesting thing occurred when µC/OS-III scheduled Task #1. It reset the time quanta for that task to four ticks so that the next time quanta will expire four ticks from this point.

F7-3(8)   Task #1 executes for its full time quanta.

µC/OS-III allows the user to change the default time quanta at run time through the **OSSchedRoundRobinCfg( )** function (see Appendix A, "µC/OS-III API Reference" on page 443). This function also allows round robin scheduling to be enabled/disabled, and the ability to change the default time quanta.

µC/OS-III also enables the user to specify the time quanta on a per-task basis. One task could have a time quanta of 1 tick, another 12, another 3, and yet another 7, etc. The time quanta of a task is specified when the task is created. The time quanta of a task may also be changed at run time through the function **OSTaskTimeQuantaSet( )**.

7-4 SCHEDULING INTERNALS

Scheduling is performed by two functions: **OSSched( )** and **OSIntExit( )**. **OSSched( )** is called by task level code while **OSIntExit( )** is called by ISRs. Both functions are found in **os_core.c**.

Figure 7-1 illustrates the two sets of data structures that the scheduler uses; the priority ready bitmap and the ready list as described in Chapter 6, "The Ready List" on page 141.

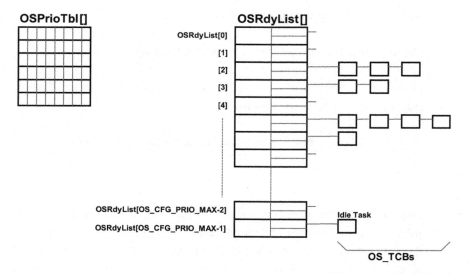

Figure 7-4 **Priority ready bitmap and Ready list**

7-4-1 OSSched()

The pseudo code for the task level scheduler, **OSSched()** (see **os_core.c**) is shown in Listing 7-1.

```
void  OSSched (void)
{
    Disable interrupts;
    if (OSIntNestingCtr > 0) {                              (1)
        return;
    }
    if (OSSchedLockNestingCtr > 0) {                        (2)
        return;
    }
    Get highest priority ready;                             (3)
    Get pointer to OS_TCB of next highest priority task;   (4)
    if (OSTCBNHighRdyPtr != OSTCBCurPtr) {                  (5)
        Perform task level context switch;
    }
    Enable interrupts;
}
```

Listing 7-1 **OSSched() pseudocode**

L7-1(1)   **OSSched()** starts by making sure it is not called from an ISR as **OSSched()** is the task level scheduler. Instead, an ISR must call **OSIntExit()**. If **OSSched()** is called by an ISR, **OSSched()** simply returns.

L7-1(2)   The next step is to make sure the scheduler is not locked. If your code called **OSSchedLock()** then the user does not want to run the scheduler and **OSSchedLock()** just returns.

L7-1(3)   **OSSched()** determines the priority of the highest priority task ready by scanning the bitmap **OSPrioTbl[]** as described in Chapter 6, "The Ready List" on page 141.

L7-1(4)   Once it is known which priority is ready, the priority is used as an index into the **OSRdyList[]** and we extract the **OS_TCB** at the head of the list (i.e., **OSRdyList[highest priority].HeadPtr**). At this point, we know which

OS_TCB to switch to and which OS_TCB to save to as this was the task that called OSSched(). Specifically, OSTCBCurPtr points to the current task's OS_TCB and OSTCBHighRdyPtr points to the new OS_TCB to switch to.

L7-1(5)   If the user is not attempting to switch to the same task that is currently running, OSSched() calls the code that will perform the context switch (see Chapter 8, "Context Switching" on page 165). As the code indicates, however, the task level scheduler calls a task-level function to perform the context switch.

Notice that the scheduler and the context switch runs with interrupts disabled. This is necessary because this process needs to be atomic.

7-4-2 OSIntExit()

The pseudo code for the ISR level scheduler, OSIntExit() (see os_core.c) is shown in Listing 7-2. Note that interrupts are assumed to be disabled when OSIntExit() is called.

```
void  OSIntExit (void)
{
    if (OSIntNestingCtr == 0) {                          (1)
        return;
    }
    OSIntNestingCtr--;
    if (OSIntNestingCtr > 0) {                           (2)
        return;
    }
    if (OSSchedLockNestingCtr > 0) {                     (3)
        return;
    }
    Get highest priority ready;                          (4)
    Get pointer to OS_TCB of next highest priority task; (5)
    if (OSTCBHighRdyPtr != OSTCBCurPtr) {                (6)
        Perform ISR level context switch;
    }
}
```

Listing 7-2 **OSIntExit() pseudocode**

L7-2(1)   OSIntExit() starts by making sure that the call to OSIntExit() will not cause OSIntNestingCtr to wrap around. This would be an unlikely occurrence, but not worth verifying that it's not.

L7-2(2)   `OSIntExit()` decrements the nesting counter as `OSIntExit()` is called at the end of an ISR. If all ISRs have not nested, the code simply returns. There is no need to run the scheduler since there are still interrupts to return to.

L7-2(3)   `OSIntExit()` checks to see that the scheduler is not locked. If it is, `OSIntExit()` does not run the scheduler and simply returns to the interrupted task that locked the scheduler.

L7-2(4)   Finally, this is the last nested ISR (we are returning to task-level code) and the scheduler is not locked. Therefore, we need to find the highest priority task that needs to run.

L7-2(5)   Again, we extract the highest priority `OS_TCB` from `OSRdyList[]`.

L7-2(6)   If the highest-priority task is not the current task, µC/OS-III performs an ISR level context switch. The ISR level context switch is different as it is assumed that the interrupted task's context was saved at the beginning of the ISR and we only need to restore the context of the new task to run. This is described in Chapter 8, "Context Switching" on page 165.

7-4-3 OS_SchedRoundRobin()

When the time quanta for a task expires and there are multiple tasks at the same priority, µC/OS-III will select and run the next task that is ready-to-run at the current priority. `OS_SchedRoundRobin()` is the code used to perform this operation. `OS_SchedRoundRobin()` is either called by `OSTimeTick()` or `OS_IntQTask()`. `OS_SchedRoundRobin()` is found in `os_core.c`.

`OS_SchedRoundRobin()` is called by `OSTimeTick()` if you selected the Direct Method of posting (see Chapter 9, "Interrupt Management" on page 175). `OS_SchedRoundRobin()` is called by `OS_IntQTask()` if you selected the Deferred Post Method of posting, described in Chapter 8.

The pseudo code for the round-robin scheduler is shown in Listing 7-3.

```
void  OS_SchedRoundRobin (void)
{
    if (OSSchedRoundRobinEn != TRUE) {                          (1)
        return;
    }
    if (Time quanta counter > 0) {                              (2)
        Decrement time quanta counter;
    }
    if (Time quanta counter > 0) {
        return;
    }
    if (Number of OS_TCB at current priority level < 2) {      (3)
        return;
    }
    if (OSSchedLockNestingCtr > 0) {                            (4)
        return;
    }
    Move OS_TCB from head of list to tail of list;             (5)
    Reload time quanta for current task;                       (6)
}
```

Listing 7-3 **OS_SchedRoundRobin() pseudocode**

L7-3(1)   OS_SchedRoundRobin() starts by making sure that round robin scheduling is enabled. Recall that to enable round robin scheduling, your code must call OSSchedRoundRobinCfg().

L7-3(2)   The time quanta counter, which resides inside the OS_TCB of the running task, is decremented. If the value is still non-zero then OS_SchedRoundRobin() returns.

L7-3(3)   Once the time quanta counter reaches zero, OS_SchedRoundRobin() checks to see that there are other ready-to-run tasks at the current priority. If there are none, the function returns. Round robin scheduling only applies when there are multiple tasks at the same priority and the task doesn't completes its work within its time quanta.

L7-3(4)   OS_SchedRoundRobin() also returns if the scheduler is locked.

L7-3(5)   Next, OS_SchedRoundRobin() moves the OS_TCB of the current task from the head of the ready list to the end.

L7-3(6)   The time quanta for the task at the head of the list is loaded. Each task may specify its own time quanta when the task is created or through `OSTaskTimeQuantaSet()`. If you set the task time quanta to 0 then µC/OS-III assumes the default time quanta, which corresponds to the value in the variable `OSSchedRoundRobinDfltTimeQuanta`.

7-5 SUMMARY

µC/OS-III is a preemptive scheduler so it will always execute the highest priority task that is ready-to-run.

µC/OS-III allows for multiple tasks at the same priority. If there are multiple ready-to-run tasks, µC/OS-III will round robin between these tasks.

Scheduling occurs at specific scheduling points when the application calls µC/OS-III functions.

µC/OS-III has two schedulers: `OSSched()`, which is called by task-level code, and `OSIntExit()` called at the end of each ISR.

Context Switching

When μC/OS-III decides to run a different task (see Chapter 7, "Scheduling" on page 151), it saves the current task's context, which typically consists of the CPU registers, onto the current task's stack and restores the context of the new task and resumes execution of that task. This process is called a *Context Switch*.

Context switching adds overhead. The more registers a CPU has, the higher the overhead. The time required to perform a context switch is generally determined by how many registers must be saved and restored by the CPU.

The context switch code is generally part of a processor's *port* of μC/OS-III. A port is the code needed to adapt μC/OS-III to the desired processor. This code is placed in special C and assembly language files: **os_cpu.h**, **os_cpu_c.c** and **os_cpu_a.asm** Chapter 18, "Porting μC/OS-III" on page 355, Porting μC/OS-III provides more details on the steps needed to port μC/OS-III to different CPU architectures.

In this chapter, we will discuss the context switching process in generic terms using a fictitious CPU as shown in Figure 8-1. Our fictitious CPU contains 16 integer registers (R0 to R15), a separate ISR stack pointer, and a separate status register (SR). Every register is 32 bits wide and each of the 16 integer registers can hold either data or an address. The program counter (or instruction pointer) is R15 and there are two separate stack pointers labeled R14 and R14'. R14 represents a task stack pointer (TSP), and R14' represents an ISR stack pointer (ISP). The CPU automatically switches to the ISR stack when servicing an exception or interrupt. The task stack is accessible from an ISR (i.e., we can push and pop elements onto the task stack when in an ISR), and the interrupt stack is also accessible from a task.

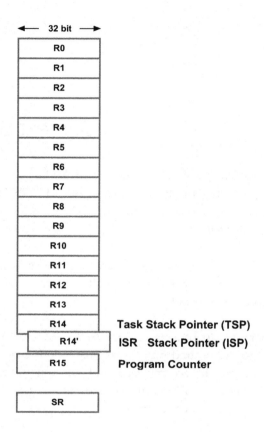

Figure 8-1 **Fictitious CPU**

In µC/OS-III, the stack frame for a ready task is always setup to look as if an interrupt has just occurred and all processor registers were saved onto it. Tasks enter the ready state upon creation and thus their stack frames are pre-initialized by software in a similar manner. Using our fictitious CPU, we'll assume that a stack frame for a task that is ready to be restored is shown in Figure 8-2.

The task stack pointer points to the last register saved onto the task's stack. The program counter (**PC** or **R15**) and status register (**SR**) are the first registers saved onto the stack. In fact, these are saved automatically by the CPU when an exception or interrupt occurs (assuming interrupts are enabled) while the other registers are pushed onto the stack by software in the exception handler. The stack pointer (**SP** or **R14**) is not actually saved on the stack but instead is saved in the task's **OS_TCB**.

The interrupt stack pointer points to the current top-of-stack for the interrupt stack, which is a different memory area. When an ISR executes, the processor uses R14' as the stack pointer for function calls and local arguments.

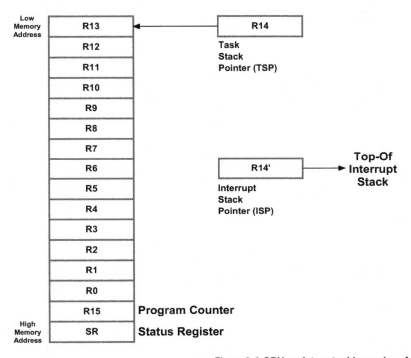

Figure 8-2 **CPU register stacking order of ready task**

There are two types of context switches: one performed from a task and another from an ISR. The task level context switch is implemented by the code in **OSCtxSw()**, which is actually invoked by the macro **OS_TASK_SW()**. A macro is used as there are many ways to invoke **OSCtxSw()** such as software interrupts, trap instructions, or simply calling the function.

The ISR context switch is implemented by **OSIntCtxSw()**. The code for both functions is typically written in assembly language and is found in a file called **os_cpu_a.asm**.

8-1 OSCtxSw()

OSCtxSw() (see **os_cpu_a.asm**) is called when the task level scheduler (OSSched()) determines that a new high priority task needs to execute. Figure 8-3 shows the state of several µC/OS-III variables and data structures just prior to calling OSCtxSw().

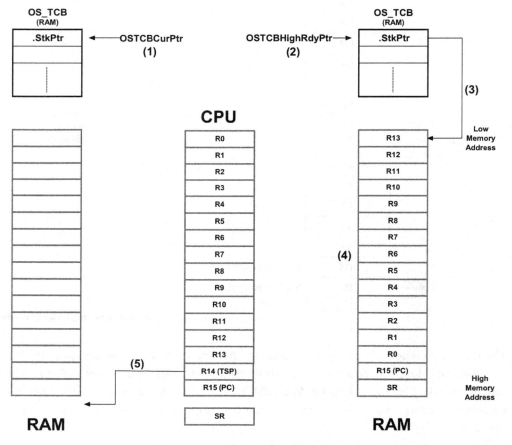

Figure 8-3 **Variables and data structures prior to calling OSCtxSw()**

F8-3(1)   OSTCBCurPtr points to the OS_TCB of the task that is currently running and that called OSSched().

F8-3(2)   OSSched() finds the new task to run by having OSTCBHighRdyPtr point to its OS_TCB.

F8-3(3)   `OSTCBHighRdyPtr->StkPtr` points to the top of stack of the new task to run.

F8-3(4)   When μC/OS-III creates or suspends a task, it always leaves the stack frame to look as if an interrupt just occurred and all the registers saved onto it. This represents the expected state of the task so it can be resumed.

F8-3(5)   The CPU's stack pointer points within the stack area (i.e., RAM) of the task that called `OSSched()`. Depending on how `OSCtxSw()` is invoked, the stack pointer may be pointing at the return address of `OSCtxSw()`.

Figure 8-4 shows the steps involved in performing the context switch as implemented by `OSCtxSw()`.

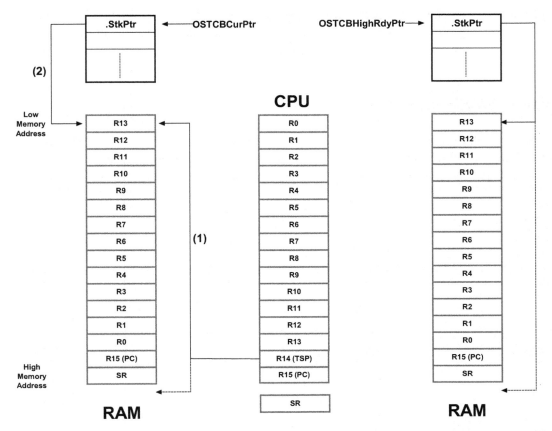

Figure 8-4 **Operations performed by OSCtxSw()**

F8-4(1)   **OSCtxSw()** begins by saving the status register and program counter of the current task onto the current task's stack. The saving order of register depends on how the CPU expects the registers on the stack frame when an interrupt occurs. In this case, it is assumed that the SR is stacked first. The remaining registers are then saved onto the stack.

F8-4(2)   **OSCtxSw()** saves the contents of the CPU's stack pointer into the **OS_TCB** of the task being context switched out. In other words, **OSTCBCurPtr->StkPtr = R14**.

F8-4(3)   **OSCtxSw()** then loads the CPU stack pointer with the saved top-of-stack from the new task's **OS_TCB**. In other words, **R14 = OSTCBHighRdyPtr->StkPtr**.

F8-4(4)   Finally, **OSCtxSw()** retrieves the CPU register contents from the new stack. The program counter and status registers are generally retrieved at the same time by executing a return from interrupt instruction.

8-2 OSIntCtxSw()

OSIntCtxSw() (see **os_cpu_a.asm**) is called when the ISR level scheduler (**OSIntExit()**) determines that a new high priority task is ready to execute. Figure 8-5 shows the state of several µC/OS-III variables and data structures just prior to calling **OSIntCtxSw()**.

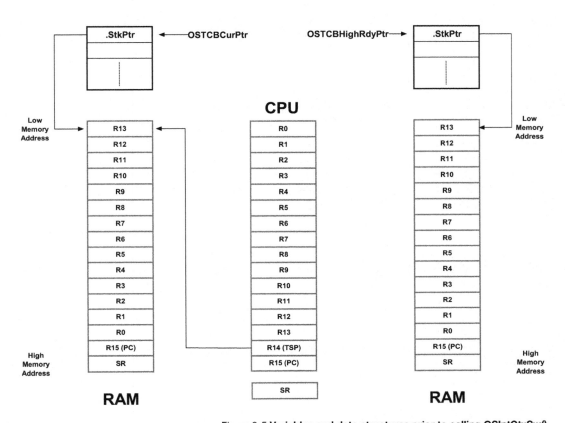

Figure 8-5 **Variables and data structures prior to calling OSIntCtxSw()**

µC/OS-III assumes that CPU registers are saved onto the task's stack at the beginning of an ISR (see Chapter 9, "Interrupt Management" on page 175). Because of this, notice that OSTCBCurPtr->StkPtr contains a pointer to the top-of-stack pointer of the task being suspended (the one on the left). OSIntCtxSw() does not have to worry about saving the CPU registers of the suspended task since that has already been done.

Figure 8-6 shows the operations performed by OSIntCtxSw() to complete the second half of the context switch. This is exactly the same process as the second half of OSCtxSw().

8

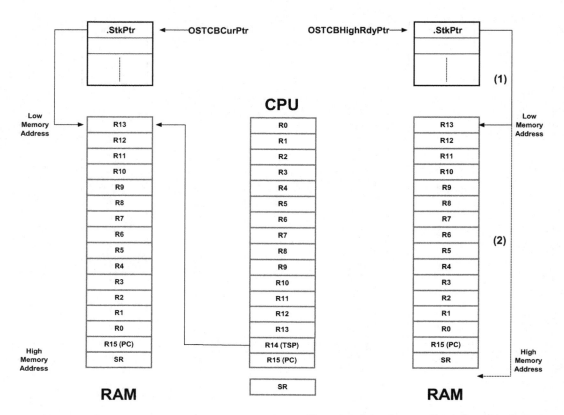

Figure 8-6 **Operations performed by OSIntCtxSw()**

F8-6(1)   OSIntCtxSw() loads the CPU stack pointer with the saved top-of-stack from the new task's OS_TCB. R14 = OSTCBHighRdyPtr->StkPtr.

F8-6(2)   OSIntCtxSw() then retrieves the CPU register contents from the new stack. The program counter and status registers are generally retrieved at the same time by executing a return from interrupt instruction.

8-3 SUMMARY

A context switch consists of saving the context (i.e., CPU registers) associated with one task and restoring the context of a new, higher-priority task.

The new task to be switched to is determined by **OSSched()** when a context switch is initiated by task level code, and **OSIntExit()** when initiated by an ISR.

OSCtxSw() performs the context switch for **OSSched()** and **OSIntCtxSw()** performs the context switch for **OSIntExit()**. However, **OSIntCtxSw()** only needs to perform the second half of the context switch because it is assumed that the ISR saved CPU registers upon entry to the ISR.

8

8

Interrupt Management

An *interrupt* is a hardware mechanism used to inform the CPU that an asynchronous event occurred. When an interrupt is recognized, the CPU saves part (or all) of its context (i.e., registers) and jumps to a special subroutine called an *Interrupt Service Routine* (ISR). The ISR processes the event, and – upon completion of the ISR – the program either returns to the interrupted task, or the highest priority task, if the ISR made a higher priority task ready-to-run.

Interrupts allow a microprocessor to process events when they occur (i.e., asynchronously), which prevents the microprocessor from continuously *polling* (looking at) an event to see if it occurred. Task level response to events is typically better using interrupt mode as opposed to polling mode. Microprocessors allow interrupts to be ignored or recognized through the use of two special instructions: disable interrupts and enable interrupts, respectively.

In a real-time environment, interrupts should be disabled as little as possible. Disabling interrupts affects interrupt latency possibly causing interrupts to be missed.

Processors generally allow interrupts to be nested, which means that while servicing an interrupt, the processor recognizes and services other (more important) interrupts.

One of the most important specifications of a real-time kernel is the maximum amount of time that interrupts are disabled. This is called *interrupt disable time*. All real-time systems disable interrupts to manipulate critical sections of code and re-enable interrupts when critical sections are completed. The longer interrupts are disabled, the higher the interrupt latency.

Interrupt response is defined as the time between the reception of the interrupt and the start of the user code that handles the interrupt. Interrupt response time accounts for the entire overhead involved in handling an interrupt. Typically, the processor's context (CPU registers) is saved on the stack before the user code is executed.

Interrupt recovery is defined as the time required for the processor to return to the interrupted code or to a higher priority task if the ISR made such a task ready-to-run.

Task latency is defined as the time it takes from the time the interrupt occurs to the time task level code resumes.

9-1 HANDLING CPU INTERRUPTS

There are many popular CPU architectures on the market today, and most processors typically handle interrupts from a multitude of sources. For example, a UART receives a character, an Ethernet controller receives a packet, a DMA controller completes a data transfer, an Analog-to-Digital Converter (ADC) completes an analog conversion, a timer expires, *etc.*

In most cases, an *interrupt controller* captures all of the different interrupts presented to the processor as shown in Figure 9-1 (note that the "CPU Interrupt Enable/Disable" is typically part of the CPU, but is shown here separately for sake of the illustration).

Interrupting devices signal the interrupt controller, which then prioritizes the interrupts and presents the highest-priority interrupt to the CPU.

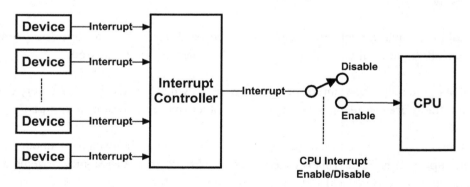

Figure 9-1 **Interrupt controllers**

Modern interrupt controllers have built-in intelligence that enable the user to prioritize interrupts, remember which interrupts are still pending and, in many cases, have the interrupt controller provide the address of the ISR (also called the vector address) directly to the CPU.

If "global" interrupts (i.e., the switch in Figure 9-1) are disabled, the CPU will ignore requests from the interrupt controller, but they will be held pending by the interrupt controller until the CPU re-enables interrupts.

CPUs deal with interrupts using one of two models:

1   All interrupts *vector* to a single interrupt handler.

2   Each interrupt *vectors* directly to an interrupt handler.

Before discussing these two methods, it is important to understand how µC/OS-III handles CPU interrupts.

9-2 TYPICAL µC/OS-III INTERRUPT SERVICE ROUTINE (ISR)

µC/OS-III requires that an interrupt service routine be written in assembly language. However, if a C compiler supports in-line assembly language, the ISR code can be placed directly into a C source file. The pseudo-code for a typical ISR when using µC/OS-III is shown in Listing 9-1.

```
MyISR:                                                        (1)
    Disable all interrupts;                                   (2)
    Save the CPU registers;                                   (3)
    OSIntNestingCtr++;                                        (4)
    if (OSIntNestingCtr == 1) {                               (5)
        OSTCBCurPtr->StkPtr = Current task's CPU stack pointer register value;
    }
    Clear interrupting device;                                (6)
    Re-enable interrupts (optional);                          (7)
    Call user ISR;                                            (8)
    OSIntExit();                                              (9)
    Restore the CPU registers;                                (10)
    Return from interrupt;                                    (11)
```

Listing 9-1 **ISRs under µC/OS-III (assembly language)**

L9-1(1)   As mentioned above, an ISR is typically written in assembly language. **MyISR** corresponds to the name of the handler that will handle the interrupting device.

L9-1(2)   It is important that all interrupts are disabled before going any further. Some processors have interrupts disabled whenever an interrupt handler starts. Others require the user to explicitly disable interrupts as shown here. This step may be tricky if a processor supports different interrupt priority levels. However, there is always a way to solve the problem.

L9-1(3)   The first thing the interrupt handler must do is save the context of the CPU onto the interrupted task's stack. On some processors, this occurs automatically. However, on most processors it is important to know how to save the CPU registers onto the task's stack. You should save the full "context" of the CPU, which may also include Floating-Point Unit (FPU) registers if the CPU used is equipped with an FPU.

Certain CPUs also automatically switch to a special stack just to process interrupts (i.e., an interrupt stack). This is generally beneficial as it avoids using up valuable task stack space. However, for µC/OS-III, the context of the interrupted task needs to be saved onto that task's stack.

If the processor does not have a dedicated stack pointer to handle ISRs then it is possible to implement one in software. Specifically, upon entering the ISR, simply save the current task stack, switch to a dedicated ISR stack, and when done with the ISR switch back to the task stack. Of course, this means that there is additional code to write, however the benefits are enormous since it is not necessary to allocate extra space on the task stacks to accommodate for worst case interrupt stack usage including interrupt nesting.

L9-1(4)   Next, either call **OSIntEnter()**, or simply increment the variable **OSIntNestingCtr** in assembly language. This is generally quite easy to do and is more efficient than calling **OSIntEnter()**. As its name implies, **OSIntNestingCtr** keeps track of the interrupt nesting level.

L9-1(5)   If this is the first nested interrupt, you need to save the current value of the stack pointer of the interrupted task into its **OS_TCB**. The global pointer **OSTCBCurPtr** conveniently points to the interrupted task's **OS_TCB**. The very first field in **OS_TCB** is where the stack pointer needs to be saved. In other words, **OSTCBCurPtr->StkPtr** happens to be at offset 0 in the **OS_TCB** (this greatly simplifies assembly language).

L9-1(6)   At this point, you need to clear the interrupting device so that it does not generate the same another interrupt. However, most people defer the clearing of the source and prefer to perform the action within the user ISR handler in "C."

L9-1(7)   At this point, it is safe to re-enable interrupts you want to support nested interrupts. This step is optional.

L9-1(8)   At this point, further processing can be deferred to a C function called from assembly language. This is especially useful if there is a large amount of processing to do in the ISR handler. However, as a general rule, keep the ISRs as short as possible. In fact, it is best to simply signal or send a message to a task and let the task handle the details of servicing the interrupting device.

The ISR must call one of the following functions: **OSSemPost( )**, **OSTaskSemPost( )**, **OSFlagPost( )**, **OSQPost( )** or **OSTaskQPost( )**. This is necessary since the ISR will notify a task, which will service the interrupting device. These are the only functions able to be called from an ISR and they are used to signal or send a message to a task. However, if the ISR does not need to call one of these functions, consider writing the ISR as a "Non Kernel-Aware Interrupt Service Routine," as described in the next section.

L9-1(9)   When the ISR completes, you must call **OSIntExit( )** to tell µC/OS-III that the ISR has completed. **OSIntExit( )** simply decrements **OSIntNestingCtr** and, if **OSIntNestingCtr** reaches 0, this indicates that the ISR is about to return to task-level code (instead of a previously interrupted ISR). µC/OS-III will need to determine whether there is a higher priority task that needs to run because of one of the nested ISRs. In other words, the ISR might have signaled or sent a message to a higher- priority task waiting for this signal or message. In this case, µC/OS-III will context switch to this higher priority task instead of returning to the interrupted task. In this latter case, **OSIntExit( )** does not actually return, but takes a different path.

9

9

L9-1(10)   If the ISR signaled or sent a message to a lower-priority task than the interrupted task, **OSIntExit( )** returns. This means that the interrupted task is still the highest-priority task to run and it is important to restore the previously saved registers.

L9-1(11)   The ISR performs a return from interrupts and so resumes the interrupted task.

NOTE: From this point on, (1) to (6) will be referred to as the *ISR Prologue* and (9) to (11) as the ISR Epilogue.

9-3 NON KERNEL-AWARE INTERRUPT SERVICE ROUTINE (ISR)

The above sequence assumes that the ISR signals or sends a message to a task. However, in many cases, the ISR may not need to notify a task and can simply perform all of its work within the ISR (assuming it can be done quickly). In this case, the ISR will appear as shown in Listing 9-2.

```
MyShortISR:                                              (1)
    Save enough registers as needed by the ISR;          (2)
    Clear interrupting device;                           (3)
    DO NOT re-enable interrupts;                         (4)
    Call user ISR;                                       (5)
    Restore the saved CPU registers;                     (6)
    Return from interrupt;                               (7)
```

Listing 9-2 **Non-Kernel Aware ISRs with µC/OS-III**

L9-2(1)   As mentioned above, an ISR is typically written in assembly language. **MyShortISR** corresponds to the name of the handler that will handle the interrupting device.

L9-2(2)   Here, you save sufficient registers as required to handle the ISR.

L9-2(3)   The user probably needs to clear the interrupting device to prevent it from generating the same interrupt once the ISR returns.

L9-2(4)   *Do not* re-enable interrupts at this point since another interrupt could make µC/OS-III calls, forcing a context switch to a higher-priority task. This means that the above ISR would complete, but at a much later time.

L9-2(5)   Now you can take care of the interrupting device in assembly language or call a C function, if necessary.

L9-2(6)   Once finished, simply restore the saved CPU registers.

L9-2(7)   Perform a return from interrupt to resume the interrupted task.

9-4 PROCESSORS WITH MULTIPLE INTERRUPT PRIORITIES

There are some processors that actually supports multiple interrupt levels as shown in Figure 9-2.

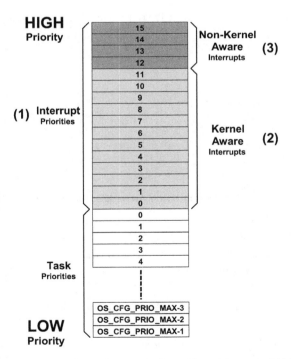

Figure 9-2 **Kernel Aware and Non-Kernel Aware Interrupts**

F9-2(1)   Here, we are assuming that the processor supports 16 different interrupt priority levels. Priority 0 is the lowest priority while 15 is the highest. As shown, interrupts are always higher in priority than tasks (assuming interrupts are enabled).

F9-2(2)   The designed of the product decided that interrupt levels 0 through 12 will be allowed to make µC/OS-III 'post' calls to notify tasks that are assigned to service these interrupts. It's important to note that disabling interrupts (when entering critical sections) for task aware interrupts means raising the interrupt mask to level 12. In other words, interrupt levels 0 through 11 would be disabled but, levels 12 and above would be allowed.

F9-2(3)   Interrupt levels 12 through 15 will **not** be allowed to make any µC/OS-III function calls and are thus implemented as shown in Listing 9-2. It's important to note that since µC/OS-III cannot disable these interrupts, interrupt latency for these interrupts is very short.

Listing 9-3 shows how to implement non-kernel aware ISRs when the processor supports multiple interrupt priorities.

```
MyNonKernelAwareISR:                                    (1)
    Save enough registers as needed by the ISR;         (2)
    Clear interrupting device;                          (3)
    Call user ISR;                                      (4)
    Restore the saved CPU registers;                    (5)
    Return from interrupt;                              (6)
```

Listing 9-3 **Non-Kernel Aware ISRs for Processors with Multiple Priority Levels**

L9-3(1)   As mentioned above, an ISR is typically written in assembly language. **MyNonKernelAwareISR** corresponds to the name of the handler that will handle the interrupting device.

L9-3(2)   Here, you save sufficient registers as required to handle the ISR.

L9-3(3)   The user probably needs to clear the interrupting device to prevent it from generating the same interrupt once the ISR returns.

L9-3(4)   Now you can take care of the interrupting device in assembly language or call a C function, if necessary.

L9-3(5)   Once finished, simply restore the saved CPU registers.

L9-3(6)   Perform a return from interrupt to resume the interrupted task.

9-5 ALL INTERRUPTS VECTOR TO A COMMON LOCATION

Even though an interrupt controller is present in most designs, some CPUs still vector to a common interrupt handler, and the ISR queries the interrupt controller to determine the source of the interrupt. At first glance, this might seem silly since most interrupt controllers are able to force the CPU to jump directly to the proper interrupt handler. It turns out, however, that for µC/OS-III, it is easier to have the interrupt controller vector to a single ISR handler than to vector to a unique ISR handler for each source. Listing 9-4 describes the sequence of events to be performed when the interrupt controller forces the CPU to vector to a single location.

```
An interrupt occurs;                                   (1)
The CPU vectors to a common location;                  (2)
The ISR code performs the "ISR prologue"               (3)
The C handler performs the following:                  (4)
    while (there are still interrupts to process) {    (5)
        Get vector address from interrupt controller;
        Call interrupt handler;
    }
The "ISR epilogue" is executed;                        (6)
```

Listing 9-4 **Single interrupt vector for all interrupts**

L9-4(1)   An interrupt occurs from any device. The interrupt controller activates the interrupt pin on the CPU. If there are other interrupts that occur after the first one, the interrupt controller will latch them and properly prioritize the interrupts.

L9-4(2)   The CPU vectors to a single interrupt handler address. In other words, all interrupts are to be handled by this one interrupt handler.

L9-4(3)   The ISR executes the "ISR prologue" code needed by μC/OS-III. as previously described. This ensures that all ISRs will be able to make μC/OS-III "post" calls.

L9-4(4)   You call a μC/OS-III C handler, which will continue processing the ISR. This makes the code easier to write (and read). Notice that interrupts are not re-enabled.

L9-4(5)   The μC/OS-III C handler then interrogates the interrupt controller and asks it: "Who caused the interrupt?" The interrupt controller will either respond with a number (**0** to **N-1**) or with the address of the interrupt handler for the highest priority interrupting device. Of course, the μC/OS-III C handler will know how to handle the specific interrupt controller since the C handler is written specifically for that controller.

If the interrupt controller provides a number between 0 and N-1, the C handler simply uses this number as an index into a table (in ROM or RAM) containing the address of the interrupt service routine associated with the interrupting device. A RAM table is handy to change interrupt handlers at run-time. For many embedded systems, however, the table may also reside in ROM.

If the interrupt controller responds with the address of the interrupt service routine, the C handler only needs to call this function.

In both of the above cases, all interrupt handlers need to be declared as follows:

```
void MyISRHandler (void);
```

There is one such handler for each possible interrupt source (obviously, each having a unique name).

The "**while**" loop terminates when there are no other interrupting devices to service.

L9-4(6)   The μC/OS-III "ISR epilogue" is executed to see if it is necessary to return to the interrupted task, or switch to a more important one.

A couple of interesting points to note:

■ If another device caused an interrupt before the C handler had a chance to query the interrupt controller, most likely the interrupt controller will capture that interrupt. In fact, if that second device happens to be a higher-priority interrupting device, it will most likely be serviced first, as the interrupt controller will prioritize the interrupts.

■ The loop will not terminate until all pending interrupts are serviced. This is similar to allowing nested interrupts, but better, since it is not necessary to redo the ISR prologue and epilogue.

The disadvantage of this method is that a high priority interrupt that occurs after the servicing of another interrupt that has already started must wait for that interrupt to complete before it will be serviced. So, the latency of any interrupt, regardless of priority, can be as long as it takes to process the longest interrupt.

9-6 EVERY INTERRUPT VECTORS TO A UNIQUE LOCATION

If the interrupt controller vectors directly to the appropriate interrupt handler, each of the ISRs must be written in assembly language as described in section 9-2 "Typical µC/OS-III Interrupt Service Routine (ISR)" on page 177. This, of course, slightly complicates the design. However, you can copy and paste the majority of the code from one handler to the other and just change what is specific to the actual device.

If the interrupt controller allows the user to query it for the source of the interrupt, it may be possible to simulate the mode in which all interrupts vector to the same location by simply setting all vectors to point to the same location. Most interrupt controllers that vector to a unique location, however, do not allow users to query it for the source of the interrupt since, by definition, having a unique vector for all interrupting devices should not be necessary.

9-7 DIRECT AND DEFERRED POST METHODS

μC/OS-III handles event posting from interrupts using two different methods: Direct and Deferred Post. The method used in the application is selected by changing the value of **OS_CFG_ISR_POST_DEFERRED_EN** in **os_cfg.h**. When set to 0, μC/OS-III uses the Direct Post Method and when set to 1, μC/OS-III uses the Deferred Post Method.

As far as application code and ISRs are concerned, these two methods are completely transparent. It is not necessary to change anything except the configuration value **OS_CFG_ISR_POST_DEFERRED_EN** to switch between the two methods. Of course, changing the configuration constant will require recompiling the product and μC/OS-III.

Before explaining why to use one versus the other, let us review their differences.

9-7-1 DIRECT POST METHOD

The Direct Post Method is used by μC/OS-II and is replicated in μC/OS-III. Figure 9-3 shows a task diagram of what takes place in a Direct Post.

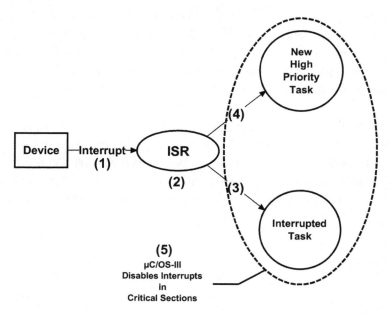

Figure 9-3 **Direct Post Method**

F9-3(1)   A device generates an interrupt.

F9-3(2)   The Interrupt Service Routine (ISR) responsible to handle the device executes (assuming interrupts are enabled). The device interrupt is generally the event a task is waiting for. The task waiting for this interrupt to occur either has a higher priority than the interrupted task, or lower (or equal) in priority.

F9-3(3)   If the ISR made a lower (or equal) priority task ready-to-run then upon completion of the ISR, µC/OS-III returns to the interrupted task exactly at the point the interrupt occurred.

F9-3(4)   If the ISR made a higher priority task ready-to-run, µC/OS-III will context switch to the new higher-priority task since the more important task was waiting for this device interrupt.

F9-3(5)   In the Direct Post Method, µC/OS-III must protect critical sections by disabling interrupts as some of these critical sections can be accessed by ISRs.

The above discussion assumed that interrupts were enabled and that the ISR could respond quickly to the interrupting device. However, if the application code makes µC/OS-III service calls (and it will at some point), it is possible that interrupts would be disabled. When `OS_CFG_ISR_POST_DEFERRED_EN` is set to 0, µC/OS-III disables interrupts while accessing critical sections. Thus, interrupts will not be responded to until µC/OS-III re-enables interrupts. Of course, everything was done to keep interrupt disable times as short as possible, but there are complex features of µC/OS-III that disable interrupts for relatively long periods of time.

The key factor in determining whether to use the Direct Post Method is generally the µC/OS-III interrupt disable time. This is fairly easy to determine since the µC/CPU files provided with the µC/OS-III port for the processor used includes code to measure maximum interrupt disable time. This code can be enabled testing purposes and removed when ready to deploy the product. The user would typically not want to leave measurement code in production code to avoid introducing measurement artifacts.

You can determine the interrupt latency, interrupt response, interrupt recovery, and task latency by adding the execution times of the code involved for each, as shown below.

Interrupt Latency   =   Maximum interrupt disable time;

Interrupt Response   =   Interrupt latency
                              + Vectoring to the interrupt handler
                              + ISR prologue;

Interrupt Recovery   =   Handling of the interrupting device
                              + Posting a signal or a message to a task
                              + `OSIntExit()`
                              + `OSIntCtxSw();`

Task Latency   =   Interrupt response
                              + Interrupt recovery
                              + Time scheduler is locked;

The execution times of the µC/OS-III ISR prologue, ISR epilogue, `OSIntExit()`, and `OSIntCtxSw()`, can be measured independently and should be fairly constant.

It should also be easy to measure the execution time of a post call by using `OS_TS_GET()`.

In the Direct Post Method, the scheduler is locked only when handling timers and therefore, task latency should be fast if there are few timers with short callbacks expiring at the same time. See Chapter 12, "Timer Management" on page 213. µC/OS-III is also able to measure the amount of time the scheduler is locked, providing task latency.

9-7-2 DEFERRED POST METHOD

In the Deferred Post Method (OS_CFG_ISR_POST_DEFERRED_EN is set to 1), instead of disabling interrupts to access critical sections, μC/OS-III locks the scheduler. This avoids having other tasks access critical sections while allowing interrupts to be recognized and serviced. In the Deferred Post Method, interrupts are almost never disabled. The Deferred Post Method is, however, a bit more complex as shown in Figure 9-4.

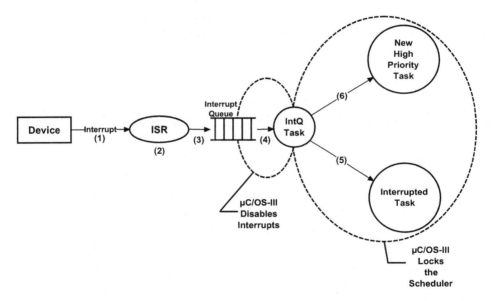

Figure 9-4 **Deferred Post Method block diagram**

F9-4(1)   A device generates an interrupt.

F9-4(2)   The ISR responsible for handling the device executes (assuming interrupts are enabled). The device interrupt is the event that a task was waiting for. The task waiting for this interrupt to occur is either higher in priority than the interrupted task, lower, or equal in priority.

F9-4(3)   The ISR calls one of the post services to signal or send a message to a task. However, instead of performing the post operation, the ISR queues the actual post call along with arguments in a special queue called the *Interrupt Queue*. The ISR then makes the *Interrupt Queue Handler Task* ready-to-run. This task is internal to µC/OS-III and is always the highest priority task (i.e., Priority 0).

F9-4(4)   At the end of the ISR, µC/OS-III always context switches to the interrupt queue handler task, which then extracts the post command from the queue. We disable interrupts to prevent another interrupt from accessing the interrupt queue while the queue is being emptied. The task then re-enables interrupts, locks the scheduler, and performs the post call as if the post was performed at the task level all along. This effectively manipulates critical sections at the task level.

F9-4(5)   When the interrupt queue handler task empties the interrupt queue, it makes itself not ready-to-run and then calls the scheduler to determine which task must run next. If the original interrupted task is still the highest priority task, µC/OS-III will resume that task.

F9-4(6)   If, however, a more important task was made ready-to-run because of the post, µC/OS-III will context switch to that task.

All the extra processing is performed to avoid disabling interrupts during critical sections of code. The extra processing time only consist of copying the post call and arguments into the queue, extracting it back out of the queue, and performing an extra context switch.

Similar to the Direct Post Method, it is easy to determine interrupt latency, interrupt response, interrupt recovery, and task latency, by adding execution times of the pieces of code involved for each as shown below.

Interrupt Latency = Maximum interrupt disable time;

Interrupt Response = Interrupt latency
+ Vectoring to the interrupt handler
+ ISR prologue;

Interrupt Recovery = Handling of the interrupting device
+ Posting a signal or a message to the Interrupt Queue
+ **OSIntExit( )**
+ **OSIntCtxSw( )** to Interrupt Queue Handler Task;

Task Latency = Interrupt response
+ Interrupt recovery
+ Re-issue the post to the object or task
+ Context switch to task
+ Time scheduler is locked;

The execution times of the µC/OS-III ISR prologue, ISR epilogue, **OSIntExit( )**, and **OSIntCtxSw( )**, can be measured independently and should be constant.

It should also be easy to measure the execution time of a post call by using **OS_TS_GET( )**. In fact, the post calls should be short in the Deferred Post Method because it only involves copying the post call and its arguments into the interrupt queue.

The difference is that in the Deferred Post Method, interrupts are disabled for a very short amount of time and thus, the first three metrics should be fast. However, task latency is higher as µC/OS-III locks the scheduler to access critical sections.

9-8 DIRECT VS. DEFERRED POST METHOD

In the Direct Post Method, μC/OS-III disables interrupts to access critical sections. In comparison, while in the Deferred Post Method, μC/OS-III locks the scheduler to access the same critical sections.

In the Deferred Post Method, μC/OS-III must still disable interrupts to access the interrupt queue. However, the interrupt disable time is very short and fairly constant.

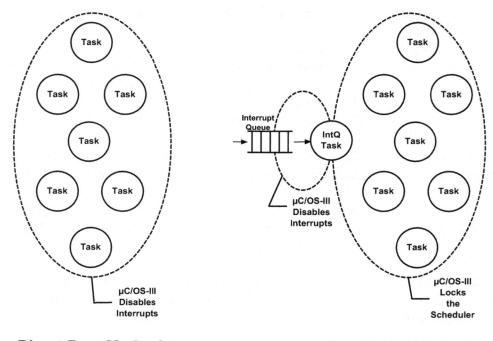

Direct Post Method   **Deferred Post Method**

Figure 9-5 **Direct vs. Deferred Post Methods**

If interrupt disable time is critical in the application because there are very fast interrupt sources and the interrupt disable time of μC/OS-III is not acceptable using the Direct Post Method, use the Deferred Post Method.

However, if you are planning on using the features listed in Table 9-1, consider using the Deferred Post Method.

Feature	Reason
Multiple tasks at the same priority	Although this is an important feature of µC/OS-III, multiple tasks at the same priority create longer critical sections. However, if there are only a few tasks at the same priority, interrupt latency will be relatively small. If the user does not create multiple tasks at the same priority, the Direct Post Method is recommended.
Event Flags Chapter 14, "Synchronization" on page 273	If multiple tasks are waiting on different events, going through all of the tasks waiting for events requires a fair amount of processing time, which means longer critical sections. If only a few tasks (approximately one to five) are waiting on an event flag group, the critical section will be short enough to use the Direct Post Method.
Pend on multiple objects Chapter 16, "Pending On Multiple Objects" on page 333	Pending on multiple objects is probably the most complex feature provided by µC/OS-III and requires interrupts to be disabled for fairly long periods of time when using the Direct Post Method. If pending on multiple objects, the Deferred Post Method is highly recommended. If the application does not use this feature, the user may select the Direct Post Method.
Broadcast on Post calls See OSSemPost() and OSQPost() descriptions.	µC/OS-III disables interrupts while processing a post to multiple tasks in a broadcast. If not using the broadcast option, use the Direct Post Method. Note that broadcasts only apply to semaphores and message queues.

Table 9-1 **µC/OS-III features to avoid when using the Direct Post Method**

9-9 THE CLOCK TICK (OR SYSTEM TICK)

µC/OS-III-based systems generally require the presence of a periodic time source called the *clock tick* or *system tick*.

A hardware timer configured to generate an interrupt at a rate between 10 and 1000 Hz provides the clock tick. A tick source may also be obtained by generating an interrupt from an AC power line (typically 50 or 60 Hz). In fact, you can easily derive 100 or 120 Hz by detecting zero crossings of the power line. That being said, if your product is subject to be used in regions that use both power line frequencies then you may need to have the user specify which frequency to use or, have the product automatically detect which region it's in.

The clock tick interrupt can be viewed as the system's heartbeat. The rate is application specific and depends on the desired resolution of this time source. However, the faster the tick rate, the higher the overhead imposed on the system.

The clock tick interrupt allows µC/OS-III to delay tasks for an integral number of clock ticks and provide timeouts when tasks are waiting for events to occur.

The clock tick interrupt must call **OSTimeTick()**. The pseudocode for **OSTimeTick()** is shown in Listing 9-5.

```
void  OSTimeTick (void)
{
    OSTimeTickHook();                               (1)
#if OS_CFG_ISR_POST_DEFERRED_EN > 0u
    Get timestamp;                                  (2)
    Post "time tick" to the Interrupt Queue;
#else
    Signal the Tick Task;                           (3)
    Run the round-robin scheduling algorithm;       (4)
    Signal the timer task;                          (5)
#endif
}
```

Listing 9-5 **OSTimeTick() pseudocode**

L9-5(1)   The time tick ISR starts by calling a hook function, **OSTimeTickHook()**. The hook function allows the implementer of the µC/OS-III port to perform additional processing when a tick interrupt occurs. In turn, the tick hook can call a user-defined tick hook if its corresponding pointer, **OS_AppTimeTickHookPtr**, is non-**NULL**. The reason the hook is called first is to give the application immediate access to this periodic time source. This can be useful to read sensors at a regular interval (not as subject to jitter), update Pulse Width Modulation (PWM) registers, and more.

L9-5(2)   If µC/OS-III is configured for the Deferred Post Method, µC/OS-III reads the current timestamp and defers the call to signal the tick task by placing an appropriate entry in the interrupt queue. The tick task will thus be signaled by the Interrupt Queue Handler Task.

L9-5(3)   If µC/OS-III is configured for the Direct Post Method, µC/OS-III signals the tick task so that it can process the time delays and timeouts.

L9-5(4)   µC/OS-III runs the round-robin scheduling algorithm to determine whether the time slot for the current task has expired.

L9-5(5)   The tick task is also used as the time base for the timers (see Chapter 13, "Resource Management" on page 231).

A common misconception is that a system tick is always needed with µC/OS-III. In fact, many low-power applications may not implement the system tick because of the power required to maintain the tick list. In other words, it is not reasonable to continuously power down and power up the product just to maintain the system tick. Since µC/OS-III is a preemptive kernel, an event other than a tick interrupt can wake up a system placed in low power mode by either a keystroke from a keypad or other means. Not having a system tick means that the user is not allowed to use time delays and timeouts on system calls. This is a decision required to be made by the designer of the low-power product.

9-10 SUMMARY

µC/OS-III provides services to manage interrupts. An ISR should be short in length, and signal or send a message to a task, which is responsible for servicing the interrupting device.

ISRs that are short and do not need to signal or send a message to a task, are not required to do so. In other words, µC/OS-III allows you to have non -kernel-aware ISRs.

µC/OS-III supports processors that vector to a single ISR for all interrupting devices, or to a unique ISR for each device.

µC/OS-III supports two methods: Direct and Deferred Post. The Direct Post Method assumes that µC/OS-III critical sections are protected by disabling interrupts. The Deferred Post Method locks the scheduler when µC/OS-III accesses critical sections of code. The method used depends greatly on your interrupt response as well as the task response needs.

µC/OS-III assumes the presence of a periodic time source for applications requiring time delays and timeouts on certain services.

9

Chapter

10

Pend Lists (or Wait Lists)

A task is placed in a *Pend List* (also called a *Wait List*) when it is waiting on a semaphore to be signaled, a mutual exclusion semaphore to be released, an event flag group to be posted, or a message queue to be posted.

See ...	For ...	Kernel Object
Chapter 13, "Resource Management" on page 231	Semaphores Mutual Exclusion Semaphores	OS_SEM OS_MUTEX
Chapter 14, "Synchronization" on page 273	Semaphores Event Flags	OS_SEM OS_FLAG_GRP
Chapter 15, "Message Passing" on page 309	Message Queues	OS_Q

Table 10-1 **Kernel objects that have Pend Lists**

A pend list is similar to the *Ready List*, except that instead of keeping track of tasks that are ready-to-run, the pend list keeps track of tasks waiting for an object to be posted. In addition, the pend list is sorted by priority; the highest priority task waiting on the object is placed at the head of the list, and the lowest priority task waiting on the object is placed at the end of the list.

A pend list is a data structure of type **OS_PEND_LIST**, which consists of three fields as shown in Figure 10-1.

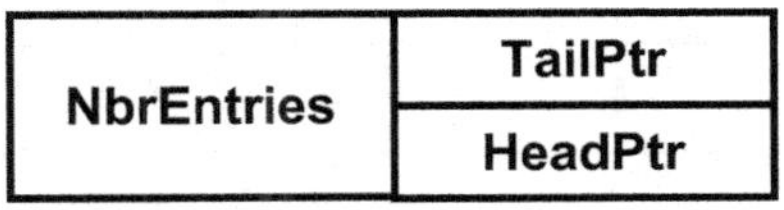

NbrEntries	TailPtr
	HeadPtr

Figure 10-1 **Pend List**

.NbrEntries	Contains the current number of entries in the pend list. Each entry in the pend list points to a task that is waiting for the kernel object to be posted.
.TailPtr	Is a pointer to the last task in the list (i.e., the lowest priority task).
.HeadPtr	Is a pointer to the first task in the list (i.e., the highest priority task).

Figure 10-2 indicates that each kernel object using a pend list contains the same three fields at the beginning of the kernel object that we called an **OS_PEND_OBJ**. Notice that the first field is always a "Type" which allows µC/OS-III to know if the kernel object is a semaphore, a mutual exclusion semaphore, an event flag group, or a message queue object.

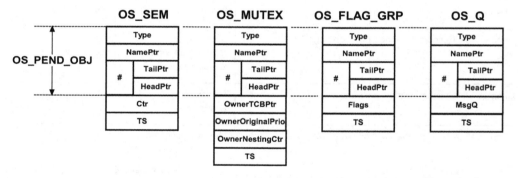

Figure 10-2 **OS_PEND_OBJ at the beginning of certain kernel objects**

Table 10-2 shows that the "Type" field of each of the above objects is initialized to contain four ASCII characters when the respective object is created. This allows the user to identify these objects when performing a memory dump using a debugger.

Kernel Object	Type
Semaphore	'S' 'E' 'M' 'A'
Mutual Exclusion Semaphore	'M' 'U' 'T' 'X'
Event Flag Group	'F' 'L' 'A' 'G'
Message Queue	'Q' 'U' 'E' 'U'

Table 10-2 **Kernel objects with initialized "Type" field**

A pend list does not actually point to a task's **OS_TCB**, but instead points to **OS_PEND_DATA** objects as shown in Figure 10-3. Also, an **OS_PEND_DATA** structure is allocated dynamically on the current task's stack when a task is placed on a pend list. This implies that a task stack needs to be able to allocate storage for this data structure.

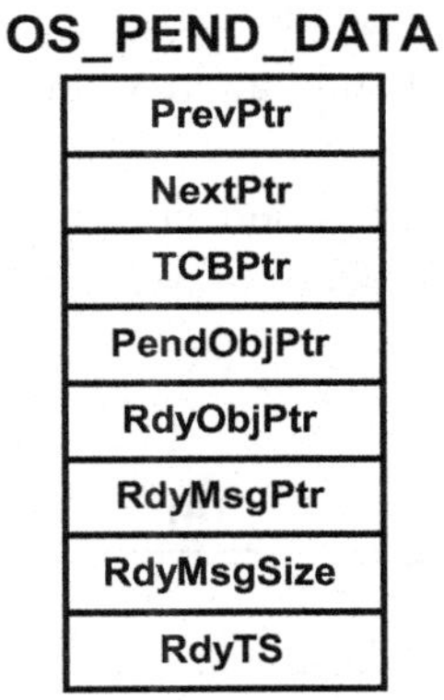

OS_PEND_DATA

PrevPtr
NextPtr
TCBPtr
PendObjPtr
RdyObjPtr
RdyMsgPtr
RdyMsgSize
RdyTS

Figure 10-3 **Pend Data**

.PrevPtr	Is a pointer to an **OS_PEND_DATA** entry in the pend list. This pointer points to a higher or equal priority task waiting on the kernel object.
.NextPtr	Is a pointer to an **OS_PEND_DATA** entry in the pend list. This pointer points to a lower or equal priority task waiting on the kernel object.
.TCBPtr	Is a pointer to the **OS_TCB** of the task waiting on the pend list.
.PendObjPtr	Is a pointer to the kernel object that the task is pending on. In other words, this pointer can point to an **OS_SEM**, **OS_MUTEX**, **OS_FLAG_GRP** or **OS_Q** by using an **OS_PEND_OBJ** as the common data structure.
.RdyObjPtr	Is a pointer to the kernel object that is ready if the task actually waits for multiple kernel objects. See Chapter 16, "Pending On Multiple Objects" on page 333 for more on this.

10

.RdyMsgPtr   Is a pointer to the message posted through OSQPost() if the task
                                    is pending on multiple kernel objects. Again, see Chapter 16,
                                    "Pending On Multiple Objects" on page 333.

.RdyTS   Is a timestamp of when the kernel object was posted. This is used
                                    when a task pends on multiple kernel objects as described in
                                    Chapter 16, "Pending On Multiple Objects" on page 333.

Figure 10-4 shows how all data structures connect to each other when tasks are inserted in
a pend list. This drawing assumes that there are two tasks waiting on a semaphore.

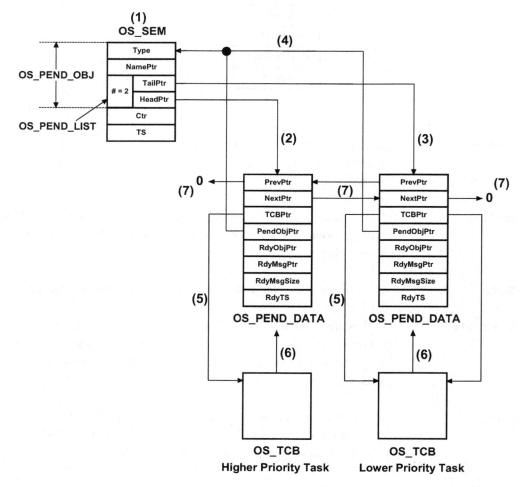

Figure 10-4 **Pend Data**

F10-4(1)   The **OS_SEM** data type contains an **OS_PEND_OBJ**, which in turn contains an **OS_PEND_LIST**. The **.NbrEntries** field in the pend list indicates that there are two tasks waiting on the semaphore.

F10-4(2)   The **.HeadPtr** field of the pend list points to the **OS_PEND_DATA** structure associated with the highest priority task waiting on the semaphore.

F10-4(3)   The **.TailPtr** field of the pend list points to the **OS_PEND_DATA** structure associated with the lowest priority task waiting on the semaphore.

F10-4(4)   Both **OS_PEND_DATA** structures in turn point back to the **OS_SEM** data structure. The pointers think they are pointing to an **OS_PEND_OBJ**. We know that the **OS_PEND_OBJ** is a semaphore by examining the **.Type** field of the **OS_PEND_OBJ**. **.Type** will contain the four (4) ASCII characters 'S', 'E', 'M' and 'A'.

F10-4(5)   Each **OS_PEND_DATA** structure points to its respective **OS_TCB**. In other words, we know which task is pending on the semaphore.

F10-4(6)   Each task points back to the **OS_PEND_DATA** structure.

F10-4(7)   Finally, the **OS_PEND_DATA** structure forms a doubly linked list so that the µC/OS-III can easily add or remove entries in this list.

Although this may seem complex, the reasoning will become apparent in Chapter 16, "Pending On Multiple Objects" on page 333. For now, you should assume that all of the links are necessary.

Table 10-3 shows the functions that µC/OS-III uses to manipulate entries in a pend list. These functions are internal to µC/OS-III and the application code must never call them. The code is found in **os_core.c**.

Function	Description
OS_PendListChangePrio( )	Change the priority of a task in a pend list
OS_PendListInit( )	Initialize a pend list
OS_PendListInsertHead( )	Insert an OS_PEND_DATA at the head of the pend list
OS_PendListInsertPrio( )	Insert an OS_PEND_DATA in priority order in the pend list
OS_PendListRemove( )	Remove multiple OS_PEND_DATA from the pend list
OS_PendListRemove1( )	Remove single OS_PEND_DATA from the pend list

Table 10-3 **Pend List access functions**

10-1 SUMMARY

µC/OS-III keeps track of tasks waiting for semaphores, mutual exclusion semaphores, event flag groups and message queues using pend lists.

A pend list consists of a data structure of type **OS_PEND_LIST**. The pend list is further encapsulated into another data type called an **OS_PEND_OBJ**.

Tasks are not directly linked to the pend list but instead are linked through an intermediate data structure called an **OS_PEND_DATA** which is allocated on the stack of the task waiting on the kernel object.

Application code must not access pend lists, since these are internal to µC/OS-III.

Chapter

11

Time Management

μC/OS-III provides time-related services to the application programmer.

In Chapter 9, "Interrupt Management" on page 175, it was established that μC/OS-III generally requires (as do most kernels) that the user provide a periodic interrupt to keep track of time delays and timeouts. This periodic time source is called a clock tick and should occur between 10 and 1000 times per second, or Hertz (see **OS_CFG_TICK_RATE_HZ** in **os_cfg_app.h**). The actual frequency of the clock tick depends on the desired tick resolution of the application. However, the higher the frequency of the ticker, the higher the overhead.

μC/OS-III provides a number of services to manage time as summarized in Table 11-1, and the code is found in **os_time.c**.

Function Name	Operation
OSTimeDly()	Delay execution of a task for "n" ticks
OSTimeDlyHMSM()	Delay a task for a user specified time in HH:MM:SS.mmm
OSTimeDlyResume()	Resume a delayed task
OSTimeGet()	Obtain the current value of the tick counter
OSTimeSet()	Set the tick counter to a new value
OSTimeTick()	Signal the occurrence of a clock tick

Table 11-1 **Time Services API summary**

The application programmer should refer to Appendix A, "μC/OS-III API Reference" on page 443 for a detailed description of these services.

11-1 OSTimeDly()

A task calls this function to suspend execution until some time expires. The calling function will not execute until the specified time expires. This function allows three modes: relative, periodic and absolute.

Listing 11-1 shows how to use OSTimeDly() in relative mode.

```
void  MyTask (void *p_arg)
{
    OS_ERR  err;
    :
    :
    while (DEF_ON) {
        :
        :
        OSTimeDly(2,                           (1)
                  OS_OPT_TIME_DLY,             (2)
                  &err);                       (3)
        /* Check "err" */                      (4)
        :
        :
    }
}
```

Listing 11-1 **OSTimeDly() - Relative**

L11-1(1)   The first argument specifies the amount of time delay (in number of ticks) from when the function is called. For the example in L11-1, if the tick rate (OS_CFG_TICK_RATE_HZ in os_cfg_app.h) is set to 1000 Hz, the user is asking to suspend the current task for approximately 2 milliseconds. However, the value is not accurate since the count starts from the next tick which could occur almost immediately. This will be explained shortly.

L11-1(2)   Specifying OS_OPT_TIME_DLY indicates that the user wants to use "relative" mode.

L11-1(3)   As with most μC/OS-III services an error return value will be returned. The example should return OS_ERR_NONE because the arguments are all valid.

L11-1(4)   You should always check the error code returned by μC/OS-III. If "**err**" does not contain **OS_ERR_NONE**, **OSTimeDly()** did not perform the intended work. For example, another task could remove the time delay suspension by calling **OSTimeDlyResume()** and when **MyTask()** returns, it would not have returned because the time had expired.

As mentioned above, the delay is not accurate. Refer to Figure 11-1 and its description below to understand why.

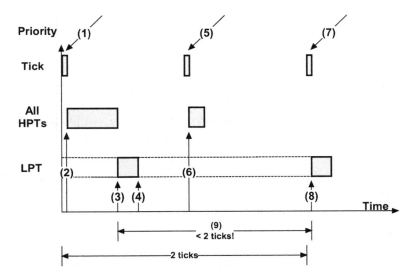

Figure 11-1 **OSTimeDly() - Relative**

F11-1(1)   We get a tick interrupt and μC/OS-III services the ISR.

F11-1(2)   At the end of the ISR, all Higher Priority Tasks (HPTs) execute. The execution time of HPTs is unknown and can vary.

F11-1(3)   Once all HPTs have executed, μC/OS-III runs the task that has called **OSTimeDly()** as shown in L11-1. For the sake of discussion, it is assumed that this task is a lower priority task (LPT).

F11-1(4)   The task calls **OSTimeDly()** and specifies to delay for two ticks in "relative" mode. At this point, µC/OS-III places the current task in the tick list where it will wait for two ticks to expire. The delayed task consumes zero CPU time while waiting for the time to expire.

F11-1(5)   The next tick occurs. If there are HPTs waiting for this particular tick, µC/OS-III will schedule them to run at the end of the ISR.

F11-1(6)   The HPTs execute.

F11-1(7)   The next tick interrupt occurs. This is the tick that the LPT was waiting for and will now be made ready-to-run by µC/OS-III.

F11-1(8)   Since there are no HPTs to execute on this tick, µC/OS-III switches to the LPT.

F11-1(9)   Given the execution time of the HPTs, the time delay is not exactly two ticks, as requested. In fact, it is virtually impossible to obtain a delay of exactly the desired number of ticks. You might ask for a delay of two ticks, but the very next tick could occur almost immediately after calling **OSTimeDly()**! Just imagine what might happen if all HPTs took longer to execute and pushed (3) and (4) further to the right. In this case, the delay would actually appear as one tick instead of two.

OSTimeDly() can also be called with the **OS_OPT_TIME_PERIODIC** option as shown in Listing 11-2. This option allows delaying the task until the tick counter reaches a certain periodic match value and thus ensures that the spacing in time is always the same as it is not subject to CPU load variations.

µC/OS-III determines the "match value" of **OSTickCtr** to determine when the task will need to wake up based on the desired period. This is shown in Figure 11-2. µC/OS-III checks to ensure that if the match is computed such that it represents a value that has already gone by then, the delay will be zero.

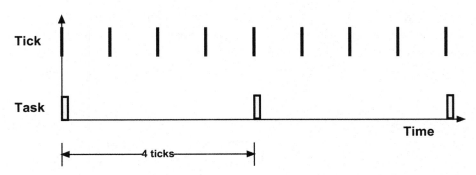

Figure 11-2 **OSTimeDly() - Periodic**

```
void  MyTask (void *p_arg)
{
    OS_ERR    err;
    :
    :
    while (DEF_ON) {
        OSTimeDly(4,                              (1)
                  OS_OPT_TIME_PERIODIC,           (2)
                  &err);
        /* Check "err" */                         (3)
        :
        :
    }
}
```

Listing 11-2 **OSTimeDly() - Periodic**

L11-2(1)   The first argument specifies the period for the task to execute, specifically every four ticks. Of course, if the task is a low-priority task, µC/OS-III only schedules and runs the task based on its priority relative to what else needs to be executed.

L11-2(2)   Specifying **OS_OPT_TIME_PERIODIC** indicates that the task is to be ready-to-run when the tick counter reaches the desired period from the previous call.

L11-2(3)   You should always check the error code returned by µC/OS-III.

11

Relative and Periodic modes might not look different, but they are. In Relative mode, it is possible to miss one of the ticks when the system is heavily loaded, missing a tick or more on occasion. In Periodic mode, the task may still execute later, but it will always be synchronized to the desired number of ticks. In fact, Periodic mode is the preferred mode to use to implement a time-of-day clock.

Finally, you can use the absolute mode to perform a specific action at a fixed time after power up. For example, turn off a light 10 seconds after the product powers up. In this case, you would specify **OS_OPT_TIME_MATCH** while "**dly**" actually corresponds to the desired value of **OSTickCtr** you want to reach.

To summarize, the task will wake up when **OSTickCtr** reaches the following value:

Value of "opt"	Task wakes up when
OS_OPT_TIME_DLY	OSTickCtr + dly
OS_OPT_TIME_PERIODIC	OSTCBCurPtr->TickCtrPrev + dly
OS_OPT_TIME_MATCH	dly

11-2 OSTimeDlyHMSM()

A task may call this function to suspend execution until some time expires by specifying the length of time in a more user-friendly way. Specifically, you can specify the delay in hours, minutes, seconds, and milliseconds (thus the **HMSM**). This function only works in "Relative" mode.

Listing 11-3 indicates how to use OSTimeDlyHMSM( ).

```
void  MyTask (void *p_arg)
{
    OS_ERR  err;
    :
    :
    while (DEF_ON) {
        :
        :
        OSTimeDlyHMSM(0,                            (1)
                      0,
                      1,
                      0,
                      OS_OPT_TIME_HMSM_STRICT,      (2)
                      &err);                        (3)
        /* Check "err" */
        :
        :
    }
}
```

Listing 11-3 **OSTimeDlyHMSM()**

L11-3(1)   The first four arguments specify the amount of time delay (in hours, minutes, seconds, and milliseconds) from this point in time. In the above example, the task should delay for 1 second. The resolution greatly depends on the tick rate. For example, if the tick rate (**OS_CFG_TICK_RATE_HZ** in **os_cfg_app.h**) is set to 1000 Hz there is technically a resolution of 1 millisecond. If the tick rate is 100 Hz then the delay of the current task is in increments of 10 milliseconds. Again, given the relative nature of this call, the actual delay may not be accurate.

L11-3(2)   Specifying **OS_OPT_TIME_HMSM_STRICT** verifies that the user strictly passes valid values for hours, minutes, seconds and milliseconds. Valid hours are 0 to 99, valid minutes are 0 to 59, valid seconds are 0 to 59, and valid milliseconds are 0 to 999.

If specifying **OS_OPT_TIME_HMSM_NON_STRICT**, the function will accept nearly any value for hours (between 0 to 999), minutes (from 0 to 9999), seconds (any value, up to **65,535**), and milliseconds (any value, up to **4,294,967,295**). **OSTimeDlyHMSM(203, 101, 69, 10000)** may be accepted. Whether or not this makes sense is a different story.

The reason hours is limited to 999 is that time delays typically use 32-bit values to keep track of ticks. If the tick rate is set at 1000 Hz then, it is possible to only track 4,294,967 seconds, which corresponds to 1,193 hours, and therefore 999 is a reasonable limit.

L11-3(3)   As with most μC/OS-III services the user will receive an error return value. The example should return **OS_ERR_NONE** since the arguments in L11-3 are all valid. Refer to Appendix A, "μC/OS-III API Reference" on page 443 for a list of possible error codes.

Even though μC/OS-III allows for very long delays for tasks, it is actually not recommended to delay tasks for a long time. The reason is that there is no indication that the task is actually "alive" unless it is possible to monitor the amount of time remaining for the delay. It is better to have the task wake up approximately every minute or so, and have it "tell you" that it is still ok.

OSTimeDly() is often used to create periodic tasks (tasks that execute periodically). For example, it is possible to have a task that scans a keyboard every 50 milliseconds and another task that reads analog inputs every 10 milliseconds, etc.

11-3 OSTimeDlyResume()

A task can resume another task that called **OSTimeDly()** or **OSTimeDlyHMSM()** by calling **OSTimeDlyResume()**. Listing 11-4 shows how to use **OSTimeDlyResume()**. The task that delayed itself will not know that it was resumed, but will think that the delay expired. Because of this, use this function with great care.

```
OS_TCB  MyTaskTCB;


void  MyTask (void *p_arg)
{
    OS_ERR  err;
    :
    :
    while (DEF_ON) {
        :
        :
        OSTimeDly(10,
                  OS_OPT_TIME_DLY,
                  &err);
        /* Check "err" */
        :
        :
    }
}


void  MyOtherTask (void *p_arg)
{
    OS_ERR  err;
    :
    :
    while (DEF_ON) {
        :
        :
        OSTimeDlyResume(&MyTaskTCB,
                        &err);
        /* Check "err" */
        :
        :
    }
}
```

Listing 11-4 **OSTimeDlyResume()**

11-4 OSTimeSet() AND OSTimeGet()

µC/OS-III increments a tick counter every time a tick interrupt occurs. This counter allows the application to make coarse time measurements and have some notion of time (after power up).

OSTimeGet() allows the user to take a snapshot of the tick counter. You can use this value to delay a task for a specific number of ticks and repeat this periodically without losing track of time.

OSTimeSet() allows the user to change the current value of the tick counter. Although µC/OS-III allows for this, it is recommended to use this function with great care.

11-5 OSTimeTick()

The tick Interrupt Service Routine (ISR) must call this function every time a tick interrupt occurs. µC/OS-III uses this function to update time delays and timeouts used by other system calls. OSTimeTick() is considered an internal function to µC/OS-III.

11-6 SUMMARY

µC/OS-III provides services to applications so that tasks can suspend their execution for user-defined time delays. Delays are either specified by a number of clock ticks or hours, minutes, seconds, and milliseconds.

Application code can resume a delayed task by calling OSTimeDlyResume(). However, its use is not recommended because resumed task will not know that they were resumed as opposed to the time delay expired.

µC/OS-III keeps track of the number of ticks that occurred since power up or since the number of ticks counter was last changed by OSTimeSet(). The counter may be read by the application code using OSTimeGet().

Chapter

12

Timer Management

μC/OS-III provides timer services to the application programmer and code to handle timers is found in **os_tmr.c**. Timer services are enabled when setting **OS_CFG_TMR_EN** to 1 in **os_cfg.h**.

Timers are down counters that perform an *action* when the counter reaches zero. The user provides the action through a *callback* function (or simply *callback*). A callback is a user-declared function that will be called when the timer expires. The callback can be used to turn a light on or off, start a motor, or perform other actions. However, it is important to never make blocking calls within a callback function (i.e., call **OSTimeDly()**, **OSTimeDlyHMSM()**, **OS???Pend()**, or anything that causes the timer task to block or be deleted).

Timers are useful in protocol stacks (retransmission timers, for example), and can also be used to poll I/O devices at predefined intervals.

An application can have any number of timers (limited only by the amount of RAM available). Timer services (i.e. functions) in μC/OS-III start with the **OSTmr???()** prefix, and the services available to the application programmer are described in Appendix A, "μC/OS-III API Reference" on page 443.

The resolution of all the timers managed by μC/OS-III is determined by the configuration constant: **OS_CFG_TMR_TASK_RATE_HZ**, which is expressed in Hertz (Hz). So, if the timer task (described later) rate is set to 10, all timers have a resolution of 1/10th of a second (ticks in the diagrams to follow). In fact, this is the typical recommended value for the timer task. Timers are to be used with "coarse" granularity.

μC/OS-III provides a number of services to manage timers as summarized in Table 12-1.

Function Name	Operation
OSTmrCreate()	Create and specify the operating mode of the timer.
OSTmrDel()	Delete a timer.
OSTmrRemainGet()	Obtain the remaining time left before the timer expires.
OSTmrStart()	Start (or restart) a timer.
OSTmrStateGet()	Obtain the current state of a timer.
OSTmrStop()	Stop the countdown process of a timer.

Table 12-1 **Timer API summary**

A timer needs to be created before it can be used. You create a timer by calling **OSTmrCreate()** and specify a number of arguments to this function based on how the timer is to operate. Once the timer operation is specified, its operating mode cannot be changed unless the timer is deleted and recreated. The function prototype for **OSTmrCreate()** is shown below as a quick reference:

```
void  OSTmrCreate (OS_TMR               *p_tmr,           /* Pointer to timer    */
                   CPU_CHAR             *p_name,          /* Name of timer, ASCII */
                   OS_TICK              dly,              /* Initial delay       */
                   OS_TICK              period,           /* Repeat period       */
                   OS_OPT               opt,              /* Options             */
                   OS_TMR_CALLBACK_PTR  p_callback,       /* Fnct to call at 0   */
                   void                 *p_callback_arg,  /* Arg. to callback    */
                   OS_ERR               *p_err)
```

Once created, a timer can be started (or restarted) and stopped as often as is necessary. Timers can be created to operate in one of three modes: One-shot, Periodic (no initial delay), and Periodic (with initial delay).

12-1 ONE-SHOT TIMERS

As its name implies, a one-shot timer will countdown from its initial value, call the callback function when it reaches zero, and stop. Figure 12-1 shows a timing diagram of this operation. The countdown is initiated by calling OSTmrStart(). At the completion of the time delay, the callback function is called, assuming a callback function was provided when the timer was created. Once completed, the timer does not do anything unless restarted by calling OSTmrStart(), at which point the process starts over.

You terminate the countdown process of a timer (before it reaches zero) by calling OSTmrStop(). In this case, you can specify that the callback function be called or not.

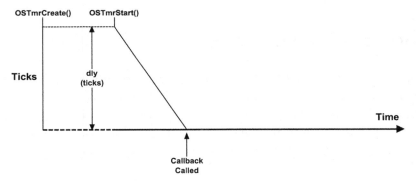

Figure 12-1 **One Shot Timers (dly > 0, period == 0)**

As shown in Figure 12-2, a one-shot timer can be retriggered by calling OSTmrStart() before the timer reaches zero. This feature can be used to implement watchdogs and similar safeguards.

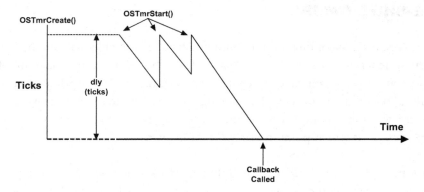

Figure 12-2 **Retriggering a One Shot Timer**

12-2 PERIODIC (NO INITIAL DELAY)

As indicated in Figure 12-3, timers can be configured for periodic mode. When the countdown expires, the callback function is called, the timer is automatically reloaded, and the process is repeated. If specifying a delay of zero (i.e., **dly == 0**) when the timer is created and, when started, the timer immediately uses the "**period**" as the reload value. You can call **OSTmrStart()** at any point in the countdown to restart the process.

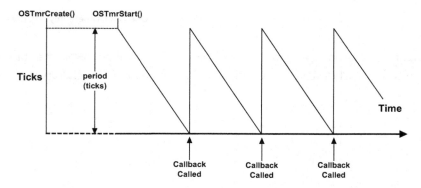

Figure 12-3 **Periodic Timers (dly == 0, period > 0)**

12-3 PERIODIC (WITH INITIAL DELAY)

As shown in Figure 12-4, timers can be configured for periodic mode with an initial delay that is different than its period. The first countdown count comes from the "**dly**" argument passed in the **OSTmrCreate()** call, and the reload value is the "**period**". You can call **OSTmrStart()** to restart the process including the initial delay.

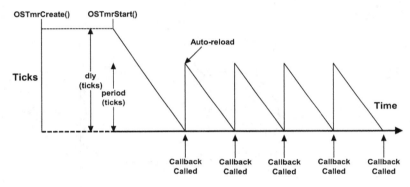

Figure 12-4 **Periodic Timers (dly > 0, period > 0)**

12-4 TIMER MANAGEMENT INTERNALS

12-4-1 TIMER MANAGEMENT INTERNALS - TIMERS STATES

Figure 12-5 shows the state diagram of a timer.

Tasks can call **OSTmrStateGet()** to find out the state of a timer. Also, at any time during the countdown process, the application code can call **OSTmrRemainGet()** to find out how much time remains before the timer reaches zero (0). The value returned is expressed in "timer ticks." If timers are decremented at a rate of 10 Hz then a count of 50 corresponds to 5 seconds. If the timer is in the stop state, the time remaining will correspond to either the initial delay (one shot or periodic with initial delay), or the period if the timer is configured for periodic without initial delay.

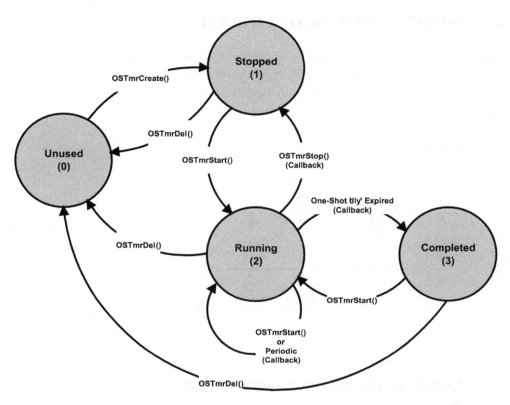

Figure 12-5 **Timer State Diagram**

F12-5(0)   The "Unused" state is a timer that has not been created or has been "deleted." In other words, µC/OS-III does not know about this timer.

F12-5(1)   When creating a timer or calling **OSTmrStop()**, the timer is placed in the "stopped" state.

F12-5(2)   A timer is placed in running state when calling **OSTmrStart()**. The timer stays in that state unless it's stopped, deleted, or completes its one shot.

F12-5(3)   The "Completed" state is the state a one-shot timer is in when its delay expires.

12-4-2 TIMER MANAGEMENT INTERNALS - OS_TMR

A timer is a kernel object as defined by the **OS_TMR** data type (see **os.h**) as shown in Listing 12-1.

The services provided by µC/OS-III to manage timers are implemented in the file **os_tmr.c**. Timer services are enabled at compile time by setting the configuration constant **OS_CFG_TMR_EN** to 1 in **os_cfg.h**.

```
typedef  struct  os_tmr  OS_TMR;              (1)


struct  os_tmr {
    OS_OBJ_TYPE          Type;               (2)
    CPU_CHAR            *NamePtr;            (3)
    OS_TMR_CALLBACK_PTR  CallbackPtr;        (4)
    void                *CallbackPtrArg;     (5)
    OS_TMR              *NextPtr;            (6)
    OS_TMR              *PrevPtr;
    OS_TICK              Match;              (7)
    OS_TICK              Remain;             (8)
    OS_TICK              Dly;                (9)
    OS_TICK              Period;             (10)
    OS_OPT               Opt;                (11)
    OS_STATE             State;              (12)
};
```

Listing 12-1 **OS_TMR data type**

L12-1(1)   In µC/OS-III, all structures are given a data type. In fact, all data types start with "**OS_**" and are all uppercase. When a timer is declared, you simply use **OS_TMR** as the data type of the variable used to declare the timer.

L12-1(2)   The structure starts with a "**Type**" field, which allows it to be recognized by µC/OS-III as a timer. Other kernel objects will also have a "**Type**" as the first member of the structure. If a function is passed a kernel object, µC/OS-III is able to confirm that it is passed the proper data type (assuming **OS_CFG_OBJ_TYPE_CHK_EN** is set to 1 in **os_cfg.h**). For example, if passing a message queue (**OS_Q**) to a timer service (for example **OSTmrStart()**) then µC/OS-III will be able to recognize that an invalid object was passed, and return an error code accordingly.

L12-1(3)   Each kernel object can be given a name for easier recognition by debuggers or µC/Probe. This member is simply a pointer to an ASCII string which is assumed to be NUL terminated.

L12-1(4)   The **.CallbackPtr** member is a pointer to a function that is called when the timer expires. If a timer is created and passed a **NULL** pointer, a callback would not be called when the timer expires.

L12-1(5)   If there is a non-**NULL** **.CallbackPtr** then the application code could have also specified that the callback be called with an argument when the timer expires. This is the argument that would be passed in this call.

L12-1(6)   **.NextPtr** and **.PrevPtr** are pointers used to link a timer in a doubly linked list. These are described later.

L12-1(7)   A timer expires when the timer manager variable **OSTmrTickCtr** reaches the value stored in a timer's **.Match** field. This is also described later.

L12-1(8)   The **.Remain** field contains the amount of time remaining for the timer to expire. This value is updated once per **OS_CFG_TMR_WHEEL_SIZE** (see **os_cfg_app.h**) that the timer task executes (described later). The value is expressed in multiples of **1/OS_CFG_TMR_TASK_RATE_HZ** of a second (see **os_cfg_app.h**).

L12-1(9)   The **.Dly** field contains the one-shot time when the timer is configured (i.e., created) as a one-shot timer and the initial delay when the timer is created as a periodic timer. The value is expressed in multiples of **1/OS_CFG_TMR_TASK_RATE_HZ** of a second (see **os_cfg_app.h**).

L12-1(10)   The **.Period** field is the timer period when the timer is created to operate in periodic mode. The value is expressed in multiples of **1/OS_CFG_TMR_TASK_RATE_HZ** of a second (see **os_cfg_app.h**).

L12-1(11)   The **.Opt** field contains options that are passed to **OSTmrCreate()**.

L12-1(12)   The **.State** field represents the current state of the timer (see Figure 12-5).

Even if the internals of the **OS_TMR** data type are understood, the application code should never access any of the fields in this data structure directly. Instead, you should always use the Application Programming Interfaces (APIs) provided with µC/OS-III.

12-4-3 TIMER MANAGEMENT INTERNALS - TIMER TASK

OS_TmrTask() is a task created by µC/OS-III (assumes setting **OS_CFG_TMR_EN** to 1 in **os_cfg.h**) and its priority is configurable by the user through µC/OS-III's configuration file **os_cfg_app.h** (see **OS_CFG_TMR_TASK_PRIO**). **OS_TmrTask()** is typically set to a medium priority.

OS_TmrTask() is a periodic task and uses the same interrupt source used to generate clock ticks. However, timers are generally updated at a slower rate (i.e., typically 10 Hz or so) and thus, the timer tick rate is divided down in software. If the tick rate is 1000 Hz and the desired timer rate is 10 Hz then the timer task will be signaled every 100th tick interrupt as shown in Figure 12-6.

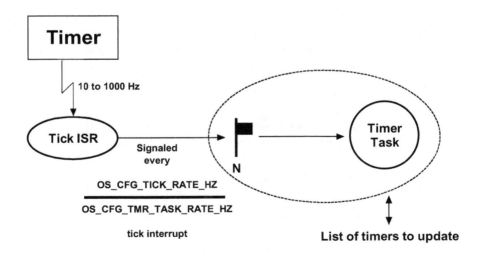

Figure 12-6 **Tick ISR and Timer Task relationship**

Figure 12-7 shows timing diagram associated with the timer management task.

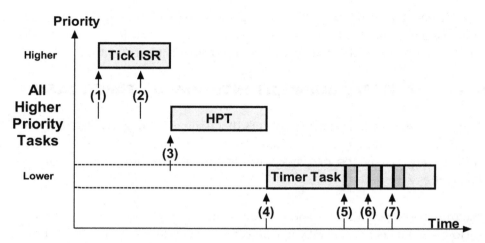

Figure 12-7 **Timing Diagram**

F12-7(1)   The tick ISR occurs and assumes interrupts are enabled and executes.

F12-7(2)   The tick ISR signals the tick task that it is time for it to update timers.

F12-7(3)   The tick ISR terminates, however there might be higher priority tasks that need to execute (assuming the timer task has a lower priority). Therefore, μC/OS-III runs the higher priority task(s).

F12-7(4)   When all higher priority tasks have executed, μC/OS-III switches to the timer task and determines that there are three timers that expired.

F12-7(5)   The callback for the first timer is executed.

F12-7(6)   The callback for the second expired timer is executed.

F12-7(7)   The callback for the third expired timer is executed.

There are a few interesting things to notice:

■   Execution of the callback functions is performed within the context of the timer task. This means that the application code will need to make sure there is sufficient stack space for the timer task to handle these callbacks.

- The callback functions are executed one after the other based on the order they are found in the timer list.

- The execution time of the timer task greatly depends on how many timers expire and how long each of the callback functions takes to execute. Since the callbacks are provided by the application code they have a large influence on the execution time of the timer task.

- The timer callback functions must never wait on events because this would delay the timer task for excessive amounts of time, if not forever.

- Callbacks are called with the scheduler locked, so you should ensure that callbacks execute as quickly as possible.

12-4-4 TIMER MANAGEMENT INTERNALS - TIMER LIST

µC/OS-III might need to literally maintain hundreds of timers (if an application requires that many). The timer list management needs to be implemented such that it does not take too much CPU time to update the timers. The timer list works similarly to a tick list as shown in Figure 12-8.

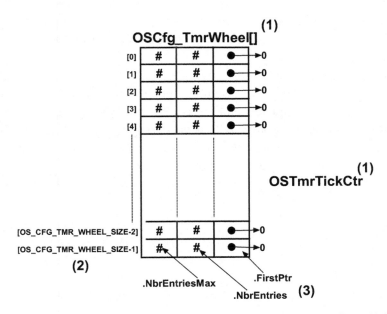

Figure 12-8 **Empty Timer List**

F12-8(1)   The timer list consists of a table (**OSCfg_TmrWheel[]**, declared in **os_cfg_app.c**) and a counter (**OSTmrTickCtr**, declared on **os.h**).

F12-8(2)   The table contains up to **OS_CFG_TMR_WHEEL_SIZE** entries, which is a compile time configuration value (see **os_cfg_app.h**). The number of entries depends on the amount of RAM available to the processor and the maximum number of timers in the application. A good starting point for **OS_CFG_TMR_WHEEL_SIZE** might be: **#Timers/4**. It is not recommended to make **OS_CFG_TMR_WHEEL_SIZE** an even multiple of the timer task rate. In other words, if the timer task is 10 Hz, avoid setting **OS_CFG_TMR_WHEEL_SIZE** to 10 or 100 (use 11 or 101 instead). Also, use prime numbers for the timer wheel size. Although it is not really possible to plan at compile time what will happen at run time, ideally the number of timers waiting in each entry of the table is distributed uniformly.

F12-8(3)   Each entry in the table contains three fields: **.NbrEntriesMax**, **.NbrEntries** and **.FirstPtr**. **.NbrEntries** indicates how many timers are linked to this table entry. **.NbrEntriesMax** keeps track of the highest number of entries in the table. Finally, **.FirstPtr** contains a pointer to a doubly linked list of timers (through the tasks **OS_TMR**) belonging into the list at that table position.

OSTmrTickCtr is incremented by **OS_TmrTask()** every time the tick ISR signals the task.

Timers are inserted in the timer list by calling **OSTmrStart()**. However, a timer must be created before it can be used.

An example to illustrate the process of inserting a timer in the timer list is as follows. Let's assume that the timer list is completely empty, **OS_CFG_TMR_WHEEL_SIZE** is configured to 9, and the current value of **OSTmrTickCtr** is 12 as shown in Figure 12-9. A timer is placed in the timer list when calling **OSTmrStart()**, and assumes that the timer was created with a delay of 1 and that this timer will be a one-shot timer as follows:

```
OS_TMR  MyTmr1;
OS_TMR  MyTmr2;


void MyTmrCallbackFnct1 (void *p_arg)
{
    /* Do something when timer #1 expires */
}


void MyTmrCallbackFnct2 (void *p_arg)
{
    /* Do something when timer #2 expires */
}


void MyTask (void *p_arg)
{
    OS_ERR  err;


    while (DEF_ON) {
        :
        OSTmrCreate((OS_TMR              *)&MyTmr1,
                    (OS_CHAR             *)"My Timer #1",
                    (OS_TICK             )1,
                    (OS_TICK             )0,
                    (OS_OPT              )OS_OPT_TMR_ONE_SHOT,
                    (OS_TMR_CALLBACK_PTR)MyTmrCallbackFnct1,
                    (void                *)0,
                    (OS_ERR              *)&err);
        /* Check 'err" */
        OSTmrStart ((OS_TMR *)&MyTmr1,
                    (OS_ERR *)&err);
        /* Check "err" */
        // Continues in the next code listing!
```

Listing 12-2 **Creating and Starting a timer**

Since **OSTmrTickCtr** has a value of 12, the timer will expire when **OSTmrTickCtr** reaches 13, or during the next time the timer task is signaled. Timers are inserted in the **OSCfg_TmrWheel[]** table using the following equation:

```
MatchValue                      = OSTmrTickCtr + dly
Index into OSCfg_TmrWheel[]      = MatchValue % OS_CFG_TMR_WHEEL_SIZE
```

Where "**dly**" (in this example) is the value passed in the third argument of **OSTmrCreate()** (i.e., 1 in this example). Again, using the example, we arrive at the following:

```
MatchValue                      = 12 + 1
Index into OSCfg_TickWheel[]     = 13 % 9
```

or,

```
MatchValue                      = 13
Index into OSCfg_TickWheel[]     = 4
```

Because of the "circular" nature of the table (a modulo operation using the size of the table), the table is referred to as a timer wheel, and each entry is a spoke in the wheel.

The timer is entered at index 4 in the timer wheel, **OSCfg_TmrWheel[]**. In this case, the **OS_TMR** is placed at the head of the list (i.e., pointed to by **OSCfg_TmrWheel[4].FirstPtr**), and the number of entries at index 4 is incremented (i.e., **OSCfg_TmrWheel[4].NbrEntries** will be 1). "**MatchValue**" is placed in the **OS_TMR** field **.Match**. Since this is the first timer inserted in the timer list at index 4, the **.NextPtr** and **.PrevPtr** both point to **NULL**.

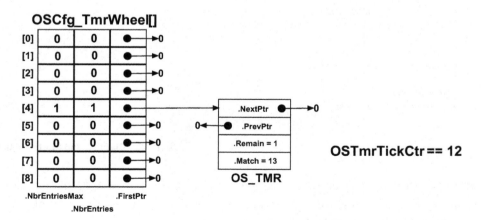

Figure 12-9 **Inserting a timer in the timer list**

The code below shows creating and starting another timer. This is performed "before" the timer task is signaled.

```
           // Continuation of code from previous code listing.
           :
           :
       OSTmrCreate((OS_TMR             *)&MyTmr2,
                   (OS_CHAR            *)"My Timer #2",
                   (OS_TICK            )10,
                   (OS_TICK            )0,
                   (OS_OPT             )OS_OPT_TMR_ONE_SHOT,
                   (OS_TMR_CALLBACK_PTR)MyTmrCallbackFnct2,
                   (void               *)0,
                   (OS_ERR             *)&err);
           /* Check 'err" */
       OSTmrStart ((OS_TMR *)&MyTmr,
                   (OS_ERR *)&err);
           /* Check 'err" */
       }
   }
```

Listing 12-3 **Creating and Starting a timer - continued**

µC/OS-III will calculate the match value and index as follows:

```
MatchValue                  = 12 + 10
Index into OSCfg_TmrWheel[] = 22 % 9
```

or,

```
MatchValue                  = 22
Index into OSCfg_TickWheel[] =  4
```

The "second timer" will be inserted at the same table entry as shown in Figure 12-10, but sorted so that the timer with the least amount of time remaining before expiration is placed at the head of the list, and the timer with the longest to wait at the end.

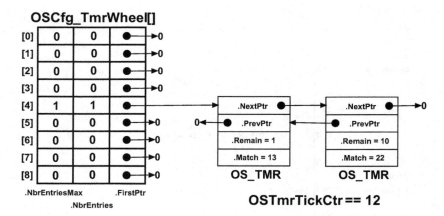

Figure 12-10 **Inserting a second timer in the tick list**

When the timer task executes (see **OS_TmrTask()** in **os_tmr.c**), it starts by incrementing **OSTmrTickCtr** and determines which table entry (i.e., spoke) it needs to update. Then, if there are timers in the list at this entry (i.e., **.FirstPtr** is not **NULL**), each **OS_TMR** is examined to determine whether the **.Match** value "matches" **OSTmrTickCtr** and, if so, the **OS_TMR** is removed from the list and **OS_TmrTask()** calls the timer callback function, assuming one was defined when the timer was created. The search through the list terminates as soon as **OSTmrTickCtr** does not match the timer's **.Match** value. In other words, there is no point in looking any further in the list since the list is already sorted.

Note that **OS_TmrTask()** does most of its work with the scheduler locked. However, because the list is sorted, and the search through the list terminates as soon as there no longer is a match, the critical section should be fairly short.

12-5 SUMMARY

Timers are down counters that perform an action when the counter reaches zero. The action is provided by the user through a callback function.

µC/OS-III allows application code to create any number of timers (limited only by the amount of RAM available).

The callback functions are executed in the context of the timer task with the scheduler locked. You must keep callback functions as short and as fast as possible and do not have the callbacks make blocking calls.

_____

12

13

Resource Management

This chapter will discuss services provided by µC/OS-III to manage shared resources. A shared resource is typically a variable (static or global), a data structure, table (in RAM), or registers in an I/O device.

When protecting a shared resource it is preferred to use mutual exclusion semaphores, as will be described in this chapter. Other methods are also presented.

Tasks can easily share data when all tasks exist in a single address space and can reference global variables, pointers, buffers, linked lists, ring buffers, etc. Although sharing data simplifies the exchange of information between tasks, it is important to ensure that each task has exclusive access to the data to avoid contention and data corruption.

For example, when implementing a module that performs a simple time-of-day algorithm in software, the module obviously keeps track of hours, minutes and seconds. The **TimeOfDay()** task may appear as shown in Listing 13-1.

Imagine if this task was preempted by another task because an interrupt occurred, and, the other task was more important than the **TimeOfDay()** task) after setting the Minutes to 0. Now imagine what will happen if this higher priority task wants to know the current time from the time-of-day module. Since the Hours were not incremented prior to the interrupt, the higher-priority task will read the time incorrectly and, in this case, it will be incorrect by a whole hour.

The code that updates variables for the **TimeOfDay()** task must treat all of the variables indivisibly (or atomically) whenever there is possible preemption. Time-of-day variables are considered shared resources and any code that accesses those variables must have exclusive access through what is called a critical section. µC/OS-III provides services to protect shared resources and enables the easy creation of critical sections.

```
CPU_INT08U  Hours;
CPU_INT08U  Minutes;
CPU_INT08U  Seconds;


void  TimeOfDay (void *p_arg)
{
    OS_ERR  err;


    (void)&p_arg;
    while (DEF_ON) {
        OSTimeDlyHMSM(0,
                      0,
                      1,
                      0,
                      OS_OPT_TIME_HMSM_STRICT,
                      &err);
        /* Examine "err" to make sure the call was successful */
        Seconds++;
        if (Seconds > 59) {
            Seconds = 0;
            Minutes++;
            if (Minutes > 59) {
                Minutes = 0;
                Hours++;
                if (Hours > 23) {
                    Hours = 0;
                }
            }
        }
    }
}
```

Listing 13-1 **Faulty Time-Of-Day clock task**

The most common methods of obtaining exclusive access to shared resources and to create *critical sections* are:

- disabling interrupts

- disabling the scheduler

- using semaphores

- using mutual exclusion semaphores (a.k.a. a mutex)

The mutual exclusion mechanism used depends on how fast the code will access a shared resource, as shown in Table 13-1.

Resource Sharing Method	When should you use?
Disable/Enable Interrupts	When access to shared resource is very quick (reading from or writing to few variables) and access is faster than µC/OS-III's interrupt disable time. It is highly recommended to not use this method as it impacts interrupt latency.
Locking/Unlocking the Scheduler	When access time to the shared resource is longer than µC/OS-III's interrupt disable time, but shorter than µC/OS-III's scheduler lock time. Locking the scheduler has the same effect as making the task that locks the scheduler the highest-priority task. It is recommended not to use this method since it defeats the purpose of using µC/OS-III. However, it is a better method than disabling interrupts, as it does not impact interrupt latency.
Semaphores	When all tasks that need to access a shared resource do not have deadlines. This is because semaphores may cause unbounded priority inversions (described later). However, semaphore services are slightly faster (in execution time) than mutual-exclusion semaphores.
Mutual Exclusion Semaphores	This is the preferred method for accessing shared resources, especially if the tasks that need to access a shared resource have deadlines. µC/OS-III's mutual exclusion semaphores have a built-in priority inheritance mechanism, which avoids unbounded priority inversions. However, mutual exclusion semaphore services are slightly slower (in execution time) than semaphores since the priority of the owner may need to be changed, which requires CPU processing.

Table 13-1 **Resource sharing**

13-1 DISABLE/ENABLE INTERRUPTS

The easiest and fastest way to gain exclusive access to a shared resource is by disabling and enabling interrupts, as shown in the pseudo-code in Listing 13-2.

```
Disable Interrupts;
Access the resource;
Enable  Interrupts;
```

Listing 13-2 **Disabling and Enabling Interrupts**

µC/OS-III uses this technique (as do most, if not all, kernels) to access certain internal variables and data structures, ensuring that these variables and data structures are manipulated atomically. However, disabling and enabling interrupts are actually CPU-related functions rather than OS-related functions and functions in CPU-specific files are provided to accomplish this (see the **cpu.h** file of the processor being used). The services provided in the CPU module are called µC/CPU. Each different target CPU architecture has its own set of µC/CPU-related files.

```
void YourFunction (void)
{
    CPU_SR_ALLOC();                (1)


    CPU_CRITICAL_ENTER();          (2)
    Access the resource;           (3)
    CPU_CRITICAL_EXIT();           (4)
}
```

Listing 13-3 **Using CPU macros to disable and enable interrupts**

L13-3(1)   The **CPU_SR_ALLOC()** macro is required when the other two macros that disable/enable interrupts are used. This macro simply allocates storage for a local variable to hold the value of the current interrupt disable status of the CPU. If interrupts are already disabled we do not want to enable them upon exiting the critical section.

L13-3(2)   **CPU_CRITICAL_ENTER( )** saves the current state of the CPU interrupt disable flag(s) in the local variable allocated by **CPU_SR_ALLOC( )** and disables all maskable interrupts.

L13-3(3)   The critical section of code is then accessed without fear of being changed by either an ISR or another task because interrupts are disabled. In other words, this operation is now atomic.

L13-3(4)   **CPU_CRITICAL_EXIT( )** restores the previously saved interrupt disable status of the CPU from the local variable.

CPU_CRITICAL_ENTER( ) and **CPU_CRITICAL_EXIT( )** are always used in pairs. Interrupts should be disabled for as short a time as possible as disabling interrupts impacts the response of the system to interrupts. This is known as interrupt latency. Disabling and enabling is used only when changing or copying a few variables.

Note that this is the only way that a task can share variables or data structures with an ISR.

µC/CPU provides a way to actually measure interrupt latency.

When using µC/OS-III, interrupts may be disabled for as much time as µC/OS-III does, without affecting *interrupt latency*. Obviously, it is important to know how long µC/OS-III disables interrupts, which depends on the CPU used.

Although this method works, you should avoid disabling interrupts as it affects the responsiveness of the system to real-time events.

13

13-2 LOCK/UNLOCK

If the task does not share variables or data structures with an ISR, you can disable and enable µC/OS-III's scheduler while accessing the resource, as shown in Listing 13-4.

```
void YourFunction (void)
{
    OS_ERR  err();              (1)


    OSSchedLock(&err);          (2)
    Access the resource;        (3)
    OSSchedUnlock(&err);        (4)
}
```

Listing 13-4 **Accessing a resource with the scheduler locked**

Using this method, two or more tasks share data without the possibility of contention. Note that while the scheduler is locked, interrupts are enabled and if an interrupt occurs while in the critical section, the ISR is executed immediately. At the end of the ISR, the kernel always returns to the interrupted task even if a higher priority task is made ready-to-run by the ISR. Since the ISR returns to the interrupted task, the behavior of the kernel is similar to that of a non-preemptive kernel (while the scheduler is locked).

OSSchedLock() and OSSchedUnlock() can be nested up to 250 levels deep. The scheduler is invoked only when OSSchedUnlock() is called the same number of times the application called OSSchedLock().

After the scheduler is unlocked, µC/OS-III performs a context switch if a higher priority task is ready-to-run.

µC/OS-III will not allow the user to make blocking calls when the scheduler is locked. If the application were able to make blocking calls, the application would most likely fail.

Although this method works well, you can avoid disabling the scheduler as it defeats the purpose of having a preemptive kernel. Locking the scheduler makes the current task the highest priority task.

13-3 SEMAPHORES

A semaphore was originally a mechanical signaling mechanism. The railroad industry used the device to provide a form of mutual exclusion for railroads tracks shared by more than one train. In this form, the semaphore signaled trains by closing a set of mechanical arms to block a train from a section of track that was currently in use. When the track became available, the arm would swing up and the waiting train would then proceed.

The notion of using a semaphore in software as a means of mutual exclusion was invented by the Dutch computer scientist Edgser Dijkstra in 1959. In computer software, a semaphore is a protocol mechanism offered by most multitasking kernels. Semaphores, originally used to control access to shared resources, but now they are used for synchronization as described in Chapter 14, "Synchronization" on page 273. However, it is useful to describe how semaphores can be used to share resources. The pitfalls of semaphores will be discussed in a later section.

A semaphore was originally a "lock mechanism" and code acquired the key to this lock to continue execution. Acquiring the key means that the executing task has permission to enter the section of otherwise locked code. Entering a section of locked code causes the task to wait until the key becomes available.

Typically, two types of semaphores exist: binary semaphores and counting semaphores. As its name implies, a binary semaphore can only take two values: 0 or 1. A counting semaphore allows for values between 0 and 255, 65,535, or 4,294,967,295, depending on whether the semaphore mechanism is implemented using 8, 16, or 32 bits, respectively. For µC/OS-III, the maximum value of a semaphore is determined by the data type **OS_SEM_CTR** (see **os_type.h**), which can be changed as needed. Along with the semaphore's value, µC/OS-III also keeps track of tasks waiting for the semaphore's availability.

Only tasks are allowed to use semaphores when semaphores are used for sharing resources; ISRs are not allowed.

A semaphore is a kernel object defined by the **OS_SEM** data type, which is defined by the structure **os_sem** (see **os.h**). The application can have any number of semaphores (limited only by the amount of RAM available).

There are a number of operations the application is able to perform on semaphores, summarized in Table 13-2. In this chapter, only three functions used most often are discussed: **OSSemCreate()**, **OSSemPend()**, and **OSSemPost()**. Other functions are described in Appendix A, "µC/OS-III API Reference" on page 443. When semaphores are used for sharing resources, every semaphore function must be called from a task and never from an ISR. The same limitation does not apply when using semaphores for signaling, as described later in Chapter 13.

Function Name	Operation
OSSemCreate()	Create a semaphore.
OSSemDel()	Delete a semaphore.
OSSemPend()	Wait on a semaphore.
OSSemPendAbort()	Abort the wait on a semaphore.
OSSemPost()	Release or signal a semaphore.
OSSemSet()	Force the semaphore count to a desired value.

Table 13-2 **Semaphore API summary**

13-3-1 BINARY SEMAPHORES

A task that wants to acquire a resource must perform a Wait (or Pend) operation. If the semaphore is available (the semaphore value is greater than 0), the semaphore value is set to **0**, and the task continues execution (owning the resource). If the semaphore's value is 0, the task performing a Wait on the semaphore is placed in a waiting list. μC/OS-III allows a timeout to be specified. If the semaphore is not available within a certain amount of time, the requesting task is made ready-to-run, and an error code (indicating that a timeout has occurred) is returned to the caller.

A task releases a semaphore by performing a Signal (or Post) operation. If no task is waiting for the semaphore, the semaphore value is simply set to **1**. If there is at least one task waiting for the semaphore, the highest-priority task waiting on the semaphore is made ready-to-run, and the semaphore value is not incremented. If the readied task has a higher priority than the current task (the task releasing the semaphore), a context switch occurs and the higher-priority task resumes execution. The current task is suspended until it again becomes the highest-priority task that is ready-to-run.

The operations described above are summarized using the pseudo-code shown in Listing 13-5.

```
OS_SEM  MySem;                      (1)


void  main (void)
{
    OS_ERR  err;
    :

    :

    OSInit(&err);
    :
    OSSemCreate(&MySem,             (2)
            "My Semaphore",         (3)
            1,                      (4)
            &err);                  (5)
    /* Check "err" */
    :
    /* Create task(s) */
    :
    OSStart(&err);
    (void)err;
}
```

Listing 13-5 **Using a semaphore to access a shared resource**

L13-5(1)   The application must declare a semaphore as a variable of type **OS_SEM**. This variable will be referenced by other semaphore services.

L13-5(2)   You create a semaphore by calling **OSSemCreate()** and pass the address to the semaphore allocated in (1). The semaphore must be created before it can be used by other tasks. Here, the semaphore is initialized in startup code (i.e., **main** ()), however it could also be initialized by a task (but it must be initialized before it is used).

L13-5(3)   You can assign an ASCII name to the semaphore, which can be used by debuggers or µC/Probe to easily identify the semaphore. Storage for the ASCII characters is typically in ROM, which is typically more plentiful than RAM. If it is necessary to change the name of the semaphore at runtime, you can store the characters in an array in RAM and simply pass the address of the array to **OSSemCreate()**. Of course, the array must be NUL terminated.

L13-5(4)   You specify the initial value of the semaphore. You should initialize the semaphore to 1 when the semaphore is used to access a single shared resource (as in this example).

L13-5(5)   **OSSemCreate()** returns an error code based on the outcome of the call. If all the arguments are valid, **err** will contain **OS_ERR_NONE**. Refer to the description of **OSSemCreate()** in Appendix A, "µC/OS-III API Reference" on page 443 for a list of other error codes and their meaning.

```
void  Task1 (void *p_arg)
{
    OS_ERR  err;
    CPU_TS  ts;


    while (DEF_ON) {
        :
        OSSemPend(&MySem,                              (1)
                  0,                                   (2)
                  OS_OPT_PEND_BLOCKING,                (3)
                  &ts,                                 (4)
                  &err);                               (5)
        switch (err) {
            case OS_ERR_NONE:
                Access Shared Resource;                (6)
                OSSemPost(&MySem,                      (7)
                          OS_OPT_POST_1,               (8)
                          &err);                       (9)
                /* Check "err" */
                break;

            case OS_ERR_PEND_ABORT:
                /* The pend was aborted by another task    */
                break;

            case OS_ERR_OBJ_DEL:
                /* The semaphore was deleted               */
                break;

            default:
                /* Other errors                            */
        }
        :
    }
}
```

Listing 13-6 **Using a semaphore to access a shared resource**

L13-6(1)   The task pends (or waits) on the semaphore by calling **OSSemPend()**. The application must specify the desired semaphore to wait upon, and the semaphore must have been previously created.

L13-6(2)   The next argument is a timeout specified in number of clock ticks. The actual timeout depends on the tick rate. If the tick rate (see **os_cfg_app.h**) is set to 1000, a timeout of 10 ticks represents 10 milliseconds. Specifying a timeout of zero (0) means waiting forever for the semaphore.

L13-6(3)   The third argument specifies how to wait. There are two options: OS_OPT_PEND_BLOCKING and OS_OPT_PEND_NON_BLOCKING. The blocking option means that if the semaphore is not available, the task calling OSSemPend() will wait until the semaphore is posted or until the timeout expires. The non-blocking option indicates that if the semaphore is not available, OSSemPend() will return immediately and not wait. This last option is rarely used when using a semaphore to protect a shared resource.

L13-6(4)   When the semaphore is posted, µC/OS-III reads a "timestamp" and returns this timestamp when OSSemPend() returns. This feature allows the application to know "when" the post happened and the semaphore was released. At this point, OS_TS_GET() is read to get the current timestamp and you can compute the difference, indicating the length of the wait.

L13-6(5)   OSSemPend() returns an error code based on the outcome of the call. If the call is successful, **err** will contain OS_ERR_NONE. If not, the error code will indicate the reason for the error. See Appendix A, "µC/OS-III API Reference" on page 443 for a list of possible error code for OSSemPend(). Checking for error return values is important since other tasks might delete or otherwise abort the pend. However, it is not a recommended practice to delete kernel objects at run time as the action may cause serious problems.

L13-6(6)   The resource can be accessed when OSSemPend() returns, if there are no errors.

L13-6(7)   When finished accessing the resource, you simply call OSSemPost() and specify the semaphore to be released.

L13-6(8)   OS_OPT_POST_1 indicates that the semaphore is signaling a single task, if there are many tasks waiting on the semaphore. In fact, you should always specify this option when a semaphore is used to access a shared resource.

L13-6(9)   As with most µC/OS-III functions, you specify the address of a variable that will receive an error message from the call.

```
void  Task2 (void *p_arg)
{
    OS_ERR  err;
    CPU_TS  ts;


    while (DEF_ON) {
        :
        OSSemPend(&MySem,                               (1)
                  0,
                  OS_OPT_PEND_BLOCKING,
                  &ts,
                  &err);
        switch (err) {
            case OS_ERR_NONE:
                Access Shared Resource;
                OSSemPost(&MySem,
                          OS_OPT_POST_1,
                          &err);
                /* Check "err" */
                break;

            case OS_ERR_PEND_ABORT:
                /* The pend was aborted by another task    */
                break;

            case OS_ERR_OBJ_DEL:
                /* The semaphore was deleted               */
                break;

            default:
                /* Other errors                            */
        }
        :
    }
}
```

Listing 13-7 **Using a semaphore to access a shared resource**

L13-7(1)   Another task wanting to access the shared resource needs to use the same procedure to access the shared resource.

243

Semaphores are especially useful when tasks share I/O devices. Imagine what would happen if two tasks were allowed to send characters to a printer at the same time. The printer would contain interleaved data from each task. For instance, the printout from Task 1 printing "I am Task 1," and Task 2 printing "I am Task 2," could result in "I Ia amm T Tasask k1 2". In this case, you can use a semaphore and initialize it to 1 (i.e., a binary semaphore). The rule is simple: to access the printer each task must first obtain the resource's semaphore. Figure 13-1 shows tasks competing for a semaphore to gain exclusive access to the printer. Note that a key, indicating that each task must obtain this key to use the printer, represents the semaphore symbolically.

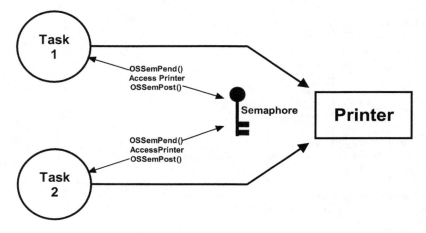

Figure 13-1 **Using a semaphore to access a printer**

The above example implies that each task knows about the existence of the semaphore to access the resource. It is almost always better to encapsulate the critical section and its protection mechanism. Each task would therefore not know that it is acquiring a semaphore when accessing the resource. For example, an RS-232C port is used by multiple tasks to send commands and receive responses from a device connected at the other end as shown in Figure 13-2.

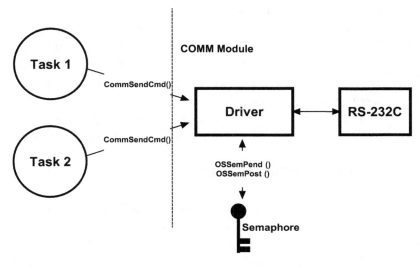

Figure 13-2 **Hiding a semaphore from a task**

The function **CommSendCmd( )** is called with three arguments: the ASCII string containing the command, a pointer to the response string from the device, and finally, a timeout in case the device does not respond within a certain amount of time. The pseudo-code for this function is shown in Listing 13-8.

```
APP_ERR  CommSendCmd (CPU_CHAR  *cmd,
                      CPU_CHAR  *response,
                      OS_TICK   timeout)
{
    Acquire serial port's semaphore;
    Send "cmd" to device;
    Wait for response with "timeout";
    if (timed out) {
        Release serial port's semaphore;
        return (error code);
    } else {
        Release serial port's semaphore;
        return (no error);
    }
}
```

Listing 13-8 **Encapsulating the use of a semaphore**

Each task that needs to send a command to the device must call this function. The semaphore is assumed to be initialized to 1 (i.e., available) by the communication driver initialization routine. The first task that calls **CommSendCmd()** acquires the semaphore, proceeds to send the command, and waits for a response. If another task attempts to send a command while the port is busy, this second task is suspended until the semaphore is released. The second task appears simply to have made a call to a normal function that will not return until the function performs its duty. When the semaphore is released by the first task, the second task acquires the semaphore and is allowed to use the RS-232C port.

13-3-2 COUNTING SEMAPHORES

A counting semaphore is used when elements of a resource can be used by more than one task at the same time. For example, a counting semaphore is used in the management of a buffer pool, as shown in Figure 13-3. Let's assume that the buffer pool initially contains 10 buffers. A task obtains a buffer from the buffer manager by calling **BufReq()**. When the buffer is no longer needed, the task returns the buffer to the buffer manager by calling **BufRel()**. The pseudo-code for these functions is shown in Listing 13-9.

The buffer manager satisfies the first 10 buffer requests because the semaphore is initialized to 10. When all buffers are used, a task requesting a buffer is suspended until a buffer becomes available. You use μC/OS-III's **OSMemGet()** and **OSMemPut()** (see Chapter 17, "Memory Management" on page 343) to obtain a buffer from the buffer pool. When a task is finished with the buffer it acquired, the task calls **BufRel()** to return the buffer to the buffer manager and the buffer is inserted into the linked list before the semaphore is signaled. By encapsulating the interface to the buffer manager in **BufReq()** and **BufRel()**, the caller does not need to be concerned with actual implementation details.

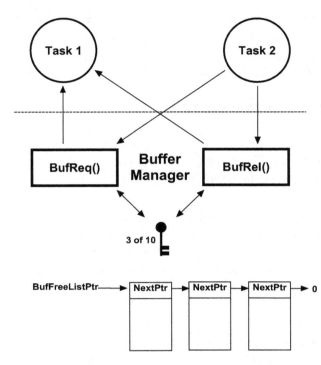

Figure 13-3 **Using a counting semaphore**

```
BUF  *BufReq (void)
{
    BUF  *ptr;


    Wait on semaphore;
    ptr = OSMemGet(...) ;                /* Get a buffer      */
    return (ptr);
}


void  BufRel (BUF *ptr)
{
    OSMemPut(..., (void *)ptr, ...);     /* Return the buffer */
    Signal semaphore;
}
```

Listing 13-9 **Buffer management using a semaphore.**

Note that the details of creating the memory partition are removed since this is discussed in Chapter 17, "Memory Management" on page 343. The semaphore is used here to extend the memory management capabilities of μC/OS-III, and to provide it with a blocking mechanism. However, only tasks can make `BufReq()` and `BufRel()` calls.

13-3-3 NOTES ON SEMAPHORES

Using a semaphore to access a shared resource does not increase interrupt latency. If an ISR or the current task makes a higher priority task ready-to-run while accessing shared data, the higher priority task executes immediately.

An application may have as many semaphores as required to protect a variety of different resources. For example, one semaphore may be used to access a shared display, another to access a shared printer, another for shared data structures, and another to protect a pool of buffers, etc. However, it is preferable to use semaphores to protect access to I/O devices rather than memory locations.

Semaphores are often overused. The use of a semaphore to access a simple shared variable is overkill in most situations. The overhead involved in acquiring and releasing the semaphore consumes valuable CPU time. You can perform the job more efficiently by disabling and enabling interrupts, however there is an indirect cost to disabling interrupts: even higher priority tasks that do not share the specific resource are blocked from using the CPU. Suppose, for instance, that two tasks share a 32-bit integer variable. The first task increments the variable, while the second task clears it. When considering how long a processor takes to perform either operation, it is easy to see that a semaphore is not required to gain exclusive access to the variable. Each task simply needs to disable interrupts before performing its operation on the variable and enable interrupts when the operation is complete. A semaphore should be used if the variable is a floating-point variable and the microprocessor does not support hardware floating-point operations. In this case, the time involved in processing the floating-point variable may affect interrupt latency if interrupts are disabled.

Semaphores are subject to a serious problem in real-time systems called priority inversion, which is described in section 13-3-5 "Priority Inversions" on page 254.

13-3-4 SEMAPHORE INTERNALS (FOR RESOURCE SHARING)

As previously mentioned, a semaphore is a kernel object as defined by the **OS_SEM** data type, which is derived from the structure **os_sem** (see **os.h**) as shown in Listing 13-10.

The services provided by μC/OS-III to manage semaphores are implemented in the file **os_sem.c**. Semaphore services are enabled at compile time by setting the configuration constant **OS_CFG_SEM_EN** to 1 in **os_cfg.h**.

```
typedef  struct  os_sem  OS_SEM;                (1)


struct  os_sem {
    OS_OBJ_TYPE          Type;                  (2)
    CPU_CHAR             *NamePtr;              (3)
    OS_PEND_LIST         PendList;              (4)
    OS_SEM_CTR           Ctr;                   (5)
    CPU_TS               TS;                    (6)
};
```

Listing 13-10 **OS_SEM data type**

L13-10(1)   In μC/OS-III, all structures are given a data type. All data types start with "**OS_**" and are uppercase. When a semaphore is declared, you simply use **OS_SEM** as the data type of the variable used to declare the semaphore.

L13-10(2)   The structure starts with a "Type" field, which allows it to be recognized by μC/OS-III as a semaphore. Other kernel objects will also have a "**.Type**" as the first member of the structure. If a function is passed a kernel object, μC/OS-III will confirm that it is being passed the proper data type (assuming **OS_CFG_OBJ_TYPE_CHK_EN** is set to **1** in **os_cfg.h**). For example, if you pass a message queue (**OS_Q**) to a semaphore service (for example **OSSemPend()**), μC/OS-III will recognize that an invalid object was passed, and return an error code accordingly.

L13-10(3)   Each kernel object can be given a name for easier recognition by debuggers or μC/Probe. This member is simply a pointer to an ASCII string, which is assumed to be NUL terminated.

L13-10(4)   Since it is possible for multiple tasks to wait (or pend) on a semaphore, the
semaphore object contains a pend list as described in Chapter 10, "Pend Lists
(or Wait Lists)" on page 197.

L13-10(5)   A semaphore contains a counter. As explained above, the counter can be
implemented as either an 8-, 16- or 32-bit value, depending on how the data
type **OS_SEM_CTR** is declared in **os_type.h**.

μC/OS-III does not make a distinction between binary and counting
semaphores. The distinction is made when the semaphore is created. If creating
a semaphore with an initial value of 1, it is a binary semaphore. When creating
a semaphore with a value > 1, it is a counting semaphore. In the next chapter,
you will discover that a semaphore is more often used as a signaling
mechanism and therefore, the semaphore counter is initialized to zero.

L13-10(6)   A semaphore contains a timestamp used to indicate the last time the semaphore
was posted. μC/OS-III assumes the presence of a free-running counter that
allows the application to make time measurements. When the semaphore is
posted, the free-running counter is read and the value is placed in this field,
which is returned when **OSSemPend()** is called. The value of this field is more
useful when a semaphore is used as a signaling mechanism (see Chapter 14,
"Synchronization" on page 273), as opposed to a resource-sharing mechanism.

Even if the user understands the internals of the **OS_SEM** data type, the application code
should never access any of the fields in this data structure directly. Instead, you should
always use the APIs provided with μC/OS-III.

As previously mentioned, semaphores must be created before they can be used by an
application.

A task waits on a semaphore before accessing a shared resource by calling **OSSemPend()** as
shown in Listing 13-11 (see Appendix A, "μC/OS-III API Reference" on page 443 for details
regarding the arguments).

```
OS_SEM  MySem;


void MyTask (void *p_arg)
{
    OS_ERR  err;
    CPU_TS  ts;

    :
    while (DEF_ON) {
        :
        OSSemPend(&MySem,                /* (1) Pointer to semaphore                    */
                  10,                    /*     Wait up until this time for the semaphore */
                  OS_OPT_PEND_BLOCKING,  /*     Option(s)                               */
                  &ts,                   /*     Returned timestamp of when sem. was released */
                  &err);                 /*     Pointer to Error returned               */
        :
        /* Check "err" */                /* (2)                                         */
        :
        OSSemPost(&MySem,                /* (3) Pointer to semaphore                    */
                  OS_OPT_POST_1,         /*     Option(s) … always OS_OPT_POST_1        */
                  &err);                 /*     Pointer to Error returned               */
        /* Check "err" */
        :
        :
    }
}
```

Listing 13-11 **Pending on and Posting to a Semaphore**

L13-11(1)   When called, **OSSemPend()** starts by checking the arguments passed to this function to make sure they have valid values (assuming **OS_CFG_ARG_CHK_EN** is set to 1 in **os_cfg.h**).

If the semaphore counter (**.Ctr** of **OS_SEM**) is greater than zero, the counter is decremented and **OSSemPend()** returns. If **OSSemPend()** returns without error, then the task now owns the shared resource.

If the semaphore counter is zero, then another task owns the semaphore, and the calling task will need to wait for the semaphore to be released. If you specify **OS_OPT_PEND_NON_BLOCKING** as the option (the application does not want the task to block), **OSSemPend()** returns immediately to the caller and the returned error code indicates that the semaphore is unavailable. You use this option if the task does not want to wait for the resource to be available, and would prefer to do something else and check back later.

If you specify the **OS_OPT_PEND_BLOCKING** option, the calling task will be inserted in the list of tasks waiting for the semaphore to become available. The task is inserted in the list by priority order and therefore, the highest priority task waiting on the semaphore is at the beginning of the list.

If you specify a non-zero timeout, the task will also be inserted in the tick list. A zero value for a timeout indicates that the user is willing to wait forever for the semaphore to be released. Most of the time, you would specify an infinite timeout when using the semaphore in resource sharing. Adding a timeout may temporarily break a deadlock, however, there are better ways of preventing deadlock at the application level (e.g., never hold more than one semaphore at the same time; resource ordering; etc.).

Assuming blocking, the scheduler is called since the current task is no longer able to run (it is waiting for the semaphore to be released). The scheduler will then run the next highest-priority task that is ready-to-run.

When the semaphore is released and the task that called **OSSemPend( )** is again the highest-priority task, μC/OS-III examines the task status to determine the reason why **OSSemPend( )** is returning to its caller. The possibilities are:

1) The semaphore was given to the waiting task. This is the preferred outcome.

2) The pend was aborted by another task

3) The semaphore was not posted within the specified timeout

4) The semaphore was deleted

When **OSSemPend( )** returns, the caller is notified of the above outcome through an appropriate error code.

L13-11(2)   If **OSSemPend( )** returns with **err** set to **OS_ERR_NONE**, your code can assume that it now has access to the resource.

If **err** contains anything else, **OSSemPend( )** either timed out (if the timeout argument was non-zero), the pend was aborted by another task, or the semaphore was deleted by another task. It is always important to examine the returned error code and not assume that everything went well.

L13-11(3)   When the task is finished accessing the resource, it needs to call **OSSemPost( )** and specify the same semaphore. Again, **OSSemPost( )** starts by checking the arguments passed to this function to make sure there are valid values (assuming **OS_CFG_ARG_CHK_EN** is set to **1** in **os_cfg.h**).

OSSemPost( ) then calls **OS_TS_GET( )** to obtain the current timestamp so it can place that information in the semaphore to be used by **OSSemPend( )**. This feature is not as useful when semaphores are used to share resources as it is when used as a signaling mechanism.

OSSemPost( ) checks to see if any tasks are waiting for the semaphore. If not, **OSSemPost( )** simply increments **p_sem->Ctr**, saves the timestamp in the semaphore, and returns.

If there are tasks waiting for the semaphore to be released, **OSSemPost( )** extracts the highest-priority task waiting for the semaphore. This is a fast operation as the pend list is sorted by priority order.

When calling **OSSemPost( )**, it is possible to specify as an option to not call the scheduler. This means that the post is performed, but the scheduler is not called even if a higher priority task waits for the semaphore to be released. This allows the calling task to perform other post functions (if needed) and make all posts take effect simultaneously without the possibility of context switching in between each post.

13-3-5 PRIORITY INVERSIONS

Priority inversion is a problem in real-time systems, and occurs only when using a priority-based preemptive kernel. Figure 13-4 illustrates a priority-inversion scenario. Task H (high priority) has a higher priority than Task M (medium priority), which in turn has a higher priority than Task L (low priority).

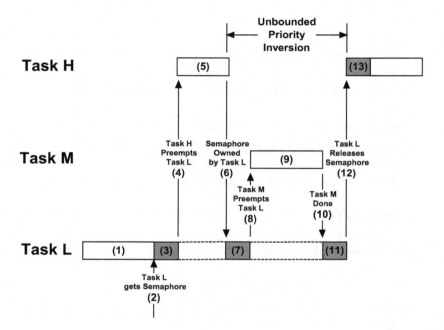

Figure 13-4 **Unbounded priority Inversion**

F13-4(1)   Task H and Task M are both waiting for an event to occur and Task L is executing.

F13-4(2)   At some point, Task L acquires a semaphore, which it needs before it can access a shared resource.

F13-4(3)   Task L performs operations on the acquired resource.

F13-4(4)   The event that Task H was waiting for occurs, and the kernel suspends Task L and start executing Task H since Task H has a higher priority.

F13-4(5)   Task H performs computations based on the event it just received.

F13-4(6)   Task H now wants to access the resource that Task L currently owns (i.e., it attempts to get the semaphore that Task L owns). Because Task L owns the resource, Task H is placed in a list of tasks waiting for the semaphore to be available.

F13-4(7)   Task L is resumed and continues to access the shared resource.

F13-4(8)   Task L is preempted by Task M since the event that Task M was waiting for occurred.

F13-4(9)   Task M handles the event.

F13-4(10)   When Task M completes, the kernel relinquishes the CPU back to Task L.

F13-4(11)   Task L continues accessing the resource.

F13-4(12)   Task L finally finishes working with the resource and releases the semaphore. At this point, the kernel knows that a higher-priority task is waiting for the semaphore, and a context switch takes place to resume Task H.

F13-4(13)   Task H has the semaphore and can access the shared resource.

So, what happened here is that the priority of Task H has been reduced to that of Task L since it waited for the resource that Task L owned. The trouble begins when Task M preempted Task L, further delaying the execution of Task H. This is called an *unbounded priority inversion*. It is unbounded because any medium priority can extend the time Task H has to wait for the resource. Technically, if all medium-priority tasks have known worst-case periodic behavior and bounded execution times, the priority inversion time is computable. This process, however, may be tedious and would need to be revised every time the medium priority tasks change.

This situation can be corrected by raising the priority of Task L, only during the time it takes to access the resource, and restore the original priority level when the task is finished. The priority of Task L should be raised up to the priority of Task H. In fact, µC/OS-III contains a special type of semaphore that does just that and is called a mutual-exclusion semaphore.

13

13-4 MUTUAL EXCLUSION SEMAPHORES (MUTEX)

µC/OS-III supports a special type of binary semaphore called a mutual exclusion semaphore (also known as a mutex) that eliminates unbounded priority inversions. Figure 13-5 shows how priority inversions are bounded using a Mutex.

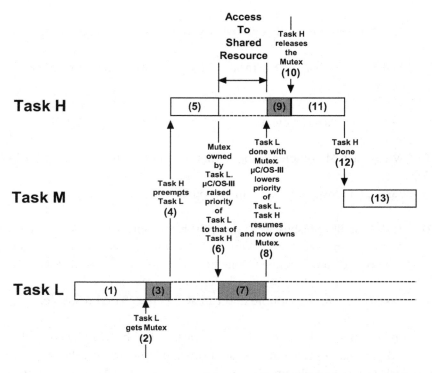

Figure 13-5 **Using a mutex to share a resource**

F13-5(1)   Task H and Task M are both waiting for an event to occur and Task L is executing.

F13-5(2)   At some point, Task L acquires a mutex, which it needs before it is able to access a shared resource.

F13-5(3)   Task L performs operations on the acquired resource.

F13-5(4)   The event that Task H waited for occurs and the kernel suspends Task L and begins executing Task H since Task H has a higher priority.

F13-5(5)   Task H performs computations based on the event it just received.

F13-5(6)   Task H now wants to access the resource that Task L currently owns (i.e., it attempts to get the mutex from Task L). Given that Task L owns the resource, μC/OS-III raises the priority of Task L to the same priority as Task H to allow Task L to finish with the resource and prevent Task L from being preempted by medium-priority tasks.

F13-5(7)   Task L continues accessing the resource, however it now does so while it is running at the same priority as Task H. Note that Task H is not actually running since it is waiting for Task L to release the mutex. In other words, Task H is in the mutex wait list.

F13-5(8)   Task L finishes working with the resource and releases the mutex. μC/OS-III notices that Task L was raised in priority and thus lowers Task L to its original priority. After doing so, μC/OS-III gives the mutex to Task H, which was waiting for the mutex to be released.

F13-5(9)   Task H now has the mutex and can access the shared resource.

F13-5(10)   Task H is finished accessing the shared resource, and frees up the mutex.

F13-5(11)   There are no higher-priority tasks to execute, therefore Task H continues execution.

F13-5(12)   Task H completes and decides to wait for an event to occur. At this point, μC/OS-III resumes Task M, which was made ready-to-run while Task H or Task L were executing. Task M was made ready-to-run because an interrupt (not shown in figure 13-5) occurred which Task M was waiting for.

F13-5(13)   Task M executes.

Note that there is no priority inversion, only resource sharing. Of course, the faster Task L accesses the shared resource and frees up the mutex, the better.

μC/OS-III implements full-priority inheritance and therefore if a higher priority requests the resource, the priority of the owner task will be raised to the priority of the new requestor.

A mutex is a kernel object defined by the **OS_MUTEX** data type, which is derived from the structure **os_mutex** (see **os.h**). An application may have an unlimited number of mutexes (limited only by the RAM available).

Only tasks are allowed to use mutual exclusion semaphores (ISRs are not allowed).

μC/OS-III enables the user to nest ownership of mutexes. If a task owns a mutex, it can own the same mutex up to 250 times. The owner must release the mutex an equivalent number of times. In several cases, an application may not be immediately aware that it called **OSMutexPend()** multiple times, especially if the mutex is acquired again by calling a function as shown in Listing 13-12.

```
OS_MUTEX          MyMutex;
SOME_STRUCT       MySharedResource;


void  MyTask (void *p_arg)
{
    OS_ERR  err;
    CPU_TS  ts;


    :
    while (DEF_ON) {
        OSMutexPend((OS_MUTEX *)&MyMutex,                     (1)
                    (OS_TICK  )0,
                    (OS_OPT   )OS_OPT_PEND_BLOCKING,
                    (CPU_TS  *)&ts,
                    (OS_ERR  *)&err);
        /* Check 'err"                           */          (2)
        /* Acquire shared resource if no error   */
        MyLibFunction();                                     (3)
        OSMutexPost((OS_MUTEX *)&MyMutex,                    (7)
                    (OS_OPT   )OS_OPT_POST_NONE,
                    (OS_ERR  *)&err);
        /* Check "err"                           */
    }
}
```

```
void  MyLibFunction (void)
{
    OS_ERR   err;
    CPU_TS   ts;


    OSMutexPend((OS_MUTEX *)&MyMutex,                         (4)
                (OS_TICK   )0,
                (OS_OPT    )OS_OPT_PEND_BLOCKING,
                (CPU_TS   *)&ts,
                (OS_ERR   *)&err);
    /* Check "err"                      */
    /* Access shared resource if no error  */               (5)
    OSMutexPost((OS_MUTEX *)&MyMutex,                        (6)
                (OS_OPT    )OS_OPT_POST_NONE,
                (OS_ERR   *)&err);
    /* Check "err"                      */
}
```

Listing 13-12 **Nesting calls to OSMutexPend()**

L13-12(1)   A task starts by pending on a mutex to access shared resources. **OSMutexPend( )** sets a nesting counter to 1.

L13-12(2)   You should check the error return value. If no errors exist, **MyTask( )** owns **MySharedResource**.

L13-12(3)   A function is called that will perform additional work.

L13-12(4)   The designer of **MyLibFunction( )** knows that, to access **MySharedResource**, it must acquire the mutex. Since the calling task already owns the mutex, this operation should not be necessary. However, **MyLibFunction( )** could have been called by yet another function that might not need access to **MySharedResource**. μC/OS-III allows nested mutex pends, so this is not a problem. The mutex nesting counter is thus incremented to 2.

L13-12(5)   **MyLibFunction( )** can access the shared resource.

L13-12(6)   The mutex is released and the nesting counter is decremented back to 1. Since this indicates that the mutex is still owned by the same task, nothing further needs to be done, and **OSMutexPost()** simply returns. **MyLibFunction()** returns to its caller.

L13-12(7)   The mutex is released again and, this time, the nesting counter is decremented back to 0 indicating that other tasks can now acquire the mutex.

You should always check the return value of **OSMutexPend()** (and any kernel call) to ensure that the function returned because you properly obtained the mutex, and not because the return from **OSMutexPend()** was caused by the mutex being deleted, or because another task called **OSMutexPendAbort()** on this mutex.

As a general rule, do not make function calls in critical sections. All mutual exclusion semaphore calls should be in the leaf nodes of the source code (e.g., in the low level drivers that actually touches real hardware or in other reentrant function libraries).

There are a number of operations that can be performed on a mutex, as summarized in Table 13-3. However, in this chapter, we will only discuss the three functions that are most often used: **OSMutexCreate()**, **OSMutexPend()**, and **OSMutexPost()**. Other functions are described in Appendix A, "µC/OS-III API Reference" on page 443.

Function Name	Operation
OSMutexCreate()	Create a mutex.
OSMutexDel()	Delete a mutex.
OSMutexPend()	Wait on a mutex.
OSMutexPendAbort()	Abort the wait on a mutex.
OSMutexPost()	Release a mutex.

Table 13-3 **Mutex API summary**

13-4-1 MUTUAL EXCLUSION SEMAPHORE INTERNALS

A mutex is a kernel object defined by the **OS_MUTEX** data type, which is derived from the structure **os_mutex** (see **os.h**) as shown in Listing 13-13:

```
typedef  struct  os_mutex  OS_MUTEX;            (1)


struct  os_mutex {
    OS_OBJ_TYPE          Type;               (2)
    CPU_CHAR             *NamePtr;           (3)
    OS_PEND_LIST         PendList;           (4)
    OS_TCB               *OwnerTCBPtr;       (5)
    OS_PRIO              OwnerOriginalPrio;  (6)
    OS_NESTING_CTR       OwnerNestingCtr;    (7)
    CPU_TS               TS;                 (8)
};
```

Listing 13-13 **OS_MUTEX data type**

L13-13(1)   In µC/OS-III, all structures are given a data type. All data types begin with "**OS_**" and are uppercase. When a mutex is declared, you simply use **OS_MUTEX** as the data type of the variable used to declare the mutex.

L13-13(2)   The structure starts with a "Type" field, which allows it to be recognized by µC/OS-III as a mutex. Other kernel objects will also have a "**.Type**" as the first member of the structure. If a function is passed a kernel object, µC/OS-III will be able to confirm that it is being passed the proper data type (assuming **OS_CFG_OBJ_TYPE_CHK_EN** is set to 1 in **os_cfg.h**). For example, if passing a message queue (**OS_Q**) to a mutex service (for example **OSMutexPend()**), µC/OS-III will recognize that the application passed an invalid object and return an error code accordingly.

L13-13(3)   Each kernel object can be given a name to make them easier to recognize by debuggers or µC/Probe. This member is simply a pointer to an ASCII string, which is assumed to be **NUL** terminated.

L13-13(4)   Because it is possible for multiple tasks to wait (or pend on a mutex), the mutex object contains a pend list as described in Chapter 10, "Pend Lists (or Wait Lists)" on page 197.

L13-13(5)   If the mutex is owned by a task, it will point to the **OS_TCB** of that task.

L13-13(6)   If the mutex is owned by a task, this field contains the "original" priority of the task that owns the mutex. This field is required in case the priority of the task must be raised to a higher priority to prevent unbounded priority inversions.

L13-13(7)   µC/OS-III allows a task to "acquire" the same mutex multiple times. In order for the mutex to be released, the owner must release the mutex the same number of times that it was acquired. Nesting can be performed up to 250-levels deep.

L13-13(8)   A mutex contains a timestamp, used to indicate the last time it was released. µC/OS-III assumes the presence of a free-running counter that allows applications to make time measurements. When the mutex is released, the free-running counter is read and the value is placed in this field, which is returned when **OSMutexPend( )** returns.

Application code should never access any of the fields in this data structure directly. Instead, you should always use the APIs provided with µC/OS-III.

A mutual exclusion semaphore (mutex) must be created before it can be used by an application. Listing 13-14 shows how to create a mutex.

```
OS_MUTEX  MyMutex;                            (1)


void  MyTask (void *p_arg)
{
    OS_ERR  err;
    :
    :
    OSMutexCreate(&MyMutex,                    (2)
                "My Mutex",                    (3)
                &err);                         (4)
    /* Check "err" */
    :
    :
}
```

Listing 13-14 **Creating a mutex**

L13-14(1)   The application must declare a variable of type **OS_MUTEX**. This variable will be referenced by other mutex services.

L13-14(2)   You create a mutex by calling **OSMutexCreate()** and pass the address to the mutex allocated in L13-14(1).

L13-14(3)   You can assign an ASCII name to the mutex, which can be used by debuggers or µC/Probe to easily identify this mutex. There are no practical limits to the length of the name since µC/OS-III stores a pointer to the ASCII string, and not to the actual characters that makes up the string.

L13-14(4)   **OSMutexCreate()** returns an error code based on the outcome of the call. If all the arguments are valid, **err** will contain **OS_ERR_NONE**.

Note that since a mutex is always a binary semaphore, there is no need to initialize a mutex counter.

A task waits on a mutual exclusion semaphore before accessing a shared resource by calling **OSMutexPend()** as shown in Listing 13-15 (see Appendix A, "µC/OS-III API Reference" on page 443 for details regarding the arguments).

13

```
OS_MUTEX  MyMutex;


void MyTask (void *p_arg)
{
    OS_ERR  err;
    CPU_TS  ts;
    :
    while (DEF_ON) {
        :
        OSMutexPend(&MyMutex,               /* (1) Pointer to mutex                          */
                    10,                     /*     Wait up until this time for the mutex     */
                    OS_OPT_PEND_BLOCKING,   /*     Option(s)                                 */
                    &ts,                    /*     Timestamp of when mutex was released      */
                    &err);                  /*     Pointer to Error returned                 */
        :
        /* Check "err"                         (2)                                           */
        :
        OSMutexPost(&MyMutex,               /* (3) Pointer to mutex                          */
                    OS_OPT_POST_NONE,
                    &err);                  /*     Pointer to Error returned                 */
        /* Check "err"                                                                       */
        :
        :
    }
}
```

Listing 13-15 **Pending (or waiting) on a Mutual Exclusion Semaphore**

L13-15(1)   When called, **OSMutexPend()** starts by checking the arguments passed to this function to make sure they have valid values. This assumes that OS_CFG_ARG_CHK_EN is set to 1 in **os_cfg.h**).

If the mutex is available, **OSMutexPend()** assumes the calling task is now the owner of the mutex and stores a pointer to the task's **OS_TCB** in **p_mutex->OwnerTCPPtr**, saves the priority of the task in **p_mutex->OwnerOriginalPrio**, and sets a mutex nesting counter to 1. **OSMutexPend()** then returns to its caller with an error code of **OS_ERR_NONE**.

If the task that calls **OSMutexPend()** already owns the mutex, **OSMutexPend()** simply increments a nesting counter. Applications can nest calls to **OSMutexPend()** up to 250-levels deep. In this case, the error returned will indicate **OS_ERR_MUTEX_OWNER**.

If the mutex is already owned by another task and **OS_OPT_PEND_NON_BLOCKING** is specified, **OSMutexPend()** returns since the task is not willing to wait for the mutex to be released by its owner.

If the mutex is owned by a lower-priority task, μC/OS-III will raise the priority of the owner to match the priority of the current task.

If you specify **OS_OPT_PEND_BLOCKING** as the option, the calling task will be inserted in the list of tasks waiting for the mutex to be available. The task is inserted in the list by priority order and thus, the highest priority task waiting on the mutex is at the beginning of the list.

If you further specify a non-zero timeout, the task will also be inserted in the tick list. A zero value for a timeout indicates a willingness to wait forever for the mutex to be released.

The scheduler is then called since the current task is no longer able to run (it is waiting for the mutex to be released). The scheduler will then run the next highest-priority task that is ready-to-run.

When the mutex is finally released and the task that called **OSMutexPend()** is again the highest-priority task, a task status is examined to determine the reason why **OSMutexPend()** is returning to its caller. The possibilities are:

1) The mutex was given to the waiting task. This is the desired outcome.

2) The pend was aborted by another task.

3) The mutex was not posted within the specified timeout.

4) The mutex was deleted.

When **OSMutexPend()** returns, the caller is notified of the outcome through an appropriate error code.

L13-15(2)   If OSMutexPend() returns with **err** set to OS_ERR_NONE, assume that the calling task now owns the resource and can proceed with accessing it. If **err** contains anything else, then OSMutexPend() either timed out (if the timeout argument was non-zero), the pend was aborted by another task, or the mutex was deleted by another task. It is always important to examine returned error codes and not assume everything went as planned.

If "**err**" is OS_ERR_MUTEX_NESTING, then the caller attempted to pend on the same mutex.

L13-15(3)   When your task is finished accessing the resource, it must call OSMutexPost() and specify the same mutex. Again, OSMutexPost() starts by checking the arguments passed to this function to make sure they contain valid values (Assuming OS_CFG_ARG_CHK_EN is set to 1 in os_cfg.h).

OSMutexPost() now calls OS_TS_GET() to obtain the current timestamp and place that information in the mutex, which will be used by OSMutexPend().

OSMutexPost() decrements the nesting counter and, if still non-zero, OSMutexPost() returns to the caller. In this case, the current owner has not fully released the mutex. The error code will be OS_ERR_MUTEX_NESTING.

If there are no tasks waiting for the mutex, OSMutexPost() sets **p_mutex->OwnerTCBPtr** to a **NULL** pointer and clears the mutex nesting counter.

If µC/OS-III had to raise the priority of the mutex owner, it is returned to its original priority at this time.

The highest-priority task waiting on the mutex is then extracted from the pend list and given the mutex. This is a fast operation since the pend list is sorted by priority.

If the option to OSMutexPost() is not OS_OPT_POST_NO_SCHED then, the scheduler is called to see if the new mutex owner has a higher priority than the current task. If so, µC/OS-III will switch context to the new mutex owner.

You should note that you should only acquire one mutex at a time. In fact, it's highly recommended that when you acquire a mutex, you don't acquire any other kernel objects.

13-5 SHOULD YOU USE A SEMAPHORE INSTEAD OF A MUTEX?

A semaphore can be used instead of a mutex if none of the tasks competing for the shared resource have deadlines to be satisfied.

However, if there are deadlines to meet, you should use a mutex prior to accessing shared resources. Semaphores are subject to unbounded priority inversions, while mutex are not.

13-6 DEADLOCKS (OR DEADLY EMBRACE)

A *deadlock*, also called a **deadly embrace**, is a situation in which two tasks are each unknowingly waiting for resources held by the other.

Assume Task T1 has exclusive access to Resource R1 and Task T2 has exclusive access to Resource R2 as shown in the pseudo-code of Listing 13-16.

```
void T1 (void *p_arg)
{
    while (DEF_ON) {
        Wait for event to occur;       (1)
        Acquire M1;                    (2)
        Access  R1;                    (3)
        :
        :
        \-------- Interrupt!           (4)
        :
        :                              (8)
        Acquire M2;                    (9)
        Access  R2;
    }
}
```

13

```
void  T2 (void *p_arg)
{
    while (DEF_ON) {
        Wait for event to occur;        (5)
        Acquire M2;                     (6)
        Access  R2;
        :
        :
        Acquire M1;                     (7)
        Access  R1;
    }
}
```

Listing 13-16 **Deadlock problem**

L13-16(1)   Assume that the event that task T1 is waiting for occurs and T1 is now the highest priority task that must execute.

L13-16(2)   Task T1 executes and acquires Mutex M1.

L13-16(3)   Resource R1 is accessed.

L13-16(4)   An interrupt occurs causing the CPU to switch to task T2 since T2 has a higher priority than task T1.

L13-16(5)   The ISR is the event that task T2 was waiting for and therefore T2 resumes execution.

L13-16(6)   Task T2 acquires mutex M2 and is able to access resource R2.

L13-16(7)   Task T2 tries to acquire mutex M1, but µC/OS-III knows that mutex M1 is owned by another task.

L13-16(8)   µC/OS-III switches back to task T1 because Task T2 can no longer continue. It needs mutex M1 to access resource R1.

L13-16(9)   Task T1 now tries to access mutex M2 but, unfortunately, mutex M2 is owned by task T2. At this point, the two tasks are deadlocked, neither one can continue because each owns a resource that the other one wants.

Techniques used to avoid deadlocks are for tasks to:

- Acquire all resources before proceeding

- Always acquire resources in the same order

- Use timeouts on pend calls

μC/OS-III allows the calling task to specify a timeout when acquiring a mutex. This feature allows a deadlock to be broken, but the same deadlock may then recur later, or many times later. If the mutex is not available within a certain period of time, the task requesting the resource resumes execution. μC/OS-III returns an error code indicating that a timeout occurred. A return error code prevents the task from thinking it has properly obtained the resource.

The pseudo-code avoids deadlocks by first acquiring all resources as shown in Listing 13-17.

```
void T1 (void *p_arg)
{
    while (DEF_ON) {
        Wait for event to occur;
        Acquire M1;
        Acquire M2;
        Access  R1;
        Access  R2;
    }
}


void  T2 (void *p_arg)
{
    while (DEF_ON) {
        Wait for event to occur;
        Acquire M1;
        Acquire M2;
        Access  R1;
        Access  R2;
    }
}
```

Listing 13-17 **Deadlock avoidance – acquire all first and in the same order**

The pseudo-code to acquire all of the mutexes in the same order is shown in Listing 13-18. This is similar to the previous example, except that it is not necessary to acquire all the mutexes first, only to make sure that the mutexes are acquired in the same order for both tasks.

```
void T1 (void *p_arg){
    while (DEF_ON) {
        Wait for event to occur;
        Acquire M1;
        Access  R1;
        Acquire M2;
        Access  R2;
    }
}


void  T2 (void *p_arg)
{
    while (DEF_ON) {
        Wait for event to occur;
        Acquire M1;
        Access  R1;
        Acquire M2;
        Access  R2;
    }
}
```

Listing 13-18 **Deadlock avoidance – acquire in the same order**

13-7 SUMMARY

The mutual exclusion mechanism used depends on how fast code will access the shared resource, as shown in Table 13-4.

Resource Sharing Method	When should you use?
Disable/Enable Interrupts	When access to shared resource is very quick (reading from or writing to just a few variables) and the access is actually faster than μC/OS-III's interrupt disable time. It is highly recommended to not use this method as it impacts interrupt latency.
Locking/Unlocking the Scheduler	When access time to the shared resource is longer than μC/OS-III's interrupt disable time, but shorter than μC/OS-III's scheduler lock time. Locking the scheduler has the same effect as making the task that locks the scheduler the highest priority task. It is recommended to not use this method since it defeats the purpose of using μC/OS-III. However, it's a better method than disabling interrupts as it does not impact interrupt latency.
Semaphores	When all tasks that need to access a shared resource do not have deadlines. This is because semaphores can cause unbounded priority inversions. However, semaphore services are slightly faster (in execution time) than mutual exclusion semaphores.
Mutual Exclusion Semaphores	This is the preferred method for accessing shared resources, especially if the tasks that need to access a shared resource have deadlines. Remember that mutual exclusion semaphores have a built-in priority inheritance mechanism, which avoids unbounded priority inversions. However, mutual exclusion semaphore services are slightly slower (in execution time) than semaphores, because the priority of the owner may need to be changed, which requires CPU processing.

Table 13-4 **Resource sharing summary**

14

Synchronization

This chapter focuses on how tasks can synchronize their activities with Interrupt Service Routines (ISRs), or other tasks.

When an ISR executes, it can signal a task telling the task that an event of interest has occurred. After signaling the task, the ISR exits and, depending on the signaled task priority, the scheduler is run. The signaled task may then service the interrupting device, or otherwise react to the event. Servicing interrupting devices from task level is preferred whenever possible, since it reduces the amount of time that interrupts are disabled and the code is easier to debug.

There are two basic mechanisms for synchronizations in µC/OS-III: semaphores and event flags.

14-1 SEMAPHORES

As defined in Chapter 13, "Resource Management" on page 231, a semaphore is a protocol mechanism offered by most multitasking kernels. Semaphores were originally used to control access to shared resources. However, better mechanisms exist to protect access to shared resources, as described in Chapter 12. Semaphores are best used to synchronize an ISR to a task, or synchronize a task with another task as shown in Figure 14-1.

Note that the semaphore is drawn as a flag to indicate that it is used to signal the occurrence of an event. The initial value for the semaphore is typically zero (0), indicating the event has not yet occurred.

The value "N" next to the flag indicates that the semaphore can accumulate *events* or *credits*. An ISR (or a task) can post (or signal) multiple times to a semaphore and the semaphore will remember how many times it was posted. It is possible to initialize the semaphore with a value other than zero, indicating that the semaphore initially contains that number of events.

Also, the small hourglass close to the receiving task indicates that the task has an option to specify a timeout. This timeout indicates that the task is willing to wait for the semaphore to be signaled (or posted to) within a certain amount of time. If the semaphore is not signaled within that time, µC/OS-III resumes the task and returns an error code indicating that the task was made ready-to-run because of a timeout and not the semaphore was signaled.

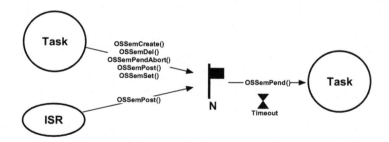

Figure 14-1 **µC/OS-III Semaphore Services**

There are a number of operations to perform on semaphores as summarized in Table 14-1 and Figure 14-1. However, in this chapter, we will only discuss the three functions used most often: **OSSemCreate( )**, **OSSemPend( )**, and **OSSemPost( )**. The other functions are described in Appendix A, "µC/OS-III API Reference" on page 443. Also note that every semaphore function is callable from a task, but only **OSSemPost( )** can be called by an ISR

Function Name	Operation
OSSemCreate()	Create a semaphore.
OSSemDel()	Delete a semaphore.
OSSemPend()	Wait on a semaphore.
OSSemPendAbort()	Abort the wait on a semaphore.
OSSemPost()	Signal a semaphore.
OSSemSet()	Force the semaphore count to a desired value.

Table 14-1 **Semaphore API summary**

When used for synchronization, a semaphore keeps track of how many times it was signaled using a counter. The counter can take values between 0 and 255, 65,535, or 4,294,967,295, depending on whether the semaphore mechanism is implemented using 8, 16, or 32 bits, respectively. For μC/OS-III, the maximum value of a semaphore is determined by the data type **OS_SEM_CTR** (see **os_type.h**), which is changeable, as needed (assuming access to μC/OS-III's source code). Along with the semaphore's value, μC/OS-III keeps track of tasks waiting for the semaphore to be signaled.

14

14-1-1 UNILATERAL RENDEZ-VOUS

Figure 14-2 shows that a task can be synchronized with an ISR (or another task) by using a semaphore. In this case, no data is exchanged, however there is an indication that the ISR or the task (on the left) has occurred. Using a semaphore for this type of synchronization is called a unilateral rendez-vous.

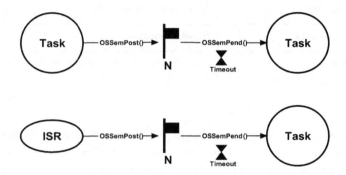

Figure 14-2 **Unilateral Rendezvous**

A unilateral rendez-vous is used when a task initiates an I/O operation and waits (i.e., call **OSSemPend()**) for the semaphore to be signaled (posted). When the I/O operation is complete, an ISR (or another task) signals the semaphore (i.e., calls **OSSemPost()**), and the task is resumed. This process is also shown on the timeline of Figure 14-3 and described below. The code for the ISR and task is shown in Listing 14-1.

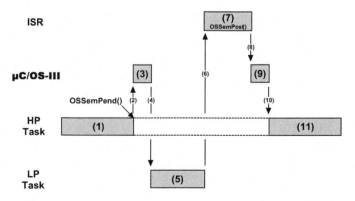

Figure 14-3 **Unilateral Rendezvous, Timing Diagram**

F14-3(1)   A high priority task is executing. The task needs to synchronize with an ISR (i.e., wait for the ISR to occur) and call **OSSemPend()**.

F14-3(2)
F14-3(3)
F14-3(4)   Since the ISR has not occurred, the task will be placed in the waiting list for the semaphore until the event occurs The scheduler in µC/OS-III will then select the next most important task and context switch to that task.

F14-3(5)   The low-priority task executes.

F14-3(6)   The event that the original task was waiting for occurs. The lower-priority task is immediately preempted (assuming interrupts are enabled), and the CPU vectors to the interrupt handler for the event.

F14-3(7)
F14-3(8)   The ISR handles the interrupting device and then calls **OSSemPost()** to signal the semaphore. When the ISR completes, µC/OS-III is called (i.e. **OSIntExit()**).

F14-3(9)
F14-3(10)   µC/OS-III notices that a higher-priority task is waiting for this event to occur and context switches back to the original task.

F14-3(11)   The original task resumes execution immediately after the call to **OSSemPend()**.

14

```
OS_SEM  MySem;


void MyISR (void)
{
    OS_ERR  err;


    /* Clear the interrupting device */
    OSSemPost(&MySem,                  (7)
              OS_OPT_POST_1,
              &err);
    /* Check "err" */
}


void MyTask (void *p_arg)
{
    OS_ERR  err;
    CPU_TS  ts;
    :
    :
    while (DEF_ON) {
        OSSemPend(&MySem,              (1)
                  10,
                  OS_OPT_PEND_BLOCKING,
                  &ts,
                  &err);
        /* Check "err" */             (11)
        :
        :
    }
}
```

Listing 14-1 **Pending (or waiting) on a Semaphore**

A few interesting things are worth noting about this process. First, the task does not need to know about the details of what happens behind the scenes. As far as the task is concerned, it called a function (**OSSemPend()**) that will return when the event it is waiting for occurs. Second, µC/OS-III maximizes the use of the CPU by selecting the next most important task, which executes until the ISR occurs. In fact, the ISR may not occur for many milliseconds and, during that time, the CPU will work on other tasks. As far as the task that is waiting for the semaphore is concerned, it does not consume CPU time while it is waiting. Finally, the task waiting for the semaphore will execute immediately after the event occurs (assuming it is the most important task that needs to run).

14-1-2 CREDIT TRACKING

As previously mentioned, a semaphore "remembers" how many times it was signaled (or posted to). In other words, if the ISR occurs multiple times before the task waiting for the event becomes the highest-priority task, the semaphore will keep count of the number of times it was signaled. When the task becomes the highest priority ready-to-run task, it will execute without blocking as many times as there were ISRs signaled. This is called *Credit Tracking* and is illustrated in Figure 14-4 and described below.

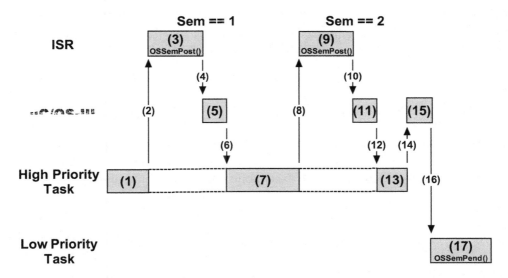

Figure 14-4 **Semaphore Credit Tracking**

F14-4(1)   A high-priority task is executing.

F14-4(2)

F14-4(3)   An event meant for a lower-priority task occurs which preempts the task (assuming interrupts are enabled). The ISR executes and posts the semaphore. At this point the semaphore count is 1.

F14-4(4)

F14-4(5)

F14-4(6)   µC/OS-III is called at the end of the ISR to see if the ISR caused a higher-priority task to be ready-to-run. Since the ISR was an event that a lower-priority task was waiting for, µC/OS-III will resume execution of the higher-priority task at the exact point where it was interrupted.

F14-4(7)   The high-priority task is resumed and continues execution.

F14-4(8)

F14-4(9)   The interrupt occurs a second time. The ISR executes and posts the semaphore. At this point the semaphore count is 2.

F14-4(10)

F14-4(11)

F14-4(12)   µC/OS-III is called at the end of the ISR to see if the ISR caused a higher-priority task to be ready-to-run. Since the ISR was an event that a lower-priority task was waiting for, µC/OS-III resumes execution of the higher-priority task at the exact point where it was interrupted.

F14-4(13)

F14-4(14)   The high-priority task resumes execution and actually terminates the work it was doing. This task will then call one of the µC/OS-III services to wait for "its" event to occur.

F14-4(15)

F14-4(16)   µC/OS-III will then select the next most important task, which happens to be the task waiting for the event and will context switch to that task.

F14-4(17)   The new task executes and will know that the ISR occurred twice since the semaphore count is two. The task will handle this accordingly.

14-1-3 MULTIPLE TASKS WAITING ON A SEMAPHORE

It is possible for more than one task to wait on the same semaphore, each with its own timeout as illustrated in Figure 14-5.

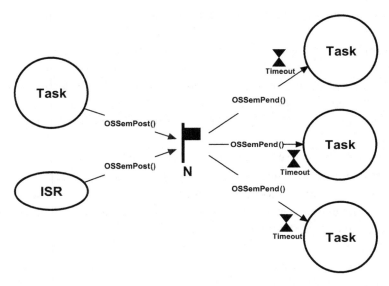

Figure 14-5 **Multiple Tasks waiting on a Semaphore**

When the semaphore is signaled (whether by an ISR or task), µC/OS-III makes the highest-priority task waiting on the semaphore ready-to-run. However, it is also possible to specify that all tasks waiting on the semaphore be made ready-to-run. This is called *broadcasting* and is accomplished by specifying OS_OPT_POST_ALL as an option when calling OSSemPost(). If any of the waiting tasks has a higher priority than the previously running task, µC/OS-III will execute the highest-priority task made ready by OSSemPost().

Broadcasting is a common technique used to synchronize multiple tasks and have them start executing at the same time. However, some of the tasks that we want to synchronize might not be waiting for the semaphore. It is fairly easy to resolve this problem by combining semaphores and event flags. This will be described after examining event flags.

14-1-4 SEMAPHORE INTERNALS (FOR SYNCHRONIZATION)

Note that some of the material presented in this section is also contained in Chapter 13, "Resource Management" on page 231, as semaphores were also discussed in that chapter. However, the material presented here will be applicable to semaphores used for synchronization and thus will differ somewhat.

A counting semaphore allows values between 0 and 255, 65,535, or 4,294,967,295, depending on whether the semaphore mechanism is implemented using 8, 16, or 32 bits, respectively. For µC/OS-III, the maximum value of a semaphore is determined by the data type **OS_SEM_CTR** (see **os_type.h**), which can be changed as needed. Along with the semaphore's value, µC/OS-III keeps track of tasks waiting for the semaphore's availability.

The application programmer can create an unlimited number of semaphores (limited only by available RAM). Semaphore services in µC/OS-III start with the **OSSem???()** prefix, and services available to the application programmer are described in Appendix A, "µC/OS-III API Reference" on page 443. Semaphore services are enabled at compile time by setting the configuration constant **OS_CFG_SEM_EN** to 1 in **os_cfg.h**.

Semaphores must be created before they can be used by the application. Listing 14-3 shows how to create a semaphore.

As previously mentioned, a semaphore is a kernel object as defined by the **OS_SEM** data type, which is derived from the structure **os_sem** (see **os.h**) as shown in Listing 14-2. The services provided by µC/OS-III to manage semaphores are implemented in the file **os_sem.c**.

```
typedef  struct  os_sem  OS_SEM;              (1)


struct  os_sem {
    OS_OBJ_TYPE         Type;                 (2)
    CPU_CHAR            *NamePtr;             (3)
    OS_PEND_LIST        PendList;             (4)
    OS_SEM_CTR          Ctr;                  (5)
    CPU_TS              TS;                   (6)
};
```

Listing 14-2 **OS_SEM data type**

L14-2(1)   In µC/OS-III, all structures are given a data type. In fact, all data types start with "**OS_**" and are all uppercase. When a semaphore is declared, simply use **OS_SEM** as the data type of the variable used to declare the semaphore.

L14-2(2)   The structure starts with a "**Type**" field, which allows it to be recognized by µC/OS-III as a semaphore. In other words, other kernel objects will also have a "**Type**" as the first member of the structure. If a function is passed a kernel object, µC/OS-III will confirm that it is being passed the proper data type (assuming **OS_CFG_OBJ_TYPE_CHK_EN** is set to 1 in **os_cfg.h**). For example, if passing a message queue (**OS_Q**) to a semaphore service (for example **OSSemPend( )**), µC/OS-III will recognize that an invalid object was passed, and return an error code accordingly.

L14-2(3)   Each kernel object can be given a name to make them easier to be recognized by debuggers or µC/Probe. This member is simply a pointer to an ASCII string, which is assumed to be **NUL** terminated.

L14-2(4)   Since it is possible for multiple tasks to be waiting (or pending) on a semaphore, the semaphore object contains a pend list as described in Chapter 10, "Pend Lists (or Wait Lists)" on page 197.

L14-2(5)   A semaphore contains a counter. As explained above, the counter can be implemented as either an 8-, 16- or 32-bit value, depending on how the data type **OS_SEM_CTR** is declared in **os_type.h**. µC/OS-III keeps track of how many times the semaphore is signaled with this counter and this field is typically initialized to zero by **OSSemCreate( )**.

L14-2(6)   A semaphore contains a time stamp, which is used to indicate the last time the semaphore was signaled (or posted to). µC/OS-III assumes the presence of a free-running counter that allows the application to make time measurements. When the semaphore is signaled, the free-running counter is read and the value is placed in this field, which is returned when **OSSemPend( )** is called. This value allows the application to determine either when the signal was performed, or how long it took for the task to get control of the CPU from the signal. In the latter case, you should call **OS_TS_GET( )** to determine the current timestamp and compute the difference.

Even for users who understand the internals of the **OS_SEM** data type, the application code should never access any of the fields in this data structure directly. Instead, you should always use the APIs provided with µC/OS-III.

Semaphores must be created before they can be used by an application. Listing 14-3 shows how to create a semaphore.

```
OS_SEM  MySem;                          (1)


void  MyCode (void)
{
    OS_ERR  err;
    :
    OSSemCreate(&MySem,                 (2)
                "My Semaphore",         (3)
                (OS_SEM_CTR)0,          (4)
                &err);                  (5)
    /* Check "err" */
    :

}
```

Listing 14-3 **Creating a Semaphore**

L14-3(1)   The application must declare a variable of type **OS_SEM**. This variable will be referenced by other semaphore services.

L14-3(2)   You create a semaphore by calling **OSSemCreate()** and pass the address to the semaphore allocated in L14-3(1).

L14-3(3)   You can assign an ASCII name to the semaphore, which can be used by debuggers or µC/Probe to easily identify this semaphore.

L14-3(4)   You need to initialize the semaphore to zero (0) when using a semaphore as a signaling mechanism.

L14-3(5)   **OSSemCreate()** returns an error code based on the outcome of the call. If all arguments are valid, **err** will contain **OS_ERR_NONE**.

OSSemCreate() performs a check on the arguments passed to this function (assuming **OS_CFG_ARG_CHK_EN** is set to **1** in **os_cfg.h**) and only initializes the contents of the variable of type **OS_SEM** used for signaling.

A task waits for a signal from an ISR or another task by calling **OSSemPend()** as shown in Listing 14-4 (see Appendix A, "µC/OS-III API Reference" on page 443 for details regarding the arguments).

```
void  MyTask (void *p_arg)
{
    OS_ERR   err;
    CPU_TS   ts;
    :
    while (DEF_ON) {
        OSSemPend(&MySem,                      (1)
                  0,
                  OS_OPT_PEND_BLOCKING,
                  &ts,
                  &err);
        /* Check "err" */                      (2)
        :
    }
}
```

Listing 14-4 **Pending (or waiting) on a Semaphore**

L14-4(1)   When called, **OSSemPend()** starts by checking the arguments passed to this function to make sure they have valid values (assuming **OS_CFG_OBJ_TYPE_CHK_EN** is set to **1** in **os_cfg.h**).

If the semaphore counter (**.Ctr** of **OS_SEM**) is greater than zero, the counter is decremented and **OSSemPend()** returns, which indicates that the signal occurred. This is the outcome that the caller expects.

If the semaphore counter is zero, this indicates that the signal has not occurred and the calling task might need to wait for the semaphore to be released. If you specify **OS_OPT_PEND_NON_BLOCKING** as the option (the task is not to block), **OSSemPend()** returns immediately to the caller and the returned error code will indicate that the signal did not occur.

If you specify **OS_OPT_PEND_BLOCKING** as the option, the calling task will be inserted in the list of tasks waiting for the semaphore to be signaled. The task is inserted in the list by priority order with the highest priority task waiting on the semaphore at the beginning of the list as shown in Figure 14-6.

If you further specify a non-zero timeout, the task will also be inserted in the tick list. A zero value for a timeout indicates that the calling task is willing to wait forever for the semaphore to be signaled.

The scheduler is then called since the current task is not able to run (it is waiting for the semaphore to be signaled). The scheduler will then run the next highest-priority task that is ready-to-run.

When the semaphore is signaled and the task that called **OSSemPend()** is again the highest-priority task, a task status is examined to determine the reason why **OSSemPend()** is returning to its caller. The possibilities are:

1) The semaphore was signaled which is the desired outcome

2) The pend was aborted by another task

3) The semaphore was not signaled within the specified timeout

4) The semaphore was deleted

When **OSSemPend()** returns, the caller is notified of the above outcome through an appropriate error code.

L14-4(2)   If **OSSemPend()** returns with **err** set to **OS_ERR_NONE**, you can assume that the semaphore was signaled and the task can proceed with servicing the ISR or task that caused the signal. If **err** contains anything else, **OSSemPend()** either timed out (if the timeout argument was non-zero), the pend was aborted by another task, or the semaphore was deleted by another task. It is always important to examine returned error code and not assume everything went as expected.

To signal a task (either from an ISR or a task), simply call **OSSemPost()** as shown in Listing 14-5.

```
OS_SEM  MySem;


void MyISR (void)
{
    OS_ERR  err;
    :
    OSSemPost(&MySem,                 (1)
              OS_OPT_POST_1,          (2)
              &err);                  (3)
    /* Check "err" */
    :
    :
}
```

Listing 14-5 **Posting (or signaling) a Semaphore**

L14-5(1)   Your task signals (or posts to) the semaphore by calling **OSSemPost()**. You specify the semaphore to post by passing its address. The semaphore must have been previously created.

L14-5(2)   The next argument specifies how the task wants to post. There are a number of options to choose from.

When you specify **OS_OPT_POST_1**, you are indicating that you want to post to only one task (in case there are multiple tasks waiting on the semaphore). The task that will be made ready-to-run will be the highest-priority task waiting on the semaphore. If there are multiple tasks at the same priority, only one of them will be made ready-to-run. As shown in Figure 14-6, tasks waiting are in priority order (HPT means High Priority Task and LPT means Low Priority Task). So, it is a fast operation to extract the HPT from the list.

If specifying **OS_OPT_POST_ALL**, all tasks waiting on the semaphore will be posted and made ready-to-run.

The calling task can "add" the option **OS_OPT_POST_NO_SCHED** to either of the two previous options to indicate that the scheduler is not to be called at the end of **OSSemPost()**, possibly because additional postings will be performed, and rescheduling should only take place when finished. This means that the signal is performed, but the scheduler is not called even if a higher-priority task was waiting for the semaphore to be signaled. This allows the calling task to perform other post functions (if needed) and make all the posts take effect simultaneously. Note that **OS_OPT_POST_NO_SCHED** is "additive," meaning that it can be used with either of the previous options. You can thus specify:

```
OS_OPT_POST_1
OS_OPT_POST_ALL
OS_OPT_POST_1    + OS_OPT_POST_NO_SCHED
OS_OPT_POST_ALL + OS_OPT_POST_NO_SCHED
```

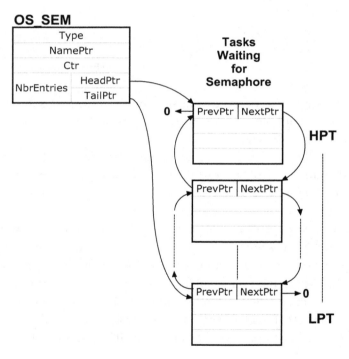

Figure 14-6 **Tasks waiting for semaphore**

L14-5(3) **OSSemPost()** returns an error code based on the outcome of the call. If the call was successful, **err** will contain **OS_ERR_NONE**. If not, the error code will indicate the reason for the error (see Appendix A, "μC/OS-III API Reference" on page 443 for a list of possible error codes for **OSSemPost()**.

14-2 TASK SEMAPHORE

Signaling a task using a semaphore is a very popular method of synchronization and, in µC/OS-III, each task has its own built-in semaphore. This feature not only simplifies code, but is also more efficient than using a separate semaphore object. The semaphore, which is built into each task, is shown in Figure 14-7.

Task semaphore services in µC/OS-III start with the **OSTaskSem???()** prefix, and the services available to the application programmer are described in Appendix A, "µC/OS-III API Reference" on page 443. Task semaphores are built into µC/OS-III and cannot be disabled at compile time as can other services. The code for task semaphores is found in **os_task.c**.

You can use this feature if your code knows which task to signal when the event occurs. For example, if you receive an interrupt from an Ethernet controller, you can signal the task responsible for processing the received packet as it is preferable to perform this processing using a task instead of the ISR.

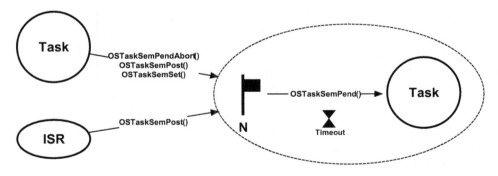

Figure 14-7 **Semaphore built-into a Task**

There is a variety of operations to perform on task semaphores, summarized in Table 14-2.

Function Name	Operation
OSTaskSemPend()	Wait on a task semaphore.
OSTaskSemPendAbort()	Abort the wait on a task semaphore.
OSTaskSemPost()	Signal a task.
OSTaskSemSet()	Force the semaphore count to a desired value.

Table 14-2 **Task Semaphore API summary**

14-2-1 PENDING (i.e., WAITING) ON A TASK SEMAPHORE

When a task is created, it automatically creates an internal semaphore with an initial value of zero (0). Waiting on a task semaphore is quite simple, as shown in Listing 14-6.

```
void MyTask (void *p_arg)
{
    OS_ERR   err;
    CPU_TS   ts;
    :
    while (DEF_ON) {
        OSTaskSemPend(10,                    (1)
                      OS_OPT_PEND_BLOCKING,  (2)
                      &ts,                   (3)
                      &err);                 (4)
        /* Check "err" */
        :
        :
    }
}
```

Listing 14-6 **Pending (or waiting) on Task's internal semaphore**

L14-6(1)   A task pends (or waits) on the task semaphore by calling **OSTaskSemPend( )**. There is no need to specify which task, as the current task is assumed. The first argument is a timeout specified in number of clock ticks. The actual timeout obviously depends on the tick rate. If the tick rate (see **os_cfg_app.h**) is set to 1000, a timeout of 10 ticks represents 10 milliseconds. Specifying a timeout of zero (0) means that the task will wait forever for the task semaphore.

L14-6(2)   The second argument specifies how to pend. There are two options: **OS_OPT_PEND_BLOCKING** and **OS_OPT_PEND_NON_BLOCKING**. The blocking option means that, if the task semaphore has not been signaled (or posted to), the task will wait until the semaphore is signaled, the pend is aborted by another task or, until the timeout expires.

L14-6(3)   When the semaphore is signaled, µC/OS-III reads a "timestamp" and places it in the receiving task's **OS_TCB**. When **OSTaskSemPend( )** returns, the value of the timestamp is placed in the local variable "**ts**". This feature captures "when" the signal actually happened. You can **call OS_TS_GET( )** to read the current timestamp and compute the difference. This establishes how long it took for the task to receive the signal from the posting task or ISR.

L14-6(4)   OSTaskSemPend() returns an error code based on the outcome of the call. If the call was successful, **err** will contain OS_ERR_NONE. If not, the error code will indicate the reason of the error (see Appendix A, "µC/OS-III API Reference" on page 443 for a list of possible error code for OSTaskSemPend().

14-2-2 POSTING (i.e., SIGNALING) A TASK SEMAPHORE

An ISR or a task signals a task by calling OSTaskSemPost(), as shown in Listing 14-7.

```
OS_TCB  MyTaskTCB;


void MyISR (void *p_arg)
{
    OS_ERR  err;
    :
    OSTaskSemPost(&MyTaskTCB,           (1)
                  OS_OPT_POST_NONE,     (2)
                  &err);                (3)
    /* Check "err" */
    :
    :
}
```

Listing 14-7 **Posting (or signaling) a Semaphore**

L14-7(1)   A task posts (or signals) the task by calling OSTaskSemPost(). It is necessary to pass the address of the desired task's OS_TCB and of course, the task must exist.

L14-7(2)   The next argument specifies how the user wants to post. There are only two choices.

Specify OS_OPT_POST_NONE, which indicates the use of the default option of calling the scheduler after posting the semaphore.

Or, specify OS_OPT_POST_NO_SCHED to indicate that the scheduler is not to be called at the end of OSTaskSemPost(), possibly because there will be additional postings, and rescheduling would take place when finished (the last post would not specify this option).

L14-7(3)   **OSTaskSemPost()** returns an error code based on the outcome of the call. If the call was successful, **err** will contain **OS_ERR_NONE**. If not, the error code will indicate the reason of the error (see Appendix A, "µC/OS-III API Reference" on page 443 for a list of possible error codes for **OSTaskSemPost()**.

14-2-3 BILATERAL RENDEZ-VOUS

Two tasks can synchronize their activities by using two task semaphores, as shown in Figure 14-8, and is called a *bilateral rendez-vous*. A bilateral rendez-vous is similar to a unilateral rendez-vous, except that both tasks must synchronize with one another before proceeding. A bilateral rendez-vous cannot be performed between a task and an ISR because an ISR cannot wait on a semaphore.

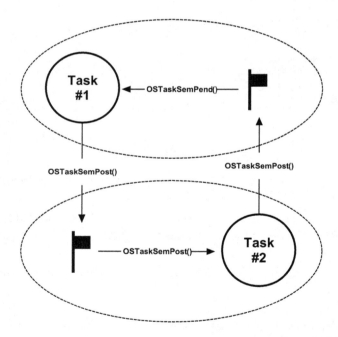

Figure 14-8 **Bilateral Rendezvous**

The code for a bilateral rendez-vous is shown in Listing 14-8. Of course, a bilateral rendez-vous can use two separate semaphores, but the built-in task semaphore makes setting up this type of synchronization quite straightforward.

```
OS_TCB  MyTask1_TCB;
OS_TCB  MyTask2_TCB;


void Task1 (void *p_arg)
{
    OS_ERR  err;
    CPU_TS  ts;

    while (DEF_ON) {
        :
        OSTaskSemPost(&MyTask2_TCB,              (1)
                    OS_OPT_POST_NONE,
                    &err);
        /* Check 'err" */
        OSTaskSemPend(0,                         (2)
                    OS_OPT_PEND_BLOCKING,
                    &ts,
                    &err);
        /* Check 'err" */
        :
    }
}


void Task2 (void *p_arg)
{
    OS_ERR  err;
    CPU_TS  ts;

    while (DEF_ON) {
        :
        OSTaskSemPost(&MyTask1_TCB,              (3)
                    OS_OPT_POST_NONE,
                    &err);
        /* Check 'err" */
        OSTaskSemPend(0,                         (4)
                    OS_OPT_PEND_BLOCKING,
                    &ts,
                    &err);
        /* Check 'err" */
        :
    }
}
```

Listing 14-8 **Tasks synchronizing their activities**

L14-8(1)   Task #1 is executing and signals Task #2's semaphore.

L14-8(2)   Task #1 pends on its internal semaphore to synchronize with Task #2. Because Task #2 has not executed yet, Task #1 is blocked waiting on its semaphore to be signaled. µC/OS-III context switches to Task #2.

L14-8(3)   Task #2 executes, and signals Task #1's semaphore.

L14-8(4)   Since it has already been signaled, Task #2 is now synchronized to Task #1. If Task #1 is higher in priority than Task #2, µC/OS-III will switch back to Task #1. If not, Task #2 continues execution.

14-3 EVENT FLAGS

Event flags are used when a task needs to synchronize with the occurrence of multiple events. The task can be synchronized when any of the events have occurred, which is called disjunctive synchronization (logical OR). A task can also be synchronized when all events have occurred, which is called conjunctive synchronization (logical AND). Disjunctive and conjunctive synchronization are shown in Figure 14-9.

The application programmer can create an unlimited number of event flag groups (limited only by available RAM). Event flag services in µC/OS-III start with the **OSFlag???()** prefix. The services available to the application programmer are described in Appendix A, "µC/OS-III API Reference" on page 443.

The code for event flag services is found in the file **os_flag.c**, and is enabled at compile time by setting the configuration constant **OS_CFG_FLAG_EN** to 1 in **os_cfg.h**.

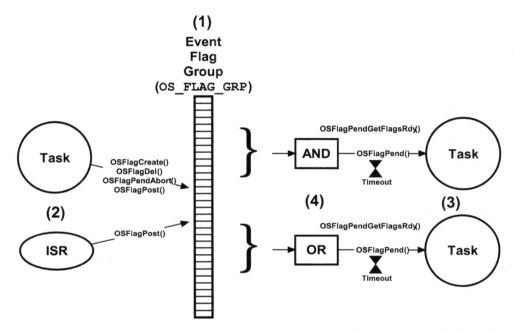

Figure 14-9 **Event Flags**

F14-9(1)   A μC/OS-III "event flag group" is a kernel object of type OS_FLAG_GRP (see os.h), and consists of a series of bits (8-, 16- or 32-bits, based on the data type OS_FLAGS defined in os_type.h). The event flag group also contains a list of tasks waiting for some (or all) of the bits to be set (1) or clear (0). An event flag group must be created before it can be used by tasks and ISRs. You need to create event flags prior to starting μC/OS-III, or by a startup task in the application code.

F14-9(2)   Tasks or ISRs can post to event flags. In addition, only tasks can create, delete, and stop other task from pending on event flag groups.

F14-9(3)   A task can wait (i.e., pend) on any number of bits in an event flag group (i.e., a subset of all the bits). As with all μC/OS-III pend calls, the calling task can specify a timeout value such that if the desired bits are not posted within a specified amount of time (in ticks), the pending task is resumed and informed about the timeout.

F14-9(4)   The task can specify whether it wants to wait for "any" subset of bits (OR) to be set (or clear), or wait for "all" bits in a subset of bit (AND) to be set (or clear).

There are a number of operations to perform on event flags, as summarized in Table 14-3.

Function Name	Operation
OSFlagCreate()	Create an event flag group
OSFlagDel()	Delete an event flag group
OSFlagPend()	Pend (i.e., wait) on an event flag group
OSFlagPendAbort()	Abort waiting on an event flag group
OSFlagPendGetFlagsRdy()	Get flags that caused task to become ready
OSFlagPost()	Post flag(s) to an event flag group

Table 14-3 **Event Flags API summary**

14-3-1 USING EVENT FLAGS

When a task or an ISR posts to an event flag group, all tasks that have their wait conditions satisfied will be resumed.

It's up to the application to determine what each bit in an event flag group means and it is possible to use as many event flag groups as needed. In an event flag group you can, for example, define that bit #0 indicates that a temperature sensor is too low, bit #1 may indicate a low battery voltage, bit #2 could indicate that a switch was pressed, etc. The code (tasks or ISRs) that detects these conditions would set the appropriate event flag by calling **OSFlagPost()** and the task(s) that would respond to those conditions would call **OSFlagPend()**.

Listing 14-9 shows how to use event flags.

```
#define     TEMP_LOW    (OS_FLAGS)0x0001                         (1)
#define     BATT_LOW    (OS_FLAGS)0x0002
#define     SW_PRESSED  (OS_FLAGS)0x0004

OS_FLAG_GRP  MyEventFlagGrp;                                     (2)

void main (void)
{
    OS_ERR  err;

    OSInit(&err);
    :
    OSFlagCreate(&MyEventFlagGrp,                                (3)
              "My Event Flag Group",
              (OS_FLAGS)0,
              &err);
    /* Check 'err" */
    :
    OSStart(&err);
}


void  MyTask (void *p_arg)                                       (4)
{
    OS_ERR  err;
    CPU_TS  ts;

    while (DEF_ON) {
        OSFlagPend(&MyEventFlagGrp,                              (5)
              TEMP_LOW + BATT_LOW,
              (OS_TICK )0,
              (OS_OPT)OS_OPT_PEND_FLAG_SET_ANY,
              &ts,
              &err);
        /* Check 'err" */
        :
    }
}
```

14

```
void  MyISR (void)                                           (6)
{
    OS_ERR  err;
    :
    OSFlagPost(&MyEventFlagGrp,                               (7)
            BAT_LOW,
            (OS_OPT)OS_OPT_POST_FLAG_SET,
            &err);
    /* Check 'err" */
    :
}
```

Listing 14-9 **Using Event Flags**

L14-9(1)   You need to define some bits in the event flag group.

L14-9(2)   You have to declare an object of type **OS_FLAG_GRP**. This object will be referenced in all subsequent μC/OS-III calls that apply to this event flag group. For the sake of discussions, assume that event flags are declared to be 16-bits in **os_type.h** (i.e., of type **CPU_INT16U**).

L14-9(3)   Event flag groups must be "created" before they can be used. The best place to do this is in your startup code as it ensures that no tasks, or ISR, will be able to use the event flag group until μC/OS-III is started. In other words, the best place is to create the event flag group is in **main()**. In the example, the event flag was given a name and all bits start in their cleared state (i.e., all zeros).

L14-9(4)   You can assume here that the application created "**MyTask()**" which will be pending on the event flag group.

L14-9(5)   To pend on an event flag group, you call **OSFlagPend()** and pass it the address of the desired event flag group.

The second argument specifies which bits the task will be waiting to be set (assuming the task is triggered by set bits instead of cleared bits).

You also need to specify how long to wait for these bits to be set. A timeout value of zero (0) indicates that the task will wait forever. A non-zero value indicates the number of ticks the task will wait until it is resumed if the desired bits are not set.

Specifying **OS_OPT_FLAG_SET_ANY** indicates that the task will wake up if either of the two bits specified is set.

A timestamp is read and saved when the event flag group is posted to. This timestamp can be used to determine the response time to the event.

OSFlagPend( ) performs a number of checks on the arguments passed (i.e., did you pass **NULL** pointers, invalid options, etc.), and returns an error code based on the outcome of the call (assuming **OS_CFG_ARG_CHK_EN** is set to 1 in **os_cfg.h**). If the call was successful "**err**" will be set to **OS_ERR_NONE**.

L14-9(6) An ISR (it can also be a task) is setup to detect when the battery voltage of the product goes low (assuming the product is battery operated). The ISR signals the task, letting the task perform whatever corrective action is needed.

L14-9(7) The desired event flag group is specified in the post call as well as which flag the ISR is setting. The third option specifies that the error condition will be "flagged" as a set bit. Again, the function sets "err" based on the outcome of the call.

Event flags are generally used for two purposes: status and transient events. Typically you would use different event flag groups to handle each of these as shown in Listing 14-10.

Tasks or ISRs can report status information such as a temperature that has exceeded a certain value, that RPM is zero on an engine or motor, or there is fuel in the tank, and more. This status information cannot be "consumed" by the tasks waiting for these events, because the status is managed by other tasks or ISRs. Event flags associated with status information are monitored by other task by using non-blocking wait calls.

Tasks will report transient events such as a switch was pressed, an object was detected by a motion sensor, an explosion occurred, etc. The task that responds to these events will typically block waiting for any of those events to occur and "consume" the event.

14

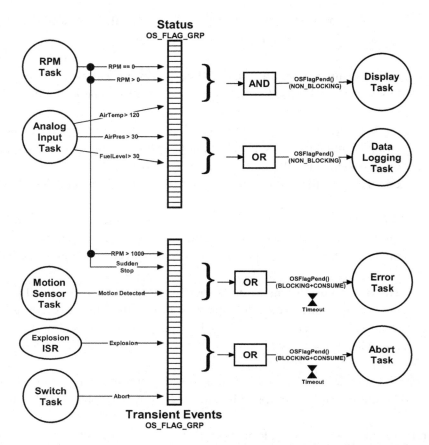

Figure 14-10 **Event Flags used for Status and Transient Events**

14-3-2 EVENT FLAGS INTERNALS

The application programmer can create an unlimited number of event flag groups (limited only by available RAM). Event flag services in µC/OS-III start with **OSFlag** and the services available to the application programmer are described in Appendix A, "µC/OS-III API Reference" on page 443. Event flag services are enabled at compile time by setting the configuration constant **OS_CFG_FLAG_EN** to 1 in **os_cfg.h**.

An event flag group is a kernel object as defined by the **OS_FLAG_GRP** data type, which is derived from the structure **os_flag_grp** (see **os.h**) as shown in Listing 14-10.

The services provided by µC/OS-III to manage event flags are implemented in the file **os_flag.c**.

```
typedef  struct  os_flag_grp  OS_FLAG_GRP;    (1)


struct  os_flag_grp {
    OS_OBJ_TYPE          Type;              (2)
    CPU_CHAR             *NamePtr;          (3)
    OS_PEND_LIST         PendList;          (4)
    OS_FLAGS             Flags;             (5)
    CPU_TS               TS;                (6)
};
```

Listing 14-10 **OS_FLAG_GRP data type**

L14-10(1)   In µC/OS-III, all structures are given a data type. In fact, all data types start with "**OS_**" and are uppercase. When an event flag group is declared, you simply use **OS_FLAG_GRP** as the data type of the variable used to declare the event flag group.

L14-10(2)   The structure starts with a "**Type**" field, which allows it to be recognized by µC/OS-III as an event flag group. In other words, other kernel objects will also have a "**Type**" as the first member of the structure. If a function is passed a kernel object, µC/OS-III will be able to confirm that it is being passed the proper data type (assuming **OS_CFG_OBJ_TYPE_CHK_EN** is set to 1 in **os_cfg.h**). For example, if passing a message queue (**OS_Q**) to an event flag service (for example **OSFlagPend()**), µC/OS-III will be able to recognize that an invalid object was passed, and return an error code accordingly.

L14-10(3)   Each kernel object can be given a name to make them easier to be recognized by debuggers or µC/Probe. This member is simply a pointer to an ASCII string, which is assumed to be **NUL** terminated.

L14-10(4)   Because it is possible for multiple tasks to be waiting (or pending) on an event flag group, the event flag group object contains a pend list as described in Chapter 10, "Pend Lists (or Wait Lists)" on page 197.

L14-10(5)   An event flag group contains a series of flags (i.e., bits), and this member contains the current state of these flags. The flags can be implemented using either an 8-, 16- or 32-bit value depending on how the data type **OS_FLAGS** is declared in **os_type.h**.

L14-10(6)   An event flag group contains a timestamp used to indicate the last time the event flag group was posted to. µC/OS-III assumes the presence of a free-running counter that allows users to make time measurements. When the event flag group is posted to, the free-running counter is read and the value is placed in this field, which is returned when **OSFlagPend( )** is called. This value allows an application to determine either when the post was performed, or how long it took for your code to obtain control of the CPU from the post. In the latter case, you can call **OS_TS_GET( )** to determine the current timestamp and compute the difference.

Even if the user understands the internals of the **OS_FLAG_GRP** data type, application code should never access any of the fields in this data structure directly. Instead, you should always use the APIs provided with µC/OS-III.

Event flag groups must be created before they can be used by an application as shown in Listing 14-11.

```
OS_FLAG_GRP  MyEventFlagGrp;              (1)


void  MyCode (void)
{
    OS_ERR  err;
    :
    OSFlagCreate(&MyEventFlagGrp,          (2)
             "My Event Flag Group",        (3)
             (OS_FLAGS)0,                   (4)
             &err);                         (5)
    /* Check 'err" */
    :

}
```

Listing 14-11 **Creating a Event Flag Group**

L14-11(1)   The application must declare a variable of type **OS_FLAG_GRP**. This variable will be referenced by other event flag services.

L14-11(2)   You create an event flag group by calling **OSFlagCreate( )** and pass the address to the event flag group allocated in (1).

L14-11(3)   You can assign an ASCII name to the event flag group, which can be used by debuggers or µC/Probe to easily identify this event flag group. µC/OS-III stores a pointer to the name so there is no practical limit to its size, except that the ASCII string needs to be **NUL** terminated.

L14-11(4)   You initialize the flags inside the event flag group to zero (0) unless the task and ISRs signal events with bits cleared instead of bits set. If using cleared bits, you should initialize all the bits to ones (1).

L14-11(5)   **OSFlagCreate()** returns an error code based on the outcome of the call. If all the arguments are valid, **err** will contain **OS_ERR_NONE**.

A task waits for one or more event flag bits either from an ISR or another task by calling **OSFlagPend()** as shown in Listing 14-12 (see Appendix A, "µC/OS-III API Reference" on page 443 for details regarding the arguments).

```
OS_FLAG_GRP  MyEventFlagGrp;


void MyTask (void *p_arg)
{
    OS_ERR    err;
    CPU_TS    ts;
    OS_FLAGS  which_flags;
    :
    while (DEF_ON) {
        :
        which_flags = OSFlagPend(&MyEventFlagGrp,      /* (1) Pointer to event flag group       */
                                 (OS_FLAGS)0x0F,       /*     Which bits to wait on              */
                                 10,                   /*     Maximum time to wait               */
                                 OS_OPT_PEND_BLOCKING +
                                 OS_OPT_PEND_FLAG_SET_ANY, /*     Option(s)                      */
                                 &ts,                  /*     Timestamp of when posted to */
                                 &err);                /*     Pointer to Error returned    */
        /* Check "err"                                 (2)                                  */
        :
        :
    }
}
```

Listing 14-12 **Pending (or waiting) on an Event Flag Group**

L14-12(1)   When called, **OSFlagPend( )** starts by checking the arguments passed to this function to ensure they have valid values (assuming **OS_CFG_ARG_CHK_EN** is set to 1 in **os_cfg.h**). If the bits the task is waiting for are set (or cleared depending on the option), **OSFlagPend( )** returns and indicate which flags satisfied the condition. This is the outcome that the caller expects.

If the event flag group does not contain the flags that the caller is looking for, the calling task might need to wait for the desired flags to be set (or cleared). If you specify **OS_OPT_PEND_NON_BLOCKING** as the option (the task is not to block), **OSFlagPend( )** returns immediately to the caller and the returned error code indicates that the bits have not been set (or cleared).

If you specify **OS_OPT_PEND_BLOCKING** as the option, the calling task will be inserted in the list of tasks waiting for the desired event flag bits. The task is not inserted in priority order but simply inserted at the beginning of the list. This is done because whenever bits are set (or cleared), it is necessary to examine all tasks in this list to see if their desired bits have been satisfied.

If you further specify a non-zero **timeout**, the task will also be inserted in the tick list. A zero value for a **timeout** indicates that the calling task is willing to wait forever for the desired bits.

The scheduler is then called since the current task is no longer able to run (it is waiting for the desired bits). The scheduler will run the next highest-priority task that is ready-to-run.

When the event flag group is posted to and the task that called **OSFlagPend( )** has its desired bits set or cleared, a task status is examined to determine the reason why **OSFlagPend( )** is returning to its caller. The possibilities are:

1) The desired bits were set (or cleared)

2) The pend was aborted by another task

3) The bits were not set (or cleared) within the specified timeout

4) The event flag group was deleted

When **OSFlagPend( )** returns, the caller is notified of the above outcome through an appropriate error code.

L14-12(2)   If **OSFlagPend( )** returns with **err** set to **OS_ERR_NONE**, you can assume that the desired bits were set (or cleared) and the task can proceed with servicing the ISR or task that created those events. If **err** contains anything else, **OSFlagPend( )** either timed out (if the timeout argument was non-zero), the pend was aborted by another task or, the event flag group was deleted by another task. It is always important to examine the returned error code and not assume everything went as planned.

To set (or clear) event flags (either from an ISR or a task), you simply call **OSFlagPost( )**, as shown in Listing 14-13.

```
OS_FLAG_GRP  MyEventFlagGrp;

void MyISR (void)
{
    OS_ERR    err;
    OS_FLAGS  flags_cur;
    :
    flags_cur = OSFlagPost(&MyEventFlagGrp,         (1)
                           (OS_FLAGS)0x0C,          (2)
                           OS_OPT_POST_FLAG_SET,    (3)
                           &err);                   (4)
    /* Check 'err" */
    :
    :
}
```

Listing 14-13 **Posting flags to an Event Flag Group**

L14-13(1)   A task posts to the event flag group by calling **OSFlagPost( )**. Specify the desired event flag group to post by passing its address. Of course, the event flag group must have been previously created. **OSFlagPost( )** returns the current value of the event flags in the event flag group after the post has been performed.

L14-13(2)   The next argument specifies which bit(s) the ISR (or task) will be setting or clearing in the event flag group.

L14-13(3)   You can specify **OS_OPT_POST_FLAG_SET** or **OS_OPT_POST_FLAG_CLR**.

If you specify **OS_OPT_POST_FLAG_SET**, the bits specified in the second arguments will set the corresponding bits in the event flag group. For example, if **MyEventFlagGrp.Flags** contains 0x03, the code in Listing 14-13 will change **MyEventFlagGrp.Flags** to 0x0F.

If you specify **OS_OPT_POST_FLAG_CLR**, the bits specified in the second arguments will clear the corresponding bits in the event flag group. For example, if **MyEventFlagGrp.Flags** contains **0x0F**, the code in Listing 14-13 will change **MyEventFlagGrp.Flags** to 0x03.

When calling **OSFlagPost()** you can specify as an option (i.e., **OS_OPT_POST_NO_SCHED**) to not call the scheduler. This means that the post is performed, but the scheduler is not called even if a higher-priority task was waiting for the event flag group. This allows the calling task to perform other post functions (if needed) and make all the posts take effect simultaneously.

L14-13(4)   **OSFlagPost()** returns an error code based on the outcome of the call. If the call was successful, **err** will contain **OS_ERR_NONE**. If not, the error code will indicate the reason of the error (see Appendix A, "µC/OS-III API Reference" on page 443 for a list of possible error codes for **OSFlagPost()**.

14-4 SYNCHRONIZING MULTIPLE TASKS

Synchronizing the execution of multiple tasks by broadcasting to a semaphore is a commonly used technique. It may be important to have multiple tasks start executing at the same time. Obviously, on a single processor, only one task will actually execute at one time. However, the start of their execution will be synchronized to the same time. This is called a multiple task rendez-vous. However, some of the tasks synchronized might not be waiting for the semaphore when the broadcast is performed. It is fairly easy to resolve this problem by combining semaphores and event flags, as shown in Figure 14-11. For this to work properly, the task on the left needs to have a lower priority than the tasks waiting on the semaphore.

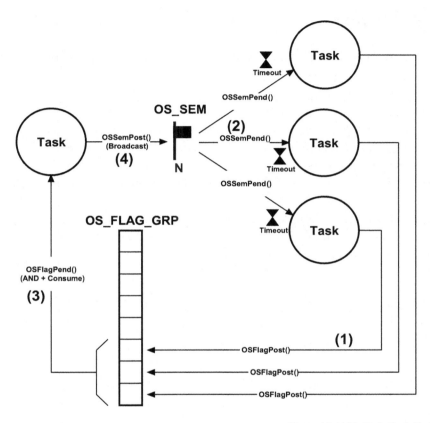

Figure 14-11 **Multiple Task Rendezvous**

F14-11(1)   Each task that needs to synchronize at the rendez-vous needs to set an event flag bit (and specify OS_OPT_POST_NO_SCHED).

F14-11(2)   The task needs to wait for the semaphore to be signaled.

F14-11(3)   The task that will be broadcasting must wait for "**all**" of the event flags corresponding to each task to be set.

F14-11(4)   When all waiting tasks are ready, the task that will synchronize the waiting task issues a broadcast to the semaphore.

14-5 SUMMARY

Three methods are presented to allow an ISR or a task to signal one or more tasks: semaphores, task semaphores, and event flags.

Both semaphores and task semaphores contain a counter allowing them to perform credit tracking and accumulate the occurrence of events. If an ISR or task needs to signal a single task (as opposed to multiple tasks when the event occurs), it makes sense to use a task semaphore since it prevents the user from having to declare an external semaphore object. Also, task semaphore services are slightly faster (in execution time) than semaphores.

Event flags are used when a task needs to synchronize with the occurrence of one or more events. However, event flags cannot perform credit tracking since a single bit (as opposed to a counter) represents each event.

Chapter

15

Message Passing

It is sometimes necessary for a task or an ISR to communicate information to another task. This information transfer is called *inter-task* communication. Information can be communicated between tasks in two ways: through global data, or by sending messages.

As seen in Chapter 13, "Resource Management" on page 231, when using global variables, each task or ISR must ensure that it has exclusive access to variables. If an ISR is involved, the only way to ensure exclusive access to common variables is to disable interrupts. If two tasks share data, each can gain exclusive access to variables either by disabling interrupts, locking the scheduler, using a semaphore, or preferably, using a mutual-exclusion semaphore. Note that a task can only communicate information to an ISR by using global variables. A task is not aware when a global variable is changed by an ISR, unless the ISR signals the task, or the task polls the contents of a variable periodically.

Messages can either be sent to an intermediate object called a *message queue*, or directly to a task since in µC/OS-III, each task has its own built-in message queue. You can use an external message queue if multiple tasks are to wait for messages. You would send a message directly to a task if only one task will process the data received.

When a task waits for a message to arrive, it does not consume CPU time.

15-1 MESSAGES

A message consists of a pointer to data, a variable containing the size of the data being pointed to, and a timestamp indicating when the message was sent. The pointer can point to a data area or even a function. Obviously, the sender and the receiver must agree as to the contents and the meaning of the message. In other words, the receiver of the message will need to know the meaning of the message received to be able to process it. For example, an Ethernet controller receives a packet and sends a pointer to this packet to a task that knows how to handle the packet.

The message contents must always remain in scope since the data is actually sent by reference instead of by value. In other words, data sent is not copied. You might consider using dynamically allocated memory as described in Chapter 17, "Memory Management" on page 343. Alternatively, you can pass a pointer to a global variable, a global data structure, a global array, or a function, etc.

15-2 MESSAGE QUEUES

A message queue is a kernel object allocated by the application. In fact, you can allocate any number of message queues. The only limit is the amount of RAM available.

There are a number of operations that the user can perform on message queues, summarized in Figure 15-1. However, an ISR can only call OSQPost(). A message queue must be created before sending messages through it.

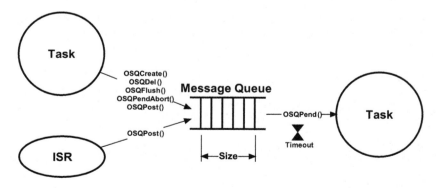

Figure 15-1 **Operations on message queue**

Message queues are drawn as a first-in, first-out pipe (FIFO). However, with µC/OS-III, it is possible to post messages in last-in, first-out order (LIFO). The LIFO mechanism is useful when a task or an ISR must send an "urgent" message to a task. In this case, the message bypasses all other messages already in the message queue. The size of the message queue is configurable at run-time.

The small hourglass close to the receiving task (F15-1) indicates that the task has an option to specify a timeout. This timeout indicates that the task is willing to wait for a message to be sent to the message queue within a certain amount of time. If the message is not sent within that time, µC/OS-III resumes the task and returns an error code indicating that the task was made ready-to-run because of a timeout, and not because the message was received. It is possible to specify an infinite timeout and indicate that the task is willing to wait forever for the message to arrive.

The message queue also contains a list of tasks waiting for messages to be sent to the message queue. Multiple tasks can wait on a message queue as shown in Figure 15-2. When a message is sent to the message queue, the highest priority task waiting on the message queue receives the message. Optionally, the sender can *broadcast* a message to all tasks waiting on the message queue. In this case, if any of the tasks receiving the message from the broadcast has a higher priority than the task sending the message (or interrupted task, if the message is sent by an ISR), µC/OS-III will run the highest-priority task that is waiting. Notice that not all tasks must specify a timeout; some tasks may want to wait forever.

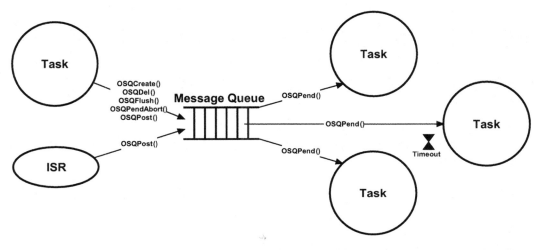

Figure 15-2 **Multiple tasks waiting on a message queue**

15-3 TASK MESSAGE QUEUE

It is fairly rare to find applications where multiple tasks wait on a single message queue. Because of this, a message queue is built into each task and the user can send messages directly to a task without going through an external message queue object. This feature not only simplifies the code but, is also more efficient than using a separate message queue object. The message queue that is built into each task is shown in Figure 15-3.

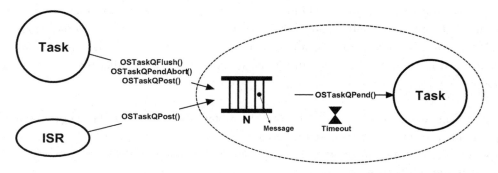

Figure 15-3 **Task message queue**

Task message queue services in μC/OS-III start with the **OSTaskQ???()** prefix, and services available to the application programmer are described in Appendix A, "μC/OS-III API Reference" on page 443. Setting **OS_CFG_TASK_Q_EN** in **os_cfg.h** enables task message queue services. The code for task message queue management is found in **os_task.c**.

You use this feature if the code knows which task to send the message(s) to. For example, if receiving an interrupt from an Ethernet controller, you can send the address of the received packet to the task that will be responsible for processing the received packet.

15-4 BILATERAL RENDEZ-VOUS

Two tasks can synchronize their activities by using two message queues, as shown in Figure 15-4. This is called a *bilateral rendez-vous* and works the same as with semaphores except that both tasks may send messages to each other. A bilateral rendez-vous cannot be performed between a task and an ISR since an ISR cannot wait on a message queue.

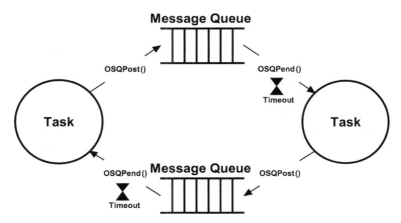

Figure 15-4 **Bilateral Rendez-vous**

In a bilateral rendez-vous, each message queue holds a maximum of one message. Both message queues are initially created empty. When the task on the left reaches the rendez-vous point, it sends a message to the top message queue and waits for a message to arrive on the bottom message queue. Similarly, when the task on the right reaches its rendez-vous point, it sends a message to the message queue on the bottom and waits for a message to arrive on the top message queue.

Figure 15-5 shows how to use task-message queues to perform a bilateral rendez-vous.

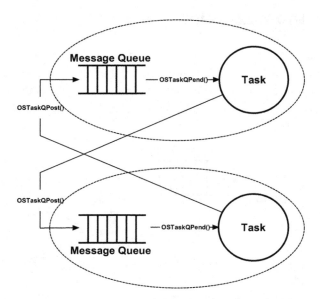

Figure 15-5 **Figure Bilateral Rendez-vous with task message queues**

15-5 FLOW CONTROL

Task-to-task communication often involves data transfer from one task to another. One task produces data while the other *consumes* it. However, data processing takes time and consumers might not consume data as fast as it is produced. In other words, it is possible for the producer to overflow the message queue if a higher-priority task preempts the consumer. One way to solve this problem is to add flow control in the process as shown in Figure 15-6.

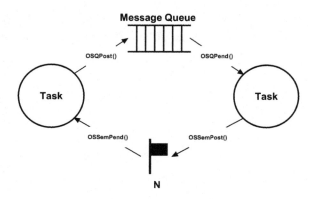

Figure 15-6 **Producer and consumer tasks with flow control**

Here, a counting semaphore is used, initialized with the number of allowable messages that can be sent by the consumer. If the consumer cannot queue more than 10 messages, the counting semaphore contains a count of 10.

As shown in the pseudo code of Listing 15-1, the producer must wait on the semaphore before it is allowed to send a message. The consumer waits for messages and, when processed, signals the semaphore.

```
Producer Task:
    Pend on Semaphore;
    Send message to message queue;

Consumer Task:
    Wait for message from message queue;
    Signal the semaphore;
```

Listing 15-1 **Producer and consumer flow control**

Combining the task message queue and task semaphores (see Chapter 14, "Synchronization" on page 273), it is easy to implement flow control as shown in Figure 15-7. In this case, however, `OSTaskSemSet()` must be called immediately after creating the task to set the value of the task semaphore to the same value as the maximum number of allowable messages in the task message queue.

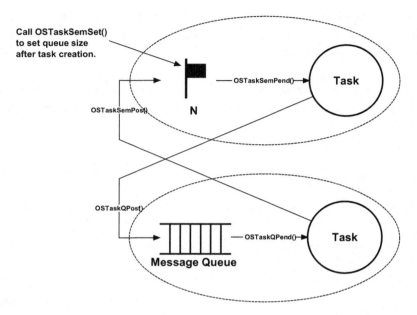

Figure 15-7 **Flow control with task semaphore and task message queue**

15-6 KEEPING THE DATA IN SCOPE

The messages sent typically point to data structures, variables, arrays, tables, etc. However, it is important to realize that the data must remain static until the receiver of the data completes its processing of the data. Once sent, the sender must not touch the sent data. This seems obvious, however it is easy to forget.

One possibility is to use the fixed-size memory partition manager provided with μC/OS-III (see Chapter 17, "Memory Management" on page 343) to dynamically allocate and free memory blocks used to pass the data. Figure 15-8 shows an example. For sake of illustration, assume that a device is sending data bytes to the UART in packets using some protocol. In this case, the first byte of a packet is unique and the end-of-packet byte is also unique.

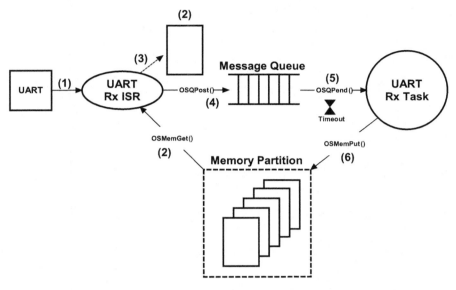

Figure 15-8 **Using memory partitions for message contents**

F15-8(1)   Here, a UART generates an interrupt when characters are received.

F15-8(2)   The pseudo-code in Listing 15-2 shows what the UART ISR code might look like. There are a lot of details omitted for sake of simplicity. The ISR reads the byte received from the UART and sees if it corresponds to a start of packet. If it is, a buffer is obtained from the memory partition.

F15-8(3)   The received byte is then placed in the buffer.

F15-8(4)   If the data received is an end-of-packet byte, you would simply post the address of the buffer to the message queue so that the task can process the received packet.

F15-8(5)   If the message sent makes the UART task the highest priority task, μC/OS-III will switch to that task at the end of the ISR instead of returning to the interrupted task. The task retrieves the packet from the message queue. Note that the **OSQPend( )** call also returns the number of bytes in the packet and a time stamp indicating when the message was sent.

F15-8(6)   When the task is finished processing the packet, the buffer is returned to the
            memory partition it came from by calling OSMemPut().

```
void  UART_ISR (void)
{
    OS_ERR  err;


    RxData = Read byte from UART;
    if (RxData == Start of Packet) {              /* See if we need a new buffer    */
        RxDataPtr = OSMemGet(&UART_MemPool,       /* Yes                            */
                             &err);
       *RxDataPtr++ = RxData;
        RxDataCtr   = 1;
    } if (RxData == End of Packet byte) {         /* See if we got a full packet    */
       *RxDataPtr++ = RxData;
        RxDataCtr++;
        OSQPost((OS_Q       *)&UART_Q,            /* Yes, post to task for processing */
                (void        *)RxDataPtr,
                (OS_MSG_SIZE)RxDataCtr,
                (OS_OPT      )OS_OPT_POST_FIFO,
                (OS_ERR      *)&err);
        RxDataPtr = NULL;                         /* Don't point to sent buffer     */
        RxDataCtr = 0;
    } else; {
       *RxDataPtr++ = RxData;                      /* Save the byte received         */
        RxDataCtr++;
    }
}
```

Listing 15-2 **UART ISR Pseudo-code**

15-7 USING MESSAGE QUEUES

Table 15-1 shows a summary of message-queue services available from µC/OS-III. Refer to Appendix A, "µC/OS-III API Reference" on page 443 for a full description on their use.

Function Name	Operation
OSQCreate()	Create a message queue.
OSQDel()	Delete a message queue.
OSQFlush()	Empty the message queue.
OSQPend()	Wait for a message.
OSQPendAbort()	Abort waiting for a message.
OSQPost()	Send a message through a message queue.

Table 15-1 **Message queue API summary**

Table 15-2 is a summary of task message queue services available from µC/OS-III. Refer to Appendix A, "µC/OS-III API Reference" on page 443, for a full description of their use.

Function Name	Operation
OSTaskQPend()	Wait for a message.
OSTaskQPendAbort()	Abort the wait for a message.
OSTaskQPost()	Send a message to a task.
OSTaskQFlush()	Empty the message queue.

Table 15-2 **Task message queue API summary**

Figure 15-9 shows an example of using a message queue when determining the speed of a rotating wheel.

15

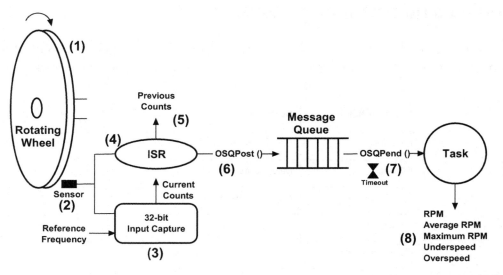

Figure 15-9 **Measuring RPM**

F15-9(1)   The goal is to measure the RPM of a rotating wheel.

F15-9(2)   A sensor is used to detect the passage of a hole in the wheel. In fact, to receive additional resolution, the wheel could contain multiple holes that are equally spaced.

F15-9(3)   A 32-bit input capture register is used to capture the value of a free-running counter when the hole is detected.

F15-9(4)   An interrupt is generated when the hole is detected. The ISR reads the current count of the input capture register and subtracts the value of the previous capture to determine the time it took for one rotation (assuming only a single hole).

```
Delta Counts    = Current Counts - Previous Counts;
Previous Counts = Current Counts;
```

F15-9(5)

F15-9(6)   The delta counts are sent to a message queue. Since a message is actually a pointer, if the pointer is 32-bits wide on the processor in use, you can simply cast the 32-bit delta counts to a pointer and send this through the message queue. A safer and more portable approach is to dynamically allocate storage to hold the delta counts using a memory block from μC/OS-III's memory management services (see Chapter 17, "Memory Management" on page 343) and send the address of the allocated memory block. The counts read are then saved in 'Previous Counts' to be used on the next interrupt.

F15-9(7)   When the message is sent, the RPM measurement task wakes up and computes the RPM as follows:

```
RPM = 60 * Reference Frequency / Delta Counts;
```

The user may specify a timeout on the pend call and the task will wake up if a message is not sent within the timeout period. This allows the user to easily detect that the wheel is not rotating and therefore, the RPM is 0.

F15-9(8)   Along with computing RPM, the task can also compute average RPM, maximum RPM, and whether the speed is above or below thresholds, etc.

A few interesting things are worth noting about the above example. First, the ISR is very short; it reads the input capture and post the delta counts to the task so it can computer the time-consuming math. Second, with the timeout on the pend, it is easy to detect that the wheel is stopped. Finally, the task can perform additional calculations and can further detect such errors as the wheel spinning too fast or too slow. In fact, the task can notify other tasks about these errors, if needed.

Listing 15-3 shows how to implement the RPM measurement example using μC/OS-III's message queue services. Some of the code is pseudo-code, while the calls to μC/OS-III services are actual calls with their appropriate arguments.

```
OS_Q        RPM_Q;                                          (1)
CPU_INT32U  DeltaCounts;
CPU_INT32U  CurrentCounts;
CPU_INT32U  PreviousCounts;


void main (void)
{
    OS_ERR  err ;
    :
    OSInit(&err) ;                                          (2)
    :
    OSQCreate((OS_Q      *)&RPM_Q,
              (CPU_CHAR *)"My Queue",
              (OS_MSG_QTY)10,
              (OS_ERR    *)&err);
    :
    OSStart(&err);
}


void RPM_ISR (void)                                         (3)
{
    OS_ERR  err;


    Clear the interrupt from the sensor;
    CurrentCounts  = Read the input capture;
    DeltaCounts    = CurrentCounts - PreviousCounts;
    PreviousCounts = CurrentCounts;
    OSQPost((OS_Q      *)&RPM_Q,                            (4)
            (void      *)DeltaCounts,
            (OS_MSG_SIZE)sizeof(void *),
            (OS_OPT     )OS_OPT_POST_FIFO,
            (OS_ERR    *)&err);
}
```

```
void RPM_Task (void *p_arg)
{
    CPU_INT32U   delta;
    OS_ERR       err;
    OS_MSG_SIZE  size;
    CPU_TS       ts;


    DeltaCounts    = 0;
    PreviousCounts = 0;
    CurrentCounts  = 0;
    while (DEF_ON) {
        delta = (CPU_INT32U)OSQPend((OS_Q        *)&RPM_Q,            (5)
                                    (OS_TICK      )OS_CFG_TICK_RATE_HZ * 10,
                                    (OS_OPT       )OS_OPT_PEND_BLOCKING,
                                    (OS_MSG_SIZE *)&size,
                                    (CPU_TS       *)&ts,
                                    (OS_ERR       *)&err);
        if (err == OS_ERR_TIMEOUT) {                                 (6)
            RPM = 0;
        } else {
            if (delta > 0u) {
                RPM = 60 * Reference Frequency / delta;              (7)
            }
        }
        Compute average RPM;                                         (8)
        Detect maximum RPM;
        Check for overspeed;
        Check for underspeed;
        :
        :

    }
}
```

Listing 15-3 **Pseudo-code of RPM measurement**

L15-3(1) Variables are declared. Notice that it is necessary to allocate storage for the message queue itself.

L15-3(2) You need to call **OSInit()** and create the message queue before it is used. The best place to do this is in startup code.

L15-3(3)   The RPM ISR clears the sensor interrupt and reads the value of the 32-bit input capture. Note that it is possible to read RPM if there is only a 16-bit input capture. The problem with a 16-bit input capture is that it is easy for it to overflow, especially at low RPMs.

The RPM ISR also computes delta counts directly in the ISR. It is just as easy to post the current counts and let the task compute the delta. However, the subtraction is a fast operation and does not significantly increase ISR processing time.

L15-3(4)   The code then sends the delta counts to the RPM task, which is responsible for computing the RPM and perform additional computations. Note that the message gets lost if the queue is full when the user attempts to post. This happens if data is generated faster than it is processed. Unfortunately, it is not possible to implement flow control in the example because we are dealing with an ISR.

L15-3(5)   The RPM task starts by waiting for a message from the RPM ISR by pending on the message queue. The third argument specifies the timeout. In this case, ten seconds worth of timeout is specified. However, the value chosen depends on the requirements of an application.

Also notice that the **ts** variable contains the timestamp of when the post was completed. You can determine the time it took for the task to respond to the message received by calling **OS_TS_GET( )**, and subtract the value of **ts**:

```
response_time = OS_TS_GET() - ts;
```

L15-3(6)   If a timeout occurs, you can assume the wheel is no longer spinning.

L15-3(7)   The RPM is computed from the delta counts received, and from the reference frequency of the free-running counter.

L15-3(8)   Additional computations are performed as needed. In fact, messages can be sent to different tasks in case error conditions are detected. The messages would be processed by the other tasks. For example, if the wheel spins too fast, another task can initiate a shutdown on the device that is controlling the wheel speed.

In Listing 15-4, **OSQPost()** and **OSQPend()** are replaced with **OSTaskQPost()** and **OSTaskQPend()** for the RPM measurement example. Notice that the code is slightly simpler to use and does not require creating a separate message queue object. However, when creating the RPM task, it is important to specify the size of the message queue used by the task and compile the application code with **OS_CFG_TASK_Q_EN** set to 1. The differences between using message queues and the task's message queue will be explained.

```
OS_TCB       RPM_TCB;                                           (1)
OS_STK       RPM_Stk[1000];
CPU_INT32U   DeltaCounts ;
CPU_INT32U   CurrentCounts ;
CPU_INT32U   PreviousCounts ;


void main (void)
{
    OS_ERR  err ;
    :
    OSInit(&err) ;
    :
    void  OSTaskCreate ((OS_TCB        *)&RPM_TCB,              (2)
                        (CPU_CHAR      *)"RPM Task",
                        (OS_TASK_PTR   )RPM_Task,
                        (void          *)0,
                        (OS_PRIO       )10,
                        (CPU_STK       *)&RPM_Stk[0],
                        (CPU_STK_SIZE  )100,
                        (CPU_STK_SIZE  )1000,
                        (OS_MSG_QTY    )10,
                        (OS_TICK       )0,
                        (void          *)0,
                        (OS_OPT        )(OS_OPT_TASK_STK_CHK + OS_OPT_TASK_STK_CLR),
                        (OS_ERR        *)&err);
    :
    OSStart(&err);
}
```

1

```
void RPM_ISR (void)
{
    OS_ERR  err;

    Clear the interrupting from the sensor;
    CurrentCounts  = Read the input capture;
    DeltaCounts    = CurrentCounts — PreviousCounts;
    PreviousCounts = CurrentCounts;
    OSTaskQPost((OS_TCB    *)&RPM_TCB,                                    (3)
                (void       *)DeltaCounts,
                (OS_MSG_SIZE)sizeof(DeltaCounts),
                (OS_OPT     )OS_OPT_POST_FIFO,
                (OS_ERR     *)&err);
}

void RPM_Task (void *p_arg)
{
    CPU_INT32U   delta;
    OS_ERR       err;
    OS_MSG_SIZE  size;
    CPU_TS       ts;

    DeltaCounts    = 0;
    PreviousCounts = 0;
    CurrentCounts  = 0;
    while (DEF_ON) {
        delta = (CPU_INT32U)OSTaskQPend((OS_TICK      )OS_CFG_TICK_RATE * 10,  (4)
                                        (OS_OPT       )OS_OPT_PEND_BLOCKING,
                                        (OS_MSG_SIZE *)&size,
                                        (CPU_TS      *)&ts,
                                        (OS_ERR      *)&err);
        if (err == OS_ERR_TIMEOUT) {
            RPM = 0;
        } else {
            if (delta > 0u) {
                RPM = 60 * ReferenceFrequency / delta;
            }
        }
        Compute average RPM;
        Detect maximum RPM;
        Check for overspeed;
        Check for underspeed;
        :
        :
    }
}
```

Listing 15-4 **Pseudo-code of RPM measurement**

15

L15-4(1)   Instead of declaring a message queue, it is important to know the **OS_TCB** of the task that will be receiving messages.

L15-4(2)   The RPM task is created and a queue size of 10 entries is specified. Of course, hard-coded values should not be specified in a real application, but instead, you should use **#defines**. Fixed numbers are used here for sake of illustration.

L15-4(3)   Instead of posting to a message queue, the ISR posts the message directly to the task, specifying the address of the **OS_TCB** of the task. This is known since the **OS_TCB** is allocated when creating the task.

L15-4(4)   The RPM task starts by waiting for a message from the RPM ISR by calling **OSTaskQPend()**. This is an inherent call so it is not necessary to specify the address of the **OS_TCB** to pend on as the current task is assumed. The second argument specifies the timeout. Here, ten seconds worth of timeout is specified, which corresponds to 6 RPM.

15-8 CLIENTS AND SERVERS

Another interesting use of message queues is shown in Figure 15-10. Here, a task (the server) is used to monitor error conditions that are sent to it by other tasks or ISRs (clients). For example, a client detects whether the RPM of the rotating wheel has been exceeded, another client detects whether an over-temperature exists, and yet another client detects that a user pressed a shutdown button. When the clients detect error conditions, they send a message through the message queue. The message sent indicates the error detected, which threshold was exceeded, the error code that is associated with error conditions, or even suggests the address of a function that will handle the error, and more.

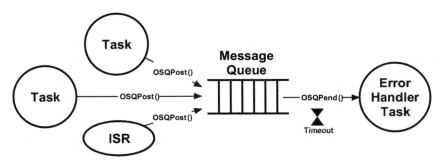

Figure 15-10 **Clients and Servers**

327

15-9 MESSAGE QUEUES INTERNALS

As previously described, a message consists of a pointer to actual data, a variable indicating the size of the data being pointed to and a timestamp indicating when the message was actually sent. When sent, a message is placed in a data structure of type OS_MSG, shown in Figure 15-11.

The sender and receiver are unaware of this data structure since everything is hidden through the APIs provided by μC/OS-III.

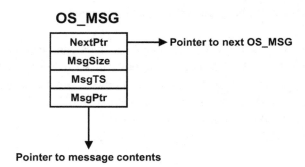

Figure 15-11 **OS_MSG structure**

μC/OS-III maintains a pool of free OS_MSGs. The total number of available messages in the pool is determined by the value of OS_CFG_MSG_POOL_SIZE found in **os_cfg_app.h**. When μC/OS-III is initialized, OS_MSGs are linked in a single linked list as shown in Figure 15-12. Notice that the free list is maintained by a data structure of type OS_MSG_POOL, which contains four (4) fields: **.NextPtr**, which points to the free list; **.NbrFree**, which contains the number of free OS_MSGs in the pool, **.NbrUsed**, which contains the number of OS_MSGs allocated to the application and, **.NbrUsedMax** which detects the maximum number of messages allocated to the application.

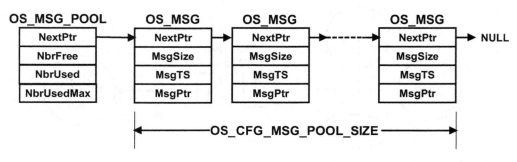

Figure 15-12 **Pool of free OS_MSGs**

Messages are queued using a data structure of type **OS_MSG_Q**, as shown in Figure 15-13.

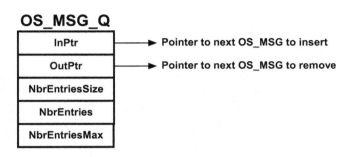

Figure 15-13 **OS_MSG_Q structure**

.InPtr   This field contains a pointer to where the next **OS_MSG** will be inserted in the queue. In fact, the **OS_MSG** will be inserted "after" the **OS_MSG** pointed to.

.OutPtr   This field contains a pointer to where the next **OS_MSG** will be extracted.

.NbrEntriesSize   This field contains the maximum number of **OS_MSGs** that the queue will hold. If an application attempts to send a message and the **.NbrEntries** matches this value, the queue is considered to be full and the **OS_MSG** will not be inserted.

.NbrEntries   This field contains the current number of **OS_MSGs** in the queue.

.NbrEntriesMax   This field contains the highest number of **OS_MSGs** existing in the queue at any given time.

A number of internal functions are used by µC/OS-III to manipulate the free list and messages. Specifically, **OS_MsgQPut()** inserts an **OS_MSG** in an **OS_MSG_Q**, **OS_MsgQGet()** extracts an **OS_MSG** from an **OS_MSG_Q**, and **OS_MsgQFreeAll()** returns all **OS_MSGs** in an **OS_MSG_Q** to the pool of free **OS_MSGs**. There are other **OS_MsgQ??()** functions in **os_msg.c** that are used during initialization.

Figure 15-14 shows an example of an OS_MSG_Q when four OS_MSGs are inserted.

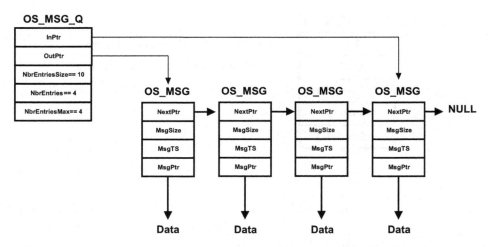

Figure 15-14 **OS_MSG_Q with four OS_MSGs**

OS_MSG_Qs are used inside two additional data structures: OS_Q and OS_TCB. Recall that an OS_Q is declared when creating a message queue object. An OS_TCB is a task control block and, as previously mentioned, each OS_TCB can have its own message queue when the configuration constant OS_CFG_TASK_Q_EN is set to 1 in os_cfg.h. Figure 15-15 shows the contents of an OS_Q and partial contents of an OS_TCB containing an OS_MSG_Q. The OS_MSG_Q data structure is shown as an "exploded view" to emphasize the structure within the structure.

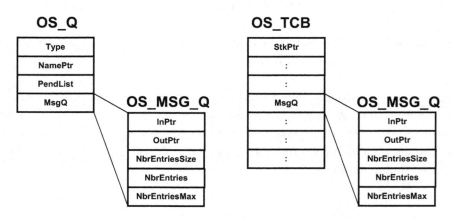

Figure 15-15 **OS_Q and OS_TCB each contain an OS_MSG_Q**

15-10 SUMMARY

Message queues are useful when a task or an ISR needs to send data to another task. The data sent must remain in scope as it is actually sent by reference instead of by value. In other words, the data sent is not copied.

The task waiting for the data will not consume CPU time while waiting for a message to be sent to it.

If it is known which task is responsible for servicing messages sent by producers, then you should use task message queue (i.e., **OSTaskQ???( )**) services since they are simple and fast. Task message queue services are enabled when **OS_CFG_TASK_Q_EN** is set to 1 in **os_cfg.h**.

If multiple tasks must wait for messages from the same message queue, you need to allocate an **OS_Q** and have the tasks wait for messages to be sent to the queue. Alternatively, you can broadcast special messages to all tasks waiting on a message queue. Regular message queue services are enabled when **OS_CFG_Q_EN** is set to 1 in **os_cfg.h**.

Messages are sent using an **OS_MSG** data structure obtained by μC/OS-III from a pool. You need to set the maximum number of messages that can be sent to a message queue, or as many messages as are available in the pool.

15

15

16

Pending On Multiple Objects

In Chapter 10, "Pend Lists (or Wait Lists)" on page 197 we saw how multiple tasks can pend (or wait) on a single kernel object such as a semaphore, mutual exclusion semaphore, event flag group, or message queue. In this chapter, we will see how tasks can pend on multiple objects. However, µC/OS-III only allows for pend on multiple semaphores and/or message queues. In other words, it is not possible to pend on multiple event flag groups or mutual exclusion semaphores.

As shown in Figure 16-1, a task can pend on any number of semaphores or message queues at the same time. The first semaphore or message queue posted will make the task ready-to-run and compete for CPU time with other tasks in the ready list. As shown, a task pends on multiple objects by calling **OSPendMulti()** and specifies an optional timeout value. The timeout applies to all of the objects. If none of the objects are posted within the specified timeout, the task resumes with an error code indicating that the pend timed out.

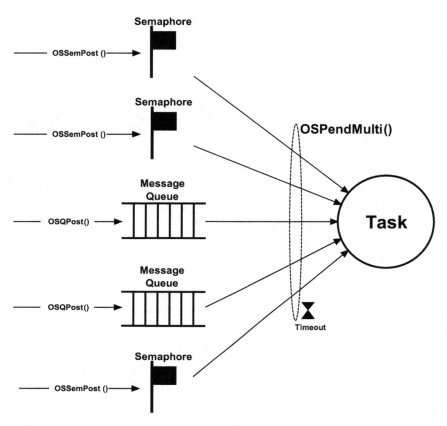

Figure 16-1 **Task pending on multiple objects**

Table 16-1 shows the function prototype of **OSPendMulti()** and Figure 16-2 shows an array of **OS_PEND_DATA** elements.

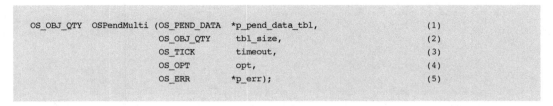

```
OS_OBJ_QTY  OSPendMulti (OS_PEND_DATA  *p_pend_data_tbl,        (1)
                         OS_OBJ_QTY     tbl_size,               (2)
                         OS_TICK        timeout,                (3)
                         OS_OPT         opt,                    (4)
                         OS_ERR        *p_err);                 (5)
```

Table 16-1 **OSPendMulti() prototype**

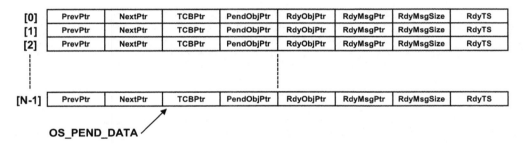

OS_PEND_DATA

Figure 16-2 **Array of OS_PEND_DATA**

L16-0(1)   **OSPendMulti()** is passed an array of **OS_PEND_DATA** elements. The caller must instantiate an array of **OS_PEND_DATA**. The size of the array depends on the total number of kernel objects that the task wants to pend on. For example, if the task wants to pend on three semaphores and two message queues then the array contains five **OS_PEND_DATA** elements as shown below:

```
OS_PEND_DATA   my_pend_multi_tbl[5];
```

The calling task needs to initialize the **.PendObjPtr** of each element of the array to point to each of the objects to be pended on. For example:

```
OS_SEM   MySem1;
OS_SEM   MySem2;
OS_SEM   MySem3;
OS_Q     MyQ1;
OS_Q     MyQ2;


void  MyTask (void)
{
    OS_ERR          err;
    OS_PEND_DATA  my_pend_multi_tbl[5];
    :
    while (DEF_ON) {
        :
        my_pend_multi_tbl[0].PendObjPtr = (OS_PEND_OBJ)&MySem1;      (6)
        my_pend_multi_tbl[1].PendObjPtr = (OS_PEND_OBJ)&MySem2;
        my_pend_multi_tbl[2].PendObjPtr = (OS_PEND_OBJ)&MySem3;
        my_pend_multi_tbl[3].PendObjPtr = (OS_PEND_OBJ)&MyQ1;
        my_pend_multi_tbl[4].PendObjPtr = (OS_PEND_OBJ)&MyQ2;
        OSPendMulti((OS_PEND_DATA *)&my_pend_multi_tbl[0],
                    (OS_OBJ_QTY    )5,
                    (OS_TICK       )0,
                    (OS_OPT        )OS_OPT_PEND_BLOCKING,
                    (OS_ERR       *)&err);
        /* Check 'err" */
        :
    }
}
```

L16-0(2)   This argument specifies the size of the **OS_PEND_DATA** table. In the above example, this is 5.

L16-0(3)   You specify whether or not to timeout in case none of the objects are posted within a certain amount of time. A non-zero value indicates the number of ticks to timeout. Specifying zero indicates the task will wait forever for any of the objects to be posted.

L16-0(4)   The "**opt**" argument specifies whether to wait for objects to be posted (you would set **opt** to **OS_OPT_PEND_BLOCKING**) or, not block if none of the objects have already been posted (you would set **opt** to **OS_OPT_PEND_NON_BLOCKING**).

F16-2(1) As with most µC/OS-III function calls, you specify the address of a variable that will receive an error code based on the outcome of the function call. See Appendix A, "µC/OS-III API Reference" on page 443 for a list of possible error codes. As always, it is highly recommended to examine the error return code.

F16-2(2) Note that all objects are cast to **OS_PEND_OBJ** data types.

When called, **OSPendMulti()** first starts by validating that all of the objects specified in the **OS_PEND_DATA** table are either an **OS_SEM** or an **OS_Q**. If not, an error code is returned.

Next, **OSPendMulti()** goes through the **OS_PEND_DATA** table to see if any of the objects have already posted. If so, **OSPendMulti()** fills the following fields in the table: **.RdyObjPtr**, **.RdyMsgPtr**, **.RdyMsgSize** and **.RdyTS**.

.RdyObjPtr   is a pointer to the object if the object has been posted. For example, if the first object in the table is a semaphore and the semaphore has been posted to, **my_pend_multi_tbl[0].RdyObjPtr** is set to **my_pend_multi_tbl[0].PendObjPtr**.

.RdyMsgPtr   is a pointer to a message if the object in the table at this entry is a message queue and a message was received from the message queue.

.RdyMsgSize   is the size of the message received if the object in the table at this entry is a message queue and a message was received from the message queue.

.RdyTS   is the timestamp of when the object posted. This allows the user to know when a semaphore or message queue was posted.

If there are no objects posted, then **OSPendMulti()** places the current task in the wait list of all the objects that it is pending on. This is a complex and tedious process for **OSPendMulti()** since there can be other tasks in the pend list of some of these objects we are pending on.

To indicate how tricky things get, Figure 16-3 is an example of a task pending on two semaphores.

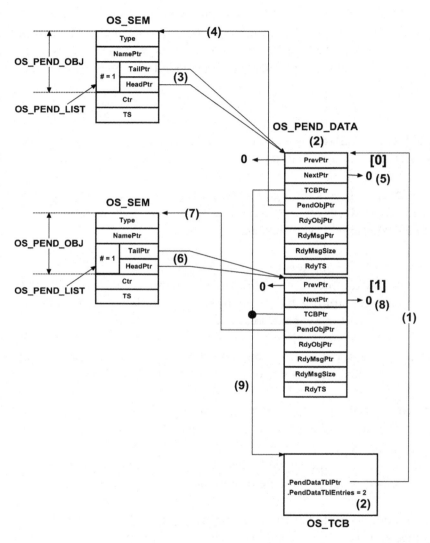

Figure 16-3 **Task pending on two semaphores**

F16-3(1)   A pointer to the base address of the **OS_PEND_DATA** table is placed in the **OS_TCB** of the task placed in the pend list of the two semaphores.

F16-3(2)   The number of entries in the **OS_PEND_DATA** table is also placed in the **OS_TCB**. Again, this task is waiting on two semaphores and therefore there are two entries in the table.

F16-3(3)   The first semaphore is linked to the first entry in the **OS_PEND_DATA** array.

F16-3(4)   Entry [0] of the **OS_PEND_DATA** table is linked to the semaphore object specified by that entry's **.PendObjPtr**. This pointer was specified by the caller of **OSPendMulti()**.

F16-3(5)   Since there is only one task in the pend list of the semaphore, the **.PrevPtr** and **.NextPtr** are pointing to **NULL**.

F16-3(6)   The second semaphore points to the second entry in the **OS_PEND_DATA** table.

F16-3(7)   The second entry in the **OS_PEND_DATA** array points to the second semaphore. This pointer was specified by the caller of **OSPendMulti()**.

F16-3(8)   The second semaphore only has one entry in its pend list. Therefore the **.PrevPtr** and **.NextPtr** both point to **NULL**.

F16-3(9)   **OSPendMulti()** links back each **OS_PEND_DATA** entry to the task that is waiting on the two semaphores.

Figure 16-4 is a more complex example where one task is pending on two semaphores while another task also pends on one of the two semaphores. The examples presented so far only show semaphores, but they could be combinations of semaphores and message queues.

16

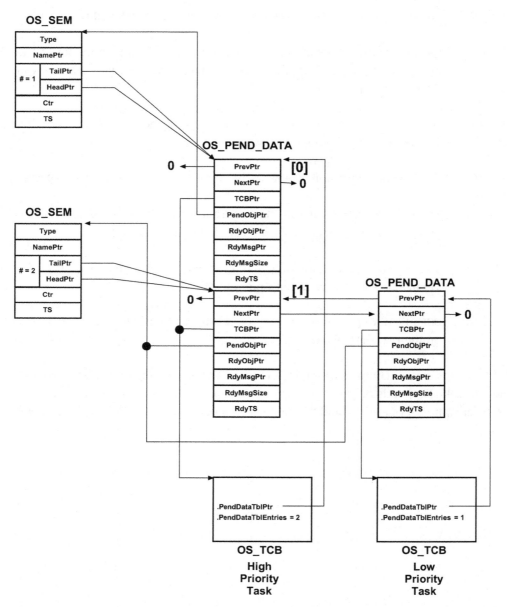

Figure 16-4 **Tasks pending on semaphores**

When either an ISR or a task signals or sends a message to one of the objects that the task is pending on, OSPendMulti() returns, indicating in the OS_PEND_DATA table which object was posted. This is done by only filling in "one" of the .RdyObjPtr entries, the one that corresponds to the object posted.

Only one of the entries in the OS_PEND_DATA table will have a .RdyObjPtr with a non-NULL value while all the other entries have the .RdyObjPtr set to NULL. Going back to the case where a task waits on five semaphores and two message queues, if the first message queue is posted while the task is pending on all those objects, the OS_PEND_DATA table will be as shown in Figure 16-5.

	.PrevPtr	.NextPtr	.TCBPtr	.PendObjPtr	.RdyObjPtr	.RdyMsgPtr	.RdyMsgSize	.RdyTS
[0]	0	0	TCBPtr	PendObjPtr	0	0	0	0
[1]	0	0	TCBPtr	PendObjPtr	0	0	0	0
[2]	0	0	TCBPtr	PendObjPtr	0	0	0	0
[3]	0	0	TCBPtr	&MyQ1	&MyQ1	Msg Ptr	Msg Size	Timestamp
[4]	0	0	TCBPtr	PendObjPtr	0	0	0	0

Figure 16-5 **Message queue #1 posted before timeout expired**

16-1 SUMMARY

μC/OS-III allows tasks to pend on multiple kernel objects.

OSPendMulti() can only pend on multiple semaphores and message queues, not event flags and mutual-exclusion semaphores.

If the objects are already posted when OSPendMulti() is called, μC/OS-III will specify which of the objects (can be more than one) in the list of objects have already been posted.

If none of the objects are posted, OSPendMulti() will place the calling task in the pend list of all the desired objects. OSPendMulti() will return as soon as one of the objects is posted. In this case, OSPendMulti() will indicate which object was posted.

OSPendMulti() is a complex function that has potentially long critical sections.

Chapter

17

Memory Management

An application can allocate and free dynamic memory using any ANSI C compiler's **malloc()** and **free()** functions, respectively. However, using **malloc()** and **free()** in an embedded real-time system may be dangerous. Eventually, it might not be possible to obtain a single contiguous memory area due to fragmentation. Fragmentation is the development of a large number of separate free areas (i.e., the total free memory is fragmented into small, non-contiguous pieces). Execution time of **malloc()** and **free()** is generally nondeterministic given the algorithms used to locate a contiguous block of free memory large enough to satisfy a **malloc()** request.

µC/OS-III provides an alternative to **malloc()** and **free()** by allowing an application to obtain fixed-sized memory blocks from a partition made from a contiguous memory area, as illustrated in Figure 17-1. All memory blocks are the same size, and the partition contains an integral number of blocks. Allocation and deallocation of these memory blocks is performed in constant time and is deterministic. The partition itself is typically allocated statically (as an array), but can also be allocated by using **malloc()** as long as it is never freed.

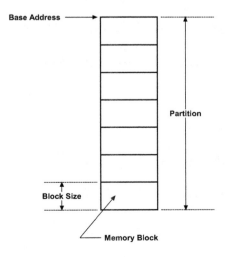

Figure 17-1 **Memory Partition**

As indicated in Figure 17-2, more than one memory partition may exist in an application and each one may have a different number of memory blocks and be a different size. An application can obtain memory blocks of different sizes based upon requirements. However, a specific memory block must always be returned to the partition that it came from. This type of memory management is not subject to fragmentation except that it is possible to run out of memory blocks. It is up to the application to decide how many partitions to have and how large each memory block should be within each partition.

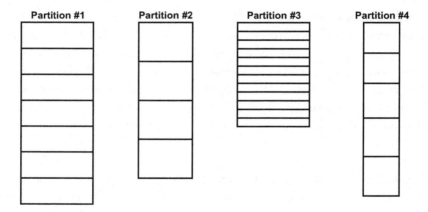

Figure 17-2 **Multiple Memory Partitions**

17-1 CREATING A MEMORY PARTITION

Before using a memory partition, it must be created. This allows µC/OS-III to know something about the memory partition so that it can manage their allocation and deallocation. Once created, a memory partition is as shown in Figure 17-3. Calling OSMemCreate() creates a memory partition.

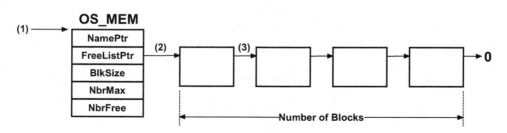

Figure 17-3 **Created Memory Partition**

F17-3(1)   When creating a partition, the application code supplies the address of a
            memory partition control block (**OS_MEM**). Typically, this memory control block
            is allocated from static memory, however it can also be obtained from the heap
            by calling **malloc()**. The application code should however never deallocate it.

F17-3(2)   **OSMemCreate()** organizes the continuous memory provided into a singly
            linked list and stores the pointer to the beginning of the list in the **OS_MEM**
            structure.

F17-3(3)   Each memory block must be large enough to hold a pointer. Given the nature
            of the linked list, a block needs to be able to point to the next block.

Listing 17-1 indicates how to create a memory partition with µC/OS-III.

```
OS_MEM        MyPartition;                              (1)
CPU_INT08U    MyPartitionStorage[12][100];             (2)


void  main (void)                                       (3)
{
    OS_ERR  err;
    :

    :

    OSInit(&err);
    :
    OSMemCreate((OS_MEM     *)&MyPartition,            (4)
               (CPU_CHAR   *)"My Partition",           (5)
               (void       *)&MyPartitionStorage[0][0], (6)
               (OS_MEM_QTY ) 12,                        (7)
               (OS_MEM_SIZE)100,                        (8)
               (OS_ERR     *)&err);                     (9)
    /* Check 'err' */
    :

    :

    OSStart(&err);
}
```

Listing 17-1 **Creating a memory partition**

L17-1(1) An application needs to allocate storage for a memory partition control block (i.e. **OS_MEM** structure). This can be a static allocation as shown here or **malloc()** can be used in the code. However, the application code must not deallocate the memory control block.

L17-1(2) The application also needs to allocate storage for the memory that will be split into memory blocks. This can also be a static allocation or **malloc()** can be used. The same reasoning applies. Do not deallocate this storage since other tasks may rely on the existence of this storage.

L17-1(3) Memory partition must be created before allocating and deallocating blocks from the partition. One of the best places to create memory partitions is in **main()** prior to starting the multitasking process. Of course, an application can call a function from **main()** to do this instead of actually placing the code directly in **main()**.

L17-1(4) You pass the address of the memory partition control block to **OSMemCreate()**. You should never reference any of the internal members of the **OS_MEM** data structure. Instead, you should always use µC/OS-III's API.

L17-1(5) You can aAssign a name to the memory partition. There is no limit to the length of the ASCII string as µC/OS-III saves a pointer to the ASCII string in the partition control block and not the actual characters.

L17-1(6) You then need to pass the base address of the storage area reserved for the memory blocks.

L17-1(7) Here, you specify how many memory blocks are available from this memory partition. Hard coded numbers are used for the sake of the illustration but you should instead use **#define** constants.

L17-1(8) You need to specify the size of each memory block in the partition. Again, a hard coded value is used for illustration, which is not recommended in real code.

L17-1(9) As with most µC/OS-III services, **OSMemCreate()** returns an error code indicating the outcome of the service. The call is successful if "**err**" contains **OS_ERR_NONE**.

17

Listing 17-2 shows how to create a memory partition with μC/OS-III, but this time, using **malloc()** to allocate storage. Do not deallocate the memory control block or the storage for the partition.

```
OS_MEM      *MyPartitionPtr;                                    (1)


void  main (void)
{
    OS_ERR   err;
    void    *p_storage;
    :
    OSInit(&err);
    :
    MyPartitionPtr = (OS_MEM *)malloc(sizeof(OS_MEM));          (2)
    if (MyPartitionPtr != (OS_MEM *)0) {
        p_storage = malloc(12 * 100);                           (3)
        if (p_storage != (void *)0) {
            OSMemCreate((OS_MEM    *)MyPartitionPtr,            (4)
                        (CPU_CHAR  *)"My Partition",
                        (void      *)p_storage,                 (5)
                        (OS_MEM_QTY ) 12,                       (6)
                        (OS_MEM_SIZE)100,                       (6)
                        (OS_ERR    *)&err);
            /* Check 'err" */
        }
    }
    :
    OSStart(&err);
}
```

Listing 17-2 **Creating a memory partition**

L17-2(1)   Instead of allocating static storage for the memory partition control block, you can assign a pointer that receives the **OS_MEM** allocated using **malloc()**.

L17-2(2)   The application allocates storage for the memory control block.

L17-2(3)   We then allocate storage for the memory partition.

L17-2(4)   A pointer is passed to the allocated memory control block to **OSMemCreate()**.

L17-2(5)   The base address of the storage used for the partition is passed to `OSMemCreate()`.

L17-2(6)   Finally, the number of blocks and the size of each block is passed so that µC/OS-III can create the linked list of 12 blocks of 100 bytes each. Again, hard coded numbers are used, but these would typically be replaced by **#defines**.

17-2 GETTING A MEMORY BLOCK FROM A PARTITION

Application code can request a memory block from a partition by calling `OSMemGet()` as shown in Listing 17-3. The code assumes that the partition was already created.

```
OS_MEM      MyPartition;                                              (1)
CPU_INT08U  *MyDataBlkPtr;


void  MyTask (void *p_arg)
{
    OS_ERR  err;


    :
    while (DEF_ON) {
        :
        MyDataBlkPtr = (CPU_INT08U *)OSMemGet((OS_MEM    *)&MyPartition,  (2)
                                              (OS_ERR    *)&err);
        if (err == OS_ERR_NONE) {                                     (3)
            /* You have a memory block from the partition */
        }
        :
        :
    }
}
```

Listing 17-3 **Obtaining a memory block from a partition**

L17-3(1)   The memory partition control block must be accessible by all tasks or ISRs that will be using the partition.

L17-3(2)   Simply call **OSMemGet()** to obtain a memory block from the desired partition. A pointer to the allocated memory block is returned. This is similar to **malloc()**, except that the memory block comes from a pool that is guaranteed to not fragment. Also, it's assumed that your application knows the size of each block so it doesn't overflow the block with data.

L17-3(3)   It is important to examine the returned error code to ensure that there are free memory blocks and that the application can start putting content in the memory blocks.

17-3 RETURNING A MEMORY BLOCK TO A PARTITION

The application code must return an allocated memory block back to the proper partition when finished. You do this by calling **OSMemPut()** as shown in Listing 17-4. The code assumes that the partition was already created.

```
OS_MEM       MyPartition;                                    (1)
CPU_INT08U  *MyDataBlkPtr;


void  MyTask (void *p_arg)
{
    OS_ERR  err;


    :
    while (DEF_ON) {
        :
        OSMemPut((OS_MEM  *)&MyPartition,                    (2)
                 (void     *)MyDataBlkPtr,                   (3)
                 (OS_ERR   *)&err);
        if (err == OS_ERR_NONE) {                            (4)
            /* You properly returned the memory block to the partition */
        }
        :
        :

    }
}
```

Listing 17-4 **Returning a memory block to a partition**

L17-4(1)   The memory partition control block must be accessible by all tasks or ISRs that will be using the partition.

L17-4(2)   You simply call **OSMemPut()** to return the memory block back to the memory partition. Note that there is no check to see whether the proper memory block is being returned to the proper partition (assuming you have multiple different partitions). It is therefore important to be careful (as is necessary when designing embedded systems).

L17-4(3)   You pass the pointer to the data area that is allocated so that it can be returned to the pool. Note that a "**void ***" is assumed.

L17-4(4)   You would examine the returned error code to ensure that the call was successful.

17-4 USING MEMORY PARTITIONS

Memory management services are enabled at compile time by setting the configuration constant OS_CFG_MEM_EN to 1 in **os_cfg.h**.

There are a number of operations to perform on memory partitions as summarized in Table 13-1.

Function Name	Operation
OSMemCreate()	Create a memory partition.
OSMemGet()	Obtain a memory block from a memory partition.
OSMemPut()	Return a memory block to a memory partition.

Table 17-1 **Memory Partition API summary**

OSMemCreate() can only be called from task-level code, but **OSMemGet()** and **OSMemPut()** can be called by Interrupt Service Routines (ISRs).

Listing 17-4 shows an example of how to use the dynamic memory allocation feature of µC/OS-III, as well as message-passing capabilities (see Chapter 15, "Message Passing" on page 309). In this example, the task on the left reads and checks the value of analog inputs (pressures, temperatures, and voltage) and sends a message to the second task if any of the

17

analog inputs exceed a threshold. The message sent contains information about which channel had the error, an error code, an indication of the severity of the error, and other information.

Error handling in this example is centralized. Other tasks, or even ISRs, can post error messages to the error-handling task. The error-handling task could be responsible for displaying error messages on a monitor (a display), logging errors to a disk, or dispatching other tasks to take corrective action based on the error.

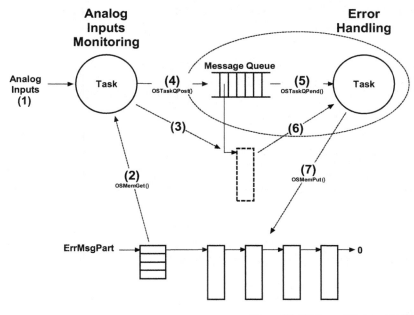

Figure 17-4 **Using a Memory Partition – non blocking**

F17-4(1)   The analog inputs are read by the task. The task determines that one of the inputs is outside a valid range and an error message needs to be sent to the error handler.

F17-4(2)   The task then obtains a memory block from a memory partition so that it can place information regarding the detected error.

F17-4(3)   The task writes this information to the memory block. As mentioned above, the task places the analog channel that is at fault, an error code, an indication of the severity, possible solutions, and more. There is no need to store a timestamp in the message, as time stamping is a built-in feature of µC/OS-III so the receiving task will know when the message was posted.

F17-4(4)   Once the message is complete, it is posted to the task that will handle such error messages. Of course the receiving task needs to know how the information is placed in the message. Once the message is sent, the analog input task is no longer allowed (by convention) to access the memory block since it sent it out to be processed.

F17-4(5)   The error handler task (on the right) normally pends on the message queue. This task will not execute until a message is sent to it.

F17-4(6)   When a message is received, the error handler task reads the contents of the message and performs necessary action(s). As indicated, once sent, the sender will not do anything else with the message.

F17-4(7)   Once the error handler task is finished processing the message, it simply returns the memory block to the memory partition. The sender and receiver therefore need to know about the memory partition or, the sender can pass the address of the memory partition as part of the message and the error handler task will know where to return the memory block to.

Sometimes it is useful to have a task wait for a memory block in case a partition runs out of blocks. µC/OS-III does not support pending on partitions, but it is possible to support this requirement by adding a counting semaphore (see Chapter 13, "Resource Management" on page 231) to guard the memory partition. The initial value of the counting semaphore would be set to the number of blocks in the partition. This is illustrated in Figure 17-5.

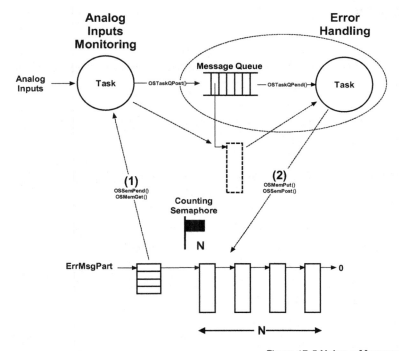

Figure 17-5 **Using a Memory Partition - blocking**

F17-5(1)   To obtain a memory block, your code simply obtain the semaphore by calling
            OSSemPend() and then calls OSMemGet() to receive the memory block.

F17-5(2)   To release a block, you simply return the memory block by calling OSMemPut()
            and then signal the semaphore by calling OSSemPost().

The above operations must be performed in order.

Note that the user may call OSMemGet() and OSMemPut() from an ISR since these functions
do not block and in fact, execute very quickly. However, you cannot use blocking calls from
ISRs.

17-5 SUMMARY

Do not use `malloc()` and `free()` in embedded systems since they lead to fragmentation. However, it is possible to use `malloc()` to allocate memory from the heap, but do not deallocate the memory.

The application programmer can create an unlimited number of memory partitions (limited only by the amount of available RAM).

Memory partition services in µC/OS-III start with the `OSMem???()` prefix, and the services available to the application programmer are described in Appendix A, "µC/OS-III API Reference" on page 443.

Memory management services are enabled at compile time by setting the configuration constant `OS_CFG_MEM_EN` to 1 in `os_cfg.h`.

`OSMemGet()` and `OSMemPut()` can be called from ISRs.

18

Porting µC/OS-III

This chapter describes how to adapt µC/OS-III to different processors. Adapting µC/OS-III to a microprocessor or a microcontroller is called porting. Most of µC/OS-III is written in C for portability. However, it is still necessary to write processor-specific code in C and assembly language. µC/OS-III manipulates processor registers, which can only be done using assembly language unless the C compiler supports inline assembly language extensions. Porting µC/OS-III to different processors is relatively easy as µC/OS-III was designed to be portable and, since µC/OS-III is similar to µC/OS-II, the user can start from a µC/OS-II port. In fact, this is the easiest way to do a µC/OS-III port.

If there is already a port for the processor to be used, it is not necessary to read this chapter unless, of course, there is an interest in knowing how µC/OS-III processor-specific code works.

µC/OS-III can run on a processor if it satisfies the following general requirements:

■ The processor has an ANSI C compiler that generates reentrant code. In fact, the toolchain used must contain an assembler, C compiler and linker/locator. Finding such a toolchain is generally not an issue since there are a number of good toolchains available on the market.

■ The processor supports interrupts and can provide an interrupt that occurs at regular intervals (typically between 10 and 1000 Hz). Most processors (especially MCUs) provide timer that can be used for this purpose. Some processors even have dedicated timers for use by an RTOS.

■ Interrupts can be disabled and enabled. All current processors that we've worked with offer this. Ideally, the processor allows you to save the current state of the interrupt mask so that it can be restored.

- The processor supports a hardware stack that accommodates a fair amount of data (possibly many kilobytes).

- The processor has instructions to save and restore the stack pointer and other CPU registers, either on the stack or in memory.

- The processor has access to sufficient RAM for µC/OS-III's variables and data structures as well as internal task stacks.

- The compiler should support 32-bit data types. For some fast 32-bit processors, the compiler should also support 64-bit data types (typically "`long long`").

Figure 18-1 shows the µC/OS-III architecture and its relationship with other software components and hardware. When using µC/OS-III in an application, the user is responsible for providing application software and the µC/OS-III configuration sections.

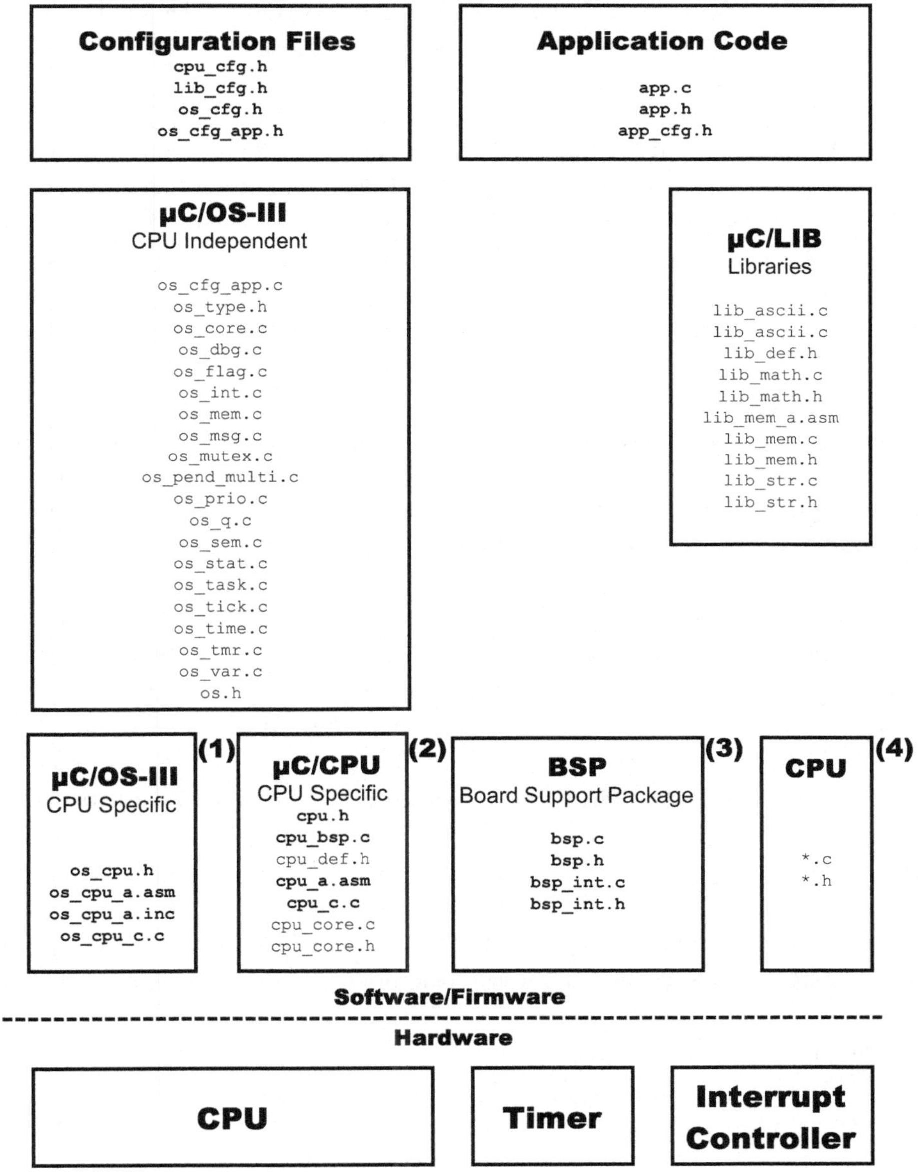

Figure 18-1 **µC/OS-III architecture**

F18-1(1)   The port developer is responsible for providing the **µC/OS-III CPU Specific** portion. A µC/OS-III port consists of writing or changing the contents of four kernel-specific files: **os_cpu.h, os_cpu_a.asm, os_cpu_a.inc** and **os_cpu_c.c**.

F18-1(2)   A port also involves writing or changing the contents of two CPU specific files: **cpu.h** and **cpu_a.asm**. **cpu_core.c** is generally generic and should not require modifications.

F18-1(3)   A Board Support Package (BSP) is generally necessary to interface µC/OS-III to a timer (which is used for the clock tick) and an interrupt controller.

F18-1(4)   Some semiconductor manufacturers provide source and header files to access on-chip peripherals. These are contained in CPU/MCU specific files. You generally don't need to modify any of these and thus, you can use them as-is.

Porting µC/OS-III is quite straightforward once the subtleties of the target processor and the C compiler/assembler are understood. Depending on the processor, a port consists of writing or changing between 100 and 400 lines of code, which takes a few hours to a few days to accomplish. The easiest thing to do, however, is to modify an existing port from a processor that is similar to the one intended for use.

A µC/OS-III port looks very much like a µC/OS-II port. Since µC/OS-II was ported to well over 45 different CPU architectures it is easy to start from a µC/OS-II port. Converting a µC/OS-II port to µC/OS-III takes approximately an hour. The process is described in Appendix C, "Migrating from µC/OS-II to µC/OS-III" on page 689.

A port involves three aspects: CPU, OS and board-specific code. The board-specific code is often called a *Board Support Package* (BSP) and from µC/OS-III's point of view, requires very little.

In this chapter, we'll present the steps needed to do a port from scratch. Actually, you'll be starting from *templates* files that already contain placeholders for the code you'll need to insert.

The following is the layout for this chapter:

- Conventions

- µC/CPU Port Files

- µC/OS-III Port Files

- BSP Files

- Testing a Port

18

18-1 CONVENTIONS

µC/CPU and µC/OS-III are provided in source form and include template files (C and assembly language) which contain instructions about what code needs to be inserted and where. Specifically, you will need to search the source files for four dollar signs (i.e., $$$$) which are used as placeholders and replace those with the necessary code.

It is assumed that assembly language code use a file extension of **.asm**. Other assembler might require that the extension be **.s** or **.src**. If that's the case with your tools, simply name the assembly language files using the proper extension.

It is assumed that comments in an assembly language file starts with a semicolon, '**;**'.

In assembly language, there are a number of 'directives' that tell the assembler how to process certain pieces of information. Below is a list of such directives and their meaning. The assembler you use may use different syntax for these directives but overall, they should work and mean the same.

- The **PUBLIC** directive indicates that you are declaring a symbol to be globally available. In other words, it's public for all files to see.

- The **EXTERN** directive indicates that the definition of a symbol is found in another file (external to this file).

- The **CODE** directive indicates that what follows needs to be linked with the rest of your executable code. In other words, we are not declaring any variables.

- The **MACRO** directive is used to define an assembly language macro. A macro is basically a series of assembly language instructions that will be replacing the macro name. In other words, when the assembler sees the macro name being invoked in your code, it will replace the macro name with the instructions that are associated with the macro. Macros are useful to avoid repeating sequences of assembly language instructions.

- The **END** directive is generally the last assembly language statement in an assembly language file. The END directive should not appear at the end of a file that defines macros because macro files are generally included in other assembly language files.

18-2 µC/CPU

µC/CPU is a module that provides CPU-specific functionality that is independent of µC/OS-III. Specifically, µC/CPU defines compiler and CPU dependent data types, the word width of the stack, whether the stack grows from high-to-low memory or from low-to-high memory, functions for disabling and enabling interrupts and more. Additional information about this module is provided in the µC/CPU User's Manual (**uC-CPU-Manual.pdf**) which is found in the **\Micrium\Software\uC-CPU\Doc** folder.

Table 18-1 shows the name of µC/CPU files and where they should be placed on the computer used to develop a µC/OS-III-based application. The file names in **bold** are files you will need to create or modify for your own port.

File	Directory
cpu_bsp.c	\Micrium\Software\uC-CPU\BSP\Template\cpu_bsp.c
cpu_def.h	\Micrium\Software\uC-CPU\
cpu_cfg.h	\Micrium\Software\uC-CPU\CFG\Template
cpu_core.c	\Micrium\Software\uC-CPU\
cpu_core.h	\Micrium\Software\uC-CPU\
cpu.h	\Micrium\Software\uC-CPU\<processor>\<compiler>
cpu_c.c	\Micrium\Software\uC-CPU\<processor>\<compiler>
cpu_a.asm	\Micrium\Software\uC-CPU\<processor>\<compiler>

Table 18-1 **µC/CPU files and directories**

<processor> is the name of the processor that the **cpu*.*** files apply to.

<compiler> is the name of the toolchain (compiler, assembler, linker/locator) used. Each has its own directory because they may have different features that makes them different from one another.

18-2-1 CPU_BSP.H

This file contains skeleton functions for **CPU_TS_TmrInit()**, **CPU_TS_TmrRd()** and other time stamp related functions. You can copy this file to your Board Support Package (BSP) directory, modify its content and add it to your build.

18-2-2 CPU_DEF.H

This file should not require any changes. **cpu_def.h** declares **#define** constants that are used by Micriµm software components.

18-2-3 CPU_CFG.H

This is a configuration file to be copied into the product directory and changed based on the options to exercise in µC/CPU. **cpu_cfg.h** is not considered a 'port file' but more an application specific file. However, it's discussed here for completeness. The file contains **#define** constants that may need to be changed based on the desired use of µC/CPU.

CPU_CFG_NAME_EN

This **#define** determines whether you will be assigning a 'name' to the CPU port. This name can then be read by application code.

CPU_CFG_NAME_SIZE

This **#define** specifies the length of the ASCII string used to assign a name to the CPU.

CPU_CFG_TS_32_EN

This **#define** specifies whether 32-bit time stamps are available for this CPU. A 32-bit timestamp is typically the value of a free-running 32-bit counter that is used to make accurate time measurements. The application code can obtain the current value of this free-running timer at any point in time and use such value to determine when an event occurred or, measure the time difference between two events. The free-running counter is generally incremented at a fairly high rate, for example 1 MHz or more.

CPU_CFG_TS_64_EN

This **#define** specifies whether 64-bit time stamps are available for this CPU. A 64-bit timestamp is typically the value of a free-running 64-bit counter (possibly made up by counting overflows of a 32-bit counter) that is used to make accurate time measurements. The application code can obtain the current value of this free-running timer at any point in time and use such value to determine when an event occurred or, measure the time difference between two events. The free-running counter is generally incremented at a fairly high rate, for example 100 MHz or more.

CPU_CFG_TS_TMR_SIZE

This **#define** specifies the size, in number of bytes, of a timestamp. A 32-bit timestamp is 4 bytes long while a 64-bit timestamp is 8 bytes long.

CPU_CFG_INT_DIS_MEAS_EN

This **#define** specifies whether extra code will be inserted to measure interrupt disable time when the code uses **CPU_CRITICAL_ENTER( )** and **CPU_CRITICAL_EXIT( )**. This extra code obviously adds additional interrupt latency because of the measurement artifacts.

CPU_CFG_INT_DIS_MEAS_OVRHD_NBR

This **#define** is used to account for the interrupt disable time measurement artifacts. The value should typically be 1.

CPU_CFG_LEAD_ZEROS_ASM_PRESENT

This **#define** specifies whether or not your processor offers assembly language instructions to count the number of consecutive zeros from the left most bit position of an integer.

CPU_CFG_TRAIL_ZEROS_ASM_PRESENT

This **#define** specifies whether or not your processor offers assembly language instructions to count the number of consecutive zeros from the right most bit position of an integer.

18

18-2-4 CPU_CORE.C

This file is generic and does not need to be changed. However it must be included in all builds. **cpu_core.c** defines such functions as **CPU_Init()**, **CPU_CntLeadZeros()**, and code to measure maximum CPU interrupt disable time. A few functions are explained here since they are used in µC/OS-III-based applications.

CPU_Init()

CPU_Init() must be called before calling **OSInit()**.

CPU_CntLeadZeros()

CPU_CntLeadZeros() is used by the µC/OS-III scheduler to find the highest priority ready task (see Chapter 7, "Scheduling" on page 151). **cpu_core.c** implements a count leading zeros in C. However, if the processor used provides a built-in instruction to count leading zeros, define **CPU_CFG_LEAD_ZEROS_ASM_PRESENT**, and replace this function by an assembly language equivalent (in **cpu_a.asm**). It is important to properly declare **CPU_CFG_DATA_SIZE** in **cpu.h** for this function to work.

CPU_TS_TmrFreqSet()

CPU_TS_TmrFreqSet() is a function that needs to be called by the application code to notify µC/CPU about the increment frequency of the timer used for timestamps. In other words, if the timestamp timer is incremented at a rate of 1 MHz then your application code would need to call **CPU_TS_TmrFreqSet()** and pass **1000000**.

CPU_TS_Get32()

CPU_TS_Get32() is a function that returns a 32-bit timestamp. The macro **OS_TS_GET()** **(see os_cpu.h)** generally maps to this function.

18-2-5 CPU_CORE.H

This header file is required by **cpu_core.c** to define function prototypes.

Table 18-2 shows the name of μC/CPU 'template' files you should use as a starting point should you decide to start a μC/CPU port from scratch. It's highly recommended that you copy these files to folders that matches the layout shown in Table 18-1. You would then edit these files to build up your own μC/CPU port files. Again, refer to the μC/CPU User's Manual (**uC-CPU-Manual.pdf**) found in **\Micrium\Software\uC-CPU\Doc**.

File	Directory
cpu.h	\Micrium\Software\uC-CPU\Template
cpu_c.c	\Micrium\Software\uC-CPU\Template
cpu_a.asm	\Micrium\Software\uC-CPU\Template

Table 18-2 **μC/CPU template files**

18-2-6 CPU.H

Many CPUs have different word lengths and **cpu.h** declares a series of type definitions that ensure portability. Specifically, we don't use the C data types **int**, **short**, **long**, **char**, etc. at Micrium. Instead, clearer data types are defined. Consult your compiler documentation to determine whether the standard declarations described below need to be changed for the CPU/compiler you are using. You should note that the **typedef**s below are not all grouped together in **cpu.h** and also, **cpu.h** contains additional comments about these data types.

```
typedef             void      CPU_VOID;
typedef  unsigned   char      CPU_CHAR;
typedef  unsigned   char      CPU_BOOLEAN;
typedef  unsigned   char      CPU_INT08U;
typedef    signed   char      CPU_INT08S;
typedef  unsigned   short     CPU_INT16U;
typedef    signed   short     CPU_INT16S;
typedef  unsigned   int       CPU_INT32U;
typedef    signed   int       CPU_INT32S;
typedef  unsigned   long long CPU_INT64U;
typedef    signed   long long CPU_INT64S;
typedef             float     CPU_FP32;
typedef             double    CPU_FP64;
typedef  volatile   CPU_INT08U  CPU_REG08;
typedef  volatile   CPU_INT16U  CPU_REG16;
typedef  volatile   CPU_INT32U  CPU_REG32;
typedef  volatile   CPU_INT64U  CPU_REG64;
typedef             void      (*CPU_FNCT_VOID)(void);
typedef             void      (*CPU_FNCT_PTR )(void *);
typedef  CPU_INT32U           CPU_ADDR;
typedef  CPU_INT32U           CPU_DATA;
typedef  CPU_DATA             CPU_ALIGN;
typedef  CPU_ADDR             CPU_SIZE_T;
typedef  CPU_INT32U           CPU_STK;            (1)
typedef  CPU_ADDR             CPU_STK_SIZE;
typedef  CPU_INT16U           CPU_ERR;
typedef  CPU_INT32U           CPU_SR;             (2)
typedef  CPU_INT32U           CPU_TS;             (3)
```

Listing 18-1 **µC/CPU Data Types**

L18-1(1)   Especially important for µC/OS-III is the definition of the **CPU_STK** data type, which sets the width of a stack entry. Specifically, is the width of data pushed to and popped from the stack 8 bits, 16 bits, 32 bits or 64 bits?

L18-1(2)   **CPU_SR** defines the data type for the processor's status register (SR) that generally holds the interrupt disable status.

L18-1(3)   The **CPU_TS** is a time stamp used to determine when an operation occurred, or to measure the execution time of code.

cpu.h also declares macros to disable and enable interrupts: **CPU_CRITICAL_ENTER( )** and **CPU_CRITICAL_EXIT( )**, respectively. The documentation in the template file explains how to declare these macros.

cpu.h is also where you need to define configuration constants:

CPU_CFG_ENDIAN_TYPE

This **#define** specifies whether your CPU is a little-endian machine or a big-endian machine. **cpu_def.h** offers the following choices:

```
CPU_ENDIAN_TYPE_BIG
CPU_ENDIAN_TYPE_LITTLE
```

CPU_CFG_ADDR_SIZE

This **#define** specifies the size of an address for the processor, in number of bytes. **cpu_def.h** offers the following choices:

```
CPU_WORD_SIZE_08
CPU_WORD_SIZE_16
CPU_WORD_SIZE_32
CPU_WORD_SIZE_64
```

CPU_CFG_DATA_SIZE

This **#define** specifies the 'natural' data width of the processor, in number of bytes. **cpu_def.h** offers the following choices:

```
CPU_WORD_SIZE_08
CPU_WORD_SIZE_16
CPU_WORD_SIZE_32
CPU_WORD_SIZE_64
```

CPU_DATA_SIZE_MAX

This **#define** specifies the maximum word size of the processor, in number of bytes. **cpu_def.h** offers the following choices:

```
CPU_WORD_SIZE_08
CPU_WORD_SIZE_16
CPU_WORD_SIZE_32
CPU_WORD_SIZE_64
```

CPU_CFG_STK_GROWTH

This **#define** specifies whether the stack grows from high to low memory or from low to high memory addresses. **cpu_def.h** offers the following choices:

```
CPU_STK_GROWTH_LO_TO_HI
CPU_STK_GROWTH_HI_TO_LO
```

CPU_CFG_CRITICAL_METHOD

This **#define** establishes how interrupts will be disabled when processing critical sections. Specifically, will we simply disable interrupts when entering a critical section, irrespective of whether or not interrupts were already disabled? Will we save the status of the interrupt disable state before we disable interrupts? **cpu_def.h** offers the following choices:

```
CPU_CRITICAL_METHOD_INT_DIS_EN
CPU_CRITICAL_METHOD_STATUS_STK
CPU_CRITICAL_METHOD_STATUS_LOCAL
```

cpu.h also declares function prototypes for a number of functions found in either **cpu_c.c** or **cpu_a.asm**.

18

18-2-7 CPU_C.C

This is an optional file containing CPU-specific functions to set the interrupt controller, timer prescalers, and more. Most implementations will not contain this file.

18-2-8 CPU_A.ASM

This file contains assembly language code to implement such functions as disabling and enabling interrupts, a more efficient count leading zeros function, and more. At a minimum, this file should implement CPU_SR_Save() and CPU_SR_Restore().

CPU_SR_Save()

CPU_SR_Save() reads the current value of the CPU status register where the current interrupt disable flag resides and returns this value to the caller. However, before returning, CPU_SR_Save() must disable all interrupts. CPU_SR_Save() is actually called by the macro CPU_CRITICAL_ENTER().

CPU_SR_Restore()

CPU_SR_Restore() restores the CPU's status register to a previously saved value. CPU_SR_Restore() is called from the macro CPU_CRITICAL_EXIT().

18

18-3 µC/OS-III PORT

Table 18-3 shows the name of µC/OS-III files and where they are typically found.

For the purpose of demonstrating how to do a port, we will assume the generic 32-bit processor as described in Chapter 8, "Context Switching" on page 165 and shown in Figure 18-2.

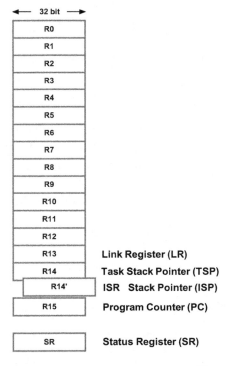

Figure 18-2 **Generic 32-bit CPU**

Our generic CPU contains 16 integer registers (R0 to R15), a separate ISR stack pointer, and a separate status register (SR). Every register is 32 bits wide and each of the 16 integer registers can hold either data or an address. The return address of a function call is placed in the Link Register (**LR**). The program counter (or instruction pointer) is R15 and there are two separate stack pointers labeled R14 and R14'. R14 represents a task stack pointer (TSP), and R14' represents an ISR stack pointer (ISP). The CPU automatically switches to the ISR stack when servicing an exception or interrupt. The task stack is accessible from an ISR (i.e., we can push and pop elements onto the task stack when in an ISR), and the interrupt stack is also accessible from a task. The Status Register (SR) contains the interrupt mask as well as various status such as the Carry, Zero, Sign, Overflow, Parity, etc.

File	Directory
os_cpu.h	\Micrium\Software\uCOS-III\Ports\<processor>\<compiler>\
os_cpu_a.asm	\Micrium\Software\uCOS-III\Ports\<processor>\<compiler>\
os_cpu_a.inc	\Micrium\Software\uCOS-III\Ports\<processor>\<compiler>
os_cpu_c.c	\Micrium\Software\uCOS-III\Ports\<processor>\<compiler>\

Table 18-3 **µC/OS-III files and directories**

Here, <processor> is the name of the processor that the **os_cpu*.*** files apply to, and <compiler> is the name of the compiler that these files assume because of the different assembly language directives that different toolchain uses.

Table 18-4 shows where you can find template files that will help you create a µC/OS-III port from scratch. You would simply copy these files in a folder specific to your processor/compiler as shown in Table 18-3 and then change the contents of these files per your processor/compiler.

File	Directory
os_cpu.h	\Micrium\Software\uCOS-III\Ports\Template\
os_cpu_a.asm	\Micrium\Software\uCOS-III\Ports\Template\
os_cpu_a.inc	\Micrium\Software\uCOS-III\Ports\Template\
os_cpu_c.c	\Micrium\Software\uCOS-III\Ports\Template\

Table 18-4 **µC/OS-III template files**

18-3-1 OS_CPU.H

OS_TASK_SW()

OS_TASK_SW() is a macro that is called by OSSched() to perform a task-level context switch. The macro can translate directly to a call to OSCtxSw(), trigger a software interrupt, or a TRAP. If a software interrupt or TRAP is used then you would most likely need to add the address of OSCtxSw() in the interrupt vector table. The choice depends on the CPU architecture.

OS_TS_GET()

OS_TS_GET() is a macro that obtains the current time stamp. It is expected that the time stamp is type CPU_TS, which is typically declared as at least a 32-bit value.

OSCtxSw(), OSIntCtxSw() and OSStartHighRdy()

os_cpu.h declares function prototypes for OSCtxSw(), OSIntCtxSw(), OSStartHighRdy() and possibly other functions required by the port.

18

18-3-2 OS_CPU_C.C

The functions are described in Appendix A, "µC/OS-III API Reference" on page 443. **os_cpu_c.c** can declare other functions as needed by the port, however the functions described below are mandatory. These functions are already implemented in the template file but those can certainly be extended as needed. However, you should not need to change this file unless you have specific needs.

OSIdleTaskHook()

This function is called repeatedly when µC/OS-III doesn't have any task ready-to-run. The port implemented might choose to put the processor in low power mode if the product being designed is battery operated. However, it would be preferable, in this case to defer this to the application level. This can be easily accomplished by putting the processor in low power mode in a function called **App_OS_IdleTaskHook()** and let the product designed decide whether or not this product requires to place the processor in low power mode. The template file contains the following code:

```
void   OSIdleTaskHook (void)
{
#if OS_CFG_APP_HOOKS_EN > 0u
    if (OS_AppIdleTaskHookPtr != (OS_APP_HOOK_VOID)0) {
        (*OS_AppIdleTaskHookPtr)();
    }
#endif
}
```

Listing 18-2 **Typical OSIdleTaskHook()**

OSInitHook()

This function is called by **OSInit()** as the very beginning of **OSInit()**. This is done to allow the port implemented to add functionality to the port while hiding the details from the µC/OS-III user. For one thing, the port implementer could setup an ISR stack in **OSInitHook()**. The template file contains the following code:

```
void  OSInitHook (void)
{
}
```

Listing 18-3 **Typical OSInitHook()**

OSStatTaskHook()

This function is called when the statistic task executes. This hook allows the port developer the opportunity to add his or her own statistics. The template file contains the following code:

```
void  OSStatTaskHook (void)
{
#if OS_CFG_APP_HOOKS_EN > 0u
    if (OS_AppStatTaskHookPtr != (OS_APP_HOOK_VOID)0) {
        (*OS_AppStatTaskHookPtr)();
    }
#endif
}
```

Listing 18-4 **Typical OSStatTaskHook()**

18

373

OSTaskCreateHook()

This function is called by **OSTaskCreate( )** and is passed the address of the **OS_TCB** of the newly created task. **OSTaskCreateHook( )** is called by **OSTaskCreate( )** after initializing the **OS_TCB** fields and setting up the stack frame for the task. The template file contains the following code:

```
void OSTaskCreateHook (OS_TCB *p_tcb)
{
#if OS_CFG_APP_HOOKS_EN > 0u
    if (OS_AppTaskCreateHookPtr != (OS_APP_HOOK_TCB)0) {
        (*OS_AppTaskCreateHookPtr)(p_tcb);
    }
#else
    (void)p_tcb;
}
```

Listing 18-5 **Typical OSTaskCreateHook()**

OSTaskDelHook()

This function is called by **OSTaskDel( )** after the task to delete has been removed either from the ready list or a wait list. The template file contains the following code:

```
void OSTaskDelHook (OS_TCB *p_tcb)
{
#if OS_CFG_APP_HOOKS_EN > 0u
    if (OS_AppTaskDelHookPtr != (OS_APP_HOOK_TCB)0) {
        (*OS_AppTaskDelHookPtr)(p_tcb);
    }
#else
    (void)p_tcb;
#endif
}
```

Listing 18-6 **Typical OSTaskDelHook()**

OSTaskReturnHook()

This function is called by **OS_TaskReturn()** if the user accidentally returns from the task code. The template file contains the following code:

```
void  OSTaskReturnHook (OS_TCB  *p_tcb)
{
#if OS_CFG_APP_HOOKS_EN > 0u
    if (OS_AppTaskReturnHookPtr != (OS_APP_HOOK_TCB)0) {
        (*OS_AppTaskReturnHookPtr)(p_tcb);
    }
#else
    (void)p_tcb;
}
```

Listing 18-7 **Typical OSTaskReturnHook()**

18

375

OSTaskStkInit()

OSTaskStkInit() is called by OSTaskCreate() and is one of the most difficult port functions to create because it establishes the stack frame of every task created. The template file contains the following code:

```
CPU_STK  *OSTaskStkInit (OS_TASK_PTR    p_task,
                         void          *p_arg,
                         CPU_STK       *p_stk_base,
                         CPU_STK       *p_stk_limit,
                         CPU_STK_SIZE   stk_size,
                         OS_OPT         opt)
{
    CPU_STK  *p_stk;


    (void)opt;

    p_stk    = &p_stk_base[stk_size];                (1)

    *--p_stk = (CPU_STK)0x00000000u;                 (2)
    *--p_stk = (CPU_STK)p_task;                      (3)
    *--p_stk = (CPU_STK)p_arg;                       (4)
    *--p_stk = (CPU_STK)0x01010101u;                 (5)
    *--p_stk = (CPU_STK)0x02020202u;
    *--p_stk = (CPU_STK)0x03030303u;
    *--p_stk = (CPU_STK)0x04040404u;
    *--p_stk = (CPU_STK)0x05050505u;
    *--p_stk = (CPU_STK)0x06060606u;
    *--p_stk = (CPU_STK)0x07070707u;
    *--p_stk = (CPU_STK)0x08080808u;
    *--p_stk = (CPU_STK)0x09090909u;
    *--p_stk = (CPU_STK)0x10101010u;
    *--p_stk = (CPU_STK)0x11111111u;
    *--p_stk = (CPU_STK)0x12121212u;
    *--p_stk = (CPU_STK)OS_TaskReturn;               (6)

    return (p_stk);                                  (7)
}
```

Listing 18-8 **Generic OSTaskStkInit()**

L18-8(1)   You need to initialize the top-of-stack. For our 'generic 32-bit CPU, the top-of-stack (TOS) points at one location beyond the area reserved for the stack. This is because we will decrement the TOS pointer before storing a value into the stack.

If the stack for the processor grew from low memory to high memory, most likely you would have setup the TOS to point at the base of the memory or, **&p_stk_base[0]**.

L18-8(2)   Since we are simulating an interrupt and the stacking of registers in the same order as an ISR would place them on the stack, we start by putting the **SR** (Status Register, also called the Program Status Word) of the CPU onto the stack first.

Also, the value stored at this location must be such that, once restored into the CPU, the **SR** must enable ALL interrupts. Here we assumed that a value of **0x00000000** would do this. However, you need to check with the processor you are using to find out how this works on that processor.

L18-8(3)   The address of the task code is then placed onto the next stack location. This way, when you perform a return from interrupt (or exception) instruction the PC will automatically be loaded with the address of the task to run.

L18-8(4)   You should recall that a task is passed an argument, **p_arg**. **p_arg** is a pointer to some user define storage or function and its use is application specific. In the assumptions above, we indicated that a function called with a single argument gets this argument passed in **R0**. You will need to check the compiler documentation to determine where '**p_arg**' is placed for your processor.

L18-8(5)   The remaining registers are placed onto the stack. You will notice that we initialized the value of those registers with a hexadecimal number that corresponds to the register number. In other words, **R12** should have the value **0x12121212** when the task starts, **R11** should have the value **0x11111111** when the task starts and so on. This makes it easy to determine whether the stack frame was setup properly when you test the port. You would simply look at the register contents with a debugger and confirm that all registers have the proper values.

L18-8(6)   Here we place the return address of the task into the location where the Link Register (**LR**) will be retrieved from. In this case, we force the return address to actually be **OS_TaskReturn()** allowing µC/OS-III to catch a task that is attempting to return. You should recall that this is not allowed with µC/OS-III.

L18-8(7)   **OSTaskStkInit()** needs to return the new top-of-stack location. In this case, the top-of-stack points at the last element placed onto the stack.

Figure 18-3 shows how the stack frame looks like just before the function returns. **OSTaskCreate()** will actually save the new top-of-stack (**p_stk**) into the **OS_TCB** of the task being created.

Figure 18-3 **Stack frame created by OSTaskStkInit()**

OSTaskSwHook()

The typical code for µC/OS-III's context switch hook is shown below. What **OSTaskSwHook()** does is highly dependent on a number of configuration options.

```
void  OSTaskSwHook (void)
{
#if OS_CFG_TASK_PROFILE_EN > 0u
    CPU_TS  ts;
#endif
#ifdef  CPU_CFG_INT_DIS_MEAS_EN
    CPU_TS  int_dis_time;
#endif


#if OS_CFG_APP_HOOKS_EN > 0u
    if (OS_AppTaskSwHookPtr != (OS_APP_HOOK_VOID)0) {                        (1)
        (*OS_AppTaskSwHookPtr)();
    }
#endif

#if OS_CFG_TASK_PROFILE_EN > 0u
    ts = OS_TS_GET();                                                        (2)
    if (OSTCBCurPtr != OSTCBHighRdyPtr) {
        OSTCBCurPtr->CyclesDelta  = ts - OSTCBCurPtr->CyclesStart;
        OSTCBCurPtr->CyclesTotal += (OS_CYCLES)OSTCBCurPtr->CyclesDelta;
    }

    OSTCBHighRdyPtr->CyclesStart = ts;
#endif

#ifdef  CPU_CFG_INT_DIS_MEAS_EN
    int_dis_time = CPU_IntDisMeasMaxCurReset();                             (3)
    if (OSTCBCurPtr->IntDisTimeMax < int_dis_time) {
        OSTCBCurPtr->IntDisTimeMax = int_dis_time;
    }
#endif

#if OS_CFG_SCHED_LOCK_TIME_MEAS_EN > 0u
    if (OSTCBCurPtr->SchedLockTimeMax < OSSchedLockTimeMaxCur) {            (4)
        OSTCBCurPtr->SchedLockTimeMax = OSSchedLockTimeMaxCur;
    }
    OSSchedLockTimeMaxCur = (CPU_TS)0;
#endif
}
```

Listing 18-9 **Typical OSTaskSwHook()**

18

379

L18-9(1)   If the application code defined a hook function to be called during a context switch then this function is called first. You application hook function can assume that **OSTCBCurPtr** points to the **OS_TCB** of the task being switched out while **OSTCBHighRdyPtr** points to the **OS_TCB** of the task being switched in.

L18-9(2)   **OSTaskSwHook()** then computes the amount of time the current task ran. However, this includes the execution time of all the ISRs that happened while the task was running.

            We then take a timestamp to mark the beginning of the task being switched in.

L18-9(3)   **OSTaskSwHook()** then stores the highest interrupt disable time into the **OS_TCB** of the task being switched out. This allows a debugger or µC/Probe to display maximum interrupt disable time on a per-task basis.

L18-9(4)   **OSTaskSwHook()** then captures the highest scheduler lock time and stores that in the **OS_TCB** of the task being switched out.

OSTimeTickHook()

This function is called by **OSTimeTick()** and is called before any other code is executed in **OSTimeTick()**. The template file contains the following code. If the application code defines an application hook function then it is called as shown.

```
void  OSTimeTickHook (void)
{
#if OS_CFG_APP_HOOKS_EN > 0u
    if (OS_AppTimeTickHookPtr != (OS_APP_HOOK_VOID)0) {
        (*OS_AppTimeTickHookPtr)();
    }
#endif
}
```

Listing 18-10 **Typical OSTimeTickHook()**

18-3-3 OS_CPU_A.ASM

This file contains the implementation of the following assembly language functions:

OSStartHighRdy()

This function is called by **OSStart()** to start multitasking. **OSStart()** will have determined the highest priority task (**OSTCBHighRdyPtr** will point to the **OS_TCB** of that task) that was created prior to calling **OSStart()** and will start executing that task. The pseudo code for this function is shown below (the C-like code needs to be implemented in assembly language):

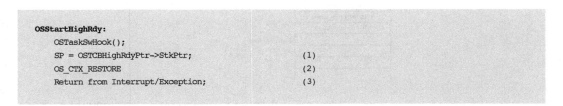

```
OSStartHighRdy:
    OSTaskSwHook();
    SP = OSTCBHighRdyPtr->StkPtr;              (1)
    OS_CTX_RESTORE                             (2)
    Return from Interrupt/Exception;           (3)
```

Listing 18-11 **OSStartHighRdy() Pseudo Code**

L18-11(1)   The Stack Pointer **(SP)** for the first task to execute is retrieved from the **OS_TCB** of the highest priority task that was created prior to calling **OSStart()**. Figure 18-4 shows the stack frame as pointed to by **OSTCBHighRdy->StkPtr**.

L18-11(2)   **OS_CTX_RESTORE** is a macro (see **os_cpu_a.inc**) that restores the context of the CPU (**R0** through **R13**) from the new task's stack.

L18-11(3)   The Return from Interrupt/Exception restores the Program Counter (**PC**) and the Status Register (**SR**) in a single instruction. At this point, the task will start executing. In fact, the task will think it was called by another function and thus, will receive '**p_arg**' as its argument. Of course, the task *must not* return.

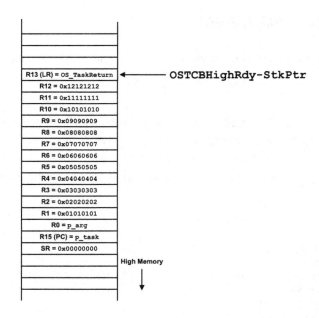

Figure 18-4 **Stack Frame pointed to by OSTCBHighRdy->StkPtr**

OSCtxSw()

This function implements the task level context switch which is invoked by the **OS_TASK_SW()** macro declared in **os_cpu.h**. The pseudo code for this function is shown below (the C-like code needs to be implemented in assembly language). You should also refer to Chapter 8, on page 168.

```
OSCtxSw:                                                 (1)
    OS_CTX_SAVE                                          (2)
    OSTCBCurPtr->StkPtr = SP;                            (3)
    OSTaskSwHook();
    OSPrioCur   = OSPrioHighRdy;
    OSTCBCurPtr = OSTCBHighRdyPtr;
    SP          = OSTCBCurPtr->StkPtr;                   (4)
    OS_CTX_RESTORE                                       (5)
    Return from Interrupt/Exception;                     (6)
```

Listing 18-12 **OSCtxSw() Pseudo Code**

L18-12(1)   OSCtxSw() is invoked by OS_TASK_SW() which is typically implemented as a *software interrupt* instruction or, a *trap* instruction. These types of instructions generally simulate the behavior of an interrupt, but is synchronous with the code. OSCtxSw() is thus the *entry point* for this instruction. In other words, if a software interrupt or TRAP is used then you would most likely need to add the address of OSCtxSw() in the interrupt vector table.

L18-12(2)   OS_CTX_SAVE is a macro (see os_cpu_a.inc) that saves the CPU context onto the current task's stack. For our generic 32-bit CPU, OS_CTX_SAVE would push R0 through R13 onto the stack, in that order.

L18-12(3)   OSCtxSw() then needs to save the current top-of-stack pointer (i.e. R14 or SP) into the OS_TCB of the current task.

L18-12(4)   The stack pointer for the new task is retrieved from the OS_TCB of the new current task.

L18-12(5)   OS_CTX_RESTORE is a macro (see os_cpu_a.inc) that restores the context of the CPU from the new task's stack. For our generic 32-bit CPU, OS_CTX_RESTORE would pop CPU registers R13 through R0 from the stack, in that order.

L18-12(6)   The Return from Interrupt/Exception restores the Program Counter (PC) and the Status Register (SR) in a single instruction. At this point, the new task will resume execution, exactly where it was preempted.

18

___

OSIntCtxSw()

This function implements the interrupt level context switch which is called by **OSIntExit()** (see **os_core.c**). The pseudo code for this function is shown below (the C-like code needs to be implemented in assembly language). Refer also to Chapter 8, on page 170.

```
OSIntCtxSw:                                              (1)
    OSTaskSwHook();
    OSPrioCur   = OSPrioHighRdy;
    OSTCBCurPtr = OSTCBHighRdyPtr;
    SP          = OSTCBCurPtr->StkPtr;                   (2)
    OS_CTX_RESTORE                                       (3)
    Return from Interrupt/Exception;                     (4)
```

Listing 18-13 **OSIntCtxSw() Pseudo Code**

L18-13(1)   **OSIntCtxSw()** is called by **OSIntExit()** at the end of all nested ISRs. The ISR is assumed to have saved the context of the interrupted task onto that task's stack. Also, the ISR is assumed to have saved the new top-of-stack of the interrupted task into the **OS_TCB** of that task.

L18-13(2)   The stack pointer for the new task is then retrieved from the **OS_TCB** of the new current task.

L18-13(3)   **OS_CTX_RESTORE** is a macro (see **os_cpu_a.inc**) that restores the context of the CPU from the new task's stack. For our generic 32-bit CPU, **OS_CTX_RESTORE** would pop CPU registers **R13** through **R0** from the stack, in that order.

L18-13(4)   The Return from Interrupt/Exception restores the Program Counter (**PC**) and the Status Register (**SR**) in a single instruction. At this point, the new task will resume execution, exactly where it was preempted.

OSTickISR()

This function may or may not reside in **os_cpu_a.asm** It's presence in **os_cpu_a.asm** depends on whether the tick ISR is generic for the CPU and, whether it needs to be implemented in assembly language. In other words, if the CPU or MCU has a dedicated timer that can be assigned for the tick ISR so that it's the same, irrespective of the target application then **OSTickISR()** can be placed in **os_cpu_a.asm** The pseudo code for this function is shown below (the C-like code needs to be implemented in assembly language). You should note that all ISRs should be modeled after **OSTickISR()**.

```
OSTickISR:                              (1)
    OS_CTX_SAVE                         (2)
    Disable Interrupts;                 (3)
    OSIntNestingCtr++;                  (4)
    if (OSIntNestingCtr == 1) {         (5)
        OSTCBCurPtr->StkPtr = SP;
    }
    Clear tick interrupt;               (6)
    OSTimeTick();                       (7)
    OSIntExit();                        (8)
    OS_CTX_RESTORE                      (9)
    Return from Interrupt/Exception;    (10)
```

Listing 18-14 **OSTickISR() Pseudo Code**

L18-14(1)   **OSTickISR()** is generally invoked automatically by the interrupt controller when the tick interrupt occurs. Assuming again our generic 32-bit CPU, it's assumed here that the **SR** and **PC** of the interrupted task are pushed automatically onto the stack of the interrupted task.

L18-14(2)   Again, **OS_CTX_SAVE** saves the CPU context onto the current task's stack. For our generic 32-bit CPU, **OS_CTX_SAVE** would push **R0** through **R13** onto the stack, in that order.

L18-14(3) Interrupts should be disabled here. On some processors, interrupts are automatically disabled when the processor accepts the interrupt. Some processors support multiple interrupt levels. In fact, some interrupts are allowed to make kernel calls while others are not. Typically, interrupts that do not make kernel calls (called *Non-Kernel Aware Interrupts*) would generally be high priority interrupts and kernel aware interrupts would all be grouped (in priority) below these. For example, if a processor has **16** different interrupt levels and level **0** is the lowest priority interrupt then, all kernel aware interrupts would be assigned from 0 to some number **N** (let's say **12**) and **N+1** to **15** would be assigned to be non-kernel aware interrupts.

L18-14(4) **OSTickISR()** then needs to increment the interrupt nesting counter. This tells µC/OS-III that the code is servicing an interrupt. The nesting counter indicates how many levels of interrupts we are currently servicing (in case the application supports nested interrupts).

L18-14(5) If this interrupt interrupts a task then we need to save the stack pointer of that task into the **OS_TCB** of that task.

L18-14(6) You need to clear the interrupting device so that it doesn't re-issue the same interrupt upon returning from interrupts. This can be done here or, in the device handler (see below).

L18-14(7) At this point, **OSTickISR()** calls **OSTimeTick()** which is reponsible for notifying the tick task that a tick occurred.

If you model your ISR like **OSTickISR()** then you would call your own C function to service the interrupting device.

L18-14(8) **OSIntExit()** is then called at the end of the ISR to notify µC/OS-III that you are done processing the ISR. µC/OS-III decrements the nesting counter and if **OSIntNestingCtr** reaches **0**, µC/OS-III knows it's returning to task level code. So, if the ISR made a more important task ready-to-run (more important than the interrupted task), µC/OS-III will context switch to that task instead of returning to the interrupted task.

18

L18-14(9)   If the interrupted task is still the most important task then **OSIntExit( )** returns and the ISR will needs to restore the saved registers. **OS_CTX_RESTORE** does just that. For our generic 32-bit CPU, **OS_CTX_RESTORE** would pop CPU registers **R13** through **R0** from the stack, in that order.

L18-14(10) Finally, the Return from Interrupt/Exception restores the Program Counter (**PC**) and the Status Register (**SR**) in a single instruction. At this point, the interrupted task will resume execution, exactly where it was interrupted.

It is actually possible to simplify the code for **OSTickISR( )** or any of your ISRs. Notice that the code at the beginning and end of the ISR is common for all ISRs. Because of that, it's possible to create two assembly language macros, **OS_ISR_ENTER** and **OS_ISR_EXIT** in **os_cpu_a.inc**. The new **OSTickISR( )** code would now look as shown below:

```
OSTickISR:
    OS_ISR_ENTER
    Clear tick interrupt;
    OSTimeTick();
    OS_ISR_EXIT
```

Listing 18-15 **OSTickISR() Pseudo Code using the OS_ISR_ENTER and OS_ISR_EXIT macros**

18

18-3-4 OS_CPU_A.INC

This file contains the implementation of assembly language macros that are used to simplify the implementation of os_cpu_a.asm. A macro replaces many assembly language instructions with a single macro invocation.

OS_CTX_SAVE

This macro is used to save the CPU context onto the current stack. **OS_CTX_SAVE** needs to save the CPU registers in the same order as they are pushed in **OSTaskStkInit()** which is described later. **OS_CTX_SAVE** only saves the CPU registers that are not automatically saved by the CPU when the CPU accepts an interrupt. In other words, if the CPU automatically saves the **PSW** and **PC** onto the stack upon initiating an ISR then **OS_CTX_SAVE** only needs to save the remaining CPU registers.

```
OS_CTX_SAVE
        Save all the CPU registers onto the current task stack
        (in the same order as in OSTaskStkInit())
```

Listing 18-16 **OS_CTX_SAVE macro Pseudo Code**

Assuming our generic 32-bit CPU, **OS_CTX_SAVE** would be implemented as follows.

```
OS_CTX_SAVE  MACRO
        PUSH  R0
        PUSH  R1
        PUSH  R2
        PUSH  R3
        PUSH  R4
        PUSH  R5
        PUSH  R6
        PUSH  R7
        PUSH  R8
        PUSH  R9
        PUSH  R10
        PUSH  R11
        PUSH  R12
        PUSH  R13
ENDM
```

Listing 18-17 **OS_CTX_SAVE assuming generic 32-bit CPU**

OS_CTX_RESTORE

This macro is used to reverse the process done by **OS_CTX_SAVE**. In other words, **OS_CTX_RESTORE** loads the CPU registers from the stack in the reverse order..

```
OS_CTX_RESTORE
    Restore all the CPU registers from the new task's stack
        (in the reverse order that they were in OSTaskStkInit())
```

Listing 18-18 **OS_CTX_SAVE macro Pseudo Code**

Assuming our generic 32-bit CPU, **OS_CTX_RESTORE** would be implemented as follows.

```
OS_CTX_RESTORE   MACRO
    POP R13
    POP R12
    POP R11
    POP R10
    POP R9
    POP R8
    POP R7
    POP R6
    POP R5
    POP R4
    POP R3
    POP R2
    POP R1
    POP R0
ENDM
```

Listing 18-19 **OS_CTX_RESTORE assuming generic 32-bit CPU**

OS_ISR_ENTER

This macro allows you to simplify your assembly language ISRs. **OS_ISR_ENTER** is basically the first line of code you would add to the ISR. The pseudo code for **OS_ISR_ENTER** is shown below.

```
OS_ISR_ENTER
    OS_CTX_SAVE
    OSIntNestingCtr++;
    if (OSIntNestingCtr == 1) {
        OSTCBCurPtr->StkPtr = SP;
    }
```

Listing 18-20 **OS_ISR_ENTER macro Pseudo Code**

Assuming our generic 32-bit CPU, **OS_ISR_ENTER** would be implemented as follows. You should note that the C-like code would actually be implemented in assembly language.

```
OS_ISR_ENTER    MACRO
    PUSH R0
    PUSH R1
    PUSH R2
    PUSH R3
    PUSH R4
    PUSH R5
    PUSH R6
    PUSH R7
    PUSH R8
    PUSH R9
    PUSH R10
    PUSH R11
    PUSH R12
    PUSH R13
    OSIntNestingCtr++;
    if (OSIntNestingCtr == 1) {
        OSTCBCurPtr->StkPtr = SP;
    }
ENDM
```

Listing 18-21 **OS_ISR_ENTER assuming generic 32-bit CPU**

OS_ISR_EXIT

This macro allows you to simplify your assembly language ISRs. OS_ISR_EXIT is basically the last line of code you would add to the ISR. The pseudo code for OS_ISR_EXIT is shown below.

```
OS_ISR_EXIT
    OSIntExit();
    OS_CTX_RESTORE
    Return from Interrupt/Exception
```

Listing 18-22 **OS_ISR_EXIT macro Pseudo Code**

Assuming our generic 32-bit CPU, OS_ISR_EXIT would be implemented as follows. You should note that the C-like code would actually be implemented in assembly language.

```
OS_ISR_EXIT  MACRO
    OSIntExit();
    POP R13
    POP R12
    POP R11
    POP R10
    POP R9
    POP R8
    POP R7
    POP R6
    POP R5
    POP R4
    POP R3
    POP R2
    POP R1
    POP R0
    Return from Interrupt/Exception;
ENDM
```

Listing 18-23 **OS_ISR_EXIT assuming generic 32-bit CPU**

18

391

18-4 BOARD SUPPORT PACKAGE (BSP)

A board support package refers to code associated with the actual evaluation board or the target board used. For example, the BSP defines functions to turn LEDs on or off, reads push-button switches, initializes peripheral clocks, etc., providing nearly any functionality to multiple products/projects.

Names of typical BSP files include:

```
bsp.c
bsp.h
bsp_int.c
bsp_int.h
```

All files are generally placed in a directory as follows:

`\Micrium\Software\EvalBoards\<manufacturer>\<board_name>\<compiler>\BSP\`

Here, **<manufacturer>** is the name of the evaluation board or target board manufacturer, **<board_name>** is the name of the evaluation or target board and <compiler> is the name of the compiler that these files assume, although most should be portable to different compilers since the BSP is typically written in C.

18-4-1 BSP.C AND BSP.H

These files normally contain functions and their definitions such as:

BSP_Init()

This function is called by application code to initialize the BSP functionality. **BSP_Init()** could initialize I/O ports, setup timers, serial ports, SPI ports and so on.

BSP_LED_On(), BSP_LED_Off() and BSP_LED_Toggle()

This code allows the user to control LEDs by referring to them as 'logical' devices as opposed to controlling ports directly from application code. **BSP_LED_On()** allows your application to turn a specific LED, **BSP_LED_Off()** turn off a specific LED and **BSP_LED_Toggle()** to change the state of a specific LED. The argument to these functions is an ID number 0..N. Each ID refers to a specific LED on the board. It's up to the BSP implementer to define which ID corresponds to what LED. By convention, however, ID 0 refers to all LEDs. In other words, you can turn on all LEDs on the board by calling **BSP_LED_On(0)**.

BSP_PB_Rd()

BSP_PB_Rd() is a function that reads the state of push button switches on the board. Each push button is identified by an ID. It's up to the BSP developer to assign the IDs to the push button switches.

Note: It is up to you to decide if the functions in this file start with the prefix **BSP_**. In other words, you can use **LED_On()** and **PB_Rd()** if this is clearer to you. However, it is a good practice to encapsulate this type of functionality in a BSP type file.

CPU_TS_TmrInit()

CPU_TS_TmrInit() is a function that µC/CPU expects to have in order to initialize the timer that will be used for timestamps. Note that a skeleton of **CPU_TS_TmrInit()** is can be found in the template file **\Micrium\Software\uC-CPU\BSP\Template\cpu_bsp.c**.

CPU_TS_TmrRd()

CPU_TS_TmrRd() is responsible for reading the value of a 16-, 32- or 64-bit free-running timer. **CPU_TS_TmrRd()** returns a **CPU_TS_TMR** data type which can be configured to be either a **CPU_TS32** or a **CPU_TS64**. If a 16-bit timer is used, the implementer of this function must accumulate 16-bit values into a 32-bit accumulator in order to always have 32-bit timestamps. The timer used for timestamps must count up (0, 1, 2, 3, ...) and must rollover automatically when the maximum count for the resolution of the timer is reached. In other words, a 16-bit counter should go from **0x0000** to **0xFFFF** and then roll back to 0x0000. Note that a skeleton of **CPU_TS_TmrRd()** is can be found in the template file **\Micrium\Software\uC-CPU\BSP\Template\cpu_bsp.c**.

18-4-2 BSP_INT.C AND BSP_INT.H

These files are typically used to declare interrupt controller related functions. For example, code that enables or disables specific interrupts from the interrupt controller, acknowledges the interrupt controller, and code to handle all interrupts if the CPU vectors to a single location when an interrupt occurs (see Chapter 9, "Interrupt Management" on page 175).

The pseudo code below shows an example of the latter.

```
void  BSP_IntHandler (void)                                          (1)
{
    CPU_FNCT_VOID   p_isr;

    while (interrupts being asserted) {                             (2)
        p_isr = Read the highest priority interrupt from the controller; (3)
        if (p_isr != (CPU_FNCT_VOID)0) {                           (4)
            (*p_isr)();                                            (5)
        }
        Acknowledge interrupt controller;                         (6)
    }
}
```

Listing 18-24 **Generic Interrupt Handler**

L18-24(1)   Here we assume that the handler for the interrupt controller is called from the assembly language code that saves the CPU registers upon entering an ISR (see Chapter 9, "Interrupt Management" on page 175).

L18-24(2)   The handler queries the interrupt controller to ask it for the address of the ISR that needs to be executed in response to the interrupt. Some interrupt controllers return an integer value that corresponds to the source. In this case, you would simply use this integer value as an index into a table (RAM or ROM) where those vectors are placed.

L18-24(3)   The interrupt controller is then asked to provide the highest priority interrupt pending. It is assumed here that the CPU may receive multiple simultaneous interrupts (or closely spaced interrupts), and that the interrupt controller will prioritize the interrupts received. The CPU will then service each interrupt in priority order instead of on a first-come basis. However, the scheme used greatly depends on the interrupt controller itself.

L18-24(4)   Here we check to ensure that the interrupt controller did not return a **NULL** pointer.

L18-24(5)   We then simply call the ISR associated with the interrupt device.

L18-24(6)   The interrupt controller generally needs to be acknowledged so that it knows that the interrupt presented is taken care of.

18-5 TESTING A PORT

Testing a port is fairly easy to do if you have the proper tools. Here we will assume that you have access to a good debugging tool, preferably built around an Integrated Development Environment (IDE). The debugger should allow you to load your code into your target, single step through your code, set breakpoint, examine CPU registers, look at memory contents and more.

18-5-1 CREATING A SIMPLE TEST PROJECT

At this point, you should have the µC/CPU and µC/OS-III port file created. To test the port files, you need to create a simple project. When you download and unzip the µC/OS-III source code you will have a directory structure similar to what is shown on the next page. When you see 'My' in front of a directory name it means a directory you will need to create for your tests of the port.

The filenames that are in **bold** are the files you will need to provide for the tests. As you will see, you can start with the template files provided with µC/CPU and µC/OS-III with little or no modifications.

```
\Micrium
  \Software
    \EvalBoards
      \MyBoardManufacturer
        \MyBoardName
          \MyToolsName
            \MyBSP
              bsp.c                <- Created in Section 18-4
              bsp.h                <- Created in Section 18-4
              bsp_int.c            <- Created in Section 18-4
            \MyTest          (1)
              app.c          (2)
              includes.h     (3)
              app_cfg.h      (4)
              app_vect.c     (5)
              cpu_cfg.h      (6) <- Copied from \Micrium\Software\uC-CPU\Cfg\Template
              lib_cfg.h          <- Copied from \Micrium\Software\uC-LIB\Cfg\Template
              os_app_hooks.c     <- Copied from \Micrium\Software\uCOS-III\Cfg\Template
              os_app_hooks.h     <- Copied from \Micrium\Software\uCOS-III\Cfg\Template
              os_cfg.h       (7) <- Copied from \Micrium\Software\uCOS-III\Cfg\Template
              os_cfg_app.h       <- Copied from \Micrium\Software\uCOS-III\Cfg\Template
              os_type.h          <- Copied from \Micrium\Software\uCOS-III\Source
\Micrium
  \Software
    \uC-CPU
      cpu_core.c
      cpu_core.h
      cpu_def.h
      \MyCPUName
        \MyToolsName
          cpu.h                  <- Created in Section 18-2
          cpu_a.asm              <- Created in Section 18-2
\Micrium
  \Software
    \uC-LIB
      lib_ascii.c
      lib_ascii.h
      lib_def.h
      lib_math.c
      lib_math.h
      lib_mem.c
      lib_mem.h
      lib_str.c
      lib_str.h
```

18

```
\Micrium
  \Software
    \uC/OS-III
      \Cfg
        os_app_hooks.c
        os_app_hooks.h
        os_cfg.h
        os_cfg_app.h
      \Ports
        \MyCPUName
          \MyToolsName
            os_cpu.h               <- Created in Section 18-3
            os_cpu_a.asm           <- Created in Section 18-3
            os_cpu_a.inc           <- Created in Section 18-3
            os_cpu_c.c         (8) <- Created in Section 18-3
      \Source
        os.h
        os_cfg_app.c
        os_core.c
        os_dbg.c
        os_flag.c
        os_int.c
        os_mem.c
        os_msg.c
        os_mutex.c
        os_pend_multi.c
        os_prio.c
        os_q.c
        os_sem.c
        os_stat.c
        os_task.c
        os_tick.c
        os_time.c
        os_tmr.c
        os_type.h
        os_var.c
```

Listing 18-25 **Test Code Directory Structure**

L18-25(1)   **MyTest** is the name of the directory that will contain the project source files.

L18-25(2)   **app.c** is the test file that contains **main()** and should look as shown below.

```
/* app.c */

#include  "includes.h"

void  main (void)
{
    OS_ERR  err;

    OSInit(&err);
    OSStart(&err);
}
```

L18-25(3)   **includes.h** is a master include file that app.c and other files assume. The contents of this file should be as shown below.

```
/* includes.h */

#include  <stdarg.h>
#include  <stdio.h>
#include  <stdlib.h>
#include  <math.h>

#include  <cpu.h>
#include  <lib_def.h>
#include  <lib_ascii.h>
#include  <lib_math.h>
#include  <lib_mem.h>
#include  <lib_str.h>

#include  <app_cfg.h>
#include  <os_cfg_app.h>
#include  <bsp.h>

#include  <os.h>
```

L18-25(4)   **app_cfg.**h must exist but should be an 'empty' file for now.

L18-25(5)   **app_vect.c** is a file that contains the processor's interrupt vector table. The file must exist but it is should be 'empty' for now.

L18-25(6)   The remaining files are copied from the directories shown in Listing 18-25 and should not be changed at this point.

L18-25(7)   You need to edit **os_cfg.h** and set the following **#define**s to the values shown below:

OS_CFG_ISR_POST_DEFERRED_EN   0u
OS_CFG_PRIO_MAX   16u
OS_CFG_STAT_TASK_EN   0u
OS_CFG_TMR_EN   0u
OS_CFG_SCHED_ROUNDROBIN_EN   0u

This is done to ensure that we only have two tasks in the test application, **OS_IdleTask()** and **OS_TickTask()**.

For this test, you need to add *one* line of code in **OSIdleTaskHook()** as shown in **bold** below. Once we verify **OSInit()**, **OSTaskStkInit()**, **OSCtxSw()**, **OS_CTX_SAVE** and **OS_CTX_RESTORE**, we'll remove this code:

```
void  OSIdleTaskHook (void)
{
    OSTimeTick();
#if OS_CFG_APP_HOOKS_EN > 0u
    if (OS_AppIdleTaskHookPtr != (OS_APP_HOOK_VOID)0) {
        (*OS_AppIdleTaskHookPtr)();
    }
#endif
}
```

18-5-2 VERIFYING TASK CONTEXT SWITCHES

In this section, we will verify the proper operation of the following functions/macros:

OSInit( )	(os_core.c)
OSStartHighRdy( )	(os_cpu_a.asm)
OSTaskStkInit( )	(os_cpu_c.c)
OSCtxSw( )	(os_cpu_a.asm)
OS_CTX_SAVE	(os_cpu_a.inc)
OS_CTX_RESTORE	(os_cpu_a.inc)
CPU_SR_Save( )	(cpu_a.asm)
CPU_SR_Restore( )	(cpu_a.asm)

Our first test is to verify that µC/OS-III gets properly initialized and that the code in **OSTaskStkInit( )** properly initializes a task's stack.

Recall that our application consist of **app.c** which contains the code shown below:

```
void  main (void)
{
    OS_ERR  err;

    OSInit(&err);
    OSStart(&err);                        <- Set a BREAKPOINT here!
}
```

STEP 1

You now need to build and download this project to your target. Building is obviously highly toolchain specific. Of course, if you encounter errors during the build, you will need to resolve those before being able to move to the next step.

Once all build errors have been resolved, you need to download the target code onto the evaluation board you selected for the tests.

STEP 2

You then need to set a breakpoint at the **OSStart()** line. In other words, have your target stop AFTER executing **OSInit()**. You should then examine the contents of '**err**' and confirm that it has the value **OS_ERR_NONE** (or, 0). If you get anything other than **OS_ERR_NONE**, the error code will tell you where the problem is (see section A-20 on page 476).

STEP 3

If **err** is **OS_ERR_NONE** then you can 'Step Into' **OSStart()** (file **os_core.c**). You should see the following code:

```
void  OSStart (OS_ERR  *p_err)
{
#ifdef OS_SAFETY_CRITICAL
    if (p_err == (OS_ERR *)0) {
        OS_SAFETY_CRITICAL_EXCEPTION();
        return;
    }
#endif

    if (OSRunning == OS_STATE_OS_STOPPED) {
        OSPrioHighRdy   = OS_PrioGetHighest();                    (1)
        OSPrioCur       = OSPrioHighRdy;
        OSTCBHighRdyPtr = OSRdyList[OSPrioHighRdy].HeadPtr;       (2)
        OSTCBCurPtr     = OSTCBHighRdyPtr;
        OSRunning       = OS_STATE_OS_RUNNING;
        OSStartHighRdy();                                         (3)
        *p_err          = OS_ERR_FATAL_RETURN;
    } else {
        *p_err          = OS_ERR_OS_RUNNING;
    }
}
```

18

STEP 4

Step into the code and stop just before executing **OSStartHighRdy()**. You should confirm that **OSPrioCur** is the same value as **OS_CFG_TICK_TASK_PRIO** (see **os_cfg_app.h**) and that **OSTCBHighRdyPtr** point at **OSTickTaskTCB**. In other words, the highest priority task should be the tick task because we should only have two task created after **OSInit()** and the tick task always has a higher priority than the idle task.

STEP 5

Now, 'Step Into' **OSStartHighRdy()** (file **os_cpu_a.asm**). You should see the assembly language shown below.

```
OSStartHighRdy:
    OSTaskSwHook();
    SP = OSTCBHighRdyPtr->StkPtr;
    OS_CTX_RESTORE
    Return from Interrupt/Exception;
```

You can 'Step Over' **OSTaskSwHook()** and the code to load the stack pointer. However, you should set a breakpoint at the 'Return from Interrupt/Exception' instruction. Once you executed the **OS_CTX_RESTORE** macro, you should look at the CPU registers and confirm that they all have their expected value (**0x12121212** for **R12**, **0x05050505** for **R5**, etc.). If not then something is not quite right with either **OSTaskStkInit()** or the **OS_CTX_RESTORE** macro. Basically, **OSTaskStkInit()** sets up the stack and **OS_CTX_RESTORE** sets up the registers based on what's on the stack.

STEP 6

If the CPU registers appear to have their proper value then you can 'Single Step' and execute the 'Return from Interrupt/Exception' instruction. If all is well, you should be looking at the OS_TickTask() code which should look something like this:

```
void  OS_TickTask (void  *p_arg)
{
    OS_ERR  err;
    CPU_TS  ts;


    p_arg = p_arg;
    while (DEF_ON) {
        (void)OSTaskSemPend((OS_TICK  )0,
                            (OS_OPT   )OS_OPT_PEND_BLOCKING,
                            (CPU_TS  *)&ts,
                            (OS_ERR  *)&err);
        if (err == OS_ERR_NONE) {                     <- Set a BREAKPOINT here!
            if (OSRunning == OS_STATE_OS_RUNNING) {
                OS_TickListUpdate();
            }
        }
    }
}
```

If the debugger doesn't show you this code then it's possible that the **PC** and **PSW** are not properly setup on the task stack by OSTaskStkInit().

If you end up in OS_TickTask() your code for OSTaskStkInit() and the macro OS_CTX_RESTORE is correct.

You should now set a breakpoint on the line following OSTaskSemPend().

STEP 7

You need to set another breakpoint in **OSCtxSw( )** as shown below.

```
OSCtxSw:                                              <- Set a BREAKPOINT here!
    OS_CTX_SAVE
    OSTCBCurPtr->StkPtr = SP;
    OSTaskSwHook();
    OSPrioCur    = OSPrioHighRdy;
    OSTCBCurPtr = OSTCBHighRdyPtr;
    SP          = OSTCBCurPtr->StkPtr;
    OS_CTX_RESTORE
    Return from Interrupt/Exception;
```

You can now run the code at full speed. Because of the breakpoint in **OSCtxSw( )**, the debugger should stop and show you the code for **OSCtxSw( )**.

Basically, what's happening here is that **OS_TickTask( )** will be waiting for the tick ISR to signal the task that a tick has expired. Since we haven't setup the tick interrupt (not yet anyway), **OS_TickTask( )** would never get to execute. However, I had you modify the idle task hook to simulate signaling the tick task so µC/OS-III will eventually switch back to this code. In the meantime, µC/OS-III will switch to the next task that's ready-to-run. This happens to be the idle task. We'll be following the code until we get to **OS_IdleTask( )**.

STEP 8

You can 'Step Over' **OS_CTX_SAVE** and verify that the stack (pointed to by **SP**) contains the value of the CPU registers saved in the same order as they are in **OSTaskStkInit( )**. In fact, you can verify this when context switches back out of the idle task in just a few more steps.

STEP 9

'Step Into' the code one more time and verify that the **SP** was saved in **OSTickTaskTCB.StkPtr**.

STEP 10

'Step Into' the code and stop just before executing the 'Return from Interrupt/Exception' instruction. At this point, the CPU registers should contain the proper register values (similar to what we had when we restored the CPU registers for **OSTickTask( )** (but this time it's for **OS_IdleTask( )**).

STEP 11

'Step Into' the return from interrupt/exception instruction and the CPU should now jump into the idle task (**os_core.c**) as shown below. You should then set a breakpoint as shown.

```
void  OS_IdleTask (void  *p_arg)
{
    CPU_SR_ALLOC();


    p_arg = p_arg;
    while (DEF_ON) {
        CPU_CRITICAL_ENTER();                          <- Set a BREAKPOINT here!
        OSIdleTaskCtr++;
#if OS_CFG_STAT_TASK_EN > 0u
        OSStatTaskCtr++;
#endif
        CPU_CRITICAL_EXIT();

        OSIdleTaskHook();
    }
}
```

STEP 12

'Step Into' the idle task and then, 'Step Into' **OSIdleTaskHook()**. Recall that I had you modify the idle task hook as shown below. What we're doing here is simulate the occurrence of the tick interrupt.

```
void  OSIdleTaskHook (void)
{
    OSTimeTick();
#if OS_CFG_APP_HOOKS_EN > 0u
    if (OS_AppIdleTaskHookPtr != (OS_APP_HOOK_VOID)0) {
        (*OS_AppIdleTaskHookPtr)();
    }
#endif
}
```

STEP 13

Have your debugger run the code at full speed. You should actually hit the breakpoint in **OSCtxSw( )** as shown below. What happened here is that µC/OS-III signaled the tick task and since the tick task is more important than the idle task, µC/OS-III is switching back to the tick task.

```
OSCtxSw:                                          <- BREAKPOINT here.
    OS_CTX_SAVE
    OSTCBCurPtr->StkPtr = SP;
    OSTaskSwHook();
    OSPrioCur    = OSPrioHighRdy;
    OSTCBCurPtr = OSTCBHighRdyPtr;
    SP           = OSTCBCurPtr->StkPtr;
    OS_CTX_RESTORE
    Return from Interrupt/Exception;
```

STEP 14

You can run the target at full speed and the debugger should bring you back at the breakpoint in **OS_TickTask( )**.

If you were to repeatedly run the target at full speed, your debugger should now stop at the following places:

OSCtxSw( )
OS_IdleTask( )
OSCtxSw( )
OS_TickTask( )
OSCtxSw( )
OS_IdleTask( )
OSCtxSw( )
etc.

18-5-3 VERIFYING INTERRUPT CONTEXT SWITCHES

In this section, we will verify the proper operation of the following functions/macros:

```
OSTickISR()         (os_cpu_a.asm)
OSIntCtxSw()        (os_cpu_a.asm)
OS_ISR_ENTER        (os_cpu_a.inc)
OS_ISR_EXIT         (os_cpu_a.inc)
CPU_INT_EN()        (cpu.h)
CPU_IntEn()         (cpu_a.asm)
```

You can now remove the code we added in **OSIdleTaskHook()**. The code should now be as shown below.

```
void  OSIdleTaskHook (void)
{
#if OS_CFG_APP_HOOKS_EN > 0u
    if (OS_AppIdleTaskHookPtr != (OS_APP_HOOK_VOID)0) {
        (*OS_AppIdleTaskHookPtr)();
    }
#endif
}
```

You should now setup the tick interrupt in **main()** (**app.c**) as shown below.

```
/* app.c */

#include  "includes.h"

void  main (void)
{
    OS_ERR  err;

    OSInit(&err);
    /* (1) Install interrupt vector for OSTickISR()              */
    /* (2) Initialize the tick timer to generate interrupts every millisecond */
    CPU_INT_EN();       /* (3) Enable interrupts                 */
    OSStart(&err);
}
```

L18-25(8)   You need to setup the interrupt vector for the tick ISR. Where this is done greatly depends on the CPU architecture. On some processors, you would simply insert a pointer to **OSTickISR()** in the interrupt vector table while on others, you would need to call a function to install the vector in a RAM table.

L18-25(9)   You can setup the timer you will use to generate interrupts here. You need to make sure that the interrupt will not occur immediately but instead 1 millisecond after the timer is initialized. You may recall that I told you to always initialize the tick interrupt from the first task that executes when we start multitasking. However, since we are testing the port, it's safe to initialize the timer here since we have control over when the first interrupt will actually occur.

L18-25(10)   This macro is used to enable global CPU interrupts. It's assumed that the startup code runs with interrupts disabled and thus, those need to be explicitly enabled.

At this point, you need to remove all breakpoints you inserted to test the task level context switch code and insert the following breakpoints. You should note that the C-like code should actually be replaced with assembly language instructions for your processor.

```
OSIntCtxSw:                                    <- Set BREAKPOINT here!
    OSTaskSwHook();
    OSPrioCur   = OSPrioHighRdy;
    OSTCBCurPtr = OSTCBHighRdyPtr;
    SP          = OSTCBCurPtr->StkPtr;
    OS_CTX_RESTORE
    Return from Interrupt/Exception;


OSTickISR:                                     <- Set BREAKPOINT here!
    OS_ISR_ENTER
    Clear tick interrupt;
    OSTimeTick();
    OS_ISR_EXIT
```

STEP 1

Reset the CPU and run the code until you hit the first breakpoint. If you properly initialized the tick timer then you should be looking at the **OSTickISR()** code. If not, you need to determine why you are not getting the tick interrupt.

If the tick interrupt is properly setup then you should verify that is pointing at **OSIdleTaskTCB** since your application should have been looping around the idle task until the tick interrupt occurred.

STEP 2

You should step into the **OSTickISR()** code and verify that **OS_ISR_ENTER** increments **OSIntNestingCtr** (you should be able to look at that variable with the debugger and notice that it should have a value of 1). Also, you should verify that the current **SP** is saved in **OSTCBCurPtr->StkPtr** (it should be the same as **OSIdleTaskTCB.StkPtr**).

STEP 3

You should now step through the code that clears the tick interrupt and verify that it's doing the proper thing.

STEP 4

You can now 'Step Over' the call to **OSTimeTick()**. **OSTimeTick()** basically signals the tick task and thus makes it ready-to-run. Instead of returning from interrupt from **OSTickISR()**, µC/OS-III will instead exit through **OSIntCtxSw()** because the tick ISR has a higher priority than the idle task.

STEP 5

You should now 'Step Into' the code for **OS_ISR_EXIT** and 'Step Over' **OSIntExit()** (**os_core.c**). **OSIntExit()** should not return to its caller but instead, call **OSIntCtxSw()** (**os_cpu_a.asm**) as shown below. At this point, **OSTCBHighRdyPtr** should point at **OSTickTaskTCB**.

```
OSIntCtxSw:
    OSTaskSwHook();
    OSPrioCur   = OSPrioHighRdy;
    OSTCBCurPtr = OSTCBHighRdyPtr;
    SP          = OSTCBCurPtr->StkPtr;
    OS_CTX_RESTORE
    Return from Interrupt/Exception;
```

STEP 6

Before going any further in the code, you should set a breakpoint in OS_TickTask()
(os_tick.c) as shown below.

```
void  OS_TickTask (void  *p_arg)
{
    OS_ERR  err;
    CPU_TS  ts;


    p_arg = p_arg;
    while (DEF_ON) {
        (void)OSTaskSemPend((OS_TICK  )0,                     <- Set BREAKPOINT here!
                            (OS_OPT   )OS_OPT_PEND_BLOCKING,
                            (CPU_TS  *)&ts,
                            (OS_ERR  *)&err);
        if (err == OS_ERR_NONE) {
            if (OSRunning == OS_STATE_OS_RUNNING) {
                OS_TickListUpdate();
            }
        }
    }
}
```

STEP 7

You should then go back to os_cpu_a.asm and 'Step Into' the code for OS_CTX_RESTORE
and then execute the Return from Interrupt/Exception instruction.

This should cause the code to context switch into OS_TickTask(). In fact, you will be in
the context of OS_TickTask() but you will not be in the OS_TickTask() code itself. This is
because µC/OS-III is actually returning to the point where it invoked the scheduler to

switch to the idle task. μC/OS-III is simply returning to that point. You can step through code to see the path μC/OS-III is taking. However, this corresponds to quite a few lines of code. It's probably simpler to simply run the CPU at full speed and have the debugger stop when you hit the breakpoint in **OS_TickTask()**.

If you were to repeatedly run the target at full speed, your debugger should now stop at the following breakpoints:

```
OSTickISR()
OSIntCtxSw()
OS_TickTask()
OSTickISR()
OSIntCtxSw()
etc.
```

At this point, the port tests are complete. You should be able to use the μC/OS-III port in your target application.

18-6 SUMMARY

A port involves three aspects: CPU, OS and board specific (BSP) code.

μC/OS-III port consists of writing or changing the contents of four kernel specific files: **os_cpu.h, os_cpu_a.asm, os_cpu_a.inc** and **os_cpu_c.c**.

It is also necessary to write or change the content of three CPU specific files: **cpu.h, cpu_a.asm** and **cpu_c.c**.

Finally, you can create or change a Board Support Package (BSP) for the evaluation board or target board being used.

A μC/OS-III port is similar to a μC/OS-II port, therefore you can start from one of the many μC/OS-II ports already available (see Appendix C, "Migrating from μC/OS-II to μC/OS-III" on page 689).

19

Run-Time Statistics

µC/OS-III performs substantial run-time statistics that can be displayed by kernel-aware debuggers and/or µC/Probe. Specifically, it is possible to ascertain the total number of context switches, maximum interrupt disable time, maximum scheduler lock time, CPU usage, stack space used on a per-task basis, the RAM used by µC/OS-III, and much more.

No other real-time kernel provides as much run-time information as µC/OS-III. This information is quite useful during debugging as it provides a sense of how well an application is running and the resources being used.

µC/OS-III also provides information about the configuration of the system. Specifically, the amount of RAM used by µC/OS-III, including all internal variables and task stacks.

The µC/OS-III variables described in this chapter should be displayed and never changed.

19-1 GENERAL STATISTICS – RUN-TIME

The following is a list of µC/OS-III variables that are not associated to any specific task:

TICK WHEEL

OSCfg_TickWheel[i].NbrEntries
The tick wheel contains up to OS_CFG_TICK_WHEEL_SIZE "spokes" (see **os_cfg_app.h**), and each spoke contains the **.NbrEntries** field, which holds the current number of entries in that spoke.

OSCfg_TickWheel[i].NbrEntriesMax
The **.NbrEntriesMax** field holds the maximum (i.e., peak) number of entries in a spoke.

TIMER WHEEL

OSCfg_TmrWheel[i].NbrEntries
The tick wheel contains up to OS_CFG_TMR_WHEEL_SIZE "spokes" (see **os_cfg_app.h**), and each spoke contains the **.NbrEntries** field, which holds the current number of entries in that spoke.

OSCfg_TmrWheel[i].NbrEntriesMax
The **.NbrEntriesMax** field holds the maximum (i.e., peak) number of entries in a spoke.

INTERRUPTS

OSIntNestingCtr
This variable contains the interrupt nesting level. 1 means servicing the first level of interrupt nesting, 2 means the interrupt was interrupted by another interrupt, etc.

OSIntDisTimeMax
This variable contains the maximum interrupt disable time (in **CPU_TS** units).

INTERRUPT QUEUE

OSIntQNbrEntries
This variable indicates the current number of entries in the interrupt handler queue.

OSIntQOvfCtr

This variable shows the number of attempts to post a message from an interrupt to the interrupt handler queue, and there was not enough room to place the post call. In other words, how many times an interrupt was not being able to be serviced by its corresponding task. This value should always be 0 if the interrupt handler queue is sized large enough. If the value is non-zero, you should increase the size of the interrupt handler queue. A non-zero value may also indicate that the processor is not fast enough.

OSIntQTaskTimeMax

This variable contains the maximum execution time of the Interrupt Queue Handler Task (in **CPU_TS** units). The total time also includes the time of any ISR that occurred while the Interrupt Handler task was running.

NUMBER OF KERNEL OBJECTS

OSFlagQty

This variable indicates the number of event flag groups created. This variable is only declared if OS_CFG_FLAG_EN is set to 1 in **os_cfg.h**.

OSMemQty

This variable indicates the number of fixed-sized memory partitions created by the application. This variable is only declared if OS_CFG_MEM_EN is set to 1 in **os_cfg.h**.

OSMutexQty

This variable indicates the number of mutual exclusion semaphores created by the application. This variable is only declared if OS_CFG_MUTEX_EN is set to 1 in **os_cfg.h**.

OSSemQty

This variable indicates the number of semaphores created by your application. This variable is only declared if OS_CFG_SEM_EN is set to 1 in **os_cfg.h**.

OSTaskQty

The variable contains the total number of tasks created in the application.

OSTmrQty

This variable indicates the number of timers created by the application. It is only declared if OS_CFG_TMR_EN is set to 1 in **os_cfg.h**.

MESSAGE POOL

OSMsgPool.NbrFree

The variable indicates the number of free OS_MSGs in the message pool. This number should never be zero since that indicate that the application is no longer able to send messages. This variable is only declared if OS_CFG_Q_EN is set to 1, or OS_CFG_TASK_Q_EN is set to 1 in os_cfg.h.

OSMsgPool.NbrUsed

This variable indicates the number of OS_MSGs currently used by the application. This variable is only declared if OS_CFG_Q_EN is set to 1, or OS_CFG_TASK_Q_EN is set to 1 in os_cfg.h.

OSMsgPool.NbrUsedMax

This variable indicates the maximum (i.e. peak) number of OS_MSGs that was ever used by the application. This variable is only declared if OS_CFG_Q_EN is set to 1, or OS_CFG_TASK_Q_EN is set to 1 in os_cfg.h.

READY LIST

OSRdyList[i].NbrEntries

These variable are used to examine how many entries there are in the ready list at each priority.

SCHEDULER

OSSchedLockTimeMax

This variable indicates the maximum amount of time the scheduler was locked irrespective of which task did the locking. It represents the global scheduler lock time. This value is expressed in CPU_TS units. The variable is only declared if OS_CFG_SCHED_LOCK_TIME_MEAS_EN is set to 1 in os_cfg.h.

OSSchedLockTimeMaxCur

This variable indicates the maximum amount of time the scheduler was locked. This value is expressed in CPU_TS units and is reset by the context switch code so that it can track the scheduler lock time on a per-task basis. This variable is only declared if OS_CFG_SCHED_LOCK_TIME_MEAS_EN is set to 1 in os_cfg.h.

OSSchedLockNestingCtr

This variable keeps track of the nesting level of the scheduler lock.

OSSchedRoundRobinEn

When set to 1, this variable indicates that round robin scheduling is enabled.

STATISTICS TASK

OSStatTaskCPUUsage

This variable indicates the CPU usage of the application expressed as a percentage (multiplied by 100). A value of 1000 indicates that 10.00% of the CPU is used, while 90.00% of the time the CPU is idling. This variable is only declared if OS_CFG_STAT_TASK_EN is set to 1 in os_cfg.h.

OSStatTaskCtr

This variable contains a counter that is incremented every time the idle task infinite loop runs. This variable is only declared if OS_CFG_STAT_TASK_EN is set to 1 in os_cfg.h.

OSStatTaskCtrMax

This variable contains the maximum number of times the idle task loop runs in 0.1 second. This value is used to measure the CPU usage of the application. This variable is only declared if OS_CFG_STAT_TASK_EN is set to 1 in os_cfg.h.

OSStatTaskTimeMax

This variable contains the maximum execution time of the statistic task (in CPU_TS units). It is only declared if OS_CFG_STAT_TASK_EN is set to 1 in os_cfg.h. The total time also includes the time of any ISR that occurred while the statistic task was running.

TICK TASK

OSTickCtr

This variable is incremented every time the tick task executes.

OSTickTaskTimeMax

This variable contains the maximum execution time of the tick task (in CPU_TS units). The total time also includes the time of any ISR that occurred while the tick task was running.

TIMER TASK

OSTmrCtr

This variable is incremented every time the timer task executes.

OSTmrTaskTimeMax

This variable contains the maximum execution time of the timer task (in **CPU_TS** units). It is only declared if **OS_CFG_TMR_EN** is set to 1 in **os_cfg.h**. The total time also includes the time of any ISR that occurred while the timer task was running.

MISCELLANEOUS

OSIdleTaskCtr

This variable contains a counter that is incremented every time the idle task infinite loop runs.

OSRunning

When non-zero, this variable indicates that multitasking has started.

OSTaskCtxSwCtr

This variable accumulates the number of context switches performed by µC/OS-III.

19-2 PER-TASK STATISTICS – RUN-TIME

µC/OS-III maintains statistics for each task at run-time. This information is saved in the task's **OS_TCB**.

.CPUUsage

This variable keeps track of CPU usage of the task (multiplied by 100). For example if the task's **.CPUUsage** is 200 then the task consumes 2.00% of total CPU usage.

The variable is only declared when **OS_CFG_TASK_PROFILE_EN** is set to 1 in **os_cfg.h**.

.CtxSwCtr

This variable keeps track of the number of times a task is context switched-in. This variable should increment. If it does not increment, the task is not running. At a minimum, the counter should at least have a value of one since a task is always created ready-to-run. However, if higher priority tasks prevent the task from ever running, the value would be 0.

This variable is only declared when **OS_CFG_TASK_PROFILE_EN** is set to 1 in **os_cfg.h**.

.IntDisTimeMax

This variable keeps track of the maximum interrupt disable time of a task (in **CPU_TS** units). This variable shows how each task affects interrupt latency.

The variable is only declared when **CPU_CFG_INT_DIS_MEAS_EN** in **cpu_cfg.h** is set to 1.

.MsgQ.NbrEntries

This variable indicates the number of entries currently waiting in the message queue of a task. This variable is only declared when **OS_CFG_TASK_Q_EN** is set to 1 in **os_cfg.h**.

.MsgQ.NbrEntriesMax

This variable indicates the maximum number of entries placed in the message queue of a task. This variable is only declared when **OS_CFG_TASK_Q_EN** is set to 1 in **os_cfg.h**.

.MsgQ.NbrEntriesSize

This variable indicates the maximum number of entries that a task message queue is able to accept before it is full.

This variable is only declared when **OS_CFG_TASK_Q_EN** is set to 1 in **os_cfg.h**.

.MsgQ.PendTime

This variable indicates the amount of time it took for a task or an ISR to send a message to the task (in **CPU_TS** units).

The variable is only declared when **OS_CFG_TASK_PROFILE_EN** is set to 1 in **os_cfg.h**.

.MsgQ.PendTimeMax

This variable indicates the maximum amount of time it took for a task or an ISR to send a message to the task (in **CPU_TS** units).

This variable is only declared when **OS_CFG_TASK_PROFILE_EN** is set to 1 in **os_cfg.h**.

.PendOn

This variable indicates what a task is pending on if the task is in a pend state. Possible values are:

0	Nothing
1	Pending on an event flag group
2	Pending on the task's message queue
3	Pending on multiple objects
4	Pending on a mutual exclusion semaphore
5	Pending on a message queue
6	Pending on a semaphore
7	Pending on a task's semaphore

.Prio

This corresponds to the priority of the task. This might change at run time depending on whether or not the task owns a mutual exclusion semaphore, or the user changes the priority of the task by calling **OSTaskChangePrio()**.

.SchedLockTimeMax

This variable keeps track of the maximum time a task locks the scheduler (in **CPU_TS** units). This variable allows the application to see how each task affects task latency. The variable is declared only when **OS_CFG_SCHED_LOCK_TIME_MEAS_EN** is set to 1 in **os_cfg.h**.

.SemPendTime

This variable indicates the amount of time it took for a task or ISR to signal the task (in **CPU_TS** units).

This variable is only declared when **OS_CFG_TASK_PROFILE_EN** is set to 1 in **os_cfg.h**.

.SemPendTimeMax

This variable indicates the maximum amount of time it took for a task or an ISR to signal the task (in **CPU_TS** units).

This variable is only declared when **OS_CFG_TASK_PROFILE_EN** is set to 1 in **os_cfg.h**.

.State

This variable indicates the current state of a task. The possible values are:

0	Ready
1	Delayed
2	Pending
3	Pending with Timeout
4	Suspended
5	Delayed and Suspended
6	Pending and Suspended
7	Pending, Delayed and Suspended

.StkFree

This variable indicates the amount of stack space (in number of stack entries) unused by a task. This value is determined by the statistic task if **OS_CFG_TASK_STAT_STK_CHK_EN** is set to 1 in **os_cfg.h**.

.StkUsed

This variable indicates the maximum stack usage (in number of stack entries) of a task. This value is determined by the statistic task if **OS_CFG_TASK_STAT_STK_CHK_EN** is set to 1 in **os_cfg.h**.

.TickRemain

This variable indicates the amount of time left (in clock ticks) until a task time delay expires, or the task times out waiting on a kernel object such as a semaphore, message queue, or other.

19

19-3 KERNEL OBJECT – RUN-TIME

It is possible to examine the run-time values of certain kernel objects as described below.

SEMAPHORES

.NamePtr

This is a pointer to an ASCII string used to provide a name to the semaphore. The ASCII string can have any length as long as it is NUL terminated.

.PendList.NbrEntries

Each semaphore contains a wait list of tasks waiting for the semaphore to be signaled. The variable represents the number of entries in the wait list.

.Ctr

This variable represents the current count of the semaphore.

.TS

This variable contains the timestamp of when the semaphore was last signaled.

MUTUAL EXCLUSION SEMAPHORES

.NamePtr

This is a pointer to an ASCII string used to provide a name to the mutual exclusion semaphore. The ASCII string can have any length as long as it is **NUL** terminated.

.PendList.NbrEntries

Each mutual exclusion semaphore contains a list of tasks waiting for the semaphore to be released. The variable represents the number of entries in the wait list.

.OwnerOriginalPrio

This variable holds the original priority of the task that owns the mutual exclusion semaphore.

.OwnerTCBPtr->Prio

Dereferencing the pointer to the **OS_TCB** of the mutual exclusion semaphore owner allows the application to determine whether a task priority was changed.

.OwnerNestingCtr

This variable indicates how many times the owner of the mutual exclusion semaphore requested the semaphore.

.TS

This variable contains the timestamp of when the mutual exclusion semaphore was last released.

MESSAGE QUEUES

.NamePtr

This is a pointer to an ASCII string used to provide a name to the message queue. The ASCII string can have any length, as long as it is NUL terminated.

.PendList.NbrEntries

Each message queue contains a wait list of tasks waiting for messages to be sent to the queue. The variable represents the number of entries in the wait list.

.MsgQ.NbrEntries

This variable represents the number of messages currently in the message queue.

.MsgQ.NbrEntriesMax

This variable represents the maximum number of messages ever placed in the message queue.

.MsgQ.NbrEntriesSize

This variable represents the maximum number of messages that can be placed in the message queue.

EVENT FLAGS

.NamePtr

This is a pointer to an ASCII string used to provide a name to the event flag group. The ASCII string can have any length, as long as it is NUL terminated.

.PendList.NbrEntries

Each event flag group contains a wait list of tasks waiting for event flags to be set or cleared. This variable represents the number of entries in the wait list.

.Flags

This variable contains the current value of the event flags in an event flag group.

.TS

This variable contains the timestamp of when the event flag group was last posted.

MEMORY PARTITIONS

.NamePtr

This is a pointer to an ASCII string that is used to provide a name to the memory partition. The ASCII string can have any length as long as it is **NUL** terminated.

.BlkSize

This variable contains the block size (in bytes) for the memory partition.

.NbrMax

This variable contains the maximum number of memory blocks belonging to the memory partition.

.NbrFree

This variable contains the number of memory blocks that are available from memory partition. The number of memory blocks in use is given by:

.NbrMax – .NbrFree

19-4 OS_DBG.C – STATIC

os_dbg.c is provided in μC/OS-III as some debuggers are not able to read the values of #define constants. Specifically, os_dbg.c contains ROM variables initialized to #define constants so that users can read them with any debugger.

Below is a list of ROM variables provided in os_dbg.c, along with their descriptions. These variables use approximately 100 bytes of code space.

The application code can examine these variables and you do not need to access them in a critical region as they reside in code space and are therefore not changeable.

ROM Variable	Data Type	Value
OSDbg_DbgEn	CPU_INT08U	OS_CFG_DBG_EN

When 1, this variable indicates that ROM variables in os_dbg.c will be compiled. This value is set in os_cfg.h.

ROM Variable	Data Type	Value
OSDbg_ArgChkEn	CPU_INT08U	OS_CFG_ARG_CHK_EN

When 1, this variable indicates that run-time argument checking is enabled. This means that μC/OS-III will check the validity of the values of arguments passed to functions. The feature is enabled in os_cfg.h.

ROM Variable	Data Type	Value
OSDbg_AppHooksEn	CPU_INT08U	OS_CFG_APP_HOOKS_EN

When 1, the variable indicates whether application hooks will be available to the application programmer, and the pointers listed below are declared. This value is set in **os_cfg.h**.

```
OS_AppTaskCreateHookPtr;
OS_AppTaskDelHookPtr;
OS_AppTaskReturnHookPtr;
OS_AppIdleTaskHookPtr;
OS_AppStatTaskHookPtr;
OS_AppTaskSwHookPtr;
OS_AppTimeTickHookPtr;
```

ROM Variable	Data Type	Value
OSDbg_EndiannessTest	CPU_INT32U	0x12345678

This variable allows a kernel awareness debugger or µC/Probe to determine the endianness of the CPU. This is easily done by looking at the lowest address in memory where this variable is saved. If the value is 0x78 then the CPU is a little endian machine. If it's 0x12, it is a big endian machine.

ROM Variable	Data Type	Value
OSDbg_CalledFromISRChkEn	CPU_INT08U	OS_CFG_CALLED_FROM_ISR_CHK_EN

When 1, this variable indicates that µC/OS-III will perform run-time checking to see if a function that is not supposed to be called from an ISR, is called from an ISR. This value is set in **os_cfg.h**.

ROM Variable	Data Type	Value
OSDbg_FlagEn	CPU_INT08U	OS_CFG_FLAG_EN

When 1, this variable indicates that μC/OS-III's event flag services are available to the application programmer. This value is set in **os_cfg.h**.

ROM Variable	Data Type	Value
OSDbg_FlagDelEn	CPU_INT08U	OS_CFG_FLAG_DEL_EN

When 1, this variable indicates that the **OSFlagDel()** function is available to the application programmer. This value is set in **os_cfg.h**.

ROM Variable	Data Type	Value
OSDbg_FlagModeClrEn	CPU_INT08U	OS_CFG_FLAG_MODE_CLR_EN

When 1, this variable indicates that you can either clear or set flags when posting and pending on event flags. This value is set in **os_cfg.h**.

ROM Variable	Data Type	Value
OSDbg_FlagPendAbortEn	CPU_INT08U	OS_CFG_FLAG_PEND_ABORT_EN

When 1, this variable indicates that the **OSFlagPendAbort()** function is available to the application programmer. This value is set in **os_cfg.h**.

ROM Variable	Data Type	Value
OSDbg_FlagGrpSize	CPU_INT16U	sizeof(OS_FLAG_GRP)

This variable indicates the memory footprint (in RAM) of an event flag group (in bytes). This data type is declared in **os.h**.

19

ROM Variable	Data Type	Value
OSDbg_FlagWidth	CPU_INT16U	sizeof(OS_FLAGS)

This variable indicates the word width (in bytes) of event flags. If event flags are declared as **CPU_INT08U**, this variable will be 1, if declared as a **CPU_INT16U**, this variable will be 2, etc. This **OS_FLAGS** data type is declared in **os_type.h**.

ROM Variable	Data Type	Value
OSDbg_IntQ	CPU_INT16U	sizeof(OS_INT_Q)

This variable indicates the size (in bytes) of the **OS_INT_Q** data type, which is used to queue up deferred posts. The value of this variable is zero if **OS_CFG_ISR_POST_DEFERRED_EN** is 0 in **os_cfg.h**.

ROM Variable	Data Type	Value
OSDbg_ISRPostDeferredEn	CPU_INT08U	OS_CFG_ISR_POST_DEFERRED_EN

When 1, this variable indicates that an ISR will defer posts to task-level code. This value is set in **os_cfg.h**.

ROM Variable	Data Type	Value
OSDbg_MemEn	CPU_INT08U	OS_CFG_MEM_EN

When 1, this variable indicates that µC/OS-III's memory management services are available to the application. This value is set in **os_cfg.h**.

ROM Variable	Data Type	Value
OSDbg_MemSize	CPU_INT16U	sizeof(OS_MEM)

This variable indicates the RAM footprint (in bytes) of a memory partition control block, **OS_MEM**.

ROM Variable	Data Type	Value
OSDbg_MsgEn	CPU_INT08U	OS_MSG_EN

When 1, this variable indicates that the application either enabled message queues, or task message queues, or both. This value is set in **os_cfg.h** by ORing the value of OS_CFG_Q_EN and OS_CFG_TASK_Q_EN.

ROM Variable	Data Type	Value
OSDbg_MsgSize	CPU_INT16U	sizeof(OS_MSG)

This variable indicates the RAM footprint (in bytes) of an **OS_MSG** data structure.

ROM Variable	Data Type	Value
OSDbg_MsgPoolSize	CPU_INT16U	sizeof(OS_MSG_POOL)

This variable indicates the RAM footprint (in bytes) of an **OS_MSG_POOL** data structure.

ROM Variable	Data Type	Value
OSDbg_MsgQSize	CPU_INT16U	sizeof(OS_MSG_Q)

This variable indicates the RAM footprint (in number of bytes) of an **OS_MSG_Q** data type.

ROM Variable	Data Type	Value
OSDbg_MutexEn	CPU_INT08U	OS_CFG_MUTEX_EN

When 1, this variable indicates that µC/OS-III's mutual exclusion semaphore management services are available to the application. This value is set in **os_cfg.h**.

ROM Variable	Data Type	Value
OSDbg_MutexDelEn	CPU_INT08U	OS_CFG_MUTEX_DEL_EN

When 1, this variable indicates that the function **OSMutexDel()** is available to the application. This value is set in **os_cfg.h**.

ROM Variable	Data Type	Value
OSDbg_MutexPendAbortEn	CPU_INT08U	OS_CFG_MUTEX_PEND_ABORT_EN

When 1, the variable indicates that the function **OSMutexPendAbort()** is available to the application. This value is set in **os_cfg.h**.

ROM Variable	Data Type	Value
OSDbg_MutexSize	CPU_INT16U	sizeof(OS_MUTEX)

This variable indicates the RAM footprint (in number of bytes) of an **OS_MUTEX** data type.

ROM Variable	Data Type	Value
OSDbg_ObjTypeChkEn	CPU_INT08U	OS_CFG_OBJ_TYPE_CHK_EN

When 1, this variable indicates that µC/OS-III will check for valid object types at run time. µC/OS-III will make sure the application is accessing a semaphore if calling **OSSem???()** functions, accessing a message queue when calling **OSQ???()** functions, etc. This value is set in **os_cfg.h**.

ROM Variable	Data Type	Value
OSDbg_PendMultiEn	CPU_INT08U	OS_CFG_PEND_MULTI_EN

When 1, this variable indicates that µC/OS-III's service to pend on multiple objects (semaphores or message queues) is available to the application. This value is set in **os_cfg.h**.

ROM Variable	Data Type	Value
OSDbg_PendDataSize	CPU_INT16U	sizeof(OS_PEND_DATA)

This variable indicates the RAM footprint (in bytes) of an **OS_PEND_DATA** data type.

ROM Variable	Data Type	Value
OSDbg_PendListSize	CPU_INT16U	sizeof(OS_PEND_LIST)

This variable indicates the RAM footprint (in bytes) of an **OS_PEND_LIST** data type.

ROM Variable	Data Type	Value
OSDbg_PendObjSize	CPU_INT16U	sizeof(OS_PEND_OBJ)

This variable indicates the RAM footprint (in bytes) of an **OS_PEND_OBJ** data type.

ROM Variable	Data Type	Value
OSDbg_PrioMax	CPU_INT16U	OS_CFG_PRIO_MAX

This variable indicates the maximum number of priorities that the application will support.

ROM Variable	Data Type	Value
OSDbg_PtrSize	CPU_INT16U	sizeof(void *)

This variable indicates the size (in bytes) of a pointer.

ROM Variable	Data Type	Value
OSDbg_QEn	CPU_INT08U	OS_CFG_Q_EN

When 1, this variable indicates that µC/OS-III's message queue services are available to the application. This value is set in **os_cfg.h**.

19

ROM Variable	Data Type	Value
OSDbg_QDelEn	CPU_INT08U	OS_CFG_Q_DEL_EN

When 1, this variable indicates that the function OSQDel() is available to the application. This value is set in os_cfg.h.

ROM Variable	Data Type	Value
OSDbg_QFlushEn	CPU_INT08U	OS_CFG_Q_FLUSH_EN

When 1, this variable indicates that the function OSQFlush() is available to the application. This value is set in os_cfg.h.

ROM Variable	Data Type	Value
OSDbg_QPendAbortEn	CPU_INT08U	OS_CFG_Q_PEND_ABORT_EN

When 1, this variable indicates that the function OSQPendAbort() is available to the application. This value is set in os_cfg.h.

ROM Variable	Data Type	Value
OSDbg_QSize	CPU_INT16U	

This variable indicates the RAM footprint (in number of bytes) of an OS_Q data type.

ROM Variable	Data Type	Value
OSDbg_SchedRoundRobinEn	CPU_INT08U	OS_CFG_SCHED_ROUND_ROBIN_EN

When 1, this variable indicates that the µC/OS-III round-robin scheduling feature is available to the application. This value is set in os_cfg.h.

ROM Variable	Data Type	Value
OSDbg_SemEn	CPU_INT08U	OS_CFG_SEM_EN

When 1, this variable indicates that µC/OS-III's semaphore management services are available to the application. This value is set in **os_cfg.h**.

ROM Variable	Data Type	Value
OSDbg_SemDelEn	CPU_INT08U	OS_CFG_SEM_DEL_EN

When 1, this variable indicates that the function **OSSemDel()** is available to the application. This value is set in **os_cfg.h**.

ROM Variable	Data Type	Value
OSDbg_SemPendAbortEn	CPU_INT08U	OS_CFG_SEM_PEND_ABORT_EN

When 1, this variable indicates that the function **OSSemPendAbort()** is available to the application. This value is set in **os_cfg.h**.

ROM Variable	Data Type	Value
OSDbg_SemSetEn	CPU_INT08U	OS_CFG_SEM_SET_EN

When 1, this variable indicates that the function **OSSemSet()** is available to the application. This value is set in **os_cfg.h**.

ROM Variable	Data Type	Value
OSDbg_SemSize	CPU_INT16U	sizeof(OS_SEM)

This variable indicates the RAM footprint (in bytes) of an **OS_SEM** data type.

ROM Variable	Data Type	Value
OSDbg_RdyList	CPU_INT16U	sizeof(OS_RDY_LIST)

This variable indicates the RAM footprint (in bytes) of the **OS_RDY_LIST** data type.

ROM Variable	Data Type	Value
OSDbg_RdyListSize	CPU_INT32U	sizeof(OSRdyList)

This variable indicates the RAM footprint (in bytes) of the ready list.

ROM Variable	Data Type	Value
OSDbg_StkWidth	CPU_INT08U	sizeof(CPU_STK)

This variable indicates the word size of a stack entry (in bytes). If a stack entry is declared as **CPU_INT08U**, this value will be 1, if a stack entry is declared as **CPU_INT16U**, the value will be 2, etc.

ROM Variable	Data Type	Value
OSDbg_StatTaskEn	CPU_INT08U	OS_CFG_STAT_TASK_EN

When 1, this variable indicates that µC/OS-III's statistic task is enabled. This value is set in **os_cfg.h**.

ROM Variable	Data Type	Value
OSDbg_StatTaskStkChkEn	CPU_INT08U	OS_CFG_STAT_TASK_STK_CHK_EN

When 1, this variable indicates that µC/OS-III will perform run-time stack checking by walking the stack of each task to determine the usage of each. This value is set in **os_cfg.h**.

ROM Variable	Data Type	Value
OSDbg_TaskChangePrioEn	CPU_INT08U	OS_CFG_TASK_CHANGE_PRIO_EN

When 1, this variable indicates that the function **OSTaskChangePrio()** is available to the application. This value is set in **os_cfg.h**.

ROM Variable	Data Type	Value
OSDbg_TaskDelEn	CPU_INT08U	OS_CFG_TASK_DEL_EN

When 1, this variable indicates that the function **OSTaskDel()** is available to the application. This value is set in **os_cfg.h**.

ROM Variable	Data Type	Value
OSDbg_TaskQEn	CPU_INT08U	OS_CFG_TASK_Q_EN

When 1, this variable indicates that **OSTaskQ???()** services are available to the application. This value is set in **os_cfg.h**.

ROM Variable	Data Type	Value
OSDbg_TaskQPendAbortEn	CPU_INT08U	OS_CFG_TASK_Q_PEND_ABORT_EN

When 1, this variable indicates that the function **OSTaskQPendAbort()** is available to the application. This value is set in **os_cfg.h**.

ROM Variable	Data Type	Value
OSDbg_TaskProfileEn	CPU_INT08U	OS_CFG_TASK_PROFILE_EN

When 1, this variable indicates that task profiling is enabled, and that μC/OS-III will perform run-time performance measurements on a per-task basis. Specifically, when 1, μC/OS-III will keep track of how many context switches each task makes, how long a task disables interrupts, how long a task locks the scheduler, and more. This value is set in **os_cfg.h**.

ROM Variable	Data Type	Value
OSDbg_TaskRegTblSize	CPU_INT16U	OS_CFG_TASK_REG_TBL_SIZE

This variable indicates how many entries each task register table can accept.

ROM Variable	Data Type	Value
OSDbg_TaskSemPendAbortEn	CPU_INT08U	OS_CFG_TASK_SEM_PEND_ABORT_EN

When 1, this variable indicates that the function **OSTaskSemPendAbort()** is available to the application. This value is set in **os_cfg.h**.

ROM Variable	Data Type	Value
OSDbg_TaskSuspendEn	CPU_INT08U	OS_CFG_TASK_SUSPEND_EN

When 1, this variable indicates that the function **OSTaskSuspend()** is available to the application. This value is set in **os_cfg.h**.

ROM Variable	Data Type	Value
OSDbg_TCBSize	CPU_INT16U	sizeof(OS_TCB)

This variable indicates the RAM footprint (in bytes) of an **OS_TCB** data structure.

ROM Variable	Data Type	Value
OSDbg_TickSpokeSize	CPU_INT16U	sizeof(OS_TICK_SPOKE)

This variable indicates the RAM footprint (in bytes) of an **OS_TICK_SPOKE** data structure.

ROM Variable	Data Type	Value
OSDbg_TimeDlyHMSMEn	CPU_INT08U	OS_CFG_TIME_DLY_HMSM_EN

When 1, this variable indicates that the function **OSTimeDlyHMSM()** is available to the application. This value is set in **os_cfg.h**.

ROM Variable	Data Type	Value
OSDbg_TimeDlyResumeEn	CPU_INT08U	OS_CFG_TIME_DLY_RESUME_EN

When 1, this variable indicates that the function **OSTimeDlyResume()** is available to the application. This value is set in **os_cfg.h**.

ROM Variable	Data Type	Value
OSDbg_TmrEn	CPU_INT08U	OS_CFG_TMR_EN

When 1, this variable indicates that **OSTmr???()** services are available to the application. This value is set in **os_cfg.h**.

ROM Variable	Data Type	Value
OSDbg_TmrDelEn	CPU_INT08U	OS_CFG_TMR_DEL_EN

When 1, this variable indicates that the function **OSTmrDel()** is available to the application. This value is set in **os_cfg.h**.

ROM Variable	Data Type	Value
OSDbg_TmrSize	CPU_INT16U	sizeof(OS_TMR)

This variable indicates the RAM footprint (in bytes) of an **OS_TMR** data structure.

19

ROM Variable	Data Type	Value
OSDbg_TmrSpokeSize	CPU_INT16U	sizeof(OS_TMR_SPOKE)

This variable indicates the RAM footprint (in bytes) of an **OS_TMR_SPOKE** data structure.

ROM Variable	Data Type	Value
OSDbg_VersionNbr	CPU_INT16U	OS_VERSION

This variable indicates the current version of µC/OS-III multiplied by 10000. For example version 3.02.00 will show as 30200.

ROM Variable	Data Type	Value
OSDbg_DataSize	CPU_INT32U	Size of all RAM variables

This variable indicates the RAM footprint (in bytes) of the internal µC/OS-III variables for the current configuration.

19-5 OS_CFG_APP.C – STATIC

As with **os_dbg.c**, **os_cfg_app.c** defines a number of ROM variables. These variables, however, reflect the run-time configuration of an application. Specifically, the user will be able to know the RAM footprint (in bytes) of µC/OS-III task stacks, the message pool, and more.

Below is a list of ROM variables provided in **os_app_cfg.c**, along with their descriptions. These variables represent approximately 100 bytes of code space.

Application code can examine these variables and the application does not need to access them in a critical region since they reside in code space and are therefore not changeable.

ROM Variable	Data Type	Value
OSCfg_IdleTaskStkSizeRAM	CPU_INT32U	sizeof(OSCfg_IdleTaskStk)

This variable indicates the RAM footprint (in bytes) of the µC/OS-III idle task stack.

ROM Variable	Data Type	Value
OSCfg_IntQSizeRAM	CPU_INT32U	sizeof(OSCfg_IntQ)

This variable indicates the RAM footprint (in bytes) of the µC/OS-III interrupt handler task queue.

ROM Variable	Data Type	Value
OSCfg_IntQTaskStkSizeRAM	CPU_INT32U	sizeof(OSCfg_IntQTaskStk)

This variable indicates the RAM footprint (in bytes) of the µC/OS-III interrupt queue handler task stack.

ROM Variable	Data Type	Value
OSCfg_ISRStkSizeRAM	CPU_INT32U	sizeof(OSCfg_ISRStk)

This variable indicates the RAM footprint (in bytes) of the dedicated Interrupt Service Routine (ISR) stack.

19

ROM Variable	Data Type	Value
OSCfg_MsgPoolSizeRAM	CPU_INT32U	sizeof(OSCfg_MsgPool)

This variable indicates the RAM footprint (in bytes) of the message pool.

ROM Variable	Data Type	Value
OSCfg_StatTaskStkSizeRAM	CPU_INT32U	sizeof(OSCfg_StatTaskStk)

This variable indicates the RAM footprint (in bytes) of the µC/OS-III statistic task stack.

ROM Variable	Data Type	Value
OSCfg_TickTaskStkSizeRAM	CPU_INT32U	sizeof(OSCfg_TickTaskStk)

This variable indicates the RAM footprint (in bytes) of the µC/OS-III tick task stack.

ROM Variable	Data Type	Value
OSCfg_TickWheelSizeRAM	CPU_INT32U	sizeof(OSCfg_TickWheel)

This variable indicates the RAM footprint (in bytes) of the tick wheel.

ROM Variable	Data Type	Value
OSCfg_TmrWheelSizeRAM	CPU_INT32U	sizeof(OSCfg_TmrWheel)

This variable indicates the RAM footprint (in bytes) of the timer wheel.

ROM Variable	Data Type	Value
OSCfg_DataSizeRAM	CPU_INT32U	Total of all configuration RAM

This variable indicates the RAM footprint (in bytes) of all of the configuration variables declared in **os_cfg_app.c**.

19-6 SUMMARY

This chapter presented a number of variables that can be read by a debugger and/or µC/Probe.

These variables provide run-time and compile-time (static) information regarding µC/OS-III-based applications. The µC/OS-III variables allow users to monitor RAM footprint, task stack usage, context switches, CPU usage, the execution time of many operations, and more.

The application must never change (i.e., write to) any of these variables.

19

µC/OS-III API Reference

This chapter provides a reference to µC/OS-III services. Each of the user-accessible kernel services is presented in alphabetical order. The following information is provided for each entry:

- A brief description of the service

- The function prototype

- The filename of the source code

- The **#define** constant required to enable code for the service

- A description of the arguments passed to the function

- A description of returned value(s)

- Specific notes and warnings regarding use of the service

- One or two examples of how to use the function

Most µC/OS-III API functions return an error code. In fact, when present, the error return value is done through the last argument of the API function, as a pointer to an error code. These error codes should be checked by the application to ensure that the µC/OS-III function performed its operation as expected. Also, some of the error codes are conditional based on configuration constants. For example, argument checking error codes are returned only if **OS_CFG_ARG_CHK_EN** is set to **1** in **os_cfg.h**.

The next few pages summarizes most of the services provided by µC/OS-III. The function calls in bold are commonly used.

A-1 Task Management

```
void
OSTaskChangePrio  (OS_TCB        *p_tcb,
                   OS_PRIO        prio_new,
                   OS_ERR        *p_err);
```

```
void
OSTaskCreate      (OS_TCB        *p_tcb,
                   CPU_CHAR      *p_name,
                   OS_TASK_PTR    p_task,
                   void          *p_arg,
                   OS_PRIO        prio,
                   CPU_STK       *p_stk_base,
                   CPU_STK_SIZE   stk_limit,
                   CPU_STK_SIZE   stk_size,
                   OS_MSG_QTY     q_size,
                   OS_TICK        time_quanta,
                   void          *p_ext,
                   OS_OPT         opt,
                   OS_ERR        *p_err);
```

Values for "opt":
   OS_OPT_TASK_NONE
   OS_OPT_TASK_STK_CHK
   OS_OPT_TASK_STK_CLR
   OS_OPT_TASK_SAVE_FP

```
void
OSTaskDel         (OS_TCB        *p_tcb,
                   OS_ERR        *p_err);
```

```
OS_REG
OSTaskRegGet      (OS_TCB        *p_tcb,
                   OS_REG_ID      id,
                   OS_ERR        *p_err);
```

```
void
OSTaskRegSet      (OS_TCB        *p_tcb,
                   OS_REG_ID      id,
                   OS_REG         value,
                   OS_ERR        *p_err);
```

```
void
OSTaskResume      (OS_TCB        *p_tcb,
                   OS_ERR        *p_err);
```

```
void
OSTaskSuspend     (OS_TCB        *p_tcb,
                   OS_ERR        *p_err);
```

```
void
OSTaskStkChk      (OS_TCB        *p_tcb,
                   CPU_STK_SIZE  *p_free,
                   CPU_STK_SIZE  *p_used,
                   OS_ERR        *p_err);
```

```
void
OSTaskTimeQuantaSet (OS_TCB      *p_tcb,
                     OS_TICK      time_quanta,
                     OS_ERR      *p_err);
```

A-2 Time Management

```
void
OSTimeDly       (OS_TICK    dly,
                 OS_OPT     opt,
                 OS_ERR     *p_err);
```

```
void
OSTimeDlyHMSM   (CPU_INT16U hours,
                 CPU_INT16U minutes,
                 CPU_INT16U seconds
                 CPU_INT32U milli,
                 OS_OPT     opt,
                 OS_ERR     *p_err);
```

Values for "opt":
   OS_OPT_TIME_HMSM_STRICT
   OS_OPT_TIME_HMSM_NON_STRICT

```
void
OSTimeDlyResume (OS_TCB     *p_tcb,
                 OS_ERR     *p_err);
```

```
OS_TICK
OSTimeGet       (OS_ERR     *p_err);
```

```
void
OSTimeSet       (OS_TICK    ticks,
                 OS_ERR     *p_err);
```

A-3 Mutual Exclusion Semaphores – Resource Management

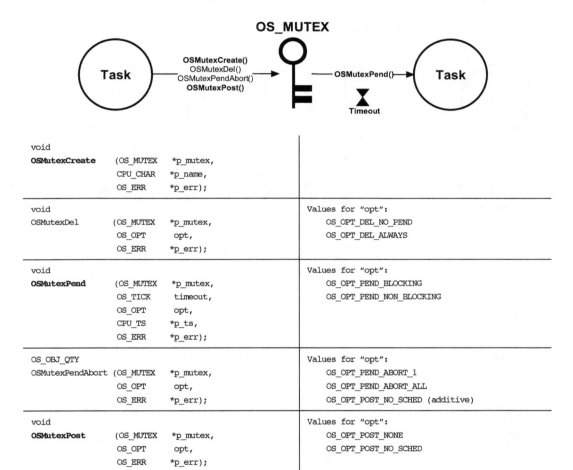

void			
OSMutexCreate	(OS_MUTEX	*p_mutex,	
	CPU_CHAR	*p_name,	
	OS_ERR	*p_err);	

			Values for "opt":
void			
OSMutexDel	(OS_MUTEX	*p_mutex,	OS_OPT_DEL_NO_PEND
	OS_OPT	opt,	OS_OPT_DEL_ALWAYS
	OS_ERR	*p_err);	

			Values for "opt":
void			
OSMutexPend	(OS_MUTEX	*p_mutex,	OS_OPT_PEND_BLOCKING
	OS_TICK	timeout,	OS_OPT_PEND_NON_BLOCKING
	OS_OPT	opt,	
	CPU_TS	*p_ts,	
	OS_ERR	*p_err);	

			Values for "opt":
OS_OBJ_QTY			
OSMutexPendAbort	(OS_MUTEX	*p_mutex,	OS_OPT_PEND_ABORT_1
	OS_OPT	opt,	OS_OPT_PEND_ABORT_ALL
	OS_ERR	*p_err);	OS_OPT_POST_NO_SCHED (additive)

			Values for "opt":
void			
OSMutexPost	(OS_MUTEX	*p_mutex,	OS_OPT_POST_NONE
	OS_OPT	opt,	OS_OPT_POST_NO_SCHED
	OS_ERR	*p_err);	

A-4 Event Flags – Synchronization

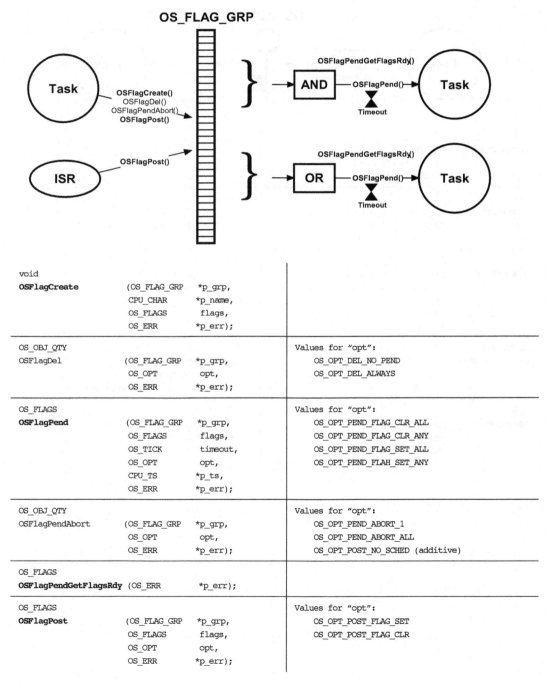

```
void
OSFlagCreate        (OS_FLAG_GRP   *p_grp,
                     CPU_CHAR      *p_name,
                     OS_FLAGS       flags,
                     OS_ERR        *p_err);
```

```
OS_OBJ_QTY
OSFlagDel           (OS_FLAG_GRP   *p_grp,
                     OS_OPT         opt,
                     OS_ERR        *p_err);
```

Values for "opt":
　OS_OPT_DEL_NO_PEND
　OS_OPT_DEL_ALWAYS

```
OS_FLAGS
OSFlagPend          (OS_FLAG_GRP   *p_grp,
                     OS_FLAGS       flags,
                     OS_TICK        timeout,
                     OS_OPT         opt,
                     CPU_TS        *p_ts,
                     OS_ERR        *p_err);
```

Values for "opt":
　OS_OPT_PEND_FLAG_CLR_ALL
　OS_OPT_PEND_FLAG_CLR_ANY
　OS_OPT_PEND_FLAG_SET_ALL
　OS_OPT_PEND_FLAH_SET_ANY

```
OS_OBJ_QTY
OSFlagPendAbort     (OS_FLAG_GRP   *p_grp,
                     OS_OPT         opt,
                     OS_ERR        *p_err);
```

Values for "opt":
　OS_OPT_PEND_ABORT_1
　OS_OPT_PEND_ABORT_ALL
　OS_OPT_POST_NO_SCHED (additive)

```
OS_FLAGS
OSFlagPendGetFlagsRdy (OS_ERR      *p_err);
```

```
OS_FLAGS
OSFlagPost          (OS_FLAG_GRP   *p_grp,
                     OS_FLAGS       flags,
                     OS_OPT         opt,
                     OS_ERR        *p_err);
```

Values for "opt":
　OS_OPT_POST_FLAG_SET
　OS_OPT_POST_FLAG_CLR

A-5 Semaphores – Synchronization

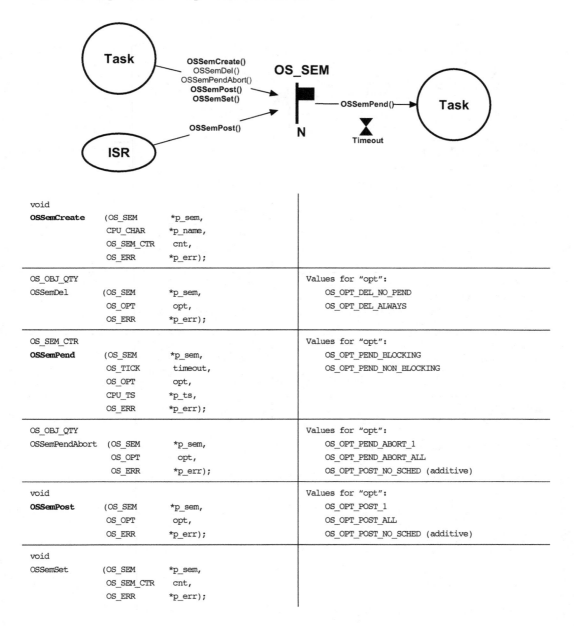

```
void
OSSemCreate    (OS_SEM        *p_sem,
                CPU_CHAR      *p_name,
                OS_SEM_CTR    cnt,
                OS_ERR        *p_err);
```

```
OS_OBJ_QTY
OSSemDel       (OS_SEM        *p_sem,
                OS_OPT        opt,
                OS_ERR        *p_err);
```
Values for "opt":
   OS_OPT_DEL_NO_PEND
   OS_OPT_DEL_ALWAYS

```
OS_SEM_CTR
OSSemPend      (OS_SEM        *p_sem,
                OS_TICK       timeout,
                OS_OPT        opt,
                CPU_TS        *p_ts,
                OS_ERR        *p_err);
```
Values for "opt":
   OS_OPT_PEND_BLOCKING
   OS_OPT_PEND_NON_BLOCKING

```
OS_OBJ_QTY
OSSemPendAbort (OS_SEM        *p_sem,
                OS_OPT        opt,
                OS_ERR        *p_err);
```
Values for "opt":
   OS_OPT_PEND_ABORT_1
   OS_OPT_PEND_ABORT_ALL
   OS_OPT_POST_NO_SCHED (additive)

```
void
OSSemPost      (OS_SEM        *p_sem,
                OS_OPT        opt,
                OS_ERR        *p_err);
```
Values for "opt":
   OS_OPT_POST_1
   OS_OPT_POST_ALL
   OS_OPT_POST_NO_SCHED (additive)

```
void
OSSemSet       (OS_SEM        *p_sem,
                OS_SEM_CTR    cnt,
                OS_ERR        *p_err);
```

A-6 Task Semaphores – Synchronization

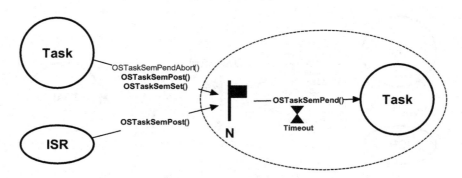

```
OS_SEM_CTR
OSTaskSemPend       (OS_TICK      timeout,
                     OS_OPT       opt,
                     CPU_TS       *p_ts,
                     OS_ERR       *p_err);
```

Values for "opt":
    OS_OPT_PEND_BLOCKING
    OS_OPT_PEND_NON_BLOCKING

```
CPU_BOOLEAN
OSTaskSemPendAbort  (OS_TCB       *p_tcb,
                     OS_OPT       opt,
                     OS_ERR       *p_err);
```

Values for "opt":
    OS_OPT_POST_NONE
    OS_OPT_POST_NO_SCHED

```
OS_SEM_CTR
OSTaskSemPost       (OS_TCB       *p_tcb,
                     OS_OPT       opt,
                     OS_ERR       *p_err);
```

Values for "opt":
    OS_OPT_POST_NONE
    OS_OPT_POST_NO_SCHED

```
OS_SEM_CTR
OSTaskSemSet        (OS_TCB       *p_tcb,
                     OS_SEM_CTR   cnt,
                     OS_ERR       *p_err);
```

A-7 Message Queues – Message Passing

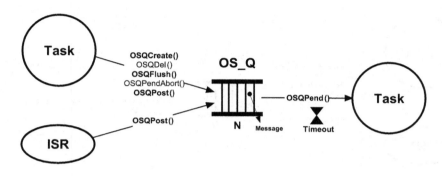

```
void
OSQCreate      (OS_Q          *p_q,
                CPU_CHAR      *p_name,
                OS_MSG_QTY    max_qty,
                OS_ERR        *p_err);
```

```
OS_OBJ_QTY,
OSQDel         (OS_Q          *p_q,
                OS_OPT        opt,
                OS_ERR        *p_err);
```

Values for "opt":
  OS_OPT_DEL_NO_PEND
  OS_OPT_DEL_ALWAYS

```
OS_MSG_QTY
OSQFlush       (OS_Q          *p_q,
                OS_ERR        *p_err);
```

```
void *
OSQPend        (OS_Q          *p_q,
                OS_TICK       timeout,
                OS_OPT        opt,
                OS_MSG_SIZE   *p_msg_size,
                CPU_TS        *p_ts,
                OS_ERR        *p_err);
```

Values for "opt":
  OS_OPT_PEND_BLOCKING
  OS_OPT_PEND_NON_BLOCKING

```
OS_OBJ_QTY
OSQPendAbort (OS_Q           *p_q,
                OS_OPT        opt,
                OS_ERR        *p_err);
```

Values for "opt":
  OS_OPT_PEND_ABORT_1
  OS_OPT_PEND_ABORT_ALL
  OS_OPT_POST_NO_SCHED (additive)

```
void
OSQPost        (OS_Q          *p_q,
                void          *p_void,
                OS_MSG_SIZE   msg_size,
                OS_OPT        opt,
                OS_ERR        *p_err);
```

Values for "opt":
  OS_OPT_POST_ALL
  OS_OPT_POST_FIFO
  OS_OPT_POST_LIFO
  OS_OPT_POST_NO_SCHED (additive)

A-8 Task Message Queues – Message Passing

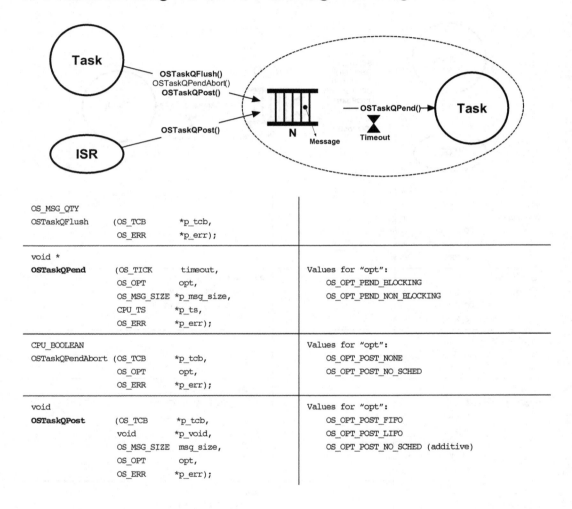

```
OS_MSG_QTY
OSTaskQFlush    (OS_TCB       *p_tcb,
                 OS_ERR       *p_err);

void *
OSTaskQPend     (OS_TICK       timeout,            Values for "opt":
                 OS_OPT        opt,                     OS_OPT_PEND_BLOCKING
                 OS_MSG_SIZE  *p_msg_size,              OS_OPT_PEND_NON_BLOCKING
                 CPU_TS       *p_ts,
                 OS_ERR       *p_err);

CPU_BOOLEAN                                         Values for "opt":
OSTaskQPendAbort (OS_TCB      *p_tcb,                   OS_OPT_POST_NONE
                 OS_OPT        opt,                     OS_OPT_POST_NO_SCHED
                 OS_ERR       *p_err);

void                                               Values for "opt":
OSTaskQPost     (OS_TCB       *p_tcb,                   OS_OPT_POST_FIFO
                 void         *p_void,                  OS_OPT_POST_LIFO
                 OS_MSG_SIZE   msg_size,                OS_OPT_POST_NO_SCHED (additive)
                 OS_OPT        opt,
                 OS_ERR       *p_err);
```

A-9 Pending on Multiple Objects

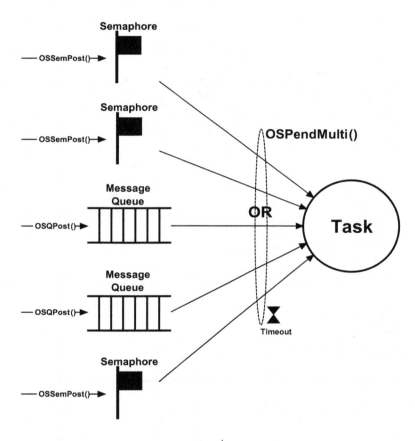

```
OS_OBJ_QTY
OSPendMulti (OS_PEND_DATA  *p_pend_data_tbl,
             OS_OBJ_QTY     tbl_size,
             OS_TICK        timeout,
             OS_OPT         opt,
             OS_ERR        *p_err);
```

```
Values for "opt":
   OS_OPT_PEND_BLOCKING
   OS_OPT_PEND_NON_BLOCKING
```

A-10 Timers

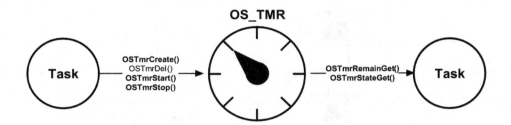

```
void
OSTmrCreate      (OS_TMR             *p_tmr,
                 CPU_CHAR           *p_name,
                 OS_TICK            dly,
                 OS_TICK            period,
                 OS_OPT             opt,
                 OS_TMR_CALLBACK_PTR p_callback,
                 void               *p_callback_arg,
                 OS_ERR             *p_err);


CPU_BOOLEAN
OSTmrDel         (OS_TMR             *p_tmr,
                 OS_ERR             *p_err);


OS_TICK
OSTmrRemainGet   (OS_TMR             *p_tmr,
                 OS_ERR             *p_err);


OS_STATE
OSTmrStateGet    (OS_TMR             *p_tmr,
                 OS_ERR             *p_err);


CPU_BOOLEAN
OSTmrStart       (OS_TMR             *p_tmr,
                 OS_ERR             *p_err);


CPU_BOOLEAN
OSTmrStop        (OS_TMR             *p_tmr,
                 OS_OPT             opt,
                 void               *p_callback_arg,
                 OS_ERR             *p_err);
```

```
Values for "opt":
   OS_OPT_TMR_ONE_SHOT
   OS_OPT_TMR_PERIODIC
```

A-11 Fixed-Size Memory Partitions – Memory Management

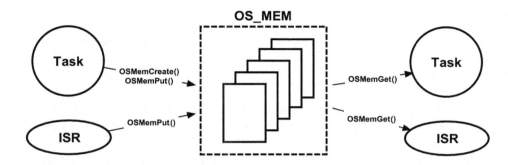

```
void
OSMemCreate (OS_MEM      *p_mem,
             CPU_CHAR    *p_name,
             void        *p_addr,
             OS_MEM_QTY  n_blks,
             OS_MEM_SIZE blk_size,
             OS_ERR      *p_err);
```

```
void *
OSMemGet    (OS_MEM      *p_mem,
             OS_ERR      *p_err);
```

```
void
OSMemPut    (OS_MEM      *p_mem,
             void        *p_blk,
             OS_ERR      *p_err);
```

A-12 OSCtxSw()

void   OSCtxSw (void)

File	Called from	Code enabled by
os_cpu_a.asm	OSSched()	N/A

OSCtxSw() is called from the macro OS_TASK_SW(), which in turn is called from OSSched() to perform a task-level context switch. Interrupts are disabled when OSCtxSw() is called.

Prior to calling OSCtxSw(), OSTCBCurPtr to point at the OS_TCB of the task that is being switched out, and OSSched() sets OSTCBHighRdyPtr to point at the OS_TCB of the task being switched in.

ARGUMENTS

None

RETURNED VALUES

None

NOTES/WARNINGS

None

EXAMPLE

The pseudocode for OSCtxSw() follows:

```
void  OSCtxSw (void)
{
    Save all CPU registers;                          (1)
    OSTCBCurPtr->StkPtr = SP;                         (2)
    OSTaskSwHook();                                   (3)
    OSPrioCur           = OSPrioHighRdy;              (4)
    OSTCBCurPtr         = OSTCBHighRdyPtr;            (5)
    SP                  = OSTCBHighRdyPtr->StkPtr;    (6)
    Restore all CPU registers;                        (7)
    Return from interrupt;                            (8)
}
```

(1)   OSCtxSw() must save all of the CPU registers onto the current task's stack. OSCtxSw() is called from the context of the task being switched out. Therefore, the CPU stack pointer is pointing to the proper stack. The user must save all of the registers in the same order as if an ISR started and all the CPU registers were saved on the stack. The stacking order should therefore match that of OSTaskStkInit().

(2)   The current task's stack pointer is then saved into the current task's OS_TCB.

(3)   Next, OSCtxSw() must call OSTaskSwHook().

(4)   OSPrioHighRdy is copied to OSPrioCur.

(5)   OSTCBHighRdyPtr is copied to OSTCBCurPtr since the current task is now the task being switched in.

(6)   The stack pointer of the new task is restored from the OS_TCB of the new task.

(7)   All the CPU registers from the new task's stack are restored.

(8)   Finally, OSCtxSw() must execute a return from interrupt instruction.

A-13 OSFlagCreate()

```
void  OSFlagCreate (OS_FLAG_GRP  *p_grp,
                    CPU_CHAR     *p_name,
                    OS_FLAGS      flags,
                    OS_ERR       *p_err)
```

File	Called from	Code enabled by
os_flag.c	Task or startup code	OS_CFG_FLAG_EN

OSFlagCreate() is used to create and initialize an event flag group. μC/OS-III allows the user to create an unlimited number of event flag groups (limited only by the amount of RAM in the system).

ARGUMENTS

p_grp   This is a pointer to an event flag group that must be allocated in the application. The user will need to declare a "global" variable as shown, and pass a pointer to this variable to OSFlagCreate():

    OS_FLAG_GRP MyEventFlag;

p_name   This is a pointer to an ASCII string used for the name of the event flag group. The name can be displayed by debuggers or by μC/Probe.

flags   This contains the initial value of the flags to store in the event flag group. Typically, you would set all flags to 0 events correspond to set bits and all 1s if events correspond to cleared bits.

p_err   This is a pointer to a variable that is used to hold an error code. The error code can be one of the following:

    OS_ERR_NONE   If the call is successful and the event flag group has been created.

    OS_ERR_CREATE_ISR   if OS_CFG_CALLED_FROM_ISR_CHK_EN set to 1 in os_cfg.h: If attempting to create an event flag group from an ISR, w is not allowed.

    OS_ERR_OBJ_CREATED   If the object passed has already been created.

OS_ERR_OBJ_PTR_NULL	if OS_CFG_ARG_CHK_EN is set to 1 in os_cfg.h: If p_grp is a NULL pointer.
OS_ERR_ILLEGAL_CREATE_RUN_TIME	if OS_SAFETY_CRITICAL_IEC61508 is defined: you called this after calling OSSafetyCriticalStart() and thus you are no longer allowed to create additional kernel objects.

RETURNED VALUES

None

NOTES/WARNINGS

Event flag groups must be created by this function before they can be used by the other event flag group services.

EXAMPLE

```
OS_FLAG_GRP  EngineStatus;


void main (void)
{
    OS_ERR  err;

    OSInit(&err);                       /* Initialize µC/OS-III                         */
    :
    :
    OSFlagCreate(&EngineStatus,
                "Engine Status",
                (OS_FLAGS)0,
                &err);                  /* Create a flag grp containing the engine's status */
    /* Check "err" */
    :
    :
    OSStart();                          /* Start Multitasking                           */
}
```

A-14 OSFlagDel()

```
void OSFlagDel (OS_FLAG_GRP  *p_grp,
                OS_OPT        opt,
                OS_ERR       *p_err);
```

File	Called from	Code enabled by
os_flag.c	Task only	OS_CFG_FLAG_EN and OS_CFG_FLAG_DEL_EN

OSFlagDel() is used to delete an event flag group. This function should be used with care since multiple tasks may be relying on the presence of the event flag group. Generally, before deleting an event flag group, first delete all of the tasks that access the event flag group. Also, it is recommended that the user not delete kernel objects at run time.

ARGUMENTS

p_grp   is a pointer to the event flag group to delete.

opt   specifies whether the user wants to delete the event flag group only if there are no pending tasks (**OS_OPT_DEL_NO_PEND**), or whether the event flag group should always be deleted regardless of whether or not tasks are pending (**OS_OPT_DEL_ALWAYS**). In this case, all pending task are readied.

p_err   is a pointer to a variable used to hold an error code. The error code can be one of the following:

OS_ERR_NONE	if the call is successful and the event flag group has been deleted.
OS_ERR_DEL_ISR	if **OS_CFG_CALLED_FROM_ISR_CHK_EN** set to 1 in **os_cfg.h**: if the user attempts to delete an event flag group from an ISR.
OS_ERR_OBJ_PTR_NULL	if **OS_CFG_ARG_CHK_EN** is set to 1 in **os_cfg.h**: if **p_grp** is a **NULL** pointer.
OS_ERR_OBJ_TYPE	if **OS_CFG_OBJ_TYPE_CHK_EN** is set to 1 in **os_cfg.h**: if **p_grp** is not pointing to an event flag group.

| OS_ERR_OPT_INVALID | if OS_CFG_ARG_CHK_EN is set to 1 in os_cfg.h: if the user does not specify one of the options mentioned in the opt argument. |
| OS_ERR_TASK_WAITING | if one or more tasks are waiting on the event flag group and OS_OPT_DEL_NO_PEND is specified. |

RETURNED VALUES

0 if no task was waiting on the event flag group, or an error occurs.

> 0 if one or more tasks waiting on the event flag group are now readied and informed

NOTES/WARNINGS

You should use this call with care as other tasks might expect the presence of the event flag group.

EXAMPLE

```
OS_FLAG_GRP  EngineStatusFlags;


void Task (void *p_arg)
{
    OS_ERR      err;
    OS_OBJ_QTY  qty;

    (void)&p_arg;
    while (DEF_ON) {
        :
        :
        qty = OSFlagDel(&EngineStatusFlags,
                       OS_OPT_DEL_ALWAYS,
                       &err);
        /* Check "err" */
        :
        :
    }
}
```

A-15 OSFlagPend()

```
OS_FLAGS   OSFlagPend (OS_FLAG_GRP *p_grp,
                       OS_FLAGS      flags,
                       OS_TICK       timeout,
                       OS_OPT        opt,
                       CPU_TS       *p_ts,
                       OS_ERR       *p_err)
```

File	Called from	Code enabled by
os_flag.c	Task only	OS_CFG_FLAG_EN

OSFlagPend() allows the task to wait for a combination of conditions or events (i.e. bits) to be set (or cleared) in an event flag group. The application can wait for any condition to be set or cleared, or for all conditions to be set or cleared. If the events that the calling task desires are not available, the calling task is blocked (optional) until the desired conditions or events are satisfied, the specified timeout expires, the event flag is deleted, or the pend is aborted by another task.

ARGUMENTS

p_grp   is a pointer to the event flag group.

flags   is a bit pattern indicating which bit(s) (i.e., flags) to check. The bits wanted are specified by setting the corresponding bits in flags. If the application wants to wait for bits 0 and 1 to be set, specify 0x03. The same applies if you'd want to wait for the same 2 bits to be cleared (you'd still specify which bits by passing 0x03).

timeout   allows the task to resume execution if the desired flag(s) is (are) not received from the event flag group within the specified number of clock ticks. A timeout value of 0 indicates that the task wants to wait forever for the flag(s). The timeout value is not synchronized with the clock tick. The timeout count begins decrementing on the next clock tick, which could potentially occur immediately.

opt	specifies whether all bits are to be set/cleared or any of the bits are to be set/cleared. Here are the options:

OS_OPT_PEND_FLAG_CLR_ALL	Check all bits in flags to be clear (0)
OS_OPT_PEND_FLAG_CLR_ANY	Check any bit in flags to be clear (0)
OS_OPT_PEND_FLAG_SET_ALL	Check all bits in flags to be set (1)
OS_OPT_PEND_FLAG_SET_ANY	Check any bit in flags to be set (1)

The caller may also specify whether the flags are consumed by "adding" OS_OPT_PEND_FLAG_CONSUME to the **opt** argument. For example, to wait for any flag in a group and then clear the flags that satisfy the condition, you would set **opt** to:

OS_OPT_PEND_FLAG_SET_ANY + OS_OPT_PEND_FLAG_CONSUME

Finally, you can specify whether you want the caller to block if the flag(s) are available or not. You would then "add" the following options:

OS_OPT_PEND_BLOCKING
OS_OPT_PEND_NON_BLOCKING

Note that the **timeout** argument should be set to **0** when specifying OS_OPT_PEND_NON_BLOCKING, since the timeout value is irrelevant using this option. Having a non-zero value could simply confuse the reader of your code.

p_ts   is a pointer to a timestamp indicating when the flags were posted, the pend was aborted, or the event flag group was deleted. Passing a **NULL** pointer (i.e., (**CPU_TS** *)0) indicates that the caller does not desire the timestamp. In other words, passing a **NULL** pointer is valid, and indicates that the caller does not need the timestamp.

A timestamp is useful when the task desires to know when the event flag group was posted or how long it took for the task to resume after the event flag group was posted. In the latter case, the user must call OS_TS_GET() and compute the difference between the current value of the timestamp and *p_ts, as shown:

delta = OS_TS_GET() - *p_ts;

p_err   is a pointer to an error code and can be:

OS_ERR_NONE	No error.
OS_ERR_OBJ_PTR_NULL	if **OS_CFG_ARG_CHK_EN** is set to 1 in **os_cfg.h**: if **p_grp** is a **NULL** pointer.
OS_ERR_OBJ_TYPE	if **OS_CFG_OBJ_TYPE_CHK_EN** is set to 1 in **os_cfg.h**: **p_grp** is not pointing to an event flag group.
OS_ERR_OPT_INVALID	if **OS_CFG_ARG_CHK_EN** is set to 1 in **os_cfg.h**: the caller specified an invalid option.
OS_ERR_PEND_ABORT	the wait on the flags was aborted by another task that called **OSFlagPendAbort()**.
OS_ERR_PEND_ISR	if **OS_CFG_CALLED_FROM_ISR_CHK_EN** set to 1 in **os_cfg.h**: An attempt was made to call **OSFlagPend()** from an ISR, which is not allowed.
OS_ERR_SCHED_LOCKED	When calling this function while the scheduler was locked.
OS_ERR_PEND_WOULD_BLOCK	**if** specifying non-blocking but the flags were not available and the call would block if the caller had specified **OS_OPT_PEND_BLOCKING**.
OS_ERR_TIMEOUT	the flags are not available within the specified amount of time.

RETURNED VALUES

The flag(s) that cause the task to be ready, **0** if either none of the flags are ready, or indicate an error occurred.

NOTES/WARNINGS

The event flag group must be created before it is used.

EXAMPLE

```c
#define   ENGINE_OIL_PRES_OK   0x01
#define   ENGINE_OIL_TEMP_OK   0x02
#define   ENGINE_START         0x04

OS_FLAG_GRP  EngineStatus;

void Task (void *p_arg)
{
    OS_ERR   err;
    OS_FLAGS value;
    CPU_TS   ts;


    (void)&p_arg;
    while (DEF_ON) {
        value = OSFlagPend(&EngineStatus,
                           ENGINE_OIL_PRES_OK   + ENGINE_OIL_TEMP_OK,
                           OS_FLAG_WAIT_SET_ALL + OS_FLAG_CONSUME,
                           10,
                           OS_OPT_PEND_BLOCKING,
                           &ts,
                           &err);
        /* Check "err" */
        :
        :
    }
}
```

A-16 OSFlagPendAbort()

```
OS_OBJ_QTY  OSFlagPendAbort (OS_SEM  *p_grp,
                             OS_OPT   opt,
                             OS_ERR  *p_err)
```

File	Called from	Code enabled by
os_flag.c	Task only	OS_CFG_FLAG_EN and OS_CFG_FLAG_PEND_ABORT_EN

OSFlagPendAbort() aborts and readies any tasks currently waiting on an event flag group. This function would be used by another task to fault abort the wait on the event flag group, rather than to normally signal the event flag group via OSFlagPost().

ARGUMENTS

p_grp   is a pointer to the event flag group for which pend(s) must be aborted.

opt   determines the type of abort performed.

OS_OPT_PEND_ABORT_1	Aborts the pend of only the highest priority task waiting on the event flag group.
OS_OPT_PEND_ABORT_ALL	Aborts the pend of all the tasks waiting on the event flag group.
OS_OPT_POST_NO_SCHED	Specifies that the scheduler should not be called even if the pend of a higher priority task is aborted. Scheduling will need to occur from another function.
	You would use this option if the task calling OSFlagPendAbort() will perform additional pend aborts, rescheduling will take place at completion, and when multiple pend aborts are to take effect simultaneously.

p_err	is a pointer to a variable that holds an error code. OSFlagPendAbort() sets *p_err to one of the following:

OS_ERR_NONE	at least one task waiting on the event flag group was readied and informed of the aborted wait. The return value indicates the number of tasks where a wait on the event flag group was aborted.
OS_ERR_OBJ_PTR_NULL	if OS_CFG_ARG_CHK_EN is set to 1 in os_cfg.h: if p_grp is a NULL pointer.
OS_ERR_OBJ_TYPE	if OS_CFG_OBJ_TYPE_CHK_EN is set to 1 in os_cfg.h: if p_grp is not pointing to an event flag group.
OS_ERR_OPT_INVALID	if OS_CFG_ARG_CHK_EN is set to 1 in os_cfg.h: if specifying an invalid option.
OS_ERR_PEND_ABORT_ISR	if OS_CFG_CALLED_FROM_ISR_CHK_EN set to 1 in os_cfg.h: This function cannot be called from an ISR.
OS_ERR_PEND_ABORT_NONE	No task was aborted since no task was waiting.

RETURNED VALUE

OSFlagPendAbort() returns the number of tasks made ready-to-run by this function. Zero indicates that no tasks were pending on the event flag group and thus this function had no effect.

NOTES/WARNINGS

Event flag groups must be created before they are used.

EXAMPLE

```
OS_FLAG_GRP  EngineStatus;


void Task (void *p_arg)
{
    OS_ERR      err;
    OS_OBJ_QTY  nbr_tasks;


    (void)&p_arg;
    while (DEF_ON) {
        :
        :
        nbr_tasks = OSFlagPendAbort(&EngineStatus,
                                    OS_OPT_PEND_ABORT_ALL,
                                    &err);
        /* Check "err" */
        :
        :
    }
}
```

A-17 OSFlagPendGetFlagsRdy()

```
OS_FLAGS  OSFlagPendGetFlagsRdy (OS_ERR  *p_err)
```

File	Called from	Code enabled by
os_flag.c	Task only	OS_CFG_FLAG_EN

OSFlagPendGetFlagsRdy() is used to obtain the flags that caused the current task to be ready-to-run. This function allows the user to know "Who did it!"

ARGUMENTS

p_err   is a pointer to an error code and can be:

> OS_ERR_NONE   No error.
>
> OS_ERR_PEND_ISR   if OS_CFG_CALLED_FROM_ISR_CHK_EN set to 1 in os_cfg.h: When attempting to call this function from an ISR.

RETURNED VALUE

The value of the flags that caused the current task to become ready-to-run.

NOTES/WARNINGS

The event flag group must be created before it is used.

Appendix A

EXAMPLE

```
#define   ENGINE_OIL_PRES_OK    0x01
#define   ENGINE_OIL_TEMP_OK    0x02
#define   ENGINE_START          0x04

OS_FLAG_GRP   EngineStatus;


void Task (void *p_arg)
{
    OS_ERR    err;
    OS_FLAGS  value;
    OS_FLAGS  flags_rdy;


    (void)&p_arg;
    while (DEF_ON) {
        value    = OSFlagPend(&EngineStatus,
                              ENGINE_OIL_PRES_OK    + ENGINE_OIL_TEMP_OK,
                              OS_FLAG_WAIT_SET_ALL + OS_FLAG_CONSUME,
                              10,
                              &err);
        /* Check "err" */
        flags_rdy = OSFlagPendGetFlagsRdy(&err);
        /* Check "err" */
        :
        :
    }
}
```

A-18 OSFlagPost()

```
OS_FLAGS  OSFlagPost (OS_FLAG_GRP  *p_grp,
                      OS_FLAGS      flags,
                      OS_OPT        opt,
                      OS_ERR        *p_err)
```

File	Called from	Code enabled by
os_flag.c	Task or ISR	OS_CFG_FLAG_EN

You can set or clear event flag bits by calling **OSFlagPost()**. The bits set or cleared are specified in a bit mask (i.e., the flags argument). **OSFlagPost()** readies each task that has its desired bits satisfied by this call. The caller can set or clear bits that are already set or cleared.

ARGUMENTS

p_grp   is a pointer to the event flag group.

flags   specifies which bits to be set or cleared. If **opt** is **OS_OPT_POST_FLAG_SET**, each bit that is set in **flags** will set the corresponding bit in the event flag group. For example to set bits 0, 4, and 5, you would set **flags** to **0x31** (note that bit 0 is the least significant bit). If opt is **OS_OPT_POST_FLAG_CLR**, each bit that is set in **flags** will clear the corresponding bit in the event flag group. For example to clear bits 0, 4, and 5, you would specify **flags** as **0x31** (again, bit 0 is the least significant bit).

opt   indicates whether the flags are set (**OS_OPT_POST_FLAG_SET**) or cleared (**OS_OPT_POST_FLAG_CLR**).

The caller may also "add" **OS_OPT_POST_NO_SCHED** so that µC/OS-III will not call the scheduler after the post.

p_err   is a pointer to an error code and can be:

OS_ERR_NONE	the call is successful.
OS_ERR_FLAG_INVALID_OPT	if OS_CFG_ARG_CHK_EN is set to 1 in os_cfg.h: if you specified an invalid option.
OS_ERR_OBJ_PTR_NULL	if OS_CFG_ARG_CHK_EN is set to 1 in os_cfg.h: if the caller passed a NULL pointer.
OS_ERR_OBJ_TYPE	if OS_CFG_OBJ_TYPE_CHK_EN is set to 1 in os_cfg.h: p_grp is not pointing to an event flag group.

RETURNED VALUE

The new value of the event flags.

NOTES/WARNINGS

1   Event flag groups must be created before they are used.

2   The execution time of this function depends on the number of tasks waiting on the event flag group. However, the execution time is still deterministic.

3   Although the example below shows that we are posting from a task, OSFlagPost() can also be called from an ISR.

EXAMPLE

```
#define   ENGINE_OIL_PRES_OK   0x01
#define   ENGINE_OIL_TEMP_OK   0x02
#define   ENGINE_START         0x04

OS_FLAG_GRP  EngineStatusFlags;


void  TaskX (void *p_arg)
{
    OS_ERR    err;
    OS_FLAGS  flags;


    (void)&p_arg;
    while (DEF_ON) {
        :
        :
        flags = OSFlagPost(&EngineStatusFlags,
                           ENGINE_START,
                           OS_OPT_POST_FLAG_SET,
                           &err);
        /* Check 'err" */
        :
        :
    }
}
```

A-19 OSIdleTaskHook()

```
void  OSIdleTaskHook (void);
```

File	Called from	Code enabled by
os_cpu_c.c	OS_IdleTask() ONLY	N/A

This function is called by OS_IdleTask().

OSIdleTaskHook() is part of the CPU port code and this function *must not* be called by the application code. OSIdleTaskHook() is used by the µC/OS-III port developer.

OSIdleTaskHook() runs in the context of the idle task and thus it is important to make sure there is sufficient stack space in the idle task. OSIdleTaskHook() *must not* make any OS???Pend() calls, call OSTaskSuspend() or OSTimeDly???(). In other words, this function must never be allowed to make a blocking call.

ARGUMENTS

None

RETURNED VALUE

None

NOTES/WARNINGS

■ Never make blocking calls from OSIdleTaskHook().

■ *Do not* call this function from you application.

EXAMPLE

The code below calls an application-specific hook that the application programmer can define. The user can simply set the value of OS_AppIdleTaskHookPtr to point to the desired hook function which in this case is assumed to be defined in os_app_hooks.c. The idle task calls OSIdleTaskHook() which in turns calls App_OS_IdleTaskHook() through OS_AppIdleTaskHookPtr.

This feature is very useful when there is a processor that can enter low-power mode. When µC/OS-III has no other task to run, the processor can be put to sleep waiting for an interrupt to wake it up.

```
void  App_OS_IdleTaskHook (void)                        /* See os_app_hooks.c   */
{
    /* Your code goes here! */
    /* Put the CPU in low power mode (optional) */
}


void App_OS_SetAllHooks (void)                          /* os_app_hooks.c       */
{
    CPU_SR_ALLOC();

    CPU_CRITICAL_ENTER();
    :
    OS_AppIdleTaskHookPtr = App_OS_IdleTaskHook;
    :
    CPU_CRITICAL_EXIT();
}


void  OSIdleTaskHook (void)                             /* See os_cpu_c.c       */
{
#if OS_CFG_APP_HOOKS_EN > 0u
    if (OS_AppIdleTaskHookPtr != (OS_APP_HOOK_VOID)0) {  /* Call application hook */
        (*OS_AppIdleTaskHookPtr)();
    }
#endif
}
```

A-20 OSInit()

```
void OSInit (OS_ERR *p_err);
```

File	Called from	Code enabled by
os_core.c	Startup code only	N/A

OSInit() initializes µC/OS-III and it must be called prior to calling any other µC/OS-III function. Including OSStart() which will start multitasking. OSInit() returns as soon as an error is detected.

ARGUMENTS

p_err   is a pointer to an error code. Some of the error codes below are issued only if the associated feature is enabled.

OS_ERR_NONE	initialization was successful.
OS_ERR_INT_Q	if OS_CFG_ISR_POST_DEFERRED_EN is set to 1 in os_cfg.h: OSCfg_IntQBasePtr is NULL. The error is detected by OS_IntQTaskInit() in os_int.c.
OS_ERR_INT_Q_SIZE	if OS_CFG_ISR_POST_DEFERRED_EN is set to 1 in os_cfg.h: OSCfg_IntQSize must have at least 2 elements. The error is detected by OS_IntQTaskInit() in os_int.c.
OS_ERR_INT_Q_STK_INVALID	if OS_CFG_ISR_POST_DEFERRED_EN is set to 1 in os_cfg.h: OSCfg_IntQTaskStkBasePtr is NULL. The error is detected by OS_IntQTaskInit() in os_int.c
OS_ERR_INT_Q_STK_SIZE_INVALID	if OS_CFG_ISR_POST_DEFERRED_EN is set to 1 in os_cfg.h: OSCfg_IntQTaskStkSize is less than OSCfg_StkSizeMin. The error is detected by OS_IntQTaskInit() in os_int.c.

OS_ERR_MSG_POOL_EMPTY	if OS_CFG_ARG_CHK_EN and OS_CFG_Q_EN or OS_CFG_TASK_Q_EN are set to 1 in os_cfg.h: OSCfg_MsgPoolSize is zero. The error is detected by OS_MsgPoolInit() in os_msg.c.
OS_ERR_MSG_POOL_NULL_PTR	if OS_CFG_ARG_CHK_EN and OS_CFG_Q_EN or OS_CFG_TASK_Q_EN are set to 1 in os_cfg.h: OSCfg_MsgPoolBasePtr is NULL in os_msg.c. The error is detected by OS_MsgPoolInit() in os_msg.c.
OS_ERR_STAT_PRIO_INVALID	if OS_CFG_STAT_TASK_EN is set to 1 in os_cfg.h: OSCfg_StatTaskPrio is invalid. The error is detected by OS_StatTaskInit() in os_stat.c.
OS_ERR_STAT_STK_INVALID	if OS_CFG_STAT_TASK_EN is set to 1 in os_cfg.h: OSCfg_StatTaskStkBasePtr is NULL. The error is detected by OS_StatTaskInit() in os_stat.c.
OS_ERR_STAT_STK_SIZE_INVALID	ifOS_CFG_STAT_TASK_EN is set to 1 in os_cfg.h: OSCfg_StatTaskStkSize is less than OSCfg_StkSizeMin. The error is detected by OS_StatTaskInit() in os_stat.c.
OS_ERR_TICK_PRIO_INVALID	if OSCfg_TickTaskPrio is invalid, The error is detected by OS_TickTaskInit() in os_tick.c.
OS_ERR_TICK_STK_INVALID	OSCfg_TickTaskStkBasePtr is NULL. The error is detected by OS_TickTaskInit() in os_tick.c.
OS_ERR_TICK_STK_SIZE_INVALID	OSCfg_TickTaskStkSize is less than OSCfg_StkSizeMin. This error was detected by OS_TickTaskInit() in os_tick.c.
OS_ERR_TMR_PRIO_INVALID	if OS_CFG_TMR_EN is set to 1 in os_cfg.h: OSCfg_TmrTaskPrio is invalid. The error is detected by see OS_TmrInit() in os_tmr.c.

| OS_ERR_TMR_STK_INVALID | if OS_CFG_TMR_EN is set to 1 in **os_cfg.h**: OSCfg_TmrTaskBasePtr is pointing at NULL. The error is detected by OS_TmrInit() in **os_tmr.c**. |
| OS_ERR_TMR_STK_SIZE_INVALID | if OS_CFG_TMR_EN is set to 1 in **os_cfg.h**: OSCfg_TmrTaskStkSize is less than OSCfg_StkSizeMin. The error is detected by OS_TmrInit() in **os_tmr.c**. |

RETURNED VALUES

None

NOTES/WARNINGS

■ OSInit() must be called before OSStart().

■ OSInit() returns as soon as it detects an error in any of the sub-functions it calls. For example, if OSInit() encounters a problem initializing the task manager, an appropriate error code will be returned and OSInit() will not go any further. It is therefore important that the user checks the error code before starting multitasking.

EXAMPLE

```
void main (void)
{
    OS_ERR  err;

        :

    OSInit(&err);               /* Initialize µC/OS-III         */
    /* Check "err" */
        :
        :
    OSStart(&err);              /* Start Multitasking           */
    /* Check "err" */          /* Code not supposed to end up here! */
}
```

A-21 OSInitHook()

void OSInitHook (void);

File	Called from	Code enabled by
os_cpu_c.c	OSInit()	Always enabled

OSInitHook() is a function that is called by µC/OS-III's initialization code, OSInit(). OSInitHook() is typically implemented by the port implementer for the processor used. This hook allows the port to be extended to do such tasks as setup exception stacks, floating-point registers, and more. OSInitHook() is called at the beginning of OSInit(), before any µC/OS-III task and data structure have been initialized.

ARGUMENTS

None

RETURNED VALUES

None

NOTES/WARNINGS

None

EXAMPLE

```
void  OSInitHook (void)                          /* See os_cpu_c.c       */
{
    /* Perform any initialization code necessary by the port */
}
```

A-22 OSIntCtxSw()

`void  OSIntCtxSw (void)`

File	Called from	Code enabled by
os_cpu_a.asm	OSIntExit()	N/A

OSIntCtxSw() is called from OSIntExit() to perform a context switch when all nested interrupts have returned.

Interrupts are disabled when OSIntCtxSw() is called.

OSTCBCurPtr points at the OS_TCB of the task that is switched out when OSIntCtxSw() is called and OSIntExit() sets OSTCBHighRdyPtr to point at the OS_TCB of the task that is switched in.

ARGUMENTS

None

RETURNED VALUES

None

NOTES/WARNINGS

None

EXAMPLE

The pseudocode for OSIntCtxSw() is shown below. Notice that the code does only half of what OSCtxSw() did. The reason is that OSIntCtxSw() is called from an ISR and it is assumed that all of the CPU registers of the interrupted task were saved at the beginning of the ISR. OSIntCtxSw() therefore must only restore the context of the new, high-priority task.

```
void  OSIntCtxSw (void)
{
    OSTaskSwHook();                                  (1)
    OSPrioCur           = OSPrioHighRdy;             (2)
    OSTCBCurPtr         = OSTCBHighRdyPtr;           (3)
    SP                  = OSTCBHighRdyPtr->StkPtr;   (4)
    Restore all CPU registers;                       (5)
    Return from interrupt;                           (6)
}
```

(1)   OSIntCtxSw() must call OSTaskSwHook().

(2)   OSPrioHighRdy needs to be copied to OSPrioCur.

(3)   OSTCBHighRdyPtr needs to be copied to OSTCBCurPtr because the current task will now be the new task.

(4)   The stack pointer of the new task is restored from the OS_TCB of the new task.

(5)   All the CPU registers need to be restored from the new task's stack.

(6)   A return from interrupt instruction must be executed.

A-23 OSIntEnter()

void OSIntEnter (void);

File	Called from	Code enabled by
os_core.c	ISR only	N/A

OSIntEnter() notifies µC/OS-III that an ISR is being processed. This allows µC/OS-III to keep track of interrupt nesting. OSIntEnter() is used in conjunction with OSIntExit(). This function is generally called at the beginning of ISRs. Note that on some CPU architectures, it must be written in assembly language (shown below in pseudo code):

```
MyISR:
    Save CPU registers;
    OSIntEnter();              /* Or, OSIntNestingCtr++ */
        :
    Process ISR;
        :
    OSIntExit();
    Restore CPU registers;
    Return from interrupt;
```

ARGUMENTS

None

RETURNED VALUES

None

NOTES/WARNINGS

■ This function must not be called by task-level code.

■ You can also increment the interrupt-nesting counter (**OSIntNestingCtr**) directly in the ISR to avoid the overhead of the function call/return. It is safe to increment **OSIntNestingCtr** in the ISR since interrupts are assumed to be disabled when **OSIntNestingCtr** is incremented. However, that is not true for all CPU architectures. You need to make sure that interrupts are disabled in the ISR before directly incrementing **OSIntNestingCtr**.

■ It is possible to nest interrupts up to 250 levels deep.

A-24 OSIntExit()

```
void OSIntExit (void);
```

File	Called from	Code enabled by
os_core.c	ISR only	N/A

OSIntExit() notifies µC/OS-III that an ISR is complete. This allows µC/OS-III to keep track of interrupt nesting. **OSIntExit()** is used in conjunction with **OSIntEnter()**. When the last nested interrupt completes, **OSIntExit()** determines if a higher priority task is ready-to-run. If so, the interrupt returns to the higher priority task instead of the interrupted task.

This function is typically called at the end of ISRs as follows, and on some CPU architectures, it must be written in assembly language (shown below in pseudo code):

```
MyISR:
    Save CPU registers;
    OSIntEnter();
        :
    Process ISR;
        :
    OSIntExit();
    Restore CPU registers;
    Return from interrupt;
```

ARGUMENTS

None

RETURNED VALUE

None

NOTES/WARNINGS

This function must not be called by task-level code. Also, if you decide to directly increment **OSIntNestingCtr**, instead of calling **OSIntEnter()**, you must still call **OSIntExit()**.

A-25 OSMemCreate()

```
void   OSMemCreate (OS_MEM      *p_mem,
                    CPU_CHAR    *p_name,
                    void        *p_addr,
                    OS_MEM_QTY   n_blks,
                    OS_MEM_SIZE  blk_size,
                    OS_ERR      *p_err)
```

File	Called from	Code enabled by
os_mem.c	Task or startup code	OS_CFG_MEM_EN

OSMemCreate() creates and initializes a memory partition. A memory partition contains a user-specified number of fixed-size memory blocks. An application may obtain one of these memory blocks and, when completed, release the block back to the same partition where the block originated.

ARGUMENTS

p_mem   is a pointer to a memory partition control block that must be allocated in the application. It is assumed that storage will be allocated for the memory control blocks in the application. In other words, the user will declare a "global" variable as follows, and pass a pointer to this variable to OSMemCreate():

```
OS_MEM  MyMemPartition;
```

p_name   is a pointer to an ASCII string to provide a name to the memory partition. The name can be displayed by debuggers or μC/Probe.

p_addr   is the address of the start of a memory area used to create fixed-size memory blocks. Memory partitions may be created using either static arrays or malloc() during startup. Note that the partition *must* align on a pointer boundary. Thus, if a pointer is 16-bits wide. the partition must start on a memory location with an address that ends with 0, 2, 4, 6, 8, etc. If a pointer is 32-bits wide, the partition must start on a memory location with an address that ends in 0, 4, 8 or C. The easiest way to ensure this is to create a static array as follows:

```
void *MyMemArray[N][M]
```

You should never deallocate memory blocks that were allocated from the heap to prevent fragmentation of your heap. It is quite acceptable to allocate memory blocks from the heap as long as the user does not deallocate them.

n_blks   contains the number of memory blocks available from the specified partition. You need to specify at least two memory blocks per partition.

blk_size   specifies the size (in bytes) of each memory block within a partition. A memory block must be large enough to hold at least a pointer. Also, the size of a memory block must be a multiple of the size of a pointer. If a pointer is 32-bits wide then the block size must be 4, 8, 12, 16, 20, etc. bytes (i.e., a multiple of 4 bytes).

p_err   is a pointer to a variable that holds an error code:

OS_ERR_NONE	if the memory partition is created successfully
OS_ERR_MEM_CREATE_ISR	if OS_CFG_CALLED_FROM_ISR_CHK_EN is set to 1 in os_cfg.h: if you called OSMemCreate() from an ISR.
OS_ERR_MEM_INVALID_BLKS	if OS_CFG_ARG_CHK_EN is set to 1 in os_cfg.h: if the user does not specify at least two memory blocks per partition
OS_ERR_MEM_INVALID_P_ADDR	if OS_CFG_ARG_CHK_EN is set to 1 in os_cfg.h: if specifying an invalid address (i.e., **p_addr** is a **NULL** pointer) or the partition is not properly aligned.
OS_ERR_MEM_INVALID_SIZE	if OS_CFG_ARG_CHK_EN is set to 1 in os_cfg.h: if the user does not specify a block size that can contain at least a pointer variable, and if it is not a multiple of a pointer-size variable.
OS_ERR_ILLEGAL_CREATE_RUN_TIME	if OS_SAFETY_CRITICAL_IEC61508 is defined: you called this after calling OSSafetyCriticalStart() and thus you are no longer allowed to create additional kernel objects.

RETURNED VALUE

None

NOTES/WARNINGS

Memory partitions must be created before they are used.

EXAMPLE

```
OS_MEM      CommMem;
CPU_INT32U  *CommBuf[16][32];          /* 16 buffers of 32 words of 32 bits */


void  main (void)
{
    OS_ERR  err;


    OSInit(&err);                      /* Initialize µC/OS-III              */
    :
    :
    OSMemCreate(&CommMem,
                "Comm Buffers",
                &CommBuf[0][0],
                16,
                32 * sizeof(CPU_INT32U),
                &err);
    /* Check "err" */
    :
    :
    OSStart(&err);                     /* Start Multitasking               */
}
```

A-26 OSMemGet()

```
void  *OSMemGet (OS_MEM   *p_mem,
                 OS_ERR   *p_err)
```

File	Called from	Code enabled by
os_mem.c	Task or ISR	OS_CFG_MEM_EN

OSMemGet() obtains a memory block from a memory partition. It is assumed that the application knows the size of each memory block obtained. Also, the application must return the memory block [using OSMemPut()] to the same memory partition when it no longer requires it. OSMemGet() may be called more than once until all memory blocks are allocated.

ARGUMENTS

p_mem   is a pointer to the desired memory partition control block.

p_err   is a pointer to a variable that holds an error code:

> OS_ERR_NONE   if a memory block is available and returned to the application.
>
> OS_ERR_MEM_INVALID_P_MEM   if OS_CFG_ARG_CHK_EN is set to 1 in os_cfg.h: if p_mem is a NULL pointer.
>
> OS_ERR_MEM_NO_FREE_BLKS   if the memory partition does not contain additional memory blocks to allocate.

RETURNED VALUE

OSMemGet() returns a pointer to the allocated memory block if one is available. If a memory block is not available from the memory partition, OSMemGet() returns a NULL pointer. It is up to the application to "cast" the pointer to the proper data type since OSMemGet() returns a void *.

NOTES/WARNINGS

■ Memory partitions must be created before they are used.

■ This is a non-blocking call and this function can be called from an ISR.

EXAMPLE

```
OS_MEM   CommMem;


void Task (void *p_arg)
{
    OS_ERR      err;
    CPU_INT32U *p_msg;


    (void)&p_arg;
    while (DEF_ON) {
        p_msg = (CPU_INT32U *)OSMemGet(&CommMem,
                                      &err);
        /* Check "err" */
        :
        :
    }
}
```

A-27 OSMemPut()

```
void  OSMemPut (OS_MEM  *p_mem,
               void     *p_blk,
               OS_ERR   *p_err)
```

File	Called from	Code enabled by
os_mem.c	Task or ISR	OS_CFG_MEM_EN

OSMemPut() returns a memory block back to a memory partition. It is assumed that the user will return the memory block to the same memory partition from which it was allocated.

ARGUMENTS

p_mem   is a pointer to the memory partition control block.

p_blk   is a pointer to the memory block to be returned to the memory partition.

p_err   is a pointer to a variable that holds an error code:

OS_ERR_NONE	if a memory block is available and returned to the application.
OS_ERR_MEM_INVALID_P_BLK	if OS_CFG_ARG_CHK_EN is set to 1 in os_cfg.h: if the user passed a NULL pointer for the memory block being returned to the memory partition.
OS_ERR_MEM_INVALID_P_MEM	if OS_CFG_ARG_CHK_EN is set to 1 in os_cfg.h: if p_mem is a NULL pointer.
OS_ERR_MEM_MEM_FULL	if returning a memory block to an already full memory partition. This would indicate that the user freed more blocks that were allocated and potentially did not return some of the memory blocks to the proper memory partition.

RETURNED VALUE

None

NOTES/WARNINGS

- Memory partitions must be created before they are used.

- You must return a memory block to the proper memory partition.

- You can call this function from an ISR or a task.

EXAMPLE

```
OS_MEM        CommMem;
CPU_INT32U    *CommMsg;


void Task (void *p_arg)
{
    OS_ERR err;


    (void)&p_arg;
    while (DEF_ON) {
        OSMemPut(&CommMem,
                 (void *)CommMsg,
                 &err);
        /* Check "err" */
        :
        :
    }
}
```

A-28 OSMutexCreate()

```
void  OSMutexCreate (OS_MUTEX    *p_mutex,
                     CPU_CHAR    *p_name,
                     OS_ERR      *p_err)
```

File	Called from	Code enabled by
os_mutex.c	Task or startup code	OS_CFG_MUTEX_EN

OSMutexCreate() is used to create and initialize a mutex. A mutex is used to gain exclusive access to a resource.

ARGUMENTS

p_mutex   is a pointer to a mutex control block that must be allocated in the application. The user will need to declare a "global" variable as follows, and pass a pointer to this variable to **OSMutexCreate()**:

        OS_MUTEX MyMutex;

p_name   is a pointer to an ASCII string used to assign a name to the mutual exclusion semaphore. The name may be displayed by debuggers or µC/Probe.

p_err   is a pointer to a variable that is used to hold an error code:

OS_ERR_NONE	if the call is successful and the mutex has been created.
OS_ERR_CREATE_ISR	if OS_CFG_CALLED_FROM_ISR_CHK_EN set to 1 in os_cfg.h: if attempting to create a mutex from an ISR.
OS_ERR_OBJ_PTR_NULL	if OS_CFG_ARG_CHK_EN is set to 1 in os_cfg.h: if p_mutex is a NULL pointer.
OS_ERR_ILLEGAL_CREATE_RUN_TIME	if OS_SAFETY_CRITICAL_IEC61508 is defined: you called this after calling OSSafetyCriticalStart() and thus you are no longer allowed to create additional kernel objects.

RETURNED VALUE

None

NOTES/WARNINGS

Mutexes must be created before they are used.

EXAMPLE

```
OS_MUTEX  DispMutex;


void main (void)
{
    OS_ERR  err;



    :
    OSInit(&err);                        /* Initialize µC/OS-III       */
    :
    :
    OSMutexCreate(&DispMutex,            /* Create Display Mutex        */
                  "Display Mutex",
                  &err);
    /* Check "err" */


    :
    :
    OSStart(&err);                       /* Start Multitasking          */
}
```

A-29 OSMutexDel()

```
void  OSMutexDel (OS_MUTEX  *p_mutex,
                  OS_OPT     opt,
                  OS_ERR    *p_err)
```

File	Called from	Code enabled by
os_mutex.c	Task only	OS_CFG_MUTEX_EN and OS_CFG_MUTEX_DEL_EN

OSMutexDel() is used to delete a mutex. This function should be used with care because multiple tasks may rely on the presence of the mutex. Generally speaking, before deleting a mutex, first delete all the tasks that access the mutex. However, as a general rule, do not delete kernel objects at run-time.

ARGUMENTS

p_mutex   is a pointer to the mutex to delete.

opt   specifies whether to delete the mutex only if there are no pending tasks (**OS_OPT_DEL_NO_PEND**), or whether to always delete the mutex regardless of whether tasks are pending or not (**OS_OPT_DEL_ALWAYS**). In this case, all pending tasks are readied.

p_err   is a pointer to a variable that is used to hold an error code:

OS_ERR_NONE	if the call is successful and the mutex has been deleted.
OS_ERR_DEL_ISR	if OS_CFG_CALLED_FROM_ISR_CHK_EN set to 1 in os_cfg.h: if attempting to delete a mutex from an ISR.
OS_ERR_OBJ_PTR_NULL	if OS_CFG_ARG_CHK_EN is set to 1 in os_cfg.h: if p_mutex is a NULL pointer.
OS_ERR_OBJ_TYPE	if OS_CFG_OBJ_TYPE_CHK_EN is set to 1 in os_cfg.h: if p_mutex is not pointing to a mutex.
OS_ERR_OPT_INVALID	if the user does not specify one of the two options mentioned in the opt argument.

OS_ERR_TASK_WAITING   if one or more task are waiting on the mutex and **OS_OPT_DEL_NO_PEND** is specified.

RETURNED VALUE

The number of tasks that were waiting for the mutex and 0 if an error occurred.

NOTES/WARNINGS

Use this call with care as other tasks may expect the presence of the mutex.

EXAMPLE

```
OS_MUTEX  DispMutex;


void Task (void *p_arg)
{
    OS_ERR  err;


    (void)&p_arg;
    while (DEF_ON) {
        :
        :
        OSMutexDel(&DispMutex,
                   OS_OPT_DEL_ALWAYS,
                   &err);
        /* Check "err" */
        :
        :
    }
}
```

A-30 OSMutexPend()

```
void  OSMutexPend (OS_MUTEX    *p_mutex,
                   OS_TICK      timeout,
                   OS_OPT       opt,
                   CPU_TS      *p_ts,
                   OS_ERR      *p_err)
```

File	Called from	Code enabled by
os_mutex.c	Task only	OS_CFG_MUTEX_EN

OSMutexPend() is used when a task requires exclusive access to a resource. If a task calls OSMutexPend() and the mutex is available, OSMutexPend() gives the mutex to the caller and returns to its caller. Note that nothing is actually given to the caller except that if **p_err** is set to **OS_ERR_NONE**, the caller can assume that it owns the mutex.

However, if the mutex is already owned by another task, OSMutexPend() places the calling task in the wait list for the mutex. The task waits until the task that owns the mutex releases the mutex and therefore the resource, or until the specified timeout expires. If the mutex is signaled before the timeout expires, µC/OS-III resumes the highest-priority task that is waiting for the mutex.

Note that if the mutex is owned by a lower-priority task, OSMutexPend() raises the priority of the task that owns the mutex to the same priority as the task requesting the mutex. The priority of the owner will be returned to its original priority when the owner releases the mutex (see OSMutexPost()).

OSMutexPend() allows nesting. The same task can call OSMutexPend() multiple times. However, the same task must then call OSMutexPost() an equivalent number of times to release the mutex.

ARGUMENTS

p_mutex   is a pointer to the mutex.

timeout   specifies a timeout value (in clock ticks) and is used to allow the task to resume execution if the mutex is not signaled (i.e., posted to) within the specified timeout. A timeout value of 0 indicates that the task wants to wait forever for the mutex. The timeout value is not synchronized with the clock tick. The timeout count is decremented on the next clock tick, which could potentially occur immediately.

opt   determines whether the user wants to block if the mutex is not available or not. This argument must be set to either:

OS_OPT_PEND_BLOCKING, or

OS_OPT_PEND_NON_BLOCKING

Note that the timeout argument should be set to 0 when specifying OS_OPT_PEND_NON_BLOCKING since the timeout value is irrelevant using this option.

p_ts   is a pointer to a timestamp indicating when the mutex was posted, the pend was aborted, or the mutex was deleted. If passing a **NULL** pointer (i.e., (**CPU_TS** *)0), the caller will not receive the timestamp. In other words, passing a **NULL** pointer is valid and indicates that the timestamp is not required.

A timestamp is useful when it is important for a task to know when the mutex was posted, or how long it took for the task to resume after the mutex was posted. In the latter case, the user must call **OS_TS_GET( )** and compute the difference between the current value of the timestamp and ***p_ts**. In other words:

delta = OS_TS_GET() - *p_ts;

p_err   is a pointer to a variable that is used to hold an error code:

OS_ERR_NONE	if the call is successful and the mutex is available.
OS_ERR_MUTEX_NESTING	if the calling task already owns the mutex and it has not posted all nested values.
OS_ERR_MUTEX_OWNER	if the calling task already owns the mutex.
OS_ERR_OBJ_PTR_NULL	if OS_CFG_ARG_CHK_EN is set to 1 in os_cfg.h: if p_mutex is a NULL pointer.
OS_ERR_OBJ_TYPE	if OS_CFG_OBJ_TYPE_CHK_EN is set to 1 in os_cfg.h: if the user did not pass a pointer to a mutex.
OS_ERR_OPT_INVALID	if OS_CFG_ARG_CHK_EN is set to 1 in os_cfg.h: if a valid option is not specified.
OS_ERR_PEND_ISR	if OS_CFG_CALLED_FROM_ISR_CHK_EN set to 1 in os_cfg.h: if attempting to acquire the mutex from an ISR.
OS_ERR_SCHED_LOCKED	if calling this function when the scheduler is locked
OS_ERR_TIMEOUT	if the mutex is not available within the specified timeout.

RETURNED VALUE

None

NOTES/WARNINGS

■   Mutexes must be created before they are used.

■   Do not suspend the task that owns the mutex. Also, do not have the mutex owner wait on any other µC/OS-III objects (i.e., semaphore, event flag, or queue), and delay the task that owns the mutex. The code should release the resource as quickly as possible.

EXAMPLE

```
OS_MUTEX  DispMutex;


void  DispTask (void *p_arg)
{
    OS_ERR  err;
    CPU_TS  ts;


    (void)&p_arg;
    while (DEF_ON) {
        :
        OSMutexPend(&DispMutex,
                    0,
                    OS_OPT_PEND_BLOCKING,
                    &ts,
                    &err);
        /* Check "err" */
    }
}
```

A-31 OSMutexPendAbort()

```
void OSMutexPendAbort (OS_MUTEX    *p_mutex,
                       OS_OPT       opt,
                       OS_ERR      *p_err)
```

File	Called from	Code enabled by
os_mutex.c	Task only	OS_CFG_MUTEX_EN and OS_CFG_MUTEX_PEND_ABORT_EN

OSMutexPendAbort() aborts and readies any tasks currently waiting on a mutex. This function should be used to fault-abort the wait on the mutex rather than to normally signal the mutex via OSMutexPost().

ARGUMENTS

p_mutex   is a pointer to the mutex.

opt   specifies whether to abort only the highest-priority task waiting on the mutex or all tasks waiting on the mutex:

OS_OPT_PEND_ABORT_1	to abort only the highest-priority task waiting on the mutex.
OS_OPT_PEND_ABORT_ALL	to abort all tasks waiting on the mutex.
OS_OPT_POST_NO_SCHED	specifies that the scheduler should not be called even if the pend of a higher-priority task has been aborted. Scheduling will need to occur from another function. The user would select this option if the task calling OSMutexPendAbort() will be doing additional pend aborts, rescheduling should not take place until all tasks are completed, and multiple pend aborts should take place simultaneously.

p_err   is a pointer to a variable that is used to hold an error code:

OS_ERR_NONE	if at least one task was aborted. Check the return value for the number of tasks aborted.
OS_ERR_OBJ_PTR_NULL	if OS_CFG_ARG_CHK_EN is set to 1 in os_cfg.h: if p_mutex is a NULL pointer.
OS_ERR_OBJ_TYPE	if OS_CFG_OBJ_TYPE_CHK_EN is set to 1 in os_cfg.h: if the caller does not pass a pointer to a mutex.
OS_ERR_OPT_INVALID	if OS_CFG_ARG_CHK_EN is set to 1 in os_cfg.h: if the caller specified an invalid option.
OS_ERR_PEND_ABORT_ISR	if OS_CFG_CALLED_FROM_ISR_CHK_EN set to 1 in os_cfg.h: if attempting to call this function from an ISR
OS_ERR_PEND_ABORT_NONE	if no tasks were aborted.

RETURNED VALUE

OSMutexPendAbort() returns the number of tasks made ready-to-run by this function. Zero indicates that no tasks were pending on the mutex and therefore this function had no effect.

NOTES/WARNINGS

Mutexes must be created before they are used.

EXAMPLE

```
OS_MUTEX  DispMutex;


void  DispTask (void *p_arg)
{
    OS_ERR      err;
    OS_OBJ_QTY  qty;


    (void)&p_arg;
    while (DEF_ON) {
        :
        :
        qty = OSMutexPendAbort(&DispMutex,
                               OS_OPT_PEND_ABORT_ALL,
                               &err);
        /* Check "err" */
    }
}
```

A-32 OSMutexPost()

```
void OSMutexPost (OS_MUTEX   *p_mutex,
                  OS_OPT      opt,
                  OS_ERR      *p_err);
```

File	Called from	Code enabled by
os_mutex.c	Task only	OS_CFG_MUTEX_EN

A mutex is signaled (i.e., released) by calling **OSMutexPost()**. You should call this function only if you acquired the mutex by first calling **OSMutexPend()**. If the priority of the task that owns the mutex has been raised when a higher priority task attempted to acquire the mutex, at that point, the original task priority of the task is restored. If one or more tasks are waiting for the mutex, the mutex is given to the highest-priority task waiting on the mutex. The scheduler is then called to determine if the awakened task is now the highest-priority task ready-to-run, and if so, a context switch is performed to run the readied task. If no task is waiting for the mutex, the mutex value is simply set to available.

ARGUMENTS

p_mutex   is a pointer to the mutex.

opt   determines the type of POST performed.

OS_OPT_POST_NONE	No special option selected.
OS_OPT_POST_NO_SCHED	Do not call the scheduler after the post, therefore the caller is resumed even if the mutex was posted and tasks of higher priority are waiting for the mutex.
	Use this option if the task calling **OSMutexPost()** will be doing additional posts, if the user does not want to reschedule until all is complete, and multiple posts should take effect simultaneously.

p_err   is a pointer to a variable that is used to hold an error code:

OS_ERR_NONE	if the call is successful and the mutex is available.
OS_ERR_MUTEX_NESTING	if the owner of the mutex has the mutex nested and it has not fully un-nested.
OS_ERR_MUTEX_NOT_OWNER	if the caller is not the owner of the mutex and therefore is not allowed to release it.
OS_ERR_OBJ_PTR_NULL	if OS_CFG_ARG_CHK_EN is set to 1 in os_cfg.h: if p_mutex is a NULL pointer.
OS_ERR_OBJ_TYPE	if OS_CFG_OBJ_TYPE_CHK_EN is set to 1 in os_cfg.h: if not passing a pointer to a mutex.
OS_ERR_POST_ISR	if OS_CFG_CALLED_FROM_ISR_CHK_EN set to 1 in os_cfg.h: if attempting to post the mutex from an ISR.

RETURNED VALUE

None

NOTES/WARNINGS

- Mutexes must be created before they are used.

- Do not call this function from an ISR.

EXAMPLE

```
OS_MUTEX  DispMutex;


void  TaskX (void *p_arg)
{
    OS_ERR  err;


    (void)&p_arg;
    while (DEF_ON) {
        :
        OSMutexPost(&DispMutex,
                    OS_OPT_POST_NONE,
                    &err);
        /* Check "err" */
        :
    }
}
```

A-33 OSPendMulti()

```
OS_OBJ_QTY  OSPendMulti(OS_PEND_DATA  *p_pend_data_tbl,
                        OS_OBJ_QTY     tbl_size,
                        OS_TICK        timeout,
                        OS_OPT         opt,
                        OS_ERR         *p_err);
```

File	Called from	Code enabled by
os_pend_multi.c	Task only	OS_CFG_PEND_MULTI_EN && (OS_CFG_Q_EN || OS_CFG_SEM_EN)

OSPendMulti() is used when a task expects to wait on multiple kernel objects, specifically semaphores or message queues. If more than one such object is ready when OSPendMulti() is called, then all available objects and messages, if any, are returned as ready to the caller. If no objects are ready, OSPendMulti() suspends the current task until either:

■ an object becomes ready,

■ a timeout occurs,

■ one or more of the tasks are deleted or pend aborted or,

■ one or more of the objects are deleted.

If an object becomes ready, and multiple tasks are waiting for the object, μC/OS-III resumes the highest-priority task waiting on that object.

A pended task suspended with OSTaskSuspend() can still receive a message from a multi-pended message queue, or obtain a signal from a multi-pended semaphore. However, the task remains suspended until it is resumed by calling OSTaskResume().

ARGUMENTS

p_pend_data_tbl   is a pointer to an **OS_PEND_DATA** table. This table will be used by the caller to understand the outcome of this call. Also, the caller *must* initialize the **.PendObjPtr** field of the **OS_PEND_DATA** field for each object that the caller wants to pend on (see example below).

tbl_size is the number of entries in the **OS_PEND_DATA** table pointed to by **p_pend_data_tbl**. This value indicates how many objects the task will be pending on.

timeout specifies the amount of time (in clock ticks) that the calling task is willing to wait for objects to be posted. A timeout value of 0 indicates that the task wants to wait forever for any of the multi-pended objects. The timeout value is not synchronized with the clock tick. The timeout count begins decrementing on the next clock tick, which could potentially occur immediately.

opt specifies options:

    OS_OPT_PEND_BLOCKING if the caller desired to wait until any of the objects is posted to, a timeout, the pend is aborted or an object is deleted.

    OS_OPT_PEND_NON_BLOCKING if the caller is not willing to wait if none of the objects have not already been posted.

p_err is a pointer to a variable that holds an error code:

    OS_ERR_NONE if any of the multi-pended objects are ready.

    OS_ERR_OBJ_TYPE if **OS_CFG_OBJ_TYPE_CHK_EN** is set to 1 in **os_cfg.h**: if any of the **.PendObjPtr** in the **p_pend_data_tbl** is a **NULL** pointer (i.e. is not a semaphore or not a message queue).

    OS_ERR_OPT_INVALID if **OS_CFG_ARG_CHK_EN** is set to 1 in **os_cfg.h**: if specifying an invalid option.

    OS_ERR_PEND_ABORT indicates that a multi-pended object was aborted; check the **.RdyObjPtr** of the **p_pend_data_tbl** to know which object was aborted. The first non-**NULL** **.RdyObjPtr** is the object that was aborted.

    OS_ERR_PEND_DEL indicates that a multi-pended object was deleted; check the **.RdyObjPtr** of the **p_pend_data_tbl** to know which object was deleted. The first non-**NULL** **.RdyObjPtr** is the object that was deleted.

OS_ERR_PEND_ISR	if OS_CFG_CALLED_FROM_ISR_CHK_EN set to 1 in **os_cfg.h**: if calling this function from an ISR.
OS_ERR_PEND_LOCKED	if calling this function when the scheduler is locked.
OS_ERR_PEND_WOULD_BLOCK	if the caller does not want to block and no object is ready and **opt** was OS_OPT_PEND_NON_BLOCKING.
OS_ERR_PTR_INVALID	if OS_CFG_ARG_CHK_EN is set to 1 in **os_cfg.h**: if **p_pend_data_tbl** is a **NULL** pointer.
OS_ERR_TIMEOUT	if no multi-pended object is ready within the specified timeout.

RETURNED VALUE

OSPendMulti() returns the number of multi-pended objects that are ready. If an object is pend aborted or deleted, the return value will be 1. You should examine the value of ***p_err** to know the exact outcome of this call. If no multi-pended object is ready within the specified timeout period, or because of any error, the **.RdyObjPtr** in the **p_pend_data_tbl** array will all be **NULL**.

When objects are posted, the **OS_PEND_DATA** fields of **p_pend_data_tbl** contains additional information about the posted objects:

.RdyObjPtr	Contains a pointer to the object ready or posted to, or **NULL** pointer if the object was not ready or posted to.
.RdyMsgPtr	If the object pended on was a message queue and the queue was posted to, this field contains the message.
.RdyMsgSize	If the object pended on was a message queue and the queue was posted to, this field contains the size of the message (in number of bytes).

.RdyTS   If the object pended on was posted to, this field contains the timestamp as to when the object was posted. Note that if the object is deleted or pend-aborted, this field contains the timestamp of when this occurred.

NOTES/WARNINGS

■ Message queue or semaphore objects must be created before they are used.

■ You cannot call **OSPendMulti()** from an ISR.

■ The user cannot multi-pend on event flags and mutexes.

EXAMPLE

```
OS_SEM   Sem1;
OS_SEM   Sem2;
OS_Q     Q1;
OS_Q     Q2;


void Task(void *p_arg)
{
    OS_PEND_DATA   pend_data_tbl[4];
    OS_ERR         err;
    OS_OBJ_QTY     nbr_rdy;


    (void)&p_arg;
    while (DEF_ON) {
        :
        pend_data_tbl[0].PendObjPtr = (OS_PEND_OBJ *)Sem1;
        pend_data_tbl[1].PendObjPtr = (OS_PEND_OBJ *)Sem2;
        pend_data_tbl[2].PendObjPtr = (OS_PEND_OBJ *)Q1;
        pend_data_tbl[3].PendObjPtr = (OS_PEND_OBJ *)Q2;
        nbr_rdy = OSPendMulti(&pend_data_tbl[0],
                              4,
                              0,
                              OS_OPT_PEND_BLOCKING,
                              &err);
        /* Check "err" */
        :
        :
    }
}
```

A-34 OSQCreate()

```
void  OSQCreate (OS_Q        *p_q,
                 CPU_CHAR     *p_name,
                 OS_MSG_QTY   max_qty,
                 OS_ERR       *p_err)
```

File	Called from	Code enabled by
os_q.c	Task or startup code	OS_CFG_Q_EN and OS_CFG_MSG_EN

OSQCreate() creates a message queue. A message queue allows tasks or ISRs to send pointer-sized variables (messages) to one or more tasks. The meaning of the messages sent are application specific.

ARGUMENTS

p_q   is a pointer to the message queue control block. It is assumed that storage for the message queue will be allocated in the application. The user will need to declare a "global" variable as follows, and pass a pointer to this variable to OSQCreate():

        OS_Q MyMsgQ;

p_name   is a pointer to an ASCII string used to name the message queue. The name can be displayed by debuggers or µC/Probe.

msg_qty   indicates the maximum size of the message queue (must be non-zero). If the user intends to not limit the size of the queue, simply pass a very large number. Of course, if there are not enough OS_MSGs in the pool of OS_MSGs, the post call (i.e., OSQPost()) will simply fail and an error code will indicate that there are no more OS_MSGs to use.

___

p_err   is a pointer to a variable that is used to hold an error code:

OS_ERR_NONE	if the call is successful and the mutex has been created.
OS_ERR_CREATE_ISR	if **OS_CFG_CALLED_FROM_ISR_CHK_EN** set to 1 in **os_cfg.h**: if attempting to create the message queue from an ISR.
OS_ERR_OBJ_PTR_NULL	if **OS_CFG_ARG_CHK_EN** is set to 1 in **os_cfg.h**: if **p_q** is a **NULL** pointer.
OS_ERR_Q_SIZE	if **OS_CFG_ARG_CHK_EN** is set to 1 in **os_cfg.h**: if the size specified is 0.
OS_ERR_ILLEGAL_CREATE_RUN_TIME	if **OS_SAFETY_CRITICAL_IEC61508** is defined: you called this after calling **OSSafetyCriticalStart()** and thus you are no longer allowed to create additional kernel objects.

RETURNED VALUE

None

NOTES/WARNINGS

Queues must be created before they are used.

EXAMPLE

```
OS_Q    CommQ;


void main (void)
{
    OS_ERR    err;


    OSInit(&err);                    /* Initialize µC/OS-III  */
    :
    :
    OSQCreate(&CommQ,
            "Comm Queue",
            10,
            &err);                   /* Create COMM Q          */
    /* Check "err" */
    :
    :
    OSStart();                       /* Start Multitasking    */
}
```

A-35 OSQDel()

```
OS_OBJ_QTY  OSQDel (OS_Q     *p_q,
                    OS_OPT    opt,
                    OS_ERR    *p_err)
```

File	Called from	Code enabled by
os_q.c	Task only	OS_CFG_Q_EN and OS_CFG_Q_DEL_EN

OSQDel() is used to delete a message queue. This function should be used with care since multiple tasks may rely on the presence of the message queue. Generally speaking, before deleting a message queue, first delete all the tasks that can access the message queue. However, it is highly recommended that you do not delete kernel objects at run time.

ARGUMENTS

p_q   is a pointer to the message queue to delete.

opt   specifies whether to delete the queue only if there are no pending tasks (OS_OPT_DEL_NO_PEND), or always delete the queue regardless of whether tasks are pending or not (OS_OPT_DEL_ALWAYS). In this case, all pending task are readied.

p_err   is a pointer to a variable that is used to hold an error code. The error code can be one of the following:

OS_ERR_NONE	if the call is successful and the message queue has been deleted.
OS_ERR_DEL_ISR	if OS_CFG_CALLED_FROM_ISR_CHK_EN set to 1 in os_cfg.h: if the user attempts to delete the message queue from an ISR.
OS_ERR_OBJ_PTR_NULL	if OS_CFG_ARG_CHK_EN is set to 1 in os_cfg.h: if passing a NULL pointer for p_q.
OS_ERR_OBJ_TYPE	if OS_CFG_OBJ_TYPE_CHK_EN is set to 1 in os_cfg.h: if p_q is not pointing to a queue.
OS_ERR_OPT_INVALID	if not specifying one of the two options mentioned in the opt argument.

| OS_ERR_TASK_WAITING | if one or more tasks are waiting for messages at the message queue and it is specified to only delete if no task is pending. |

RETURNED VALUE

The number of tasks that were waiting on the message queue and **0** if an error is detected.

NOTES/WARNINGS

- Message queues must be created before they can be used.

- This function must be used with care. Tasks that would normally expect the presence of the queue *must* check the return code of **OSQPend( )**.

EXAMPLE

```
OS_Q  DispQ;


void Task (void *p_arg)
{
    OS_ERR  err;


    (void)&p_arg;
    while (DEF_ON) {
        :
        :
        OSQDel(&DispQ,
               OS_OPT_DEL_ALWAYS,
               &err);
        /* Check "err" */
        :
        :
    }
}
```

A-36 OSQFlush()

```
OS_MSG_QTY  OSQFlush (OS_Q    *p_q,
                      OS_ERR  *p_err)
```

File	Called from	Code enabled by
os_q.c	Task only	OS_CFG_Q_EN and OS_CFG_Q_FLUSH_EN

OSQFlush() empties the contents of the message queue and eliminates all messages sent to the queue. This function takes the same amount of time to execute regardless of whether tasks are waiting on the queue (and thus no messages are present), or the queue contains one or more messages. **OS_MSGs** from the queue are simply returned to the free pool of OS_MSGs.

ARGUMENTS

p_q   is a pointer to the message queue.

p_err   is a pointer to a variable that will contain an error code returned by this function.

OS_ERR_NONE	if the message queue is flushed.
OS_ERR_FLUSH_ISR	if OS_CFG_CALLED_FROM_ISR_CHK_EN set to 1 in os_cfg.h: if calling this function from an ISR
OS_ERR_OBJ_PTR_NULL	if OS_CFG_ARG_CHK_EN is set to 1 in os_cfg.h: if p_q is a **NULL** pointer.
OS_ERR_OBJ_TYPE	if OS_CFG_OBJ_TYPE_CHK_EN is set to 1 in os_cfg.h: if you attempt to flush an object other than a message queue.

RETURNED VALUE

The number of **OS_MSG** entries freed from the message queue. Note that the **OS_MSG** entries are returned to the free pool of **OS_MSGs**.

NOTES/WARNINGS

■ Queues must be created before they are used.

■ Use this function with great care. When flushing a queue, you lose the references to what the queue entries are pointing to, potentially causing 'memory leaks'. The data that the user is pointing to that is referenced by the queue entries should, most likely, be de-allocated (i.e., freed).

EXAMPLE

```
OS_Q   CommQ;


void Task (void *p_arg)
{
    OS_ERR   err;


    (void)&p_arg;
    while (DEF_ON) {
        :
        :
        entries = OSQFlush(&CommQ,
                           &err);
        /* Check "err" */
        :
        :
    }
}
```

or, to flush a queue that contains entries, instead you can use OSQPend( ) and specify the OS_OPT_PEND_NON_BLOCKING option.

```
OS_Q  CommQ;


void Task (void *p_arg)
{
    OS_ERR      err;
    CPU_TS      ts;
    OS_MSG_SIZE msg_size;


    (void)&p_arg;
    :
    do {
        OSQPend(&CommQ,
                0,
                OS_OPT_PEND_NON_BLOCKING,
                &msg_size,
                &ts,
                &err);
    } while (err != OS_ERR_PEND_WOULD_BLOCK);
    :
    :
}
```

A-37 OSQPend()

```
void  *OSQPend (OS_Q          *p_q,
               OS_TICK         timeout,
               OS_OPT          opt,
               OS_MSG_SIZE    *p_msg_size,
               CPU_TS         *p_ts,
               OS_ERR         *p_err)
```

File	Called from	Code enabled by
os_q.c	Task only	OS_CFG_Q_EN and OS_CFG_MSG_EN

OSQPend() is used when a task wants to receive messages from a message queue. The messages are sent to the task via the message queue either by an ISR, or by another task using the OSQPost() call. The messages received are pointer-sized variables, and their use is application specific. If at least one message is already present in the message queue when OSQPend() is called, the message is retrieved and returned to the caller.

If no message is present in the message queue and OS_OPT_PEND_BLOCKING is specified for the opt argument, OSQPend() suspends the current task until either a message is received, or a user-specified timeout expires. If a message is sent to the message queue and multiple tasks are waiting for such a message, µC/OS-III resumes the highest priority task that is waiting.

A pended task suspended with OSTaskSuspend() can receive a message. However, the task remains suspended until it is resumed by calling OSTaskResume().

If no message is present in the queue and OS_OPT_PEND_NON_BLOCKING is specifed for the opt argument, OSQPend() returns to the caller with an appropriate error code, and returns a NULL pointer.

ARGUMENTS

p_q   is a pointer to the queue from which the messages are received.

timeout   allows the task to resume execution if a message is not received from the message queue within the specified number of clock ticks. A **timeout** value of 0 indicates that the task is willing to wait forever for a message. The timeout value is not synchronized with the clock tick. The timeout count starts decrementing on the next clock tick, which could potentially occur immediately.

opt   determines whether or not to block if a message is not available in the queue. This argument must be set to either:

OS_OPT_PEND_BLOCKING, or

OS_OPT_PEND_NON_BLOCKING

Note that the **timeout** argument should be set to **0** when specifying OS_OPT_PEND_NON_BLOCKING, since the timeout value is irrelevant using this option.

p_msg_size is a pointer to a variable that will receive the size of the message (in number of bytes).

p_ts   is a pointer to a variable that will receive the timestamp of when the message was received. Passing a **NULL** pointer is valid, and indicates that the user does not need the timestamp.

A timestamp is useful when the user wants the task to know when the message queue was posted, or how long it took for the task to resume after the message queue was posted. In the latter case, you would call **OS_TS_GET()** and compute the difference between the current value of the timestamp and ***p_ts**. In other words:

delta = OS_TS_GET() - *p_ts;

p_err	is a pointer to a variable used to hold an error code.	
	OS_ERR_NONE	if a message is received.
	OS_ERR_OBJ_PTR_NULL	if OS_CFG_ARG_CHK_EN is set to 1 in os_cfg.h: if p_q is a NULL pointer.
	OS_ERR_OBJ_TYPE	if OS_CFG_OBJ_TYPE_CHK_EN is set to 1 in os_cfg.h: if p_q is not pointing to a message queue.
	OS_ERR_OPT_INVALID	if OS_CFG_ARG_CHK_EN is set to 1 in os_cfg.h: if you specified invalid options.
	OS_ERR_PEND_ABORT	if the pend was aborted because another task called OSQPendAbort().
	OS_ERR_PEND_ISR	if OS_CFG_CALLED_FROM_ISR_CHK_EN set to 1 in os_cfg.h: if the function is called from an ISR.
	OS_ERR_PEND_WOULD_BLOCK	if this function is called with the opt argument set to OS_OPT_PEND_NON_BLOCKING, and no message is in the queue.
	OS_ERR_PTR_INVALID	if OS_CFG_ARG_CHK_EN is set to 1 in os_cfg.h: if p_msg_size is a NULL pointer.
	OS_ERR_SCHED_LOCKED	if calling this function when the scheduler is locked.
	OS_ERR_TIMEOUT	if a message is not received within the specified timeout.

RETURNED VALUE

The message (i.e., a pointer) or a NULL pointer if no messages has been received. Note that it is possible for the actual message to be a NULL pointer, so you should check the returned error code instead of relying on the returned value.

NOTES/WARNINGS

- Queues must be created before they are used.

- The user cannot call OSQPend() from an ISR.

EXAMPLE

```
OS_Q   CommQ;


void CommTask (void *p_arg)
{
    OS_ERR      err;
    void        *p_msg;
    OS_MSG_SIZE msg_size;
    CPU_TS      ts;


    (void)&p_arg;
    while (DEF_ON) {
        :
        :
        p_msg = OSQPend(CommQ,
                        100,
                        OS_OPT_PEND_BLOCKING,
                        &msg_size,
                        &ts,
                        &err);
        /* Check "err" */
        :
        :
    }
}
```

A-38 OSQPendAbort()

```
OS_OBJ_QTY   OSQPendAbort (OS_Q    *p_q,
                           OS_OPT   opt,
                           OS_ERR  *p_err)
```

File	Called from	Code enabled by
os_q.c	Task only	OS_CFG_Q_EN and OS_CFG_Q_PEND_ABORT_EN

OSQPendAbort() aborts and readies any tasks currently waiting on a message queue. This function should be used to fault-abort the wait on the message queue, rather than to signal the message queue via OSQPost().

ARGUMENTS

p_q   is a pointer to the queue for which pend(s) need to be aborted.

opt   determines the type of abort to be performed.

OS_OPT_PEND_ABORT_1	Aborts the pend of only the highest-priority task waiting on the message queue.
OS_OPT_PEND_ABORT_ALL	Aborts the pend of all tasks waiting on the message queue.
OS_OPT_POST_NO_SCHED	specifies that the scheduler should not be called, even if the pend of a higher-priority task has been aborted. Scheduling will need to occur from another function.
	You would use this option if the task calling OSQPendAbort() is doing additional pend aborts, rescheduling is not performed until completion, and multiple pend aborts are to take effect simultaneously.

p_err   is a pointer to a variable that holds an error code:

OS_ERR_NONE	at least one task waiting on the message queue was readied and informed of the aborted wait. Check the return value for the number of tasks whose wait on the message queue was aborted.
OS_ERR_PEND_ABORT_ISR	if OS_CFG_CALLED_FROM_ISR_CHK_EN set to 1 in os_cfg.h: if called from an ISR
OS_ERR_PEND_ABORT_NONE	if no task was pending on the message queue
OS_ERR_OBJ_PTR_NULL	if OS_CFG_ARG_CHK_EN is set to 1 in os_cfg.h: if p_q is a NULL pointer.
OS_ERR_OBJ_TYPE	if OS_CFG_OBJ_TYPE_CHK_EN is set to 1 in os_cfg.h: if p_q is not pointing to a message queue.
OS_ERR_OPT_INVALID	if OS_CFG_ARG_CHK_EN is set to 1 in os_cfg.h: if an invalid option is specified.

RETURNED VALUE

OSQPendAbort() returns the number of tasks made ready-to-run by this function. Zero indicates that no tasks were pending on the message queue, therefore this function had no effect.

NOTES/WARNINGS

Queues must be created before they are used.

EXAMPLE

```
OS_Q   CommQ;


void CommTask(void *p_arg)
{
    OS_ERR      err;
    OS_OBJ_QTY  nbr_tasks;


    (void)&p_arg;
    while (DEF_ON) {
        :
        :
        nbr_tasks = OSQPendAbort(&CommQ,
                                 OS_OPT_PEND_ABORT_ALL,
                                 &err);
        /* Check "err" */
        :
        :
    }
}
```

A-39 OSQPost()

```
void  OSQPost (OS_Q        *p_q,
               void         *p_void,
               OS_MSG_SIZE  msg_size,
               OS_OPT       opt,
               OS_ERR       *p_err)
```

File	Called from	Code enabled by
os_q.c	Task or ISR	OS_CFG_Q_EN

OSQPost() sends a message to a task through a message queue. A message is a pointer-sized variable, and its use is application specific. If the message queue is full, an error code is returned to the caller. In this case, OSQPost() immediately returns to its caller, and the message is not placed in the message queue.

If any task is waiting for a message to be posted to the message queue, the highest-priority task receives the message. If the task waiting for the message has a higher priority than the task sending the message, the higher-priority task resumes, and the task sending the message is suspended; that is, a context switch occurs. Message queues can be first-in first-out (OS_OPT_POST_FIFO), or last-in-first-out (OS_OPT_POST_LIFO) depending of the value specified in the **opt** argument.

If any task is waiting for a message at the message queue, OSQPost() allows the user to either post the message to the highest-priority task waiting at the queue (**opt** set to OS_OPT_POST_FIFO or OS_OPT_POST_LIFO), or to all tasks waiting at the message queue (**opt** is set to OS_OPT_POST_ALL). In either case, scheduling occurs unless **opt** is also set to OS_OPT_POST_NO_SCHED.

ARGUMENTS

p_q   is a pointer to the message queue being posted to.

p_void   is the actual message posted. **p_void** is a pointer-sized variable. Its meaning is application specific.

msg_size specifies the size of the message (in number of bytes).

opt   determines the type of POST performed. The last two options may be added to either **OS_OPT_POST_FIFO** or **OS_OPT_POST_LIFO** to create different combinations:

OS_OPT_POST_FIFO	POST message to the end of the queue (FIFO), or send message to a single waiting task.
OS_OPT_POST_LIFO	POST message to the front of the queue (LIFO), or send message to a single waiting task
OS_OPT_POST_ALL	POST message to ALL tasks that are waiting on the queue. This option can be added to either **OS_OPT_POST_FIFO** or **OS_OPT_POST_LIFO**.
OS_OPT_POST_NO_SCHED	This option specifies to not call the scheduler after the post and therefore the caller is resumed, even if the message was posted to a message queue with tasks having a higher priority than the caller. You would use this option if the task (or ISR) calling **OSQPost()** will do additional posts, in this case, the caller does not want to reschedule until finished, and, multiple posts are to take effect simultaneously.

p_err   is a pointer to a variable that will contain an error code returned by this function.

OS_ERR_NONE	if no tasks were waiting on the queue. In this case, the return value is also 0.
OS_ERR_MSG_POOL_EMPTY	if there are no more **OS_MSG** structures to use to store the message.
OS_ERR_OBJ_PTR_NULL	if **OS_CFG_ARG_CHK_EN** is set to 1 in **os_cfg.h**: if **p_q** is a **NULL** pointer.
OS_ERR_OBJ_TYPE	if **OS_CFG_OBJ_TYPE_CHK_EN** is set to 1 in **os_cfg.h**: if **p_q** is not pointing to a message queue.
OS_ERR_Q_MAX	if the queue is full and therefore cannot accept more messages.

RETURNED VALUE

None

NOTES/WARNINGS

■ Queues must be created before they are used.

■ Possible combinations of options are:

```
OS_OPT_POST_FIFO
OS_OPT_POST_LIFO
OS_OPT_POST_FIFO + OS_OPT_POST_ALL
OS_OPT_POST_LIFO + OS_OPT_POST_ALL
OS_OPT_POST_FIFO + OS_OPT_POST_NO_SCHED
OS_OPT_POST_LIFO + OS_OPT_POST_NO_SCHED
OS_OPT_POST_FIFO + OS_OPT_POST_ALL + OS_OPT_POST_NO_SCHED
OS_OPT_POST_LIFO + OS_OPT_POST_ALL + OS_OPT_POST_NO_SCHED
```

■ Although the example below shows calling **OSQPost()** from a task, it can also be called from an ISR.

EXAMPLE

```
OS_Q        CommQ;
CPU_INT08U  CommRxBuf[100];


void CommTaskRx (void *p_arg)
{
    OS_ERR  err;


    (void)&p_arg;
    while (DEF_ON) {
        :
        :
        OSQPost(&CommQ,
                &CommRxBuf[0],
                sizeof(CommRxBuf),
                OS_OPT_POST_OPT_FIFO + OS_OPT_POST_ALL + OS_OPT_POST_NO_SCHED,
                &err);
        /* Check "err" */
        :
        :
    }
}
```

A-40 OSSafetyCriticalStart()

void OSSafetyCriticalStart (void)

File	Called from	Code enabled by
os_core.c	Task only	OS_SAFETY_CRITICAL_IEC61508

OSSafetyCriticalStart() allows your code to notify µC/OS-III that you are done initializing and creating kernel objects. After calling **OSSafetyCriticalStart()**, your application code will no longer be allowed to create kernel objects. In other words, once your code has called OSSafetyCriticalStart(), you will not be allowed to create tasks, semaphores, mutexes, message queues, event flags and timers.

ARGUMENTS

None

RETURNED VALUE

None

NOTES/WARNINGS

None

EXAMPLE

```
void AppStartTask (void *p_arg)
{
    (void)&p_arg;
    /* Create tasks and other kernel objects                          */
    OSSafetyCriticalStart();
    /* Your code is no longer allowed to create any additional kernel objects */
    while (DEF_ON) {
        :
        :
    }
}
```

A-41 OSSched()

```
void OSSched (void)
```

File	Called from	Code enabled by
os_core.c	Task only	N/A

OSSched() allows a task to call the scheduler. You would use this function after doing a series of "posts" where you specified OS_OPT_POST_NO_SCHED as a post option.

OSSched() can only be called by task-level code. Also, if the scheduler is locked (i.e., OSSchedLock() was previously called), then OSSched() will have no effect.

If a higher-priority task than the calling task is ready-to-run, OSSched() will context switch to that task.

ARGUMENTS

None

RETURNED VALUE

None

NOTES/WARNINGS

None

EXAMPLE

```
void TaskX (void *p_arg)
{
    (void)&p_arg;
    while (DEF_ON) {
        :
        OS??Post(…);           /* Posts with OS_OPT_POST_NO_SCHED option        */
        /* Check "err" */
        OS??Post(…);
        /* Check "err" */
        OS??Post(…);
        /* Check "err" */
        :
        OSSched();             /* Run the scheduler                             */
        :
    }
}
```

A-42 OSSchedLock()

```
void OSSchedLock (OS_ERR   *p_err)
```

File	Called from	Code enabled by
os_core.c	Task only	N/A

OSSchedLock() prevents task rescheduling until its counterpart, OSSchedUnlock(), is called. The task that calls OSSchedLock() retains control of the CPU, even though other higher-priority tasks are ready-to-run. However, interrupts are still recognized and serviced (assuming interrupts are enabled). OSSchedLock() and OSSchedUnlock() must be used in pairs.

µC/OS-III allows OSSchedLock() to be nested up to 250 levels deep. Scheduling is enabled when an equal number of OSSchedUnlock() calls have been made.

ARGUMENTS

p_err   is a pointer to a variable that will contain an error code returned by this function.

OS_ERR_NONE	the scheduler is locked.
OS_ERR_LOCK_NESTING_OVF	if the user called this function too many times.
OS_ERR_OS_NOT_RUNNING	if the function is called before calling OSStart().
OS_ERR_SCHED_LOCK_ISR	if OS_CFG_CALLED_FROM_ISR_CHK_EN set to 1 in os_cfg.h: if you attempted to call OSSchedLock() from an ISR.

RETURNED VALUE

None

NOTES/WARNINGS

After calling **OSSchedLock( )**, the application must not make system calls that suspend execution of the current task; that is, the application cannot call **OSTimeDly( )**, **OSTimeDlyHMSM( )**, **OSFlagPend( )**, **OSSemPend( )**, **OSMutexPend( )**, or **OSQPend( )**. Since the scheduler is locked out, no other task is allowed to run, and the system will lock up.

EXAMPLE

```c
void TaskX (void *p_arg)
{
    OS_ERR   err;


    (void)&p_arg;
    while (DEF_ON) {
        :
        OSSchedLock(&err);      /* Prevent other tasks to run            */
        /* Check "err" */
        :                       /* Code protected from context switch */
        OSSchedUnlock(&err);    /* Enable other tasks to run             */
        /* Check "err" */
        :
    }
}
```

A-43 OSSchedRoundRobinCfg()

```
void  OSSchedRoundRobinCfg (CPU_BOOLEAN  en,
                            OS_TICK      dflt_time_quanta,
                            OS_ERR       *p_err)
```

File	Called from	Code enabled by
os_core.c	Task or startup code	OS_CFG_SCHED_ROUND_ROBIN_EN

OSSchedRoundRobinCfg() is used to enable or disable round-robin scheduling.

ARGUMENTS

en   when set to **DEF_ENABLED** enables round-robin scheduling, and when set to **DEF_DISABLED** disables it.

dflt_time_quanta   is the default time quanta given to a task. This value is used when a task is created and you specify a value of 0 for the time quanta. In other words, if the user did not specify a non-zero for the task's time quanta, this is the value that will be used. If passing 0 for this argument, µC/OS-III will assume a time quanta of 1/10 the tick rate. For example, if the tick rate is 1000 Hz and 0 is passed for **dflt_time_quanta** then, µC/OS-III will set the time quanta to 10 milliseconds.

p_err   is a pointer to a variable that is used to hold an error code:

OS_ERR_NONE   if the call is successful.

RETURNED VALUE

None

NOTES/WARNINGS

None

EXAMPLE

```
void main (void)
{
    OS_ERR   err;


    :
    OSInit(&err);                   /* Initialize µC/OS-III          */
    :
    :
    OSSchedRoundRobinCfg(DEF_ENABLED,
                         10,
                         &err);
    /* Check "err" */
    :
    :
    OSStart(&err);                  /* Start Multitasking            */
}
```

A-44 OSSchedRoundRobinYield()

void OSSchedRoundRobinYield (OS_ERR *p_err);

File	Called from	Code enabled by
os_core.c	Task only	OS_CFG_SCHED_ROUND_ROBIN_EN

OSSchedRoundRobinYield() is used to voluntarily give up a task's time slot, assuming that there are other tasks running at the same priority.

ARGUMENTS

p_err   is a pointer to a variable used to hold an error code:

OS_ERR_NONE   if the call was successful.

OS_ERR_ROUND_ROBIN_1   if there is only one task at the current priority level that is ready-to-run.

OS_ERR_ROUND_ROBIN_DISABLED   if round-robin scheduling has not been enabled. See OSSchedRoundRobinCfg() to enable or disable.

OS_ERR_SCHED_LOCKED   if the scheduler is locked and μC/OS-III cannot switch tasks.

OS_ERR_YIELD_ISR   if OS_CFG_CALLED_FROM_ISR_CHK_EN set to 1 in os_cfg.h: if calling this function from an ISR.

RETURNED VALUE

None

NOTES/WARNINGS

None

EXAMPLE

```
void Task (void *p_arg)
{
    OS_ERR  err;


    (void)&p_arg;
    while (DEF_ON) {
        :
        :
        OSSchedRoundRobinYield(&err); /* Give up the CPU to the next task at same priority */
        /* Check "err" */
        :
        :
    }
}
```

A-45 OSSchedUnlock()

```
void OSSchedUnlock(OS_ERR  *p_err);
```

File	Called from	Code enabled by
os_core.c	Task only	N/A

OSSchedUnlock() re-enables task scheduling whenever it is paired with OSSchedLock().

ARGUMENTS

p_err   is a pointer to a variable that will contain an error code returned by this function.

OS_ERR_NONE	the call is successful and the scheduler is no longer locked.
OS_ERR_OS_NOT_RUNNING	if calling this function before calling OSStart().
OS_ERR_SCHED_LOCKED	if the scheduler is still locked. This would indicate that scheduler lock has not fully unnested
OS_ERR_SCHED_NOT_LOCKED	if the user did not call OSSchedLock().
OS_ERR_SCHED_UNLOCK_ISR	if OS_CFG_CALLED_FROM_ISR_CHK_EN set to 1 in os_cfg.h: if you attempted to unlock scheduler from an ISR.

RETURNED VALUE

None

NOTES/WARNINGS

None

EXAMPLE

```
void TaskX (void *p_arg)
{
    OS_ERR  err;


    (void)&p_arg;
    while (DEF_ON) {
        :
        OSSchedLock(&err);      /* Prevent other tasks to run      */
        /* Check "err" */
        :                       /* Code protected from context switch */
        OSSchedUnlock(&err);    /* Enable other tasks to run       */
        /* Check "err" */
        :
    }
}
```

A-46 OSSemCreate()

```
void   OSSemCreate (OS_SEM      *p_sem,
                    CPU_CHAR    *p_name,
                    OS_SEM_CTR  cnt,
                    OS_ERR      *p_err)
```

File	Called from	Code enabled by
os_sem.c	Task or startup code	OS_CFG_SEM_EN

OSSemCreate() initializes a semaphore. Semaphores are used when a task wants exclusive access to a resource, needs to synchronize its activities with an ISR or a task, or is waiting until an event occurs. You would use a semaphore to signal the occurrence of an event to one or multiple tasks, and use mutexes to guard share resources. However, technically, semaphores allow for both.

ARGUMENTS

p_sem   is a pointer to the semaphore control block. It is assumed that storage for the semaphore will be allocated in the application. In other words, you need to declare a "global" variable as follows, and pass a pointer to this variable to OSSemCreate():

OS_SEM MySem;

p_name   is a pointer to an ASCII string used to assign a name to the semaphore. The name can be displayed by debuggers or µC/Probe.

cnt   specifies the initial value of the semaphore.

If the semaphore is used for resource sharing, you would set the initial value of the semaphore to the number of identical resources guarded by the semaphore. If there is only one resource, the value should be set to 1 (this is called a binary semaphore). For multiple resources, set the value to the number of resources (this is called a counting semaphore).

If using a semaphore as a signaling mechanism, you should set the initial value to 0.

p_err   is a pointer to a variable used to hold an error code:

OS_ERR_NONE	if the call is successful and the semaphore has been created.
OS_ERR_CREATE_ISR	if OS_CFG_CALLED_FROM_ISR_CHK_EN set to 1 in os_cfg.h: if you attempted to create a semaphore from an ISR.
OS_ERR_OBJ_PTR_NULL	if OS_CFG_ARG_CHK_EN is set to 1 in os_cfg.h: if p_sem is a NULL pointer.
OS_ERR_OBJ_TYPE	if OS_CFG_OBJ_TYPE_CHK_EN is set to 1 in os_cfg.h: if p_sem has been initialized to a different object type.
OS_ERR_ILLEGAL_CREATE_RUN_TIME	if OS_SAFETY_CRITICAL_IEC61508 is defined: you called this after calling OSSafetyCriticalStart() and thus you are no longer allowed to create additional kernel objects.

RETURNED VALUE

None

NOTES/WARNINGS

Semaphores must be created before they are used.

EXAMPLE

```
OS_SEM  SwSem;


void main (void)
{
    OS_ERR  err;


    :
    OSInit(&err);                /* Initialize µC/OS-III        */
    :
    :
    OSSemCreate(&SwSem,          /* Create Switch Semaphore     */
            "Switch Semaphore",
            0,
            &err);
    /* Check "err" */
    :
    :
    OSStart(&err);               /* Start Multitasking          */
}
```

A-47 OSSemDel()

```
void  OSSemDel (OS_SEM  *p_sem,
               OS_OPT   opt,
               OS_ERR   *p_err)
```

File	Called from	Code enabled by
os_sem.c	Task only	OS_CFG_SEM_EN and OS_CFG_SEM_DEL_EN

OSSemDel() is used to delete a semaphore. This function should be used with care as multiple tasks may rely on the presence of the semaphore. Generally speaking, before deleting a semaphore, first delete all the tasks that access the semaphore. As a rule, it is highly recommended to not delete kernel objects at run time.

Deleting the semaphore will not de-allocate the object. In other words, storage for the variable will still remain at the same location unless the semaphore is allocated dynamically from the heap. The dynamic allocation of objects has its own set of problems. Specifically, it is not recommended for embedded systems to allocate (and de-allocate) objects from the heap given the high likelihood of fragmentation.

ARGUMENTS

p_sem   is a pointer to the semaphore.

opt   specifies one of two options: OS_OPT_DEL_NO_PEND or OS_OPT_DEL_ALWAYS.

OS_OPT_DEL_NO_PEND specifies to delete the semaphore only if no task is waiting on the semaphore. Because no task is "currently" waiting on the semaphore does not mean that a task will not attempt to wait for the semaphore later. How would such a task handle the situation waiting for a semaphore that was deleted? The application code will have to deal with this eventuality.

OS_OPT_DEL_ALWAYS specifies deleting the semaphore, regardless of whether tasks are waiting on the semaphore or not. If there are tasks waiting on the semaphore, these tasks will be made ready-to-run and informed (through an appropriate error code) that the reason the task is readied is that the semaphore it was waiting on was deleted. The same reasoning applies with the other option, how will the tasks handle the fact that the semaphore they want to wait for is no longer available?

p_err   is a pointer to a variable used to hold an error code. The error code may be one of the following:

OS_ERR_NONE	if the call is successful and the semaphore has been deleted.
OS_ERR_DEL_ISR	if OS_CFG_CALLED_FROM_ISR_CHK_EN set to 1 in os_cfg.h: if attempting to delete the semaphore from an ISR.
OS_ERR_OBJ_PTR_NULL	if OS_CFG_ARG_CHK_EN is set to 1 in os_cfg.h: if p_sem is a NULL pointer.
OS_ERR_OBJ_TYPE	if OS_CFG_OBJ_TYPE_CHK_EN is set to 1 in os_cfg.h: if p_sem is not pointing to a semaphore.
OS_ERR_OPT_INVALID	if OS_CFG_ARG_CHK_EN is set to 1 in os_cfg.h: if one of the two options mentioned in the opt argument is not specified.
OS_ERR_TASK_WAITING	if one or more tasks are waiting on the semaphore.

RETURNED VALUE

None

NOTES/WARNINGS

Use this call with care because other tasks might expect the presence of the semaphore.

EXAMPLE

```
OS_SEM  SwSem;


void Task (void *p_arg)
{
    OS_ERR  err;


    (void)&p_arg;
    while (DEF_ON) {
        :
        :
        OSSemDel(&SwSem,
                 OS_OPT_DEL_ALWAYS,
                 &err);
        /* Check "err" */
        :
        :
    }
}
```

A-48 OSSemPend()

```
OS_SEM_CTR   OSSemPend (OS_SEM     *p_sem,
                        OS_TICK     timeout,
                        OS_OPT      opt,
                        CPU_TS      *p_ts,
                        OS_ERR      *p_err)
```

File	Called from	Code enabled by
os_sem.c	Task only	OS_CFG_SEM_EN

OSSemPend() is used when a task wants exclusive access to a resource, needs to synchronize its activities with an ISR or task, or is waiting until an event occurs.

When the semaphore is used for resource sharing, if a task calls OSSemPend() and the value of the semaphore is greater than 0, OSSemPend() decrements the semaphore and returns to its caller. However, if the value of the semaphore is 0, OSSemPend() places the calling task in the waiting list for the semaphore. The task waits until the owner of the semaphore (which is always a task in this case) releases the semaphore by calling OSSemPost(), or the specified timeout expires. If the semaphore is signaled before the timeout expires, µC/OS-III resumes the highest-priority task waiting for the semaphore.

When the semaphore is used as a signaling mechanism, the calling task waits until a task or an ISR signals the semaphore by calling OSSemPost(), or the specified timeout expires. If the semaphore is signaled before the timeout expires, µC/OS-III resumes the highest-priority task waiting for the semaphore.

A pended task that has been suspended with OSTaskSuspend() can obtain the semaphore. However, the task remains suspended until it is resumed by calling OSTaskResume().

OSSemPend() also returns if the pend is aborted or, the semaphore is deleted.

ARGUMENTS

p_sem   is a pointer to the semaphore.

---

timeout   allows the task to resume execution if a semaphore is not posted within the specified number of clock ticks. A timeout value of 0 indicates that the task waits forever for the semaphore. The timeout value is not synchronized with the clock tick. The timeout count begins decrementing on the next clock tick, which could potentially occur immediately.

opt   specifies whether the call is to block if the semaphore is not available, or not block.

        OS_OPT_PEND_BLOCKING   to block the caller until the semaphore is available or a timeout occurs.

        OS_OPT_PEND_NON_BLOCKING   if the semaphore is not available, **OSSemPend()** will not block but return to the caller with an appropriate error code.

p_ts   is a pointer to a variable that will receive a timestamp of when the semaphore was posted, pend aborted, or deleted. Passing a **NULL** pointer is valid and indicates that a timestamp is not required.

    A timestamp is useful when the task must know when the semaphore was posted or, how long it took for the task to resume after the semaphore was posted. In the latter case, call **OS_TS_GET()** and compute the difference between the current value of the timestamp and ***p_ts**. In other words:

    delta = OS_TS_GET() - *p_ts;

p_err   is a pointer to a variable used to hold an error code:

        OS_ERR_NONE   if the semaphore is available.

        OS_ERR_OBJ_DEL   if the semaphore was deleted.

        OS_ERR_OBJ_PTR_NULL   if **OS_CFG_ARG_CHK_EN** is set to 1 in **os_cfg.h**: if **p_sem** is a **NULL** pointer.

        OS_ERR_OBJ_TYPE   if **OS_CFG_OBJ_TYPE_CHK_EN** is set to 1 in **os_cfg.h**: if **p_sem** is not pointing to a semaphore.

OS_ERR_OPT_INVALID	if OS_CFG_ARG_CHK_EN is set to 1 in os_cfg.h: if opt is not OS_OPT_PEND_NON_BLOCKING or OS_OPT_PEND_BLOCKING.
OS_ERR_PEND_ABORT	if the pend was aborted
OS_ERR_PEND_ISR	if OS_CFG_CALLED_FROM_ISR_CHK_EN set to 1 in os_cfg.h: if this function is called from an ISR.
OS_ERR_PEND_WOULD_BLOCK	if this function is called as specified OS_OPT_PEND_NON_BLOCKING, and the semaphore was not available.
OS_ERR_SCHED_LOCKED	if calling this function when the scheduler is locked.
OS_ERR_TIMEOUT	if the semaphore is not signaled within the specified timeout.

RETURNED VALUE

The new value of the semaphore count.

NOTES/WARNINGS

Semaphores must be created before they are used.

EXAMPLE

```
OS_SEM   SwSem;


void DispTask (void *p_arg)
{
    OS_ERR   err;
    CPU_TS   ts;


    (void)&p_arg;
    while (DEF_ON) {
        :
        :
        (void)OSSemPend(&SwSem,
                        0,
                        OS_OPT_PEND_BLOCKING,
                        &ts,
                        &err);
        /* Check "err" */
    }
}
```

A-49 OSSemPendAbort()

```
OS_OBJ_QTY  OSSemPendAbort (OS_SEM  *p_sem,
                            OS_OPT   opt,
                            OS_ERR  *p_err)
```

File	Called from	Code enabled by
os_sem.c	Task only	OS_CFG_SEM_EN and OS_CFG_SEM_PEND_ABORT_EN

OSSemPendAbort() aborts and readies any task currently waiting on a semaphore. This function should be used to fault-abort the wait on the semaphore, rather than to normally signal the semaphore via **OSSemPost()**.

ARGUMENTS

p_sem   is a pointer to the semaphore for which pend(s) need to be aborted.

opt   determines the type of abort performed.

OS_OPT_PEND_ABORT_1	Aborts the pend of only the highest-priority task waiting on the semaphore.
OS_OPT_PEND_ABORT_ALL	Aborts the pend of all the tasks waiting on the semaphore.
OS_OPT_POST_NO_SCHED	Specifies that the scheduler should not be called, even if the pend of a higher-priority task has been aborted. Scheduling will need to occur from another function.
	You would use this option if the task calling **OSSemPendAbort()** will be doing additional pend aborts, reschedule takes place when finished, and multiple pend aborts are to take effect simultaneously.

p_err   Is a pointer to a variable that holds an error code:

OS_ERR_NONE	At least one task waiting on the semaphore was readied and informed of the aborted wait. Check the return value for the number of tasks whose wait on the semaphore was aborted.
OS_ERR_OBJ_PTR_NULL	if OS_CFG_ARG_CHK_EN is set to 1 in os_cfg.h: if p_sem is a NULL pointer.
OS_ERR_OBJ_TYPE	if OS_CFG_OBJ_TYPE_CHK_EN is set to 1 in os_cfg.h: if p_sem is not pointing to a semaphore.
OS_ERR_OPT_INVALID	if OS_CFG_ARG_CHK_EN is set to 1 in os_cfg.h: if an invalid option is specified.
OS_ERR_PEND_ABORT_ISR	if OS_CFG_CALLED_FROM_ISR_CHK_EN set to 1 in os_cfg.h: if you called this function from an ISR.
OS_ERR_PEND_ABORT_NONE	No task was aborted because no task was waiting.

RETURNED VALUE

OSSemPendAbort() returns the number of tasks made ready-to-run by this function. Zero indicates that no tasks were pending on the semaphore and therefore, the function had no effect.

NOTES/WARNINGS

Semaphores must be created before they are used.

EXAMPLE

```
OS_SEM  SwSem;


void CommTask(void *p_arg)
{
    OS_ERR     err;
    OS_OBJ_QTY  nbr_tasks;


    (void)&p_arg;
    while (DEF_ON) {
        :
        :
        nbr_tasks = OSSemPendAbort(&SwSem,
                                   OS_OPT_PEND_ABORT_ALL,
                                   &err);
        /* Check "err" */
        :
        :
    }
}
```

A-50 OSSemPost()

```
OS_SEM_CTR  OSSemPost (OS_SEM  *p_sem,
                       OS_OPT   opt,
                       OS_ERR  *p_err)
```

File	Called from	Code enabled by
os_sem.c	Task or ISR	OS_CFG_SEM_EN

A semaphore is signaled by calling **OSSemPost()**. If the semaphore value is 0 or more, it is incremented, and **OSSemPost()** returns to its caller. If tasks are waiting for the semaphore to be signaled, **OSSemPost()** removes the highest-priority task pending for the semaphore from the waiting list and makes this task ready-to-run. The scheduler is then called to determine if the awakened task is now the highest-priority task that is ready-to-run.

ARGUMENTS

p_sem   is a pointer to the semaphore.

opt   determines the type of post performed.

OS_OPT_POST_1	Post and ready only the highest-priority task waiting on the semaphore.
OS_OPT_POST_ALL	Post to all tasks waiting on the semaphore. You should only use this option if the semaphore is used as a signaling mechanism and never when the semaphore is used to guard a shared resource. It does not make sense to tell all tasks that are sharing a resource that they can all access the resource.
OS_OPT_POST_NO_SCHED	This option indicates that the caller does not want the scheduler to be called after the post. This option can be used in combination with one of the two previous options.
	You should use this option if the task (or ISR) calling **OSSemPost()** will be doing additional posting and, the user does not want to

reschedule until all done, and multiple posts are to take effect simultaneously.

p_err   is a pointer to a variable that holds an error code:

OS_ERR_NONE   if no tasks are waiting on the semaphore. In this case, the return value is also 0.

OS_ERR_OBJ_PTR_NULL   if OS_CFG_ARG_CHK_EN is set to 1 in os_cfg.h: if p_sem is a NULL pointer.

OS_ERR_OBJ_TYPE   if OS_CFG_OBJ_TYPE_CHK_EN is set to 1 in os_cfg.h: if p_sem is not pointing to a semaphore.

OS_ERR_SEM_OVF   if the post would have caused the semaphore counter to overflow.

RETURNED VALUE

The current value of the semaphore count

NOTES/WARNINGS

■ Semaphores must be created before they are used.

■ You can also post to a semaphore from an ISR but the semaphore must be used as a signaling mechanism and not to protect a shared resource.

EXAMPLE

```
OS_SEM   SwSem;


void TaskX (void *p_arg)
{
    OS_ERR       err;
    OS_SEM_CTR   ctr;


    (void)&p_arg;
    while (DEF_ON) {
        :
        :
        ctr = OSSemPost(&SwSem,
                        OS_OPT_POST_1 + OS_OPT_POST_NO_SCHED,
                        &err);
        /* Check "err" */
        :
        :
    }
}
```

A-51 OSSemSet()

```
void   OSSemSet (OS_SEM       *p_sem,
                 OS_SEM_CTR    cnt,
                 OS_ERR       *p_err)
```

File	Called from	Code enabled by
os_sem.c	Task only	OS_CFG_SEM_EN and OS_CFG_SEM_SET_EN

OSSemSet() is used to change the current value of the semaphore count. This function is normally selected when a semaphore is used as a signaling mechanism. OSSemSet() can then be used to reset the count to any value. If the semaphore count is already 0, the count is only changed if there are no tasks waiting on the semaphore.

ARGUMENTS

p_sem   is a pointer to the semaphore that is used as a signaling mechanism.

cnt   is the desired count that the semaphore should be set to.

p_err   is a pointer to a variable used to hold an error code:

OS_ERR_NONE	if the count was changed or, not changed, because one or more tasks was waiting on the semaphore.
OS_ERR_OBJ_PTR_NULL	if OS_CFG_ARG_CHK_EN is set to 1 in os_cfg.h: if p_sem is a NULL pointer.
OS_ERR_OBJ_TYPE	if OS_CFG_OBJ_TYPE_CHK_EN is set to 1 in os_cfg.h: if p_sem is not pointing to a semaphore.
OS_ERR_SET_ISR	if OS_CFG_CALLED_FROM_ISR_CHK_EN set to 1 in os_cfg.h: if this function was called from an ISR.
OS_ERR_TASK_WAITING	if tasks are waiting on the semaphore.

RETURNED VALUE

None

NOTES/WARNINGS

Do not use this function if the semaphore is used to protect a shared resource.

EXAMPLE

```
OS_SEM   SwSem;


void Task (void *p_arg)
{
    OS_ERR   err;


    (void)&p_arg;
    while (DEF_ON) {
        OSSemSet(&SwSem,       /* Reset the semaphore count */
                 0,
                 &err);
        /* Check "err" */
        :
        :
    }
}
```

A-52 OSStart()

```
void  OSStart (OS_ERR  *p_err)
```

File	Called from	Code enabled by
os_core.c	Startup code only	N/A

OSStart() starts multitasking under µC/OS-III. This function is typically called from startup code after calling OSInit() and creating at least one application task. OSStart() will not return to the caller. Once µC/OS-III is running, calling OSStart() again will have no effect.

ARGUMENTS

p_err   is a pointer to a variable used to hold an error code:

OS_ERR_FATAL_RETURN   if we ever return to this function.

OS_ERR_OS_RUNNING   if the kernel is already running. In other words, if this function has already been called.

RETURNED VALUE

None

NOTES/WARNINGS

OSInit() must be called prior to calling OSStart(). OSStart() should only be called once by the application code. However, if you called OSStart() more than once, nothing happens on the second and subsequent calls.

EXAMPLE

```
void main (void)
{
    OS_ERR  err;

                                    /* User Code          */
    :
    OSInit(&err);                   /* Initialize µC/OS-III */
    /* Check "err" */
    :                               /* User Code          */
    :
    OSStart(&err);                  /* Start Multitasking  */
    /* Any code here should NEVER be executed! */
}
```

A-53 OSStartHighRdy()

void OSStartHighRdy (void)

File	Called from	Code enabled by
os_cpu_a.asm	OSStart()	N/A

OSStartHighRdy() is responsible for starting the highest-priority task that was created prior to calling OSStart(). OSStartHighRdy() is a μC/OS-III port function that is generally written in assembly language.

ARGUMENTS

None

RETURNED VALUES

None

NOTES/WARNINGS

None

EXAMPLE

The pseudocode for OSStartHighRdy() is shown below.

```
OSStartHighRdy:
    OSTaskSwHook();                           (1)
    SP = OSTCBHighRdyPtr->StkPtr;             (2)
    Pop CPU registers off the task's stack;   (3)
    Return from interrupt;                    (4)
```

(1)   OSStartHighRdy() must call OSTaskSwHook().

When called, OSTCBCurPtr and OSTCBHighRdyPtr both point to the OS_TCB of the highest-priority task created.

OSTaskSwHook() should check that OSTCBCurPtr is not equal to OSTCBHighRdyPtr as this is the first time OSTaskSwHook() is called and there is not a task being switched out.

(2)   The CPU stack pointer register is loaded with the top-of-stack (TOS) of the task being started. The TOS is found in the .StkPtr field of the OS_TCB. For convenience, the .StkPtr field is the very first field of the OS_TCB data structure. This makes it easily accessible from assembly language.

(3)   The registers are popped from the task's stack frame. Recall that the registers should have been placed on the stack frame in the same order as if they were pushed at the beginning of an interrupt service routine.

(4)   You must execute a return from interrupt. This starts the task as if it was resumed when returning from a real interrupt.

A-54 OSStatReset()

```
void OSStatReset (OS_ERR *p_err)
```

File	Called from	Code enabled by
os_stat.c	Task only	OS_CFG_STAT_TASK_EN

OSStatReset() is used to reset statistical variables maintained by µC/OS-III. Specifically, the per-task maximum interrupt disable time, maximum scheduler lock time, maximum amount of time a message takes to reach a task queue, the maximum amount of time it takes a signal to reach a task and more.

ARGUMENTS

p_err   is a pointer to a variable used to hold an error code:

OS_ERR_NONE   the call was successful.

OS_ERR_STAT_RESET_ISR   if OS_CFG_CALLED_FROM_ISR_CHK_EN set to 1 in os_cfg.h: if the call was attempted from an ISR.

RETURNED VALUE

None

NOTES/WARNINGS

None

EXAMPLE

```
void TaskX (void *p_arg)
{
    OS_ERR   err;

    (void)&p_arg;
    while (DEF_ON) {
        :
        :
        if (statistics reset switch is pressed) {
            OSStatReset(&err);
            /* Check "err" */
        }
        :
        :
    }
}
```

A-55 OSStatTaskCPUUsageInit()

```
void  OSStatTaskCPUUsageInit (OS_ERR *p_err)
```

File	Called from	Code enabled by
os_stat.c	Startup code only	OS_CFG_TASK_STAT_EN

OSStatTaskCPUUsageInit() determines the maximum value that a 32-bit counter can reach when no other task is executing. This function must be called when only one task is created in the application and when multitasking has started. This function must be called from the first and only task created by the application.

ARGUMENTS

p_err   is a pointer to a variable used to hold an error code:

   OS_ERR_NONE   Always returns this value.

RETURNED VALUE

None

NOTES/WARNINGS

None

EXAMPLE

```
void FirstAndOnlyTask (void *p_arg)
{
    OS_ERR   err;
    :
    :
#if OS_CFG_TASK_STAT_EN > 0
    OSStatTaskCPUUsageInit(&err); /* Compute CPU capacity with no task running */
#endif
    :
    OSTaskCreate(_);                /* Create the other tasks                    */
    OSTaskCreate(_);
    :
    while (DEF_ON) {
        :
        :
    }
}
```

A-56 OSStatTaskHook()

```
void OSStatTaskHook (void);
```

File	Called from	Code enabled by
os_cpu_c.c	OSStatTask()	Always enabled

OSStatTaskHook() is a function called by µC/OS-III's statistic task, OSStatTask(). OSStatTaskHook() is generally implemented by the port implementer for the processor used. This hook allows the port to perform additional statistics.

ARGUMENTS

None

RETURNED VALUES

None

NOTES/WARNINGS

None

EXAMPLE

The code below calls an application-specific hook that an application programmer can define. For this, the user can simply set the value of OS_AppStatTaskHookPtr to point to the desired hook function (see App_OS_SetAllHooks() in os_app_hooks.c).

In the example below, OSStatTaskHook() calls App_OS_StatTaskHook() if the pointer OS_AppStatTaskHookPtr is set to that function.

```
void  App_OS_StatTaskHook (void)                        /* os_app_hooks.c      */
{
    /* Your code goes here! */
}


void App_OS_SetAllHooks (void)                          /* os_app_hooks.c      */
{
    CPU_SR_ALLOC();

    CPU_CRITICAL_ENTER();
    :
    OS_AppStatTaskHookPtr = App_OS_StatTaskHook;
    :
    CPU_CRITICAL_EXIT();
}


void  OSStatTaskHook (void)                             /* os_cpu_c.c          */
{
#if OS_CFG_APP_HOOKS_EN > 0u
    if (OS_AppStatTaskHookPtr != (OS_APP_HOOK_VOID)0) {   /* Call application hook */
        (*OS_AppStatTaskHookPtr)();
    }
#endif
}
```

A-57 OSTaskChangePrio()

```
void  OSTaskChangePrio (OS_TCB    *p_tcb,
                        OS_PRIO   prio_new,
                        OS_ERR    *p_err)
```

File	Called from	Code enabled by
os_task.c	Task only	OS_CFG_TASK_CHANGE_PRIO_EN

When you creating a task (see **OSTaskCreate()**), you specify the priority of the task being created. In most cases, it is not necessary to change the priority of the task at run time. However, it is sometimes useful to do so, and **OSTaskChangePrio()** allows this to take place.

If the task is ready-to-run, **OSTaskChangePrio()** simply changes the position of the task in µC/OS-III's ready list. If the task is waiting on an event, **OSTaskChangePrio()** will change the position of the task in the pend list of the corresponding object, so that the pend list remains sorted by priority.

Because µC/OS-III supports multiple tasks at the same priority, there are no restrictions on the priority that a task can have, except that task priority zero (0) is reserved by µC/OS-III, and priority **OS_PRIO_MAX-1** is used by the idle task.

Note that a task priority cannot be changed from an ISR.

ARGUMENTS

p_tcb   is a pointer to the **OS_TCB** of the task for which the priority is being changed. If you pass a **NULL** pointer, the priority of the current task is changed.

prio_new is the new task's priority. This value must never be set to **OS_CFG_PRIO_MAX-1**, or higher and you must not use priority 0 since they are reserved for µC/OS-III.

p_err   is a pointer to a variable that will receive an error code:

OS_ERR_NONE	if the task's priority is changed.
OS_ERR_TASK_CHANGE_PRIO_ISR	if OS_CFG_CALLED_FROM_ISR_CHK_EN set to 1 in **os_cfg.h**: if attempting to change the task's priority from an ISR.
OS_ERR_PRIO_INVALID	if the priority of the task specified is invalid. By specifying a priority greater than or equal to **OS_PRIO_MAX-1**, or 0.

RETURNED VALUE

None

NOTES/WARNINGS

None

EXAMPLE

```
OS_TCB  MyTaskTCB;


void TaskX (void *p_arg)
{
    OS_ERR  err;


    while (DEF_ON) {
        :
        :
        OSTaskChangePrio(&MyTaskTCB,      /* Change the priority of "MyTask" to 10 */
                         10,
                         &err);
        /* Check "err" */
        :
    }
}
```

A-58 OSTaskCreate()

```
void  OSTaskCreate (OS_TCB          *p_tcb,
                    CPU_CHAR        *p_name,
                    OS_TASK_PTR      p_task,
                    void            *p_arg,
                    OS_PRIO          prio,
                    CPU_STK         *p_stk_base,
                    CPU_STK_SIZE     stk_limit,
                    CPU_STK_SIZE     stk_size,
                    OS_MSG_QTY       q_size,
                    OS_TICK          time_quanta,
                    void            *p_ext,
                    OS_OPT           opt,
                    OS_ERR          *p_err)
```

File	Called from	Code enabled by
os_task.c	Task or startup code	N/A

Tasks must be created in order for µC/OS-III to recognize them as tasks. You create a task by calling **OSTaskCreate()** and by providing arguments specifying to µC/OS-III how the task will be managed. Tasks are always created in the ready-to-run state.

Tasks can be created either prior to the start of multitasking (i.e., before calling **OSStart()**), or by a running task. A task cannot be created by an ISR. A task must either be written as an infinite loop, or delete itself once completed. If the task code returns by mistake, µC/OS-III will terminate the task by calling **OSTaskDel((OS_TCB *)0, &err))**. At Micrium, we like the "**while (DEF_ON)**" to implement infinite loops because, by convention, we use a **while** loop when we don't know how many iterations a loop will do. This is the case of an infinite loop. We prefer to use **for** loops when we know how many iterations a loop will do.

Task as an infinite loop:

```
void MyTask (void *p_arg)
{
    /* Local variables                                      */


    /* Do something with 'p_arg'                            */
    /* Task initialization                                  */
    while (DEF_ON) {      /* Task body, as an infinite loop.  */
        :
        :
        /* Must call one of the following services:          */
        /*     OSFlagPend()                                  */
        /*     OSMutexPend()                                 */
        /*     OSQPend()                                     */
        /*     OSSemPend()                                   */
        /*     OSTimeDly()                                   */
        /*     OSTimeDlyHMSM()                               */
        /*     OSTaskQPend()                                 */
        /*     OSTaskSemPend()                               */
        /*     OSTaskSuspend()      (Suspend self)           */
        /*     OSTaskDel()          (Delete  self)           */
        :
        :
    }
}
```

Run to completion task:

```
void MyTask (void *p_arg)
{
    OS_ERR  err;
    /* Local variables                                      */


    /* Do something with 'p_arg'                            */
    /* Task initialization                                  */
    /* Task body (do some work)                             */
    OSTaskDel((OS_TCB *)0, &err);
    /* Check 'err" ... you code should never end up here!   */
}
```

ARGUMENTS

p_tcb   is a pointer to the task's **OS_TCB** to use. It is assumed that storage for the TCB of the task will be allocated by the user code. You can declare a "global" variable as follows, and pass a pointer to this variable to **OSTaskCreate()**:

             OS_TCB MyTaskTCB;

p_name   is a pointer to an ASCII string (NUL terminated) to assign a name to the task. The name can be displayed by debuggers or by µC/Probe.

p_task   is a pointer to the task (i.e., the name of the function that defines the task).

p_arg   is a pointer to an optional data area which is used to pass parameters to the task when it is created. When µC/OS-III runs the task for the first time, the task will think that it was invoked, and passed the argument **p_arg**. For example, you could create a generic task that handles an asynchronous serial port. **p_arg** can be used to pass task information about the serial port it will manage: the port address, baud rate, number of bits, parity, and more. **p_arg** is the argument received by the task shown below.

```
void MyTask (void *p_arg)
{
    while (DEF_ON) {
        Task code;
    }
}
```

prio   is the task priority. The lower the number, the higher the priority (i.e., the importance) of the task. If **OS_CFG_ISR_POST_DEFERRED_EN** is set to 1, the user cannot use priority **0.**

             Task priority must also have a lower number than **OS_CFG_PRIO_MAX**–Priorities 0, 1, **OS_CFG_PRIO_MAX-2** and **OS_CFG_PRIO_MAX-1** are reserved. In other words, a task should have a priority between **2** and **OOS_CFG_PRIO_MAX-3**, inclusively.

p_stk_base is a pointer to the task's stack base address. The task's stack is used to store local variables, function parameters, return addresses, and possibly CPU registers during an interrupt.

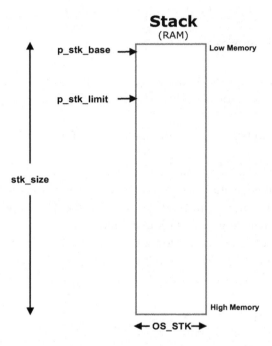

The task stack must be declared as follows:

```
CPU_STK MyTaskStk[???];
```

The user would then pass **p_stk_base** the address of the first element of this array or, **&MyTaskStk[0]**. "???" represents the size of the stack.

The size of this stack is determined by the task's requirements and the anticipated interrupt nesting (unless the processor has a separate stack just for interrupts). Determining the size of the stack involves knowing how many bytes are required for storage of local variables for the task itself, all nested functions, as well as requirements for interrupts (accounting for nesting).

Note that you can allocate stack space for a task from the heap but, in this case, we don't recommend to ever delete the task and free the stack space as this can cause the heap to fragment, which is not desirable in embedded systems.

stk_limit is used to locate, within the task's stack, a watermark limit that can be used to monitor and ensure that the stack does not overflow.

If the processor does not have hardware stack overflow detection, or this feature is not implemented in software by the port developer, this value may be used for other purposes. For example, some processors have two stacks, a hardware and a software stack. The hardware stack typically keeps track of function call nesting and the software stack is used to pass function arguments. **stk_limit** may be used to set the size of the hardware stack as shown below.

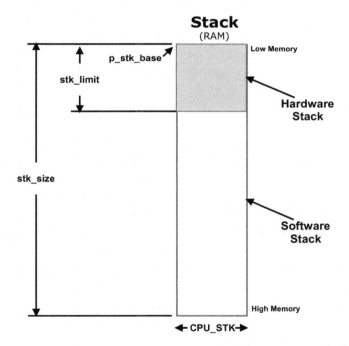

stk_size specifies the size of the task's stack in number of elements. If **CPU_STK** is set to **CPU_INT08U** (see **os_type.h**), **stk_size** corresponds to the number of bytes available on the stack. If **CPU_STK** is set to **CPU_INT16U**, then **stk_size** contains the number of 16-bit entries available on the stack. Finally, if **CPU_STK** is set to **CPU_INT32U**, **stk_size** contains the number of 32-bit entries available on the stack.

q_size   A µC/OS-III task contains an optional internal message queue (if OS_CFG_TASK_Q_EN > 0). This argument specifies the maximum number of messages that the task can receive through this message queue. The user may specify that the task is unable to receive messages by setting this argument to 0.

time_quanta   the amount of time (in clock ticks) for the time quanta when round robin is enabled. If you specify 0, then the default time quanta will be used which is the tick rate divided by 10.

p_ext   is a pointer to a user-supplied memory location (typically a data structure) used as a TCB extension. For example, the user memory can hold the contents of floating-point registers during a context switch.

opt   contains task-specific options. Each option consists of one bit. The option is selected when the bit is set. The current version of µC/OS-III supports the following options:

OS_OPT_TASK_NONE	specifies that there are no options.
OS_OPT_TASK_STK_CHK	specifies whether stack checking is allowed for the task.
OS_OPT_TASK_STK_CLR	specifies whether the stack needs to be cleared.
OS_OPT_TASK_SAVE_FP	specifies whether floating-point registers are saved. This option is only valid if the processor has floating-point hardware and the processor-specific code saves the floating-point registers.

p_err   is a pointer to a variable that will receive an error code:

OS_ERR_NONE	if the function is successful.
OS_ERR_PRIO_INVALID	if OS_CFG_ARG_CHK_EN is set to 1 in os_cfg.h: if prio is higher than the maximum value allowed (i.e., > OS_PRIO_MAX-1). Also, you will get this error if the user set OS_CFG_ISR_POST_DEFERRED_EN to 1 and tried to use priority 0.

OS_ERR_STK_INVALID	if OS_CFG_ARG_CHK_EN is set to 1 in os_cfg.h: if specifying a NULL pointer for p_stk_base.
OS_ERR_STK_SIZE_INVALID	if OS_CFG_ARG_CHK_EN is set to 1 in os_cfg.h: if specifying a stack size smaller than what is currently specified by OS_CFG_STK_SIZE_MIN (see the os_cfg.h).
OS_ERR_TASK_CREATE_ISR	if OS_CFG_CALLED_FROM_ISR_CHK_EN set to 1 in os_cfg.h: if attempting to create the task from an ISR.
OS_ERR_TASK_INVALID	if OS_CFG_ARG_CHK_EN is set to 1 in os_cfg.h: if specifying a NULL pointer for p_task
OS_ERR_TCB_INVALID	if OS_CFG_ARG_CHK_EN is set to 1 in os_cfg.h: if specifying a NULL pointer for p_tcb.
OS_ERR_ILLEGAL_CREATE_RUN_TIME	if OS_SAFETY_CRITICAL_IEC61508 is defined: you called this after calling OSSafetyCriticalStart() and thus you are no longer allowed to create additional kernel objects.

RETURNED VALUE

None

NOTES/WARNINGS

■ The stack must be declared with the CPU_STK type.

■ A task must always invoke one of the services provided by µC/OS-III to wait for time to expire, suspend the task, or wait on an object (wait on a message queue, event flag, mutex, semaphore, a signal or a message to be sent directly to the task). This allows other tasks to gain control of the CPU.

■ You should not use task priorities 0, 1, OS_CFG_PRIO_MAX-2 and OS_CFG_PRIO_MAX-1 because they are reserved for use by µC/OS-III.

EXAMPLE

`OSTaskCreate()` can be called from **main()** (in C), or a previously created task.

```
OS_TCB  MyTaskTCB;                        /* (1) Storage for task's TCB                    */
CPU_STK MyTaskStk[200];


void  MyTask (void *p_arg)                /* (3) The address of the task is its name       */
{
    while (DEF_ON) {
        /* Wait for an event */
        /* My task body      */
    }
}


void SomeCode (void)
{
    OS_ERR  err;
    :
    :
    OSTaskCreate (&MyTaskTCB,             /* (1) Address of TCB assigned to the task       */
                  "My Task",              /* (2) Name you want to give the task            */
                  MyTask,                 /* (3) Address of the task itself                */
                  (void *)0,              /* (4) "p_arg" is not used                       */
                  12,                     /* (5) Priority you want to assign to the task   */
                  &MyTaskStk[0],          /* (6) Base address of task's stack              */
                  10,                     /* (7) Watermark limit for stack growth          */
                  200,                    /* (8) Stack size in number of CPU_STK elements  */
                  5,                      /* (9) Size of task message queue                */
                  10,                     /* (10) Time quanta (in number of ticks)         */
                  (void *)0,              /* (11) Extension pointer is not used            */
                  OS_OPT_TASK_STK_CHK + OS_OPT_TASK_STK_CLR, /* (12) Options               */
                  &err);                                     /* (13) Error code            */
    /* Check "err"                                              (14)                        */
    :
    :
}
```

(1)   In order to create a task, you need to allocate storage for a TCB and pass a pointer to this TCB to `OSTaskCreate()`.

(2) You can assign an ASCII name to the task by passing a pointer to an ASCII string. The ASCII string may be allocated in code space (i.e., ROM), or data space (i.e., RAM). In either case, it is assumed that the code can access that memory. The ASCII string must be **NUL** terminated.

(3) You pass the address of the task to **OSTaskCreate()**. In C, the address of a function is simply the name of that function.

(4) To provide additional data to **MyTask()**, you can pass a pointer to such data. In this case, **MyTask()** did not need such data and therefore, a **NULL** pointer is passed.

(5) The user must assign a priority to the task. The priority specifies the importance of this task with respect to other tasks. A low-priority value indicates a high priority. Priority **0** is the highest priority (reserved for an internal task) and a priority up to **OS_CFG_PRIO_MAX-3** can be specified (see **os_cfg.h**). Note that **OS_CFG_PRIO_MAX-1** is also reserved for an internal task, the idle task.

(6) The next argument specifies the "base address" of the task's stack. In this case, it is simply the base address of the array **MyTaskStk[ ]**. Note that it is possible to simply specify the name of the array. I prefer to make it clear by writing **&MyTaskStk[0]**.

(7) This argument sets the watermark limit for stack growth. If the processor port does not use this field then you can set this value to **0**.

(8) µC/OS-III also needs to know the size of the stack for the task. This allows µC/OS-III to perform stack checking at run time. This argument represents the number of **CPU_STK** elements, not the number of bytes.

(9) µC/OS-III allows tasks or ISRs to send messages directly to a task. This argument specifies how many such messages can be received by this task.

(10) This argument specifies how much time (in number of ticks) this task will run on the CPU before µC/OS-III will force the CPU away from this task and run the next task at the same priority (if there are more than one task at the same priority that is ready-to-run).

(11)   µC/OS-III allows the user to "extend" the capabilities of the TCB by allowing passing a pointer to some memory location that could contain additional information about the task. For example, there may be a CPU that supports floating-point math and the user would likely need to save the floating-point registers during a context switch. This pointer could point to the storage area for these registers.

(12)   When creating a task, options must be specified. Specifically, such options as, whether the stack of the task will be cleared (i.e., filled with 0x00) when the task is created (**OS_OPT_TASK_STK_CLR**), whether µC/OS-III will be allowed to check for stack usage (**OS_OPT_TASK_STK_CHK**), whether the CPU supports floating-point math, and whether the task will make use of the floating-point registers and therefore need to save and restore them during a context switch (**OS_OPT_TASK_SAVE_FP**). The options are additive.

(13)   Most of µC/OS-III's services return an error code indicating the outcome of the call. The error code is always returned as a pointer to a variable of type **OS_ERR**. The user must allocate storage for this variable prior to calling **OSTaskCreate()**.

(14)   It is highly recommended that the user examine the error code whenever calling a µC/OS-III function. If the call is successful, the error code will always be **OS_ERR_NONE**. If the call is not successful, the returned code will indicate the reason for the failure (see **OS_ERR_???** in **os.h**).

A-59 OSTaskCreateHook()

```
void  OSTaskCreateHook (OS_TCB  *p_tcb)
```

File	Called from	Code enabled by
os_cpu_c.c	OSTaskCreate() ONLY	N/A

This function is called by **OSTaskCreate()** after initializing the **OS_TCB** fields and setting up the stack frame for the task, just before adding the task to the ready list. When **OSTaskCreateHook()** is called, all of the **OS_TCB** fields are assumed to be initialized.

OSTaskCreateHook() is part of the CPU port code and this function *must not* be called by the application code. **OSTaskCreateHook()** is actually used by the µC/OS-III port developer.

You can use this hook to initialize and store the contents of floating-point registers, MMU registers, or anything else that can be associated with a task. Typically, you would store this additional information in memory allocated by the application.

ARGUMENTS

p_tcb   is a pointer to the TCB of the task being created. Note that the **OS_TCB** has been validated by **OSTaskCreate()** and is guaranteed to not be a **NULL** pointer when **OSTaskCreateHook()** is called.

RETURNED VALUE

None

NOTES/WARNINGS

Do not call this function from the application.

EXAMPLE

The code below calls an application-specific hook that the application programmer can define. The user can simply set the value of **OS_AppTaskCreateHookPtr** to point to the desired hook function as shown in the example. **OSTaskCreate()** calls

`OSTaskCreateHook()` which in turns calls **App_OS_TaskCreateHook()** through `OS_AppTaskCreateHookPtr`. As can be seen, when called, the application hook is passed the address of the **OS_TCB** of the newly created task.

```c
void  App_OS_TaskCreateHook (OS_TCB *p_tcb)                    /* os_app_hooks.c        */
{
    /* Your code goes here! */
}


void App_OS_SetAllHooks (void)                                /* os_app_hooks.c        */
{
    CPU_SR_ALLOC();

    CPU_CRITICAL_ENTER();
    :
    OS_AppTaskCreateHookPtr = App_OS_TaskCreateHook;
    :
    CPU_CRITICAL_EXIT();
}


void  OSTaskCreateHook (OS_TCB *p_tcb)                         /* os_cpu_c.c            */
{
#if OS_CFG_APP_HOOKS_EN > 0u
    if (OS_AppTaskCreateHookPtr != (OS_APP_HOOK_TCB)0) {   /* Call application hook */
        (*OS_AppTaskCreateHookPtr)(p_tcb);
    }
#endif
}
```

A-60 OSTaskDel()

```
void  OSTaskDel (OS_TCB  *p_tcb,
                 OS_ERR  *p_err)
```

File	Called from	Code enabled by
os_task.c	Task only	OS_CFG_TASK_DEL_EN

When a task is no longer needed, it can be deleted. Deleting a task does not mean that the code is removed, but that the task code is no longer managed by µC/OS-III. **OSTaskDel()** can be used when creating a task that will only run once. In this case, the task must not return but instead call **OSTaskDel((OS_TCB *)0, &err)** which specifies to µC/OS-III to delete the currently running task.

A task may also delete another task by specifying to **OSTaskDel()** the address of the **OS_TCB** of the task to delete.

Once a task is deleted, its **OS_TCB** and stack may be reused to create another task. This assumes that the task's stack requirement of the new task is satisfied by the stack size of the deleted task.

Even though µC/OS-III allows the user to delete tasks at run time, it is recommend that such actions be avoided. Why? Because a task can "own" resources that are shared with other tasks. Deleting the task that owns resource(s) without first relinquishing the resources could lead to strange behaviors and possible deadlocks.

ARGUMENTS

p_tcb is a pointer to the TCB of the task to delete or, you can pass a **NULL** pointer to specify that the calling task delete itself. If deleting the calling task, the scheduler will be invoked so that the next highest-priority task is executed.

p_err is a pointer to a variable that will receive an error code:

OS_ERR_NONE	'p_err' gets set to **OS_ERR_NONE** before **OSSched()** to allow the returned error code to be monitored (by another task) even for a task that is deleting itself. In this case, **p_err** *must*

	point to a global variable that can be accessed by that other task and, you should initialize that variable to **OS_ERR_TASK_RUNNING** prior to deleting the task.
OS_ERR_TASK_DEL_IDLE	if attempting to delete the idle task.
OS_ERR_TASK_DEL_ISR	if **OS_CFG_CALLED_FROM_ISR_CHK_EN** set to 1 in **os_cfg.h**: if you called **OSTaskDel()** from an ISR.
OS_ERR_TASK_DEL_INVALID	if attempting to delete the ISR Handler task while **OS_CFG_ISR_POST_DEFERRED_EN** is set to 1.

RETURNED VALUE

None

NOTES/WARNINGS

■ **OSTaskDel()** verifies that the user is not attempting to delete the µC/OS-III idle task and the ISR handler task.

■ Be careful when deleting a task that owns resources.

EXAMPLE

```
OS_TCB  MyTaskTCB;


void TaskX (void *p_arg)
{
    OS_ERR  err;


    while (DEF_ON) {
        :
        :
        OSTaskDel(&MyTaskTCB,
                  &err);
        /* Check "err" */
        :
        :
    }
}
```

A-61 OSTaskDelHook()

```
void  OSTaskDelHook (OS_TCB  *p_tcb);
```

File	Called from	Code enabled by
os_cpu_c.c	OSTaskDel() only	N/A

This function is called by **OSTaskDel()** after the task is removed from the ready list or any pend list.

You can use this hook to deallocate storage assigned to the task.

OSTaskDelHook() is part of the CPU port code and this function *must not* be called by the application code. **OSTaskDelHook()** is actually used by the µC/OS-III port developer.

ARGUMENTS

p_tcb   is a pointer to the TCB of the task being created. Note that the **OS_TCB** has been validated by **OSTaskDel()** and is guaranteed to not be a **NULL** pointer when **OSTaskDelHook()** is called.

RETURNED VALUE

None

NOTES/WARNINGS

Do not call this function from the application.

EXAMPLE

The code below calls an application-specific hook that the application programmer can define. The user can simply set the value of **OS_AppTaskDelHookPtr** to point to the desired hook function. **OSTaskDel()** calls **OSTaskDelHook()** which in turns calls **App_OS_TaskDelHook()** through **OS_AppTaskDelHookPtr**. As can be seen, when called, the application hook is passed the address of the **OS_TCB** of the task being deleted.

```
void  App_OS_TaskDelHook (OS_TCB *p_tcb)                    /* os_app_hooks.c      */
{
    /* Your code goes here! */
}


void App_OS_SetAllHooks (void)                             /* os_app_hooks.c      */
{
    CPU_SR_ALLOC();

    CPU_CRITICAL_ENTER();
    :
    OS_AppTaskDelHookPtr = App_OS_TaskDelHook;
    :
    CPU_CRITICAL_EXIT();
}



void  OSTaskDelHook (OS_TCB *p_tcb)                        /* os_cpu_c.c          */
{
#if OS_CFG_APP_HOOKS_EN > 0u
    if (OS_AppTaskDelHookPtr != (OS_APP_HOOK_TCB)0) {     /* Call application hook */
        (*OS_AppTaskDelHookPtr)(p_tcb);
    }
#endif
}
```

A-62 OSTaskQFlush()

```
OS_MSG_QTY  OSTaskQFlush (OS_TCB   *p_tcb,
                          OS_ERR   *p_err)
```

File	Called from	Code enabled by
os_task.c	Task only	OS_CFG_TASK_Q_EN

OSTaskQFlush() empties the contents of the task message queue and eliminates all messages sent to the queue. OS_MSGs from the queue are simply returned to the free pool of OS_MSGs.

ARGUMENTS

p_tcb   is a pointer to the TCB of the task that contains the queue to flush. Specifying a NULL pointer tells OSTaskQFlush() to flush the queue of the calling task's built-in message queue.

p_err   is a pointer to a variable that will contain an error code returned by this function.

OS_ERR_NONE	if the message queue is flushed.
OS_ERR_FLUSH_ISR	if OS_CFG_CALLED_FROM_ISR_CHK_EN set to 1 in os_cfg.h: if calling this function from an ISR

RETURNED VALUE

The number of OS_MSG entries freed from the message queue. Note that the OS_MSG entries are returned to the free pool of OS_MSGs.

NOTES/WARNINGS

■   Use this function with great care. When flushing a queue, you lose the references to what the queue entries are pointing to, potentially causing 'memory leaks'. The data that the user is pointing to that is referenced by the queue entries should, most likely, be de-allocated (i.e., freed).

EXAMPLE

```
void Task (void *p_arg)
{
    OS_ERR  err;


    (void)&p_arg;
    while (DEF_ON) {
        :
        :
        entries = OSTaskQFlush((OS_TCB *)0,
                               &err);
        /* Check "err" */
        :
        :
    }
}
```

or, to flush a queue that contains entries, instead you can use **OSTaskQPend()** and specify the **OS_OPT_PEND_NON_BLOCKING** option.

```
void Task (void *p_arg)
{
    OS_ERR       err;
    CPU_TS       ts;
    OS_MSG_SIZE  msg_size;


    (void)&p_arg;
    :
    do {
        OSTaskQPend(0,
                    OS_OPT_PEND_NON_BLOCKING,
                    &msg_size,
                    &ts,
                    &err);
    } while (err != OS_ERR_PEND_WOULD_BLOCK);
    :
    :
}
```

A-63 OSTaskQPend()

```
void  *OSTaskQPend (OS_TICK       timeout,
                    OS_OPT        opt,
                    OS_MSG_SIZE   *p_msg_size,
                    CPU_TS        *p_ts,
                    OS_ERR        *p_err)
```

File	Called from	Code enabled by
os_task.c	Task only	OS_CFG_TASK_Q_EN and OS_CFG_MSG_EN

OSTaskQPend( ) allows a task to receive messages directly from an ISR or another task, without going through an intermediate message queue. In fact, each task has a built-in message queue if the configuration constant **OS_CFG_TASK_Q_EN** is set to The messages received are pointer-sized variables, and their use is application specific. If at least one message is already present in the message queue when OSTaskQPend( ) is called, the message is retrieved and returned to the caller.

If no message is present in the task's message queue and **OS_OPT_PEND_BLOCKING** is specified for the **opt** argument, OSTaskQPend( ) suspends the current task (assuming the scheduler is not locked) until either a message is received, or a user-specified timeout expires. A pended task that is suspended with **OSTaskSuspend( )** can receive messages. However, the task remains suspended until it is resumed by calling **OSTaskResume( )**.

If no message is present in the task's message queue and **OS_OPT_PEND_NON_BLOCKING** is specified for the **opt** argument, OSTaskQPend( ) returns to the caller with an appropriate error code and returns a **NULL** pointer.

ARGUMENTS

timeout   allows the task to resume execution if a message is not received from a task or an ISR within the specified number of clock ticks. A timeout value of 0 indicates that the task wants to wait forever for a message. The timeout value is not synchronized with the clock tick. The timeout count starts decrementing on the next clock tick, which could potentially occur immediately.

opt   determines whether or not the user wants to block if a message is not available in the task's queue. This argument must be set to either:

OS_OPT_PEND_BLOCKING, or
OS_OPT_PEND_NON_BLOCKING

Note that the timeout argument should be set to 0 when OS_OPT_PEND_NON_BLOCKING is specified, since the timeout value is irrelevant using this option.

p_msg_size is a pointer to a variable that will receive the size of the message.

p_ts   is a pointer to a timestamp indicating when the task's queue was posted, or the pend aborted. Passing a **NULL** pointer is valid and indicates that the timestamp is not necessary.

A timestamp is useful when the task must know when the task message queue was posted, or how long it took for the task to resume after the task message queue was posted. In the latter case, call OS_TS_GET() and compute the difference between the current value of the timestamp and ***p_ts**. In other words:

delta = OS_TS_GET() - *p_ts;

p_err   is a pointer to a variable used to hold an error code.

OS_ERR_NONE	if a message is received.
OS_ERR_OPT_INVALID	if OS_CFG_ARG_CHK_EN set to 1 in **os_cfg.h**: if you specified an invalid option.
OS_ERR_PEND_ABORT	if the pend was aborted because another task called OSTaskQPendAbort().
OS_ERR_PEND_ISR	if OS_CFG_CALLED_FROM_ISR_CHK_EN set to 1 in **os_cfg.h**: if calling this function from an ISR.
OS_ERR_PEND_WOULD_BLOCK	if calling this function with the opt argument set to OS_OPT_PEND_NON_BLOCKING and no message is in the task's message queue.

OS_ERR_PTR_INVALID	if OS_CFG_ARG_CHK_EN set to 1 in os_cfg.h: if p_msg_size is a NULL pointer.
OS_ERR_SCHED_LOCKED	if calling this function when the scheduler is locked and the user wanted to block.
OS_ERR_TIMEOUT	if a message is not received within the specified timeout.

RETURNED VALUE

The message if no error or a NULL pointer upon error. You should examine the error code since it is possible to send NULL pointer messages. In other words, a NULL pointer does not mean an error occurred. *p_err must be examined to determine the reason for the error.

NOTES/WARNINGS

Do not call OSTaskQPend() from an ISR.

EXAMPLE

```
void CommTask (void *p_arg)
{
    OS_ERR       err;
    void         *p_msg;
    OS_MSG_SIZE  msg_size;
    CPU_TS       ts;


    (void)&p_arg;
    while (DEF_ON) {
        :
        :
        p_msg = OSTaskQPend(100,
                            OS_OPT_PEND_BLOCKING,
                            &msg_size,
                            &ts,
                            &err);
        /* Check "err" */
        :
        :
    }
}
```

A-64 OSTaskQPendAbort()

```
CPU_BOOLEAN  OSTaskQPendAbort (OS_TCB  *p_tcb,
                               OS_OPT   opt,
                               OS_ERR  *p_err)
```

File	Called from	Code enabled by
os_q.c	Task only	OS_CFG_TASK_Q_EN and OS_CFG_TASK_Q_PEND_ABORT_EN

OSTaskQPendAbort() aborts and readies a task currently waiting on its built-in message queue. This function should be used to fault-abort the wait on the task's message queue, rather than to normally signal the message queue via OSTaskQPost().

ARGUMENTS

p_tcb   is a pointer to the task for which the pend needs to be aborted. Note that it doesn't make sense to pass a **NULL** pointer or the address of the calling task's TCB since, by definition, the calling task cannot be pending.

opt   provides options for this function.

OS_OPT_POST_NONE	No option specified.
OS_OPT_POST_NO_SCHED	specifies that the scheduler should not be called even if the pend of a higher priority task has been aborted. Scheduling will need to occur from another function.
	Use this option if the task calling **OSTaskQPendAbort()** will do additional pend aborts, rescheduling will take place when completed, and multiple pend aborts should take effect simultaneously.

p_err   is a pointer to a variable that holds an error code:

OS_ERR_NONE	the task was readied by another task and it was informed of the aborted wait.

OS_ERR_PEND_ABORT_ISR	if OS_CFG_CALLED_FROM_ISR_CHK_EN set to 1 in **os_cfg.h**: if called from an ISR
OS_ERR_PEND_ABORT_NONE	if the task was not pending on the task's message queue.
OS_ERR_PEND_ABORT_SELF	if **OS_CFG_ARG_CHK_EN** is set to 1 in **os_cfg.h**: if **p_tcb** is a **NULL** pointer. The user is attempting to pend abort the calling task which makes no sense as the caller, by definition, is not pending.

RETURNED VALUE

OSTaskQPendAbort() returns **DEF_TRUE** if the task was made ready-to-run by this function. **DEF_FALSE** indicates that the task was not pending, or an error occurred.

NOTES/WARNINGS

None

EXAMPLE

```
OS_TCB   CommRxTaskTCB;


void CommTask (void *p_arg)
{
    OS_ERR       err;
    CPU_BOOLEAN  aborted;


    (void)&p_arg;
    while (DEF_ON) {
        :
        :
        aborted = OSTaskQPendAbort(&CommRxTaskTCB,
                                   OS_OPT_POST_NONE,
                                   &err);
        /* Check "err" */
        :
        :
    }
}
```

A-65 OSTaskQPost()

```
void  OSTaskQPost (OS_TCB      *p_tcb,
                   void        *p_void,
                   OS_MSG_SIZE  msg_size,
                   OS_OPT       opt,
                   OS_ERR      *p_err)
```

File	Called from	Code enabled by
os_q.c	Task or ISR	OS_CFG_TASK_Q_EN and OS_CFG_MSG_EN

OSTaskQPost() sends a message to a task through its local message queue. A message is a pointer-sized variable, and its use is application specific. If the task's message queue is full, an error code is returned to the caller. In this case, OSTaskQPost() immediately returns to its caller, and the message is not placed in the message queue.

If the task receiving the message is waiting for a message to arrive, it will be made ready-to-run. If the receiving task has a higher priority than the task sending the message, the higher-priority task resumes, and the task sending the message is suspended; that is, a context switch occurs. A message can be posted as first-in first-out (FIFO), or last-in-first-out (LIFO), depending on the value specified in the **opt** argument. In either case, scheduling occurs unless **opt** is set to OS_OPT_POST_NO_SCHED.

ARGUMENTS

p_tcb   is a pointer to the TCB of the task. Note that it is possible to post a message to the calling task (i.e., self) by specifying a **NULL** pointer, or the address of its TCB.

p_void   is the actual message sent to the task. **p_void** is a pointer-sized variable and its meaning is application specific.

msg_size   specifies the size of the message posted (in number of bytes).

opt		determines the type of POST performed. Of course, it does not make sense to post LIFO and FIFO simultaneously, so these options are exclusive:

OS_OPT_POST_FIFO	POST message to task and place at the end of the queue if the task is not waiting for messages.
OS_OPT_POST_LIFO	POST message to task and place at the front of the queue if the task is not waiting for messages.
OS_OPT_POST_NO_SCHED	This option prevents calling the scheduler after the post and therefore the caller is resumed. You should use this option if the task (or ISR) calling **OSTaskQPost()** will be doing additional posts, the user does not want to reschedule until all done, and multiple posts are to take effect simultaneously.

p_err	is a pointer to a variable that will contain an error code returned by this function.

OS_ERR_NONE	if the call was successful and the message was posted to the task's message queue.
OS_ERR_MSG_POOL_EMPTY	if running out of **OS_MSG** to hold the message being posted.
OS_ERR_Q_MAX	if the task's message queue is full and cannot accept more messages.

RETURNED VALUE

None

NOTES/WARNINGS

None

EXAMPLE

```
OS_TCB      CommRxTaskTCB;
CPU_INT08U  CommRxBuf[100];


void CommTaskRx (void *p_arg)
{
    OS_ERR  err;


    (void)&p_arg;
    while (DEF_ON) {
        :
        OSTaskQPost(&CommRxTaskTCB,
                    (void *)&CommRxBuf[0],
                    sizeof(CommRxBuf),
                    OS_OPT_POST_FIFO,
                    &err);
        /* Check "err" */
        :
    }
}
```

A-66 OSTaskRegGet()

```
OS_REG   OSTaskRegGet (OS_TCB      *p_tcb,
                       OS_REG_ID   id,
                       OS_ERR      *p_err)
```

File	Called from	Code enabled by
os_task.c	Task only	OS_CFG_TASK_REG_TBL_SIZE > 0

µC/OS-III allows the user to store task-specific values in task registers. Task registers are different than CPU registers and are used to save such information as "**errno**," which are common in software components. Task registers can also store task-related data to be associated with the task at run time such as I/O register settings, configuration values, etc. A task may have as many as **OS_CFG_TASK_REG_TBL_SIZE** registers, and all registers have a data type of **OS_REG**. However, **OS_REG** can be declared at compile time (see **os_type.h**) to be nearly anything (8-, 16-, 32-, 64-bit signed or unsigned integer, or floating-point).

As shown below, a task register is changed by calling **OSTaskRegSet()** and read by calling **OSTaskRegGet()**. The desired task register is specified as an argument to these functions and can take a value between 0 and **OS_CFG_TASK_REG_TBL_SIZE-1**.

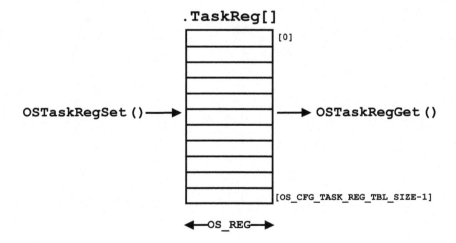

ARGUMENTS

p_tcb   is a pointer to the TCB of the task the user is receiving a task-register value from. A **NULL** pointer indicates that the user wants the value of a task register of the calling task.

id   is the identifier of the task register and valid values are from **0** to **OS_CFG_TASK_REG_TBL_SIZE-1**.

p_err   is a pointer to a variable that will contain an error code returned by this function.

OS_ERR_NONE	if the call was successful and the function returned the value of the desired task register.
OS_ERR_REG_ID_INVALID	if **OS_CFG_ARG_CHK_EN** is set to **1** in **os_cfg.h**: if a valid task register identifier is not specified.

RETURNED VALUE

The current value of the task register.

NOTES/WARNINGS

None

EXAMPLE

```
OS_TCB  MyTaskTCB;


void TaskX (void *p_arg)
{
    OS_ERR  err;
    OS_REG  reg;


    while (DEF_ON) {
        :
        reg = OSTaskRegGet(&MyTaskTCB,
                           5,
                           &err);
        /* Check "err" */
        :
    }
}
```

A-67 OSTaskRegSet()

```
void   OSTaskRegSet (OS_TCB      *p_tcb,
                     OS_REG_ID   id,
                     OS_REG      value,
                     OS_ERR      *p_err)
```

File	Called from	Code enabled by
os_task.c	Task only	OS_CFG_TASK_REG_TBL_SIZE > 0

µC/OS-III allows the user to store task-specific values in task registers. Task registers are different than CPU registers and are used to save such information as "**errno**," which are common in software components. Task registers can also store task-related data to be associated with the task at run time such as I/O register settings, configuration values, etc. A task may have as many as **OS_CFG_TASK_REG_TBL_SIZE** registers, and all registers have a data type of **OS_REG**. However, **OS_REG** can be declared at compile time to be nearly anything (8-, 16-, 32-, 64-bit signed or unsigned integer, or floating-point).

As shown below, a task register is changed by calling **OSTaskRegSet()**, and read by calling **OSTaskRegGet()**. The desired task register is specified as an argument to these functions and can take a value between 0 and **OS_CFG_TASK_REG_TBL_SIZE**-1.

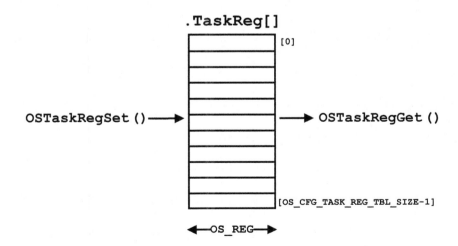

ARGUMENTS

p_tcb   is a pointer to the TCB of the task you are setting. A **NULL** pointer indicates that the user wants to set the value of a task register of the calling task.

id   is the identifier of the task register and valid values are from **0** to **OS_CFG_TASK_REG_TBL_SIZE-1**.

value   is the new value of the task register specified by **id**

p_err   is a pointer to a variable that will contain an error code returned by this function.

           OS_ERR_NONE   if the call was successful, and the function set the value of the desired task register.

           OS_ERR_REG_ID_INVALID   if **OS_CFG_ARG_CHK_EN** is set to **1** in **os_cfg.h**: if a valid task register identifier is not specified.

RETURNED VALUE

None

NOTES/WARNINGS

None

EXAMPLE

```
OS_TCB  MyTaskTCB;


void TaskX (void *p_arg)
{
    OS_ERR  err;


    while (DEF_ON) {
        :
        reg = OSTaskRegSet(&MyTaskTCB,
                           5,
                           23,
                           &err);
        /* Check "err" */
        :
    }
}
```

A-68 OSTaskReturnHook()

```
void  OSTaskReturnHook (void);
```

File	Called from	Code enabled by
os_cpu_c.c	OS_TaskReturn() ONLY	N/A

This function is called by OS_TaskReturn(). OS_TaskReturn() is called if the user accidentally returns from the task code. In other words, the task should either be implemented as an infinite loop and never return, or the task must call OSTaskDel((OS_TCB *)0, &err) to delete itself to prevent it from exiting.

OSTaskReturnHook() is part of the CPU port code and this function *must not* be called by the application code. OSTaskReturnHook() is actually used by the µC/OS-III port developer.

Note that after calling OSTaskReturnHook(), OS_TaskReturn() will actually delete the task by calling:

```
OSTaskDel((OS_TCB *)0,
          &err)
```

ARGUMENTS

p_tcb is a pointer to the TCB of the task that is not behaving as expected. Note that the OS_TCB is validated by OS_TaskReturn(), and is guaranteed to not be a NULL pointer when OSTaskReturnHook() is called.

RETURNED VALUE

None

NOTES/WARNINGS

Do not call this function from the application.

EXAMPLE

The code below calls an application-specific hook that the application programmer can define. For this, the user can simply set the value of **OS_AppTaskReturnHookPtr** to point to the desired hook function as shown in the example. If a task returns and forgets to call **OSTaskDel((OS_TCB *)0, &err)** then µC/OS-III will call **OSTaskReturnHook()** which in turns calls **App_OS_TaskReturnHook()** through **OS_AppTaskReturnHookPtr**. When called, the application hook is passed the address of the **OS_TCB** of the task returning.

```c
void  App_OS_TaskReturnHook (OS_TCB  *p_tcb)              /* os_app_hooks.c        */
{
    /* Your code goes here! */
}


void App_OS_SetAllHooks (void)                            /* os_app_hooks.c        */
{
    CPU_SR_ALLOC();

    CPU_CRITICAL_ENTER();
    :
    OS_AppTaskReturnHookPtr = App_OS_TaskReturnHook;
    :
    CPU_CRITICAL_EXIT();
}


void  OSTaskReturnHook (OS_TCB *p_tcb)                    /* os_cpu_c.c            */
{
#if OS_CFG_APP_HOOKS_EN > 0u
    if (OS_AppTaskReturnHookPtr != (OS_APP_HOOK_TCB)0) {  /* Call application hook */
        (*OS_AppTaskReturnHookPtr)(p_tcb);
    }
#endif
}
```

A-69 OSTaskResume()

```
void  OSTaskResume (OS_TCB  *p_tcb,
                    OS_ERR  *p_err)
```

File	Called from	Code enabled by
os_task.c	Task only	OS_CFG_TASK_SUSPEND_EN

OSTaskResume() resumes a task suspended through the **OSTaskSuspend()** function. In fact, **OSTaskResume()** is the only function that can unsuspend a suspended task. Obviously, the suspended task can only be resumed by another task. If the suspended task is also waiting on another kernel object such as an event flag, semaphore, mutex, message queue etc., the suspension will simply be lifted (i.e., removed), but the task will continue waiting for the object.

The user can "nest" suspension of a task by calling **OSTaskSuspend()** and therefore must call **OSTaskResume()** an equivalent number of times to resume such a task. In other words, if suspending a task five times, it is necessary to unsuspend the same task five times to remove the suspension of the task.

ARGUMENTS

p_tcb is a pointer to the TCB of the task that is resuming. A **NULL** pointer is not a valid value as one cannot resume the calling task because, by definition, the calling task is running and is not suspended.

p_err is a pointer to a variable that will contain an error code returned by this function.

> **OS_ERR_NONE** if the call was successful and the desired task is resumed.
>
> **OS_ERR_TASK_RESUME_ISR** if **OS_CFG_CALLED_FROM_ISR_CHK_EN** set to 1 in **os_cfg.h**: if calling this function from an ISR.

| OS_ERR_TASK_RESUME_SELF | if OS_CFG_ARG_CHK_EN is set to 1 in os_cfg.h: if passing a NULL pointer for p_tcb or, a pointer to the current TCB. It is not possible to resume the calling task since, if suspended, it cannot be executing. |
| OS_ERR_TASK_NOT_SUSPENDED | if the task attempting to be resumed is not suspended. |

RETURNED VALUE

None

NOTES/WARNINGS

None

EXAMPLE

```
OS_TCB    TaskY;


void TaskX (void *p_arg)
{
    OS_ERR err;


    while (DEF_ON) {
        :
        :
        OSTaskResume(&TaskY,
                     &err);              /* Resume suspended task        */
        /* Check "err" */
        :
        :
    }
}
```

A-70 OSTaskSemPend()

```
OS_SEM_CTR   OSTaskSemPend (OS_TICK    timeout,
                            OS_OPT     opt,
                            CPU_TS     *p_ts,
                            OS_ERR     *p_err)
```

File	Called from	Code enabled by
os_task.c	Task only	Always enabled

OSTaskSemPend() allows a task to wait for a signal to be sent by another task or ISR without going through an intermediate object such as a semaphore. If the task was previously signaled when OSTaskSemPend() is called then, the caller resumes.

If no signal was received by the task and OS_OPT_PEND_BLOCKING is specified for the opt argument, OSTaskSemPend() suspends the current task until either a signal is received, or a user-specified timeout expires. A pended task suspended with OSTaskSuspend() can receive signals. However, the task remains suspended until it is resumed by calling OSTaskResume().

If no signals were sent to the task and OS_OPT_PEND_NON_BLOCKING was specified for the opt argument, OSTaskSemPend() returns to the caller with an appropriate error code and returns a signal count of 0.

ARGUMENTS

timeout   allows the task to resume execution if a signal is not received from a task or an ISR within the specified number of clock ticks. A timeout value of 0 indicates that the task wants to wait forever for a signal. The timeout value is not synchronized with the clock tick. The timeout count starts decrementing on the next clock tick, which could potentially occur immediately.

opt   determines whether the user wants to block or not, if a signal was not sent to the task. Set this argument to either:

            OS_OPT_PEND_BLOCKING, or
            OS_OPT_PEND_NON_BLOCKING

Note that the **timeout** argument should be set to 0 when specifying OS_OPT_PEND_NON_BLOCKING, since the timeout value is irrelevant using this option.

p_ts   is a pointer to a timestamp indicating when the task's semaphore was posted, or the pend was aborted. Passing a **NULL** pointer is valid and indicates that the timestamp is not necessary.

A timestamp is useful when the task is to know when the semaphore was posted, or how long it took for the task to resume after the semaphore was posted. In the latter case, call **OS_TS_GET()** and compute the difference between the current value of the timestamp and ***p_ts**. In other words:

delta = OS_TS_GET() - *p_ts;

p_err   is a pointer to a variable used to hold an error code.

OS_ERR_NONE	if a signal is received.
OS_ERR_PEND_ABORT	if the pend was aborted because another task called OSTaskSemPendAbort().
OS_ERR_PEND_ISR	if OS_CFG_CALLED_FROM_ISR_CHK_EN set to 1 in os_cfg.h: if calling this function from an ISR.
OS_ERR_PEND_WOULD_BLOCK	if calling this function with the opt argument set to OS_OPT_PEND_NON_BLOCKING, and no signal was received.
OS_ERR_SCHED_LOCKED	if calling this function when the scheduler is locked and the user wanted the task to block.
OS_ERR_TIMEOUT	if a signal is not received within the specified timeout.

RETURNED VALUE

The current value of the signal counter after it has been decremented. In other words, the number of signals still remaining in the signal counter.

NOTES/WARNINGS

Do not call **OSTaskSemPend( )** from an ISR.

EXAMPLE

```c
void CommTask(void *p_arg)
{
    OS_ERR      err;
    OS_SEM_CTR  ctr;
    CPU_TS      ts;


    (void)&p_arg;
    while (DEF_ON) {
        :
        ctr = OSTaskSemPend(100,
                            OS_OPT_PEND_BLOCKING,
                            &ts,
                            &err);
        /* Check "err" */
        :
    }
}
```

A-71 OSTaskSemPendAbort()

```
CPU_BOOLEAN  OSTaskSemPendAbort (OS_TCB   *p_tcb,
                                 OS_OPT    opt,
                                 OS_ERR   *p_err)
```

File	Called from	Code enabled by
os_task.c	Task only	OS_CFG_TASK_SEM_PEND_ABORT_EN

OSTaskSemPendAbort() aborts and readies a task currently waiting on its built-in semaphore. This function should be used to fault-abort the wait on the task's semaphore, rather than to normally signal the task via OSTaskSemPost().

ARGUMENTS

p_tcb   is a pointer to the task for which the pend must be aborted. Note that it does not make sense to pass a **NULL** pointer or the address of the calling task's TCB since, by definition, the calling task cannot be pending.

opt   provides options for this function.

OS_OPT_POST_NONE	no option specified, call the scheduler by default.
OS_OPT_POST_NO_SCHED	specifies that the scheduler should not be called even if the pend of a higher-priority task has been aborted. Scheduling will need to occur from another function. Use this option if the task calling OSTaskSemPendAbort() will be doing additional pend aborts, rescheduling will not take place until finished, and multiple pend aborts are to take effect simultaneously.
p_err	is a pointer to a variable that holds an error code:
OS_ERR_NONE	the pend was aborted for the specified task.
OS_ERR_PEND_ABORT_ISR	if OS_CFG_CALLED_FROM_ISR_CHK_EN set to 1 in os_cfg.h: if called from an ISR
OS_ERR_PEND_ABORT_NONE	if the task was not waiting for a signal.

OS_ERR_PEND_ABORT_SELF	if **p_tcb** is a **NULL** pointer or the TCB of the calling task is specified. The user is attempting to pend abort the calling task, which makes no sense since, by definition, the calling task is not pending.

RETURNED VALUE

OSTaskSemPendAbort() returns **DEF_TRUE** if the task was made ready-to-run by this function. **DEF_FALSE** indicates that the task was not pending, or an error occurred.

NOTES/WARNINGS

None

EXAMPLE

```
OS_TCB   CommRxTaskTCB;


void CommTask (void *p_arg)
{
    OS_ERR       err;
    CPU_BOOLEAN  aborted;


    (void)&p_arg;
    while (DEF_ON) {
        :
        :
        aborted = OSTaskSemPendAbort(&CommRxTaskTCB,
                                     OS_OPT_POST_NONE,
                                     &err);
        /* Check "err" */
        :
        :
    }
}
```

A-72 OSTaskSemPost()

```
OS_SEM_CTR  OSTaskSemPost (OS_TCB    *p_tcb,
                           OS_OPT     opt,
                           OS_ERR    *p_err)
```

File	Called from	Code enabled by
os_task.c	Task or ISR	Always enabled

OSTaskSemPost() sends a signal to a task through it's local semaphore.

If the task receiving the signal is actually waiting for a signal to be received, it will be made ready-to-run and, if the receiving task has a higher priority than the task sending the signal, the higher-priority task resumes, and the task sending the signal is suspended; that is, a context switch occurs. Note that scheduling only occurs if opt is set to OS_OPT_POST_NONE, because the OS_OPT_POST_NO_SCHED option does not cause the scheduler to be called.

ARGUMENTS

p_tcb   is a pointer to the TCB of the task being signaled. A NULL pointer indicates that the user is sending a signal to itself.

opt   provides options to the call.

OS_OPT_POST_NONE	No option, by default the scheduler will be called.
OS_OPT_POST_NO_SCHED	Do not call the scheduler after the post, therefore the caller is resumed. You would use this option if the task (or ISR) calling OSTaskSemPost() will be doing additional posts, reschedule waits until all is done, and multiple posts are to take effect simultaneously.

p_err   is a pointer to a variable that will contain an error code returned by this function.

OS_ERR_NONE   if the call was successful and the signal was sent.

OS_ERR_SEM_OVF   the post would have caused the semaphore counter to overflow.

RETURNED VALUE

The current value of the task's signal counter, or **0** if called from an ISR and **OS_CFG_ISR_POST_DEFERRED_EN** is set to 1.

NOTES/WARNINGS

None

EXAMPLE

```
OS_TCB        CommRxTaskTCB;


void CommTaskRx (void *p_arg)
{
    OS_ERR      err;
    OS_SEM_CTR  ctr;


    (void)&p_arg;
    while (DEF_ON) {
        :
        ctr = OSTaskSemPost(&CommRxTaskTCB,
                            OS_OPT_POST_NONE,
                            &err);
        /* Check "err" */
        :
    }
}
```

A-73 OSTaskSemSet()

```
OS_SEM_CTR   OSTaskSemSet (OS_TCB      *p_tcb,
                           OS_SEM_CTR  cnt;
                           OS_ERR      *p_err)
```

File	Called from	Code enabled by
os_task.c	Task or ISR	Always Enabled

OSTaskSemSet() allows the user to set the value of the task's signal counter. You would set the signal counter of the calling task by passing a **NULL** pointer for **p_tcb**.

ARGUMENTS

p_tcb   is a pointer to the task's **OS_TCB** to clear the signal counter. A **NULL** pointer indicates that the user wants to clear the caller's signal counter.

cnt   the desired value for the task semaphore counter.

p_err   is a pointer to a variable that will contain an error code returned by this function.

> **OS_ERR_NONE**   if the call was successful and the signal counter was cleared.
>
> **OS_ERR_SET_ISR**   if OS_CFG_CALLED_FROM_ISR_CHK_EN set to 1 in **os_cfg.h**: if calling this function from an ISR

RETURNED VALUE

The value of the signal counter prior to setting it.

NOTES/WARNINGS

None

EXAMPLE

```
OS_TCB   TaskY;


void TaskX (void *p_arg)
{
    OS_ERR err;


    while (DEF_ON) {
        :
        :
        OSTaskSemSet(&TaskY,
                     0,
                     &err);
        /* Check "err" */
        :
        :
    }
}
```

A-74 OSStatTaskHook()

```
void  OSStatTaskHook (void);
```

File	Called from	Code enabled by
os_cpu_c.c	OS_StatTask() ONLY	OS_CFG_TASK_STAT_EN

This function is called by OS_StatTask().

OSStatTaskHook() is part of the CPU port code and *must not* be called by the application code. OSStatTaskHook() is actually used by the µC/OS-III port developer.

ARGUMENTS

None

RETURNED VALUE

None

NOTES/WARNINGS

Do not call this function from the application.

EXAMPLE

The code below calls an application-specific hook that the application programmer can define. The user can simply set the value of OS_AppStatTaskHookPtr to point to the desired hook function as shown in the example. The statistic task calls OSStatTaskHook() which in turns calls App_OS_StatTaskHook() through OS_AppStatTaskHookPtr.

```
void  App_OS_StatTaskHook (void)                    /* os_app_hooks.c        */
{
    /* Your code goes here! */
}


void App_OS_SetAllHooks (void)                      /* os_app_hooks.c        */
{
    CPU_SR_ALLOC();

    CPU_CRITICAL_ENTER();
    :
    OS_AppStatTaskHookPtr = App_OS_StatTaskHook;
    :
    CPU_CRITICAL_EXIT();
}


void  OSStatTaskHook (void)                         /* os_cpu_c.c            */
{
#if OS_CFG_APP_HOOKS_EN > 0u
    if (OS_AppStatTaskHookPtr != (OS_APP_HOOK_VOID)0) {   /* Call application hook */
        (*OS_AppStatTaskHookPtr)();
    }
#endif
}
```

A-75 OSTaskStkChk()

```
void   OSTaskStkChk (OS_TCB        *p_tcb,
                     CPU_STK_SIZE  *p_free,
                     CPU_STK_SIZE  *p_used,
                     OS_ERR        *p_err)
```

File	Called from	Code enabled by
os_task.c	Task only	OS_CFG_TASK_STAT_CHK_EN

OSTaskStkChk() determines a task's stack statistics. Specifically, it computes the amount of free stack space, as well as the amount of stack space used by the specified task. This function requires that the task be created with the OS_TASK_OPT_STK_CHK and OS_TASK_OPT_STK_CLR options.

Stack sizing is accomplished by walking from the bottom of the stack and counting the number of 0 entries on the stack until a non-zero value is found.

It is possible to not set the OS_TASK_OPT_STK_CLR when creating the task if the startup code clears all RAM, and tasks are not deleted (this reduces the execution time of OSTaskCreate()).

μC/OS-III's statistic task calls OSTaskStkChk() for each task created and stores the results in each task's OS_TCB so your application doesn't need to call this function if the statistic task is enabled.

ARGUMENTS

p_tcb   is a pointer to the TCB of the task where the stack is being checked. A NULL pointer indicates that the user is checking the calling task's stack.

p_free   is a pointer to a variable of type CPU_STK_SIZE and will contain the number of free CPU_STK elements on the stack of the task being inquired about.

p_used   is a pointer to a variable of type CPU_STK_SIZE and will contain the number of used CPU_STK elements on the stack of the task being inquired about.

p_err   is a pointer to a variable that will contain an error code returned by this function.

OS_ERR_NONE	if the call was successful.
OS_ERR_PTR_INVALID	if **OS_CFG_ARG_CHK_EN** is set to **1** in **os_cfg.h**: if either **p_free** or **p_used** are **NULL** pointers.
OS_ERR_TASK_NOT_EXIST	if the stack pointer of the task is a **NULL** pointer.
OS_ERR_TASK_OPT	if **OS_OPT_TASK_STK_CHK** is not specifed whencreating the task being checked.
OS_ERR_TASK_STK_CHK_ISR	if **OS_CFG_CALLED_FROM_ISR_CHK_EN** set to 1 in **os_cfg.h**: if calling this function from an ISR.

RETURNED VALUE

None

NOTES/WARNINGS

■ Execution time of this task depends on the size of the task's stack.

■ The application can determine the total task stack space (in number of **CPU_STK** elements) by adding the value of **p_free* and **p_used*. This number should add up to the task's stack size which is stored in the **.StkSize** field of the **OS_TCB** of the task.

■ The **#define CPU_CFG_STK_GROWTH** must be declared (typically from **os_cpu.h**). When this **#define** is set to **CPU_STK_GROWTH_LO_TO_HI**, the stack grows from low memory to high memory. When this **#define** is set to **CPU_STK_GROWTH_HI_TO_LO**, the stack grows from high memory to low memory.

EXAMPLE

```
OS_TCB  MyTaskTCB;


void Task (void *p_arg)
{
    OS_ERR       err;
    CPU_STK_SIZE n_free;
    CPU_STK_SIZE n_used;


    (void)&p_arg;
    while (DEF_ON) {
        :
        :
        OSTaskStkChk(&MyTaskTCB,
                     &n_free,
                     &n_used,
                     &err);
        /* Check "err" */
        :
        :
    }
}
```

A-76 OSTaskStkInit()

```
void OSTaskStkInit (OS_TASK_PTR    p_task,
                    void          *p_arg,
                    CPU_STK       *p_stk_base,
                    CPU_STK       *p_stk_limit,
                    CPU_STK_SIZE   stk_size,
                    OS_OPT         opt);
```

File	Called from	Code enabled by
os_cpu_c.c	OSTaskCreate() ONLY	N/A

This function is called by **OSTaskCreate()** to setup the stack frame of the task being created. Typically, the stack frame will look as if an interrupt just occurred, and all CPU registers were pushed onto the task's stack. The stacking order of CPU registers is very CPU specific.

OSTaskStkInit() is part of the CPU port code and this function *must not* be called by the application code. **OSTaskStkInit()** is actually defined by the µC/OS-III port developer.

ARGUMENTS

p_task   is the address of the task being created (see **MyTask()** below). Tasks must be declared as follows:

```
void   MyTask (void  *p_arg)
{
    /* Do something with "p_arg" (optional) */
    while (DEF_ON) {
        /* Wait for an event to occur */
        /* Do some work              */
    }
}
```

Or,

```
void   MyTask (void  *p_arg)
{
    OS_ERR  err;


    /* Do something with "p_arg" (optional) */
    /* Do some work                          */
    OSTaskDel((OS_TCB *)0,
              &err);
}
```

p_arg   is the argument that the task will receive when the task first start (see code above).

p_stk_base is the base address of the task's stack. This is typically the lowest address of the area of storage reserved for the task stack. In other words, if declaring the task's stack as follows:

```
CPU_STK  MyTaskStk[100];
```

OSTaskCreate() would pass **&OSMyTaskStk[0]** to **p_stk_base**.

p_stk_limit is the address of the task's stack limit watermark. This pointer is computed by **OSTaskCreate()** prior to calling **OSTaskStkInit()**.

stk_size   is the size of the task's stack in number of **CPU_STK** elements. In the example above, the stack size is 100.

opt   is the options passed to **OSTaskCreate()** for the task being created.

RETURNED VALUE

The new top of stack after the task's stack is initialized. **OSTaskStkInit()** will place values on the task's stack and will return the new pointer for the stack pointer for the task. The value returned is very processor specific. For some processors, the returned value will point to the last value placed on the stack while, with other processors, the returned value will point at the next free stack entry.

NOTES/WARNINGS

Do not call this function from the application.

EXAMPLE

The pseudo code below shows the typical steps performed by this function. Consult an existing µC/OS-III port for examples. Here it is assumed that the stack grows from high memory to low memory.

```
CPU_STK  *OSTaskStkInit (OS_TASK_PTR   p_task,
                         void          *p_arg,
                         CPU_STK       *p_stk_base,
                         CPU_STK       *p_stk_limit,
                         CPU_STK_SIZE  stk_size,
                         OS_OPT        opt)
{
    CPU_STK  *p_stk;


    p_stk    = &p_stk_base[stk_size - 1u];                      (1)
    *p_stk-- = Initialize the stack as if an interrupt just occurred; (2)
    return (p_stk);                                            (3)
}
```

(1)   **p_stk** is set to the top-of-stack. It is assumed that the stack grows from high memory locations to lower ones. If the stack of the CPU grew from low memory locations to higher ones, the user would simply set **p_stk** to point at the base. However, this also means that it would be necessary to initialize the stack frame in the opposite direction.

(2)   The CPU registers are stored onto the stack using the same stacking order as used when an interrupt service routine (ISR) saves the registers at the beginning of the ISR. The value of the register contents on the stack is typically not important. However, there are some values that are critical. Specifically, you need to place the address of the task in the proper location on the stack frame and it may be important to load the value of the CPU register and possibly pass the value of **p_arg** in one of the CPU registers. Finally, if the task is to return by mistake, it is a good idea to place the address of **OS_TaskReturn()** in the proper location on the stack frame. This ensures that a faulty returning task is intercepted by μC/OS-III.

(3)   Finally, your code will need to return the value of the stack pointer at the new top-of-stack frame. Some processors point to the last stored location, while others point to the next empty location. You should consult the processor documentation so that the return value points at the proper location.

Below is an example showing which arguments **OSTaskCreate()** passes to **OSTaskStkInit()**.

```
CPU_STK  MyTaskStk[100];
OS_TCB   MyTaskTCB;


void  MyTask (void *p_arg)
{
    /* Do something with "parg" (optional) */
}


void  main (void)
{
    OS_ERR  err;
    :
    :
    OSInit(&err);
    /* Check "err" */
    :
    OSTaskCreate ((OS_TCB       *)&MyTaskTCB,
                  (CPU_CHAR     *)"My Task",
                  (OS_TASK_PTR   )MyTask,              /* "p_task"     of OSTaskStkInit() */
                  (void         *)0,                   /* "p_arg"      of OSTaskStkInit() */
                  (OS_PRIO       )prio,
                  (CPU_STK      *)&MyTaskStk[0],       /* "p_stk_base" of OSTaskStkInit() */
                  (CPU_STK_SIZE  )10,                  /* "p_stk_limit" of OSTaskStkInit() */
                  (CPU_STK_SIZE  )100,                 /* "stk_size"   of OSTaskStkInit() */
                  (OS_MSG_QTY    )0,
                  (OS_TICK       )0,
                  (void         *)0,
                  (OS_OPT        )(OS_OPT_TASK_STK_CLR + OS_OPT_TASK_STK_CHK),   /* "opt" */
                  (OS_ERR       *)&err);
    /* Check "err" */
    :
    :
    OSStart(&err);
    /* Check "err" */
}
```

A-77 OSTaskSuspend()

```
void    OSTaskSuspend (OS_TCB   *p_tcb,
                       OS_ERR    *p_err)
```

File	Called from	Code enabled by
os_task.c	Task only	OS_CFG_TASK_SUSPEND_EN

OSTaskSuspend() suspends (or blocks) execution of a task unconditionally. The calling task may be suspended by specifying a NULL pointer for p_tcb, or simply by passing the address of its OS_TCB. In this case, another task needs to resume the suspended task. If the current task is suspended, rescheduling occurs, and μC/OS-III runs the next highest priority task ready-to-run. The only way to resume a suspended task is to call OSTaskResume().

Task suspension is additive, which means that if the task being suspended is delayed until N ticks expire, the task is resumed only when both the time expires and the suspension is removed. Also, if the suspended task is waiting for a semaphore and the semaphore is signaled, the task is removed from the semaphore wait list (if it is the highest-priority task waiting for the semaphore), but execution is not resumed until the suspension is removed.

The user can "nest" suspension of a task by calling OSTaskSuspend() and therefore it is important to call OSTaskResume() an equivalent number of times to resume the task. If suspending a task five times, it is necessary to unsuspend the same task five times to remove the suspension of the task.

ARGUMENTS

p_tcb   is a pointer to the TCB of the task the user is suspending. A NULL pointer indicates suspension of the calling task.

p_err   is a pointer to a variable that will contain an error code returned by this function.

OS_ERR_NONE	if the call was successful and the desired task was suspended.
OS_ERR_TASK_SUSPEND_ISR	if OS_CFG_CALLED_FROM_ISR_CHK_EN set to 1 in os_cfg.h: if the function is called from an ISR.

OS_ERR_TASK_SUSPEND_IDLE   if attempting to suspend the idle task. This is not allowed since the idle task must always exist.

OS_ERR_TASK_SUSPEND_INT_HANDLER if attempting to suspend the ISR handler task. This is not allowed since the ISR handler task is a µC/OS-III internal task.

RETURNED VALUE

None

NOTES/WARNINGS

■ OSTaskSuspend() and OSTaskResume() must be used in pairs.

■ A suspended task can only be resumed by OSTaskResume().

EXAMPLE

```
void TaskX (void *p_arg)
{
    OS_ERR  err;

    (void)&p_arg;
    while (DEF_ON) {
        :
        :
        OSTaskSuspend((OS_TCB *)0,
                      &err);        /* Suspend current task                */
        /* Check "err" */
        :
    }
}
```

A-78 OSTaskSwHook()

```
void  OSTaskSwHook (void)
```

File	Called from	Code enabled by
os_cpu_c.c	OSCtxSw() or OSIntCtxSw()	N/A

OSTaskSwHook() is always called by either OSCtxSw() or OSIntCtxSw() (see os_cpu_a.asm), just after saving the CPU registers onto the task being switched out. This hook function allows the port developer to perform additional operations (if needed) when µC/OS-III performs a context switch.

Before calling OSTaskSwHook(), OSTCBCurPtr points at the OS_TCB of the task being switched out, and OSTCBHighRdyPtr points at the OS_TCB of the new task being switched in.

The code shown in the example below should be included in all implementations of OSTaskSwHook(), and is used for performance measurements. This code is written in C for portability.

ARGUMENTS

None

RETURNED VALUES

None

NOTES/WARNINGS

None

EXAMPLE

The code below calls an application specific hook that the application programmer can define. The user can simply set the value of OS_AppTaskSwHookPtr to point to the desired hook function. When µC/OS-III performs a context switch, it calls OSTaskSwHook() which in turn calls App_OS_TaskSwHook() through OS_AppTaskSwHookPtr.

```
void  App_OS_TaskSwHook (void)                              /* os_app_hooks.c       */
{
    /* Your code goes here! */
}


void App_OS_SetAllHooks (void)                             /* os_app_hooks.c       */
{
    CPU_SR_ALLOC();

    CPU_CRITICAL_ENTER();
    :
    OS_AppTaskSwHookPtr = App_OS_TaskSwHook;
    :
    CPU_CRITICAL_EXIT();
}
```

```
void  OSTaskSwHook (void)                              /* os_cpu_c.c         */
{
#if OS_CFG_TASK_PROFILE_EN > 0u
    CPU_TS    ts;
#endif
#ifdef  CPU_CFG_TIME_MEAS_INT_DIS_EN
    CPU_TS    int_dis_time;
#endif


#if OS_CFG_APP_HOOKS_EN > 0u
    if (OS_AppTaskSwHookPtr != (OS_APP_HOOK_VOID)0) {
        (*OS_AppTaskSwHookPtr)();
    }
#endif
#if OS_CFG_TASK_PROFILE_EN > 0u
    ts = OS_TS_GET();
    if (OSTCBCurPtr != OSTCBHighRdyPtr) {
        OSTCBCurPtr->CyclesDelta  = ts - OSTCBCurPtr->CyclesStart;
        OSTCBCurPtr->CyclesTotal += OSTCBCurPtr->CyclesDelta;
    }
    OSTCBHighRdyPtr->CyclesStart = ts;
#endif
#ifdef  CPU_CFG_INT_DIS_MEAS_EN
    int_dis_time = CPU_IntDisMeasMaxCurReset();
    if (int_dis_time > OSTCBCurPtr->IntDisTimeMax) {
        OSTCBCurPtr->IntDisTimeMax = int_dis_time;
    }
#endif
#if OS_CFG_SCHED_LOCK_TIME_MEAS_EN > 0u
    if (OSTCBCurPtr->SchedLockTimeMax < OSSchedLockTimeMaxCur) {
        OSTCBCurPtr->SchedLockTimeMax = OSSchedLockTimeMaxCur;
    }
    OSSchedLockTimeMaxCur          = (CPU_TS)0;
#endif
}
```

A-79 OSTaskTimeQuantaSet()

```
void    OSTaskTimeQuantaSet (OS_TCB   *p_tcb,
                             OS_TICK  time_quanta,
                             OS_ERR   *p_err)
```

File	Called from	Code enabled by
os_task.c	Task only	OS_CFG_SCHED_ROUND_ROBIN_EN

OSTaskTimeQuantaSet() is used to change the amount of time a task is given when time slicing multiple tasks running at the same priority.

ARGUMENTS

p_tcb   is a pointer to the TCB of the task for which the time quanta is being set. A NULL pointer indicates that the user is changing the time quanta for the calling task.

time_quanta specifies the amount of time (in ticks) that the task will run when μC/OS-III is time slicing between tasks at the same priority. Specifying 0 indicates that the default time as specified will be used when calling the function OSSchedRoundRobinCfg(), or OS_CFG_TICK_RATE_HZ / 10 if you never called OSSchedRoundRobinCfg().

You should not specify a "large" value for this argument as this means that the task will execute for that amount of time when multiple tasks are ready-to-run at the same priority. The concept of time slicing is to allow other equal-priority tasks a chance to run. Typical time quanta periods should be approximately 10 mS. A too small value results in more overhead because of the additional context switches.

p_err   is a pointer to a variable that will contain an error code returned by this function.

OS_ERR_NONE   if the call was successful and the time quanta for the task was changed.

OS_ERR_SET_ISR   if **OS_CFG_CALLED_FROM_ISR_CHK_EN** set to 1 in **os_cfg.h**: if calling this function from an ISR.

RETURNED VALUE

None

NOTES/WARNINGS

Do not specify a large value for **time_quanta**.

EXAMPLE

```
void TaskX (void *p_arg)
{
    OS_ERR  err;


    while (DEF_ON) {
        :
        :
        OSTaskTimeQuantaSet((OS_TCB *)0,
                            OS_CFG_TICK_RATE_HZ / 4;
                            &err);
        /* Check "err" */
        :
    }
}
```

A-80 OSTickISR()

```
void  OSTickISR (void)
```

File	Called from	Code enabled by
os_cpu_a.asm	Tick interrupt	N/A

OSTickISR() is invoked by the tick interrupt, and the function is generally written in assembly language. However, this depends on how interrupts are handled by the processor. (see Chapter 9, "Interrupt Management" on page 175).

ARGUMENTS

None

RETURNED VALUES

None

NOTES/WARNINGS

None

EXAMPLE

The code below indicates how to write OSTickISR() if all interrupts vector to a common location, and the interrupt handler simply calls OSTickISR(). As indicated, this code can be written completely in C and can be placed either in **os_cpu_c.c** of the µC/OS-III port, or in the board support package (**bsp.c**) and be reused by applications using the same BSP.

```
void  OSTickISR (void)
{
    Clear the tick interrupt;
    OSTimeTick();
}
```

The pseudo code below shows how to write **OSTickISR( )** if each interrupt directly vectors to its own interrupt handler. The code, in this case, would be written in assembly language and placed either in **os_cpu_a.asm** of the µC/OS-III port, or in the board support package (**bsp.c**).

```
void  OSTickISR (void)
{
    Save all the CPU registers onto the current task's stack;
    if (OSIntNestingCtr == 0) {
        OSTCBCurPtr->StkPtr = SP;
    }
    OSIntNestingCtr++;
    Clear the tick interrupt;
    OSTimeTick();
    OSIntExit();
    Restore the CPU registers from the stack;
    Return from interrupt;
}
```

A-81 OSTimeDly()

```
void OSTimeDly (OS_TICK   dly,
                OS_OPT    opt,
                OS_ERR    *p_err)
```

File	Called from	Code enabled by
os_time.c	Task only	N/A

OSTimeDly() allows a task to delay itself for an integral number of clock ticks. The delay can either be relative (delay from current time), periodic (delay occurs at fixed intervals) or absolute (delay until we reach some time).

In relative mode, rescheduling always occurs when the number of clock ticks is greater than zero. A delay of **0** means that the task is not delayed, and OSTimeDly() returns immediately to the caller.

In periodic mode, you must specify a non-zero period otherwise the function returns immediately with an appropriate error code. The period is specified in "ticks".

In absolute mode, rescheduling always occurs since all delay values are valid.

The actual delay time depends on the tick rate (see **OS_CFG_TICK_RATE_HZ** if os_cfg_app.h).

ARGUMENTS

dly   is the desired delay expressed in number of clock ticks. Depending on the value of the **opt** field, delays can be relative or absolute.

A relative delay means that the delay is started from the "**current time + dly**".

A periodic delay means the period (in number of ticks). µC/OS-III saves the current time + **dly** in **.TcikCtrPrev** so the next time OSTimeDly() is called, we use **.TickDlyPrev + dly**.

An absolute delay means that the task will wake up when OSTickCtr reaches the value specified by **dly**.

opt   is used to indicate whether the delay is absolute or relative:

     OS_OPT_TIME_DLY   Specifies a relative delay.
     OS_OPT_TIME_PERIODIC   Specifies periodic mode.
     OS_OPT_TIME_MATCH   Specifies that the task will wake up when OSTickCtr reaches the value specified by dly

p_err   is a pointer to a variable that will contain an error code returned by this function.

     OS_ERR_NONE   if the call was successful, and the task has returned from the desired delay.
     OS_ERR_OPT_INVALID   if OS_CFG_ARG_CHK_EN is set to 1 in os_cfg.h: if a valid option is not specified.
     OS_ERR_TIME_DLY_ISR   if OS_CFG_CALLED_FROM_ISR_CHK_EN set to 1 in os_cfg.h: if calling this function from an ISR.
     OS_ERR_TIME_ZERO_DLY   if specifying a delay of 0 when the option was set to OS_OPT_TIME_DLY. Note that a value of 0 is valid when setting the option to OS_OPT_TIME_MATCH.

RETURNED VALUE

None

NOTES/WARNINGS

None

EXAMPLE

```
void TaskX (void *p_arg)
{
  OS_ERR  err;


  while (DEF_ON) {
    :
    :
    OSTimeDly(10,
              OS_OPT_TIME_PERIODIC,
              &err);
    /* Check "err" */
    :
    :
  }
}
```

A-82 OSTimeDlyHMSM()

```
void  OSTimeDlyHMSM (CPU_INT16U  hours,
                     CPU_INT16U  minutes,
                     CPU_INT16U  seconds,
                     CPU_INT32U  milli,
                     OS_OPT      opt,
                     OS_ERR      *p_err)
```

File	Called from	Code enabled by
os_time.c	Task only	OS_CFG_TIME_DLY_HMSM_EN

OSTimeDlyHMSM() allows a task to delay itself for a user-specified period that is specified in hours, minutes, seconds, and milliseconds. This format is more convenient and natural than simply specifying ticks as in OSTimeDly(). Rescheduling always occurs when at least one of the parameters is non-zero. The delay is relative from the time this function is called.

µC/OS-III allows the user to specify nearly any value when indicating that this function is not to be strict about the values being passed (opt == OS_OPT_TIME_HMSM_NON_STRICT). This is a useful feature, for example, to delay a task for thousands of milliseconds.

ARGUMENTS

hours   is the number of hours the task is delayed. Depending on the opt value, the valid range is 0..99 (OS_OPT_TIME_HMSM_STRICT), or 0..999 (OS_OPT_TIME_HMSM_NON_STRICT). Please note that it *not* recommended to delay a task for many hours because feedback from the task will not be available for such a long period of time.

minutes   is the number of minutes the task is delayed. The valid range of values is 0 to 59 (OS_OPT_TIME_HMSM_STRICT), or 0..9,999 (OS_OPT_TIME_HMSM_NON_STRICT). Please note that it *not* recommended to delay a task for tens to hundreds of minutes because feedback from the task will not be available for such a long period of time.

seconds   is the number of seconds the task is delayed. The valid range of values is 0 to 59 (OS_OPT_TIME_HMSM_STRICT), or 0..65,535 (OS_OPT_TIME_HMSM_NON_STRICT).

milli   is the number of milliseconds the task is delayed. The valid range of values is 0 to 999 (OS_OPT_TIME_HMSM_STRICT), or 0..4,294,967,295 (OS_OPT_TIME_HMSM_NON_STRICT). Note that the resolution of this argument is in multiples of the tick rate. For instance, if the tick rate is set to 100Hz, a delay of 4 ms results in no delay because the delay is rounded to the nearest tick. Thus, a delay of 15 ms actually results in a delay of 20 ms.

opt   is the desired mode and can be either:

OS_OPT_TIME_HMSM_STRICT   (see above)
OS_OPT_TIME_HMSM_NON_STRICT (see above)

p_err   is a pointer to a variable that contains an error code returned by this function.

OS_ERR_NONE	if the call was successful and the task has returned from the desired delay.
OS_ERR_TIME_DLY_ISR	if OS_CFG_CALLED_FROM_ISR_CHK_EN set to 1 in os_cfg.h: if calling this function from an ISR.
OS_ERR_TIME_INVALID_HOURS	if OS_CFG_ARG_CHK_EN is set to 1 in os_cfg.h: if not specifying a valid value for hours.
OS_ERR_TIME_INVALID_MINUTES	if OS_CFG_ARG_CHK_EN is set to 1 in os_cfg.h: if not specifying a valid value for minutes.
OS_ERR_TIME_INVALID_SECONDS	if OS_CFG_ARG_CHK_EN is set to 1 in os_cfg.h: if not specifying a valid value for seconds.
OS_ERR_TIME_INVALID_MILLISECONDS	if OS_CFG_ARG_CHK_EN is set to 1 in os_cfg.h: if not specifying a valid value for milliseconds.
OS_ERR_TIME_ZERO_DLY	if specifying a delay of 0 because all the time arguments are 0.

RETURNED VALUE

None

NOTES/WARNINGS

- Note that `OSTimeDlyHMSM(0,0,0,0,OS_OPT_TIME_HMSM_???,&err)` (i.e., hours, minutes, seconds, milliseconds are 0) results in no delay, and the function returns to the caller.

- The total delay (in ticks) must not exceed the maximum acceptable value that an `OS_TICK` variable can hold. Typically `OS_TICK` is a 32-bit value.

EXAMPLE

```
void TaskX (void *p_arg)
{
    OS_ERR  err;


    while (DEF_ON) {
        :
        :
        OSTimeDlyHMSM(0,
                      0,
                      1,
                      0,
                      OS_OPT_TIME_HMSM_STRICT,
                      &err);              /* Delay task for 1 second */
        /* Check "err" */
        :
        :
    }
}
```

A-83 OSTimeDlyResume()

```
void  OSTimeDlyResume (OS_TCB  *p_tcb,
                       OS_ERR  *p_err)
```

File	Called from	Code enabled by
os_time.c	Task only	OS_CFG_TIME_DLY_RESUME_EN

OSTimeDlyResume() resumes a task that has been delayed through a call to either OSTimeDly(), or OSTimeDlyHMSM().

ARGUMENTS

p_tcb   is a pointer to the TCB of the task that is resuming. A **NULL** pointer is not valid since it would indicate that the user is attempting to resume the current task and that is not possible as the caller cannot possibly be delayed.

p_err   is a pointer to a variable that contains an error code returned by this function.

OS_ERR_NONE	if the call was successful and the task was resumed.
OS_ERR_STATE_INVALID	if the task is in an invalid state.
OS_ERR_TIME_DLY_RESUME_ISR	if **OS_CFG_CALLED_FROM_ISR_CHK_EN** set to 1 in **os_cfg.h**: if calling this function from an ISR.
OS_ERR_TIME_NOT_DLY	if **OS_CFG_ARG_CHK_EN** is set to 1 in **os_cfg.h**: if the task was not delayed or, you passed a NULL pointer for the TCB.
OS_ERR_TASK_SUSPENDED	if the task to resume is suspended and will remain suspended.

RETURNED VALUE

None

NOTES/WARNINGS

Do not call this function to resume a task that is waiting for an event with timeout.

EXAMPLE

```
OS_TCB  AnotherTaskTCB;


void TaskX (void *p_arg)
{
    OS_ERR  err;


    while (DEF_ON) {
        :
        OSTimeDlyResume(&AnotherTaskTCB,
                        &err);
        /* Check "err" */
        :
    }
}
```

A-84 OSTimeGet()

OS_TICK   OSTimeGet (OS_ERR   *p_err)

File	Called from	Code enabled by
os_time.c	Task or ISR	N/A

OSTimeGet() obtains the current value of the system clock. Specifically, it returns a snapshot of the variable OSTickCtr. The system clock is a counter of type OS_TICK that counts the number of clock ticks since power was applied, or since OSTickCtr was last set by OSTimeSet().

ARGUMENTS

p_err   is a pointer to a variable that contains an error code returned by this function.

OS_ERR_NONE   if the call was successful.

RETURNED VALUE

The current value of OSTickCtr (in number of ticks).

NOTES/WARNINGS

None

EXAMPLE

```
void TaskX (void *p_arg)
{
    OS_TICK  clk;
    OS_ERR   err;


    while (DEF_ON) {
        :
        :
        clk = OSTimeGet(&err);  /* Get current value of system clock */
        /* Check "err" */
        :
        :
    }
}
```

A-85 OSTimeSet()

```
void OSTimeSet (OS_TICK ticks,
               OS_ERR *p_err)
```

File	Called from	Code enabled by
os_time.c	Task or ISR	N/A

OSTimeSet() sets the system clock. The system clock (OSTickCtr) is a counter, which has a data type of OS_TICK, and it counts the number of clock ticks since power was applied, or since the system clock was last set.

ARGUMENTS

ticks   is the desired value for the system clock, in ticks.

p_err   is a pointer to a variable that will contain an error code returned by this function.

OS_ERR_NONE   if the call was successful.

RETURNED VALUE

None

NOTES/WARNINGS

You should be careful when using this function because other tasks may depend on the current value of the tick counter (OSTickCtr). Specifically, a task may delay itself (see OSTimeDly()) and specify to wake up when OSTickCtr reaches a specific value.

EXAMPLE

```
void TaskX (void *p_arg)
{
    OS_ERR  err;


    while (DEF_ON) {
        :
        :
        OSTimeSet(0,
                  &err);        /* Reset the system clock  */
        /* Check "err" */
        :
        :
    }
}
```

A-86 OSTimeTick()

```
void  OSTimeTick (void)
```

File	Called from	Code enabled by
os_time.c	ISR only	N/A

OSTimeTick() "announces" that a tick has just occurred, and that time delays and timeouts need to be updated. This function must be called from the tick ISR.

ARGUMENTS

None

RETURNED VALUE

None

NOTES/WARNINGS

None

EXAMPLE

```
void MyTickISR (void)
{
    /* Clear interrupt source */
    OSTimeTick();
    :
    :
}
```

A-87 OSTimeTickHook()

```
void  OSTimeTickHook (void);
```

File	Called from	Code enabled by
os_cpu_c.c	OSTimeTick() ONLY	N/A

This function is called by **OSTimeTick()**, which is assumed to be called from an ISR. **OSTimeTickHook()** is called at the very beginning of **OSTimeTick()** to give priority to user or port-specific code when the tick interrupt occurs.

If the **#define OS_CFG_APP_HOOKS_EN** is set to 1 in **os_cfg.h**, **OSTimeTickHook()** will call **App_OS_TimeTickHook()**.

OSTimeTickHook() is part of the CPU port code and the function *must not* be called by the application code. **OSTimeTickHook()** is actually used by the μC/OS-III port developer.

ARGUMENTS

None

RETURNED VALUE

None

NOTES/WARNINGS

Do not call this function from the application.

EXAMPLE

The code below calls an application-specific hook that the application programmer can define. The user can simply set the value of **OS_AppTimeTickHookPtr** to point to the desired hook function **OSTimeTickHook()** is called by **OSTimeTick()** which in turn calls **App_OS_TimeTickHook()** through the pointer **OS_AppTimeTickHookPtr**.

```
void  App_OS_TimeTickHook (void)                          /* os_app_hooks.c      */
{
    /* Your code goes here! */
}


void App_OS_SetAllHooks (void)                            /* os_app_hooks.c      */
{
    CPU_SR_ALLOC();

    CPU_CRITICAL_ENTER();
    :
    OS_AppTimeTickHookPtr = App_OS_TimeTickHook;
    :
    CPU_CRITICAL_EXIT();
}



void  OSTimeTickHook (void)                               /* os_cpu_c.c          */
{
#if OS_CFG_APP_HOOKS_EN > 0u
    if (OS_AppTimeTickHookPtr != (OS_APP_HOOK_VOID)0) {   /* Call application hook */
        (*OS_AppTimeTickHookPtr)();
    }
#endif
}
```

A-88 OSTmrCreate()

```
void   OSTmrCreate (OS_TMR                *p_tmr,
                    CPU_CHAR              *p_name,
                    OS_TICK               dly,
                    OS_TICK               period,
                    OS_OPT                opt,
                    OS_TMR_CALLBACK_PTR   p_callback,
                    void                  *p_callback_arg,
                    OS_ERR                *p_err)
```

File	Called from	Code enabled by
os_tmr.c	Task only	OS_CFG_TMR_EN

OSTmrCreate() allows the user to create a software timer. The timer can be configured to run continuously (opt set to OS_TMR_OPT_PERIODIC), or only once (opt set to OS_TMR_OPT_ONE_SHOT). When the timer counts down to 0 (from the value specified in period), an optional "callback" function can be executed. The callback can be used to signal a task that the timer expired, or perform any other function. However, it is recommended to keep the callback function as short as possible.

The timer is created in the "stop" mode and therefore the user *must* call OSTmrStart() to actually start the timer. If configuring the timer for ONE-SHOT mode, and the timer expires, you need to call OSTmrStart() to retrigger the timer, call OSTmrDel() to delete the timer if it is not necessary to retrigger it, or not use the timer anymore. Note: you can use the callback function to delete the timer if using the ONE-SHOT mode.

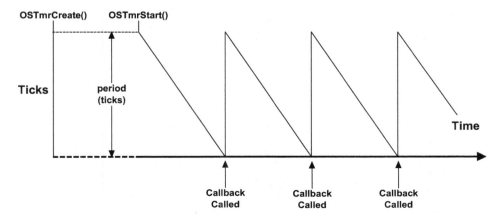

651

PERIODIC MODE (see "**opt**") – **dly** > 0, **period** > 0

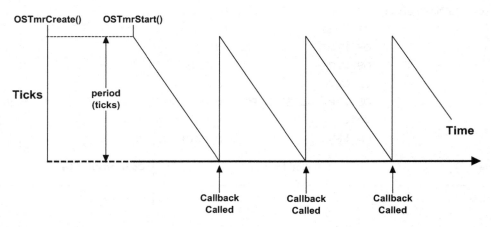

PERIODIC MODE (see "**opt**") – "**dly** == 0, period > 0

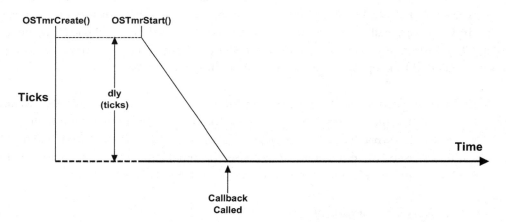

ONE-SHOT MODE (see "**opt**") – **dly** > 0, **period** == 0

ARGUMENTS

p_tmr   is a pointer to the timer-control block of the desired timer. It is assumed that storage for the timer will be allocated in the application. In other words, you should declare a "global" variable as follows, and pass a pointer to this variable to `OSTmrCreate()`:

`OS_TMR MyTmr;`

p_name   is a pointer to an ASCII string (**NUL** terminated) used to assign a name to the timer. The name can be displayed by debuggers or µC/Probe.

dly   specifies the initial delay (specified in timer tick units) used by the timer (see drawing above). If the timer is configured for ONE-SHOT mode, this is the timeout used. If the timer is configured for PERIODIC mode, this is the timeout to wait before the timer enters periodic mode. The units of this time depends on how often the user will call `OSTmrSignal()` (see `OSTimeTick()`). If `OSTmrSignal()` is called every 1/10 of a second (i.e., `OS_CFG_TMR_TASK_RATE_HZ` set to 10), **dly** specifies the number of 1/10 of a second before the delay expires.

period   specifies the period repeated by the timer if configured for PERIODIC mode. You would set the "**period**" to 0 when using ONE-SHOT mode. The units of time depend on how often `OSTmrSignal()` is called. If `OSTmrSignal()` is called every 1/10 of a second (i.e., `OS_CFG_TMR_TASK_RATE_HZ` set to 10), the period specifies the number of 1/10 of a second before the timer repeats.

opt   is used to specify whether the timer is to be ONE-SHOT or PERIODIC:

`OS_OPT_TMR_ONE_SHOT specifies   ONE-SHOT mode`
`OS_OPT_TMR_PERIODIC specifies   PERIODIC mode`

p_callback is a pointer to a function that will execute when the timer expires (ONE-SHOT mode), or every time the period expires (PERIODIC mode). A **NULL** pointer indicates that no action is to be performed upon timer expiration. The callback function must be declared as follows:

`void MyCallback (OS_TMR *p_tmr, void *p_arg);`

When called, the callback will be passed the pointer to the timer as well as an argument (**p_callback_arg**), which can be used to indicate to the callback what to do. Note that the user is allowed to call all of the timer related functions (i.e., **OSTmrCreate()**, **OSTmrDel()**, **OSTmrStateGet()**, **OSTmrRemainGet()**, **OSTmrStart()**, and **OSTmrStop()**) from the callback function.

Do not make blocking calls within callback functions.

p_callback_arg   is an argument passed to the callback function when the timer expires (ONE-SHOT mode), or every time the period expires (PERIODIC mode). The pointer is declared as a "**void ***" so it can point to any data.

p_err   is a pointer to a variable that contains an error code returned by this function.

OS_ERR_NONE	if the call was successful.
OS_ERR_OBJ_PTR_NULL	if **OS_CFG_ARG_CHK_EN** is set to 1 in **os_cfg.h**: if **p_tmr** is a **NULL** pointer
OS_ERR_TMR_INVALID_DLY	if **OS_CFG_ARG_CHK_EN** is set to 1 in **os_cfg.h**: if specifying an invalid delay in ONE-SHOT mode. In other words, it is not allowed to delay for **0** in ONE-SHOT mode.
OS_ERR_TMR_INVALID_PERIOD	if **OS_CFG_ARG_CHK_EN** is set to 1 in **os_cfg.h**: if specifying an invalid period in PERIODIC mode. It is not allowed to have a **0** period in PERIODIC.
OS_ERR_OPT_INVALID	if **OS_CFG_ARG_CHK_EN** is set to 1 in **os_cfg.h**: if not specifying a valid options.
OS_ERR_TMR_ISR	if OS_CFG_CALLED_FROM_ISR_CHK_EN set to 1 in **os_cfg.h**: if calling this function from an ISR.
OS_ERR_ILLEGAL_CREATE_RUN_TIME	if **OS_SAFETY_CRITICAL_IEC61508** is defined: you called this after calling **OSSafetyCriticalStart()** and thus you are no longer allowed to create additional kernel objects.

RETURNED VALUES

None.

NOTES/WARNINGS

- *Do not* call this function from an ISR.

- The timer is *not* started when it is created. To start the timer, simply call **OSTmrStart( )**.

- *Do not* make blocking calls within callback functions.

- Keep callback functions as short as possible.

EXAMPLE

```
OS_TMR  CloseDoorTmr;


void Task (void *p_arg)
{
    OS_ERR   err;


    (void)&p_arg;
    while (DEF_ON) {
        OSTmrCreate(&CloseDoorTmr,          /* p_tmr           */
                    "Door close",           /* p_name          */
                    10,                     /* dly             */
                    100,                    /* period          */
                    OS_OPT_TMR_PERIODIC,    /* opt             */
                    DoorCloseFnct,          /* p_callback      */
                    0,                      /* p_callback_arg  */
                    &err);                  /* p_err           */
        /* Check "err" */
    }
}


void DoorCloseFnct (OS_TMR  *p_tmr,
                    void    *p_arg)
{
    /* Close the door! */
}
```

A-89 OSTmrDel()

```
CPU_BOOLEAN   OSTmrDel(OS_TMR    *p_tmr,
                       OS_ERR     *p_err)
```

File	Called from	Code enabled by
os_tmr.c	Task only	OS_CFG_TMR_EN and OS_CFG_TMR_DEL_EN

OSTmrDel() allows the user to delete a timer. If a timer was running it will be stopped and then deleted. If the timer has already timed out and is therefore stopped, it will simply be deleted.

It is up to the user to delete unused timers. If deleting a timer, you must not reference it again.

ARGUMENTS

p_tmr   is a pointer to the timer to be deleted.

p_err   a pointer to an error code and can be any of the following:

OS_ERR_NONE	if the timer was deleted.
OS_ERR_OBJ_TYPE	if OS_CFG_OBJ_TYPE_CHK_EN is set to 1 in os_cfg.h: if the user did not pass a pointer to a timer.
OS_ERR_TMR_INVALID	if OS_CFG_ARG_CHK_EN is set to 1 in os_cfg.h: if p_tmr is a NULL pointer.
OS_ERR_TMR_ISR	if OS_CFG_CALLED_FROM_ISR_CHK_EN set to 1 in os_cfg.h: This function is called from an ISR, which is *not* allowed.
OS_ERR_TMR_INACTIVE	p_tmr is pointing to an inactive timer. In other words, this error appears when pointing to a timer that has been deleted.
OS_ERR_TMR_INVALID_STATE	the timer is in an invalid state.

RETURNED VALUES

DEF_TRUE if the timer was deleted, DEF_FALSE if not.

NOTES/WARNINGS

- *Do not* call this function from an ISR.

- When deleting a timer, *do not* reference it again unless you re-create the timer by calling OSTmrCreate().

EXAMPLE

```
OS_TMR  CloseDoorTmr;


void Task (void *p_arg)
{
    OS_ERR       err;
    CPU_BOOLEAN  deleted;


    (void)&p_arg;
    while (DEF_ON) {
        deleted = OSTmrDel(&CloseDoorTmr,
                           &err);
        /* Check "err" */
    }
}
```

A-90 OSTmrRemainGet()

```
OS_TICK  OSTmrRemainGet(OS_TMR *p_tmr,
                        OS_ERR *p_err);
```

File	Called from	Code enabled by
os_tmr.c	Task only	OS_CFG_TMR_EN

OSTmrRemainGet() allows the user to obtain the time remaining (before timeout) of the specified timer. The value returned depends on the rate (in Hz) at which the timer task is signaled (see OS_CFG_TMR_TASK_RATE_HZ). If OS_CFG_TMR_TASK_RATE_HZ is set to 10, the value returned is the number of 1/10 of a second before the timer times out. If the timer has timed out, the value returned is 0.

ARGUMENTS

p_tmr   is a pointer to the timer the user is inquiring about.

p_err   a pointer to an error code and can be any of the following:

OS_ERR_NONE	if the function returned the time remaining for the timer.
OS_ERR_OBJ_TYPE	if OS_CFG_OBJ_TYPE_CHK_EN is set to 1 in os_cfg.h: 'p_tmr" is not pointing to a timer.
OS_ERR_TMR_INVALID	if OS_CFG_ARG_CHK_EN is set to 1 in os_cfg.h: if p_tmr is a NULL pointer.
OS_ERR_TMR_ISR	if OS_CFG_CALLED_FROM_ISR_CHK_EN set to 1 in os_cfg.h: This function is called from an ISR, which is *not* allowed.
OS_ERR_TMR_INACTIVE	p_tmr is pointing to an inactive timer. In other words, this error will appear when pointing to a timer that has been deleted.
OS_ERR_TMR_INVALID_STATE	the timer is in an invalid state.

RETURNED VALUES

The time remaining for the timer. The value returned depends on the rate (in Hz) at which the timer task is signaled (see **OS_CFG_TMR_TASK_RATE_HZ**). If **OS_CFG_TMR_TASK_RATE_HZ** is set to 10 the value returned is the number of 1/10 of a second before the timer times out. If specifying an invalid timer, the returned value will be 0. If the timer expired, the returned value will be 0.

NOTES/WARNINGS

■ *Do not* call this function from an ISR.

EXAMPLE

```
OS_TICK     TimeRemainToCloseDoor;
OS_TMR      CloseDoorTmr;


void Task (void *p_arg)
{
    OS_ERR      err;


    (void)&p_arg;
    while (DEF_ON) {
        TimeRemainToCloseDoor = OSTmrRemainGet(&CloseDoorTmr,
                                               &err);
        /* Check "err" */
    }
}
```

A-91 OSTmrStart()

```
CPU_BOOLEAN  OSTmrStart (OS_TMR    *p_tmr,
                         OS_ERR    *p_err);
```

File	Called from	Code enabled by
os_tmr.c	Task only	OS_CFG_TMR_EN

OSTmrStart() allows the user to start (or restart) the countdown process of a timer. The timer *must* have previously been created.

ARGUMENTS

p_tmr   is a pointer to the timer to start (or restart).

p_err   a pointer to an error code and can be any of the following:

OS_ERR_NONE	if the timer was started.
OS_ERR_OBJ_TYPE	if OS_CFG_OBJ_TYPE_CHK_EN is set to 1 in os_cfg.h: 'p_tmr" is not pointing to a timer.
OS_ERR_TMR_INVALID	if OS_CFG_ARG_CHK_EN is set to 1 in os_cfg.h: if p_tmr is a NULL pointer.
OS_ERR_TMR_INACTIVE	p_tmr is pointing to an inactive timer. In other words, this error occurs if pointing to a timer that has been deleted or was not created.
OS_ERR_TMR_INVALID_STATE	the timer is in an invalid state.
OS_ERR_TMR_ISR	if OS_CFG_CALLED_FROM_ISR_CHK_EN set to 1 in os_cfg.h: This function was called from an ISR, which is *not* allowed.

RETURNED VALUES

DEF_TRUE   if the timer was started

DEF_FALSE if an error occurred.

NOTES/WARNINGS

■ *Do not* call this function from an ISR.

■ The timer *must* have previously been created.

EXAMPLE

```
OS_TMR      CloseDoorTmr;


void Task (void *p_arg)
{
    OS_ERR      err;
    CPU_BOOLEAN status;


    (void)&p_arg;
    while (DEF_ON) {
        status = OSTmrStart(&CloseDoorTmr,
                            &err);
        /* Check "err" */
    }
}
```

A-92 OSTmrStateGet()

```
OS_STATE  OSTmrStateGet(OS_TMR  *p_tmr,
                        OS_ERR  *p_err);
```

File	Called from	Code enabled by
os_tmr.c	Task only	OS_CFG_TMR_EN

`OSTmrStateGet()` allows the user to obtain the current state of a timer. A timer can be in one of four states:

OS_TMR_STATE_UNUSED	the timer has not been created
OS_TMR_STATE_STOPPED	the timer is created but has not yet started, or has been stopped.
OS_TMR_STATE_COMPLETED	the timer is in *one-shot* mode, and has completed its delay.
OS_TMR_STATE_RUNNING	the timer is currently running

ARGUMENTS

p_tmr   is a pointer to the timer that the user is inquiring about.

p_err   a pointer to an error code and can be any of the following:

OS_ERR_NONE	if the function returned the state of the timer.
OS_ERR_OBJ_TYPE	if OS_CFG_OBJ_TYPE_CHK_EN is set to 1 in os_cfg.h: p_tmr is not pointing to a timer.
OS_ERR_TMR_INVALID	if OS_CFG_ARG_CHK_EN is set to 1 in os_cfg.h: if p_tmr is a NULL pointer.
OS_ERR_TMR_INVALID_STATE	the timer is in an invalid state.
OS_ERR_TMR_ISR	if OS_CFG_CALLED_FROM_ISR_CHK_EN set to 1 in os_cfg.h: This function was called from an ISR, which is *not* allowed.

RETURNED VALUES

The state of the timer (see description).

NOTES/WARNINGS

■   *Do not* call this function from an ISR.

EXAMPLE

```
OS_STATE    CloseDoorTmrState;
OS_TMR      CloseDoorTmr;


void Task (void *p_arg)
{
    OS_ERR  err;


    (void)&p_arg;
    while (DEF_ON) {
        CloseDoorTmrState = OSTmrStateGet(&CloseDoorTmr,
                                          &err);

        /* Check "err" */
    }
}
```

A-93   OSTmrStop()

```
CPU_BOOLEAN    OSTmrStop (OS_TMR    *p_tmr,
                          OS_OPT     opt,
                          void      *p_callback_arg,
                          OS_ERR    *p_err)
```

File	Called from	Code enabled by
os_tmr.c	Task only	OS_CFG_TMR_EN

OSTmrStop() allows the user to stop a timer. The user may execute the callback function of the timer when it is stopped, and pass this callback function a different argument than was specified when the timer was started. This allows the callback function to know that the timer was stopped since the callback argument can be set to indicate this (this is application specific). If the timer is already stopped, the callback function is not called.

ARGUMENTS

p_tmr   is a pointer to the timer control block of the desired timer.

opt   is used to specify options:

OS_OPT_TMR_NONE	No option
OS_OPT_TMR_CALLBACK	Run the callback function with the argument specified when the timer was created.
OS_OPT_TMR_CALLBACK_ARG	Run the callback function, but use the argument passed in OSTmrStop() instead of the one specified when the task was created.

p_callback_arg   is a new argument to pass the callback functions (see options above).

p_err   is a pointer to a variable that contains an error code returned by this function.

OS_ERR_NONE	if the call was successful.
OS_ERR_OBJ_TYPE	if OS_CFG_OBJ_TYPE_CHK_EN is set to 1 in os_cfg.h: if p_tmr is not pointing to a timer object.

OS_ERR_TMR_INACTIVE	the timer cannot be stopped since it is inactive.
OS_ERR_TMR_INVALID	if **OS_CFG_ARG_CHK_EN** is set to 1 in **os_cfg.h**: if you passed a **NULL** pointer for the **p_tmr** argument.
OS_ERR_TMR_INVALID_OPT	if the user did not specify a valid option.
OS_ERR_TMR_INVALID_STATE	the timer is in an invalid state.
OS_ERR_TMR_ISR	if **OS_CFG_CALLED_FROM_ISR_CHK_EN** set to 1 in **os_cfg.h**: if calling this function from an ISR.
OS_ERR_TMR_NO_CALLBACK	if the timer lacks a callback function. This should have been specified when the timer was created.
OS_ERR_TMR_STOPPED	if the timer is currently stopped.

RETURNED VALUES

DEF_TRUE   if the timer was stopped (even if it was already stopped).

DEF_FALSE   if an error occurred.

NOTES/WARNINGS

■ *Do not* call this function from an ISR.

■ The callback function is *not* called if the timer is already stopped.

EXAMPLE

```
OS_TMR  CloseDoorTmr;


void Task (void *p_arg)
{
    OS_ERR    err;


    (void)&p_arg;
    while (DEF_ON) {
        OSTmrStop(&CloseDoorTmr,
                  OS_TMR_OPT_CALLBACK,
                  (void *)0,
                  &err);
        /* Check "err" */
    }
}
```

A-94 OSVersion()

```
CPU_INT16U OSVersion (OS_ERR  *p_err);
```

File	Called from	Code enabled by
os_core.c	Task or ISR	N/A

OSVersion() obtains the current version of µC/OS-III.

ARGUMENTS

p_err   is a pointer to a variable that contains an error code returned by this function. Currently, OSVersion() always return:

OS_ERR_NONE

RETURNED VALUE

The version is returned as **x.yy.zz** multiplied by **10,000**. For example, V3.00.00 is returned as **30000**.

NOTES/WARNINGS

None

EXAMPLE

```
void TaskX (void *p_arg)
{
    CPU_INT16U  os_version;
    OS_ERR      err;


    while (DEF_ON) {
        :
        :
        os_version = OSVersion(&err);  /* Obtain µC/OS-III's version    */
        /* Check "err" */
        :
        :
    }
}
```

μC/OS-III Configuration Manual

Three (3) files are used to configure μC/OS-III as highlighted in Figure B-1: **os_cfg.h**, **os_cfg_app.h** and **os_type.h**.

Table B-1 shows where these files are typically located on your on a computer.

File	Directory
os_cfg.h	\Micrium\Software\uCOS-III\Cfg\Template
os_cfg_app.h	\Micrium\Software\uCOS-III\Cfg\Template
os_type.h	\Micrium\Software\uCOS-III\Source

Table B-1 **Configuration files and directories**

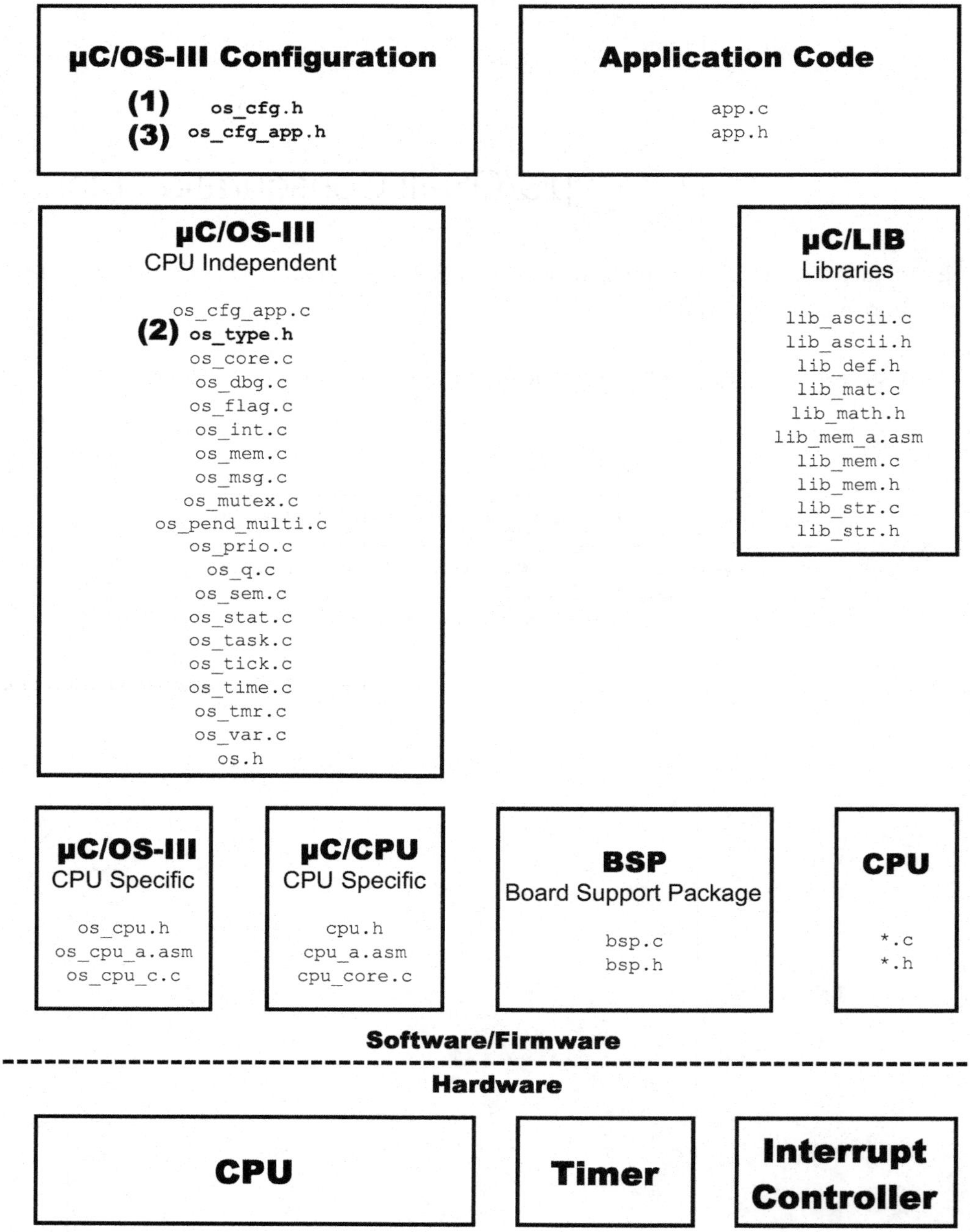

Figure B-1 µC/OS-III **File Structure**

FB-1(1)   **µC/OS-III Features (os_cfg.h):**

os_cfg.h is used to determine which features are needed from µC/OS-III for an application (i.e., product). Specifically, this file allows a user to determine whether to include semaphores, mutexes, event flags, run-time argument checking, etc.

FB-1(2)   **µC/OS-III Data Types (os_type.h):**

os_type.h establishes µC/OS-III-specific data types used when building an application. It specifies the size of variables used to represent task priorities, the size of a semaphore count, and more. This file contains recommended data types for µC/OS-III, however these can be altered to make better use of the CPU's natural word size. For example, on some 32-bit CPUs, it is better to declare boolean variables as 32-bit values for performance considerations, even though an 8-bit quantity is more space efficient (assuming performance is more important than footprint).

The port developer typically makes those decisions, since altering the contents of the file requires a deep understanding of the CPU and, most important, how data sizes affect µC/OS-III.

FB-1(3)   **µC/OS-III Stacks, Pools and other data sizes (os_cfg_app.h):**

µC/OS-III can be configured at the application level through **#define** constants in **os_cfg_app.h**. The **#defines** allows a user to specify stack sizes for all µC/OS-III internal tasks: the idle task, statistic task, tick task, timer task, and the ISR handler task. **os_cfg_app.h** also allows users to specify task priorities (except for the idle task since it is always the lowest priority), the tick rate, tick wheel size, the timer wheel size, and more.

The contents of the three configuration files will be described in the following sections.

B-1 µC/OS-III FEATURES (OS_CFG.H)

Compile-time configuration allows users to determine which features to enable and those features that are not needed. With compile-time configuration, the code and data sizes of µC/OS-III (i.e., its footprint) can be reduced by enabling only the desired functionality.

Compile-time configuration is accomplished by setting a number of **#define** constants in a file called **os_cfg.h** that the application is expected to provide. You simply copy **os_cfg.h** into the application directory and change the copied file to satisfy the application's requirements. This way, **os_cfg.h** is not recreated from scratch.

The compile-time configuration **#defines** are listed below in alphabetic order and are not necessarily found in this order in **os_cfg.h**.

OS_CFG_APP_HOOKS_EN

When set to 1, this **#define** specifies that application-defined hooks can be called from µC/OS-III's hooks. This allows the application code to extend the functionality of µC/OS-III. Specifically:

The µC/OS-III hook ...	Calls the Application-define hook through...
OSIdleTaskHook()	OS_AppIdleTaskHookPtr
OSInitHook()	None
OSStatTaskHook()	OS_AppStatTaskHookPtr
OSTaskCreateHook()	OS_AppTaskCreateHookPtr
OSTaskDelHook()	OS_AppTaskDelHookPtr
OSTaskReturnHook()	OS_AppTaskReturnHookPtr
OSTaskSwHook()	OS_AppTaskSwHookPtr
OSTimeTickHook()	OS_AppTimeTickHookPtr

Application hook functions could be declared as shown in the code below.

```
void  App_OS_TaskCreateHook (OS_TCB *p_tcb)
{
    /* Your code here */
}


void  App_OS_TaskDelHook (OS_TCB *p_tcb)
{
    /* Your code here */
}


void  App_OS_TaskReturnHook (OS_TCB *p_tcb)
{
    /* Your code here */
}


void  App_OS_IdleTaskHook (void)
{
    /* Your code here */
}


void  App_OS_StatTaskHook (void)
{
    /* Your code here */
}


void  App_OS_TaskSwHook (void)
{
    /* Your code here */
}


void  App_OS_TimeTickHook (void)
{
    /* Your code here */
}
```

It's also up to a user to set the value of the pointers so that they point to the appropriate functions as shown below. The pointers do not have to be set in **main()** but, you can set them after calling **OSInit()**.

```
void  main (void)
{
    OS_ERR  err;


    OSInit(&err);
    :
    :
    OS_AppTaskCreateHookPtr = (OS_APP_HOOK_TCB )App_OS_TaskCreateHook;
    OS_AppTaskDelHookPtr    = (OS_APP_HOOK_TCB )App_OS_TaskDelHook;
    OS_AppTaskReturnHookPtr = (OS_APP_HOOK_TCB )App_OS_TaskReturnHook;
    OS_AppIdleTaskHookPtr   = (OS_APP_HOOK_VOID)App_OS_IdleTaskHook;
    OS_AppStatTaskHookPtr   = (OS_APP_HOOK_VOID)App_OS_StatTaskHook;
    OS_AppTaskSwHookPtr     = (OS_APP_HOOK_VOID)App_OS_TaskSwHook;
    OS_AppTimeTickHookPtr   = (OS_APP_HOOK_VOID)App_OS_TimeTickHook;
    :
    :
    OSStart(&err);
}
```

Note that not every hook function need to be defined, only the ones the user wants to place in the application code.

Also, if you don't intend to extend µC/OS-III's hook through these application hooks, you can set **OS_CFG_APP_HOOKS_EN** to 0 to save RAM (i.e., the pointers).

OS_CFG_ARG_CHK_EN

OS_CFG_ARG_CHK_EN determines whether the user wants most of µC/OS-III functions to perform argument checking. When set to 1, µC/OS-III ensures that pointers passed to functions are non-**NULL**, that arguments passed are within allowable range, that options are valid, and more. When set to 0, **OS_CFG_ARG_CHK_EN** those arguments are not checked and the amount of code space and processing time required by µC/OS-III is reduced. You would set **OS_CFG_ARG_CHK_EN** to 0 if you are certain that the arguments are correct.

µC/OS-III performs argument checking in over 40 functions. Therefore, you can save a few hundred bytes of code space by disabling this check. However, you should always enable argument checking until you are certain the code can be trusted.

OS_CFG_CALLED_FROM_ISR_CHK_EN

OS_CFG_CALLED_FROM_ISR_CHK_EN determines whether most of µC/OS-III functions are to confirm that the function is not called from an ISR. In other words, most of the functions from µC/OS-III should be called by task-level code except "post" type functions (which can also be called from ISRs). By setting this **#define** to 1 μC/OS-III is told to make sure that functions that are only supposed to be called by tasks are not called by ISRs. It's highly recommended to set this **#define** to 1 until you are absolutely certain that the code is behaving correctly and that task-level functions are always called from tasks. You can set this **#define** to 0 to save code space and, of course, processing time.

μC/OS-III performs this check in approximately 50 functions. Therefore, you can save a few hundred bytes of code space by disabling this check.

OS_CFG_DBG_EN

When set to 1, this **#define** adds ROM constants located in **os_dbg.c** to help support kernel aware debuggers. Specifically, a number of named ROM variables can be queried by a debugger to find out about compiled-in options. For example, a debugger can find out the size of an **OS_TCB**, μC/OS-III's version number, the size of an event flag group (**OS_FLAG_GRP**), and much more.

OS_CFG_FLAG_EN

OS_CFG_FLAG_EN enables (when set to 1) or disables (when set to 0) code generation of event flag services and data structures. This reduces the amount of code and data space needed when an application does not require event flags. When **OS_CFG_FLAG_EN** is set to 0, it is not necessary to enable or disable any of the other **OS_CFG_FLAG_xxx #define** constants in this section.

OS_CFG_FLAG_DEL_EN

OS_CFG_FLAG_DEL_EN enables (when set to 1) or disables (when set to 0) code generation of the function **OSFlagDel()**.

OS_CFG_FLAG_MODE_CLR_EN

OS_CFG_FLAG_MODE_CLR_EN enables (when set to 1) or disables (when set to 0) code generation used to wait for event flags to be 0 instead of 1. Generally, you would wait for event flags to be set. However, the user may also want to wait for event flags to be clear and in this case, enable this option.

OS_CFG_FLAG_PEND_ABORT_EN

OS_CFG_FLAG_PEND_ABORT_EN enables (when set to 1) or disables (when set to 0) code generation of the function **OSFlagPendAbort()**.

B

OS_CFG_ISR_POST_DEFERRED_EN

When set to 1, OS_CFG_ISR_POST_DEFERRED_EN reduces interrupt latency since interrupts are not disabled during most critical sections of code within µC/OS-III. Instead, the scheduler is locked during the processing of these critical sections. The advantage of setting OS_CFG_ISR_POST_DEFERRED_EN to 1 is that interrupt latency is lower, however, ISR to task response is slightly higher. It is recommended to set OS_CFG_ISR_POST_DEFERRED_EN to 1 when enabling the following services, since setting this #define to 0 would potentially make interrupt latency unacceptably high:

µC/OS-III Services	Enabled by ...
Event Flags	OS_CFG_FLAG_EN
Multiple Pend	OS_CFG_PEND_MULTI_EN
OS???Post() with broadcast	
OS???Del() with OS_OPT_DEL_ALWAYS	
OS???PendAbort()	

The compromise to make is:

> OS_CFG_ISR_POST_DEFERRED_EN set to 1
> Short interrupt latency, longer ISR-to-task response.

> OS_CFG_ISR_POST_DEFERRED_EN set to 0
> Long interrupt latency (see table above), shorter ISR-to-task response.

OS_CFG_MEM_EN

OS_CFG_MEM_EN enables (when set to 1) or disables (when set to 0) code generation of the µC/OS-III partition memory manager and its associated data structures. This feature allows users to reduce the amount of code and data space needed when an application does not require the use of memory partitions.

OS_CFG_MUTEX_EN

OS_CFG_MUTEX_EN enables (when set to 1) or disables (when set to 0) the code generation of all mutual exclusion semaphore services and data structures. This feature allows users to reduce the amount of code and data space needed when an application does not require the use of mutexes. When OS_CFG_MUTEX_EN is set to 0, there is no need to enable or disable any of the other OS_CFG_MUTEX_XXX #define constants in this section.

OS_CFG_MUTEX_DEL_EN

OS_CFG_MUTEX_DEL_EN enables (when set to 1) or disables (when set to 0) code generation of the function OSMutexDel().

OS_CFG_MUTEX_PEND_ABORT_EN

OS_CFG_MUTEX_PEND_ABORT_EN enables (when set to 1) or disables (when set to 0) code generation of the function OSMutexPendAbort().

OS_CFG_OBJ_TYPE_CHK_EN

OS_CFG_OBJ_TYPE_CHK_EN determines whether most of µC/OS-III functions should check to see if the function is manipulating the proper object. In other words, if attempting to post to a semaphore, is the user in fact passing a semaphore object or another object by mistake? It is recommended to set this #define to 1 until absolutely certain that the code is behaving correctly and the user code is always pointing to the proper objects. You would set this #define to 0 to save code space as well as data space. µC/OS-III object type checking is done nearly 30 times, and it is possible to save a few hundred bytes of code space and processing time by disabling this check.

OS_CFG_PEND_MULTI_EN

This constant determines whether the code to support pending on multiple events (i.e., semaphores or message queues) will be enabled (1) or not (0).

OS_CFG_PRIO_MAX

OS_CFG_PRIO_MAX specifies the maximum number of priorities available in the application. Specifying OS_CFG_PRIO_MAX to just the number of priorities the user intends to use, reduces the amount of RAM needed by µC/OS-III.

In µC/OS-III, task priorities can range from 0 (highest priority) to a maximum of 255 (lowest possible priority) when the data type OS_PRIO is defined as a CPU_INT08U. However, in µC/OS-III, there is no practical limit to the number of available priorities. Specifically, if defining **OS_PRIO** as a **CPU_INT16U**, there can be up to 65536 priority levels. It is recommended to leave **OS_PRIO** defined as a **CPU_INT08U** and use only 256 different priority levels (i.e., 0..255), which is generally sufficient for every application. You should always set the value of **OS_CFG_PRIO_MAX** to even multiples of 8 (8, 16, 32, 64, 128, 256, etc.). The higher the number of different priorities, the more RAM µC/OS-III will consume.

An application cannot create tasks with a priority number higher than or equal to **OS_CFG_PRIO_MAX**. In fact, µC/OS-III reserves priority **OS_CFG_PRIO_MAX-2** and **OS_CFG_PRIO_MAX-1** for itself; **OS_CFG_PRIO_MAX-1** is reserved for the idle task **OS_IdleTask()**. Additionally, do not use priority 0 for an application since it is reserved by µC/OS-III's ISR handler task. The priorities of the application tasks can therefore take a value between 2 and **OS_CFG_PRIO_MAX-3** (inclusive).

To summarize, there are two priority levels to avoid in an application:

Priority	Reserved by µC/OS-III for ...
0	The ISR Handler Task (OS_IntQTask())
1	Reserved
OS_CFG_PRIO_MAX-2	Reserved
OS_CFG_PRIO_MAX-1	The idle task (OS_IdleTask())

OS_CFG_Q_EN

OS_CFG_Q_EN enables (when set to 1) or disables (when set to 0) code generation of message queue services and data structures. This reduces the amount of code space needed when an application does not require the use of message queues. When OS_CFG_Q_EN is set to 0, you do not need to enable or disable any of the other OS_CFG_Q_XXX **#define** constants in this section.

OS_CFG_Q_DEL_EN

OS_CFG_Q_DEL_EN enables (when set to 1) or disables (when set to 0) code generation of the function OSQDel().

OS_CFG_Q_FLUSH_EN

OS_CFG_Q_FLUSH_EN enables (when set to 1) or disables (when set to 0) code generation of the function OSQFlush().

OS_CFG_Q_PEND_ABORT_EN

OS_CFG_Q_PEND_ABORT_EN enables (when set to 1) or disables (when set to 0) code generation of the function OSQPendAbort().

OS_CFG_SCHED_LOCK_TIME_MEAS_EN

This constant enables (when set to 1) or disables (when set to 0) code generation to measure the amount of time the scheduler is locked. This is useful when determining task latency.

OS_CFG_SCHED_ROUND_ROBIN_EN

This constant enables (when set to 1) or disables (when set to 0) code generation for the round-robin feature of µC/OS-III.

OS_CFG_SEM_EN

OS_CFG_SEM_EN enables (when set to 1) or disables (when set to 0) code generation of the semaphore manager and associated data structures. This reduces the amount of code and data space needed when an application does not require the use of semaphores. When OS_CFG_SEM_EN is set to 0, it is not necessary to enable or disable any of the other OS_CFG_SEM_XXX #define constants in this section.

OS_CFG_SEM_DEL_EN

OS_CFG_SEM_DEL_EN enables (when set to 1) or disables (when set to 0) code generation of the function OSSemDel().

OS_CFG_SEM_PEND_ABORT_EN

OS_CFG_SEM_PEND_ABORT_EN enables (when set to 1) or disables (when set to 0) code generation of the function OSSemPendAbort().

OS_CFG_SEM_SET_EN

OS_CFG_SEM_SET_EN enables (when set to 1) or disables (when set to 0) code generation of the function OSSemSet().

OS_CFG_STAT_TASK_EN

OS_CFG_STAT_TASK_EN specifies whether or not to enable µC/OS-III's statistic task, as well as its initialization function. When set to 1, the statistic task OS_StatTask() and statistic task initialization function are enabled. OS_StatTask() computes the CPU usage of an application, stack usage of each task, the CPU usage of each task at run time and more.

When enabled, OS_StatTask() executes at a rate of OS_CFG_STAT_TASK_RATE_HZ (see os_cfg_app.h), and computes the value of OSStatTaskCPUUsage, which is a variable that contains the percentage of CPU used by the application. OS_StatTask() calls OSStatTaskHook() every time it executes so that the user can add their own statistics as needed. See os_stat.c for details on the statistic task. The priority of OS_StatTask() is configurable by the application code (see os_cfg_app.h).

OS_StatTask() also computes stack usage of each task created when the #define OS_CFG_STAT_TASK_STK_CHK_EN is set to 1. In this case, OS_StatTask() calls OSTaskStkChk() for each task and the result is placed in the task's TCB. The .StkFree and .StkUsed field of the task's TCB represents the amount of free space (in bytes) and amount of used space, respectively.

When OS_CFG_STAT_TASK_EN is set to 0, all variables used by the statistic task are not declared (see os.h). This, of course, reduces the amount of RAM needed by µC/OS-III when not enabling the statistic task. When setting OS_CFG_STAT_TASK_EN to 1, statistics will be determined at a rate of OS_CFG_STAT_TASK_RATE_HZ (see os_cfg_app.h).

OS_CFG_STAT_TASK_STK_CHK_EN

This constant allows the statistic task to call OSTaskStkChk() for each task created. For this to happen, OS_CFG_STAT_TASK_EN needs to be set to 1 (i.e., the statistic task needs to be enabled). However, you can call OSStatStkChk() from one of the tasks to obtain this information about the task(s).

OS_CFG_STK_SIZE_MIN

This #define specifies the minimum stack size (in CPU_STK elements) for each task. This is used by µC/OS-III to verify that sufficient stack space is provided for when each task is created. Suppose the full context of a processor consists of 16 registers of 32 bits. Also, suppose CPU_STK is declared as being of type CPU_INT32U, at a bare minimum, set OS_CFG_STK_SIZE_MIN to 16. However, it would be quite unwise to not accommodate for storage of local variables, function call returns, and possibly nested ISRs. Refer to the "port" of the processor used to see how to set this minimum. Again, this is a safeguard to make sure task stacks have sufficient stack space.

OS_CFG_TASK_CHANGE_PRIO_EN

OS_CFG_TASK_CHANGE_PRIO_EN enables (when set to 1) or disables (when set to 0) code generation of the function OSTaskChangePrio( ).

OS_CFG_TASK_DEL_EN

OS_CFG_TASK_DEL_EN enables (when set to 1) or disables (when set to 0) code generation of the function OSTaskDel( ).

OS_CFG_TASK_Q_EN

OS_CFG_TASK_Q_EN enables (when set to 1) or disables (when set to 0) code generation of the OSTaskQXXX( ) functions used to send and receive messages directly to/from tasks and ISRs. Sending messages directly to a task is more efficient than sending messages using a message queue because there is no pend list associated with messages sent to a task.

OS_CFG_TASK_Q_PEND_ABORT_EN

OS_CFG_TASK_Q_PEND_ABORT_EN enables (when set to 1) or disables (when set to 0) code generation of code for the function OSTaskQPendAbort( ).

OS_CFG_TASK_PROFILE_EN

This constant allows variables to be allocated in each task's OS_TCB to hold performance data about each task. If OS_CFG_TASK_PROFILE_EN is set to 1, each task will have a variable to keep track of the number of times a task is switched to, the task execution time, the percent CPU usage of the task relative to the other tasks and more. The information made available with this feature is highly useful when debugging, but requires extra RAM.

OS_CFG_TASK_REG_TBL_SIZE

This constant allows each task to have task context variables. Use task variables to store such elements as "errno", task identifiers and other task-specific values. The number of variables that a task contains is set by this constant. Each variable is identified by a unique identifier from 0 to OS_CFG_TASK_REG_TBL_SIZE-1. Also, each variable is declared as having an OS_REG data type (see os_type.h). If OS_REG is a CPU_INT08U, all variables in this table are of this type.

OS_CFG_TASK_SEM_PEND_ABORT_EN

OS_CFG_TASK_SEM_PEND_ABORT_EN enables (when set to 1) or disables (when set to 0) code generation of code for the function OSTaskSemPendAbort().

OS_CFG_TASK_SUSPEND_EN

OS_CFG_TASK_SUSPEND_EN enables (when set to 1) or disables (when set to 0) code generation of the functions OSTaskSuspend() and OSTaskResume(), which allows the application to explicitly suspend and resume tasks, respectively. Suspending and resuming a task is useful when debugging, especially if calling these functions via a terminal interface at run time.

OS_CFG_TIME_DLY_HMSM_EN

OS_CFG_TIME_DLY_HMSM_EN enables (when set to 1) or disables (when set to 0) the code generation of the function OSTimeDlyHMSM(), which is used to delay a task for a specified number of hours, minutes, seconds, and milliseconds.

OS_CFG_TIME_DLY_RESUME_EN

OS_CFG_TIME_DLY_RESUME_EN enables (when set to 1) or disables (when set to 0) the code generation of the function OSTimeDlyResume().

OS_CFG_TMR_EN

Enables (when set to 1) or disables (when set to 0) the code generation of timer management services.

OS_CFG_TMR_DEL_EN

OS_CFG_TMR_DEL_EN enables (when set to 1) or disables (when set to 0) the code generation of the function OSTmrDel().

B-2 DATA TYPES (OS_TYPE.H)

os_type.h contains the data types used by µC/OS-III, which should only be altered by the implementer of the µC/OS-III port. You can alter the contents of **os_type.h**. However, it is important to understand how each of the data types that are being changed will affect the operation of µC/OS-III-based applications.

The reason to change **os_type.h** is that processors may work better with specific word sizes. For example, a 16-bit processor will likely be more efficient at manipulating 16-bit values and a 32-bit processor more comfortable with 32-bit values, even at the cost of extra RAM. In other words, the user may need to choose between processor performance and RAM footprint.

If changing "any" of the data types, you should copy **os_type.h** in the project directory and change that file (not the original **os_type.h** that comes with the µC/OS-III release).

Recommended data type sizes are specified in comments in **os_type.h**.

B-3 µC/OS-III STACKS, POOLS AND OTHER (OS_CFG_APP.H)

µC/OS-III allows the user to configure the sizes of the idle task stack, statistic task stack, message pool, tick wheel, timer wheel, debug tables, and more. This is done through **os_cfg_app.h**.

OS_CFG_TASK_STK_LIMIT_PCT_EMPTY

This **#define** sets the position (as a percentage to empty) of the stack limit for the idle, statistic, tick, interrupt queue handler, and timer tasks stacks. In other words, the amount of space to leave before the stack is empty. For example if the stack contains 1000 **CPU_STK** entries and the user declares **OS_CFG_TASK_STK_LIMIT_PCT_EMPTY** to 10, the stack limit will be set when the stack reaches 90% full, or 10% empty.

If the stack of the processor grows from high memory to low memory, the limit would be set towards the "base address" of the stack, i.e., closer to element 0 of the stack.

If the processor used does not offer automatic stack limit checking, you should set this **#define** to 0.

OS_CFG_IDLE_TASK_STK_SIZE

This #define sets the size of the idle task's stack (in CPU_STK elements) as follows:

```
CPU_STK OSCfg_IdleTaskStk[OS_CFG_IDLE_TASK_STK_SIZE];
```

Note that the stack size needs to be at least greater than OS_CFG_STK_SIZE_MIN.

OS_CFG_INT_Q_SIZE

If OS_CFG_ISR_POST_DEFERRED_EN is set to 1 (see os_cfg.h), this #define specifies the number of entries that can be placed in the interrupt queue. The size of this queue depends on how many interrupts could occur in the time it takes to process interrupts by the ISR Handler Task. The size also depends on whether or not to allow interrupt nesting. A good start point is approximately 10 entries.

OS_CFG_INT_Q_TASK_STK_SIZE

If OS_CFG_ISR_POST_DEFERRED_EN is set to 1 (see os_cfg.h) then this #define sets the size of the ISR handler task's stack (in CPU_STK elements) as follows:

```
CPU_STK OSCfg_IntQTaskStk[OS_CFG_INT_Q_TASK_STK_SIZE];
```

Note that the stack size needs to be at least greater than OS_CFG_STK_SIZE_MIN.

OS_CFG_ISR_STK_SIZE

This specifies the size of μC/OS-III's interrupt stack (in CPU_STK elements). Note that the stack size needs to accommodate for worst case interrupt nesting, assuming the processor supports interrupt nesting. The ISR handler task stack is declared in os_cfg_app.c as follows:

```
CPU_STK   OSCfg_ISRStk[OS_CFG_ISR_STK_SIZE];
```

OS_CFG_MSG_POOL_SIZE

This entry specifies the number of OS_MSGs available in the pool of OS_MSGs. The size is specified in number of OS_MSG elements. The message pool is declared in **os_cfg_app.c** as follows:

```
OS_MSG   OSCfg_MsgPool[OS_CFG_MSG_POOL_SIZE];
```

OS_CFG_STAT_TASK_PRIO

This **#define** allows a user to specify the priority assigned to the µC/OS-III statistic task. It is recommended to make this task a very low priority and possibly even one priority level just above the idle task, or, **OS_CFG_PRIO_MAX-2**.

OS_CFG_STAT_TASK_RATE_HZ

This **#define** defines the execution rate (in Hz) of the statistic task. It is recommended to make this rate an even multiple of the tick rate (see **OS_CFG_TICK_RATE_HZ**).

OS_CFG_STAT_TASK_STK_SIZE

This **#define** sets the size of the statistic task's stack (in **CPU_STK** elements) as follows:

```
CPU_STK OSCfg_StatTaskStk[OS_CFG_STAT_TASK_STK_SIZE];
```

Note that the stack size needs to be at least greater than **OS_CFG_STK_SIZE_MIN**.

OS_CFG_TICK_RATE_HZ

This **#define** specifies the rate in Hertz of µC/OS-III's tick interrupt. The tick rate should be set between 10 and 1000 Hz. The higher the rate, the more overhead it will impose on the processor. The desired rate depends on the granularity required for time delays and timeouts.

OS_CFG_TICK_TASK_PRIO

This **#define** specifies the priority to assign to the µC/OS-III tick task. It is recommended to make this task a fairly high priority, but it does not need to be the highest. The priority assigned to this task must be greater than 0 and less than **OS_CFG_PRIO_MAX-1**.

OS_CFG_TICK_TASK_STK_SIZE

This entry specifies the size of µC/OS-III's tick task stack (in **CPU_STK** elements). Note that the stack size must be at least greater than **OS_CFG_STK_SIZE_MIN**. The tick task stack is declared in os_cfg_app.c as follows:

```
CPU_STK  OSCfg_TickTaskStk[OS_CFG_TICK_TASK_STK_SIZE];
```

OS_CFG_TICK_WHEEL_SIZE

This **#define** determines the number of entries in the **OSTickWheel[]** table. This "wheel" reduces the number of tasks to be updated by the tick task. The size of the wheel should be a fraction of the number of tasks expected in the application.

This value should be a number between 4 and 1024. Task management overhead is somewhat determined by the size of the wheel. A large number of entries might reduce the overhead for tick management but would require more RAM. Each entry requires a pointer and a counter of the number of entries in each "spoke" of the wheel. This counter is typically a 16-bit value. It is recommended that **OS_CFG_TICK_WHEEL_SIZE** not be a multiple of the tick rate. If the application has many tasks, a large wheel size is recommended. As a starting value, you should use a prime number (3, 5, 7, 11, 13, 17, 19, 23, etc.).

OS_CFG_TMR_TASK_PRIO

This **#define** allows a user to specify the priority to assign to the µC/OS-III timer task. It is recommended to make this task a medium-to-low priority, depending on how fast the timer task will execute (see **OS_CFG_TMR_TASK_RATE_HZ**), how many timers running in the application, and the size of the timer wheel, etc. The priority assigned to this task must be greater than 0 and less than **OS_CFG_PRIO_MAX-1**.

You should start with these simple rules:

■   The faster the timer rate, the higher the priority to assign to this task.

■   The higher the timer wheel size, the higher the priority to assign this task.

■   The higher the number of timers in the system, the lower the priority.

In other words:

High Timer Rate	Higher Priority
High Timer Wheel Size	Higher Priority
High Number of Timers	Lower Priority

OS_CFG_TMR_TASK_RATE_HZ

This #define specifies the rate in Hertz of µC/OS-III's timer task. The timer task rate should typically be set to 10 Hz. However, timers can run at a faster rate at the price of higher processor overhead. Note that OS_CFG_TMR_TASK_RATE_HZ MUST be an integer multiple of OS_CFG_TICK_TASK_RATE_HZ. In other words, if setting OS_CFG_TICK_TASK_RATE_HZ to 1000, do not set OS_CFG_TMR_TASK_RATE_HZ to 11 since 90.91 ticks would be required for every timer update, and 90.91 is not an integer multiple. Use approximately 10 Hz in this example.

OS_CFG_TMR_TASK_STK_SIZE

This #define sets the size of the timer task's stack (in CPU_STK elements) as follows:

```
CPU_STK OSCfg_TmrTaskStk[OS_CFG_TMR_TASK_STK_SIZE];
```

Note that the stack size needs to be at least greater than OS_CFG_STK_SIZE_MIN.

OS_CFG_TMR_WHEEL_SIZE

Timers are updated using a rotating wheel mechanism. This "wheel" reduces the number of timers to be updated by the timer manager task. The size of the wheel should be a fraction of the number of timers in the application.

This value should be a number between 4 and 1024. Timer management overhead is somewhat determined by the size of the wheel. A large number of entries might reduce the overhead for timer management but would require more RAM. Each entry requires a pointer and a counter of the number of entries in each "spoke" of the wheel. This counter is typically a 16-bit value. It is recommended that this value *not* be a multiple of the tick rate. If an application has many timers a large wheel size is recommended. As a starting value, you should use a prime number (3, 5, 7, 11, 13, 17, 19, 23, etc.).

Appendix

C

Migrating from µC/OS-II to µC/OS-III

µC/OS-III is a completely new real-time kernel with roots in µC/OS-II. Portions of the µC/OS-II Application Programming Interface (API) function names are the same, but the arguments passed to the functions have, in some places, drastically changed.

Appendix C explains several differences between the two real-time kernels. However, access to µC/OS-II and µC/OS-III source files best highlights the differences.

Table C-1 is a feature-comparison chart for µC/OS-II and µC/OS-III.

Feature	µC/OS-II	µC/OS-III
Year of introduction	1998	2009
Book	Yes	Yes
Source code available	Yes	Yes
Preemptive Multitasking	Yes	Yes
Maximum number of tasks	255	Unlimited
Number of tasks at each priority level	1	Unlimited
Round Robin Scheduling	No	Yes
Semaphores	Yes	Yes
Mutual Exclusion Semaphores	Yes	Yes (nestable)
Event Flags	Yes	Yes
Message Mailboxes	Yes	No (not needed)
Message Queues	**Yes**	**Yes**
Fixed Sized Memory Management	Yes	Yes
Signal a task without requiring a semaphore	No	Yes
Send messages to a task without requiring a message queue	No	Yes
Software Timers	Yes	Yes
Task suspend/resume	Yes	Yes (nestable)
Deadlock prevention	Yes	Yes
Scalable	Yes	Yes
Code Footprint	6K to 26K	6K to 24K
Data Footprint	1K+	1K+
ROMable	Yes	Yes
Run-time configurable	No	Yes
Catch a task that returns	No	Yes
Compile-time configurable	Yes	Yes

Feature	µC/OS-II	µC/OS-III
ASCII names for each kernel object	Yes	Yes
Optio to post without scheduling	No	Yes
Pend on multiple objects	Yes	Yes
Task registers	Yes	Yes
Built-in performance measurements	Limited	Extensive
User definable hook functions	Yes	Yes
Time stamps on posts	No	Yes
Built-in Kernel Awareness support	Yes	Yes
Optimizable Scheduler in assembly language	No	Yes
Tick handling at task level	No	Yes
Number of services	~90	~70
MISRA-C:1998	Yes	N/A
MISRA-C:2004	No	Yes
DO178B Level A and EUROCAE ED-12B	Yes	In progress
Medical FDA pre-market notification (510(k)) and pre-market approval (PMA)	Yes	In progress
SIL3/SIL4 IEC for transportation and nuclear systems	Yes	In progress
IEC-61508	Yes	In progress

Table C-1 **µC/OS-II and µC/OS-III features comparison chart**

C-1 DIFFERENCES IN SOURCE FILE NAMES AND CONTENTS

Table C-2 shows the source files used in both kernels. Note that a few of the files have the same or similar name.

µC/OS-II	µC/OS-III	Note
	os_app_hooks.c	(1)
	os_cfg_app.c	(2)
	os_cfg_app.h	(3)
os_cfg_r.h	os_cfg.h	(4)
os_core.c	os_core.c	
os_cpu.h	os_cpu.h	(5)
os_cpu_a.asm	os_cpu_a.asm	(5)
os_cpu_c.c	os_cpu_c.c	(5)
os_dbg_r.c	os_dbg.c	(6)
os_flag.c	os_flag.c	
	os_int.c	(7)
	os_pend_multi.c	(8)
	os_prio.c	(9)
os_mbox.c		(10)
os_mem.c	os_mem.c	
	os_msg.c	(11)
os_mutex.c	os_mutex.c	
os_q.c	os_q.c	
os_sem.c	os_sem.c	
	os_stat.c	(12)
os_task.c	os_task.c	
os_time.c	os_time.c	
os_tmr.c	os_tmr.c	
	os_var.c	(13)
	os_type.h	(14)
ucos_ii.h	os.h	(15)

Table C-2 µC/OS-II and µC/OS-III files

TC-2(1) µC/OS-II does not have this file, which is now provided for convenience so you can add application hooks. You should copy this file to the application directory and edit the contents of the file to satisfy your application requirements.

TC-2(2) **os_cfg_app.c** did not exist in µC/OS-II. This file needs to be added to a project build for µC/OS-III.

TC-2(3) In µC/OS-II, all configuration constants were placed in **os_cfg.h**. In µC/OS-III, some of the configuration constants are placed in this file, while others are in **os_cfg_app.h**. **os_cfg_app.h** contains application-specific configurations such as the size of the idle task stack, tick rate, and others.

TC-2(4) In µC/OS-III, **os_cfg.h** is reserved for configuring certain features of the kernel. For example, are any of the semaphore services required, and will the application have fixed-sized memory partition management?

TC-2(5) These are the port files and a few variables and functions will need to be changed when using a µC/OS-II port as a starting point for the µC/OS-III port.

µC/OS-II variable changes from ...	... to these in µC/OS-III
OSIntNesting	OSIntNestingCtr
OSTCBCur	OSTCBCurPtr
OSTCBHighRdy	OSTCBHighRdyPtr
µC/OS-II function changes from ...	**... to these in µC/OS-III**
OSInitHookBegin()	OSInitHook()
OSInitHookEnd()	N/A
OSTaskStatHook()	OSStatTaskHook()
OSTaskIdleHook()	OSIdleTaskHook()
OSTCBInitHook()	N/A
OSTaskStkInit()	OSTaskStkInit()

The name of **OSTaskStkInit()** is the same but it is listed here since the code for it needs to be changed slightly as several arguments passed to this function are different. Specifically, instead of passing the top-of-stack as in µC/OS-II, **OSTaskStkInit()** is passed the base address and the size of the task stack.

C

TC-2(6)   In µC/OS-III, **os_dbg.c** should always be part of the build. In µC/OS-II, the equivalent file (**os_dbg_r.c**) was optional.

TC-2(7)   **os_int.c** contains the code for the Interrupt Queue handler, which is a new feature in µC/OS-III, allowing post calls from ISRs to be deferred to a task-level handler. This is done to reduce interrupt latency (see Chapter 9, "Interrupt Management" on page 175).

TC-2(8)   Both kernels allow tasks to pend on multiple kernel objects. In µC/OS-II, this code is found in **os_core.c**, while in µC/OS-III, the code is placed in a separate file, **os_pend_multi.c**.

TC-2(9)   The code to determine the highest priority ready-to-run task is isolated in µC/OS-III and placed in **os_prio.c**. This allows the port developer to replace this file by an assembly language equivalent file, especially if the CPU used supports certain bit manipulation instructions and a count leading zeros (CLZ) instruction.

TC-2(10)   µC/OS-II provides message mailbox services. A message mailbox is identical to a message queue of size one. µC/OS-III does not have these services since they can be easily emulated by message queues.

TC-2(11)   Management of messages for message queues is encapsulated in **os_msg.c** in µC/OS-III.

TC-2(12)   The statistics task and its support functions have been extracted out of **os_core.c** and placed in **os_stat.c** for µC/OS-III.

TC-2(13)   All the µC/OS-III variables are instantiated in a file called **os_var.c**.

TC-2(14)   In µC/OS-III, the size of most data types is better adapted to the CPU architecture used. In µC/OS-II, the size of a number of these data types was assumed.

TC-2(15)   In µC/OS-II, the main header file is called **ucos_ii.h**. In µC/OS-III, it is renamed to **os.h**.

C-2 CONVENTION CHANGES

There are a number of convention changes from µC/OS-II to µC/OS-III. The most notable is the use of CPU-specific data types. Table C-3 shows the differences between the data types used in both kernels

µC/OS-II (os_cpu.h)	µC/CPU (cpu.h)	Note
BOOLEAN	CPU_BOOLEAN	
INT8S	CPU_INT08S	
INT8U	CPU_INT08U	
INT16S	CPU_INT16S	
INT16U	CPU_INT16U	
INT32S	CPU_INT32S	
INT32U	CPU_INT32U	
OS_STK	CPU_STK	(1)
OS_CPU_SR	CPU_SR	(2)
µC/OS-II (os_cfg.h)	**µC/CPU (cpu.h)**	
OS_STK_GROWTH	CPU_CFG_STK_GROWTH	(3)

Table C-3 µC/OS-II vs. µC/OS-III basic data types

TC-3(1)   A task stack in µC/OS-II is declared as an **OS_STK**, which is now replaced by a CPU specific data type **CPU_STK**. These two data types are equivalent, except that defining the width of the CPU stack in µC/CPU makes more sense.

TC-3(2)   It also makes sense to declare the CPU's status register in µC/CPU.

TC-3(3)   Stack growth (high-to-low or low-to-high memory) is declared in µC/CPU since stack growth is a CPU feature and not an OS one.

Another convention change is the use of the acronym "**CFG**" which stands for configuration. Now, all **#define** configuration constants and variables have the "**CFG**" or "**Cfg**" acronym in them as shown in Table C-4. Table C-4 shows the configuration constants that have been moved from **os_cfg.h** to **os_cfg_app.h**. This is done because µC/OS-III is configurable at the application level instead of just at compile time as with µC/OS-II.

µC/OS-II (os_cfg.h)	µC/OS-III (os_cfg_app.h)	Note
	OS_CFG_MSG_POOL_SIZE	
	OS_CFG_ISR_STK_SIZE	
	OS_CFG_TASK_STK_LIMIT_PCT_EMPTY	
OS_TASK_IDLE_STK_SIZE	OS_CFG_IDLE_TASK_STK_SIZE	
	OS_CFG_INT_Q_SIZE	
	OS_CFG_INT_Q_TASK_STK_SIZE	
	OS_CFG_STAT_TASK_PRIO	
	OS_CFG_STAT_TASK_RATE_HZ	
OS_TASK_STAT_STK_SIZE	OS_CFG_STAT_TASK_STK_SIZE	
OS_TICKS_PER_SEC	OS_CFG_TICK_RATE_HZ	(1)
	OS_CFG_TICK_TASK_PRIO	
	OS_CFG_TICK_TASK_STK_SIZE	
	OS_CFG_TICK_WHEEL_SIZE	
	OS_CFG_TMR_TASK_PRIO	
OS_TMR_CFG_TICKS_PER_SEC	OS_CFG_TMR_TASK_RATE_HZ	
OS_TASK_TMR_STK_SIZE	OS_CFG_TMR_TASK_STK_SIZE	
OS_TMR_CFG_WHEEL_SIZE	OS_CFG_TMR_WHEEL_SIZE	

Table C-4 µC/OS-III uses "CFG" in configuration

TC-4(1)   The very useful **OS_TICKS_PER_SEC** in µC/OS-II was renamed to **OS_CFG_TICK_RATE_HZ** in µC/OS-III. The "**HZ**" indicates that this **#define** represents Hertz (i.e., ticks per second).

Table C-5 shows additional configuration constants added to **os_cfg.h**, while several µC/OS-II constants were either removed or renamed.

µC/OS-II (os_cfg.h)	µC/OS-III (os_cfg.h)	Note
OS_APP_HOOKS_EN	OS_CFG_APP_HOOKS_EN	
OS_ARG_CHK_EN	OS_CFG_ARG_CHK_EN	
	OS_CFG_CALLED_FROM_ISR_CHK_EN	
OS_DEBUG_EN	OS_CFG_DBG_EN	(1)
OS_EVENT_MULTI_EN	OS_CFG_PEND_MULTI_EN	
OS_EVENT_NAME_EN		(2)
	OS_CFG_ISR_POST_DEFERRED_EN	
OS_MAX_EVENTS		(3)
OS_MAX_FLAGS		(3)
OS_MAX_MEM_PART		(3)
OS_MAX_QS		(3)
OS_MAX_TASKS		(3)
	OS_CFG_OBJ_TYPE_CHK_EN	
OS_LOWEST_PRIO	OS_CFG_PRIO_MAX	
	OS_CFG_SCHED_LOCK_TIME_MEAS_EN	
	OS_CFG_SCHED_ROUND_ROBIN_EN	
	OS_CFG_STK_SIZE_MIN	
OS_FLAG_EN	OS_CFG_FLAG_EN	
OS_FLAG_ACCEPT_EN		(6)
OS_FLAG_DEL_EN	OS_CFG_FLAG_DEL_EN	
OS_FLAG_WAIT_CLR_EN	OS_CFG_FLAG_MODE_CLR_EN	
OS_FLAG_NAME_EN		(2)
OS_FLAG_NBITS		(4)
OS_FLAG_QUERY_EN		(5)
	OS_CFG_PEND_ABORT_EN	
OS_MBOX_EN		
OS_MBOX_ACCEPT_EN		(6)

µC/OS-II (os_cfg.h)	µC/OS-III (os_cfg.h)	Note
OS_MBOX_DEL_EN		
OS_MBOX_PEND_ABORT_EN		
OS_MBOX_POST_EN		
OS_MBOX_POST_OPT_EN		
OS_MBOX_QUERY_EN		(5)
OS_MEM_EN	OS_CFG_MEM_EN	
OS_MEM_NAME_EN		(2)
OS_MEM_QUERY_EN		(5)
OS_MUTEX_EN	OS_CFG_MUTEX_EN	
OS_MUTEX_ACCEPT_EN		(6)
OS_MUTEX_DEL_EN	OS_CFG_MUTEX_DEL_EN	
	OS_CFG_MUTEX_PEND_ABORT_EN	
OS_MUTEX_QUERY_EN		(5)
OS_Q_EN	OS_CFG_Q_EN	
OS_Q_ACCEPT_EN		(6)
OS_Q_DEL_EN	OS_CFG_Q_DEL_EN	
OS_Q_FLUSH_EN	OS_CFG_Q_FLUSH_EN	
	OS_CFG_Q_PEND_ABORT_EN	
OS_Q_POST_EN		(7)
OS_Q_POST_FRONT_EN		(7)
OS_Q_POST_OPT_EN		(7)
OS_Q_QUERY_EN		(5)
OS_SCHED_LOCK_EN		
OS_SEM_EN	OS_CFG_SEM_EN	
OS_SEM_ACCEPT_EN		(6)
OS_SEM_DEL_EN	OS_CFG_SEM_DEL_EN	
OS_SEM_PEND_ABORT_EN	OS_CFG_SEM_PEND_ABORT_EN	

µC/OS-II (os_cfg.h)	µC/OS-III (os_cfg.h)	Note
OS_SEM_QUERY_EN		(5)
OS_SEM_SET_EN	OS_CFG_SEM_SET_EN	
OS_TASK_STAT_EN	OS_CFG_STAT_TASK_EN	
OS_TASK_STK_CHK_EN	OS_CFG_STAT_TASK_STK_CHK_EN	
OS_TASK_CHANGE_PRIO_EN	OS_CFG_TASK_CHANGE_PRIO_EN	
OS_TASK_CREATE_EN		
OS_TASK_CREATE_EXT_EN		
OS_TASK_DEL_EN	OS_CFG_TASK_DEL_EN	
OS_TASK_NAME_EN		(2)
	OS_CFG_TASK_Q_EN	
	OS_CFG_TASK_Q_PEND_ABORT_EN	
OS_TASK_QUERY_EN		(5)
OS_TASK_PROFILE_EN	OS_CFG_TASK_PROFILE_EN	
	OS_CFG_TASK_REG_TBL_SIZE	
	OS_CFG_TASK_SEM_PEND_ABORT_EN	
OS_TASK_SUSPEND_EN	OS_CFG_TASK_SUSPEND_EN	
OS_TASK_SW_HOOK_EN		
OS_TICK_STEP_EN		(8)
OS_TIME_DLY_HMSM_EN	OS_CFG_TIME_DLY_HMSM_EN	
OS_TIME_DLY_RESUME_EN	OS_CFG_TIME_DLY_RESUME_EN	
OS_TIME_GET_SET_EN		
OS_TIME_TICK_HOOK_EN		
OS_TMR_EN	OS_CFG_TMR_EN	
OS_TMR_CFG_NAME_EN		(2)
OS_TMR_DEL_EN	OS_CFG_TMR_DEL_EN	

Table C-5 **µC/OS-III uses "CFG" in configuration**

TC-5(1)   **DEBUG** is replaced with **DBG**.

TC-5(2)   In µC/OS-II, all kernel objects can be assigned ASCII names after creation. In µC/OS-III, ASCII names are assigned when the object is created.

TC-5(3)   In µC/OS-II, it is necessary to declare the maximum number of kernel objects (number of tasks, number of event flag groups, message queues, etc.) at compile time. In µC/OS-III, all kernel objects are allocated at run time so it is no longer necessary to specify the maximum number of these objects. This feature saves valuable RAM as it is no longer necessary to over allocate objects.

TC-5(4)   In µC/OS-II, event-flag width must be declared at compile time through **OS_FLAG_NBITS**. In µC/OS-III, this is accomplished by defining the width (i.e., number of bits) in **os_type.h** through the data type **OS_FLAG**. The default is typically 32 bits.

TC-5(5)   µC/OS-III does not provide query services to the application.

TC-5(6)   µC/OS-III does not directly provide "**accept**" function calls as with µC/OS-II. Instead, **OS???Pend()** functions provide an option that emulates the "**accept**" functionality by specifying **OS_OPT_PEND_NON_BLOCKING**.

TC-5(7)   In µC/OS-II, there are a number of "**post**" functions. The features offered are now combined in the **OS???Post()** functions in µC/OS-III.

TC-5(8)   The µC/OS-View feature **OS_TICK_STEP_EN** is not present in µC/OS-III since µC/OS-View is an obsolete product and in fact, was replaced by µC/Probe.

C-3 VARIABLE NAME CHANGES

Some of the variable names in µC/OS-II are changed for µC/OS-III to be more consistent with coding conventions. Significant variables are shown in Table C-6.

µC/OS-II (ucos_ii.h)	µC/OS-III (os.h)	Note
OSCtxSwCtr	OSTaskCtxSwCtr	
OSCPUUsage	OSStatTaskCPUUsage	(1)
OSIdleCtr	OSIdleTaskCtr	
OSIdleCtrMax	OSIdleTaskCtrMax	
OSIntNesting	OSIntNestingCtr	(2)
OSPrioCur	OSPrioCur	
OSPrioHighRdy	OSPrioHighRdy	
OSRunning	OSRunning	
OSSchedNesting	OSSchedLockNestingCtr	(3)
	OSSchedLockTimeMax	
OSTaskCtr	OSTaskQty	
OSTCBCur	OSTCBCurPtr	(4)
OSTCBHighRdy	OSTCBHighRdyPtr	(4)
OSTime	OSTickCtr	(5)
OSTmrTime	OSTmrTickCtr	

Table C-6 **Changes in variable naming**

TC-6(1)   In µC/OS-II, **OSCPUUsage** contains the total CPU utilization in percentage format. If the CPU is busy 12% of the time, **OSCPUUsage** has the value 12. In µC/OS-III, the same information is provided in **OSStatTaskCPUUsage**. However, as of µC/OS-III V3.03.00, the resolution of **OSStatTaskCPUUsage** is 1/100th of a percent or, 0.00% (value is **0**) to 100.00% (value is **10,000**).

TC-6(2)   In µC/OS-II, **OSIntNesting** keeps track of the number of interrupts nesting. µC/OS-III uses **OSIntNestingCtr**. The "**Ctr**" has been added to indicate that this variable is a counter.

TC-6(3)   **OSSchedNesting** represents the number of times **OSSchedLock()** is called. µC/OS-III renames this variable to **OSSchedLockNestingCtr** to better represent the variable's meaning.

TC-6(4)   In µC/OS-II, **OSTCBCur** and **OSTCBHighRdy** are pointers to the **OS_TCB** of the current task, and to the **OS_TCB** of the highest-priority task that is ready-to-run. In µC/OS-III, these are renamed by adding the "**Ptr**" to indicate that they are pointers.

TC-6(5)   The internal counter of the number of ticks since power up, or the last time the variable was changed through **OSTimeSet()**, has been renamed to better reflect its function.

C-4 API CHANGES

The most significant change from µC/OS-II to µC/OS-III occurs in the API. In order to port a µC/OS-II-based application to µC/OS-III, it is necessary to change the way services are invoked.

Table C-7 shows changes in the way critical sections in µC/OS-III are handled. Specifically, µC/OS-II defines macros to disable interrupts, and they are moved to µC/CPU withµC/OS-III since they are CPU specific functions.

µC/OS-II (os_cpu.h)	µC/CPU (cpu.h)	Note
OS_ENTER_CRITICAL()	CPU_CRITICAL_ENTER()	
OS_EXIT_CRITICAL()	CPU_CRITICAL_EXIT()	

Table C-7 **Changes in macro naming**

One of the biggest changes in the µC/OS-III API is its consistency. In fact, based on the function performed, it is possible to guess which arguments are needed, and in what order. For example, "***p_err**" is a pointer to an error-returned variable. When present, "***p_err**" is always the last argument of a function. In µC/OS-II, error-returned values are at times returned as a "***perr**," and at other times as the return value of the function. This inconsistency has been removed in µC/OS-III.

C-4-1 EVENT FLAGS

Table C-8 shows the API for event-flag management.

µC/OS-II (os_flag.c)	µC/OS-III (os_flag.c)	Note

OS_FLAGS
OSFlagAccept(
    OS_FLAG_GRP *pgrp,
    OS_FLAGS   flags,
    INT8U   wait_type,
    INT8U   *perr);
		(1)

OS_FLAG_GRP *
OSFlagCreate(
    OS_FLAGS   flags,
    INT8U   *perr);
	void
	OSFlagCreate(
	    OS_FLAG_GRP *p_grp,
	    CPU_CHAR *p_name,
	    OS_FLAGS flags,
	    OS_ERR *p_err);
		(2)

OS_FLAG_GRP *
OSFlagDel(
    OS_FLAG_GRP *pgrp,
    INT8U   opt,
    INT8U   *perr);
	OS_OBJ_QTY
	OSFlagDel(
	    OS_FLAG_GRP *p_grp,
	    OS_OPT opt,
	    OS_ERR *p_err);	

INT8U
OSFlagNameGet(
    OS_FLAG_GRP *pgrp,
    INT8U   **pname,
    INT8U *perr);		

void
OSFlagNameSet(
    OS_FLAG_GRP *pgrp,
    INT8U   *pname,
    INT8U   *perr);
		(3)

OS_FLAGS
OSFlagPend(
    OS_FLAG_GRP *pgrp,
    OS_FLAGS   flags,
    INT8U   wait_type,
    INT32U   timeout,
    INT8U   *perr);
	OS_FLAGS
	OSFlagPend(
	    OS_FLAG_GRP *p_grp,
	    OS_FLAGS flags,
	    OS_TICK timeout,
	    OS_OPT opt,
	    OS_TS *p_ts,
	    OS_ERR *p_err);	

µC/OS-II (os_flag.c)	µC/OS-III (os_flag.c)	Note

`OS_FLAGS`
`OSFlagPendGetFlagsRdy(`
    `void);`
	`OS_FLAGS`
	`OSFlagPendGetFlagsRdy(`
	    `OS_ERR` `*p_err);`	

`OS_FLAGS`
`OSFlagPost(`
    `OS_FLAG_GRP` `*pgrp,`
    `OS_FLAGS`   `flags,`
    `INT8U`   `opt,`
    `INT8U`   `*perr);`
	`OS_FLAGS`
	`OSFlagPost(`
	    `OS_FLAG_GRP` `*p_grp,`
	    `OS_FLAGS` `flags,`
	    `OS_OPT` `opt,`
	    `OS_ERR` `*p_err);`	

`OS_FLAGS`
`OSFlagQuery(`
    `OS_FLAG_GRP` `*pgrp,`
    `INT8U`   `*perr);`
		(4)

Table C-8 **Event Flags API**

TC-8(1)   In µC/OS-III, there is no "accept" API. This feature is actually built-in the `OSFlagPend()` by specifying the `OS_OPT_PEND_NON_BLOCKING` option.

TC-8(2)   In µC/OS-II, `OSFlagCreate()` returns the address of an `OS_FLAG_GRP`, which is used as the "handle" to the event-flag group. In µC/OS-III, the application must allocate storage for an `OS_FLAG_GRP`, which serves the same purpose as the `OS_EVENT`. The benefit in µC/OS-III is that it is not necessary to predetermine the number of event flags at compile time.

TC-8(3)   In µC/OS-II, the user may assign a name to an event-flag group after the group is created. This functionality is built-into `OSFlagCreate()` for µC/OS-III.

TC-8(4)   µC/OS-III does not provide query services, as they were rarely used in µC/OS-II.

C-4-2 MESSAGE MAILBOXES

Table C-9 shows the API for message mailbox management. Note that µC/OS-III does not directly provide services for managing message mailboxes. Given that a message mailbox is a message queue of size one, µC/OS-III can easily emulate message mailboxes.

µC/OS-II (os_mbox.c)	µC/OS-III (os_q.c)	Note
void * OSMboxAccept(OS_EVENT *pevent);		(1)

OS_EVENT *
OSMboxCreate(
    void   *pmsg);
	void
	OSQCreate(
	    OS_Q *p_q,
	    CPU_CHAR *p_name,
	    OS_MSG_QTY max_qty,
	    OS_ERR *p_err);
		(2)

void *
OSMboxDel(
    OS_EVENT   *pevent,
    INT8U   opt,
    INT8U   *perr);
	OS_OBJ_QTY,
	OSQDel(
	    OS_Q *p_q,
	    OS_OPT opt,
	    OS_ERR *p_err);	

void *
OSMboxPend(
    OS_EVENT   *pevent,
    INT32U   timeout,
    INT8U   *perr);
	void *
	OSQPend(
	    OS_Q *p_q,
	    OS_TICK timeout,
	    OS_OPT opt,
	    OS_MSG_SIZE *p_msg_size,
	    CPU_TS *p_ts,
	    OS_ERR *p_err);
		(3)

INT8U
OSMBoxPendAbort(
    OS_EVENT   *pevent,
    INT8U   opt,
    INT8U   *perr);
	OS_OBJ_QTY
	OSQPendAbort(
	    OS_Q *p_q,
	    OS_OPT opt
	    OS_ERR *p_err);	

µC/OS-II (os_mbox.c)	µC/OS-III (os_q.c)	Note

INT8U
OSMboxPost(
    OS_EVENT   *pevent,
    void   *pmsg);
	void
	OSQPost(
	    OS_Q *p_q,
	    Void *p_void,
	    OS_MSG_SIZE msg_size,
	    OS_OPT opt,
	    OS_ERR *p_err);
		(4)

INT8U
OSMboxPostOpt(
    OS_EVENT   *pevent,
    void   *pmsg,
    INT8U   opt);
		(4)

INT8U
OSMboxQuery(
    OS_EVENT   *pevent,
    OS_MBOX_DATA *p_mbox_data);
		(5)

Table C-9 **Message Mailbox API**

TC-9(1)   In µC/OS-III, there is no "accept" API since this feature is built into the **OSQPend()** by specifying the **OS_OPT_PEND_NON_BLOCKING** option.

TC-9(2)   In µC/OS-II, **OSMboxCreate()** returns the address of an **OS_EVENT**, which is used as the "handle" to the message mailbox. In µC/OS-III, the application must allocate storage for an **OS_Q**, which serves the same purpose as the **OS_EVENT**. The benefit in µC/OS-III is that it is not necessary to predetermine the number of message queues at compile time. Also, to create the equivalent of a message mailbox, you would specify 1 for the **max_qty** argument.

TC-9(3)   µC/OS-III returns additional information about the message received. Specifically, the sender specifies the size of the message as a snapshot of the current timestamp is taken and stored as part of the message. The receiver of the message therefore knows when the message was sent.

TC-9(4)   In µC/OS-III, **OSQPost()** offers a number of options that replaces the two post functions provided in µC/OS-II.

TC-9(5)   µC/OS-III does not provide query services, as they were rarely used in µC/OS-II.

C-4-3 MEMORY MANAGEMENT

Table C-10 shows the difference in API for memory management.

µC/OS-II (os_mem.c)	µC/OS-III (os_mem.c)	Note

OS_MEM *
OSMemCreate(
    void   *addr,
    INT32U   nblks,
    INT32U   blksize,
    INT8U   *perr);
	void
	OSMemCreate(
	    OS_MEM *p_mem,
	    CPU_CHAR *p_name,
	    void *p_addr,
	    OS_MEM_QTY n_blks,
	    OS_MEM_SIZE blk_size,
	    OS_ERR *p_err);
		(1)

void *
OSMemGet(
    OS_MEM   *pmem,
    INT8U   *perr);
	void *
	OSMemGet(
	    OS_MEM *p_mem,
	    OS_ERR *p_err);	

INT8U
OSMemNameGet(
    OS_MEM   *pmem,
    INT8U   **pname,
    INT8U *perr);		

void
OSMemNameSet(
    OS_MEM   *pmem,
    INT8U   *pname,
    INT8U   *perr);
	void
	OSMemPut(
	    OS_MEM *p_mem,
	    void *p_blk,
	    OS_ERR *p_err);
		(2)

INT8U
OSMemPut(
    OS_MEM   *pmem,
    void *pblk);		

INT8U
OSMemQuery(
    OS_MEM   *pmem,
    OS_MEM_DATA *p_mem_data);
		(3)

Table C-10 **Memory Management API**

TC-10(1)   In µC/OS-II, **OSMemCreate()** returns the address of an **OS_MEM** object, which is used as the "handle" to the newly created memory partition. In µC/OS-III, the application must allocate storage for an **OS_MEM**, which serves the same purpose. The benefit in µC/OS-III is that it is not necessary to predetermine the number of memory partitions at compile time.

C

TC-10(2)   µC/OS-III does not need an **OSMemNameSet()** since the name of the memory partition is passed as an argument to **OSMemCreate()**.

TC-10(3)   µC/OS-III does not support query calls.

C-4-4 MUTUAL EXCLUSION SEMAPHORES

Table C-11 shows the difference in API for mutual exclusion semaphore management.

µC/OS-II (os_mutex.c)		µC/OS-III (os_mutex.c)		Note

BOOLEAN
OSMutexAccept(
    OS_EVENT   *pevent,
    INT8U   *perr);
				(1)

OS_EVENT *
OSMutexCreate(
    INT8U   prio,
    INT8U   *perr);
		void
		OSMutexCreate(
		    OS_MUTEX *p_mutex,
		    CPU_CHAR *p_name,
		    OS_ERR *p_err);
				(2)

OS_EVENT *
OSMutexDel(
    OS_EVENT   *pevent,
    INT8U   opt,
    INT8U   *perr);
		void
		OSMutexDel(
		    OS_MUTEX *p_mutex,
		    OS_OPT opt,
		    OS_ERR *p_err);		

void
OSMutexPend(
    OS_EVENT   *pevent,
    INT32U   timeout,
    INT8U   *perr);
		void
		OSMutexPend(
		    OS_MUTEX *p_mutex,
		    OS_TICK timeout,
		    OS_OPT opt,
		    CPU_TS *p_ts,
		    OS_ERR *p_err);
				(3)

		OS_OBJ_QTY
		OSMutexPendAbort(
		    OS_MUTEX *p_mutex,
		    OS_OPT opt,
		    OS_ERR *p_err);		

µC/OS-II (os_mutex.c)	µC/OS-III (os_mutex.c)	Note

INT8U
OSMutexPost(
    OS_EVENT   *pevent);
	void
	OSMutexPost(
	    OS_MUTEX *p_mutex,
	    OS_OPT opt,
	    OS_ERR *p_err);	

INT8U
OSMutexQuery(
    OS_EVENT   *pevent,
    OS_MUTEX_DATA *p_mutex_data);
		(4)

Table C-11 **Mutual Exclusion Semaphore Management API**

TC-11(1)   In µC/OS-III, there is no "accept" API, since this feature is built into the **OSMutexPend()** by specifying the **OS_OPT_PEND_NON_BLOCKING** option.

TC-11(2)   In µC/OS-II, **OSMutexCreate()** returns the address of an **OS_EVENT**, which is used as the "handle" to the message mailbox. In µC/OS-III, the application must allocate storage for an **OS_MUTEX**, which serves the same purpose as the **OS_EVENT**. The benefit in µC/OS-III is that it is not necessary to predetermine the number of mutual-exclusion semaphores at compile time.

TC-11(3)   µC/OS-III returns additional information when a mutex is released. The releaser takes a snapshot of the current time stamp and stores it in the **OS_MUTEX**. The new owner of the mutex therefore knows when the mutex was released.

TC-11(4)   µC/OS-III does not provide query services as they were rarely used.

C-4-5 MESSAGE QUEUES

Table C-12 shows the difference in API for message-queue management.

µC/OS-II (os_q.c)	µC/OS-III (os_q.c)	Note

void *
 OSQAccept(
    OS_EVENT *pevent,
    INT8U   *perr);
		(1)

OS_EVENT *
 OSQCreate(
    void   **start,
    INT16U   size);
	void
	 OSQCreate(
	    OS_Q *p_q,
	    CPU_CHAR *p_name,
	    OS_MSG_QTY max_qty,
	    OS_ERR *p_err);
		(2)

OS_EVENT *
 OSQDel(
    OS_EVENT *pevent,
    INT8U   opt,
    INT8U   *perr);
	OS_OBJ_QTY,
	 OSQDel(
	    OS_Q *p_q,
	    OS_OPT opt,
	    OS_ERR *p_err);	

INT8U
 OSQFlush(
    OS_EVENT *pevent);
	OS_MSG_QTY
	 OSQFlush(
	    OS_Q *p_q,
	    OS_ERR *p_err);	

void *
 OSQPend(
    OS_EVENT *pevent,
    INT32U   timeout,
    INT8U   *perr);
	void *
	 OSQPend(
	    OS_Q *p_q,
	    OS_MSG_SIZE *p_msg_size,
	    OS_TICK timeout,
	    OS_OPT opt,
	    CPU_TS *p_ts,
	    OS_ERR *p_err);
		(3)

INT8U
 OSQPendAbort(
    OS_EVENT *pevent,
    INT8U   opt,
    INT8U   *perr);
	OS_OBJ_QTY
	 OSQPendAbort(
	    OS_Q *p_q,
	    OS_OPT opt,
	    OS_ERR *p_err);	

INT8U
 OSQPost(
    OS_EVENT *pevent,
    void   *pmsg);
	void
	 OSQPost(
	    OS_Q *p_q,
	    void *p_void,
	    OS_MSG_SIZE msg_size,
	    OS_OPT opt,
	    OS_ERR *p_err);
		(4)

µC/OS-II (os_q.c)	µC/OS-III (os_q.c)	Note

INT8U
OSQPostFront(
    OS_EVENT *pevent,
    void *pmsg);		

INT8U
OSQPostOpt(
    OS_EVENT *pevent,
    void   *pmsg,
    INT8U   opt);
		(4)

INT8U
OSQQuery(
    OS_EVENT *pevent,
    OS_Q_DATA *p_q_data);
		(5)

Table C-12 **Message Queue Management API**

TC-12(1)   In µC/OS-III, there is no "accept" API as this feature is built into the OSQPend() by specifying the OS_OPT_PEND_NON_BLOCKING option.

TC-12(2)   In µC/OS-II, OSQCreate() returns the address of an OS_EVENT, which is used as the "handle" to the message queue. In µC/OS-III, the application must allocate storage for an OS_Q object, which serves the same purpose as the OS_EVENT. The benefit in µC/OS-III is that it is not necessary to predetermine at compile time, the number of message queues.

TC-12(3)   µC/OS-III returns additional information when a message queue is posted. Specifically, the sender includes the size of the message and takes a snapshot of the current timestamp and stores it in the message. The receiver of the message therefore knows when the message was posted.

TC-12(4)   In µC/OS-III, OSQPost() offers a number of options that replaces the three post functions provided in µC/OS-II.

TC-12(5)   µC/OS-III does not provide query services as they were rarely used.

C-4-6 SEMAPHORES

Table C-13 shows the difference in API for semaphore management.

µC/OS-II (os_sem.c)	µC/OS-III (os_sem.c)	Note
```INT16U OSSemAccept(OS_EVENT *pevent);```		(1)
```OS_EVENT * OSSemCreate(INT16U cnt);```	```void OSSemCreate(OS_SEM *p_sem, CPU_CHAR *p_name, OS_SEM_CTR cnt, OS_ERR *p_err);```	(2)
```OS_EVENT * OSSemDel(OS_EVENT *pevent, INT8U opt, INT8U *perr);```	```OS_OBJ_QTY, OSSemDel(OS_SEM *p_sem, OS_OPT opt, OS_ERR *p_err);```	
```void OSSemPend(OS_EVENT *pevent, INT32U timeout, INT8U *perr);```	```OS_SEM_CTR OSSemPend(OS_SEM *p_sem, OS_TICK timeout, OS_OPT opt, CPU_TS *p_ts, OS_ERR *p_err);```	(3)
```INT8U OSSemPendAbort(OS_EVENT *pevent, INT8U opt, INT8U *perr);```	```OS_OBJ_QTY OSSemPendAbort(OS_SEM *p_sem, OS_OPT opt, OS_ERR *p_err);```	
```void OSSemPost(OS_EVENT *pevent);```	```void OSSemPost(OS_SEM *p_sem, OS_OPT opt, OS_ERR *p_err);```	
```INT8U OSSemQuery(OS_EVENT *pevent, OS_SEM_DATA *p_sem_data);```		(4)

µC/OS-II (os_sem.c)	µC/OS-III (os_sem.c)	Note

<pre>void
OSSemSet(
    OS_EVENT   *pevent,
    INT16U   cnt,
    INT8U   *perr);</pre>
	<pre>void
	OSSemSet(
	    OS_SEM *p_sem,
	    OS_SEM_CTR cnt,
	    OS_ERR *p_err);</pre>	

Table C-13 **Semaphore Management API**

TC-13(1)   In µC/OS-III, there is no "accept" API since this feature is built into the **OSSemPend( )** by specifying the **OS_OPT_PEND_NON_BLOCKING** option.

TC-13(2)   In µC/OS-II, **OSSemCreate( )** returns the address of an **OS_EVENT**, which is used as the "handle" to the semaphore. In µC/OS-III, the application must allocate storage for an **OS_SEM** object, which serves the same purpose as the **OS_EVENT**. The benefit in µC/OS-III is that it is not necessary to predetermine the number of semaphores at compile time.

TC-13(3)   µC/OS-III returns additional information when a semaphore is signaled. The ISR or task that signals the semaphore takes a snapshot of the current timestamp and stores this in the **OS_SEM** object signaled. The receiver of the signal therefore knows when the signal was sent.

TC-13(4)   µC/OS-III does not provide query services, as they were rarely used.

C-4-7 TASK MANAGEMENT

Table C-14 shows the difference in API for task-management services.

µC/OS-II (os_task.c)	µC/OS-III (os_task.c)	Note

INT8U
OSTaskChangePrio(
    INT8U   oldprio,
    INT8U   newprio);
	void
	OSTaskChangePrio(
	    OS_TCB *p_tcb,
	    OS_PRIO prio,
	    OS_ERR *p_err);
		(1)

INT8U
OSTaskCreate(
    void   (*task)(void *p_arg),
    void   *p_arg,
    OS_STK   *ptos,
    INT8U   prio);
	void
	OSTaskCreate(
	    OS_TCB *p_tcb,
	    CPU_CHAR *p_name,
	    OS_TASK_PTR *p_task,
	    void *p_arg,
	    OS_PRIO prio,
	    CPU_STK *p_stk_base,
	    CPU_STK_SIZE stk_limit,
	    CPU_STK_SIZE stk_size,
	    OS_MSG_QTY q_size,
	    OS_TICK time_quanta,
	    void *p_ext,
	    OS_OPT opt,
	    OS_ERR *p_err);
		(2)

INT8U
OSTaskCreateExt(
    void   (*task)(void *p_arg),
    void   *p_arg,
    OS_STK   *ptos,
    INT8U   prio,
    INT16U   id,
    OS_STK   *pbos,
    INT32U   stk_size,
    void   *pext,
    INT16U   opt);
	void
	OSTaskCreate(
	    OS_TCB *p_tcb,
	    CPU_CHAR *p_name,
	    OS_TASK_PTR *p_task,
	    void *p_arg,
	    OS_PRIO prio,
	    CPU_STK *p_stk_base,
	    CPU_STK_SIZE stk_limit,
	    CPU_STK_SIZE stk_size,
	    OS_MSG_QTY q_size,
	    OS_TICK time_quanta,
	    void *p_ext,
	    OS_OPT opt,
	    OS_ERR *p_err);
		(2)

INT8U
OSTaskDel(
    INT8U   prio);
	void
	OSTaskDel(
	    OS_TCB *p_tcb,
	    OS_ERR *p_err);	

µC/OS-II (os_task.c)	µC/OS-III (os_task.c)	Note

`INT8U`
`OSTaskDelReq(`
`    INT8U      prio);`		

`INT8U`
`OSTaskNameGet(`
`    INT8U      prio,`
`    INT8U      **pname,`
`    INT8U      *perr);`		

`void`
`OSTaskNameSet(`
`    INT8U      prio,`
`    INT8U      *pname,`
`    INT8U      *perr);`
		(3)

	`OS_MSG_QTY`
	`OSTaskQFlush(`
	`    OS_TCB      *p_tcb,`
	`    OS_ERR      *p_err);`
		(4)

	`void *`
	`OSTaskQPend(`
	`    OS_TICK     timeout,`
	`    OS_OPT      opt,`
	`    OS_MSG_SIZE *p_msg_size,`
	`    CPU_TS      *p_ts,`
	`    OS_ERR      *p_err);`
		(4)

	`CPU_BOOLEAN`
	`OSTaskQPendAbort(`
	`    OS_TCB      *p_tcb,`
	`    OS_OPT      opt,`
	`    OS_ERR      *p_err);`
		(4)

	`void`
	`OSTaskQPost(`
	`    OS_TCB      *p_tcb,`
	`    void        *p_void,`
	`    OS_MSG_SIZE msg_size,`
	`    OS_OPT      opt,`
	`    OS_ERR      *p_err);`
		(4)

`INT32U`
`OSTaskRegGet(`
`    INT8U      prio,`
`    INT8U      id,`
`    INT8U      *perr);`
	`OS_REG`
	`OSTaskRegGet(`
	`    OS_TCB      *p_tcb,`
	`    OS_REG_ID   id,`
	`    OS_ERR      *p_err);`	

µC/OS-II (os_task.c)	µC/OS-III (os_task.c)	Note
```void OSTaskRegSet(INT8U prio, INT8U id, INT32U value, INT8U *perr);```	```void OSTaskRegGet(OS_TCB *p_tcb, OS_REG_ID id, OS_REG value, OS_ERR *p_err);```	
```INT8U OSTaskResume(INT8U prio);```	```void OSTaskResume(OS_TCB *p_tcb, OS_ERR *p_err);```	
	```OS_SEM_CTR OSTaskSemPend(OS_TICK timeout, OS_OPT opt, CPU_TS *p_ts, OS_ERR *p_err);```	(5)
	```CPU_BOOLEAN OSTaskSemPendAbort(OS_TCB *p_tcb, OS_OPT opt, OS_ERR *p_err);```	(5)
	```CPU_BOOLEAN OSTaskSemPendAbort(OS_TCB *p_tcb, OS_OPT opt, OS_ERR *p_err);```	(5)
	```OS_SEM_CTR OSTaskSemPost(OS_TCB *p_tcb, OS_OPT opt, OS_ERR *p_err);```	(5)
	```OS_SEM_CTR OSTaskSemSet(OS_TCB *p_tcb, OS_SEM_CTR cnt, OS_ERR *p_err);```	(5)
```INT8U OSTaskSuspend(INT8U prio);```	```void OSTaskSuspend(OS_TCB *p_tcb, OS_ERR *p_err);```	

µC/OS-II (os_task.c)	µC/OS-III (os_task.c)	Note

`INT8U`
`OSTaskStkChk(`
    `INT8U        prio,`
    `OS_STK_DATA *p_stk_data);`
	`void`
	`OSTaskStkChk(`
	    `OS_TCB       *p_tcb,`
	    `CPU_STK_SIZE *p_free,`
	    `CPU_STK_SIZE *p_used,`
	    `OS_ERR       *p_err);`
		(6)

	`void`
	`OSTaskTimeQuantaSet(`
	    `OS_TCB     *p_tcb,`
	    `OS_TICK     time_quanta,`
	    `OS_ERR     *p_err);`
		(7)

`INT8U`
`OSTaskQuery(`
    `INT8U      prio,`
    `OS_TCB    *p_task_data);`
		(8)

Table C-14 **Task Management API**

TC-14(1)   In µC/OS-II, each task must have a unique priority. The priority of a task can be changed at run-time, however it can only be changed to an unused priority. This is generally not a problem since µC/OS-II supports up to 255 different priority levels and is rare for an application to require all levels. Since µC/OS-III supports an unlimited number of tasks at each priority, the user can change the priority of a task to any available level.

TC-14(2)   µC/OS-II provides two functions to create a task: **OSTaskCreate()** and **OSTaskCreateExt()**. **OSTaskCreateExt()** is recommended since it offers more flexibility. In µC/OS-III, only one API is used to create a task, **OSTaskCreate()**, which offers similar features to **OSTaskCreateExt()** and provides additional ones.

TC-14(3)   µC/OS-III does not need an **OSTaskNameSet()** since an ASCII name for the task is passed as an argument to **OSTaskCreate()**.

TC-14(4)   µC/OS-III allows tasks or ISRs to send messages directly to a task instead of having to pass through a mailbox or a message queue as does µC/OS-II.

TC-14(5)   µC/OS-III allows tasks or ISRs to directly signal a task instead of having to pass through a semaphore as does µC/OS-II.

TC-14(6)   In µC/OS-II, the user must allocate storage for a special data structure called **OS_STK_DATA**, which is used to place the result of a stack check of a task. This data structure contains only two fields: **.OSFree** and **.OSUsed**. In µC/OS-III, it is required that the caller pass pointers to destination variables where those values will be placed.

TC-14(7)   µC/OS-III allows users to specify the time quanta of each task on a per-task basis. This is available since µC/OS-III supports multiple tasks at the same priority, and allows for round robin scheduling. The time quanta for a task is specified when the task is created, but it can be changed by the API at run time.

TC-14(8)   µC/OS-III does not provide query services as they were rarely used.

C-4-8 TIME MANAGEMENT

Table C-15 shows the difference in API for time-management services.

µC/OS-II (os_time.c)	µC/OS-III (os_time.c)	Note

void
OSTimeDly(
    INT32U   ticks);
	void
	OSTimeDly(
	    OS_TICK dly,
	    OS_OPT opt,
	    OS_ERR *p_err);
		(1)

INT8U
OSTimeDlyHMSM(
    INT8U   hours,
    INT8U   minutes,
    INT8U   seconds,
    INT16U   ms);
	void
	OSTimeDlyHMSM(
	    CPU_INT16U hours,
	    CPU_INT16U minutes,
	    CPU_INT16U seconds
	    CPU_INT32U milli,
	    OS_OPT opt,
	    OS_ERR *p_err);
		(2)

INT8U
OSTimeDlyResume(
    INT8U   prio);
	void
	OSTimeDlyResume(
	    OS_TCB *p_tcb,
	    OS_ERR *p_err);	

INT32U OSTimeGet(void);	OS_TICK OSTimeGet(OS_ERR *p_err);	

µC/OS-II (`os_time.c`)	µC/OS-III (`os_time.c`)	Note
```void OSTimeSet(INT32U ticks);```	```void OSTimeSet(OS_TICK ticks, OS_ERR *p_err);```	
```void OSTimeTick(void)```	```void OSTimeTick(void)```	

Table C-15 **Time Management API**

TC-15(1)   µC/OS-III includes an option argument, which allows the user to delay a task for a certain number of ticks, periodic mode or wait until the tick counter reaches a certain value. In µC/OS-II, only the former is available.

TC-15(2)   **OSTimeDlyHMSM()** in µC/OS-III is more flexible as it allows a user to specify whether to be "strict" about the ranges of hours (0 to 999), minutes (0 to 59), seconds (0 to 59), and milliseconds (0 to 999), or whether to allow any values such as 200 minutes, 75 seconds, or 20,000 milliseconds (non-strict).

C-4-9 TIMER MANAGEMENT

Table C-16 shows the difference in API for timer-management services. The timer management in µC/OS-III is similar to that of µC/OS-II except for minor changes in arguments in **OSTmrCreate()**.

µC/OS-II (`os_tmr.c`)	µC/OS-III (`os_tmr.c`)	Note
```OS_TMR * OSTmrCreate(INT32U dly, INT32U period, INT8U opt, OS_TMR_CALLBACK callback, void *callback_arg, INT8U *pname, INT8U *perr);```	```void OSTmrCreate(OS_TMR *p_tmr, CPU_CHAR *p_name, OS_TICK dly, OS_TICK period, OS_OPT opt, OS_TMR_CALLBACK_PTR *p_callback, void *p_callback_arg, OS_ERR *p_err);```	

µC/OS-II (os_tmr.c)		µC/OS-III (os_tmr.c)		Note

BOOLEAN
OSTmrDel(
    OS_TMR   *ptmr,
    INT8U   *perr);
		CPU_BOOLEAN
		OSTmrDel(
		    OS_TMR *p_tmr,
		    OS_ERR *p_err);		

INT8U
OSTmrNameGet(
    OS_TMR   *ptmr,
    INT8U   **pdest,
    INT8U *perr);				

INT32U
OSTmrRemainGet(
    OS_TMR   *ptmr,
    INT8U   *perr);
		OS_TICK
		OSTmrRemainGet(
		    OS_TMR *p_tmr,
		    OS_ERR *p_err);		

INT8U
OSTmrStateGet(
    OS_TMR   *ptmr,
    INT8U   *perr);
		OS_STATE
		OSTmrStateGet(
		    OS_TMR *p_tmr,
		    OS_ERR *p_err);		

BOOLEAN
OSTmrStart(
    OS_TMR   *ptmr,
    INT8U   *perr);
		CPU_BOOLEAN
		OSTmrStart(
		    OS_TMR *p_tmr,
		    OS_ERR *p_err);		

BOOLEAN
OSTmrStop(
    OS_TMR   *ptmr,
    INT8U   opt,
    void   *callback_arg,
    INT8U   *perr);
		CPU_BOOLEAN
		OSTmrStop(
		    OS_TMR *p_tmr,
		    OS_OPT opt,
		    void *p_callback_arg,
		    OS_ERR *p_err);		

INT8U OSTmrSignal(void);				

Table C-16 **Timer Management API**

C-4-10 MISCELLANEOUS

Table C-17 shows the difference in API for miscellaneous services.

µC/OS-II (os_core.c)	µC/OS-III (os_core.c)	Note

`INT8U`
`OSEventNameGet(`
`    OS_EVENT    *pevent,`
`    INT8U       **pname,`
`    INT8U       *perr);`
		(1)

`void`
`OSEventNameSet(`
`    OS_EVENT    *pevent,`
`    INT8U       *pname,`
`    INT8U       *perr);`
		(1)

`INT16U`
`OSEventPendMulti(`
`    OS_EVENT    **pevent_pend,`
`    OS_EVENT    **pevent_rdy,`
`    void        **pmsgs_rdy,`
`    INT32U      timeout,`
`    INT8U       *perr);`
	`OS_OBJ_QTY`
	`OSPendMulti(`
	`    OS_PEND_DATA    *p_pend_data_tbl,`
	`    OS_OBJ_QTY      tbl_size,`
	`    OS_TICK         timeout,`
	`    OS_OPT          opt,`
	`    OS_ERR          *p_err);`
		(2)

`void`
`OSInit(void)`
	`void`
	`OSInit(`
	`    OS_ERR          *p_err);`
		(3)

`void` `OSIntEnter(void)`	`void` `OSIntEnter(void);`	
`void` `OSIntExit(void)`	`void` `OSIntExit(void)`	
	`void` `OSSched(void);`	

`void`
`OSSchedLock(void)`
	`void`
	`OSSchedLock(`
	`    OS_ERR          *p_err);`
		(4)

	`void`
	`OSSchedRoundRobinCfg(`
	`    CPU_BOOLEAN     en,`
	`    OS_TICK         dflt_time_quanta,`
	`    OS_ERR          *p_err);`
		(5)

	`void`
	`OSSchedRoundRobinYield(`
	`    OS_ERR          *p_err);`
		(6)

`void`
`OSSchedUnlock(void)`
	`void`
	`OSSchedUnlock(`
	`    OS_ERR          *p_err);`
		(7)

µC/OS-II (os_core.c)	µC/OS-III (os_core.c)	Note
``void
OSStart(void)```	```void
OSStart(void);```	
``void
OSStatInit(void)```	```void
OSStatTaskCPUUsageInit(
OS_ERR *p_err);```	(8)
``INT16U
OSVersion(void)```	```CPU_INT16U
OSVersion(
OS_ERR *p_err);```	(9)

Table C-17 **Miscellaneous API**

TC-17(1)   Objects in µC/OS-III are named when they are created and these functions are not required in µC/OS-III.

TC-17(2)   The implementation of the multi-pend functionality is changed from µC/OS-II. However, the purpose of multi-pend is the same, to allow a task to pend (or wait) on multiple objects. In µC/OS-III, however, it is possible to only multi-pend on semaphores and message queues and not event flags and mutexes.

TC-17(3)   µC/OS-III returns an error code for this function. Initialization is successful if **OS_ERR_NONE** is received from **OSInit( )**. In µC/OS-II, there is no way of detecting an error in the configuration that caused **OSInit( )** to fail.

TC-17(4)   An error code is returned in µC/OS-III for this function.

TC-17(5)   Enable or disable µC/OS-III's round-robin scheduling at run time, as well as change the default time quanta.

TC-17(6)   A task that completes its work before its time quanta expires may yield the CPU to another task at the same priority.

TC-17(7)   An error code is returned in µC/OS-III for this function.

TC-17(8)   Note the change in name for the function that computes the "capacity" of the CPU for the purpose of computing CPU usage at run-time.

TC-17(9)   An error code is returned in µC/OS-III for this function.

C-4-11 HOOKS AND PORT

Table C-18 shows the difference in APIs used to port µC/OS-II to µC/OS-III.

µC/OS-II (os_cpu*.c/h)	µC/OS-III (os_cpu*.c/h)	Note
	`OS_GET_TS();`	(1)
`void` `OSInitHookBegin(void);`	`void` `OSInitHook(void);`	
`void` `OSInitHookEnd(void);`		

`void`
`OSTaskCreateHook(`
`    OS_TCB    *ptcb);`
	`void`
	`OSTaskCreateHook(`
	`    OS_TCB         *p_tcb);`	

`void`
`OSTaskDelHook(`
`    OS_TCB    *ptcb);`
	`void`
	`OSTaskDelHook(`
	`    OS_TCB         *p_tcb);`	

`void` `OSTaskIdleHook(void);`	`void` `OSIdleTaskHook(void);`	

	`void`
	`OSTaskReturnHook(`
	`    OS_TCB         *p_tcb);`
		(2)

`void` `OSTaskStatHook(void)`	`void` `OSStatTaskHook(void);`	

`void`
`OSTaskStkInit(`
`    void      (*task)(void *p_arg),`
`    void      *p_arg,`
`    OS_STK    *ptos,`
`    INT16U    opt);`
	`CPU_STK *`
	`OSTaskStkInit(`
	`    OS_TASK_PTR    p_task,`
	`    void           *p_arg,`
	`    CPU_STK        *p_stk_base,`
	`    CPU_STK        *p_stk_limit,`
	`    CPU_STK_SIZE   size,`
	`    OS_OPT         opt);`
		(3)

`void` `OSTaskSwHook(void)`	`void` `OSTaskSwHook(void);`	

`void`
`OSTCBInitHook(`
`    OS_TCB    *ptcb);`
		(4)

`void` `OSTimeTickHook(void);`	`void` `OSTimeTickHook(void);`	
`void` `OSStartHighRdy(void);`	`void` `OSStartHighRdy(void);`	(5)
`void` `OSIntCtxSw(void);`	`void` `OSIntCtxSw(void);`	(5)

µC/OS-II (os_cpu*.c/h)	µC/OS-III (os_cpu*.c/h)	Note
void OSCtxSw(void);	void OSCtxSw(void);	(5)

Table C-18 **Hooks and Port API**

TC-18(1)   µC/OS-III requires that the Board Support Package (BSP) provide a 32-bit free-running counter (from **0x00000000** to **0xFFFFFFFF** and rolls back to **0x00000000**) for the purpose of performing time measurements. When a signal is sent, or a message is posted, this counter is read and sent to the recipient. This allows the recipient to know when the message was sent. If a 32-bit free-running counter is not available, you can simulate one using a 16-bit counter but, this requires more code to keep track of overflows.

TC-18(2)   µC/OS-III is able to terminate a task that returns. Recall that tasks should not return since they should be either implemented as an infinite loop, or deleted if implemented as run once.

TC-18(3)   The code for **OSTaskStkInit()** must be changed slightly in µC/OS-III since several arguments passed to this function are different than in µC/OS-II. Instead of passing the top-of-stack as in µC/OS-II, **OSTaskStkInit()** is passed the base address of the task stack, as well as the size of the stack.

TC-18(4)   This function is not needed in µC/OS-III.

TC-18(5)   These functions are a part of **os_cpu_a.asm**, and should only require name changes for the following variables:

µC/OS-II variable changes from ...	... to this in µC/OS-III
OSIntNesting	OSIntNestingCtr
OSTCBCur	OSTCBCurPtr
OSTCBHighRdy	OSTCBHighRdyPtr

MISRA-C:2004 and µC/OS-III

MISRA C is a software development standard for the C programming language developed by the Motor Industry Software Reliability Association (MISRA). Its aims are to facilitate code safety, portability, and reliability in the context of embedded systems, specifically those systems programmed in ANSI C. There is also a set of guidelines for MISRA C++.

There are now more MISRA users outside of the automotive industry than within it. MISRA has evolved into a widely accepted model of best practices by leading developers in such sectors as aerospace, telecom, medical devices, defense, railway, and others.

The first edition of the MISRA C standard, "Guidelines for the use of the C language in vehicle based software," was produced in 1998 and is officially known as MISRA-C:1998. MISRA-C:1998 had 127 rules, of which 93 were required and 34 advisory. The rules were numbered in sequence from 1 to 127.

In 2004, a second edition "Guidelines for the use of the C language in critical systems," or MISRA-C:2004 was produced with many substantial changes, including a complete renumbering of the rules.

The MISRA-C:2004 document contains 141 rules, of which 121 are "required" and 20 are "advisory," divided into 21 topical categories, from "Environment" to "Run-time failures."

µC/OS-III follows most of the MISRA-C:2004 except a few of the required rules were suppressed. The reasoning behind this is discussed within this appendix.

IAR Embedded Workbench for ARM (EWARM) V6.2x was used to verify MISRA-C:2004 compliance, which required suppressing the rules to achieve a clean build.

D

D-1 MISRA-C:2004, RULE 8.5 (REQUIRED)

Rule Description

There shall be no definitions of objects or functions in a header file.

Offending code appears as

```
OS_EXT   OS_IDLE_CTR   OSIdleTaskCtr;
```

OS_EXT allows us to declare "extern" and storage using a single declaration in **os.h** but allocation of storage actually occurs in **os_var.c**.

Rule suppressed

The method used in μC/OS-III is an improved scheme as it avoids declaring variables in multiple files.

Occurs in

os.h

D-2 MISRA-C:2004, RULE 8.12 (REQUIRED)

Rule Description:

When an array is declared with external linkage, its size shall be stated explicitly or defined implicitly by initialization.

Offending code appears as

```
extern  CPU_STK        OSCfg_IdleTaskStk[];
```

µC/OS-III can be provided in object form (linkable object), but requires that the value and size of known variables and arrays be declared in application code. It is not possible to know the size of the arrays.

Rule suppressed

There is no choice other than to suppress or add a fictitious size, which would not be proper. For example, we could specify a size of 1 and the MISRA-C:2004 would pass but, we chose not to.

Occurs in:

os.h

D

D-3 MISRA-C:2004, RULE 14.7 (REQUIRED)

Rule Description
A function shall have a single point of exit at the end of the function.

Offending code appears as

```
if (argument is invalid) {
    Set error code;
    return;
}
```

Rule suppressed
We prefer to exit immediately upon finding an invalid argument rather than create nested "if" statements.

Occurs in
os_core.c

os_flag.c

os_int.c

os_mem.c

os_msg.c

os_mutex.c

os_pend_multi.c

os_prio.c

os_q.c

os_sem.c

os_stat.c

os_task.c

os_tick.c

os_time.c

os_tmr.c

D-4 MISRA-C:2004, RULE 15.2 (REQUIRED)

Rule Description

An unconditional break statement shall terminate every non-empty **switch** clause.

Offending code appears as

```
switch (value) {
    case constant_value:
        /* Code */
        return;
}
```

Rule suppressed

The problem involves using a return statement to exit the function instead of using a **break**. When adding a "**break**" statement after the return, the compiler complains about the unreachable code of the "**break**" statement.

Occurs in

os_flag.c

os_mutex.c

os_q.c

os_tmr.c

D

D-5 MISRA-C:2004, RULE 17.4 (REQUIRED)

Rule Description

Array indexing shall be the only allowed form of pointer arithmetic.

Offending code appears as

```
        :
    p_tcb++;
        :
```

Rule suppressed

It is common practice in C to increment a pointer instead of using array indexing to accomplish the same thing. This common practice is not in agreement with this rule.

Occurs in

os_core.c

os_cpu_c.c

os_int.c

os_msg.c

os_pend_multi.c

os_prio.c

os_task.c

os_tick.c

os_tmr.c

Appendix

E

Bibliography

Bal Sathe, Dhananjay. 1988. *Fast Algorithm Determines Priority*. EDN (India), September, p. 237.

Comer, Douglas. 1984. *Operating System Design, The XINU Approach*. Englewood Cliffs, New Jersey: Prentice-Hall. ISBN 0-13-637539-1.

Kernighan, Brian W. and Dennis M. Ritchie. 1988. *The C Programming Language, 2nd edition*. Englewood Cliffs, New Jersey: Prentice Hall. ISBN 0-13-110362-8.

Klein, Mark H., Thomas Ralya, Bill Pollak, Ray Harbour Obenza, and Michael Gonzlez. 1993. *A Practioner's Handbook for Real-Time Analysis: Guide to Rate Monotonic Analysis for Real-Time Systems*. Norwell, Massachusetts: Kluwer Academic Publishers Group. ISBN 0-7923-9361-9.

Labrosse, Jean J. 2002, *MicroC/OS-II, The Real-Time Kernel*, CMP Books, 2002, ISBN 1-57820-103-9.

Li, Qing. *Real-Time Concepts for Embedded Systems*, CMP Books, July 2003, ISBN 1-57820-124-1.

The Motor Industry Software Reliability Association, *MISRA-C:2004*, Guidelines for the Use of the C Language in Critical Systems, October 2004. www.misra-c.com.

F

Licensing Policy

uC/OS-III is provided in source form for FREE short-term evaluation, for educational use or for peaceful research. If you plan or intend to use uC/OS-III in a commercial application/ product then, you need to contact Micrium to properly license uC/OS-III for its use in your application/product. We provide ALL the source code for your convenience and to help you experience uC/OS-III. The fact that the source is provided does NOT mean that you can use it commercially without paying a licensing fee.

It is necessary to purchase this license when the decision to use µC/OS-III in a design is made, not when the design is ready to go to production.

If you are unsure about whether you need to obtain a license for your application, please contact Micriµm and discuss the intended use with a sales representative.

CONTACT MICRIUM

1290 Weston Road, Suite 306
Weston, FL 33326
USA

Phone: +1 954 217 2036
Fax: +1 954 217 2037

E-mail: Licensing@Micrium.com
Web: www.Micrium.com

µC/OS-III™
The Real-Time Kernel

and the Freescale
Kinetis ARM® Cortex™-M4

Jean J. Labrosse
Juan P. Benavides
and
José Fernandez-Villaseñor, M.D.

Micriµm
Press

Weston, FL 33326

Micriµm Press
1290 Weston Road, Suite 306
Weston, FL 33326
USA
www.micrium.com

Library of Congress Control Number: 2011931642

Library of Congress subject headings:

1. Embedded computer systems
2. Real-time data processing
3. Computer software - Development

For bulk orders, please contact Micriµm Press at: +1 954 217 2036

978-0-9823375-2-3
100-uCOS-III-Freescale-Kinetis-002

Foreword

If you are reading these words I know one thing for sure: you are facing a challenge. That challenge falls within certain boundaries defined by your interest in this book. You need to learn how to use an RTOS, or you're planning to create a medical device for that rapidly growing market. You will face decisions on processor, platform, development tools, software design for life-critical systems, human machine interface, and more.

The good news is, you are in the right place for several reasons. For one thing, µC/OS has a long and storied history in the industry dating back to 1992. For another, you are smart enough to realize that writing everything from scratch is just plain dumb. With complex systems, especially those with life-critical or mission-critical applications, quality and reliability are absolutely paramount. Like any engineer, you want to use proven components. So here you are, reading and learning.

At Freescale we take an innovative approach to these problems, because we face them too. You need reliable components: processors, boards, OS, software stacks. You need them to all work together perfectly. Yet the simple fact is that your specific personal needs are not identical to everyone else. So how do we help you personally, while addressing a general market?

We take a solution approach, and this book fits perfectly into that strategy. The first component in that strategy is, of course, the processor. We've recently introduced the K50 family of microcontrollers, expanding upon our popular Kinetis ARM-Cortex M4 portfolio. This family of devices is focused on delivering the system level hardware to support a wide variety of measurement and communication requirements often found in medical devices. These are sophisticated and highly capable devices.

You need that processor on a board. What you need is not what "the other guy" needs. What peripherals should we include? What if you decide to change processors for some reason? We designed an innovative modular reference design platform called the Tower System – you can swap controller modules and various peripheral modules in and out of the system almost transparently. If you need a different peripheral, odds are excellent you can just buy a module and plug it into the tower, and not buy an entirely new piece of hardware and start over. Several of our partners are jumping into this open modular design, creating a huge community of "Tower Geeks" developing products on this highly customizable reference design.

The solution is not complete without software, and that's really where this book makes the greatest sense. There will be a lot going on in a modern medical device: continuous monitoring of an integrated measurement engine, processing of analog signals for the application and control functionality, human machine interface updates, and secure communication among devices and/or across networks. Getting all this to work together seamlessly and robustly is no easy task. Leveraging an RTOS during the system design will not only ease development, but also allow for optimal utilization of the variety of on-chip peripherals. This book will get you well started down that road.

On top of that, after introducing you to the fundamental principles of RTOS design and use, which you can apply to other RTOS designs, you have several real world examples of medical systems to build and experiment with: a heart rate monitor, a blood glucose meter, a pulse oximeter, and a blood pressure monitor.

There you have the main components of a real solution: a processor, a board with peripherals and drivers, an operating system, and the software required to put it to use to do something more than blink an LED. You still add the "secret sauce" that turns it into your product, but the Freescale solution puts you a long way up the learning curve. This book from Jean Labrosse is a big part of that.

The world of medical devices and applications continues to expand, presenting new opportunities and challenges for embedded system design. Freescale continues to innovate in this space to give the embedded designer the tools and the enablement to bring highly-capable and robust products to market in a timely and resource-efficient manner. I wish you the best of luck and trust you will find success as you tame your challenges. Thank you for choosing Freescale to help you along the way to making the world a better place.

Reza Kazerounian, Ph. D.
Senior Vice President and General Manager
Microcontroller Solutions
Freescale Semiconductor

Chapter

1

Introduction

A large percentage of the U.S. population, the baby boomers, is approaching retirement age. They are more health conscious than any previous generation, tend to continue to work longer and have substantial disposable income. They are used to demanding products and features that improve the quality of life, and most are extremely comfortable in the personal use of digital devices. In fact, a repetitive stress called "Blackberry Thumb" is no stranger to this demographic.

While the conditions on the demand side appear ripe to support a large and growing market, what about the supply side?

For healthcare providers, things do not at first blush look as rosy. Dramatic increases in the cost of healthcare means continued cuts in services. Further reductions in the average length of hospital stays, and even in the ability to offer expensive testing, are expected.

Furthermore, other factors beyond the scope of this book are driving healthcare personnel shortages. No matter the place, whether it is a large medical center in a developed country or a rural community hospital in a third world country, being a patient involves a lot of waiting around. Taking aside the time spent dealing with the bureaucracy of scheduling appointments, filling out the forms and paying the bills, most of the time is spent waiting for the limited number of healthcare personnel that can take care of you.

Unless the economics of healthcare change dramatically, the trend towards outpatient care will drive an increase in remote care options. Battery, sensor, processing and wireless technology advances will support the move from hands-on and in-person testing to remote test and monitoring. And, in some remote regions of the world, it may be the only way to provide reasonable care.

Home medical devices will play a major role as remote care catches on. And, as the evolution takes place, embedded software accuracy and accountability become even more critical in nature.

One of the main obstacles standing in the way of the development of home medical devices is the cost associated with the rigorous processes and practices mandated in safety-critical development that the medical devices manufacturers have to face in order to meet the certification needs for their products.

Appendix A describes with more detail the medical device marketplace and the conditions and factors behind its rapid growth. It also puts emphasis into the regulatory environment, especially in the U.S. and the European Union, and makes emphasis on the embedded software that provides safety-critical assurance against device failure, and the processes and regulatory criteria involved in the software's development, verification and validation.

Micriµm's µC/OS-II and several of its RTOS modules have been deployed in many medical designs and µC/OS-II has 100% of the required documentation needed to comply with the FDA 510(k)/Pre-market Approval (PMA), and also complies with IEC 62304, IEC 60601 and ISO 14971.

Part II of this book demonstrates how the Freescale's Tower System and Micriµm's µC/OS-III can be used as the cornerstone to build a home medical device that relies on a combination of proven hardware and software platforms. µC/OS-III is a certifiable real-time kernel that has gone through a very rigorous validation process. Freescale's ultra-low-power Kinetis MCUs are the core of the TWR-K53N512 that integrates precise analog components such as operational amplifiers, transimpedance amplifiers, high resolution ADCs and DACs specifically designed for low-power portable medical devices used in telemedicine.

The examples in this part of the book include home medical devices such as a *Heart Rate Monitor, Blood Glucose Meter, Pulse Oximeter* and a *Blood Pressure Monitor.*

All the four examples are based on the following key elements as shown in Figure 1-1:

- Freescale's Tower System controller TWR-K53N512 (Kinetis ARM® Cortex™-M4)

- Freescale's Medical Analog-Front-End modules: MED-EKG, MED-GLU, MED-SPO2 and MED-BPM

- IAR Systems Embedded Workbench for ARM (EWARM)

■ IAR Systems J-Link-Lite for ARM Processors

■ Micriµm's µC/OS-III

■ Micriµm's µC/Probe

The TWR-K53N512 is available from Freescale and is a Controller Module compatible with their Tower System that features the Kinetis K53 low-power microcontroller based on the ARM® Cortex™ M4 architecture. The next chapter will describe the main details of this controller as it will be used in all four examples.

In order to build the example code, you must download the IAR Systems Embedded Workbench for ARM from the IAR website.

You can download a trial version of µC/Probe from the Micriµm website in order to not only monitor the application variables at run time but also to prototype the front panel of each medical device. The source code of the examples is available for free from the same website.

Each example requires an Analog-Front-End (AFE) module that connects to the TWR-K53N512 controller via a 2x10 medical connector if you want to run the examples live with the signals coming from a human being. The AFEs contain all the circuits necessary to interface with standard medical supplies and the signal conditioning circuitry.

In the absence of these AFEs, all the examples feature a separate simulation task that generates the necessary analog signals. This type of built-in signal generator is typically used for calibration and testing in the medical industry.

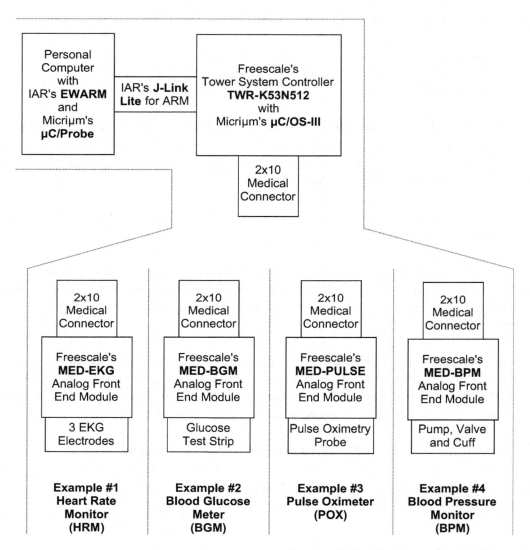

Figure 1-1 **Medical Application Examples Overview**

This book and Freescale's TWR-K53N512 make an excellent platform for hardware engineers interested in testing their own medical signal conditioning circuits as they do not have to worry about the software details. Freescale offers prototyping boards compatible with their tower system for such purpose. Software engineers interested in testing their own medical signal analysis algorithms will find this book and platform very useful too as they do not have to worry about the hardware necessary to acquire the signals. Engineers and scientists in general and those not familiar with Biomedical Engineering will find this book very interesting as they will learn some of the inner works of certainly the most advanced control system in the planet called the human body. An illustrated explanation of some of the main regulation mechanisms including the glucose level and blood pressure in the body will serve not only as inspiration for the design of any control system but also as an introduction to each example.

The medical application examples in this book are provided solely as a reference to help engineers use Micriµm and Freescale Semiconductor products.

There are no express or implied copyright licenses granted hereunder to design or fabricate any medical devices based on the information in this book.

Micriµm and Freescale Semiconductor make no warranty, representation or guarantee regarding the suitability of these examples for any particular purpose, nor does Micriµm and Freescale Semiconductor assume any liability arising out of the application or use of any example design, and specifically disclaims any and all liability, including without limitation consequential or incidental damages.

The following medical application examples are not designed, intended, or authorized for use as components in systems intended to support or sustain life, or for any other application in which the failure of the system could create a situation where personal injury or death may occur.

You should always consult your physician or other healthcare professionals for specific advice regarding any medical or health condition.

1-1 PART II CHAPTER CONTENTS

Figure 1-2 shows the layout and flow of Part II of the book. This diagram should be useful in understanding the relationship between chapters and appendices.

The first column on the left indicates chapters that should be read in order to understand µC/OS-III's structure as well as the examples. The columns to the right hand side consist of miscellaneous appendices that further expand on the information presented in the first columns on the left.

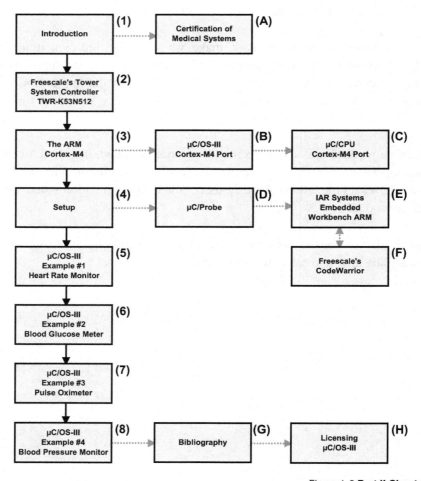

Figure 1-2 **Part II Chapter Layout**

F1-2(1)   **Chapter 1, Introduction.** This chapter.

F1-2(2)   **Chapter 2, Freescale's Tower System Controller TWR-K53N512.** This chapter provides a description of the TWR-K53N512 evaluation board that will be used for all the examples.

F1-2(3)   **Chapter 3, The ARM Cortex-M4.** This chapter provides a brief introduction to the ARM Cortex-M4 CPU.

F1-2(4)   **Chapter 4, Setup.** This chapter explains how to set up the test environment to run µC/OS-III examples. It describes how to download the 32K Kickstart version of the IAR Systems Embedded Workbench for ARM tool chain, how to obtain example code that accompanies the book, and how to connect the TWR-K53N512 tower board to a PC.

F1-2(5)   **Chapter 5, Example #1: Heart Rate Monitor.** This chapter explains how to get µC/OS-III up and running. The project features a single channel ECG monitor that calculates the heart rate. You will also see how easy it is to use µC/Probe to display the heart rate.

F1-2(6)   **Chapter 6, Example #2: Blood Glucose Meter.** This chapter shows how to read a blood glucose test strip and display the blood glucose level using µC/Probe.

F1-2(7)   **Chapter 7, Example #3: Pulse Oximeter.** This chapter shows how to drive a pulse oximetry probe's LEDs and calculate the oxygen saturation and heart rate.

F1-2(8)   **Chapter 8, Example #4: Blood Pressure Monitor.** This chapter shows how to use µC/OS-III to drive an air pump and electrical valve in order to measure the blood pressure and display the value in µC/Probe.

F1-2(A)   **Appendix A, Certification of Medical Systems.** This chapter covers general concepts that are applicable to all embedded medical systems, including the commercial development process and certification.

F1-2(B)   **Appendix B, µC/OS-III Port for the Cortex-M4.** This appendix explains how µC/OS-III was adapted to the Cortex-M4 CPU. The Cortex-M4 contains interesting features specifically designed for real-time kernels, and µC/OS-III makes good use of these.

F1-2(C)   **Appendix C, µC/CPU Port to the Cortex-M4.** This appendix describes how µC/CPU was adapted to the Cortex-M4.

F1-2(D)   **Appendix D, µC/Probe.** This appendix provides a brief description of Micriµm's award-winning µC/Probe, which easily allows users to display and change target variables at run time.

F1-2(E)   **Appendix E, IAR Systems Embedded Workbench ARM.** This appendix provides a brief description of IAR Systems Embedded Workbench for the ARM architecture (EWARM).

F1-2(F)   **Appendix F, Freescale Semiconductor's CodeWarrior for MCUs.** This appendix provides a brief description of Freescale Semiconductor's CodeWarrior 10.1 for microcontrollers.

F1-2(G)   **Appendix G, Bibliography.**

F1-2(H)   **Appendix H, Licensing µC/OS-III.**

1-2 ACKNOWLEDGEMENTS

I would like to thank Ravel Thai, from Freescale Semiconductor, who helped see the project through to completion. He made this possible by fostering collaborative relationships between Freescale and Micriµm. Thanks to Dr. José Fernandez-Villaseñor and José Santiago López from Freescale for providing their expertise in medical applications and the rest of the fine team at Freescale for designing the TWR-K53N512 evaluation board along with all the Medical Analog-Front-End plugins.

Thanks to Todd Brian from Validated Software Corporation for providing all the material related to the Certification of Medical Devices.

I would also like to thank IAR for their support and for providing access to the 32K Kickstart version of the IAR Embedded Workbench for ARM (EWARM). EWARM is an awesome tool and I'm sure readers of this book will appreciate the ability to try out µC/OS-III on the TWR-K53N512 board.

Finally, thank you to my great team at Micriµm for the help and support they provided for this project, Juan Benavides in particular who was mostly responsible for the second part of this book.

José Fernández Villaseñor is Freescale's Semiconductor Global Medical Applications lead. He is both an Electronics Systems Engineer and Medical Doctor with a Master's Degree in Plastic and Cosmetic Surgery and Medicine. He has led the technical and research activities within Freescale Semiconductor since 2007 in roles such as systems and solutions engineering and product marketing and engineering. He has collaborated with different universities in research programs for new generation medical semiconductors and microcontrollers. As a physician he has worked in Mexican Hospitals in areas involving ER, Renal and Kidney transplant surgery and cosmetic surgery.

Juan P. Benavides is an Applications Engineer at Micriµm in Florida. He received his B.S. degree in Electrical Engineering from the University of the Andes, Bogotá, Colombia in 1999 with emphasis in Biomedical Engineering and his senior research work involved the design and implementation of an Electronystagmograph (ENG) based on a microcontroller. Since then, he has held positions in the industry designing and developing multiple embedded systems using a wide variety of hardware and software architectures not only in the medical industry but also in the power generation, marine and industrial control and instrumentation. Prior to joining Micriµm he was the Lead Software Developer at Swantech, a division of the Curtiss-Wright Corporation.

2

Freescale's Tower System Controller TWR-K53N512

The TWR-K53N512 is a Tower Controller Module compatible with the Freescale Tower System. It can function as a stand-alone, low-cost platform for the evaluation of the Kinetis K53 family of microcontroller (MCU) devices.

The TWR-K53N512 features the Kinetis K53 low-power MCU based on the ARM® Cortex™-M4 architecture. As we will describe in more detail in the next chapter, the MCU comes with USB 2.0 full-speed OTG, 10/100 Mbps Ethernet MAC, a flexible, low-power segment LCD controller and analog front end capabilities specifically designed for medical devices. The K53N512 includes 256Kbytes of program flash storage and an additional 256Kbytes of FlexMemory non-volatile storage that can be used as additional program flash memory, data flash, or variable size/endurance EEPROM.

The TWR-K53N512 is the controller we used for each of the four medical application examples featured in this book. As shown in Figure 2-1 the board provides interface to the medical expansion connector that allows you to expand the capabilities of the system by connecting the following Analog Front End (AFE) plugins from Freescale:

■ MED-EKG: Electrocardiograph

■ MED-GLU: Blood glucose meter

■ MED-SPO2: Pulse oximeter

■ MED-BPM: Blood pressure monitor

We will describe in more detail each of these AFE plug-ins in their corresponding example chapters 5, 6, 7 and 8.

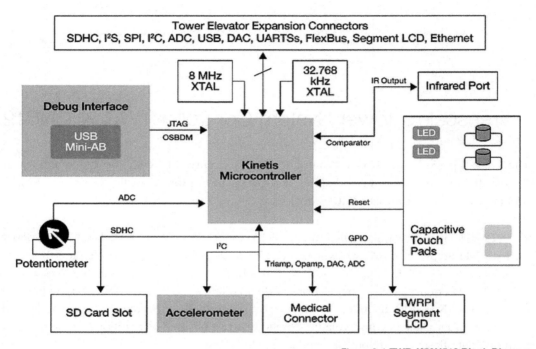

Figure 2-1 **TWR-K53N512 Block Diagram**

The following list summarizes the features of the TWR-K53N512 and Figure 2-2 and Figure 2-3 show the TWR-K53N512 with some of the key features called out:

- Tower compatible microcontroller module

- MK53N512VMD100: K53N512 in a 144 MAPBGA with 100MHz operation

- Touch Tower Plug-in Socket

- General purpose Tower Plug-In (TWRPI) socket

- On-board JTAG debug circuit (OSJTAG) with virtual serial port

- 2x10 Medical expansion connector

- Three axis accelerometer (MMA7660)

- Two (2) user-controllable LEDs

- Two (2) capacitive touch pads

- Two (2) user mechanical push buttons

- Potentiometer

- Battery Holder for 20mm lithium battery (e.g. 2032, 2025)

- SD Card slot

Primary Connector

Infrared Port

Reset Button SW3

General-purpose TWRPI socket

Power/OSJTAG Mini-B USB Connector

Push Buttons SW1 and SW2

LED/Touch Buttons E1 and E2

20-pin Medical Connector

Secondary Connector

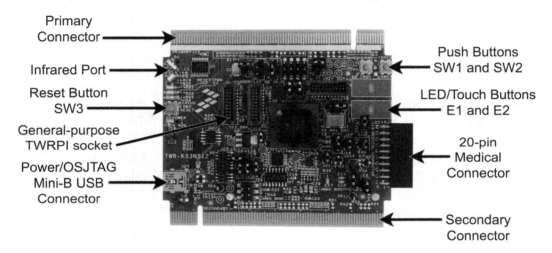

Figure 2-2 **Front side of the TWR-K53N512**

Primary Connector

Potentiometer

SD Card Socket

VBAT (RTC) Battery Holder

Secondary Connector

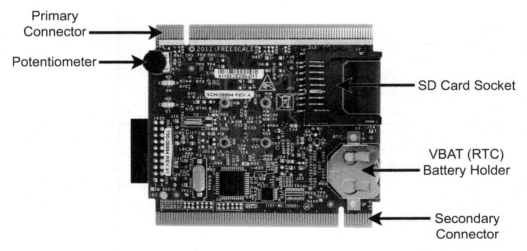

Figure 2-3 **Back side of the TWR-K53N512**

2-1 TWR-K53N512 PIN USAGE

Table 2-1 provides details on which K53N512 pins are used to communicate with the LEDs, pushbuttons, and other I/O interfaces onboard the TWR-K53N512. In order to avoid attempted simultaneous usage of mutually exclusive features, be aware that some port pins are used in multiple interfaces on-board and many are potentially connected to off-board resources via the Primary and Secondary Connectors.

TWR-K53N512 Pinout

Feature	Connection	Port Pin	Pin Function
OSJTAG USB-to-serial Bridge	OSJTAG Bridge RX Data	PTE9	UART5_RX
	OSJTAG Bridge TX Data	PTE8	UART5_TX
SD Card Slot	SD Clock	PTE2	SDHC0_DCLK
	SD Command	PTE3	SDHC0_CMD
	SD Data0	PTE1	SDHC0_D0
	SD Data1	PTE0	SDHC0_D1
	SD Data2	PTE5	SDHC0_D2
	SD Data3	PTE4	SDHC0_D3
	SD Card Detect	PTE28	PTE28
	SD Write Protect	PTC9	PTC9
Infrared Port	IR Transmit	PTD7	CMT_IRO
	IR Receive	PTC6	CMP0_IN0
Pushbuttons	SW1 (IRQ0)	PTC5	PTC5
	SW2 (IRQ1)	PTC13	PTC13
	SW3 (RESET)	RESET_b	RESET_b
Touch Pads	E1 / Touch	PTB17	TSI0_CH10
	E2 / Touch	PTB18	TSI0_CH11
LEDs	E1 / Orange LED	PTC7	PTC7
	E2 / Yellow LED	PTC8	PTC8
Potentiometer	Potentiometer (R71)	ADC1_DM1	ADC1_DM1
Accelerometer	I2C SDA	PTC11	I2C0_SDA
	I2C SCL	PTC10	I2C0_SCL
	IRQ	PTC12	PTD10

TWR-K53N512 Pinout

Feature	Connection	Port Pin	Pin Function
General Purpose TWRPI Socket	TWRPI AN0 (J9 Pin 8)	PTB6	ADC0_DP0/ADC1_DP3
	TWRPI AN1 (J9 Pin 9)	PTB7	ADC0_DM0/ADC1_DM3
	TWRPI AN2 (J9 Pin 12)	PTB5	ADC1_DP0/ADC0_DP3
	TWRPI ID0 (J9 Pin 17)	PTE0	ADC0_DP1
	TWRPI ID1 (J9 Pin 18)	PTE1	ADC0_DM1
	TWRPI I2C SCL (J10 Pin 3)	PTC10	I2C1_SCL
	TWRPI I2C SDA (J10 Pin 4)	PTC11	I2C1_SDA
	TWRPI SPI MISO (J10 Pin 9)	PTB23	SPI2_SIN
	TWRPI SPI MOSI (J10 Pin 10)	PTB22	SPI2_SOUT
	TWRPI SPI SS (J10 Pin 11)	PTB20	SPI2_PCS0
	TWRPI SPI CLK (J10 Pin 12)	PTB21	SPI2_SCK
	TWRPI GPIO0 (J10 Pin 15)	PTC12	PTC12
	TWRPI GPIO1 (J10 Pin 16)	PTB9	PTB9
	TWRPI GPIO2 (J10 Pin 17)	PTB10	PTB10
	TWRPI GPIO3 (J10 Pin 18)	PTC5	PTC5
	TWRPI GPIO4 (J10 Pin 19)	PTC13	PTC13
Touch Pad / Segment LCD TWRPI Socket	Electrode 0 (J8 Pin 3)	PTB0	TSI0_CH0
	Electrode 1 (J8 Pin 5)	PTB1	TSI0_CH6
	Electrode 2 (J8 Pin 7)	PTB2	TSI0_CH7
	Electrode 3 (J8 Pin 8)	PTB3	TSI0_CH8
	Electrode 4 (J8 Pin 9)	PTC0	TSI0_CH13
	Electrode 5 (J8 Pin 10)	PTC1	TSI0_CH14
	Electrode 6 (J8 Pin 11)	PTC2	TSI0_CH15
	Electrode 7 (J8 Pin 12)	PTA4	TSI0_CH5
	Electrode 8 (J8 Pin 13)	PTB16	TSI0_CH9
	Electrode 9 (J8 Pin 14)	PTB17	TSI0_CH10
	Electrode 10 (J8 Pin 15)	PTB18	TSI0_CH11
	Electrode 11 (J8 Pin 16)	PTB19	TSI0_CH12
	TWRPI ID0 (J8 Pin 17)	PTE2	ADC1_DP1
	TWRPI ID1 (J8 Pin 18)	ADC1_DM0	ADC1_DM0

TWR-K53N512 Pinout

Feature	Connection	Port Pin	Pin Function
Medical Connector	Voltage Supply (J19 Pin 1)	Pin3	Source of P-Channel MOSFET
	Ground (J19 Pin 2)	GND	Ground
	I2C Data (J19 Pin 3)	I2C1_SDA	PTC11/I2C1_SDA
	I2C Clock (J19 Pin 4)	I2C_SCL/FTM2_CH1	I2C1_SCL/FTM2_CH1 (J4 jpr)
	ADC0 Diff (+) Ch 0 (J19 Pin 5)	ADC0_DP0	ADC0_DP0/ADC1_DP3
	ADC0 Diff (-) Ch 0 (J19 Pin 6)	ADC0_DM0	ADC0_DM0/ADC1_DM3
	ADC1 Diff (+) Ch 0 (J19 Pin 7)	ADC1_DP0	ADC1_DP0/ADC0_DP3
	DAC0 Output (J19 Pin 8)	DAC0_OUT	DAC0_OUT
	OPAMP0 Output (J19 Pin 9)	OP0_OUT	ADC0_SE16/OP0_OUT
	OPAMP1 Output (J19 Pin 10)	OP1_OUT	ADC1_SE16/OP1_OUT
	OPAMP0 (-) Input (J19 Pin 11)	OP0_DM0	ADC0_DM1/OP0_DM0
	OPAMP1 (-) Input (J19 Pin 12)	OP1_DM0	ADC1_DM1/OP1_DM0
	OPAMP0 (+) Input (J19 Pin 13)	OP0_DP0	ADC0_DP1/OP0_DP0
	OPAMP1 (+) Input (J19 Pin 14)	OP1_DP0	ADC1_DP1/OP1_DP0/OP1_DM1
	TRIAMP0 (+) Input (J19 Pin 15)	TRI0_DP	TRI0_DP
	TRIAMP1 (+) Input (J19 Pin 16)	TRI1_DP	TRI1_DP
	TRIAMP0 (-) Input (J19 Pin 17)	TRI0_DM	TRI0_DM
	TRIAMP1 (-) Input (J19 Pin 18)	TRI1_DM	TRI1_DM
	TRIAMP0 Output (J19 Pin 19)	TRI0_OUT	TRI0_OUT/OP1_DM2
	TRIAMP1 Output (J19 Pin 20)	TRI1_OUT	TRI1_OUT

Table 2-1 **TWR-K53N512 Pinout**

2-2 TWR-K53N512 JUMPER SETTINGS

Table 2-2 provides details on the different configurations supported by the TWR-K53N512. Use the default settings shown in bold for all the medical applications featured in this book.

Jumper	Option	Setting	Description
J1	ADC1_DM1 Input Selection	ON	ADC1_DM1 reads POTENTIOMETER
		OFF	ADC1_DM1 reads MEDICAL CONNECTOR
J3	FlexBus Address Latch Selection	**2-3**	Enable FlexBus address latch
		1-2	Disable FlexBus address latch
J4	Medical Connector J19 Pin3 Selection	1-2	Select I2C1_SCL connection to MEDICAL CONNECTOR
		2-3	Select FTM2_CH1 connection to MEDICAL CONNECTOR
J5	IR Transmitter Connection	**OFF**	Disconnect PTD7/CMT_IRO from IR transmitter circuit (IRDA)
		ON	Connect PTD7/CMT_IRO to IR transmitter circuit (IRDA)
J6	FlexBus or SSIO Selection	**ON**	Use PTE7 for Flex bus
		OFF	Use PTE7 for SSIO
J7	Ethernet/TOUCH PAD TWRPI Selection	**ON**	Use PTB0 for Ethernet
		OFF	Use PTB0 for TOUCH PAD TWRPI
J11	Clock Input Source Selection	**1-2**	Connect main EXTAL to on-board 50 MHz clock
		2-3	Connect EXTAL to the CLKIN0 signal on the elevator connector
J12	SD Card/TOUCH PAD TWRPI Selection	**OFF**	Use PTE2 for SD card reader (SD/MMC SKT)
		ON	Use PTE2 for TOUCH PAD TWRPI
J14	IR Transmitter Filter Selection	**OFF**	IR input to CMP0_IN0 is not low-pass filtered by a 0.1 uF cap
		ON	IR input to CMP0_IN0 is low-pass filtered by a 0.1 uF cap

Jumper	Option	Setting	Description
J15	MCU Power Connection	**ON**	Connect on-board 3.3V supply to MCU
		OFF	Isolate MCU from power (connect an ammeter to measure current)
J16	VBAT Power Connection	**1-2**	Connect VBAT to on-board 3.3V supply
		2-3	Connect VBAT to the higher voltage between on-board 3.3V supply or coin-cell supply
J17	On-Board 50 MHz Power Connection	**ON**	Connect on-board 3.3V supply to on-board 50 MHz OSC
		OFF	Disconnect on-board 3.3V supply to on-board 50 MHz OSC
J18	VREGIN Power Connection	**ON**	Connect USB0_VBUS from Elevator to VREGIN
		OFF	Disconnect USB0_VBUS from Elevator to VREGIN
J20	SD Card/GENERAL PURPOSE TWRPI Selection	**OFF**	Use PTE1 for SD card reader (SD/MMC SKT)
		ON	Use PTE1 for GENERAL PURPOSE TWRPI
J21	Accelerometer Power Connection	**ON**	Connect accelerometer to on-board 3.3V supply
		OFF	Disconnect accelerometer from on-board 3.3V supply
J22	Off-Board Power input	OFF	J22 pin 1 can be connected to an off-board external power source. This board is only tested with 3.3V. Care should be taken not to connect to a voltage that is out of the components specification
		OFF	J22 pin 2 can be connected to the ground of the off-board external power source
J24	Off or On Board Power Input Selection	**1-2**	Board SYS_PWR is powered from on-board 3.3V regulator
		2-3	Board SYS_PWR is powered from off-board supply from J22 pin 2
J25	JTAG Board Power Connection	**OFF**	Disconnect on-board 5V supply to JTAG port
		ON	Connect on-board 5V supply to JTAG port (supports powering board from JTAG pod supporting 5V supply output)

Jumper	Option	Setting	Description
J26	SD Card/GENERAL PURPOSE TWRPI Selection	**OFF**	Use PTE0 for SD card reader (SD/MMC SKT)
		ON	Use PTE0 for GENERAL PURPOSE TWRPI
J28	OSJTAG Bootloader Selection	**OFF**	Debugger mode
		ON	OSJTAG bootloader mode (OSJTAG firmware reprogramming)
J29	Ethernet/TOUCH PAD TWRPI Selection	**ON**	Use PTB1 for Ethernet
		OFF	Use PTB1 for TOUCH PAD TWRPI
J32	TOUCH PAD/SLCD TWRPI Selection	**1-2**	PTB10_LCD_P10 pin is connected to J8 pin 3 for SLCD TWRPI
		2-3	PTB0_TSI0_CH0 pin is connected to J8 pin 3 for TOUCH PAD TWRPI. Make sure J29 and J7 are off to avoid conflict with Ethernet
J33	TOUCH PAD/SLCD TWRPI Selection	**1-2**	PTB11_LCD_P11 pin is connected to J8 pin 5 for SLCD TWRPI
		2-3	PTB1_TSI0_CH6 pin is connected to J8 pin 5 for TOUCH PAD TWRPI. Make sure J29 and J7 are off to avoid conflict with Ethernet
J34	On-Board 50 MHz Enable Source	**OFF**	On-board 50 MHz osc is enabled if J17 jumper is on. No need to have any jumper on J34
		1-2	On-board 50 MHz osc is enabled if J17 jumper is on
		2-3	On-board 50 MHz osc enable by GPIO PTA19 allowing MCU to turn off clock for lower power consumption

Table 2-2 **TWR-K53N512 Jumper Settings**

2-3 THE FREESCALE TWR-K53N512

The TWR-K53N512 is available as a stand-alone product as described in the previous sections or as a kit (TWR-K53N512-KIT) with the Tower Elevator Modules (TWR-ELEV) and the Tower Serial Module (TWR-SER). The TWR-K53N512 can also be combined with other Freescale Tower peripheral modules to create development platforms for a wide variety of applications as we will describe in the last section. Figure 2-4 provides an overview of the Freescale Tower System.

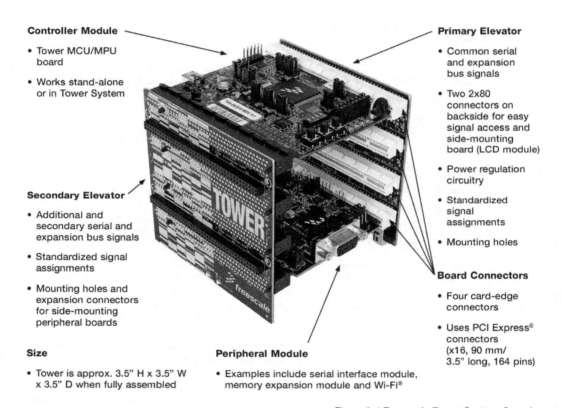

Controller Module

- Tower MCU/MPU board

- Works stand-alone or in Tower System

Secondary Elevator

- Additional and secondary serial and expansion bus signals

- Standardized signal assignments

- Mounting holes and expansion connectors for side-mounting peripheral boards

Size

- Tower is approx. 3.5" H x 3.5" W x 3.5" D when fully assembled

Peripheral Module

- Examples include serial interface module, memory expansion module and Wi-Fi®

Primary Elevator

- Common serial and expansion bus signals

- Two 2x80 connectors on backside for easy signal access and side-mounting board (LCD module)

- Power regulation circuitry

- Standardized signal assignments

- Mounting holes

Board Connectors

- Four card-edge connectors

- Uses PCI Express® connectors (x16, 90 mm/ 3.5" long, 164 pins)

Figure 2-4 **Freescale Tower System Overview**

The TWR-K53N512 features two expansion card-edge connectors that interface to the Primary and Secondary Elevator boards in a Tower System. The Primary Connector (comprised of sides A and B) is utilized by the TWR-K53N512 while the Secondary Connector (comprised of sides C and D) only makes connections to the GND pins. Table 2-3 provides the pinout for the Primary Connector.

PCI Express Tower System Elevator Connector

Primary Connector Pinout

Pin#	Side B		Pin#	Side A	
	Name	**Usage**		**Name**	**Usage**
B1	5V	5.0V Power	A1	5V	5.0V Power
B2	GND	Ground	A2	GND	Ground
B3	3.3V	3.3V Power	A3	3.3V	3.3V Power
B4	ELE_PS_SENSE	Elevator Power Sense	A4	3.3V	3.3V Power
B5	GND	Ground	A5	GND	Ground
B6	GND	Ground	A6	GND	Ground
B7	SDHC_CLK / SPI1_CLK	PTE2	A7	SCL0	PTD8
B8	SDHC_D3 / SPI1_CS1_b		A8	SDA0	PTD9
B9	SDHC_D3 / SPI1_CS0_b	PTE4	A9	GPIO9 / CTS1	PTC19
B10	SDHC_CMD / SPI1_MOSI	PTE1	A10	GPIO8 / SDHC_D2	PTE5
B11	SDHC_D0 / SPI1_MISO	PTE3	A11	GPIO7 / SD_WP_DET	PTE27
B12	ETH_COL		A12	ETH_CRS	
B13	ETH_RXER	PTA5	A13	ETH_MDC	PTB1
B14	ETH_TXCLK		A14	ETH_MDIO	PTB0
B15	ETH_TXEN	PTA15	A15	ETH_RXCLK	
B16	ETH_TXER		A16	ETH_RXDV	PTA14
B17	ETH_TXD3		A17	ETH_RXD3	
B18	ETH_TXD2		A18	ETH_RXD2	
B19	ETH_TXD1	PTA17	A19	ETH_RXD1	PTA12
B20	ETH_TXD0	PTA16	A20	ETH_RXD0	PTA13
B21	GPIO1 / RTS1	PTC18	A21	SSI_MCLK	PTE6
B22	GPIO2 / SDHC_D1	PTE0	A22	SSI_BCLK	PTE12
B23	GPIO3	PTE28	A23	SSI_FS	PTE11
B24	CLKIN0	PTA18	A24	SSI_RXD	PTE7
B25	CLKOUT1	PTE26	A25	SSI_TXD	PTE10
B26	GND	Ground	A26	GND	Ground
B27	AN7	PTB7	A27	AN3	PGA0_DP/ADC0_DP0/ ADC1_DP3
B28	AN6	PTB6	A28	AN2	PGA0_DM/ADC0_DM0/ ADC1_DM3
B29	AN5	PTB5	A29	AN1	PGA1_DP/ADC1_DP0/ ADC0_DP3

PCI Express Tower System Elevator Connector

Primary Connector Pinout

Pin#	Side B		Pin#	Side A	
	Name	Usage		Name	Usage
B30	AN4	PTB4	A30	AN0	PGA1_DM/ADC1_DM0/ADC0_DM3
B31	GND	Ground	A31	GND	Ground
B32	DAC1	DAC1_OUT	A32	DAC0	DAC0_OUT
B33	TMR3		A33	TMR1	PTA9
B34	TMR2	PTD6	A34	TMR0	PTA8
B35	GPIO4	PTB8	A35	GPIO6	PTB9
B36	3.3V	3.3V Power	A36	3.3V	3.3V Power
B37	PWM7	PTA2	A37	PWM3	PTA6
B38	PWM6	PTA1	A38	PWM2	PTC3
B39	PWM5	PTD5	A39	PWM1	PTC2
B40	PWM4	PTA7	A40	PWM0	PTC1
B41	CANRX0	PTE25	A41	RXD0	PTE25
B42	CANTX0	PTE24	A42	TXD0	PTE24
B43	1WIRE		A43	RXD1	PTC16
B44	SPI0_MISO	PTD14	A44	TXD1	PTC17
B45	SPI0_MOSI	PTD13	A45	VSS	VSSA
B46	SPI0_CS0_b	PTD11	A46	VDDA	VDDA
B47	SPI0_CS1_b	PTD15	A47	VREFA1	VREFH
B48	SPI0_CLK	PTD12	A48	VREFA2	VREFL
B49	GND	Ground	A49	GND	Ground
B50	SCL1	PTD8	A50	GPIO14	
B51	SDA1	PTD9	A51	GPIO15	
B52	GPIO5 / SD_CARD_DET	PTE28	A52	GPIO16	
B53	USB0_DP_PDOWN		A53	GPIO17	
B54	USB0_DM_PDOWN		A54	USB0_DM	USB0_DM
B55	IRQ_H	PTA24	A55	USB0_DP	USB0_DP
B56	IRQ_G	PTA24	A56	USB0_ID	
B57	IRQ_F	PTA25	A57	USB0_VBUS	VREGIN
B58	IRQ_E	PTA25	A58	TMR7	
B59	IRQ_D	PTA26	A59	TMR6	
B60	IRQ_C	PTA26	A60	TMR5	

PCI Express Tower System Elevator Connector

Primary Connector Pinout

Pin#	Side B		Pin#	Side A	
	Name	**Usage**		**Name**	**Usage**
B61	IRQ_B	PTA27	A61	TMR4	
B62	IRQ_A	PTA27	A62	RSTIN_b	RESET_b
B63	EBI_ALE / EBI_CS1_b	PTD0	A63	RSTOUT_b	RESET_b
B64	EBI_CS0_b	PTD1	A64	CLKOUT0	PTC3
B65	GND	Ground	A65	GND	Ground
B66	EBI_AD15	PTB18	A66	EBI_AD14	PTC0
B67	EBI_AD16	PTB17	A67	EBI_AD13	PTC1
B68	EBI_AD17	PTB16	A68	EBI_AD12	PTC2
B69	EBI_AD18	PTB11	A69	EBI_AD11	PTC4
B70	EBI_AD19	PTB10	A70	EBI_AD10	PTC5
B71	EBI_R/W_b	PTC11	A71	EBI_AD9	PTC6
B72	EBI_OE_b	PTB19	A72	EBI_AD8	PTC7
B73	EBI_D7	PTB20	A73	EBI_AD7	PTC8
B74	EBI_D6	PTB21	A74	EBI_AD6	PTC9
B75	EBI_D5	PTB22	A75	EBI_AD5	PTC10
B76	EBI_D4	PTB23	A76	EBI_AD4	PTD2
B77	EBI_D3	PTC12	A77	EBI_AD3	PTD3
B78	EBI_D2	PTC13	A78	EBI_AD2	PTD4
B79	EBI_D1	PTC14	A79	EBI_AD1	PTD5
B80	EBI_D0	PTC15	A80	EBI_AD0	PTD6
B81	GND	Ground	A81	GND	Ground
B82	3.3V	3.3V Power	A82	3.3V	3.3V Power

Table 2-3 **TWR-K53N512 Primary Elevator Connector Pinout**

2-4 EXPANDING THE CAPABILITIES

The modularity and affordability of the Tower System makes it simple to add new system capabilities, like Wi-Fi, Sensors, Graphical LCD, and more. Sold separately as individual development boards, these peripheral modules quickly plug into a variety of Tower System configurations for easy, quick prototyping.

Figure 2-5 shows a Prototyping Module called TWR-PROTO that provides an easy way for designers to add custom circuitry to their Tower System designs. The TWR-PROTO module is a 9 x 8 cm board with card-edge connectors that allows it to be plugged directly into the Tower System. The perfboard area provides access to all of the signals from the TWR-K53N512 as well as a generous 8.3 x 3.8 cm prototyping area where you could create your own biomedical signal conditioning circuits if you choose not to buy the Analog-Front-Ends plugins.

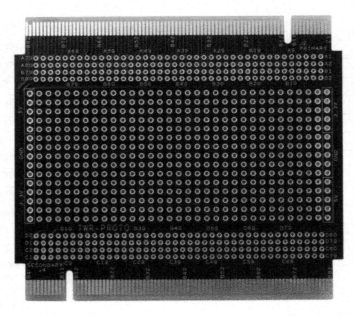

Figure 2-5 **Prototyping Board TWR-PROTO**

A graphical LCD module called TWR-LCD provides an easy way for designers to add an LCD interface to their Tower System designs. It features a 3.2" QVGA TFT LCD display and attaches to the outer edge of the Tower System elevator modules by Side Expansion Port connectors as shown in Figure 2-6. This peripheral module will not be used in these examples as we will use µC/Probe to prototype the front panel of all four medical devices but still it is a very nice option in case you want to take the examples further.

Figure 2-6 **Graphical LCD Board TWR-LCD**

Check the Freescale website at www.freescale.com/tower for more information on the TWR-PROTO, TWR-LCD and much more peripheral modules from Freescale and other partners.

Chapter

3

The ARM® Cortex™-M4 and the Kinetis K53

The ARM® Cortex™-M4 is the newest member of the Cortex™ M Series of processors targeting microcontroller cores focused on very cost sensitive, deterministic, interrupt driven environments. The Cortex M4 processor is based on the ARMv7 Architecture and Thumb®-2 ISA and is upward compatible with the Cortex M3, Cortex M1, and Cortex M0 architectures. Cortex M4 improvements include an ARMv7 Thumb-2 DSP (ported from the ARMv7-A/R profile architectures) providing 32-bit instructions with SIMD (single instruction multiple data) DSP style multiply-accumulates and saturating arithmetic.

The Private Peripheral Bus (PPB) provides access to the ARM modules such as the Nested Vector Interrupt Controller (NVIC), Embedded Trace Macrocell (ETM), Instrumentation Trace Macrocell (ITM), Data Watchpoint and Trace (DWT), Flash Patch and Breakpoint (FBP), and the ROM table as illustrated in Figure 3-1:

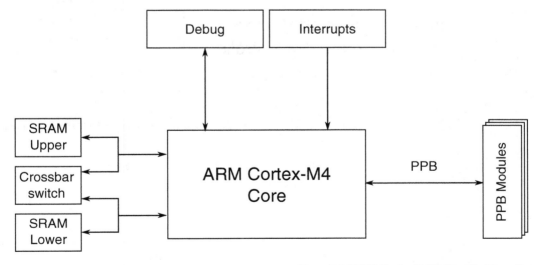

Figure 3-1 **ARM® Cortex™-M4 Core Configuration**

This chapter provides a brief summary of the Cortex-M4 architecture and other modules available on this device. Additional reference material is provided in Appendix G, "Bibliography" on page 1017.

3-1 NESTED VECTOR INTERRUPT CONTROLLER (NVIC)

The ARMv7-M exception model and nested-vectored interrupt controller (NVIC) implement a relocatable vector table supporting many external interrupts, a single nonmaskable interrupt (NMI), and priority levels. The NVIC replaces shadow registers with equivalent system and simplified programmability.

The NVIC contains the address of the function to execute for a particular handler. The address is fetched via the instruction port allowing parallel register stacking and look-up. The first sixteen entries are allocated to ARM internal sources with the others mapping to MCU-defined interrupts.

The NVIC peripheral eases the migration between Cortex-M4 processors. This is particularly true for µC/OS-III.

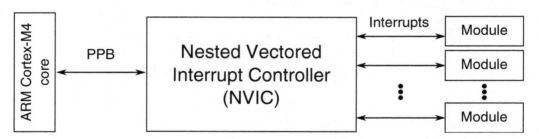

Figure 3-2 **Nested Vector Interrupt (NVIC) Configuration**

3-2 ASYNCHRONOUS WAKE-UP INTERRUPT CONTROLLER (AWIC)

The primary function of the Asynchronous Wake-up Interrupt Controller (AWIC) is to detect asynchronous wake-up events in stop modes and signal to clock control logic to resume system clocking. After clock restart, the NVIC observes the pending interrupt and performs the normal interrupt or event processing.

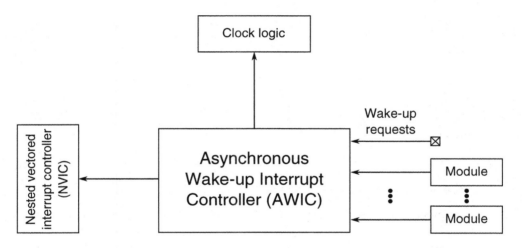

Figure 3-3 **Asynchronous Wake-up Interrupt Controller (AWIC) Configuration**

3-3 DEBUG INTERFACES

Most of this device's debug is based on the ARM CoreSight™ architecture. Four debug interfaces are supported:

- IEEE 1149.1 JTAG

- IEEE 1149.7 JTAG (cJTAG)

- Serial Wire Debug (SWD)

- ARM Real-Time Trace Interface

3-4 SYSTEM MODULES

The system modules available on this device that are specific for the Freescale K53 are:

- System integration module

- Power management and mode controllers

- 10 power modes available based on run, wait, stop, and power-down modes

- Low-leakage wakeup unit

- Miscellaneous control module

- Crossbar switch

- Memory protection unit

- Peripheral bridge

- Direct memory access (DMA) controller with multiplexer to increase available DMA requests

- Watchdog and External watchdog monitor

The System Integration Module (SIM) illustrated in Figure 3-4 provides system control and chip configuration registers to drive the integration logic and several module configuration settings. Clock gating is one of the main functions of the SIM module and you will notice when reviewing the source code in all four medical application examples that we set the SIM module registers prior to initialize all the MCU modules in order to enable their clocks.

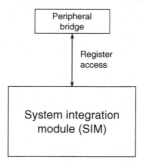

Figure 3-4 **System Integration Module (SIM) Configuration**

The peripheral bridge illustrated in Figure 3-5 converts the crossbar switch interface to an interface to access a majority of peripherals on the device.

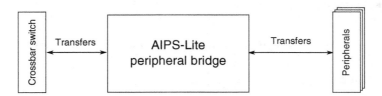

Figure 3-5 **Peripheral Bridge Configuration**

The crossbar switch illustrated in Figure 3-6 connects bus masters and bus slaves, allowing all bus masters to access different bus slaves simultaneously and providing arbitration among the bus masters when they access the same slave.

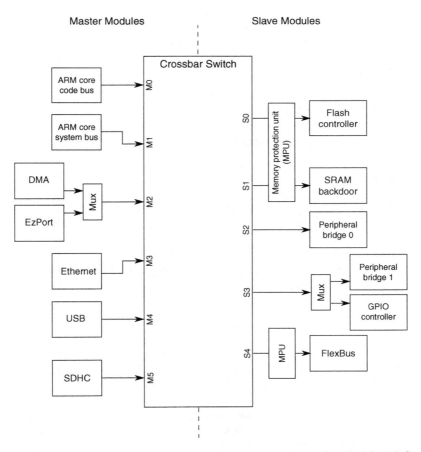

Figure 3-6 **Crossbar Switch Configuration**

3-5 MEMORIES

The following memories and memory interfaces are available on this device:

- Program flash memory

- FlexMemory (FlexNVM, FlexRAM and Programming acceleration RAM)

- Flash memory controller

- SRAM

- External memory or peripheral bus interface (FlexBus)

3-6 CLOCKS

The following clock modules are available on this device:

- Multipurpose clock generator (MCG)

- System oscillator

- Real-time clock oscillator

The Multipurpose Clock Generator (MCG) illustrated in Figure 3-7 provides several clock sources for the MCU that include PLL, FLL and Internal Reference Clocks.

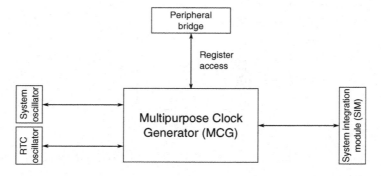

Figure 3-7 **Multipurpose Clock Generator (MCG) Configuration**

The system oscillator, in conjunction with an external crystal or resonator, generates a reference clock for the MCU.

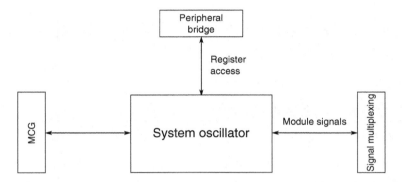

Figure 3-8 **System Oscillator Configuration**

The Real-Time Clock oscillator illustrated in Figure 3-9 has an independent power supply and supports a 32kHz crystal oscillator to feed the RTC clock.

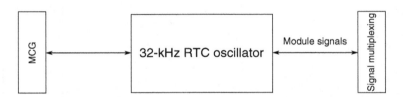

Figure 3-9 **Real-Time Clock Oscillator Configuration**

3-7 SECURITY AND INTEGRITY MODULES

The following security and integrity modules are available on this device:

- Cryptographic acceleration unit (CAU)

- Random number generator (RNG)

- Cyclic Redundancy Check (CRC)

3-8 ANALOG MODULES

The following analog modules are available on this device:

- 16-bit Analog to Digital Converter (ADC)

- Analog comparators

- 12-bit Digital to Analog Converter (DAC)

- Operational and Transimpedance Amplifiers

- Voltage Reference (VREF)

The 16-bit successive approximation ADC illustrated in Figure 3-10 is a fast, high precision ADC designed with integrated programmable gain amplifiers (PGA), high speed comparators and an internal voltage reference.

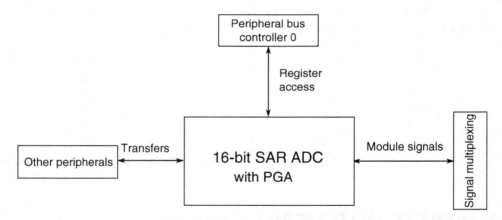

Figure 3-10 **16-bit Analog to Digital Converter (ADC) Configuration**

Figure 3-11 illustrates the low-power general-purpose DAC, whose output can be placed on an external pin or set as one of the inputs to the analog comparator, op-amps, or ADC. The DAC module will be used to generate a simulated biomedical signal to test the examples in the absence of the analog front end modules.

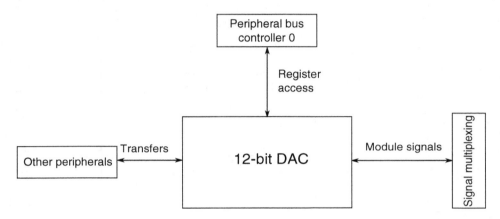

Figure 3-11 **12-bit Digital to Analog Converter (DAC) Configuration**

The op-amp illustrated in Figure 3-12 is a low-input offset voltage, low-input offset, and bias current amplifier that is designed for low-voltage, low-power operation over an input voltage range of 0 to supply. The amplifier supports inverting, non-inverting, buffer, and general-purpose modes. We will use this op-amp module to implement the signal conditioning circuits for all the four medical applications featured in this book.

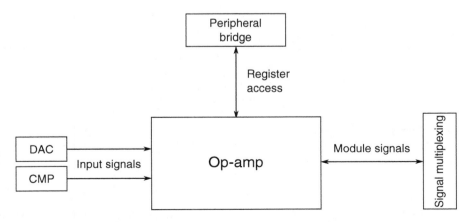

Figure 3-12 **Operational Amplifiers (OPAMP) Configuration**

The transimpedance amplifier illustrated in Figure 3-13 conditions the current input into voltages that can be read by the ADC or analog comparator. We will use the TRIAMP module to implement the signal conditioning circuit of the pulse oximetry and blood glucose meter applications featured in this book.

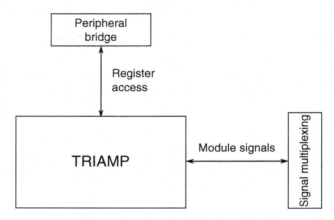

Figure 3-13 **Transimpedance Amplifiers (TRIAMP) Configuration**

The voltage reference module illustrated in Figure 3-14, supplies an accurate voltage output that is trimmable in 0.5 mV steps. The VREF can be used in medical applications, such as blood glucose meters, to provide a reference voltage to biosensors or as a reference to analog peripherals, such as the ADC, DAC, or CMP.

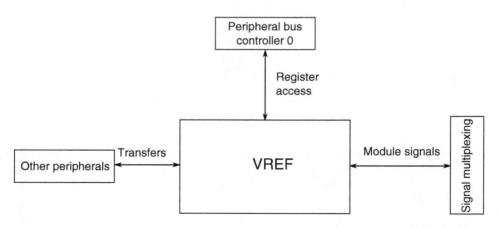

Figure 3-14 **Voltage Reference (VREF) Configuration**

3-9 TIMER MODULES

The following timer modules are available on this device:

- Programmable Delay Block (PDB)

- Flexible Timer Modules (FTM)

- Periodic Interrupt Timers (PIT)

- Low-Power Timer (LPT)

- Carrier Modulator Timer (CMT)

- Real-Time Clock (RTC)

- IEEE 1588 Timers

The Programmable Delay Block module (PDB) illustrated in Figure 3-15 provides controllable delays from either an internal or an external trigger, or a programmable interval tick, to the hardware trigger inputs of ADCs and/or generates the interval triggers to DACs, so that the precise timing between ADC conversions and/or DAC updates can be achieved.

We will use the PDB module to trigger the ADC conversions to ensure the most accurate sampling rates of each of the biomedical signals.

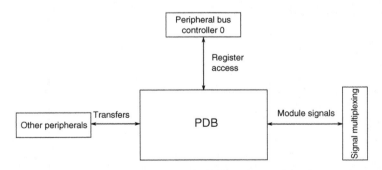

Figure 3-15 **Programmable Delay Block module (PDB) Configuration**

The FlexTimer Module (FTM) is a two-to-eight channel timer that supports input capture, output compare, and generation of PWM signals to control electric motor and power management applications. The FTM time reference is a 16-bit counter that can be used as a signed or unsigned counter.

We will use the FTM module to generate the PWM signals to drive the motor and solenoid valve in the blood pressure monitor and, to control the intensity of the red and infrared LEDs in the pulse oximetry application.

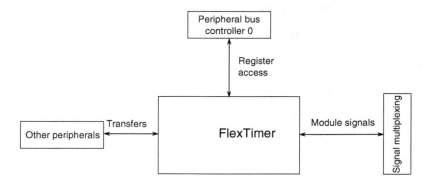

Figure 3-16 **FlexTimer (FTM) Configuration**

3-10 COMMUNICATION INTERFACES

The following communication interfaces are available on this device:

- Ethernet MAC with IEEE 1588 capability (ENET)

- USB OTG (low-/full-speed)

- USB Device Charger Detect (USBDCD)

- USB voltage regulator

- Controller Area Network (CAN)

- Serial Peripheral Interface (SPI)

- Inter-Integrated Circuit (I2C)

- Universal Asynchronous Receiver/Transmitters (UART)

- Secure Digital Host Controller (SDHC)

- Integrated Interchip Sound (I2S)

3-11 HUMAN-MACHINE INTERFACES

The following human-machine interfaces (HMI) are available on this device:

■ General Purpose Input/Output (GPIO)

■ Capacitive Touch Sense Input (TSI)

■ Segment LCD

The GPIO controller illustrated in Figure 3-17 interfaces to the processor core via a zero wait state interface for maximum pin performance. Accesses of any data size are supported to the GPIO registers.

The GPIO data direction and output data registers control the direction and output data of each pin when the pin is configured for the GPIO function. The GPIO input data register displays the logic value on each pin when the pin is configured for any digital function, provided the corresponding port control and interrupt module for that pin is enabled.

Efficient bit banging of the general purpose outputs is supported through the addition of set, clear and toggle write-only registers for each port output data register.

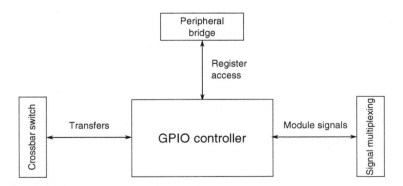

Figure 3-17 **General Purpose Input/Output (GPIO) Configuration**

The Touch Sensing Input (TSI) module in Figure 3-18 provides capacitive touch sensing detection with high sensitivity and enhanced robustness. Each TSI pin implements the capacitive measurement of an electrode having individual programmable detection thresholds and result registers. The TSI module can be functional in several low power modes with ultra low current adder and waking up the CPU in a touch event. This module is perfect for medical systems because it allows the implementation of touch keypad, rotaries and sliders that are easy to clean and sterilize.

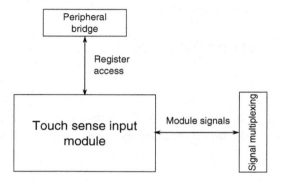

Figure 3-18 **Touch Sense Input (TSI) Configuration**

The Segment LCD (SLCD) module in Figure 3-19 is a CMOS charge pump voltage inverter that is designed for low-voltage and low-power operation. The SLCD module is designed to generate the appropriate waveforms to drive multiplexed numeric, alpha-numeric, or custom segment LCD panels.

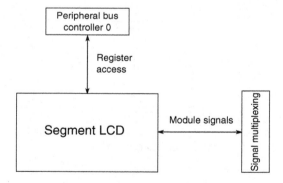

Figure 3-19 **Segment LCD (SLCD) Configuration**

4

Setup

In this chapter you will learn how to setup an environment to run the µC/OS-III-based medical application projects.

To run the examples provided with this book, it will be necessary to download a number of files from the Internet:

1   The µC/OS-III source code and medical application sample projects for the TWR-K53N512 from the Micriµm website

2   µC/Probe from the Micriµm website

3   The IAR Embedded Workbench for ARM, 32KB KickStart edition from the IAR website

Each of these downloads will be described in detail throughout this chapter.

4-1 DOWNLOADING µC/OS-III PROJECTS FOR THIS BOOK

The µC/OS-III book does not include CDs. Instead, project files are actually downloadable from the Micrium website. This allows samples to be kept up to date.

To obtain the µC/OS-III source code and projects for the medical application examples provided in this book, simply point your favorite browser to:

> www.Micrium.com/Books/Micrium-uCOS-III

You will be required to register. This means that you'll have to provide information about yourself. This information will be used for market research purposes and will allow us to contact you should new updates of µC/OS-III for this book become available. Your information will be held in strict confidence.

Download and execute the following file:

> Micrium-Book-uCOS-III-TWR-K53N512.exe

Figure 4-1 shows the directory structure created by this executable.

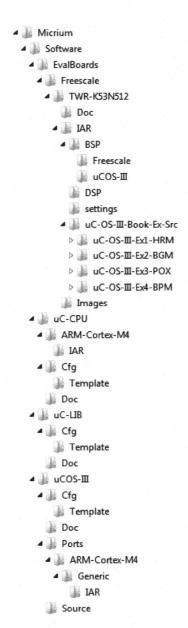

Figure 4-1 **µC/OS-III Project Directories**

All files are placed under the `\Micrium\Software` directory. There are four main sub-directories: `\EvalBoards`, `\uC-CPU`, `\uC-LIB` and `\uCOS-III` and they are described below.

4-1-1 \EvalBoards

This is the standard Micriµm sub-directory where all evaluation board examples are placed. The sub-directory contains additional sub-directories organizing evaluation boards by manufacturers. In this case, **\Freescale** is the manufacturer of the TWR-K53N512 board, and projects for this board are placed under: **\TWR-K53N512**.

The **\EvalBoards\Freescale\TWR-K53N512** sub-directory contains further directories.

\Doc contains a series of schematics and reference manuals:

```
K53 MCU Reference Manual.pdf
TWR-K53N512 Schematics.pdf
TWR-ELEV Schematics
MED-EKG Schematics.pdf
MED-GLU Schematics.pdf
MED-SPO2 Schematics.pdf
MED-BPM Schematics.pdf
```

\IAR contains the main IAR IDE workspace, which includes the four projects provided with this book. Specifically, the file **TWR-K53N512.eww** is the workspace to open with the IAR Embedded Workbench for ARM.

Projects will be described in the next four chapters. This sub-directory contains six additional sub-directories:

```
\BSP\Freescale
\BSP\uCOS-III
\DSP
\settings
\uC-OS-II-Book-Ex-Src\uC-OS-III-Ex1-HRM
\uC-OS-II-Book-Ex-Src\uC-OS-III-Ex2-BGM
\uC-OS-II-Book-Ex-Src\uC-OS-III-Ex3-POX
\uC-OS-II-Book-Ex-Src\uC-OS-III-Ex4-BPM
```

\IAR\BSP contains Board Support Package (BSP) files used to support the peripherals found on the TWR-K53N512 evaluation board. The contents of these files will be described as needed within the sample projects. This sub-directory contains the following files:

```
bsp.c
bsp.h
bsp_int.c
bsp_adc.c
bsp_dac.c
\Freescale\K53X_Flash.icf
\Freescale\MK53N512CMD100.h
\uCOS-III\bsp_os.c
\uCOS-III\bsp_os.h
```

\TWR-K53N512\IAR\uC-OS-II-Book-Ex-Src\uC-OS-III-Ex1-HRM is the directory that contains all the source code files for the Heart Rate Monitor (HRM) application.

\TWR-K53N512\IAR\uC-OS-II-Book-Ex-Src\uC-OS-III-Ex2-BGM is the directory that contains all the source code files for the Blood Glucose Meter (BGM) application.

\TWR-K53N512\IAR\uC-OS-II-Book-Ex-Src\uC-OS-III-Ex3-POX is the directory that contains all the source code files for the Pulse Oxymeter (POX) application.

\TWR-K53N512\IAR\uC-OS-II-Book-Ex-Src\uC-OS-III-Ex4-BPM is the directory that contains all the source code files for the Blood Pressure Monitor (BPM) application.

4

4-1-2 \uC-CPU

This sub-directory contains the generic and Cortex-M4-specific files for the µC/CPU module. These are described in Appendix C, "µC/CPU Port for the Cortex-M4" on page 981. This sub-directory contains the following files:

```
cpu_core.c
cpu_core.h
cpu_def.h
\Cfg\Template\cpu_cfg.h
\ARM-Cortex-M4\IAR\cpu.h
```

4-1-3 \uC-LIB

This sub-directory contains the source code of the functions used to manipulate ASCII strings, perform memory copies, and more. We refer to these files as being part of the µC/LIB module. `lib_def.h` contains a number of useful **#defines**, such as **DEF_FALSE**, **DEF_TRUE**, **DEF_ON**, **DEF_OFF**, **DEF_ENABLED**, **DEF_DISABLED**, and dozens more. µC/LIB also declares such macros as **DEF_MIN( )**, **DEF_MAX( )**, **DEF_ABS( )**, and more.

This sub-directory contains the following files:

```
lib_ascii.c
lib_ascii.h
lib_def.h
lib_math.c
lib_math.h
lib_mem.c
lib_mem.h
lib_str.c
lib_str.h
\Doc\uC-LIB_Manual.pdf
\Doc\uC-LIB-ReleaseNotes.pdf
```

4-1-4 \uCOS-III

This sub-directory contains the full source code of µC/OS-III:

```
\Cfg\Template\os_app_hooks.c
\Cfg\Template\os_app_hooks.h
\Cfg\Template\os_cfg.h
\Cfg\Template\os_cfg_app.h
\Ports\ARM-Cortex-M4\Generic\IAR\os_cpu_a.asm
\Ports\ARM-Cortex-M4\Generic\IAR\os_cpu_c.c
\Ports\ARM-Cortex-M4\Generic\IAR\os_cpu.h
\Source\os_cfg_app.c
\Source\os_core.c
\Source\os_dbg.c
\Source\os_flag.c
\Source\os_int.c
\Source\os_mem.c
\Source\os_msg.c
\Source\os_mutex.c
\Source\os_pend_multi.c
\Source\os_prio.c
\Source\os_q.c
\Source\os_sem.c
\Source\os_stat.c
\Source\os_task.c
\Source\os_tick.c
\Source\os_time.c
\Source\os_tmr.c
\Source\os.h
\Source\os_type.h
\Source\os_var.c
```

4-2 DOWNLOADING µC/PROBE

µC/Probe is an application that allows users to display or change the value (at run time) of virtually any variable or memory location on a connected embedded target. See Appendix D, "Micriµm's µC/Probe" on page 993 for a brief introduction.

µC/Probe is used in all of the examples described in Chapter 1, "Introduction" on page 739 to gain run-time visibility. There are two versions of µC/Probe:

The *Full Version* of µC/Probe is included with all µC/OS-III licenses. The Full Version supports J-Link, RS-232C, TCP/IP, USB, and other interfaces.

The *Full Version* allows users to display or change an unlimited number of variables.

The Trial Version is not time limited, but only allows users to display or change up to five application variables. However, the trial version allows users to monitor any µC/OS-III variables because µC/Probe is µC/OS-III aware.

Both versions are available from Micriµm's website. Simply point your favorite browser to:

> `www.Micrium.com/Books/Micrium-uCOS-III`

Follow the links to download the desired version (or both). If not already registered on the Micriµm website, you will be asked to do so. Once downloaded, execute the appropriate µC/Probe setup file:

> `Micrium-uC-Probe-Setup-Full.exe`
> `Micrium-uC-Probe-Setup-Trial.exe`

4-3 DOWNLOADING THE IAR EMBEDDED WORKBENCH FOR ARM

Examples provided with this book were tested using the IAR Embedded Workbench for ARM V6.10. You can download the 32K Kickstart version from the IAR website. This version allows users to create applications up to 32 Kbytes in size (excluding µC/OS-III). The file from IAR is about 400 MBytes. If you have a slow Internet connection or are planning to install a new version of Windows, you might want to consider archiving this file on a CD or even a USB drive.

You can download IAR tools from (case sensitive):

> **www.iar.com/MicriumuCOSIII**

- Click on the '*Download IAR Embedded Workbench for ARM - KickStart Edition >>*' link in the middle of the page. This will bring you to the '*KickStart edition of IAR EWARM*' page on the IAR website.

- After reading this page, simply click on '*Continue...*'.

- You will again be required to register. Unfortunately, the information you provided to register with Micrium is not transferred to IAR and vice-versa. Fill out the form and click on '*Submit*'.

- Save the file to a convenient location.

- You should receive a '*License number and Key for EWARM-KS32*' from IAR.

- Double click on the IAR executable file (**EWARM-KS-WEB-61**.exe**) (or a similar file if newer) and install the files on the disk drive of your choice, at the root.

You can use the full version of the IAR Embedded Workbench if you are already a licensee.

4-4 SETTING UP THE HARDWARE

It is assumed that the following hardware parts are available:

1   A PC running Microsoft Windows XP, Vista or 7 (32-bit or 64-bit)

2   The TWR-K53N512-KIT Tower System from Freescale

3   The MED-EKG module from Freescale for the heart rate monitoring application

4   The MED-GLU module from Freescale for the blood glucose meter application

5   The MED-SPO2 module from Freescale for the pulse oximetry application

6   The MED-BPM module from Freescale for the blood pressure monitor application

7   The J-Link Ultra debug probe from IAR

Figure 4-2 shows how to connect the TWR-K53N512 to a PC. The tower system is powered from the Mini-B USB connector in J5 of the elevator module to one of the PC's USB ports.

The J-Link Ultra debug probe is not only used to download and debug code but also to communicate with µC/Probe. Notice that a 19-pin adapter for ARM Cortex-M from IAR allows JTAG, SWD and SWO connections between IAR J-Link debug probe and Cortex-M microcontrollers. It adapts from the 20-pin 0.1" JTAG connector to the 19-pin 0.05" Samtec FTSH connector in J23 of the TWR-K53N512.

You may need to install the included battery into the battery holder in VBAT (RTC) of the TWR-K53N512 before powering up the system.

The last step to setup the environment to run the examples included in this book is to power up the tower system by turning on the switch at SW1 of the elevator module and let the PC automatically configure all the necessary USB drivers.

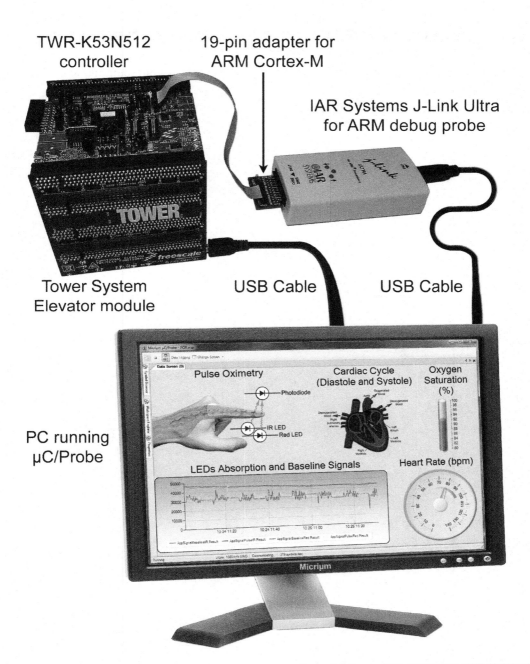

TWR-K53N512
controller

19-pin adapter for
ARM Cortex-M

IAR Systems J-Link Ultra
for ARM debug probe

Tower System
Elevator module

USB Cable

USB Cable

PC running
µC/Probe

Figure 4-2 **Connecting a PC to the TWR-K53N512**

789

4

4-5 DOWNLOADING THE TWR-K53N512 DOCUMENTATION

You can download the latest TWR-K53N512 datasheets and programming manuals from:

`http://www.freescale.com/TWR-K53N512`

Chapter

5

ECG / Heart Rate Monitor

The *electrocardiogram* (ECG or EKG) is a plot of the electrical activity of the heart over time. It is perhaps the most frequent test used at any emergency room and intensive care unit.

This chapter demonstrates a basic implementation of an ECG-based heart rate monitor built using µC/OS-III and Freescale products.

The chapter starts with an illustrated introduction to some of the anatomical and physiological fundamentals of the heart. The next section continues the introduction, but with emphasis on the acquisition of the ECG signal and presents the design of a heart rate monitor (HRM). The last part of the chapter deals with using the tools to run the example and a description of how the code works.

5-1 THE HEART

The blood carries the oxygen that the organs need to function properly.

The heart is a muscular organ responsible for pumping blood throughout the body. It is located in the middle of the thorax, slightly offset to the left and surrounded by the lungs.

The heart is composed of four chambers; two *atriums* and two *ventricles* as shown in Figure 5-1, and it is the muscular contraction of these chambers what moves the blood throughout the circulatory system as described by the arrows pointing away from the heart and towards the heart in Figure 5-2. The arteries carry blood away from the heart while the veins carry blood towards the heart. The heart valves shown in Figure 5-1 make sure the blood flows through them in only one direction.

5

The *aorta* is the largest artery in the body and carries oxygenated blood to all the body. The superior and inferior *venae cavae* are the veins that bring the deoxygenated blood from the body into the heart. The pulmonary arteries and veins allow the exchange of deoxygenated and oxygenated blood between the heart and lungs.

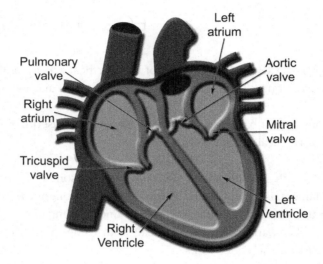

Figure 5-1 **Heart chambers and valves**

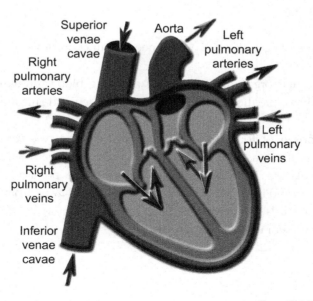

Figure 5-2 **Heart arteries and veins**

Figure 5-3 shows the principal parts of the electrical system of the heart. The electrical system of the heart is made of nodes and bundles of specialized cells capable of generating, carrying and controlling the electrical impulse that triggers the muscular contraction of the atriums and ventricles.

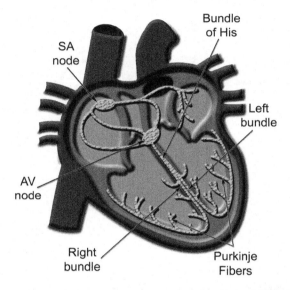

Figure 5-3 **Electrical system of the heart**

Each part of this electrical system generates its own electrical impulse and the combination of all those impulses make the typical waveform of an ECG as shown in Figure 5-4.

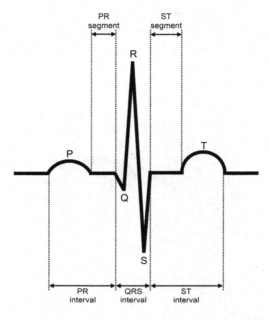

Figure 5-4 **Typical ECG waveform**

The P wave represents atrium contraction; the Q, R and S waves represent contraction of the ventricles and the T wave the repolarization of the ventricles. These waves and all the rest of time-domain features in the ECG waveform are very important when studying an ECG recording. Cardiologists are particularly interested in any deviations from a normal ECG waveform in the shape of the waves, frequency of the QRS complex, level of the segments and the duration of the intervals and segments.

The electrical activity of the heart is based on the depolarization and repolarization of the cells of the heart and the depolarization of these heart muscle cells trigger the mechanism of muscular contraction by the following coordinated series of repeated events:

(1)

(2)

(3)

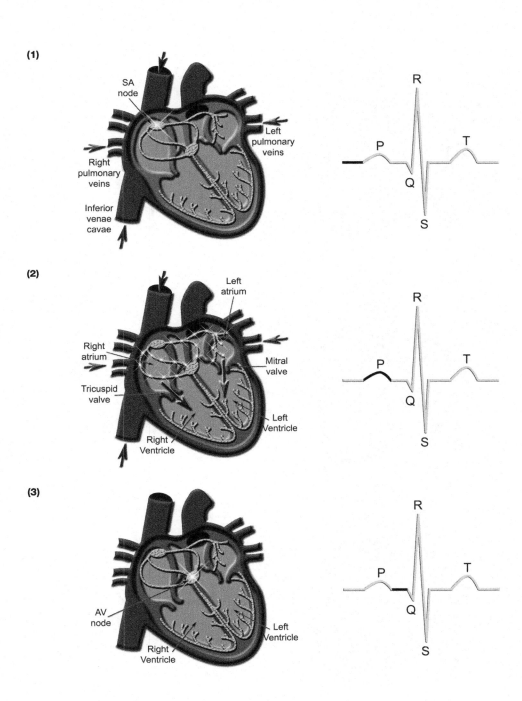

(4)

(5)

(6)

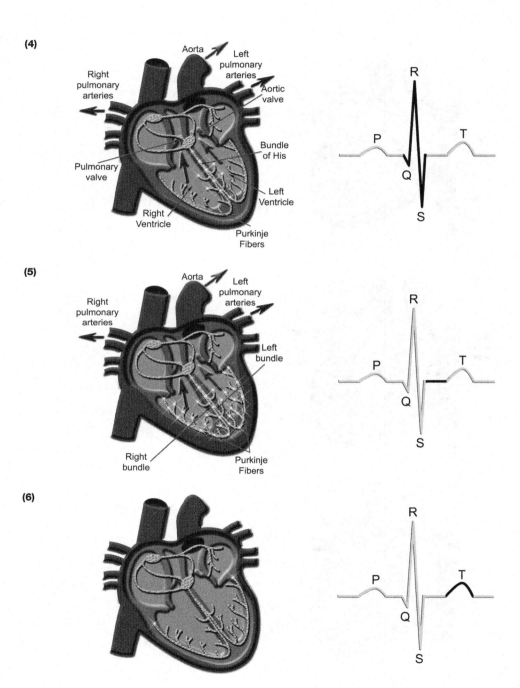

Figure 5-5 **Cardiac cycle and corresponding ECG**

F5-5(1)   The right atrium keeps filling up with the deoxygenated blood returning to the heart from the whole body through the superior and inferior venae cavae. At the same time the left atrium keeps filling up with the oxygenated blood coming from the lungs through the pulmonary veins. The electrical impulse starts at a specialized bundle of neurons called the *sinoatrial (SA)* node, located at the top of the right atrium. The SA node is considered the natural pacemaker.

F5-5(2)   The electrical impulse flows through the atriums activating the contraction of the right and then the left atrium. The blood passes to the right and left ventricles through the *tricuspid* and *mitral* valves due to the muscular contraction of the right and left atriums respectively. This event can be seen in the ECG waveform in the form of the P wave.

F5-5(3)   The electrical impulse reaches the *atrioventricular (AV) node* where it gets delayed for about 100 ms before making its way through the rest of bundles in order to give the ventricles time to fill with blood. This event can be seen in the ECG in the form of the PR segment.

F5-5(4)   The current flows through a specialized bundle of heart muscle cells known as the *bundle of His* to reach the left and right ventricles and flows through them by the *Purkinje fibers* generating the ventricular contractions.

The deoxygenated blood is pumped to the lungs through the pulmonary valve and pulmonary artery due to the muscular contraction of the right ventricle.

The left ventricle contracts and propels the oxygenated blood through the aortic valve and aorta in order to be distributed to the entire body. The QRS complex in the ECG waveform represents this event of ventricular depolarization.

F5-5(5)   Ventricles remain depolarized (contracted) for about 80 ms propelling the blood through the aorta and pulmonary arteries. This can be seen in the ECG waveform in the form of the ST segment.

F5-5(6)   The last event in the cardiac cycle is the repolarization of the heart tissue which is represented by the T wave in the ECG waveform. During this event the atriums and ventricles of the heart are relaxed to allow blood to fill them in and start the cycle again.

This series of events is repeated over and over again and it is known as the *heartbeat*. Normal resting heart rates range from 60 to 100 beats per minute. Even though for well-trained athletes, a normal resting heart rate may be closer to 40 bpm as their hearts work more efficiently.

It is important for the normal operation of the heart for these events to happen one after the other at the same rhythm. Any variation in the ECG waveform means that one or more of these events are not happening correctly and may suggest a cardiovascular disease.

The next section will explain the fundamentals of biopotentials and how to measure them. Then, section 5-3 "ECG Leads" on page 801 will describe all the different configurations used in ECG to measure the electrical activity of the heart as seen from different planes (angles).

5-2 BIOLOGICAL ELECTRICAL POTENTIALS

As we saw in the previous section 5-1 "The Heart" on page 791, the heart cells are a special type of muscle cells due to their cellular nature and function they perform. Their electrochemical activity leads to the contraction of the atriums and ventricles to make the heart pump the blood.

This electrochemical activity generates currents that flow inside the thoracic cavity and their corresponding electrical biopotentials can be measured and recorded at the body surface by using biopotential electrodes.

The electrical biopotentials generated by the heart can be represented as vector quantity. In order to understand the electrical activity of the heart, it is a common assumption that the heart can be represented as a dipole located in the thorax, with a specific polarity at one instance, and inverted polarity in the next. The potential in a specific instance is defined by the amount of charge, and the separation between charges as shown in Figure 5-6.

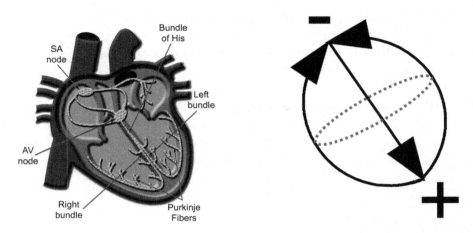

Figure 5-6 **Heart represented as an electrical dipole: cardiac vector**

In order to explain the fundamentals of medical instrumentation and how to measure the electrical activity of a muscle in general, let's consider Figure 5-7 which shows an example of acquiring signals between two points on a bicep, using biopotential electrodes and a differential operational amplifier.

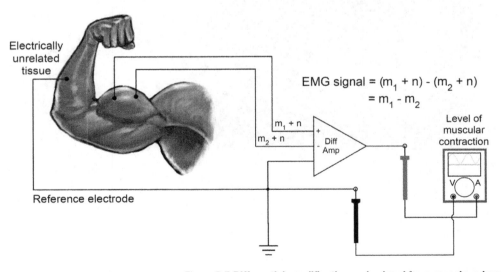

Figure 5-7 **Differential amplification: *m* is signal from muscle, *n* is noise**

The output of the operational amplifier represents the level of muscular contraction and is the difference of magnitudes of m1 and m2. Each pair of electrodes or an electrode combination is defined as a *lead* and this instrumentation principle is the same for any other muscle including the heart.

In diagnostic ECG, cardiologists are interested in looking at the electrical activity of the heart seen from different angles for a better diagnosis and that is why a typical diagnostic ECG system is comprised of 12-leads. Other ECG systems are only 3-lead or 5-lead and are used for continuous monitoring like those found in an intensive care unit or operation room (see Figure 5-8).

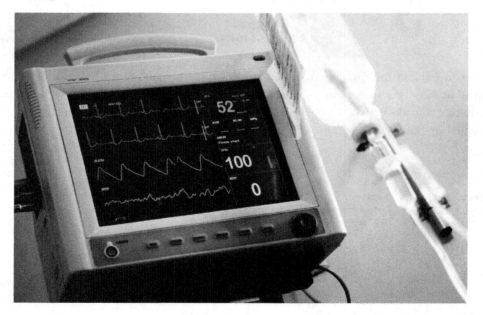

Figure 5-8 **Intensive care unit monitor**

5-3 ECG LEADS

There are three basic leads used in cardiology and the electrodes are placed on the limbs: Left Arm (LA), Right Arm (RA) and Left Leg (LL) as shown in Figure 5-9:

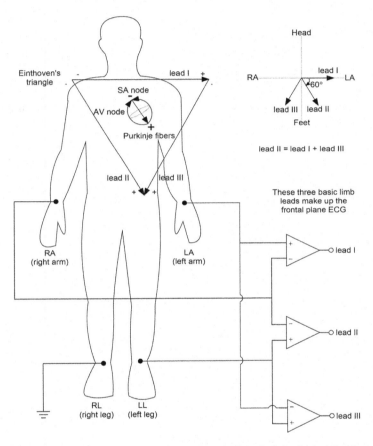

Figure 5-9 **Heart as an electrical dipole and the three basic limb leads**

Lead I is the vector at 0° and is the voltage between the left arm and right arm electrodes.

Lead II is the vector at 60° and is the voltage between the left leg and right arm electrodes.

Lead III is the vector at 120° and is the voltage between the left leg and left arm electrodes.

The three basic leads make up the frontal plane, which is known as the *Einthoven's triangle.*

5

The Einthoven's triangle is assumed to be equilateral with the heart at the center which is equivalent to the vector sum of all the electrical activity of the heart going in all directions. Assuming this triangle is equilateral, what is known as the *Einthoven's law* states that:

$$\text{lead I} + \text{lead III} = \text{lead II}$$

Figure 5-10, Figure 5-11 and Figure 5-12 show the result of combining the three basic limb leads and applying the Einthoven's law to create augmented strength versions of the vectors by combining a pair of leads and using them as a reference.

Augmented lead *aVR* represents the view of the heart from the right shoulder to the center of the heart as shown in Figure 5-10:

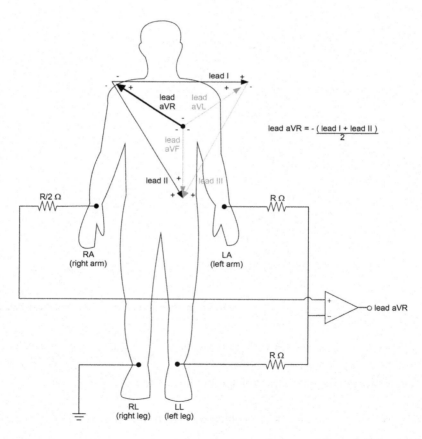

Figure 5-10 **Augmented lead aVR**

The resistive network is necessary in order to create a reference point between the electrodes such that the voltage at this reference point gets averaged out. This central reference point is known as the *Wilson's central terminal* and corresponds to the center of the heart.

Augmented lead *aVL* represents the view of the heart from the left shoulder to the center of the heart as shown in Figure 5-11.

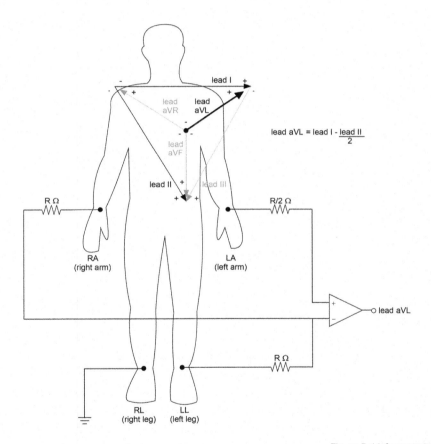

Figure 5-11 **Augmented lead aVL**

The last augmented lead is called *aVF* and it represents the view of the heart from the left hip to the center of the heart. The connections for this lead are shown in Figure 5-12.

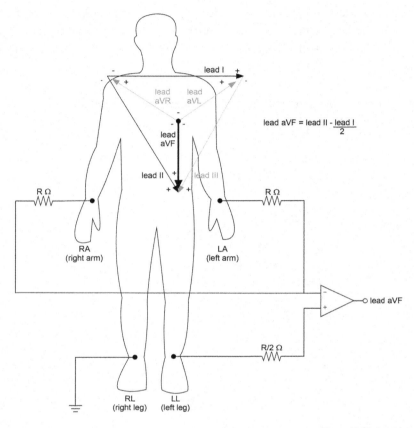

lead aVF = lead II - $\dfrac{\text{lead I}}{2}$

Figure 5-12 **Augmented lead aVF**

The last group of leads are used in diagnostic ECG when cardiologists want to see the ECG in the horizontal plane and they are called *precordial leads*.

Precordial leads are placed at certain positions on the chest. Each of the 6-precordial leads measures the potential between that specific position on the chest and the Wilson's central terminal as shown in Figure 5-13 which also shows the connections of all the 10 biopotential electrodes necessary to record a 12-lead ECG including the 3-basic limb leads (I, II and III), 3-augmented limb leads (aVR, aVL and aVF) and the 6-precordial leads (V1, V2, V3, V4, V5 and V6).

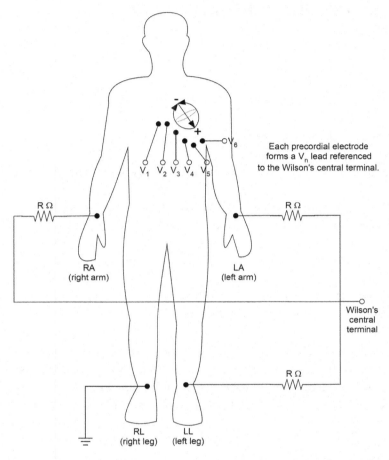

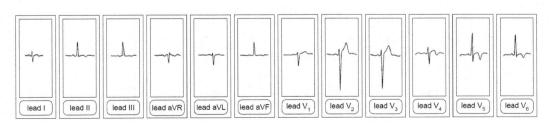

Each precordial electrode forms a V_n lead referenced to the Wilson's central terminal.

Figure 5-13 **Precordial leads**

Figure 5-14 shows an example of what is known as a 12-lead ECG strip of a healthy patient at rest that features 12 different angles of view of the heart.

Figure 5-14 **12-lead ECG strip**

5-4 CARDIOVASCULAR DISEASES (CVD)

Cardiovascular diseases or CVDs are a group of diseases of the heart and blood vessels that include:

■ Coronary heart disease: disease of the blood vessels supplying the heart muscle.

■ Cerebrovascular disease: disease of the blood vessels supplying the brain.

■ Peripheral arterial disease: disease of the blood vessels supplying the arms and legs.

■ Rheumatic heart disease: damage to the heart muscle and heart valves from inflammatory fever, caused by streptococcal bacteria among others.

■ Congenital heart disease: malformations of heart structure existing at birth.

■ Deep vein thrombosis and pulmonary embolism: blood clots in the leg veins, which can dislodge and move to the heart and lungs.

Heart attacks and strokes are usually acute events and are mainly caused by a blockage that prevents blood from flowing to the heart or brain. The most common reason for this is a build-up of fatty deposits on the inner walls of the blood vessels that supply the heart or brain. Strokes can also be caused by bleeding from a blood vessel in the brain or from blood clots.

According to the World Health Organization (WHO) and their fact sheet #317 of January 2011 these are some of the key facts regarding CVDs:

■ CVDs are the number one cause of death globally: more people die annually from CVDs than from any other cause.

■ An estimated 17.1 million people died from CVDs in 2004, representing 29% of all global deaths. Of these deaths, an estimated 7.2 million were due to coronary heart disease and 5.7 million were due to stroke.

■ Low- and middle-income countries are disproportionately affected: 82% of CVD deaths take place in low- and middle-income countries and occur almost equally in men and women.

It is well known that heart disease and stroke can be prevented through a healthy diet and physical activity but the fact that over 80% of deaths by cardiovascular diseases take place in low- and middle-income countries calls for efforts towards not only making ECG more affordable but also developing intelligent ECG algorithms to help doctors in the diagnosis in those countries where their availability can be limited.

Since survivors of a heart attack or stroke are at high risk of recurrences and at high risk of dying from them, making more affordable and intelligent ECG systems would also make them able to target the home market in developed countries. Many people at risk would find a portable ECG system very convenient if it allows them to still keep taking care of themselves without taking time off of their daily routines.

This type of portable home medical device needs low power consumption, high data processing and a wired or wireless communication interface. Freescale's Kinetis MCUs enable the development of such devices by combining the latest low-power innovations and high performance, high precision mixed-signal capabilities with a broad range of connectivity, human-machine interface, and safety and security peripherals. Kinetis MCUs are supported by Micriµm's real time kernel and this example application makes an ideal starting point for a new medical application.

5

5-5 ECG DESIGN

The preceding sections described the fundamentals of the heart, its electrical activity, how to measure the activity with skin electrodes and how important it is for physicians to have the ECG as a tool to make the right diagnosis for all the different cardiovascular diseases.

The next sections will describe the design of an Electrocardiograph and then we will take a piece of that design in order to implement an ECG-based heart rate monitor, including hardware and software.

When it comes to medical instrumentation, the signal acquisition is the first consideration. In the case of an ECG, the electrodes on the skin detect the small voltages generated by the heart activity, but the signal is weak and contains a lot of ambient noise.

First it is necessary to amplify the signal and filter the noise, so we can extract the ECG signal.

Noise and interference signals acquired by this type of systems are due to:

■   The electric power system (50Hz / 60Hz interference).

■   The common-mode voltage which is usually even higher than the ECG signal itself.

■   Muscle contraction of anything other than the heart.

■   Respiration.

■   Electromagnetic interference (EMI) and electromagnetic emissions (EME) from electronic components.

Most of the interference signals can be minimized by installing a proper grounding system in the room where the ECG is to be located, proper training of medical personnel on ECG and periodic maintenance of the power system and medical equipment. But probably one of the most important factors is the quality in the design of the ECG system.

Figure 5-15 shows the block diagram of a typical ECG signal conditioning system. The right leg electrode is connected to the system in order to minimize the effects of the common mode voltage by making adjustments to the baseline according to changes in the potential of this electrode.

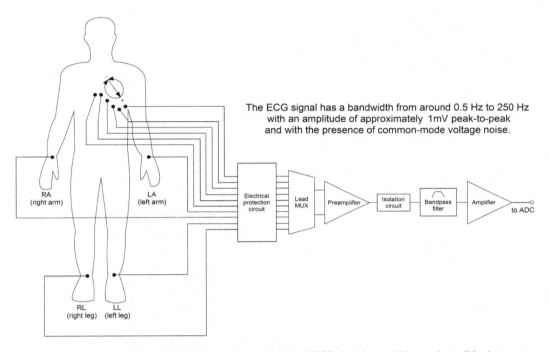

Figure 5-15 **Block diagram of a typical ECG signal acquisition and conditioning system**

Notice that the design only has a single analog channel for 12-leads and the lead MUX is used to select the lead to be recorded. Other designs feature 12 different analog channels to make an ECG system capable of recording all 12-leads simultaneously.

The example presented in this chapter is based on a single channel ECG module offered by Freescale that takes all these factors in consideration to make a high quality ECG signal conditioning system that is compatible with their popular tower development system. The MED-EKG module is designed to work with the TWR-K53N512 controller which is based on their latest Kinetis ARM® Cortex™-M4 MCU.

Figure 5-16 shows the block diagram of this heart rate monitor:

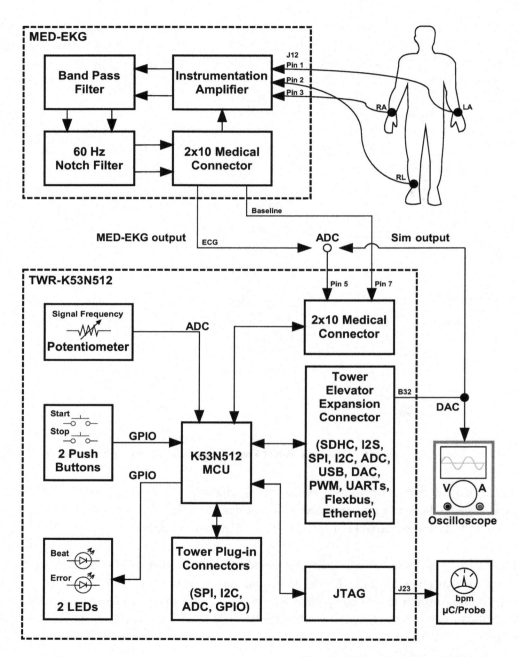

Figure 5-16 **Heart Rate Monitor Block Diagram**

The two pushbuttons onboard the TWR-K53N512 are used to either start or stop the application and the LEDs are used to indicate an error by turning on the orange LED or to indicate every heartbeat by blinking the yellow LED.

The 2x10 medical connector of the MED-EKG not only provides connectivity with the TWR-K53N512 board to make the ECG and Baseline signals available to the ADC modules but also allows the use of the on-chip op-amps and transimpedance amplifiers of the Kinetis 32-bit microcontroller to implement the required signal conditioning. The rest of the signals have been omitted from the block diagram for the sake of simplicity but Table 5-1 shows the signal present in each pin of the medical connector.

MED-EKG Signal	Pin		MED-EKG Signal
VDD	1	2	GND
ECG_IIC_SDA	3	4	ECG_IIC_SCL
ECG Signal	5	6	GND
Baseline Signal	7	8	DAC
OPAMP0 VOUT0	9	10	OPAMP1 VOUT1
OPAMP0 INN0-	11	12	OPAMP1 INN1-
OPAMP0 INP0+	13	14	OPAMP1 INP1+
TRIAMP0 INP0+	15	16	TRIAMP1 INP1+
TRIAMP0 INN0-	17	18	TRIAMP1 INN1-
TRIAMP0 VOUT0	19	20	TRIAMP1 VOUT1

Table 5-1 **Medical Connector 2x10 Pin Header Connections**

Notice from the block diagram in Figure 5-16 that in the absence of the MED-EKG module you can still run the application by using the simulated ECG signal coming out of the DAC module by connecting a jumper wire between pin 5 of the medical connector and pin B32 of the elevator module in the tower system. The potentiometer is used in such situation to increase or decrease the simulated heart rate.

The communication with µC/Probe which will be used to display the results of the heart rate monitor is via the J-Link Ultra debug probe from IAR through the JTAG connector located in J23.

The signal conditioning circuit onboard the MED-EKG module features a typical instrumentation amplifier, which is a standard differential amplifier with its two inputs buffered by two op-amps in an inverting amplifier configuration. Having the inputs buffered by these two extra op-amps provide high input impedance and high common-mode rejection to those large 60Hz voltages that exist on the body.

The band-pass filter passes all frequencies between 0.5Hz and 250Hz which eliminates the DC offset and the notch filter attenuates the 60Hz noise. The last high-pass filter and low-pass filter provide the last stage of amplification. The signal before this final stage is the baseline signal while the signal after this final stage is the actual ECG signal.

The firmware needs to monitor the baseline signal to make sure the gain is not too high such that it saturates the amplifier's output and the compensation signal is used to close the loop and provide a positive feedback for these adjustments as shown in Figure 5-17.

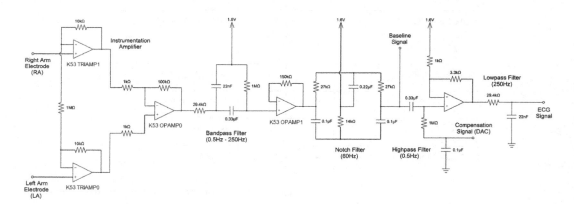

Figure 5-17 **MED-EKG Signal Conditioning Circuit**

Notice that the labels OPAMP0, OPAMP1, TRIAMP0 and TRIAMP1 in Table 5-1 and Figure 5-17 indicate the on-chip internal operational and transimpedance amplifiers in the Kinetis MCU.

Figure 5-18 shows the actual MED-EKG module connected to the TWR-K53N512 controller in a tower system configuration.

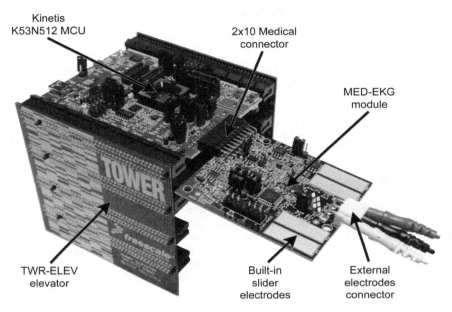

Figure 5-18 **TWR-K53N512 and MED-EKG**

The MED-EKG is powered by default through connector J1, but can also be powered by the JTAG-ONCE port (do not apply both power sources at the same time).

The power switch is controlled by the TWR-K53N512 pin PTE7 from the corresponding Tower System MCU module. To turn on the MED-EKG module in your software, make sure to set PTE7 pin to output low (active low). To turn off, set PTE7 to output high. This has already been done in the MED-EKG example software in the TWR-K53N512.

More information about the MED-EKG including user manual and schematics can be downloaded from Freescale's website at www.freescale.com by searching for part number MED-EKG.

5-6 RUNNING THE EXAMPLE PROJECT

This section describes the steps you need to follow to run the heart rate monitoring example. Start by connecting the MED-EKG module to the TWR-K53N512 controller through the 2x10 medical connector as shown in Figure 5-18.

Before powering up the system, make sure the jumper settings in the MED-EKG module are set as shown in Table 5-2. The default installed jumper settings are shown in bold.

Jumper	Option	Setting	Description
J1	Medical board connector	**open**	Connection with TWR-K53N512 medical board
J2	Connection of MM OPAMP2 INP2-	**1-2**	Directly to Vref 1.6V
		2-3	Trough R12 to OUT2
J3	Right electrode gain (must be the same as J4)	**1-2**	Gain is 100x
		2-3	Gain is 10x
J4	Left electrode gain (must be the same as J3)	**1-2**	Gain is 100x
		2-3	Gain is 10x
J5	Enabling R17 connection	**open**	R17 connection is open
		shunt	R17 is connected to Vref1.6V
J6	Right electrode connection (must be the same as J7)	1-2	Right electrode is connected to external INA input (INstrumentation Amplifier)
		2-3	Right electrode is connected to internal amplifiers
J7	Left electrode connection (must be the same as J6)	1-2	Left electrode is connected to external INA input (INstrumentation Amplifier)
		2-3	Left electrode is connected to internal amplifiers
J8	ADC input to DSC	1-2	DSC is feed from internal amplifiers output
		2-3	DSC is feed from signal selected in J9
J9	Signal selector jumper	1-2	Selected signal is the external INA circuit
		2-3	Selected signal is the output of internal amplifier OUT2

Jumper	Option	Setting	Description
J10	JTAG-ONCE header	**open**	It is used to program the DSC
J11	Reference electrodes selector	1-2	Reference electrodes are connected to ground
		2-3	Reference electrodes are connected to Vref1.6V
J12	External electrodes connector	**open**	It is used to connect external electrodes

Table 5-2 **MED-EKG Jumper Settings Table**

Notice from Table 5-2 that the MEG-EKG is configured by default to use Kinetis on-chip analog modules. The option that uses external Instrumentation Amplifier (INA) is not functional by default.

You should also notice that when J3 and J4 are set to 100x, you must use external electrodes via J12 instead of using the on-board slider contacts. This is because the on-board slider contacts yield more noise due to the non-secure connection with the finger tips and any noise at the first stage of instrumentation where high amplification occurs can easily result in a saturated output so you will not be able to see the ECG output in the final amplification stage.

Even though the on-board slider electrodes can be used when external electrodes are not available, we strongly recommend the use of standard medical grade external electrodes available from any medical supplies store. These electrodes have a conductive adhesive gel that ensures good skin contact and are shown in Figure 5-19:

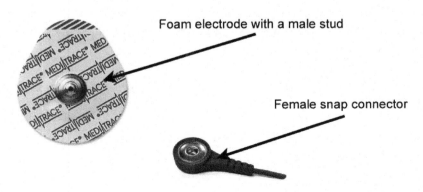

Foam electrode with a male stud

Female snap connector

Figure 5-19 **Medical grade external electrode and connector**

According to the American Heart Association, the arm electrodes may be placed on any part of the arms as long as they are below the shoulders and the left leg electrode may be placed on any part of the left leg as long as it is below the waist. We recommend placing the red wire electrode on the right wrist, the white wire electrode on the left wrist and the black wire electrode on the left side abdominal area or on the left ankle as shown in Figure 5-20:

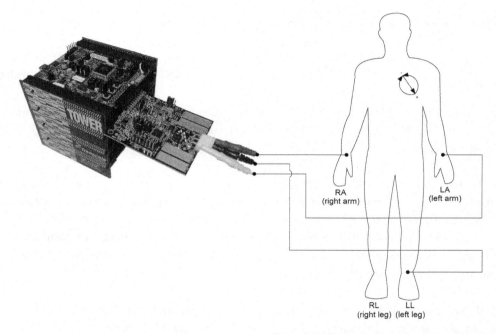

RA
(right arm)

LA
(left arm)

RL   LL
(right leg) (left leg)

Figure 5-20 **External electrodes connection example**

Assuming you have followed all the setup steps described in Chapter 4, "Setup" on page 779, proceed to connect one end of the IAR's J-Link Ultra for ARM debug probe to the JTAG connector on J23 of the TWR-K53N512 and the other end of the probe to any USB port available in your PC.

Run IAR's Embedded Workbench for ARM (EWARM) and open the workspace TWR-K53N512 at:

```
$\Micrium\Software\EvalBoards\Freescale\TWR-K53N512\IAR\
uC-OS-III-Book-Ex-Src.eww
```

In the workspace explorer window, select the tab for the project uC-OS-III-Ex1-HRM. The workspace window shows all of the files in the project which are sorted into groups represented by folder icons. Figure 5-21 shows the project files for uC-OS-III-Ex1-HRM in the workspace explorer window.

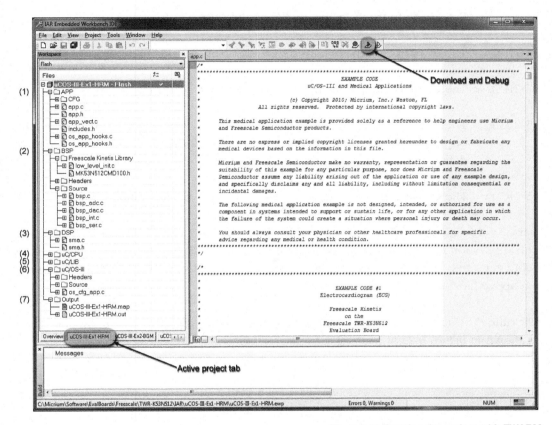

Figure 5-21 **Running the project with EWARM**

F5-21(1)   The **APP** group includes all of the application files for this example. The subgroup **CFG** includes the header files used to configure the application.

F5-21(2)   The **BSP** group contains the files that comprise the board support package. The board support package includes the code used to control the peripherals on the board. For this example, the software to control the LEDs, pushbuttons,

5

ADCs, DACs, operational amplifiers and transimpedance amplifiers will be used. The subgroup Freescale Kinetis Library includes the header files for the Kinetis K50 family of microcontrollers.

F5-21(3)   The **DSP** group contains the files that define some of the Digital Signal Processing functions called by the application.

F5-21(4)   The **uC/CPU** group contains the µC/CPU source code files.

F5-21(5)   The **uC/LIB** group contains the µC/LIB source code files.

F5-21(6)   The **µC/OS-III** group contains the µCOS-III source code. In addition, the **os_cfg_app.c** file is included in this group to allow certain behavior to be defined at compile time.

F5-21(7)   The **Output** group contains the files generated by the compiler/linker.

Start the debugger by clicking the "Download and Debug" icon as shown in Figure 5-21. The application is programmed to the internal Flash of the K53N512 microcontroller and the debugger starts. The code automatically starts executing and stops at the **main()** function in the **app.c** file.

Click the "Go" icon in IAR Embedded Workbench's debugging tools to run the application as shown in Figure 5-22.

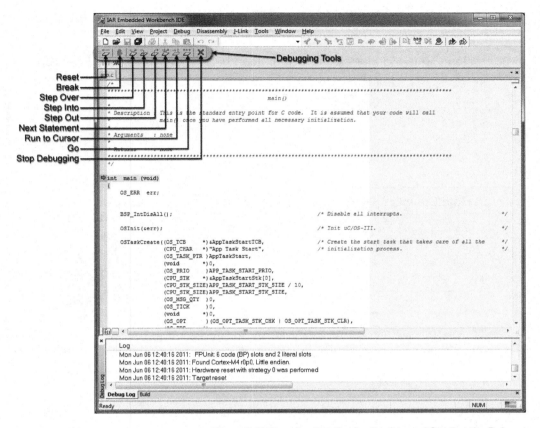

Figure 5-22 **Downloading the Application and Starting the Debugger**

You can test the application by starting µC/Probe and open the workspace for the heart rate monitor at:

```
$\Micrium\Software\EvalBoards\Freescale\TWR-K53N512\IAR\
uC-OS-III-Book-Ex-Src\uC-OS-III-Ex1-HRM\uC-OS-III-Ex1-HRM-Probe.wsp
```

After µC/Probe starts, click the run button (green triangle). Once µC/Probe is running, you will see a screen similar to the one shown in Figure 5-23.

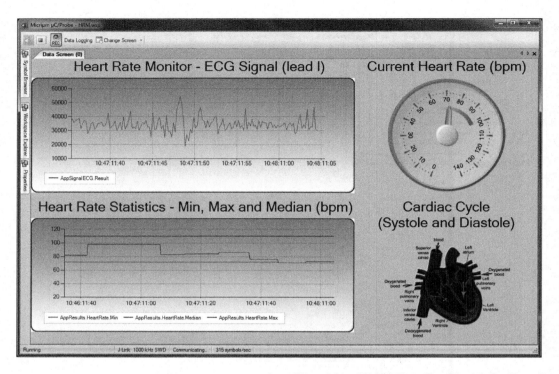

Figure 5-23 **µC/Probe Heart Rate Monitor Dashboard**

Press the pushbutton on the TWR-K53N512 board labeled as SW1 to start the application and you will start seeing the ECG tracing on the dashboard. The heart rate in beats-per-minute is calculated in real-time and displayed in the gauge. Other heart rate statistics are plotted in one of the charts as shown in Figure 5-23.

5-7 HOW THE CODE WORKS

The heart rate monitoring application consists of four different tasks:

- User IF task: The user interface task monitors the state of the two pushbuttons onboard the TWR-K53N512. The pushbuttons are used to either start or stop the application. The task is defined by `AppTaskUserIF()` in `app.c`.

- Sim task: The simulator task monitors the state of the potentiometer and updates the frequency of an ECG simulated signal generated by the DAC according to the position of the potentiometer. The task is defined by `AppTaskSim()` in `app.c`.

- DAQ task: The data acquisition task is the main task in the application and implements the state machine that processes the analog input samples to calculate the heart rate. The task is defined by `AppTaskDAQ()` in `app.c`.

- Heartbeat task: The heartbeat task is responsible for controlling the heart animation in µC/Probe by updating the value of the global variable `AppCardiacCycleState` that can take one of three states: Diastole, Systole or None. The heartbeat task is defined by `AppTaskHeartbeat()` in `app.c`

The interaction among the different tasks is facilitated by the use of µC/OS-III's task semaphores and task message queues and it is illustrated in Figure 5-24.

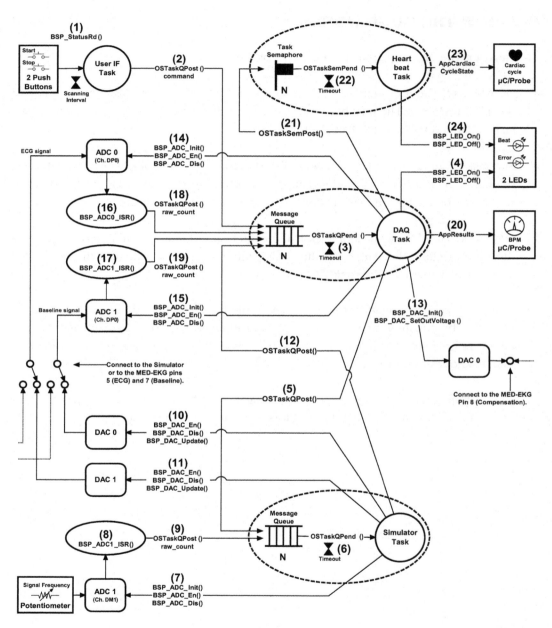

Figure 5-24 **Interaction of Application Tasks**

F5-24(1)   The state of the push buttons is monitored by the user IF task at a scanning interval defined by **BSP_STATUS_CHECK_INTERVAL**. See **AppTaskUserIF()** in **app.c** and **BSP_StatusRd()** in **bsp.c**.

F5-24(2)   Depending on the pushbutton pressed by the user a message from the user IF task to either start or stop the application is posted to the DAQ task's built-in message queue by calling **OSTaskQPost()**. See **AppTaskUserIF()** in **app.c**.

F5-24(3)   The DAQ task can receive data messages directly from the ADCs ISRs or command messages from the other two tasks. When **OSTaskQPend()** is called, the message is retrieved and processed in two different ways depending on the sender and the type of message. If the message comes from one of the ADC's ISR then the message is processed by calling the function **AppTaskDAQ_ProcessData()** and if the message comes from any other task then the message is processed by calling the function **AppTaskDAQ_ProcessCmd()** in **app.c**.

F5-24(4)   If the message retrieved by the DAQ task is a command to start the heart rate monitoring then the DAQ task turns off the LEDs by calling the function **BSP_LED_Off()** in **bsp.c**.

F5-24(5)   If the message retrieved by the DAQ task is a command to start the heart rate monitoring in simulation mode then the DAQ task posts a message to the sim task's built-in message queue to start the simulator. See **AppTaskDAQ()** in **app.c** and **AppTaskDAQ_ProcessCmd()** in **app.c**.

F5-24(6)   In similar fashion, the sim task can receive messages directly from the ADC1's ISR or from the DAQ task. When **OSTaskQPend()** is called, the message is retrieved and processed in different ways depending on the sender. The sim task retrieves the received message from its message queue and proceeds according to the command issued by the DAQ task as follows:

F5-24(7)   If the message contains a start command then the sim task starts ADC1 channel DM1 in order to read the potentiometer. See **AppTaskSim()** in **app.c**.

F5-24(8)   The CPU is interrupted by the completion of a conversion of ADC1 Channel DM1 and the interrupt is handled by **BSP_ADC1_ISR()** in **bsp_adc.c**.

F5-24(9)   The ADC1 ISR posts the result of the conversion in the form of a 16-bit raw count to the sim task's built-in message queue by calling the function `OSTaskQPost()`. See `BSP_ADC1_ISR()` in `bsp_adc.c`.

F5-24(10)   The sim task retrieves the message from the queue and configures the DAC0 to output a simulated ECG baseline waveform. See `AppTaskSim()` in `app.c`.

F5-24(11)   The sim task retrieves the message from the queue and configures the DAC1 to output a simulated ECG waveform at a rate proportional to the raw count of the ADC1 channel DM1. See `AppTaskSim()` in `app.c`.

F5-24(12)   The sim task posts a message to the DAQ task's built-in message queue notifying the DAQ task that the simulator is running. See `AppTaskSim()` in `app.c`.

F5-24(13)   The DAQ task retrieves the message from the queue and initializes DAC0 to output a voltage reference. See `AppTaskDAQ()` and `AppTaskDAQ_ProcessCmd()` in `app.c`.

F5-24(14)   The DAQ task retrieves the message from the queue and enables ADC0 channel DP0 to convert the ECG signal. See `AppTaskDAQ()`, `AppTaskDAQ_ProcessCmd()` and `AppTaskDAQ_ExecCmd()` in `app.c`.

F5-24(15)   The DAQ task retrieves the message from the queue and enables ADC1 channel DP0 to convert the Baseline signal. See `AppTaskDAQ()`, `AppTaskDAQ_ProcessCmd()` and `AppTaskDAQ_ExecCmd()` in `app.c`.

F5-24(16)   The CPU is interrupted by the completion of a conversion of ADC0 channel DP0 and the interrupt is handled by `BSP_ADC0_ISR` in `bsp_adc.c`.

F5-24(17)   About the same time, the CPU is interrupted by the completion of a conversion of ADC1 channel DP0 and the interrupt is handled by `BSP_ADC1_ISR` in `bsp_adc.c`.

F5-24(18)   The ADC0 ISR posts the result of the conversion in the form of a 16-bit raw count to the DAQ task's built-in message queue by calling the function `OSTaskQPost()`. See `BSP_ADC0_ISR()` in `bsp_adc.c`.

F5-24(19)   The ADC1 ISR posts the result of the conversion in the form of a 16-bit raw count to the DAQ task's built-in message queue by calling the function `OSTaskQPost()`. See `BSP_ADC1_ISR()` in `bsp_adc.c`.

F5-24(20)   The DAQ task retrieves the message from the queue and uses the raw counts from ADC0 and ADC1 to calculate the heart rate and display the value in µC/Probe by calling the function `AppTaskDAQ_ProcessData()` and `AppCalcResults()` in `app.c`.

F5-24(21)   The DAQ task sends a signal to the heartbeat task through its local semaphore by calling the function `OSTaskSemPost()`. The signal is to notify the heartbeat task that a new heart rate has been calculated. See `AppCalcResults()` in `app.c`.

F5-24(22)   The heartbeat task normally waits for a signal from the DAQ task in order to update a timer that drives the cardiac cycle animation in µC/Probe. See `AppTaskHeartbeat()` in `app.c`.

F5-24(23)   The heartbeat task updates the global variable `AppCardiacCycleState` toggling between diastolic and systolic states at the same rate calculated by the DAQ task. See `AppTaskHeartbeat()` in `app.c`.

F5-24(24)   The heartbeat task toggles the LED at the same rate of the heartbeat by calling the function `BSP_LED_On()` and `BSP_LED_Off()` in `bsp.c`.

5-7-1 BIOMEDICAL SIGNAL ANALYSIS

The algorithm to calculate the heart rate off the ECG signal relies on the time-domain features of the QRS complex such as the steep slope and high amplitude. The algorithm is defined by `AppTaskDAQ_DetectQRS()` in `app.c`

The DAQ task keeps a sliding window of three samples: `AppSignal1stSpl`, `AppSignal2ndSpl` and `AppSignal3rdSpl`. It also keeps a count of every sample processed in `AppSplsBtwPulsesCtr` and the counter gets reset once a QRS complex (pulse) is detected as illustrated in Figure 5-25.

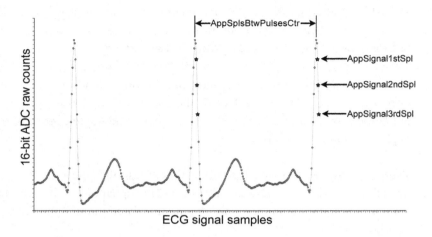

Figure 5-25 **QRS Detection Algorithm**

Assuming that the QRS complex has a high amplitude and steep slope, whenever **AppSignal1stSpl** is greater than both **AppSignal2ndSpl** and **AppSignal3rdSpl** and the difference between **AppSignal1stSpl** and **AppSignal3rdSpl** is greater than a threshold defined by **APP_MIN_PULSE_SLOPE** a QRS complex or pulse is detected.

The number of samples between pulses is kept in **AppSplsBtwPulsesCtr** and the heart rate in beats-per-minute is calculated by:

```
AppResults.HeartRate.Cur = (60 * APP_SAMPLING_RATE) / AppSplsBtwPulsesCtr;
```

Listing 5-1 **Heart Rate Calculation**

The result gets inserted into a histogram to keep running statistics of the heart rate which are stored in the following variables:

```
AppResults.HeartRate.Min
AppResults.HeartRate.Max
AppResults.HeartRate.Median
```

Listing 5-2 **Heart Rate Statistics**

5

5-8 SUMMARY

By providing the right amount of detail with simplified terminology, this chapter explained the anatomy and physiology of the heart as far as Electrocardiography is concerned. In a similar fashion, it explained the theory of operation of an Electrocardiograph including the hardware and software.

This example application demonstrated how simple it is to implement an ECG based heart rate monitor using a combination of Micrium's μC/OS-III and Freescale hardware. It also demonstrated two of the most important features of μC/OS-III: *Task Semaphores* and *Task Message Queues*.

Signaling a task through its built-in semaphore is a typical method of synchronization, and in this example we used the heartbeat task's built-in semaphore to synchronize the activities of the DAQ task and the heartbeat task. The heartbeat task is signaled by the DAQ task when a new heart rate result has been calculated and depending on the heartbeat task priority, the scheduler is run. The heartbeat task may then update the cardiac cycle animation with the new heart rate result. Synchronization through task semaphores is discussed in the first part of the book section 14-2 "Task Semaphore" on page 289.

Message queues are built into each task and the user can send messages directly to a task from another task or an ISR. Task message queues are widely used in this example because they allow the developer to encapsulate each task's functionality into a clean and simple message-based API. For example, we used the DAQ task's built-in message queue as a means to receive different types of commands from other tasks to perform an action like start or stop the simulator, start or stop the data acquisition and process samples from the ADC's ISRs. Inter-task communication via task message queues is discussed in the first part of the book, in section 15-3 "Task Message Queue" on page 312.

The need to use an RTOS in this particular example may not seem very obvious, but we hope you see that it delivers a solid platform to create a commercial medical product based on a task-oriented approach. Dividing the firmware of a medical product into different tasks in such a way that each task is responsible for some part of the application makes it easier to develop and maintain. It promotes team work and code reuse by distributing the tasks among different developers and most important, it reduces the economic impact of recertification every time you want to add new functionality or update one part of the application.

5

Imagine you want to take this design to the next level and be able to send the ECG samples to a computer via USB for display or analysis purposes. Or even, imagine you want to implement a web service client that submits the actual ECG waveform to a medical website for further diagnosis. Whether it is USB or Ethernet, chances are that you may need at least two more tasks to handle the reception and transmission of packets and one more task to handle all time-outs related to the communication protocol.

In the same way, LCD or any other type of display control is also a great candidate to encapsulate into a task and use the task message queue to receive commands to update the display.

Freescale and Micriµm support the addition of other functionality to this heart rate monitor by offering more tower system compatible peripherals and software stacks. Visit the Freescale and Micriµm websites to learn more about other products that can help you take your design to the next level.

Chapter

6

Blood Glucose Meter

The Blood Glucose Meter (BGM) is a device that measures the level of glucose in the blood. It is indispensable in the diagnosis and long-term management of diabetes.

This chapter demonstrates a basic implementation of a blood glucose meter built using µC/OS-III and Freescale products.

The chapter starts with an illustrated introduction to some of the physiological fundamentals of the system that regulates the levels of glucose in the body known as the *endocrine system*. The next section continues the introduction, but with emphasis on the measurement of the glucose concentration in the blood by using a biochemical sensor and presents the design of a Blood Glucose Meter (BGM). The last part of the chapter deals with using the tools to run the example and a description of how the code works.

6-1 GLUCOSE

Glucose is a type of sugar represented by the formula $C_6H_{12}O_6$ also known as *dextrose*. This carbohydrate is a source of energy in most living organisms including humans. It is also essential as a precursor in the creation of proteins and the production and degradation of a special group of molecules known as *lipids* as we will describe in the next paragraphs.

The levels of concentration of glucose in the bloodstream are regulated by two chemicals known as *hormones* that are released by the *pancreas*. The two hormones have opposite effects and are known as *insulin* and *glucagon*. Insulin is normally produced by a special type of cells in the pancreas called *beta cells* while glucagon is produced by *alpha cells*.

High levels of glucose in the blood trigger the pancreas to release insulin into the bloodstream, while low levels of glucose in the blood signal the pancreas to release glucagon; with the only purpose to maintain stable levels of glucose in the blood. These chemicals are the means of communication between the pancreas and the rest of the body's

6

cells to let them know that the glucose level is either high or low. The cells of the nervous system are the only cells that do not require any messages. In other words, they require a constant supply of glucose because that is the main source of energy they consume.

The key players in this closed-loop control system include the *small intestine*, the *pancreas*, the *liver*, the body tissue cells, the *adipose* tissue cells and are shown in Figure 6-1.

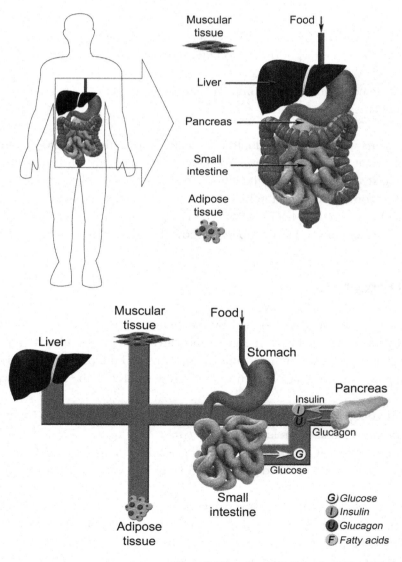

Figure 6-1 **Key players in the natural blood glucose regulation**

The regulation of glucose levels in the blood by this feedback system can be broken down into a series of events illustrated in Figure 6-2 that, for sake of illustration, takes apart all the key players and interconnects them via the circulatory system only (bloodstream):

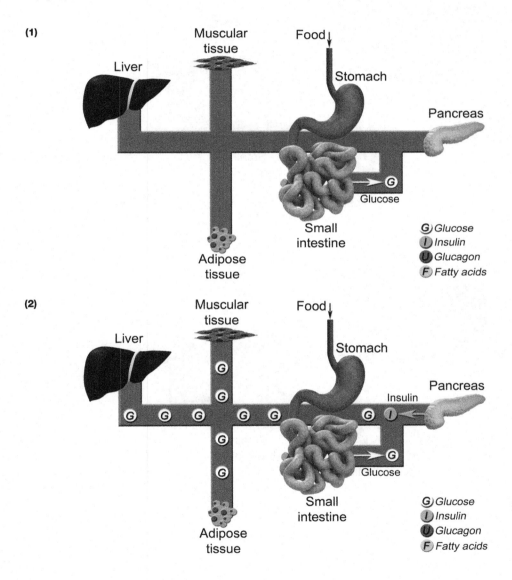

(3)

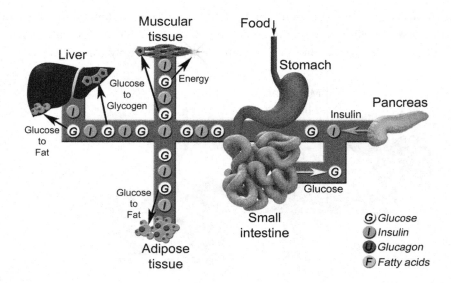

(4)

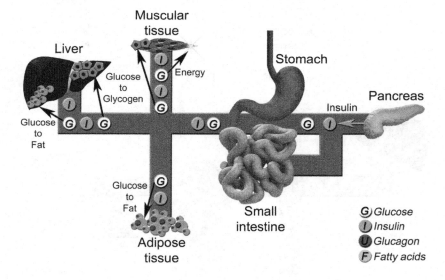

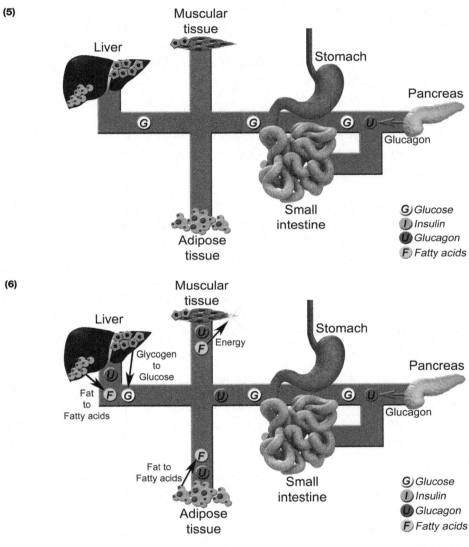

Figure 6-2 **Natural blood glucose regulation**

F6-2(1)   Food is absorbed by the small intestine and the carbohydrates in the food are digested into a type of sugar known as *monosaccharides* and more specifically glucose. The glucose gets released into the bloodstream.

F6-2(2)   The increased levels of glucose in the blood trigger the pancreas to release a type of chemical known as *insulin* into the bloodstream.

F6-2(3)   The insulin makes its way to the body cells (like muscle cells) through the circulatory system and stimulates or enables them to take glucose as their source of energy. The muscle cells also use some glucose to build molecules capable of storing energy in the form of a special type of molecule known as *glycogen*. This secondary energy storage is useful in the event the glucose level goes down in the future.

The insulin also reaches the liver cells to promote the conversion of glucose into fat and glycogen as molecules for secondary energy storage. The glycogen is stored in the liver.

In similar fashion, the insulin reaches the fat cells of the adipose tissue to stimulate the uptake of glucose and the conversion into more fat.

F6-2(4)   As long as the levels of glucose remain above a certain threshold equivalent to the amount of glucose circulating through the bloodstream when the small intestine is not absorbing anymore glucose, the pancreas will keep releasing insulin and the body, liver and fat cells will keep using the glucose. But of course, the glucose levels will eventually decrease if the stomach and intestines are empty.

F6-2(5)   When the glucose levels in the blood are low, the pancreas stops releasing insulin and instead starts releasing a chemical known as glucagon into the bloodstream. It is important to note that some glucose is still circulating but it is reserved for the nervous system.

F6-2(6)   The glucagon reaches the liver and enables it to convert their reserve energy molecules known as glycogen into glucose which is released into the bloodstream. While this glucose is mostly reserved for the cells of the nervous system the liver also converts fat into fatty acids which many body cell types like the heart can use for energy.

The glucagon gets to the body cells and enables them to switch their source of energy from glucose to fatty acids. Some cells from the body like the muscle are also capable of using the small percentage of glycogen stored in the muscle and turn it into glucose for the muscular contraction.

The body will keep burning fat from the adipose tissue in the absence of glucose and the last resource of energy is the protein of the muscles that can be degraded into glucose; certainly a non-desirable situation that is avoided by the stomach and pancreas by the release of a hormone known as *ghrelin* that stimulates hunger. The cycle completes when the glucose levels come back up by the digestion of new carbohydrate rich food.

6-2 DIABETES MELLITUS

Diabetes is a chronic disease that results either when the pancreas does not produce enough insulin or when the body cells cannot effectively respond to the insulin it produces. Either way, the effect is a high level of glucose in the bloodstream known as *hyperglycaemia* that over time, can damage the heart, blood vessels, eyes, kidneys and nerves among others.

According to the World Health Organization (WHO) and their Fact sheet # 312 of January 2011 these are some of the facts about diabetes:

■ More than 220 million people worldwide have diabetes.

■ In 2004, an estimated 3.4 million people died from consequences of high blood glucose.

■ More than 80% of diabetes deaths occur in low- and middle-income countries.

WHO recognizes three types of diabetes:

■ Type 1 diabetes is characterized by deficient insulin production and requires daily administration of insulin. The cause of type 1 diabetes is not known and it is not preventable with current knowledge. Symptoms include excessive excretion of urine, thirst, constant hunger, weight loss, vision changes and fatigue. These symptoms may occur suddenly.

■ Type 2 diabetes results from the body's ineffective use of insulin. Type 2 diabetes comprises 90% of people with diabetes around the world, and is largely the result of excess body weight and physical inactivity. Symptoms may be similar to those of Type 1 diabetes, but are often less marked. As a result, the disease may be diagnosed several

6

years after onset, once complications have already arisen. Until recently, this type of diabetes was seen only in adults but it is now also occurring in children.

■ Gestational diabetes is hyperglycaemia with onset or first recognition during pregnancy and results from the pregnancy hormones blocking the effects of insulin. Symptoms of gestational diabetes are similar to Type 2 diabetes. Gestational diabetes is most often diagnosed through prenatal screening, rather than reported symptoms.

Even though lifestyle modifications like a healthy diet, regular physical activity, maintaining a normal body weight and avoiding tobacco use can prevent or delay the onset of type 2 diabetes, the accurate measurement of the concentration of glucose in the blood is essential not only in the diagnosis but also in the long-term management of diabetes mellitus. Patients with diabetes can take a blood sample themselves and use the readings from a blood glucose meter along with their doctor's advice, to adjust their prescribed amount of insulin to administer and to make modifications in their lifestyle.

Figure 6-3 shows a commercial blood glucose meter, the patient usually inserts a disposable sensor commonly known as *test strip* into the blood glucose meter and uses a device to prick the fingertip's skin in a controlled manner known as *lancing device* in order to draw a small blood sample. The sample is then deposited into the test strip and a few seconds later the reading is displayed.

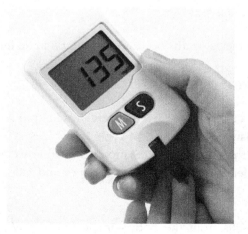

Figure 6-3 **Commercial blood glucose meter**

The next section will describe a blood glucose sensor typically used in most blood glucose meters.

6-3 BLOOD GLUCOSE SENSOR

Many biosensors are capable of generating signals that are correlated with the concentration of glucose in the blood. Some of them employ fiber-optic, laser and infrared LEDs to take an optical approach, but most blood glucose meters today take on the *electroenzymatic* approach. This section will describe the fundamentals of the electroenzymatic approach in general, considering that many sensors today use a variation of it in an effort to optimize sensitivity, stability, response time and accuracy. Some blood glucose meters are even compatible with multiple types of sensors.

The electroenzymatic sensor described here is based on a very popular chemical reaction in nature known as *glucose oxidation* and the sensor involves a very popular electrode that measures oxygen concentration developed by Leland Clark and it is known as a *Clark-type* electrode.

The sensor includes a series of membranes in order to isolate some molecules, a chemical that catalyzes a reaction known as *glucose oxidase enzyme* and two electrodes immersed in an *electrolyte*. Figure 6-4 shows the sequence of chemical reactions that take place in this type of sensor:

(1)

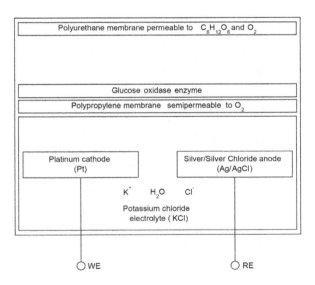

6

(2)

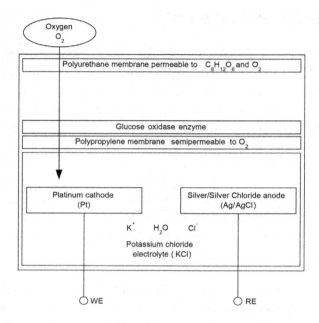

(3)

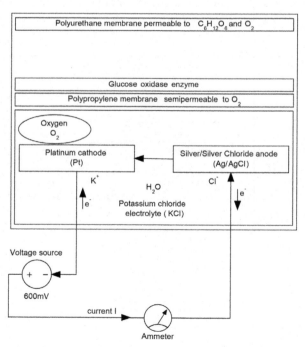

(4)

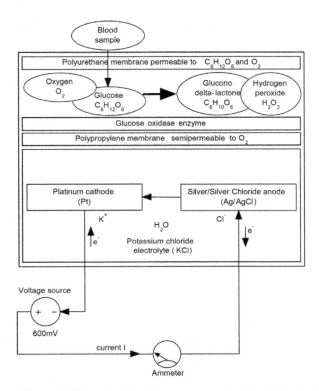

Figure 6-4 **Measuring blood glucose concentration by the electroenzymatic approach**

F6-4(1)   The Working Electrode (WE) made of platinum and the Reference Electrode (RE) made of silver are immersed in a solution of *potassium chloride* (KCl) and water (H_2O). When KCl dissolves in water, two different free ions will form: K^+ anions and Cl^- cations. This makes the electrolyte for the cell, which is nothing but a liquid that contains free ions that will be the carriers of electric current.

F6-4(2)   Without the blood sample being applied yet, the oxygen in the air makes its way through the polyurethane and polypropylene membranes to diffuse into the electrolyte.

F6-4(3)   A negative voltage of 600mV is applied to the platinum (Pt) electrode (cathode) referenced to the silver/silver chloride (Ag/AgCl) electrode (anode). Each electrode attracts ions that are of the opposite charge. That is, positively charged ions (K^+) move towards the negative cathode (Pt) that is providing the electrons whereas negatively charged ions (Cl^-) move towards the positive anode (Ag).

6

The oxygen in the vicinity of the cathode and the negative electrons supplied by the 600mV potential cause the following reaction (reduction):

$$O_2 + 2H_2O + 4e^- \rightarrow 2H_2O_2 + 4e^- \rightarrow 4OH^-$$

The four negative ions known as *hydroxides* created by the reduction are buffered by the KCl electrolyte:

$$4OH^- + 4KCl \rightarrow 4KOH + 4Cl^-$$

The four negative chloride ions will undergo their own oxidation reaction at the positive electrode (anode):

$$4Ag^0 + 4Cl^- \rightarrow 4AgCl + 4e^-$$

With this last reaction the cycle is complete, in other words, this last reaction creates the four electrons necessary in the first reaction. The cycle is complete, the circuit is closed, and the constant current is measured with an ammeter.

F6-4(4) By using a device to prick the skin in a controlled manner known as *lancing device*, a blood sample from the fingertip is applied to the sensor. The glucose in the blood sample gets in contact with the glucose oxidase enzyme through the polyurethane membrane and reacts with the oxygen from the air to produce *glucono delta-lactone* and hydrogen peroxide:

$$C_6H_{12}O_6 + O_2 \quad \boxed{\text{Glucose oxidase}} \Rightarrow \quad C_6H_{10}O_6 + H_2O_2$$

Either the consumption of oxygen or the production of hydrogen peroxide from the chemical reaction of glucose and oxygen can be detected by the cathode depending on the type of membrane used to separate the top of the sensor and the cell at the bottom. In this case it is a polypropylene membrane that is semi-permeable to the small molecules of oxygen, which lets the oxygen diffuse into the electrolyte. The oxygen consumed in the chemical reaction between glucose and oxygen can be measured as a decrease in the current that was running before the blood sample was applied, because less oxygen arrives at the cathode. The difference in the concentration of oxygen is directly proportional to the concentration of glucose.

Like we mentioned at the beginning of this section, many variations of this basic sensor have been developed over the years that include different chemicals, different type of membranes and number of electrodes, all with the purpose of improving the sensitivity, stability, response time and accuracy. But the vast majority of them share the same principle of glucose oxidation in the presence of an enzyme and a sensor that measures the changes in concentration of one or more of the participants during the chemical reaction.

Figure 6-5 shows a typical sensor commonly known as *test strip* featuring three electrodes. In this configuration the sensor is more stable than the one explained in Figure 6-4 because it adds an extra circuit that takes care of providing the voltage for the reaction leaving the reference electrode alone to create a second circuit to measure the voltage drop only. The extra electrode is called *Counter Electrode* (CE) and is made of platinum just like the Working Electrode (WE).

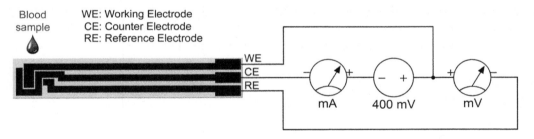

Figure 6-5 **3-electrode test strip**

In this test strip a voltage of 400mV is applied between the Working Electrode (WE) and the Counter Electrode (CE); and the output of the sensor is measured between the Working Electrode (WE) and the Reference Electrode (RE).

The transfer function can be calculated by applying a drop of two *stock glucose solutions* of known concentration as the transfer function is linear across the range of interest which is around 20 to 600 mg/dL (milligrams per deciliter). They are available in pharmacies and usually come in two bottles containing a low and high known concentration of glucose. The two readings from these solutions are enough to calculate the function transfer. The glucose solution comes in very handy too while testing your system without having to use your own blood.

6-4 BLOOD GLUCOSE METER DESIGN

As we learned in the last section, several sensor designs are available today but they all share the same fundamentals: a polarization voltage is applied and a voltage or current is read back. With the appropriate electronic circuits, the analog front end of this system is fairly simple.

Freescale's Kinetis TWR-K53N512 is an excellent part not only to drive this type of sensor, but also to acquire its output. The K53 microcontroller comes with a voltage reference module capable of providing an accurate voltage reference with a trim resolution of 0.5mV per step with a dedicated output pin. The K53 also comes with a 16-bit ADC that includes a temperature sensor whose output is connected to one of the ADC channel inputs. This allows the engineer to make adjustments to the transfer function in order to account for ambient temperature changes. Other nice features include a hardware averaging function, automatic compare functions and programmable gain amplifiers.

In order to read the three-electrode test strip you need a special circuit known as *transimpedance amplifier*. The transimpedance amplifier is nothing but an operational amplifier in the inverting configuration as shown in Figure 6-6 that converts current to voltage. The circuit also has a voltage divider in order to provide the 400mV to the reference electrode. A low-pass filter keeps the Working and Counter Electrode signals below 8Hz.

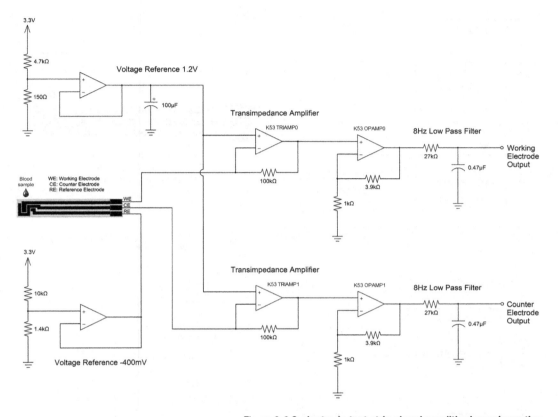

Figure 6-6 **3-electrode test strip signal conditioning schematics**

Freescale offers an analog module with a medical connector compatible with the TWR-K53N512 controller that implements this type of analog front end. The module is called MED-GLU.

The complete system including the TWR-K53N512 and MED-GLU is illustrated as a block diagram in Figure 6-7. The two pushbuttons onboard the TWR-K53N512 are used to either start or stop the application and the LEDs are used to indicate an error by turning on the orange LED or to indicate a successful reading by turning on the yellow LED.

6

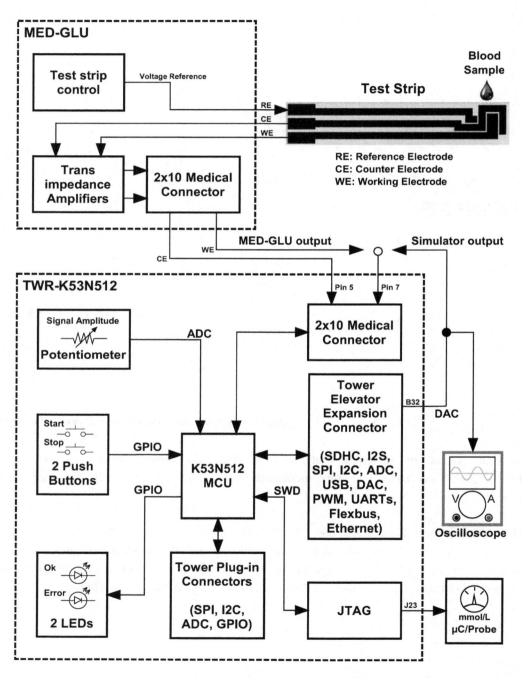

Figure 6-7 **Blood Glucose Meter Block Diagram**

The 2x10 medical connector of the MED-GLU not only provides connectivity with the TWR-K53N512 board to make the Working and Counter Electrode signals available to the ADC modules but also allows the use of the on-chip op-amps and transimpedance amplifiers of the Kinetis 32-bit microcontroller to implement the required signal conditioning. The rest of the signals have been omitted from the block diagram for the sake of simplicity but Table 6-1 shows the signal present in each pin of the medical connector.

MED-GLU Signal	Pin		MED-GLU Signal
VDD	1	2	GND
Not connected	3	4	Not connected
Counter Electrode Signal	5	6	Not connected
Working Electrode Signal	7	8	DAC (Voltage Reference)
OPAMP0 VOUT0	9	10	OPAMP1 VOUT1
OPAMP0 INN0-	11	12	OPAMP1 INN1-
OPAMP0 INP0+	13	14	OPAMP1 INP1+
TRIAMP0 INP0+	15	16	TRIAMP1 INP1+
TRIAMP0 INN0-	17	18	TRIAMP1 INN1-
TRIAMP0 VOUT0	19	20	TRIAMP1 VOUT1

Table 6-1 **Medical Connector 2x10 Pin Header Connections**

Notice from the block diagram in Figure 6-7 that in the absence of the MED-GLU module you can still run the application by using the simulated Working Electrode signal coming out of the DAC module by connecting a jumper wire between pin 7 of the medical connector and pin B32 of the elevator module in the tower system. The potentiometer is used in such situation to increase or decrease the simulated blood glucose level.

The communication with μC/Probe which will be used to display the results of the blood glucose meter is via the J-Link Ultra debug probe from IAR through the JTAG connector labeled as J23.

Figure 6-8 shows the MED-GLU module connected to the TWR-K53N512 controller in a tower system configuration.

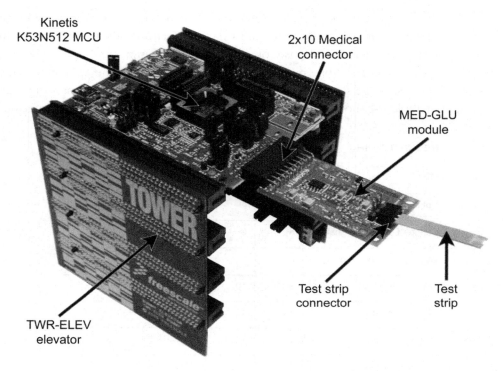

Figure 6-8 **MED-GLU and TWR-K53N512**

6-5 RUNNING THE EXAMPLE PROJECT

This section describes the steps you need to follow to run the blood glucose meter example. Start by connecting the MED-GLU module to the TWR-K53N512 controller through the 2x10 medical connector as shown in Figure 6-8.

The MED-GLU is compatible with the 3-contact-bars Optium blood glucose test strips from Abbott Diabetes Care. The test strips come individually wrapped in foil packets to avoid a reaction with oxygen in the air. *Do not unpack the test strip until you have completed all the following instructions.*

Assuming you have followed all the setup steps described in Chapter 4, "Setup" on page 779, proceed to connect one end of the IAR's J-Link Ultra for ARM debug probe to the JTAG connector on J23 of the TWR-K53N512 and the other end of the probe to any USB port available in your PC.

Run IAR's Embedded Workbench for ARM (EWARM) and open the workspace TWR-K53N512 at:

```
$\Micrium\Software\EvalBoards\Freescale\TWR-K53N512\IAR\
uC-OS-III-Book-Ex-Src.eww
```

In the workspace explorer window, select the tab for the project uC-OS-III-Ex2-BGM. The workspace window shows all of the files in the project which are sorted into groups represented by folder icons. Figure 6-9 shows the project files for uC-OS-III-Ex2-BGM in the workspace explorer window.

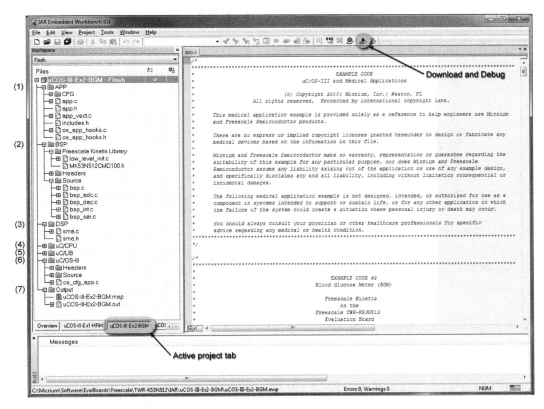

Figure 6-9 **Running the project with EWARM**

F6-9(1)   The **APP** group includes all of the application files for this example. The subgroup **CFG** includes the header files used to configure the application.

F6-9(2)   The **BSP** group contains the files that comprise the board support package. The board support package includes the code used to control the peripherals on the board. For this example, the software to control the LEDs, pushbuttons, ADCs, DACs, operational amplifiers and transimpedance amplifiers will be used. The subgroup Freescale Kinetis Library includes the header files for the Kinetis K50 family of microcontrollers.

F6-9(3)   The **DSP** group contains the files that define some of the Digital Signal Processing functions called by the application.

F6-9(4)   The **uC/CPU** group contains the µC/CPU source code.

F6-9(5)   The **uC/LIB** group contains the µC/LIB source code.

F6-9(6)   The **µC/OS-III** group contains the µCOS-III source code. In addition, the **os_cfg_app.c** file is included in this group to allow certain behavior to be defined at compile time.

F6-9(7)   The **Output** group contains the files generated by the compiler/linker.

Start the debugger by clicking the "Download and Debug" icon as shown in Figure 6-9. The application is programmed to the internal Flash of the K53N512 microcontroller and the debugger starts. The code automatically starts executing and stops at the **main()** function in the **app.c** file.

Click the "Go" icon in IAR Embedded Workbench's debugging tools to run the application as shown in Figure 6-10.

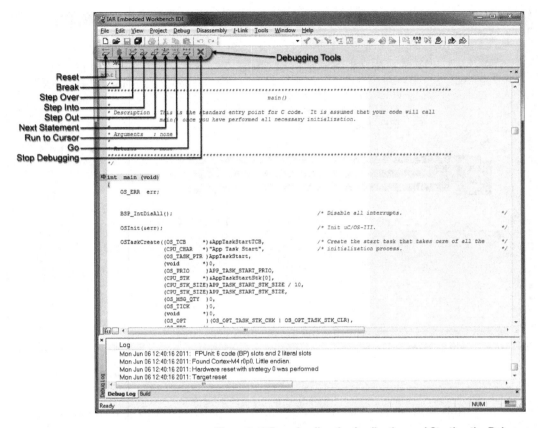

Figure 6-10 **Downloading the Application and Starting the Debugger**

You can test the application by starting µC/Probe and open the workspace for the Blood Glucose Meter at:

```
$\Micrium\Software\EvalBoards\Freescale\TWR-K53N512\IAR\
uC-OS-III-Book-Ex-Src\uC-OS-III-Ex2-BGM\uC-OS-III-Ex2-BGM-Probe.wsp
```

After µC/Probe starts, click the run button (green triangle). Once µC/Probe is running, you will see a screen similar to the one shown in Figure 6-11

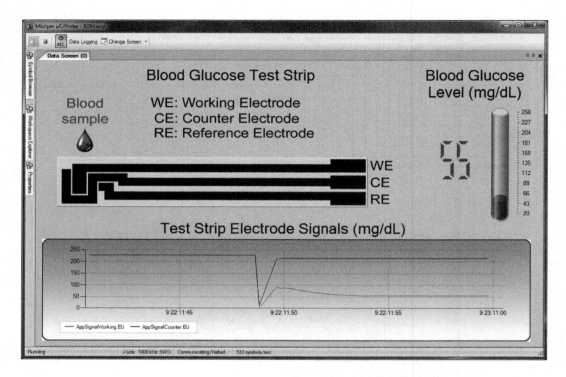

Figure 6-11 **µC/Probe Blood Glucose Meter Dashboard**

Press the pushbutton on the TWR-K53N512 board labeled as SW1 to start the application.

The application will wait for the detection of a valid test strip and a valid blood sample.

Unpack one of the test strips and insert it into the 3-contact connector in J4 of the MED-GLU as shown in Figure 6-8.

If you don't feel like lancing your finger to obtain a blood sample, you may use a control solution with a known glucose level. If you decide to test it with your own blood then first make sure your finger is clean, dry and warm. In order to help the blood flow, hang your arm down before lancing your finger and obtain the blood drop by following the instructions of the lancing device you were able to purchase. Get the blood drop to touch the white target area at the end of the test strip and the blood drop will be drawn into the test strip by capillary motion.

You will start seeing the Working and Counter Electrodes signal tracings in real time on the dashboard. The blood glucose level will be displayed in less than five seconds as shown in Figure 6-11.

According to the World Health Organization (WHO) the expected blood glucose range for a non-diabetic, non-pregnant fasting adult is 74-106 mg/dL and between one and two hours after a meal, the levels should be less than 160 mg/dL. *You should always consult your healthcare professional to determine the range that is appropriate for you.*

6-6 HOW THE CODE WORKS

The blood glucose meter application consists of three different tasks:

▪ User IF task: The user interface task monitors the state of the two pushbuttons onboard the TWR-K53N512. The pushbuttons are used to either start or stop the application. The task is defined by **AppTaskUserIF()** in **app.c**.

▪ Sim task: The simulator task monitors the state of the potentiometer and updates the amplitude of a Working Electrode simulated signal generated by the DAC according to the position of the potentiometer. The task is defined by **AppTaskSim()** in **app.c**.

▪ DAQ task: The data acquisition task is the main task in the application and implements the state machine that processes the analog input samples to calculate the blood glucose level. The task is defined by **AppTaskDAQ()** in **app.c**.

The interaction among the different tasks is facilitated by the use of μC/OS-III's task semaphores and task message queues and it is illustrated in Figure 6-12.

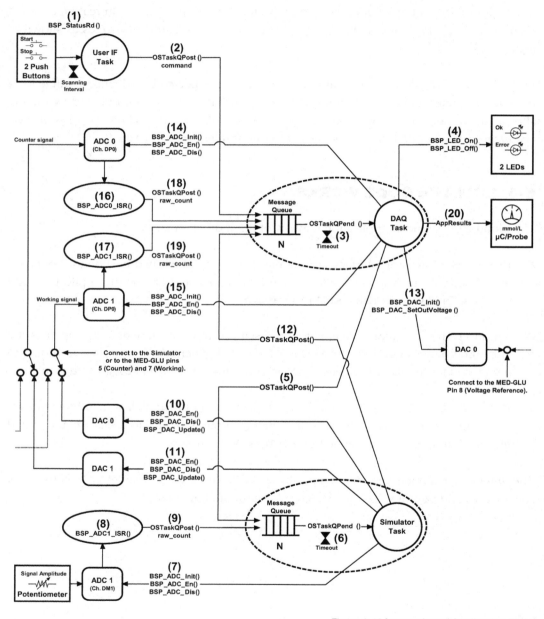

Figure 6-12 **Interaction of Application Tasks**

F6-12(1)   The state of the push buttons is monitored by the user IF task at a scanning interval defined by **BSP_STATUS_CHECK_INTERVAL**. See **AppTaskUserIF()** in **app.c** and **BSP_StatusRd()** in **bsp.c**.

F6-12(2)   Depending on the pushbutton pressed by the user a message from the user IF task to either start or stop the application is posted to the DAQ task's built-in message queue by calling **OSTaskQPost()**. See **AppTaskUserIF()** in **app.c**.

F6-12(3)   The DAQ task can receive data messages directly from the ADCs ISRs or command messages from the other two tasks. When **OSTaskQPend()** is called, the message is retrieved and processed in two different ways depending on the sender and the type of message. If the message comes from one of the ADC's ISR then the message is processed by calling the function **AppTaskDAQ_ProcessData()** and if the message comes from any other task then the message is processed by calling the function **AppTaskDAQ_ProcessCmd()** in **app.c**.

F6-12(4)   If the message retrieved by the DAQ task is a command to start the blood glucose measurement then the DAQ task turns off the LEDs by calling the function **BSP_LED_Off()** in **bsp.c**.

F6-12(5)   If the message retrieved by the DAQ task is a command to start the blood glucose measurement in simulation mode then the DAQ task posts a message to the sim task's built-in message queue to start the simulator. See **AppTaskDAQ()** in **app.c** and **AppTaskDAQ_ProcessCmd()** in **app.c**.

F6-12(6)   In similar fashion, the sim task can receive messages directly from the ADC1's ISR or from the DAQ task. When **OSTaskQPend()** is called, the message is retrieved and processed in different ways depending on the sender. The sim task retrieves the received message from its message queue and proceeds according to the command issued by the DAQ task as follows:

F6-12(7)   If the message contains a start command then the sim task starts ADC1 channel DM1 in order to read the potentiometer. See **AppTaskSim()** in **app.c**.

F6-12(8)   The CPU is interrupted by the completion of a conversion of ADC1 Channel DM1 and the interrupt is handled by **BSP_ADC1_ISR** in **bsp_adc.c**.

6

F6-12(9)   The ADC1 ISR posts the result of the conversion in the form of a 16-bit raw count to the sim task's built-in message queue by calling the function `OSTaskQPost()`. See `BSP_ADC1_ISR()` in `bsp_adc.c`.

F6-12(10)   The sim task retrieves the message from the queue and configures the DAC0 to output a simulated Working Electrode waveform at an amplitude proportional to the raw count of the ADC1 channel DM1. See `AppTaskSim()` in `app.c`.

F6-12(11)   The sim task retrieves the message from the queue and configures the DAC1 to output a simulated Counter Electrode waveform. See `AppTaskSim()` in `app.c`.

F6-12(12)   The sim task posts a message to the DAQ task's built-in message queue notifying the DAQ task that the simulator is running. See `AppTaskSim()` in `app.c`.

F6-12(13)   The DAQ task retrieves the message from the queue and initializes DAC0 to output a voltage reference to drive the test strip and trigger the chemical reaction. See `AppTaskDAQ()` and `AppTaskDAQ_ProcessCmd()` in `app.c`.

F6-12(14)   The DAQ task retrieves the message from the queue and enables ADC0 channel DP0 to convert the Counter Electrode signal. See `AppTaskDAQ()`, `AppTaskDAQ_ProcessCmd()` and `AppTaskDAQ_ExecCmd()` in `app.c`.

F6-12(15)   The DAQ task retrieves the message from the queue and enables ADC1 channel DP0 to convert the Working Electrode signal. See `AppTaskDAQ()`, `AppTaskDAQ_ProcessCmd()` and `AppTaskDAQ_ExecCmd()` in `app.c`.

F6-12(16)   The CPU is interrupted by the completion of a conversion of ADC0 channel DP0 and the interrupt is handled by `BSP_ADC0_ISR` in `bsp_adc.c`.

F6-12(17)   About the same time, the CPU is interrupted by the completion of a conversion of ADC1 channel DP0 and the interrupt is handled by `BSP_ADC1_ISR()` in `bsp_adc.c`.

F6-12(18)   The ADC0 ISR posts the result of the conversion in the form of a 16-bit raw count to the DAQ task's built-in message queue by calling the function `OSTaskQPost()`. See `BSP_ADC0_ISR()` in `bsp_adc.c`.

F6-12(19)   The ADC1 ISR posts the result of the conversion in the form of a 16-bit raw count to the DAQ task's built-in message queue by calling the function `OSTaskQPost()`. See `BSP_ADC1_ISR()` in `bsp_adc.c`.

F6-12(20)   The DAQ task retrieves the message from the queue and uses the raw counts from ADC0 and ADC1 to calculate the blood glucose level and display the value in µC/Probe by calling the function **AppTaskDAQ_ProcessData()** and **AppCalcResults()** in **app.c**.

The state machine that processes every sample in **AppTaskDAQ_ProcessData()** is illustrated in Figure 6-13.

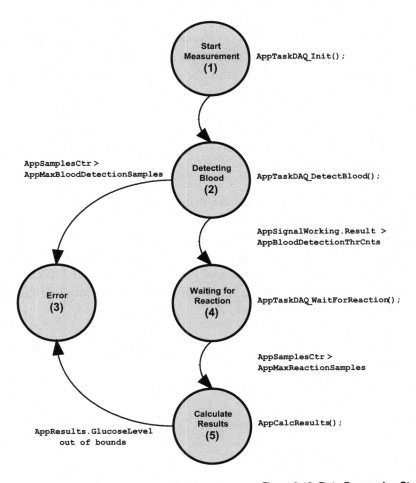

Figure 6-13 **Data Processing State Machine**

F6-13(1)   Once the start button is pressed, the application starts the blood glucose level measurement by calling **AppTaskDAQ_Init()** to initialize some global variables.

F6-13(2)   The next state keeps monitoring the amplitude of the signal coming out of the Working Electrode until the amplitude is above a threshold that indicates the presence of a valid test strip and a valid blood sample. This threshold is defined in millivolts by **APP_BLOOD_DETECT_THR_MVOLTS**. The function that smooths the signal and detects the blood sample is called **AppTaskDAQ_DetectBlood()**.

F6-13(3)   An error occurs in case the test strip is not valid or the blood sample is not enough. Such conditions can be detected by monitoring the amplitude of both, the Working and Counter Electrodes. The same error condition occurs if the calculated blood glucose level is out of the valid ranges defined in mg/dL by **APP_MIN_GLUCOSE_LEVEL_MGDL** and **APP_MAX_GLUCOSE_LEVEL_MGDL**.

F6-13(4)   The chemical reaction takes place in about five seconds and in this state, every sample from the Working Electrode is inserted into a simple moving average filter with a window size of about one second defined in number of samples by **APP_SMA_WIN_SIZE**.

F6-13(5)   The algorithm to calculate the actual blood glucose level is quite simple. A Simple Moving Average (SMA) of the voltage at the Working Electrode with a window sized at **APP_SMA_WIN_SIZE** samples is calculated over the five seconds following the beginning of the chemical reaction. The result of the SMA filter is stored in **AppSignalWorking.Result**. The blood glucose level in mg/dL is calculated in terms of the voltage at the Working Electrode by the following transfer function:

Blood Glucose Level = 90.2643 * Working Electrode Voltage - 75.2758

6-7 SUMMARY

This chapter explained the anatomy and physiology of the organs involved in the regulation of glucose in the blood and the theory of operation of a blood glucose meter including the hardware and software.

This example application demonstrated how simple it is to implement a blood glucose meter using a combination of Micrium's µC/OS-III and Freescale hardware. It also demonstrated one of the most important features of µC/OS-III: *Task Message Queues.*

Message queues are built into each task and the user can send messages directly to a task from another task or an ISR. You will notice that task message queues are used not only in this example but all the rest of examples because they allow the developer to encapsulate each task's functionality into a clean and simple message-based API. For example, we used the DAQ task's built-in message queue as a means to receive different types of commands from other tasks to perform an action like start or stop the simulator, start or stop the data acquisition and process samples from the ADC's ISRs. Inter-task communication via task message queues is discussed in the first part of the book section 15-3 "Task Message Queue" on page 312.

Thanks to the task-oriented approach of this example, adding more features to the blood glucose meter is easy to accomplish. The first obvious feature to add is USB or bluetooth connectivity to make the blood glucose meter act as an accessory of computer-like devices such as smartphones or tablet PCs. This configuration takes advantage of the GUI and internet capabilities of the smartphone or tablet PC.

For a more stand-alone approach, LCD or any other type of display control is also a great candidate to encapsulate into a task and use the task message queue to receive commands to update the display.

If you want to take the design to the ultimate level you can imagine closing the control loop by not only reading the blood glucose level but also controlling an insulin infusion pump.

Freescale and Micrium support the addition of other functionality to this blood glucose meter by offering more tower system compatible peripherals and software stacks. Visit the Freescale and Micrium websites to learn more about other products that can help you take your design to the next level.

7

Pulse Oximeter

A pulse oximeter is a device that measures the amount of oxygen transported in the arterial blood. This relative measure is known as *Oxygen Saturation* (SpO_2) and is given as a percentage. Figure 7-1 shows an example of a commercial pulse oximeter displaying the SpO_2% at the top and the heart rate in beats-per-minute at the bottom.

This chapter demonstrates a basic implementation of a pulse oximeter built using µC/OS-III and Freescale products.

The chapter starts with an illustrated description of the mechanism of transport of oxygen from the air to the tissue cells known as respiration. The next section continues the introduction, but with emphasis on the acquisition and calculation of the SpO_2 and presents the design of a pulse oximeter (POX). The last part of the chapter deals with using the tools to run the example and a description of how the code works.

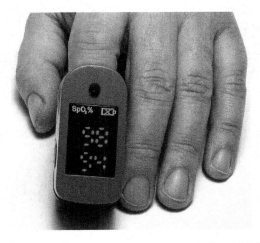

Figure 7-1 **Commercial pulse oximeter**

7-1 RESPIRATION

Every cell in the body requires oxygen to perform their function. The main role of the respiratory system is to replenish the blood with oxygen from the air in order for the blood to carry the oxygen to all the cells in the body. This is done through the exchange of two gases: oxygen and carbon dioxide. We inhale oxygen and exhale carbon dioxide by breathing as we will explain in the next paragraphs.

Figure 7-2 shows that breathing is accommodated by the muscular contraction of the *diaphragm* and other muscles in the chest and abdomen. The diaphragm is a sheet of muscles that extends across the bottom of the chest cavity. When the diaphragm contracts, it actually pulls down, lowering the internal air pressure and leaving more space for the lungs to fill with air. Since the air pressure in the exterior is higher, the air gets sucked in through the *nasal passage* (nose) and *oral cavity* (mouth) where it gets conditioned for temperature and moisture and filtered from any particles like dust.

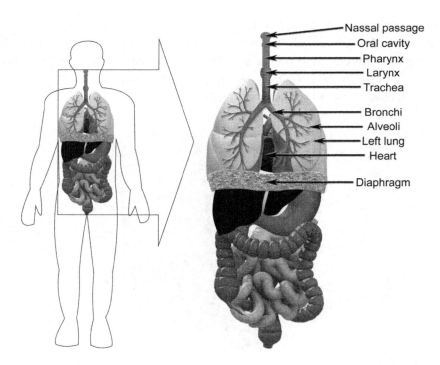

Figure 7-2 **The respiratory system**

Figure 7-3 below shows that the air then passes through a part of the throat known as *pharynx* and then to an organ in the neck known as the *larynx* which among other functions it is involved in protecting the rest of the respiratory system against food aspiration. The air continues to go down a tube that enters the chest cavity known as the *trachea*. There, the trachea divides into two smaller tubes that lead to the left and right *lungs* known as the *bronchi*. Inside the lungs the bronchi branch into millions of even smaller tubes which connect to tiny air filled sacs called *alveoli*. Each alveolus is wrapped around a mesh of *capillaries* which are the smallest blood vessels and are the point where deoxygenated and oxygenated blood meet.

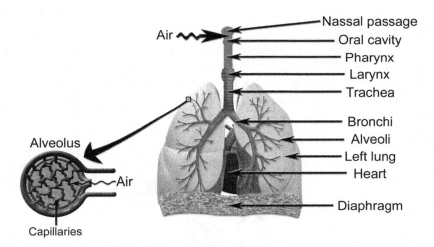

Figure 7-3 **The respiratory system, inhalation.**

Figure 7-4 shows that the air fills the alveoli and since the partial pressure of oxygen in the air is higher than the one in the blood, the oxygen diffuses into the blood and binds to a protein molecule that is carried by the *red blood cells* known as *hemoglobin* (Hb). When the hemoglobin binds to a molecule of oxygen, it forms what is known as *oxyhemoglobin* ($Hb-O_2$) which has a bright red color. At the same time, the partial pressure of carbon dioxide in the air in the alveoli is less than the partial pressure of carbon dioxide in the blood, so carbon dioxide diffuses out from the red blood cells and into the air in the alveoli.

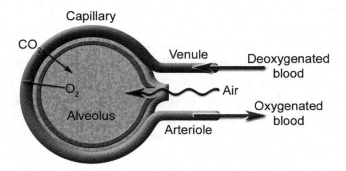

Figure 7-4 **Exchange of gases at the alveolus.**

Figure 7-5 shows how the oxygenated blood flows through the pulmonary veins into the heart where it gets handled by the left atrium and left ventricle to be pumped through the aorta to all the rest of the body. We do not mention the right atrium and ventricle on purpose because this explanation only focuses on the trip taken by the oxygen from the air to the tissue cells. But as we saw in section 5-1 "The Heart" on page 791, both pumping actions happen at the same time.

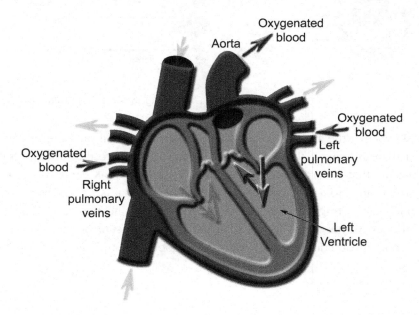

Figure 7-5 **Oxygenated blood transportation by the heart.**

Figure 7-6 shows how the blood makes its way to the body cells through the capillaries where it exchanges oxygen and carbon dioxide by diffusion; that is, the partial pressure of oxygen in the blood is higher than the one in the body tissues so the oxyhemoglobin releases its oxygen and the oxygen diffuses into the body tissues. When the oxyhemoglobin loses its bind to oxygen, it forms what is called *deoxyhemoglobin* (Hb) which has a color between blue and purple.

At the same time, the partial pressure of carbon dioxide in the blood is lower than the partial pressure of carbon dioxide in the body tissues, so carbon dioxide diffuses into the blood and binds to the hemoglobin to form *carbaminohemoglobin*.

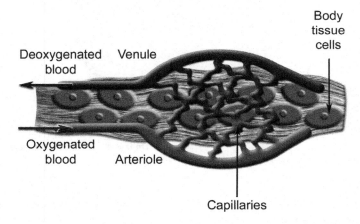

Figure 7-6 **Exchange of gases at the tissues.**

As shown in Figure 7-7, the deoxygenated blood is carried through the veins back to the heart where it gets handled by the right side chambers and pumped through the left and right pulmonary arteries back into the lungs.

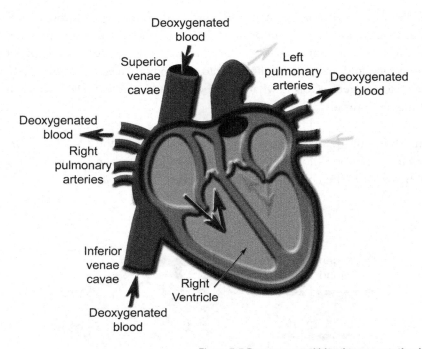

Deoxygenated
blood

Superior
venae
cavae

Left
pulmonary
arteries

Deoxygenated
blood

Deoxygenated
blood

Right
pulmonary
arteries

Inferior
venae
cavae

Right
Ventricle

Deoxygenated
blood

Figure 7-7 **Deoxygenated blood transportation by the heart.**

Figure 7-8 shows that the cycle is completed by the relaxation of the diaphragm which makes the chest cavity smaller again. The muscles squeeze the lungs and the carbonated air is pushed out of the body through the same passages it came in. The breathing cycle is repeated about 20 times per minute and the frequency is controlled by a complex system that makes sure the levels of carbon dioxide in the blood are maintained below a certain threshold. Even though the breathing frequency can also be changed voluntarily, the system is considered mostly autonomous.

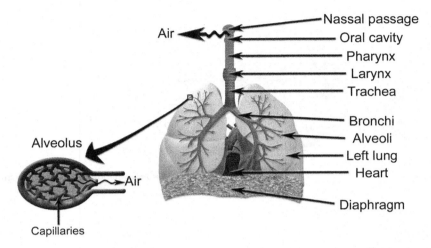

Air — Nassal passage
— Oral cavity
— Pharynx
— Larynx
— Trachea

— Bronchi
— Alveoli
— Left lung
— Heart

Alveolus

Air

— Diaphragm

Capillaries

Figure 7-8 **The respiratory system, exhalation.**

7-2 PULSE OXIMETRY

As we learned in the last section, the blood, and more specifically the hemoglobin, can be saturated with oxygen in the form of oxyhemoglobin (Hb-O_2) or desaturated of oxygen in the form of deoxyhemoglobin (Hb). The determination of the oxygen saturation level provides very important information about the efficiency of the respiratory system function in the exchange of gases and the performance of the circulatory system to carry the gases to and from the tissues. Healthy individuals show arterial oxygen saturation levels between 97% and 99% and the values can become unstable as side effects of anesthesia and / or trauma in clinical settings like an intensive care unit, operating room and emergency room. In such situations the readings off a pulse oximeter help the doctors respond appropriately like for example controlling the concentration of oxygen to be administered to the patient. For that reason, pulse oximetry is considered one of the most important monitoring tools during any procedure that involves the use of general or regional anesthesia.

A pulse oximeter is a device with two LEDs and a photodiode that analyzes the absorption of the light transmitted through the finger or the earlobe as shown in Figure 7-9.

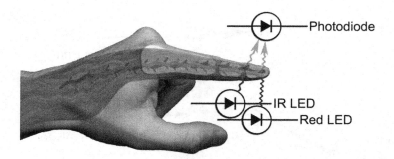

Figure 7-9 **Two-wavelength pulse oximetry in the finger**

Pulse oximetry is a technique that relies on the measurement of the absorption of electromagnetic radiation (light) due to its interaction with the hemoglobin. The *extinction coefficient* is a measure of the absorption of a solution per unit path length and concentration. In the case of oxyhemoglobin ($Hb\text{-}O_2$) and deoxyhemoglobin (Hb), the extinction coefficient is different at specific wavelengths as shown in Figure 7-10.

In pulse oximetry, when optimizing sensitivity, the best wavelengths to use are the 660 nm (red) and the 900 nm (infrared) not only because of the large difference in the extinction coefficient of oxyhemoglobin and deoxyhemoglobin at 660 nm but also because the extinction coefficients at 900 nm are about the same. Figure 7-10 clearly shows that when the blood is saturated with oxygen ($Hb\text{-}O_2$), it presents a bright red color because there is not much absorption at 660 nm. Similarly, when the blood is deoxygenated (Hb) it turns into a dark color because there is a lot of absorption at 660 nm. Meanwhile, the absorption of both oxyhemoglobin and deoxyhemoglobin at 900 nm is about the same.

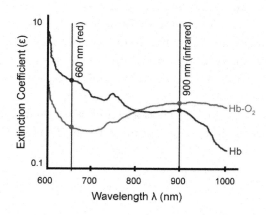

Figure 7-10 **Extinction coefficient of $Hb\text{-}O_2$ and Hb at different wavelengths**

The value calculated by a pulse oximeter is known as oxygen saturation (SpO_2) and by definition is calculated as the oxygen concentration expressed as a percentage of the maximum concentration of oxygen that can be carried by the blood:

$$SpO_2 = \frac{\text{Concentration of Oxyhemoglobin}}{\text{Total concentration of Hemoglobin}} \times 100$$

$$SpO_2 = \frac{c_{Hb\text{-}O2}}{c_{Hb\text{-}O2} + c_{Hb}} \times 100$$

Figure 7-11 shows that as the beam of light from the LEDs travels through the finger tissues, the light intensity for the most part decreases logarithmically with the path length and the concentration of the molecule in question (Hb and Hb-O_2) according to the *Beer-Lambert law*:

$$\varepsilon * c * l = - \log_{10} (I_{final} / I_{init})$$

Where:

ε: Extinction coefficient (see Figure 7-10).

c: Concentration (more molecules of Hb absorbing will result in more photons absorbed).

l: Path length (longer path lengths will result in more photons absorbed).

I_{init}: Initial intensity of the light (incident light).

I_{final}: Final intensity of the light (transmitted light).

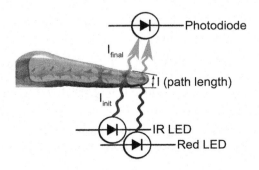

Figure 7-11 **Beer lambert law**

Because $10^c / 10^d = 10^{c-d}$ then $\log_{10} (x/y) = \log_{10} (x) - \log_{10} (y)$ and:

$$\varepsilon * c * l = - \log_{10} (I_{final}) + \log_{10} (I_{init})$$

$$c = \frac{- \log_{10} (I_{final}) + \log_{10} (I_{init})}{\varepsilon * l}$$

Thus the concentrations for the hemoglobin and oxyhemoglobin being transilluminated by the red and infrared light respectively are:

$$c_{Hb} = \frac{- \log_{10} (I_{red\text{-}final}) + \log_{10} (I_{red\text{-}init})}{\varepsilon_{Hb} * l}$$

$$c_{HbO2} = \frac{- \log_{10} (I_{ir\text{-}final}) + \log_{10} (I_{ir\text{-}init})}{\varepsilon_{Hb\text{-}O_2} * l}$$

If the oxygen saturation (SpO$_2$) is defined as the ratio:

$$SpO_2 = \frac{\text{Concentration of Oxyhemoglobin}}{\text{Total concentration of Hemoglobin}} * 100 \%$$

Then SpO$_2$ expressed in terms of the light intensities, path lengths and extinction coefficients is:

$$SpO_2 = \frac{\dfrac{- \log_{10} (I_{red\text{-}final}) + \log_{10} (I_{red\text{-}init})}{\varepsilon_{Hb\text{-}O2} * l}}{\dfrac{- \log_{10} (I_{red\text{-}final}) + \log_{10} (I_{red\text{-}init})}{\varepsilon_{Hb\text{-}O2} * l} - \dfrac{\log_{10} (I_{ir\text{-}final}) + \log_{10} (I_{ir\text{-}init})}{\varepsilon_{Hb} * l}}$$

The extinction coefficients are constants, the path length is the same, the final intensities are those measured at the output of the photodiode and the initial intensities can be assumed to be the level of the DC component just because over 90% of the absorption is due to the skin and tissues as we will explain in the next paragraph.

Let's assume we measure the final intensity of an LED that is turned on for at least two seconds and plot the initial and final intensities over time as shown in Figure 7-12. Notice that most of the absorption is due to the interaction of the light with the skin and tissue, while only a small part is due to the venous and arterial blood. Pulse oximetry relies on the

AC component of the final intensity of the light which is due to the absorption by the oxyhemoglobin that gets added at every heartbeat. This is the reason why the initial intensities can be assumed to be the level of the DC component.

That and all the assumptions mentioned before, specially the fact that the SpO_2 percentage is just a ratio can simplify the formula to:

$$SpO_2 = \frac{\log_{10}(I_{red\text{-}final})}{\log_{10}(I_{ir\text{-}final})} * 100 \%$$

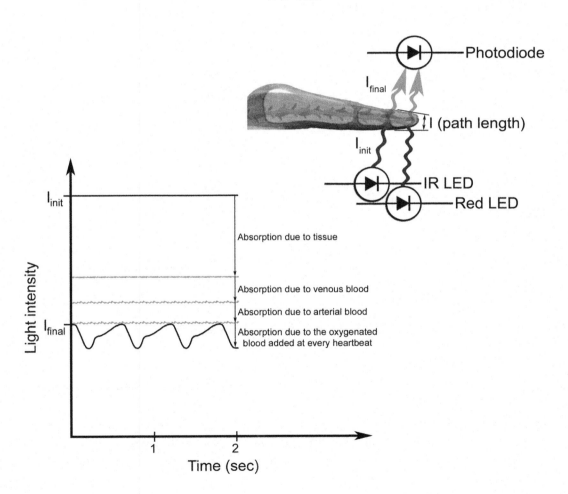

Figure 7-12 **Light intensity over time**

7-3 PULSE OXIMETER DESIGN

The analog front end of a pulse oximeter is fairly simple and includes an instrumentation circuit similar to the one used in the previous chapter which converted current to voltage known as transimpedance amplifier. The output of the photodiode (anode and cathode) is connected to the input of the transimpedance amplifier and an analog signal multiplexor routes the output to one of two channels (Red or IR LED).

Each analog channel has a low pass filter with a cutoff frequency of 6Hz in order to extract the DC component as shown in Figure 7-13.

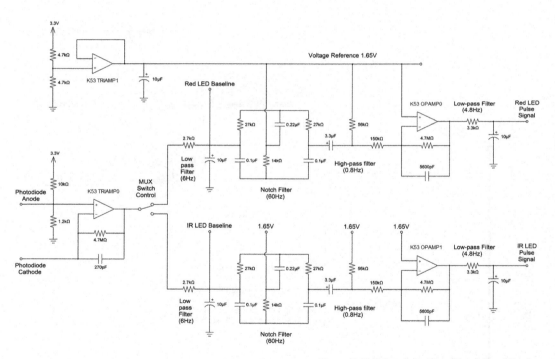

Figure 7-13 **Pulse Oximeter Signal Conditioning**

In similar fashion to the heart rate monitor's processing of the baseline signal in Chapter 5, "ECG / Heart Rate Monitor" on page 791, the signal out of the low-pass filter needs to be monitored and the intensity of the LEDs needs to be adjusted depending on the level of this baseline signal.

A notch filter attenuates any 60Hz noise and a band-pass filter not only keeps the signal within the bandwidth of interest (0.8Hz - 4.8Hz) but also provides the last stage of amplification.

The other part of the analog front includes an H-Bridge based LED driver circuit shown in Figure 7-14.

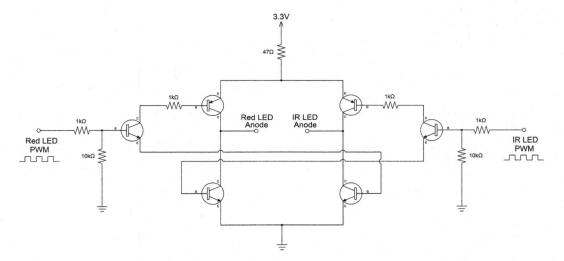

Figure 7-14 **H-Bridge LED driver**

The intensity of the LEDs is controlled by the duty cycle of a PWM signal that feeds this H-Bridge circuit. This set of bipolar transistors is arranged in such a way that a change in the PWM signal's duty cycle results in a proportional change in the current sourced to the anode of the LEDs.

Freescale offers an analog module with a medical connector compatible with the TWR-K53N512 medical board that implements this type of analog front end called MED-SPO2.

The complete system including the TWR-K53N512 and MED-SPO2 is illustrated as a block diagram in Figure 7-15. The two pushbuttons onboard the TWR-K53N512 are used to either start or stop the application and the LEDs are used to indicate an error by turning on the orange LED and to indicate the detection of the heartbeat by blinking the yellow LED.

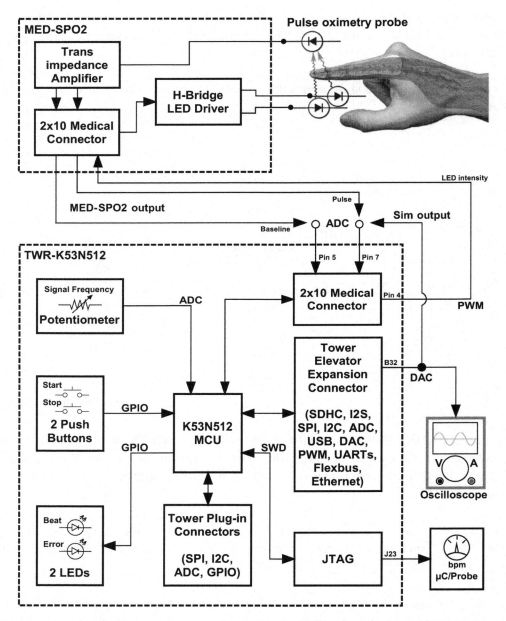

Figure 7-15 **Pulse Oximeter Block Diagram**

The 2x10 medical connector of the MED-SPO2 not only provides connectivity with the TWR-K53N512 board to make the Baseline and Pulse signals available to the ADC modules but also allows the use of the on-chip op-amps and transimpedance amplifiers of the Kinetis 32-bit microcontroller to implement the required signal conditioning. The rest of the signals have been omitted from the block diagram for the sake of simplicity but Table 7-1 shows the signal present in each pin of the medical connector.

MED-SPO2 Signal	Pin		MED-SPO2 Signal
VDD	1	2	GND
MUX Switch Control	3	4	PWM Signal
Baseline Signal	5	6	Not connected
Pulse Signal	7	8	Not connected
OPAMP0 VOUT0	9	10	OPAMP1 VOUT1
OPAMP0 INN0-	11	12	OPAMP1 INN1-
OPAMP0 INP0+	13	14	OPAMP1 INP1+
TRIAMP0 INP0+	15	16	TRIAMP1 INP1+
TRIAMP0 INN0-	17	18	TRIAMP1 INN1-
TRIAMP0 VOUT0	19	20	TRIAMP1 VOUT1

Table 7-1 **Medical Connector 2x10 Pin Header Connections**

Notice from the block diagram in Figure 7-15 that in the absence of the MED-SPO2 module you can still run the application by using the simulated pulse signal coming out of the DAC module by connecting a jumper wire between pin 7 of the medical connector and pin B32 of the elevator module in the tower system. The potentiometer is used in such situation to increase or decrease the simulated heart rate.

The communication with μC/Probe which will be used to display the results of the pulse oximeter is via the J-Link Ultra debug probe from IAR through the JTAG connector labeled as J23.

Figure 7-16 shows the MED-SPO2 module connected to the TWR-K53N512 controller in a tower system configuration.

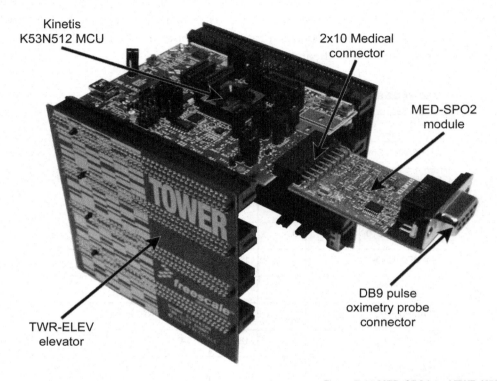

Figure 7-16 **MED-SPO2 and TWR-K53N512**

7-4 RUNNING THE EXAMPLE PROJECT

This section describes the steps you need to follow to run the pulse oximeter example. Start by connecting the MED-SPO2 module to the TWR-K53N512 controller through the 2x10 medical connector as shown in Figure 7-16.

The MED-SPO2 module is compatible with the 9-pin D-SUB male connector pulse oximeter probe from Nellcor shown in Figure 7-17. The wavelengths of the light emitted by this sensor are 660 nm for the Red LED and 900 nm for the IR LED just as previously illustrated in Figure 7-10.

Figure 7-17 **9-pin connector Pulse Oximetry Probe from Nellcor**

Assuming you have followed all the setup steps described in Chapter 4, "Setup" on page 779, proceed to connect one end of the IAR's J-Link Ultra for ARM debug probe to the JTAG connector on J23 of the TWR-K53N512 and the other end of the probe to any USB port available in your PC.

Run IAR's Embedded Workbench for ARM (EWARM) and open the workspace TWR-K53N512 at:

```
$\Micrium\Software\EvalBoards\Freescale\TWR-K53N512\IAR\
uC-OS-III-Book-Ex-Src.eww
```

In the workspace explorer window, select the tab for the project uC-OS-III-Ex3-POX. The workspace window shows all of the files in the project which are sorted into groups represented by folder icons. Figure 7-18 shows the project files for uC-OS-III-Ex3-POX in the workspace explorer window.

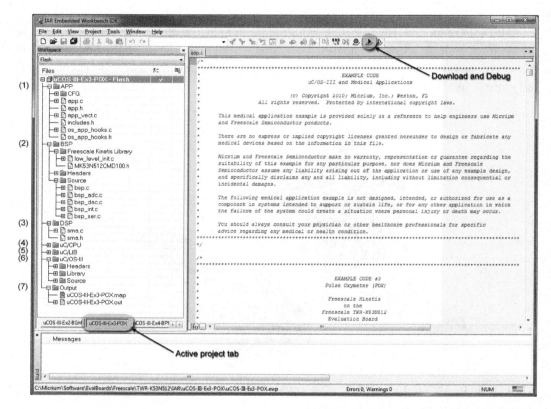

Figure 7-18 **Running the project with EWARM**

F7-18(1)   The **APP** group includes all of the application files for this example. The subgroup **CFG** includes the header files used to configure the application.

F7-18(2)   The **BSP** group contains the files that comprise the board support package. The board support package includes the code used to control the peripherals on the board. For this example, the software to control the LEDs, pushbuttons, ADCs, DACs, operational amplifiers and transimpedance amplifiers will be used. The subgroup Freescale Kinetis Library includes the header files for the Kinetis K50 family of microcontrollers.

F7-18(3)   The **DSP** group contains the files that define some of the Digital Signal Processing functions called by the application.

F7-18(4)   The **uC/CPU** group contains the µC/CPU source code.

F7-18(5)   The **uC/LIB** group contains the µC/LIB source code.

F7-18(6)   The **µC/OS-III** group contains the µCOS-III source code. In addition, the **os_cfg_app.c** file is included in this group to allow certain behavior to be defined at compile time.

F7-18(7)   The **Output** group contains the files generated by the compiler/linker.

Start the debugger by clicking the "Download and Debug" icon as shown in Figure 7-18. The application is programmed to the internal Flash of the K53N512 microcontroller and the debugger starts. The code automatically starts executing and stops at the **main()** function in the **app.c** file.

Click the "Go" icon in IAR Embedded Workbench's debugging tools to run the application as shown in Figure 7-19.

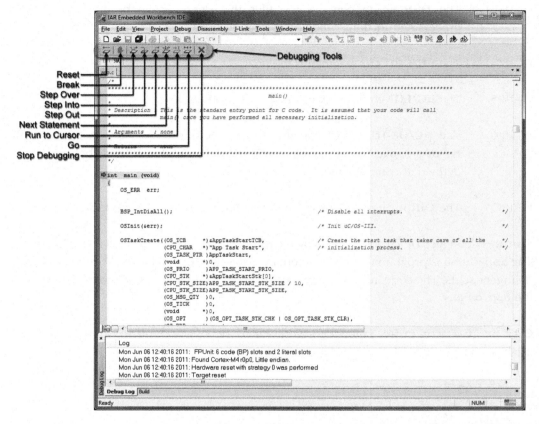

Figure 7-19 **Downloading the Application and Starting the Debugger**

You can test the application by starting µC/Probe and open the workspace for the Pulse Oximeter at:

`$\Micrium\Software\EvalBoards\Freescale\TWR-K53N512\IAR\`
`uC-OS-III-Book-Ex-Src\uC-OS-III-Ex3-POX\uC-OS-III-Ex3-POX-Probe.wsp`

After µC/Probe starts, click the run button (green triangle). Once µC/Probe is running, you will see a screen similar to the one shown in Figure 7-20.

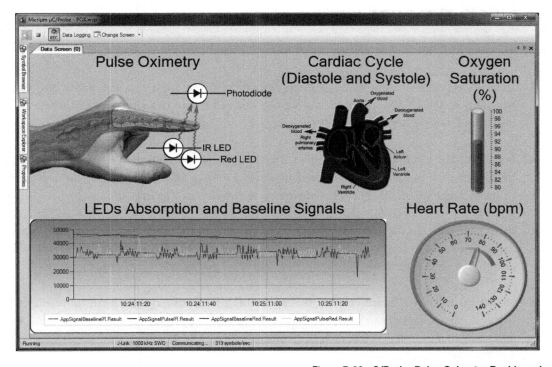

Figure 7-20 **µC/Probe Pulse Oximeter Dashboard**

Press the pushbutton on the TWR-K53N512 board labeled as SW1 to start the application.

The application will run indefinitely until you press the pushbutton on the TWR-K53N512 board labeled as SW2 to stop the application.

Place your finger in the pulse oximetry probe and watch in real time how the baseline signals for the Red and IR LEDs move around in an effort to optimize the intensity of the LEDs for the color of your skin and the size of your finger. It takes a few seconds for the system to adjust the intensities and then you should be able to see your heart rate displayed in the gauge and your oxygen saturation in the vertical meter. An animation of the heart during the systole and diastole phases of your own heart is shown to demonstrate one of the features of µC/Probe.

7-5 HOW THE CODE WORKS

The pulse oximeter application consists of four different tasks:

- User IF task: The user interface task monitors the state of the two pushbuttons onboard the TWR-K53N512. The pushbuttons are used to either start or stop the application. The task is defined by `AppTaskUserIF()` in `app.c`.

- Sim task: The simulator task monitors the state of the potentiometer and updates the frequency of a pulse simulated signal generated by the DAC according to the position of the potentiometer. The task is defined by `AppTaskSim()` in `app.c`.

- DAQ task: The data acquisition task is the main task in the application and implements the state machine that processes the analog input samples to calculate the heart rate and the oxygen saturation. The task is defined by `AppTaskDAQ()` in `app.c`.

- Heartbeat task: The heartbeat task is responsible for controlling the heart animation in μC/Probe by updating the value of the global variable `AppCardiacCycleState` that can take one of three states: Diastole, Systole or None. The heartbeat task is defined by `AppTaskHeartbeat()` in `app.c`

The interaction among the different tasks is facilitated by the use of μC/OS-III's task semaphores and task message queues and it is illustrated in Figure 7-21.

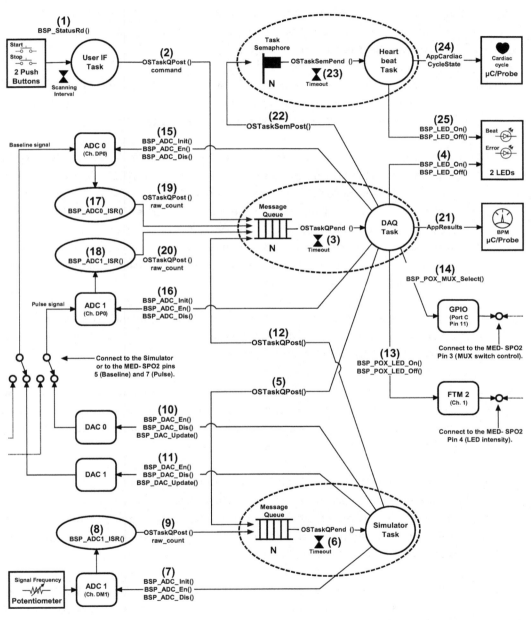

Figure 7-21 **Interaction of Application Tasks**

F7-21(1)   The state of the push buttons is monitored by the user IF task at a scanning interval defined by **BSP_STATUS_CHECK_INTERVAL**. See **AppTaskUserIF()** in **app.c** and **BSP_StatusRd()** in **bsp.c**.

F7-21(2)   Depending on the pushbutton pressed by the user a message from the user IF task to either start or stop the application is posted to the DAQ task's built-in message queue by calling **OSTaskQPost()**. See **AppTaskUserIF()** in **app.c**.

F7-21(3)   The DAQ task can receive data messages directly from the ADCs ISRs or command messages from the other two tasks. When **OSTaskQPend()** is called, the message is retrieved and processed in two different ways depending on the sender and the type of message. If the message comes from one of the ADC's ISR then the message is processed by calling the function **AppTaskDAQ_ProcessData()** and if the message comes from any other task then the message is processed by calling the function **AppTaskDAQ_ProcessCmd()** in **app.c**.

F7-21(4)   If the message retrieved by the DAQ task is a command to start the pulse oximetry monitoring then the DAQ task turns off the LEDs by calling the function **BSP_LED_Off()** in **bsp.c**.

F7-21(5)   If the message retrieved by the DAQ task is a command to start the pulse oximetry monitoring in simulation mode then the DAQ task posts a message to the sim task's built-in message queue to start the simulator. See **AppTaskDAQ()** in **app.c** and **AppTaskDAQ_ProcessCmd()** in **app.c**.

F7-21(6)   In similar fashion, the sim task can receive messages directly from the ADC1's ISR or from the DAQ task. When **OSTaskQPend()** is called, the message is retrieved and processed in different ways depending on the sender. The sim task retrieves the received message from its message queue and proceeds according to the command issued by the DAQ task as follows:

F7-21(7)   If the message contains a start command then the sim task starts ADC1 channel DM1 in order to read the potentiometer. See **AppTaskSim()** in **app.c**.

F7-21(8)   The CPU is interrupted by the completion of a conversion of ADC1 Channel DM1 and the interrupt is handled by **BSP_ADC1_ISR()** in **bsp_adc.c**.

F7-21(9)   The ADC1 ISR posts the result of the conversion in the form of a 16-bit raw count to the sim task's built-in message queue by calling the function **OSTaskQPost()**. See **BSP_ADC1_ISR()** in **bsp_adc.c**.

F7-21(10) The sim task retrieves the message from the queue and configures the DAC0 to output a simulated pulse waveform. See **AppTaskSim()** in **app.c**.

F7-21(11) The sim task retrieves the message from the queue and configures the DAC1 to output a simulated baseline waveform at a rate proportional to the raw count of the ADC1 channel DM1. See **AppTaskSim()** in **app.c**.

F7-21(12) The sim task posts a message to the DAQ task's built-in message queue notifying the DAQ task that the simulator is running. See **AppTaskSim()** in **app.c**.

F7-21(13) The DAQ task retrieves the message from the queue and initializes FlexTimer FTM2 to output a PWM signal to drive the Red and IR LEDs. See **AppTaskDAQ()** and **AppTaskDAQ_ProcessCmd()** in **app.c**.

F7-21(14) The DAQ task retrieves the message from the queue and sets/clears pin 11 of the GPIO in Port C to control the selection of either the Red or IR analog channel in the MUX onboard the MED-SPO2 module. See **AppTaskDAQ()** and **AppTaskDAQ_ProcessCmd()** in **app.c**.

F7-21(15) The DAQ task retrieves the message from the queue and enables ADC0 channel DP0 to convert the baseline signal. See **AppTaskDAQ()**, **AppTaskDAQ_ProcessCmd()** and **AppTaskDAQ_ExecCmd()** in **app.c**.

F7-21(16) The DAQ task retrieves the message from the queue and enables ADC1 channel DP0 to convert the pulse signal. See **AppTaskDAQ()**, **AppTaskDAQ_ProcessCmd()** and **AppTaskDAQ_ExecCmd()** in **app.c**.

F7-21(17) The CPU is interrupted by the completion of a conversion of ADC0 channel DP0 and the interrupt is handled by **BSP_ADC0_ISR** in **bsp_adc.c**.

F7-21(18) About the same time, the CPU is interrupted by the completion of a conversion of ADC1 channel DP0 and the interrupt is handled by **BSP_ADC1_ISR()** in **bsp_adc.c**.

F7-21(19)   The ADC0 ISR posts the result of the conversion in the form of a 16-bit raw count to the DAQ task's built-in message queue by calling the function `OSTaskQPost()`. See `BSP_ADC0_ISR()` in `bsp_adc.c`.

F7-21(20)   The ADC1 ISR posts the result of the conversion in the form of a 16-bit raw count to the DAQ task's built-in message queue by calling the function `OSTaskQPost()`. See `BSP_ADC1_ISR()` in `bsp_adc.c`.

F7-21(21)   The DAQ task retrieves the message from the queue and uses the raw counts from ADC0 and ADC1 to calculate the heart rate, the oxygen saturation and display the values in µC/Probe by calling the function `AppTaskDAQ_ProcessData()` and `AppCalcResults()` in `app.c`.

F7-21(22)   The DAQ task sends a signal to the heartbeat task through its local semaphore by calling the function `OSTaskSemPost()`. The signal is to notify the heartbeat task that a new heart rate has been calculated. See `AppCalcResults()` in `app.c`.

F7-21(23)   The heartbeat task normally waits for a signal from the DAQ task in order to update a timer that drives the cardiac cycle animation in µC/Probe. See `AppTaskHeartbeat()` in `app.c`.

F7-21(24)   The heartbeat task updates the global variable `AppCardiacCycleState` toggling between diastolic and systolic states at the same rate calculated by the DAQ task. See `AppTaskHeartbeat()` in `app.c`.

F7-21(25)   The heartbeat task toggles the LED at the same rate of the heartbeat by calling the function `BSP_LED_On()` and `BSP_LED_Off()` in `bsp.c`.

7-5-1 BIOMEDICAL SIGNAL ANALYSIS

The algorithm to detect pulses relies on the presence in the signals coming out of the Red and Infrared pulse of consecutive summit and valley peaks that represent every heartbeat (pulse).

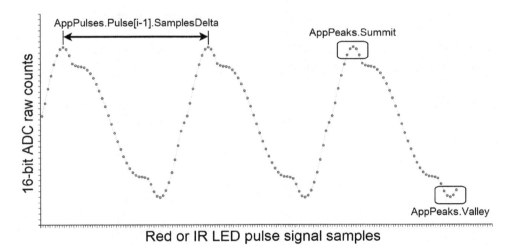

Figure 7-22 **Pulse Detection Algorithm**

As illustrated in Figure 7-22, the DAQ task keeps two sliding windows of five samples:

```
AppPeaks.Summit.Point[5]
AppPeaks.Valley.Point[5]
```

Listing 7-1 **DAQ task's sliding windows for peak detection**

The DAQ tasks keeps monitoring the first 5-point sliding window until a summit is detected. The number of samples between pulses counter at `AppPulses.Pulse[i-1].SamplesDelta` gets reset every time a summit is detected. The counter keeps counting samples and monitoring the second 5-point sliding window until a valley gets detected. At that point, it is assumed that a pulse has been detected and the time-domain features of the pulse are stored into an array of pulses for each signal (Red and Infrared):

```
AppPulses.Pulse[i].Pk2PkAmplitudeCnt
AppPulses.Pulse[i].SamplesDelta
```

Listing 7-2 **DAQ task's arrays of Red and IR pulses**

Whenever a minimum number of pulses threshold defined by **APP_MIN_HEARTBEATS_PER_CALC** is reached, the heart rate and oxygen saturation is calculated by inserting all the time domain features into a histogram and calculating the *mode*, which in statistics it is defined as the value that occurs most frequently in a data set.

The calculation of the most frequent peak-to-peak amplitude and the most frequent number of samples between pulses eliminates any errors due to artifacts and the heart rate and oxygen saturation can be calculated by:

```
AppResults.HeartRate = 60 * (APP_SAMPLING_RATE) / SamplesDeltaMode;


AppResults.OxygenSaturation = log10(Peak2PeakRedMode) / log10(Peak2PeakIRMode);
```

Listing 7-3 **Heart Rate and SpO$_2$ Calculation**

7-5-2 DATA PROCESSING STATE MACHINE

The state machine that processes every sample in **AppTaskDAQ_ProcessData()** is illustrated in Figure 7-23:

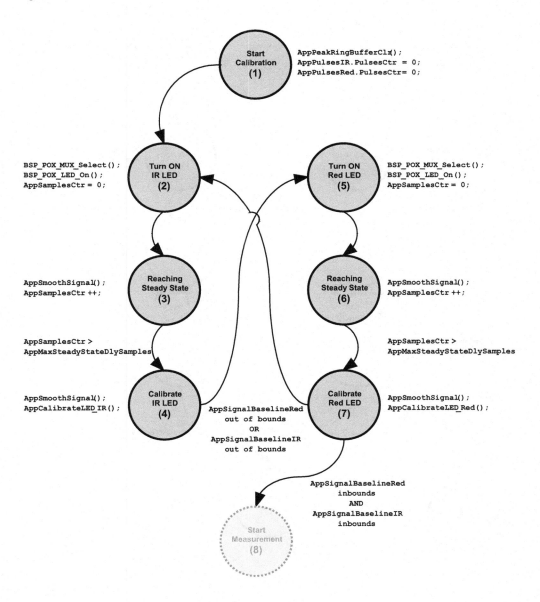

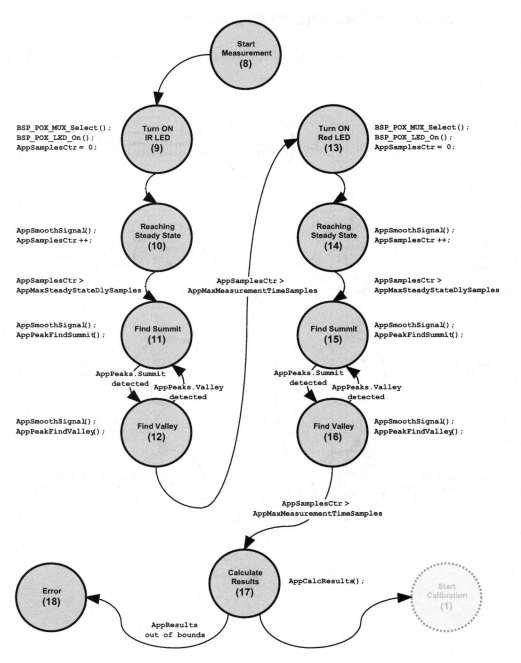

Figure 7-23 **Data Processing State Machine**

F7-23(1)   The first set of states from (1) to (7) are meant for calibration of the intensity of the IR and Red LEDs. In this state, the calibration process gets started by calling **AppPeakRingBufferClr()** with the appropriate arguments to initialize the global variables used by the peak detection algorithm.

F7-23(2)   In this state, the IR LED analog channel illustrated in Figure 7-13 is selected from the multiplexor by calling **BSP_MUX_Select()** with the appropriate arguments and the IR LED is turned on by calling **BSP_POX_LED_On()** with the right arguments.

F7-23(3)   It takes some time for the signal conditioning circuit shown in Figure 7-13 to reach a steady state condition and in this state, both the Baseline and Pulse signals for the IR LED are smoothed by applying a simple moving average filter. The number of samples processed is kept in **AppSamplesCtr** in order to count the number of samples until it reaches the steady state threshold time.

F7-23(4)   In this state, the intensity of the IR LED is optimized for the skin color and the size of the finger by calling the function **AppCalibrateLED_IR()**. The function makes adjustments to the duty cycle of the PWM signal that drives the IR LED in such a way that the Baseline signal falls in the middle of a range of amplitudes defined in volts by **APP_BASELINE_UPPER_LIMIT_MIN_VOLTS** and **APP_BASELINE_UPPER_LIMIT_MAX_VOLTS**. That ensures that the Pulse signal from the IR LED does not get clipped due to over amplification.

F7-23(5)   In a similar fashion to the IR LED, in this state, the Red LED analog channel is selected from the multiplexor by calling **BSP_MUX_Select()** with the appropriate arguments and the Red LED is turned on by calling **BSP_POX_LED_On()** with the corresponding arguments.

F7-23(6)   In order to reach a steady state condition, in this state, both the Baseline and Pulse signals for the Red LED are smoothed by applying a simple moving average filter. The number of samples processed is kept in **AppSamplesCtr** in order to count the number of samples until it reaches the steady state threshold time.

F7-23(7)   In this state, the intensity of the Red LED is optimized for the skin color and the size of the finger by calling the function **AppCalibrateLED_Red()**. The function makes adjustments to the duty cycle of the PWM signal that drives the

Red LED in such a way that the Baseline signal falls in the middle of a range of amplitudes defined in volts by **APP_BASELINE_UPPER_LIMIT_MIN_VOLTS** and **APP_BASELINE_UPPER_LIMIT_MAX_VOLTS**. That ensures that the Pulse signal from the Red LED does not get clipped due to over amplification. The process continues to calibrate the intensities by going back and forth between the IR and Red LEDs until both are within the appropriate thresholds.

F7-23(8)   The next state after the intensities of the LEDs are optimized is to start the measurement.

F7-23(9)   In this state, the IR LED analog channel illustrated in Figure 7-13 is selected from the multiplexor by calling **BSP_MUX_Select()** with the appropriate arguments and the IR LED is turned on by calling **BSP_POX_LED_On()** with the right arguments.

F7-23(10)   It takes some time for the signal conditioning circuit illustrated in Figure 7-13 to reach a steady state condition and in this state, both the Baseline and Pulse signals for the IR LED are smoothed by applying a simple moving average filter. The number of samples processed is kept in **AppSamplesCtr** in order to count the number of samples until it reaches the steady state threshold time.

F7-23(11)   Because a pulse is defined as a consecutive summit and valley as illustrated in Figure 7-22, in this state, every sample is inserted into the 5-sample sliding window in order to detect a summit.

F7-23(12)   In this state, every sample is inserted into the 5-sample sliding window in order to detect a valley. If the consecutive summit and valley form a valid pulse as illustrated in Figure 7-22, then the time-domain features of the pulse are inserted into the array of pulses **AppPulsesIR**. The process goes back and forth between finding summits and valleys for the IR LED until the maximum measurement time is reached.

F7-23(13)   In this state, the Red LED analog channel is selected from the multiplexor by calling **BSP_MUX_Select()** with the appropriate arguments and the Red LED is turned on by calling **BSP_POX_LED_On()** with the right arguments.

F7-23(14)   It is necessary to wait some time in order to reach a steady state condition and in this state, both the Baseline and Pulse signals for the Red LED are smoothed by applying a simple moving average filter. The number of samples processed is kept in **AppSamplesCtr** in order to count the number of samples until it reaches the steady state threshold time.

F7-23(15)   In a similar fashion to the IR LED, in this state, every sample is inserted into the 5-sample sliding window in order to detect a summit.

F7-23(16)   In this state, every sample is inserted into the 5-sample sliding window in order to detect a valley. If the consecutive summit and valley form a valid pulse as illustrated in Figure 7-22, then the time-domain features of the pulse are inserted into the array of pulses for the Red LED **AppPulsesRed**. The process goes back and forth between finding summits and valleys for the Red LED until the maximum measurement time is reached.

F7-23(17)   The results are calculated based on the two sets of pulses stored in **AppPulsesIR** and **AppPulsesRed** by calling **AppCalcResults()** which implements the algorithm described in section 7-5-1 "Biomedical Signal Analysis" on page 885. The results are stored in **AppResults** and the whole process is repeated over again starting from the calibration states.

F7-23(18)   An error occurs if the results are out of the valid ranges defined in beats-per-minute by **APP_MIN_HEARTRATE_BPM** and **APP_MAX_HEARTRATE_BPM** for the heart rate and the ranges defined by **APP_MIN_OXYGEN_SATURATION** and **APP_MAX_OXYGEN_SATURATION** for the oxygen saturation.

7-6 SUMMARY

Similar to the examples presented in Chapter 5, "ECG / Heart Rate Monitor" on page 791 and Chapter 6, "Blood Glucose Meter" on page 829 this chapter provides an easy to follow explanation of the anatomy and physiology of the respiratory system as far as the exchange of gases is concerned. In a similar fashion, it explained the theory of operation of a pulse oximeter including the hardware and software.

This example application demonstrated how simple it is to implement a pulse oximeter using a combination of Micrium's µC/OS-III and Freescale hardware. It also demonstrated two of the most important features of µC/OS-III: *Task Semaphores* and *Task Message Queues*.

Signaling a task through its built-in semaphore is a typical method of synchronization, and in this example we used the heartbeat task's built-in semaphore to synchronize the activities of the DAQ task and the heartbeat task in the same way we did in Chapter 5, "ECG / Heart Rate Monitor" on page 791. The heartbeat task is signaled by the DAQ task when a new heart rate result has been calculated and depending on the heartbeat task priority, the scheduler is run. The heartbeat task may then update the cardiac cycle animation with the new heart rate result. Synchronization through task semaphores is discussed in the first part of the book section 14-2 "Task Semaphore" on page 289.

Message queues are built into each task and the user can send messages directly to a task from another task or an ISR. Task message queues allow the developer to encapsulate each task's functionality into a clean and simple message-based API. For example, we used the DAQ task's built-in message queue as a means to receive different types of commands from other tasks to perform an action like start or stop the simulator, start or stop the data acquisition and process samples from the ADC's ISRs. Inter-task communication via task message queues is discussed in the first part of the book section 15-3 "Task Message Queue" on page 312.

This example delivers a solid platform to create a commercial medical product based on a task-oriented approach. You can add as many tasks as memory resources permit in order to support new features. Imagine you want to be able to send the oxygen saturation and heart rate readings to a fitness equipment, smartphone or tablet PC for display and monitoring purposes. Whether it is USB or bluetooth, chances are that you may need at least two more tasks to handle the reception and transmission of packets and one more task to handle all time-outs related to the communication protocol.

Most commercial pulse oximeters are stand-alone and come with a built-in OLED display. This type of display control is also a great candidate to encapsulate into a task and use the task message queue to receive commands to update the display.

Freescale and Micrium support the addition of other functionality to this pulse oximeter by offering more tower system compatible peripherals and software stacks. Visit the Freescale and Micrium websites to learn more about other products that can help you take your design to the next level.

8

Blood Pressure Monitor

A blood pressure monitor is a device that measures the arterial blood pressure at the phase during the cardiac cycle when the blood is pumped out of the heart (*systolic pressure*) and when the blood fills the heart (*diastolic pressure*). The device is also capable of measuring the heart rate as a byproduct of the blood pressure measurement process. Figure 8-1 shows an example of a commercial blood pressure monitor displaying the systolic and diastolic blood pressures in millimeters of mercury (mmHg) at the top and the heart rate in beats per minute at the bottom.

This chapter demonstrates a basic implementation of a blood pressure monitor built using µC/OS-III and Freescale products.

In a similar manner to the previous examples, this chapter starts with an illustrated description of the natural mechanism of blood pressure regulation. The next section continues the introduction, but with emphasis on the acquisition and calculation of the arterial blood pressure and presents the design of a blood pressure monitor (BPM). The last part of the chapter deals with using the tools to run the example and a description of how the code works.

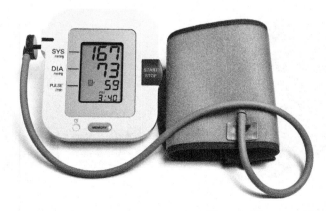

Figure 8-1 **Commercial blood pressure monitor**

8-1 BLOOD PRESSURE

Section 4-01 described the heart as a four-chambered pump responsible for pumping blood throughout the body. A series of coordinated and repeating electrical and mechanical events known as the cardiac cycle include two phases known as *systole* and *diastole*.

Figure 8-2 shows the heart during systole. The pressure generated by the ventricular contraction forces blood out of the heart through the aortic valve and into the aorta. The pressure gets distributed throughout the walls of the arteries as the blood flows through them.

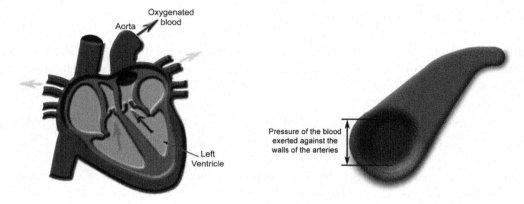

Figure 8-2 **Heart during systole**

Figure 8-3 shows the heart during diastole. The pressure inside the ventricles decreases as the ventricles relax and start filling with blood.

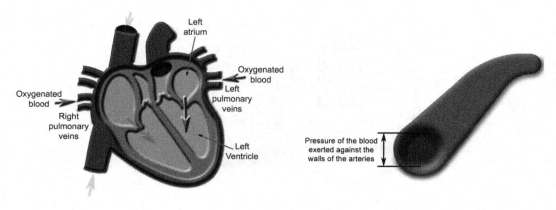

Figure 8-3 **Heart during diastole**

Systole marks the time of maximum arterial pressure while diastole marks the time of minimum arterial pressure. Determining an individual's systolic and diastolic arterial blood pressures is a standard clinical measurement and the values help to determine the functional integrity of the cardiovascular system.

Furthermore, a third important metric is called *Mean Arterial Pressure* (MAP) which is defined as the average arterial pressure over a cardiac cycle (heartbeat) and can be estimated from the systolic and diastolic pressures as:

$$MAP \approx \frac{DIA + (SYS - DIA)}{3}$$

Fluctuations in the Mean Arterial Pressure (MAP) are due to many factors including the heart rate, blood volume, blood viscosity and the resistance to the flow of blood by the blood vessels. These factors are affected by age, diet, obesity, physical activity, alcohol, drugs, stress and diseases among others.

Some of the key players in the natural regulation of the arterial blood pressure in the body are shown in Figure 8-4.

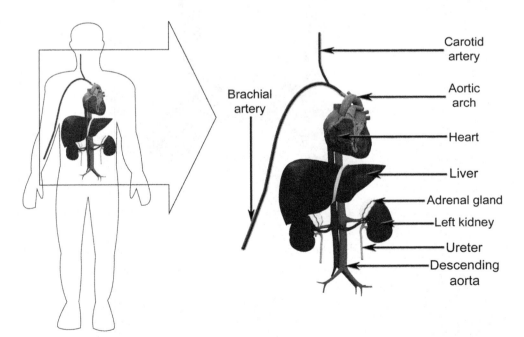

Figure 8-4 **Key players in the regulation of the arterial blood pressure**

8

The arterial blood pressure in the body is controlled by two mechanisms known as the baroreceptor reflex and the *Renin-Angiotensin-Aldosterone System* (RAAS) that work in parallel as briefly described in the next two sections.

8-2 THE BARORECEPTOR REFLEX

The baroreceptor reflex is a negative feedback control system that regulates short-term changes in the mean arterial pressure (MAP) by detecting them with a set of pressure sensors known as arterial *baroreceptors* located in the *aortic arch* and the *carotid sinuses* as shown in Figure 8-5.

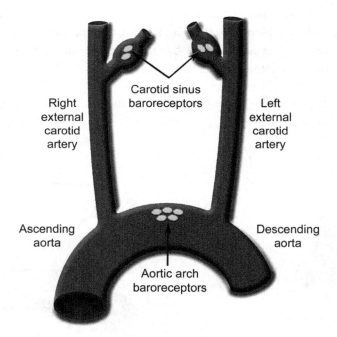

Right external carotid artery

Carotid sinus baroreceptors

Left external carotid artery

Ascending aorta

Descending aorta

Aortic arch baroreceptors

Figure 8-5 **Baroreceptors at the aortic arch and carotid sinuses**

These baroreceptors respond to the stretch caused by the force of the blood exerted against them. The baroreceptors generate an electrical signal with a frequency that is directly proportional to the stretch (blood pressure) and the signal activates and inhibits two of the main divisions of the *autonomic nervous system* known as *sympathetic* and *parasympathetic* nervous system.

If the blood pressure decreases, the frequency of the signal generated by the baroreceptors decreases proportionally and the signal activates the sympathetic nervous system and inhibits the parasympathetic nervous system. The activation of the sympathetic nervous system has the effect on the heart of increasing the heart rate and increasing the force of the ventricular contraction, and the effect on the arteries of narrowing their walls also known as *vasoconstriction*, which in turn, raises the blood pressure as illustrated in Figure 8-6.

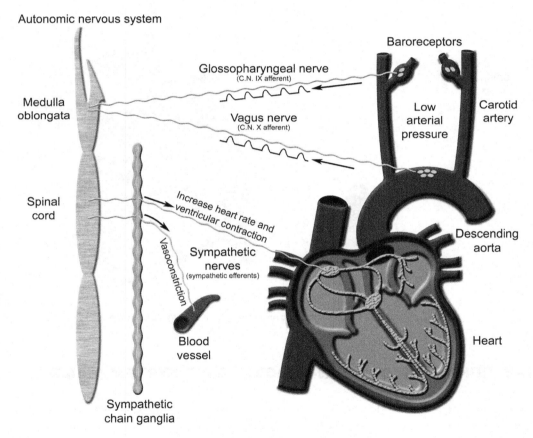

Figure 8-6 **Sympathetic nervous system effect when the blood pressure decreases**

In a similar manner, when the blood pressure increases, the frequency of the signal generated by the baroreceptors increases proportionally and the signal activates the parasympathetic nervous system and inhibits the sympathetic nervous system. The activation of the parasympathetic nervous system has the effect on the heart of decreasing the heart rate and decreasing the force of the ventricular contraction, which in turn, lowers the blood pressure as illustrated in Figure 8-7.

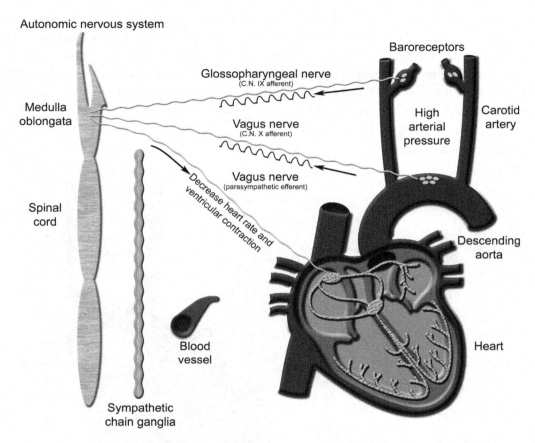

Autonomic nervous system

Baroreceptors

Glossopharyngeal nerve
(C.N. IX afferent)

Medulla
oblongata

Vagus nerve
(C.N. X afferent)

High
arterial
pressure

Carotid
artery

Vagus nerve
(parasympathetic efferent)

Decrease heart rate and
ventricular contraction

Spinal
cord

Descending
aorta

Blood
vessel

Heart

Sympathetic
chain ganglia

Figure 8-7 **Parasympathetic nervous system effect when the blood pressure increases**

8-3 RENIN-ANGIOTENSIN-ALDOSTERONE SYSTEM (RAAS)

The Renin-Angiotensin-Aldosterone System (RAAS) is a regulatory system that controls the levels of blood pressure and the levels of fluids. The system gets activated when a decrease in blood volume is detected in the kidneys by a special type of cells known as *juxtaglomerular cells*. The juxtaglomerular cells work in a similar way to the baroreceptors discussed in the last section. If the blood pressure decreases, there is a decrease in the stretch of the juxtaglomerular cells that is interpreted as a decrease in the volume of blood. The juxtaglomerular cells in the kidneys respond directly by releasing an enzyme known as *renin* into the bloodstream as shown in Figure 8-8.

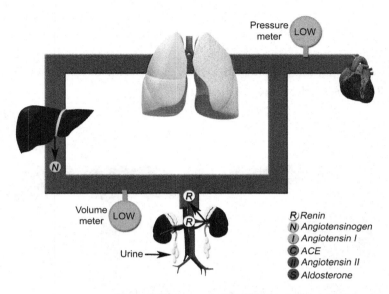

Figure 8-8 **Response of the kidneys to the detection of low blood volume**

Once the renin is flowing in the bloodstream, it encounters a chemical compound known as *angiotensinogen* which is produced and released mainly by the liver. Renin splits the angiotensinogen to form another chemical known as *angiotensin I* as shown in Figure 8-9.

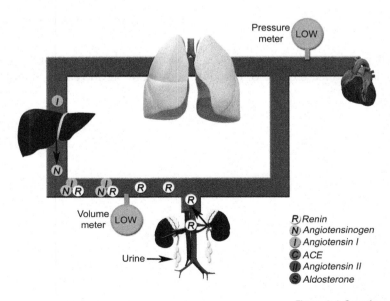

Figure 8-9 **Creation of Angiotensin I**

Angiotensin I has no biological effect other than reacting with another enzyme known as *Angiotensin-Converting Enzyme (ACE)* which is mainly secreted by a special type of cells in the lungs. When angiotensin I makes its way to the lungs, it encounters the Angiotensin-Converting Enzyme which catalyzes the conversion of Angiontensin I to *angiotensin II* as illustrated in Figure 8-10.

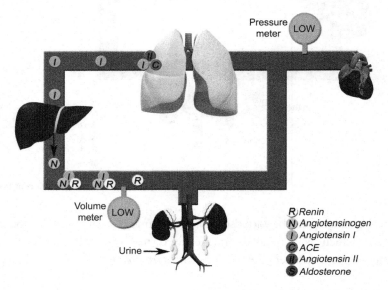

Figure 8-10 **Conversion of Angiotensin I to Angiotensin II**

Angiotensin II has three effects in response to the initial detection of low blood pressure. One of them is to reduce the size of blood vessels, therefore increasing the blood pressure as shown in Figure 8-11.

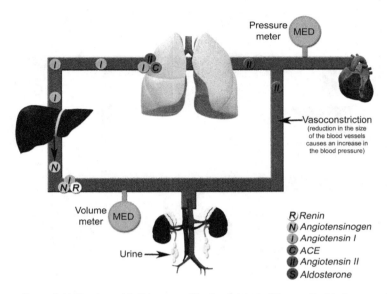

R Renin
N Angiotensinogen
I Angiotensin I
C ACE
II Angiotensin II
S Aldosterone

Figure 8-11 **Vasoconstriction caused by Angiotensin II in an effort to increase blood pressure**

The second effect of the Angiotensin II in response to the initial detection of low blood volume is to increase the sensation of thirst through the brain in an effort to increase the blood volume and therefore the blood pressure following the ingestion of liquids.

The third effect of the Angiotensin II in response to the initial detection of low blood pressure is to stimulate the release of a hormone known as *aldosterone* as explained in the next paragraph.

Once the Angiotensin II has been created in the lungs, it advances down to the *adrenal glands* which sit on top of the kidneys and stimulate the release of a hormone known as *aldosterone*. Aldosterone is a hormone that affects kidney function by increasing the reabsorption of sodium ions and water from the urine commonly known as fluid retention, and by releasing potassium and hydrogen ions. This increases blood volume, which in turn leads to an increase in blood pressure. Figure 8-12 illustrates the effect of Angiotensin II on the adrenal glands.

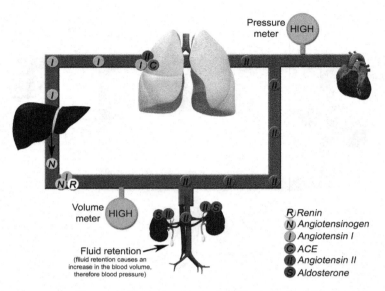

Figure 8-12 **Fluid retention by the kidneys activated by the Aldosterone hormone**

8-4 HYPERTENSION

High blood pressure or *hypertension* is a very common condition that may lead to health problems, like heart attack and stroke if uncontrolled.

Most individuals with hypertension have no signs or symptoms. A few may experience headaches, dizziness or nosebleeds but it is only when pressure has reached very dangerous levels and it is almost too late to start a treatment to control it.

Table 8-1 shows the classification of hypertension as defined by the American Heart Association for adults 18 years of age and older.

Classification	Systolic Pressure (mmHg)	Diastolic Pressure (mmHg)
Normal	90-119	60-79
Prehypertension	120-139	80-89
Stage I	140-159	90-99
Stage II	≥160	≥100
Isolated systolic hypertension	≥140	<90

Table 8-1 **Hypertension classification**

There are two types of hypertension depending on the root cause. *Primary hypertension* also known as essential hypertension accounts for 90% of all cases and it is diagnosed when there is no direct cause for the condition other than natural aging. The second type of hypertension is known as *secondary hypertension* and it is diagnosed among those patients whose high blood pressure is caused as a side effect of a different health condition like:

- Kidney disease.

- Adrenal glands tumors.

- Defects in blood vessels dating from birth.

- Certain medications such as birth control pills, cold medicines, antidepressants, prescription drugs and recreational drugs.

Major risk factors to develop hypertension according to the Mayo Clinic include:

- Chronic diseases: diabetes, high cholesterol and kidney disease among others.

- Age: the cardiovascular and renal system function declines as we age.

- Gender: more common among men, but incidence increases among women after menopause.

- Race: hypertension is common among blacks.

- Family history of hypertension.

- Overweight or obesity: larger size demands more oxygen for the tissues therefore more blood. An increase in the volume of blood causes an increase in the blood pressure as described in the last section.

- Diet: too much salt can cause fluid retention, therefore an increase in blood pressure also described in the last section.

- Lack of physical activity: a weak heart needs to work harder by increasing the heart rate, therefore the blood pressure.

8

- Alcohol.

- Tobacco.

- Stress.

According to the World Health Organization (WHO), hypertension is a disease with the largest incidence rates. Hypertension is mostly a result of the increased life expectancy and modern treatments for chronic degenerative diseases.

Not only people suffering from hypertension need to control their blood pressure levels, but also people suffering from other cardiovascular diseases like: aneurism, coronary artery disease, kidney disease, stroke and diabetes.

Furthermore, those people undergoing surgical procedures need to have a strict control of blood pressure in order to avoid *hypoxia* (lack of oxygen in the tissues), heart arrest or heart stroke due to the anesthesia, loss of blood and the mechanical manipulation of blood vessels during surgery.

8-5 INDIRECT MEASUREMENT OF ARTERIAL BLOOD PRESSURE

A number of different kinds of techniques are used by doctors to measure arterial blood pressure. Some of them are invasive and are designed to measure the arterial blood pressure by directly placing the sensor element in touch with the vascular system through the insertion of a catheter. Others try to make an attempt to measure arterial blood pressure noninvasively and are the type of technique described in this section.

The traditional manual technique used by doctors employs a *sphygmomanometer* and a *stethoscope*. The sphygmomanometer consists of an inflatable cuff for occlusion of the blood vessel, a rubber bulb for inflation of the cuff, a mechanical valve for deflation of the cuff and a mercury or mechanical *manometer* for the detection of pressure as shown in Figure 8-13.

Blood pressure is measured by using the stethoscope for the auditory detection of the systole and diastole phases in a technique known as the *oscillometric method* that will be described in the next paragraphs.

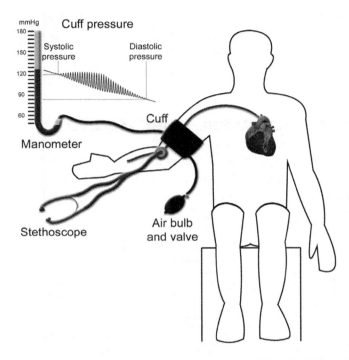

Figure 8-13 **Manual sphygmomanometer**

The oscillometric method is illustrated in Figure 8-13 and it is based on the assumption that the pressure applied by the blood to the artery wall is the same pressure inside the cuff. The cuff is placed at heart level wrapped around the upper arm and over the brachial artery while the stethoscope is placed in the joint of the arm where the brachial artery is also quite accessible and superficial.

The cuff is inflated until the pressure is above the expected systolic pressure (Table 8-1) and then the valve is opened in order to deflate the cuff at a slow regular rate of 2 mmHg/sec. As long as the systolic blood pressure is below the cuff pressure only silence is detected with the stethoscope because the cuff is preventing the passage of blood through the artery. As the cuff keeps deflating, the systolic blood pressure will eventually be higher than the cuff pressure. It is at that point when the blood is able to spurt under the cuff and cause and audible sound that can be detected through a stethoscope. The manometer reading at this point indicates the systolic pressure and as the pressure in the cuff keeps decreasing the audible sounds will keep pounding at the same rate of the heart. The audible sounds will be detected until the pressure cuff falls below the diastolic pressure and of course at that time the reading from the manometer indicates the diastolic pressure.

8

The blood pressure monitor presented in the next section is based on the same method except that the manometer is replaced with a solid state pressure sensor and a microcontroller not only to determine the systolic and diastolic pressures but also to control an air pump and solenoid valve to inflate and deflate the cuff automatically.

8-6 DESIGN OF A BLOOD PRESSURE MONITOR

Figure 8-14 shows the block diagram of the blood pressure monitor presented in this chapter. The design includes two boards from Freescale and a series of third party parts that connect through hoses as explained in the next pages..

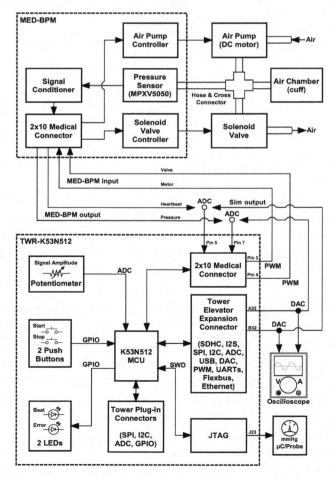

Figure 8-14 **Block diagram of the blood pressure monitor**

8

One of the key components is the pressure sensor manufactured by Freescale. The MPXx5050 series of piezoresistive transducers provide an accurate, high level analog output signal that is proportional to the applied pressure. The sensor is offered in different packages and the part used in this design is shown in Figure 8-15.

Figure 8-15 **Pressure sensor from Freescale: Part # MPXV5050GP**

The cuff can be purchased from any pharmacy or medical equipment store that carries replacement parts for commercial blood pressure monitors. The cuff used in this design was purchased from Walgreens pharmacy and it is shown in Figure 8-16.

Figure 8-16 **Blood pressure cuff**

The air pump is distributed by Cole-Parmer (www.coleparmer.com). The part used in this design provides 0.5 liter-per-minute, maximum pressure of 6.8 psi, it runs at 3 VDC and has a 3 mm barbed port. Figure 8-17 shows part # EW-79600-08:

8

Figure 8-17 **Miniature OEM pressure pump by Cole-Parmer: Part # EW-79600-08**

The solenoid valve is manufactured by Gems Sensors & Controls (www.gemssensors.com). The part used in this design runs at 3 VDC, has 3 mm barbed ports and it is part # MB202-VB30-L200 shown in Figure 8-18.

Figure 8-18 **Solenoid valve by Gems Sensors & Controls: Part # MB202-VB30-L200**

A flexible air hose or vacuum hose with an inside diameter of 3 mm and a 3 mm barbed cross connector from Cole-Parmer allows you to connect the cuff, pressure sensor, air pump and solenoid valve. Figure 8-19 shows part # WU-30705-06.

Figure 8-19 **3 mm barbed cross connector from Cole-Parmer**

Depending on the inside diameter of the hose or the port outside diameter of the parts you were able to find you may need a barbed reducing connector like the one shown in Figure 8-20, also from Cole-Parmer that connects a 3 mm hose to a ¼" hose.

Figure 8-20 **¼" to 3 mm barbed reducing connector from Cole-Parmer**

The analog front end that contains the pressure sensor along with the circuits to filter and amplify the signal is offered by Freescale. The board also includes the circuits necessary to drive the air pump and solenoid valve. The part number is MED-BPM and it is shown in Figure 8-21 connected to the TWR-K53N512 controller through the 2x10 medical connector.

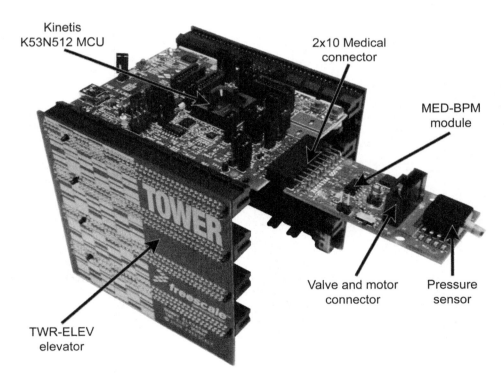

Figure 8-21 **TWR-K53N512 and MED-BPM**

8

The circuits to drive the air pump and solenoid valve in the MED-BPM module are identical and are shown in Figure 8-22 and Figure 8-23. They are typical MOSFET based inductive load drivers. The circuits in this design feature an optical isolator in order to allow the use of two different power sources that can be configured via the jumpers. The preferred power source used in this design is external power provided by a 3VDC 700mA AC-to-DC wall power adapter.

The PUMP_CTRL and VALVE_CTRL signals are outputs of a PWM module and the rate of inflation and deflation is controlled by adjusting the duty cycle of these two signals as we will describe in the last section of this chapter where we explain how the code works.

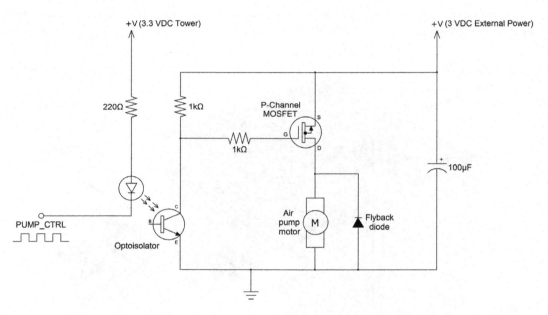

Figure 8-22 **Air pump controller**

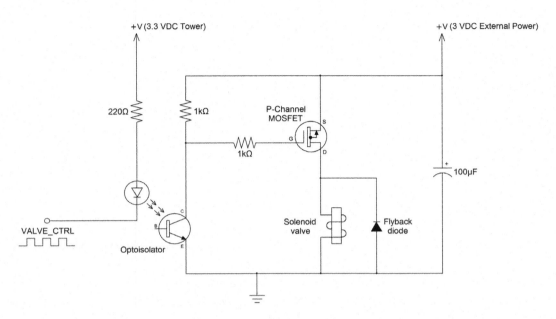

Figure 8-23 **Solenoid valve controller**

The signal conditioning circuit for the pressure sensor in the MED-BPM module is shown in Figure 8-24. It includes a series of passive low and high pass filters along with operational amplifiers to not only amplify the signals but also to avoid any loading effects common to passive filters.

The circuit has two output signals; the CUFF_PRESSURE and the HEARTBEAT signal. The HEARTBEAT signal is used to determine the time of the systolic and diastolic phases and the CUFF_PRESSURE signal indicates the actual arterial blood pressure at such phases. In other words, the HEARTBEAT signal replaces the stethoscope used in the oscillometric method discussed in section 8-5 "Indirect Measurement of Arterial Blood Pressure" on page 904.

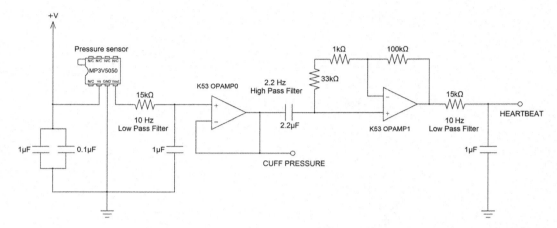

Figure 8-24 **Pressure sensor signal conditioning**

The following Figure 8-25 is provided as a supplement to the discussion of the oscillometric method in section 8-5 "Indirect Measurement of Arterial Blood Pressure" on page 904 and also to illustrate the purpose of all the different filters in the signal conditioning circuit.

The figure illustrates the raw signal at the pressure sensor output, the CUFF_PRESSURE signal at the output of the first low pass filter and the HEARTBEAT signal at the output of the last band pass filter.

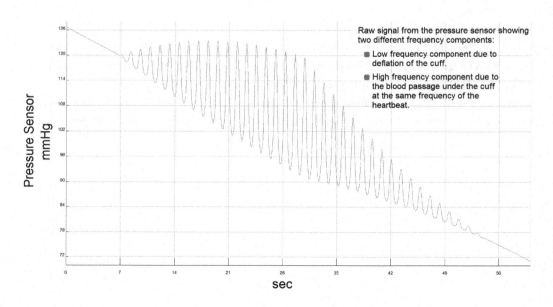

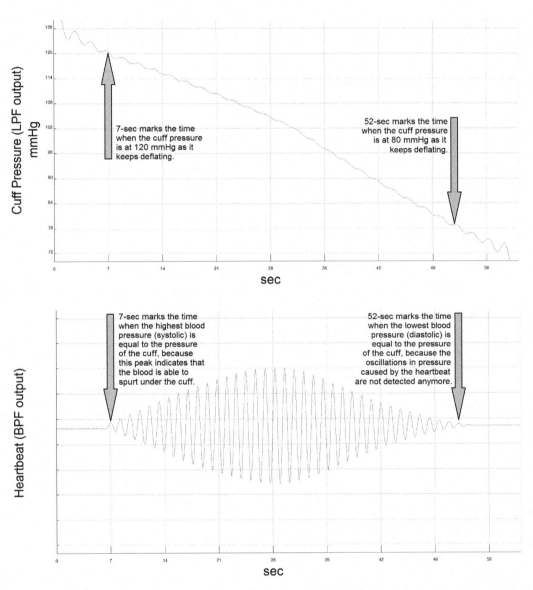

Figure 8-25 **Pressure sensor signal conditioning signals at different stages**

The 2x10 medical connector of the MED-BPM not only provides connectivity with the TWR-K53N512 board to make the heartbeat and cuff pressure signals available to the ADC modules but also allows the use of the on-chip op-amps and transimpedance amplifiers of the Kinetis 32-bit microcontroller to implement the required signal conditioning. The rest of the signals have been omitted from the block diagram for the sake of simplicity but Table 8-2 shows the signal present in each pin of the medical connector.

MED-BPM Signal	Pin		MED-BPM Signal
VDD	1	2	GND
PUMP_CTRL	3	4	VALVE_CTRL
HEARTBEAT	5	6	Not connected
CUFF_PRESSURE	7	8	Not connected
OPAMP0 VOUT0	9	10	OPAMP1 VOUT1
OPAMP0 INN0-	11	12	OPAMP1 INN1-
OPAMP0 INP0+	13	14	OPAMP1 INP1+
Not connected	15	16	Not connected
Not connected	17	18	Not connected
Not connected	19	20	Not connected

Table 8-2 **Medical Connector 2x10 Pin Header Connections**

Notice from the block diagram in Figure 8-14 that in the absence of the MED-BPM module you can still run the application by using the simulated heartbeat and pressure signals coming out of the DAC modules. You just need to connect a jumper wire between pin 5 of the medical connector and pin B32 of the elevator module in the tower system for the heartbeat signal and a jumper wire between pin 7 of the medical connector and pin A32 of the elevator module in the tower system for the cuff pressure signal. The potentiometer is used in such situation to increase or decrease the simulated blood pressure.

The communication with µC/Probe which will be used to display the results of the blood pressure monitor is via the J-Link Ultra debug probe from IAR through the JTAG connector labeled as J23.

All the rest of third party parts including the air pump motor, solenoid valve and hoses need to be put together as shown in the block diagram in Figure 8-14. We put the parts together using a perfboard and a transparent lid case as shown in Figure 8-26:

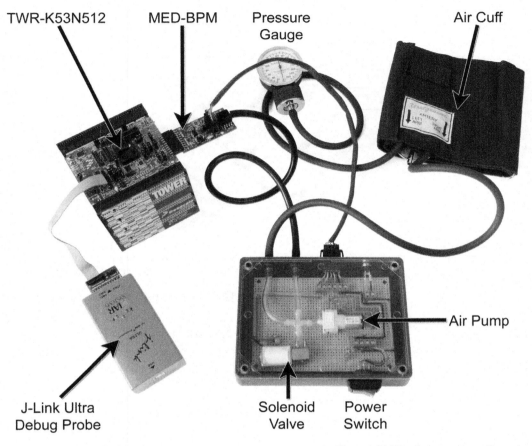

TWR-K53N512   MED-BPM   Pressure Gauge   Air Cuff

Air Pump

J-Link Ultra Debug Probe   Solenoid Valve   Power Switch

Figure 8-26 **Blood pressure monitor setup**

Connecting the solenoid valve and air pump is pretty straight forward; all you really need to pay special attention is to the 1x6 connector's pin-out that connects the MED-BPM in J1 header and your own setup (3VDC power adapter, air pump motor and solenoid valve).

The MED-BPM comes with a male header in J1 that mates with a female socket from Molex (part number 50-57-9406) shown in Figure 8-27. You need to purchase this connector separately along with the contact crimps (Molex part number 16-02-1124) also shown in Figure 8-27.

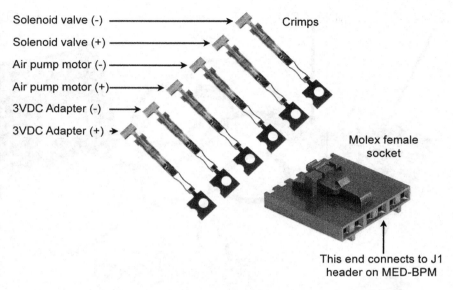

Solenoid valve (-)   Crimps

Solenoid valve (+)

Air pump motor (-)

Air pump motor (+)

3VDC Adapter (-)

3VDC Adapter (+)

Molex female socket

This end connects to J1 header on MED-BPM

Figure 8-27 **Female socket from Molex part # 50-57-9406**

Table 8-3 shows the pinout of the J1 header on the MED-BPM:

MED-BPM J1 Header Pin	MED-BPM Signal
1	3VDC (+)
2	3VDC (-)
3	Air pump motor (+)
4	Air pump motor (-)
5	Solenoid valve (+)
6	Solenoid valve (-)

Table 8-3 **Pin-out of the 1x6 MED-BPM connector in J1**

Notice from Figure 8-26 that we included a mechanical pressure gauge in the system which we found very practical in order to validate the results you get on the μC/Probe screen.

8-7 RUNNING THE EXAMPLE PROJECT

This section describes the steps you need to follow to run the blood pressure monitor example. Start by connecting the MED-BPM module to the TWR-K53N512 controller through the 2x10 medical connector as shown in Figure 8-21.

Connect the air pump, solenoid valve, cuff and pressure sensor as shown in Figure 8-26.

Assuming you have followed all the setup steps described in Chapter 4, "Setup" on page 779, proceed to connect one end of the IAR's J-Link Ultra for ARM debug probe to the JTAG connector on J23 of the TWR-K53N512 and the other end of the probe to any USB port available in your PC.

Run IAR's Embedded Workbench for ARM (EWARM) and open the workspace TWR-K53N512 at:

```
$\Micrium\Software\EvalBoards\Freescale\TWR-K53N512\IAR\
uC-OS-III-Book-Ex-Src.eww
```

In the workspace explorer window, select the tab for the project uCOS-III-Ex4-BPM. The workspace window shows all of the files in the project which are sorted into groups represented by folder icons. Figure 8-28 shows the project files for uCOS-III-Ex4-BPM in the workspace explorer window.

8

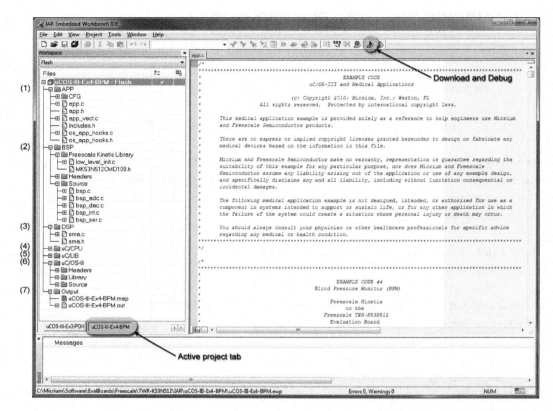

Figure 8-28 **Running the project with EWARM**

F8-28(1)   The **APP** group includes all of the application files for this example. The subgroup **CFG** includes the header files used to configure the application.

F8-28(2)   The **BSP** group contains the files that comprise the board support package. The board support package includes the code used to control the peripherals on the board. For this example, the software to control the LEDs, pushbuttons, ADCs, DACs, operational amplifiers and transimpedance amplifiers will be used. The subgroup Freescale Kinetis Library includes the header files for the Kinetis K50 family of microcontrollers.

F8-28(3)   The **DSP** group contains the files that define some of the Digital Signal Processing functions called by the application.

F8-28(4)   The **uC/CPU** group contains the µC/CPU source code.

F8-28(5)   The **uC/LIB** group contains the µC/LIB source code.

F8-28(6)   The **µC/OS-III** group contains the µCOS-III source code. In addition, the `os_cfg_app.c` file is included in this group to allow certain behavior to be defined at compile time.

F8-28(7)   The **Output** group contains the files generated by the compiler/linker.

Start the debugger by clicking the "Download and Debug" icon as shown in Figure 8-28. The application is programmed to the internal Flash of the K53N512 microcontroller and the debugger starts. The code automatically starts executing and stops at the **main( )** function in the **app.c** file.

Click the "Go" icon in IAR Embedded Workbench's debugging tools to run the application as shown in Figure 8-29.

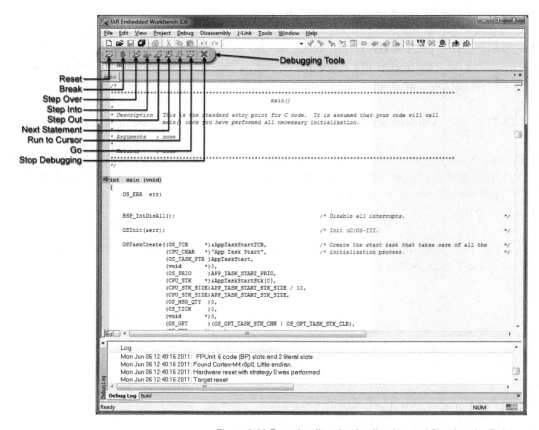

Figure 8-29 **Downloading the Application and Starting the Debugger**

You can test the application by starting μC/Probe and open the workspace for the Blood Pressure Monitor at:

```
$\Micrium\Software\EvalBoards\Freescale\TWR-K53N512\IAR\
uC-OS-III-Book-Ex-Src\uC-OS-III-Ex4-BPM\uC-OS-III-Ex4-BPM-Probe.wsp
```

After μC/Probe starts, click the run button (green triangle). Once μC/Probe is running, you will see a screen similar to the one shown in Figure 8-30

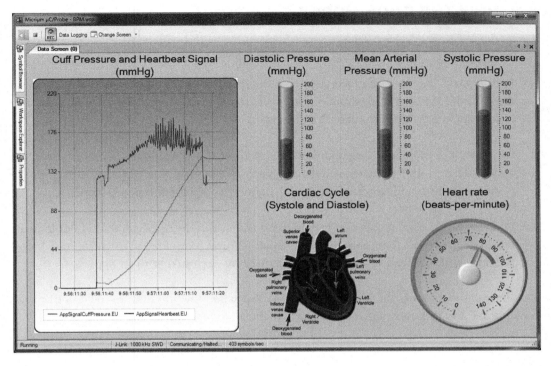

Figure 8-30 **µC/Probe Blood Pressure Monitor Dashboard**

It is important for the pressure sensor to be at the same height of your heart, take a seat, wrap your left arm around the air cuff and press the pushbutton on the TWR-K53N512 board labeled as SW1 to start the application.

The application will turn on the air pump motor, close the solenoid valve and the air cuff will start to inflate. You can press the pushbutton on the TWR-K53N512 board labeled as SW2 at anytime to stop the application (stopping the application will stop inflating and will open the solenoid valve in case of panic).

The application will inflate the cuff slowly up to a default setting of 150 mmHg and you can actually watch the pressure and heartbeat signals in real time on the dashboard. The test takes a total of 30-seconds during which you should keep your arm steady to avoid any noise in the signals. At the end of the test the solenoid valve is opened to allow deflation and your diastolic, systolic and mean arterial pressures will be displayed in the three vertical meters on the dashboard. Your heart rate will also be displayed in the gauge.

8-8 HOW THE CODE WORKS

The blood pressure monitor application consists of three different tasks:

- User IF task: The user interface task monitors the state of the two pushbuttons onboard the TWR-K53N512. The pushbuttons are used to either start or stop the application. The task is defined by `AppTaskUserIF()` in `app.c`.

- Sim task: The simulator task monitors the state of the potentiometer and updates the amplitude of a cuff pressure simulated signal generated by the DAC according to the position of the potentiometer. The task is defined by `AppTaskSim()` in `app.c`.

- DAQ task: The data acquisition task is the main task in the application and implements the state machine that processes the analog input samples to calculate the blood pressure and the heart rate. The task is defined by `AppTaskDAQ()` in `app.c`.

The interaction among the different tasks is facilitated by the use of µC/OS-III's task semaphores and task message queues and it is illustrated in Figure 8-31.

8

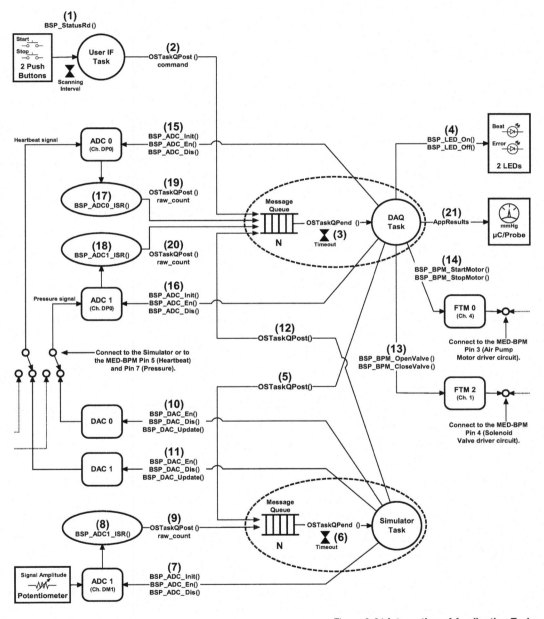

Figure 8-31 **Interaction of Application Tasks**

F8-31(1)   The state of the push buttons is monitored by the user IF task at a scanning interval defined by **BSP_STATUS_CHECK_INTERVAL**. See **AppTaskUserIF()** in **app.c** and **BSP_StatusRd()** in **bsp.c**.

F8-31(2)   Depending on the pushbutton pressed by the user a message from the user IF task to either start or stop the application is posted to the DAQ task's built-in message queue by calling **OSTaskQPost()**. See **AppTaskUserIF()** in **app.c**.

F8-31(3)   The DAQ task can receive data messages directly from the ADCs ISRs or command messages from the other two tasks. When **OSTaskQPend()** is called, the message is retrieved and processed in two different ways depending on the sender and the type of message. If the message comes from one of the ADC's ISR then the message is processed by calling the function **AppTaskDAQ_ProcessData()** and if the message comes from any other task then the message is processed by calling the function **AppTaskDAQ_ProcessCmd()** in **app.c**.

F8-31(4)   If the message retrieved by the DAQ task is a command to start the blood pressure measurement then the DAQ task turns off the LEDs by calling the function **BSP_LED_Off()** in **bsp.c**.

F8-31(5)   If the message retrieved by the DAQ task is a command to start the blood pressure measurement in simulation mode then the DAQ task posts a message to the sim task's built-in message queue to start the simulator. See **AppTaskDAQ()** in **app.c** and **AppTaskDAQ_ProcessCmd()** in **app.c**.

F8-31(6)   In similar fashion, the sim task can receive messages directly from the ADC1's ISR or from the DAQ task. When **OSTaskQPend()** is called, the message is retrieved and processed in different ways depending on the sender. The sim task retrieves the received message from its message queue and proceeds according to the command issued by the DAQ task as follows:

F8-31(7)   If the message contains a start command then the sim task starts ADC1 channel DM1 in order to read the potentiometer. See **AppTaskSim()** in **app.c**.

F8-31(8)   The CPU is interrupted by the completion of a conversion of ADC1 Channel DM1 and the interrupt is handled by **BSP_ADC1_ISR()** in **bsp_adc.c**.

F8-31(9)   The ADC1 ISR posts the result of the conversion in the form of a 16-bit raw count to the sim task's built-in message queue by calling the function `OSTaskQPost()`. See `BSP_ADC1_ISR()` in `bsp_adc.c`.

F8-31(10)   The sim task retrieves the message from the queue and configures the DAC0 to output a simulated cuff pressure waveform at an amplitude proportional to the raw count of the ADC1 channel DM1. See `AppTaskSim()` in `app.c`.

F8-31(11)   The sim task retrieves the message from the queue and configures the DAC1 to output a simulated heartbeat waveform. See `AppTaskSim()` in `app.c`.

F8-31(12)   The sim task posts a message to the DAQ task's built-in message queue notifying the DAQ task that the simulator is running. See `AppTaskSim()` in `app.c`.

F8-31(13)   The DAQ task retrieves the message from the queue and initializes FlexTimer FTM2 to output a PWM signal to drive the solenoid valve. See `AppTaskDAQ()` and `AppTaskDAQ_ProcessCmd()` in `app.c`.

F8-31(14)   The DAQ task retrieves the message from the queue and initializes FlexTimer FTM0 to output a PWM signal to drive the air pump motor. See `AppTaskDAQ()` and `AppTaskDAQ_ProcessCmd()` in `app.c`.

F8-31(15)   The DAQ task retrieves the message from the queue and enables ADC0 channel DP0 to convert the heartbeat signal. See `AppTaskDAQ()`, `AppTaskDAQ_ProcessCmd()` and `AppTaskDAQ_ExecCmd()` in `app.c`.

F8-31(16)   The DAQ task retrieves the message from the queue and enables ADC1 channel DP0 to convert the cuff pressure signal. See `AppTaskDAQ()`, `AppTaskDAQ_ProcessCmd()` and `AppTaskDAQ_ExecCmd()` in `app.c`.

F8-31(17)   The CPU is interrupted by the completion of a conversion of ADC0 channel DP0 and the interrupt is handled by `BSP_ADC0_ISR()` in `bsp_adc.c`.

F8-31(18)   About the same time, the CPU is interrupted by the completion of a conversion of ADC1 channel DP0 and the interrupt is handled by `BSP_ADC1_ISR` in `bsp_adc.c`.

F8-31(19)   The ADC0 ISR posts the result of the conversion in the form of a 16-bit raw count to the DAQ task's built-in message queue by calling the function `OSTaskQPost()`. See `BSP_ADC0_ISR()` in **bsp_adc.c**.

F8-31(20)   The ADC1 ISR posts the result of the conversion in the form of a 16-bit raw count to the DAQ task's built-in message queue by calling the function `OSTaskQPost()`. See `BSP_ADC1_ISR()` in **bsp_adc.c**.

F8-31(21)   The DAQ task retrieves the message from the queue and uses the raw counts from ADC0 and ADC1 to calculate the heart rate, the blood pressure and display the values in µC/Probe by calling the function `AppTaskDAQ_ProcessData()` and `AppCalcResults()` in **app.c**.

8-8-1 BIOMEDICAL SIGNAL ANALYSIS

The algorithm to calculate the arterial blood pressure is based on the oscillometric method described in Figure 8-13 and Figure 8-25 with just one modification: it doesn't look at the ramp-down but at the ramp-up. The reason why is because as opposed to the method that uses a manual air bulb, this digital blood pressure monitor uses an air pump motor, which means that the inflation rate can be controlled in a smooth manner. Given this advantage over the manual air bulb where the inflation rate is controlled by manually squeezing the bulb, we can spare the patient the slight pain caused by the cuff pressure during an unnecessary extended test that includes a manual inflation and a slow deflation. A digital blood pressure monitor that uses an air pump motor can instead inflate slowly while running the calculations in parallel and then deflate as fast as possible. The ramp-up algorithm is illustrated in Figure 8-32 and similar to the pulse detection algorithm for the pulse oximeter described in Chapter 7, "Pulse Oximeter" on page 859 it keeps two sliding windows of five points. One for the summit and one for the valley. A pulse is detected when a consecutive summit and valley are detected within the thresholds defined in volts by:

```
#define   APP_MIN_HEARTBEAT_PK2PK_AMP_VOLTS    0.150
#define   APP_MAX_HEARTBEAT_PK2PK_AMP_VOLTS    0.750
```

Listing 8-1 **Heartbeat's Peak-to-Peak Amplitude Detection Thresholds**

The thresholds are compared against the value of the peak to peak amplitude of each potential pulse and if it meets the requirements then the time-domain features of the pulse are stored into an array of pulses.

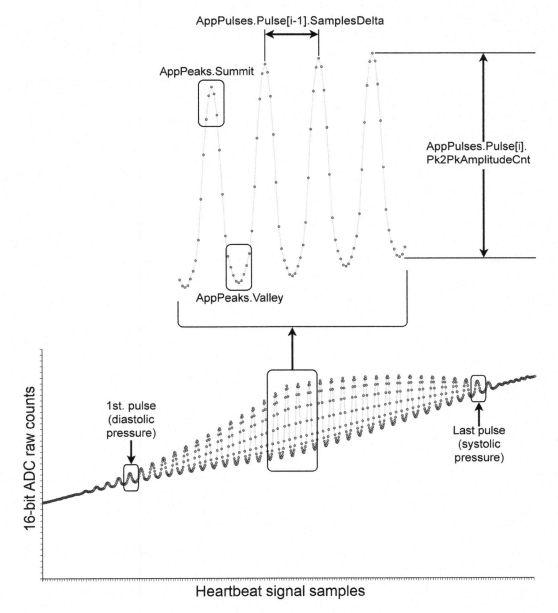

Figure 8-32 **Blood Pressures Detection Algorithm**

Similar thresholds are used to detect the diastolic and systolic pressures respectively:

```
#define  APP_MIN_HEARTBEAT_DIA_PK2PK_AMP_VOLTS     0.125
#define  APP_MAX_HEARTBEAT_DIA_PK2PK_AMP_VOLTS     0.750
#define  APP_MIN_HEARTBEAT_SYS_PK2PK_AMP_VOLTS     0.175
#define  APP_MAX_HEARTBEAT_SYS_PK2PK_AMP_VOLTS     0.750
```

Listing 8-2 **Heartbeat's Peak-to-Peak Amplitude Diastolic and Systolic Detection Thresholds**

The diastolic pressure is the one when the first pulse is detected during the ramp-up and the systolic pressure is the one when the last pulse is detected.

The mean arterial pressure is the one when the pulse reaches the maximum peak to peak amplitude.

The transfer function for the pressure sensor is linear at a temperature range between 0° F and 185° F and assuming a voltage reference of 3.3V the pressure in mmHg in function of the output voltage of the pressure sensor is given by $P = (V / 0.0079193268) - 16.66808$ and is shown in Figure 8-33:

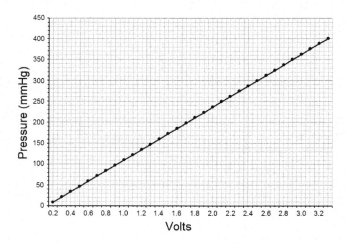

Figure 8-33 **Pressure Sensor Transfer Function**

In the next section you will learn that the algorithm has been fully implemented to support both ramp-up and ramp-down methods. Enabling both methods will slightly increase the accuracy of the results at the expense of the patient's comfort.

8-8-2 DATA PROCESSING STATE MACHINE

The state machine that processes every sample in `AppTaskDAQ_ProcessData()` is illustrated in Figure 8-34:

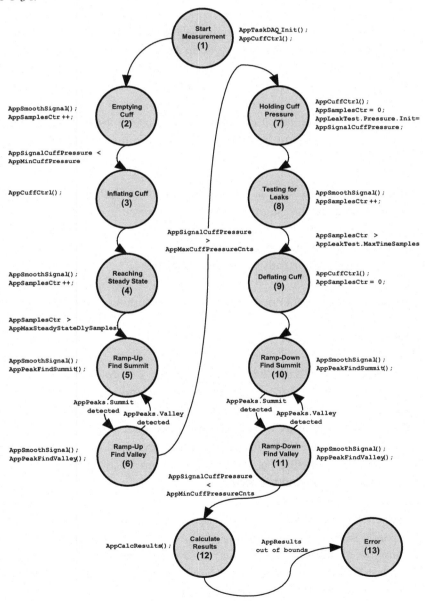

Figure 8-34 **Data Processing State Machine**

F8-34(1)   Once the start button is pressed, the application starts the blood pressure measurement by calling **AppTaskDAQ_Init()** to initialize some global variables and by calling **AppCuffCtrl()** to stop the air pump motor and open the solenoid valve which in turn will empty the cuff as fast as possible.

F8-34(2)   In this state, the cuff pressure signal is smoothed by applying a simple moving average filter and the result is stored in **AppSignalCuffPressure.Result**. This result is monitored until the cuff pressure is below a minimum threshold defined in mmHg by **APP_MIN_CUFF_PRESSURE_MMHG**.

F8-34(3)   Once the cuff is empty, it can be wrapped around the patient's arm and in this state, the cuff starts to be slowly inflated by calling **AppCuffCtrl()** with the correct arguments to start the air pump motor and close the solenoid valve.

F8-34(4)   It is necessary to wait a few seconds for the cuff and pressure sensor to stabilize and in this state, both the cuff pressure and heartbeat signals are smoothed by applying a simple moving average filter. The number of samples processed is kept in **AppSamplesCtr** in order to count the number of samples until it reaches the steady state threshold time.

F8-34(5)   Because a pulse is defined as a consecutive summit and valley as illustrated in Figure 8-32, in this state, every sample is inserted into the 5-sample sliding window in order to detect a summit.

F8-34(6)   In this state, every sample is inserted into the 5-sample sliding window in order to detect a valley. If the consecutive summit and valley form a valid pulse as illustrated in Figure 8-32, then the time-domain features of the pulse are inserted into the array of pulses **AppPulsesAtRampUp**. The process goes back and forth between finding summits and valleys until the cuff pressure is above the systolic pressure at a maximum threshold defined in mmHg by **APP_MAX_CUFF_PRESSURE_MMHG**.

F8-34(7)   Once the systolic pressure is reached, the pressure in the cuff is held for a few seconds in order to test for any leaks. The function **AppCuffCtrl()** is called with the appropriate arguments to stop the air pump motor and close the solenoid valve, which in turn will hold the cuff pressure. The initial pressure is stored in **AppLeakTest.Pressure.Init**.

F8-34(8)   In this state, the cuff pressure signal is smoothed by applying a simple moving average filter and the result is monitored for any leaks. The number of samples is counted in order to determine the amount of time to test for leaks. Such time is defined in seconds by **APP_MAX_CUFF_HOLDING_TIME**.

F8-34(9)   In this state, the cuff is deflated by calling **AppCuffCtrl()** with the right arguments to stop the air pump motor and open the solenoid valve.

F8-34(10)   In a similar fashion to the ramp-up, in this state, every sample is inserted into the 5-sample sliding window in order to detect a summit.

F8-34(11)   In this state, every sample is inserted into the 5-sample sliding window in order to detect a valley. A consecutive summit and valley may be a potential pulse. If the consecutive summit and valley form a valid pulse as illustrated in Figure 8-32, then the time-domain features of the pulse are inserted into the array of pulses **AppPulsesAtRampDown**. The process goes back and forth between finding summits and valleys until the cuff pressure is below the diastolic pressure at a minimum threshold defined in mmHg by **APP_MIN_CUFF_PRESSURE_MMHG**.

F8-34(12)   The results are calculated from the two sets of pulses, **AppPulsesAtRampUp** and **AppPulsesAtRampDown** with the algorithm described in section 8-8-1 "Biomedical Signal Analysis" on page 926. The function **AppCalcResults()** iterates through the two arrays of pulses and the results are stored in **AppResults**.

F8-34(13)   An error occurs in case any of the results are out of the ranges defined by **APP_MIN_BLOOD_PRESSURE_DIA_MMHG**, **APP_MAX_BLOOD_PRESSURE_DIA_MMHG** for the diastolic pressure result, the range defined in mmHg by **APP_MIN_BLOOD_PRESSURE_SYS_MMHG**, **APP_MAX_BLOOD_PRESSURE_SYS_MMHG** for the systolic pressure result and the range defined in beats-per-minute by **APP_MIN_HEARTRATE_BPM** and **APP_MAX_HEARTRATE_BPM** for the heart rate result.

8

8-9 SUMMARY

This chapter explained the anatomy and physiology of the organs involved in the regulation of the arterial blood pressure and the theory of operation of a blood pressure monitor including the hardware and software.

This example application demonstrated how simple it is to implement a blood pressure monitor using a combination of Micrium's µC/OS-III and Freescale hardware. It also demonstrated one of the most important features of µC/OS-III: *Task Message Queues*.

Message queues are built into each task and the user can send messages directly to a task from another task or an ISR. Similar to the rest of medical applications featured in this book, task message queues are used in this example because they allow the developer to encapsulate each task's functionality into a clean and simple message-based API. For example, we used the DAQ task's built-in message queue as a means to receive different types of commands from other tasks to perform an action like start or stop the simulator, start or stop the data acquisition and process samples from the ADC's ISRs. Inter-task communication via task message queues is discussed in the first part of the book section 15-3 "Task Message Queue" on page 312.

This example provides a solid platform to create a commercial medical product based on a task-oriented approach. Most commercial blood pressure monitors come with an LCD display and this type of display control is a great candidate to encapsulate into a task and use the task message queue to receive commands to update the display.

Other blood pressure monitors like the ones used at an Intensive Care Unit (ICU) inflate and deflate the cuff every two minutes and require some type of connectivity to report the blood pressure readings to a central station where healthcare personnel can monitor the patients. Regardless of the communication protocol, chances are that you may need at least two more tasks to handle the reception and transmission of packets and one more task to handle all time-outs related to the communication protocol.

Freescale and Micrium support the addition of other functionality to this blood pressure monitor by offering more tower system compatible peripherals and software stacks. Visit the Freescale and Micrium websites to learn more about other products that can help you take your design to the next level.

Certification of Medical Systems

For the purpose of this appendix, a medical device is defined as any electronic device that uses software to perform its intended purpose within the health-care industry; the actual product might even be "just" software.

A 2007 report titled "Future Trends in Medical Device Technologies" by Wm. A. Herman and Gilbert B. Devey [1] summarized the work of a cross functional work-group consisting of participants from the US Food and Drugs Administration (FDA), medical industry, think-tanks and academia. The group was asked to predict the direction the medical industry would take over the next 10 years. It is no surprise that many predictions were not only based on their areas of personal expertise, but also on technology convergence already seen in such commercial sectors as cellular communication, gaming, and IT.

The work-group placed a high degree of confidence that the 10-year mark would see home and tele healthcare firmly entrenched based on the assumption that a supporting host of sensor, monitors and remote devices will be sufficiently advanced to support these roles.

Other predictions include:

Devices providing full time monitoring, advanced detection, therapy, and active intervention will replace expensive tests. While many of those examples would likely be implemented in something beyond the normal embedded real-time devices, the survey included devices based on smart sensors, monitors, glucose-monitoring devices and drug delivery systems as well.

The training of doctors will benefit from Internet-based medical databases and services. Virtual reality, robotics, and computer-aided diagnostics were all mentioned as technologies that will continue to grow over the next decade.

Software needed to make these devices operable can be seen in common smartphones and such other electronics as remote control, Bluetooth, Zigbee, and other wireless protocols. Fault tolerant file system or embedded databases would be the basis for delivery of powerful chemotherapy drugs, or even sending GPS coordinates to family members in an emergency.

Let's look closer at this subject of software to be able to see its impact on medical devices, and the important choices that must be made by designers.

A-1 "OFF-THE-SHELF" SOFTWARE

Designers with experience in embedded device software know that software begets yet more software. Each line of code that enables a new "visible" feature requires 10 to 100 lines of code to support it. Let's take, for example, a new feature addition to an existing defibrillator design. The goal is to record all information that is captured from the patient during a cardiac event, the defibrillator's intervention, and post-intervention data and store it for real-time and future use.

This is not an unreasonable goal. All of this information is currently available such as information the defibrillator gathers and uses to determine the optimal intensity, frequency and duration of the electric shock it administers. However, in the past it used a simple memory file system to capture and analyze the cardiac data. Now it must convert the data to a common file system such as FAT32. Amazingly, adding what seems to be a trivial feature enhancement requires tens of thousands of lines of code.

Upgrades will not stop with a file system. Soon, a touch screen and 2-D and 3-D graphics will also be expected. In the not-too-distant future, the system should be tied into the health-care IT system using wireless communication. Now, with that level of system exposure, patient privacy and data concerns require even more software be added to protect the software that was just added. We'll look again at this concept of cost per line of code.

For even the largest companies staffing this kind of expertise is not only expensive but it can undermine the company's value-add focus. Smaller companies and startups have no choice but to turn to third party "off-the-shelf" (OTS) software.

For many consumer products such as cell phones, third party software is easily used. That is not true in medical applications. OTS software is not easy to navigate and the not-invented-here (NIH) syndrome is strong in this industry, especially given the potential for litigation. While medical device manufacturers do use third-party software, it is not always developed with their specific needs in mind. Perhaps that is a contributor to the rapid increase in recalls, as discussed in the next section.

A-2 MEDICAL DEVICE SOFTWARE – RECALLS

According to an FDA analysis of 3140 medical devices conducted between 1992 and 1998, 7.7% of them were recalled due to faulty software. Of those software related recalls, 79% were attributable to bugs introduced after the product's initial release. The FDA reports that within the subsequent years ending in 2005, nearly one in three of all medical devices containing software were recalled [2].

Just three years later, in an April 29th, 2008 presentation titled "CDRH Software Update," John F Murray Jr., an FDA software compliance expert, reported that faulty software accounted for 18% of all recalled devices. In a period of 10 years, the rate of software related recalls increased a whopping 133%.

This suggests that if the growth rate of recalls remains static, in 10 years, faulty software will account for over 40% of recalls within this industry.

The growing rate of recalls is a clear indication that the current regulatory process is inadequate. The fact that two thirds [3] of bugs found in the recalled medical device were introduced post release may be one reason that as of March 2010 [1], all but the most minor of medical devices sold within the EU must now comply with a more rigorous medical software standard known as IEC 62304.

U.S. manufacturers, along with international and domestic stakeholders participated in the creation of the international standard even though it is not adopted by the FDA. Today, IEC 62304 is the most cost effective approach in meeting the certification needs of the global market.

Before looking at the EU and U.S. regulatory climate, let's begin to look at just what safety critical means in a medical context.

A-3 SAFETY CRITICAL

Most medical software falls into a special sub-category called safety-critical. The operating environment, operators, patients, and electro-mechanical portion of the medical device comprise a safety-critical system. The failure or improper operation of such system may allow or cause:

- Injury or loss of life to a human or animal

- Environmental damage

- Damage or loss of capital equipment

The primary focus of medical software pertains to the safety of patients, operators and staff. Typical safety-critical software life cycle tasks include:

- Planning

- Requirements

- Design

- Coding and Integration

- Testing and Verification

- Configuration Management (CM)

- Quality Assurance

- Post Release Maintenance

Many of the activities that take place within software development can be likened to hardware redundancies that make up critical hardware systems. The redundant practices i.e. code reviews; traceability, code coverage, etc. remove single point failures and, while costly, are less expensive than fixing failures after the fact.

For manufacturers who have product families or products that share code, not only can code be reused but also, all of the shared artifacts (artifacts in this case include everything concerned with certification) can as well. In fact, because of the additional processes and practices mandated in safety-critical development the relative savings gained through code reuse easily exceeds that of commercial software development.

There are several areas where the pain-points of consumer electronics match those of medical device development. Scheduling, time-to-market pressures, and sufficient staff to develop and maintain software such as embedded, real-time operating system (RTOS) kernels, networking stacks, and file systems, are all examples. In many situations, it is more cost effective to leave the development and maintenance to the experts and license software as needed.

When properly vetted, the use of commercial software can be a wise choice that speeds development, improves quality (or at least does not decrease it), reduces overall development costs and reduces the stress placed on development teams allowing them to stay focused on achieving the core goals of the project rather than developing commodity software.

Off-the-shelf software intended for general-purpose devices is not the same as software that has been developed, verified and validated for use in safety-critical devices. A medical device manufacturer using OTS software generally gives up software life cycle control, but still bears the responsibility for the continued safe and effective performance of the medical device.

The manufacturer has two choices when considering the use of OTS software in their design. One is to purchase software that despite the OTS label, is designed, verified, validated and comes with the same documentation that is expected by the FDA or other certification agency. Micriµm's uC/OS and several of its RTOS components fit this category. It has been deployed in many medical designs, and has 100% of the required documentation needed to comply with the FDA 510(k)/Pre-market Approval (PMA), and also complies with IEC 62304, IEC 60601, and ISO 14971.

The second choice involves using "Software Of Unknown Provenance" (SOUP) [4]. Using this option is at first appealing, as it appears to be much less expensive than properly supported software, and in many cases, it offers great features. There are also inherent negatives. The primary negative is the code is not yet properly verified, validated and documented. The result is often a more expensive route. The References page has several links to FDA documents that provide some guidance for SOUP. One particular valuable link is: Guidance for Industry, FDA Reviewers and Compliance on Off-the-Shelf Software Use in Medical Devices, Office of Device Evaluation, Center for Devices and Radiological Health, Food and Drug Administration, September 1999.

http://www.fda.gov/downloads/MedicalDevices/DeviceRegulationandGuidance/ GuidanceDocuments/ucm073779.pdf

A-4 TRACEABILITY

The concept of traceability is used and implemented in many ways. Each requirement has an explicit attribute of traceability to its source/origin. It may evolve from a general requirement, result from a conversation with a user, result from adoption of a standard, or adhering to a new regulation. However, each requirement is present for a reason, and that reason is said to be an attribute contained within the requirement. A natural extension of this idea is to add a traceable attribute that points to the implementation and validation of the requirement, essentially documenting the path from a requirement origin thru implementation and its validation.

When traceability is not pursued with vigor, it can cause added project expense and missed schedules.

When used properly, and its role expanded to encompass and include the full gamut of software development activities including requirements specification document creation, software architecture design, detailed design, verification, validation, test and quality assurance (QA), technical publications, maintenance and other post-release activities, and software reuse, etc, it provides insight into every aspect of the project life cycle.

The concept of traceability as originally intended for validation has rapidly expanded. Some companies consider it to be a core component of the Scope of Work (SOW). It provides a way to manage and estimate the cost of changes to project requirements. Traceability is used instead of prototyping to prove understanding and to communicate to clients the nature of the design.

A-5 COST OF SAFETY CRITICAL SOFTWARE

Most developers acquainted with safety-critical software will tell you that it is anything but cheap.

Several figures are thrown out, but a rule of thumb is that commercial-grade software runs from $15 to $30 per line of code and that safety-critical software generally costs five to ten times that amount. The range of $75 to $300 per source line of software is not unrealistic. However, given that almost 20% of all recalled devices are due to software faults, adds a significant amount to that total [3] given the time to recall, fix and redistribute the solution.

Other factors to consider include:

Many software developers still follow an 80/20 rule whereby 80% of the cost is in code and debug, while 20% is attributable to design.

Results from a 2002 study indicate that 1/3 of the cost associated with faulty software could be eliminated with proactive processes [5].

Up to $59 billion (2002) of waste is attributable to faulty software, and over half of that amount is bourn by users [5].

- What is the impact of when a fault is introduced vs. when it is found?

- What is the total cost of a recall?

- What is the cost of civil litigation?

- When is a bug introduced vs. when the bug is found?

Safety-critical software standards represent a rational compromise of social and market forces. On one side is stakeholder safety, and on the other, positive economic return for investors.

There is no such thing as bug free software, as well as there is a point of investment in quality at which there will be no positive return on the investment in a safety critical device. The quality of software can be determined by comparing its characteristics (features, capabilities, behavior) with the set of requirements that govern its creation. If its characteristics satisfy the set of requirements completely, high quality is achieved. On the other hand, if its characteristics do not meet the set of requirements, low quality results. Success in documenting software requirements is a crucial factor in the successful validation of the resulting software code [6].

Requirements are often described in terms of a hierarchy of requirements i.e. high-level, and low-level.

An example of this could be system requirements that are composed of sets of hardware requirements, and software requirements. The software requirements can be broken down into even more sets of software that represent RTOS requirements, and application software requirements. This process continues until it can not be decomposed any further yet still have the attribute that it is actionable and it is measurable. Verification and validation each play an essential role in any discussion of software quality.

The terms verification and validation are often used interchangeably. Some even go as far as to use verification, validation and testing as if they mean the same thing. It is important to understand the difference of the two terms as they represent fundamental concepts in the safety-critical development processes. According to the FDA:

Verification addresses the question: "Are we making the software correctly?"

"The objective of software verification is to perform, create and document with objective evidence that the design outputs of each phase of the software development life cycle meets all of the specified requirements for that phase. Software verification looks for consistency, completeness, and correctness of the software and its supporting documentation, as it is being developed, and provides support for a subsequent conclusion that software is validated. Software testing is one of many verification activities intended to confirm that software development output meets its input requirements. Other verification activities include various static and dynamic analyses, code and document inspections, walk-through, and other techniques."

In comparison, validation addresses the question: "Are we making the correct software?"

The FDA considers software validation to be "confirmation by examination and provision of objective evidence that software specifications conform to user needs and intended uses, and that the particular requirements implemented through software can be consistently fulfilled."

A-6 MEDICAL DEVICE MARKET REGULATORY ENVIRONMENT

There are two categories of rules and regulations within the regulatory environment for medical devices: technical and non-technical. Development standards and the product cycle fall within the first category, and non-technical governance falls into the second category. The players within the medical market may be active in two or more of the following three groups, but generally take a primary role in one:

- Manufacturers – all stakeholders playing a development, manufacturing, and sales role

- Regulators – Government or Non-governmental groups responsible for compliance

- Industry and Standards Bodies – International and regional groups with goals of protection and promotion of their industry and clientele

A-6-1 THE REGULATORS

The laws, regulatory burden and constraints that apply to a domestic manufacturer of medical equipment require a substantial time and expense commitment. Manufacturers that market and sell their products internationally face a vast, convoluted, and complex morass of global laws, regulations and statutes.

Each nation has its own agency that controls its medical market. In the U.S., Congress confers power to the FDA. In the European Union, the European Parliament and the Council of the EU, empower the Competent Authorities of member states with the responsibility. Such countries as Japan, Canada, Mexico, and Great Britain have a similar approach to regulation.

A-6-2 INDUSTRY AND STANDARDS BODIES

The voluntary association of members and stakeholders from within the medical market create medical standards. While federated employees also participate in the standards groups, standards represent a consensus on best practices that will benefit the industry as a whole. The goals are focused on improving the overall industry.

There are three primary international standardization organizations for medical devices i.e. the International Organization for Standardization (ISO), the International Electrotechnical

Commission (IEC), and the International Telecommunication Union (ITU). Generally, ITU covers telecommunications, IEC covers electrical and electronic engineering, and ISO covers the remainder.

The Institute of Electrical and Electronics Engineers (IEEE), and Association for the Advancement of Medical Instrumentation (AAMI) also play a role in standards and guidance. The Global Harmonization Task Force (GHTF) is dedicated to harmonizing the different technical standards to achieve uniformity worldwide.

The next section looks at the world's largest regulatory environments, the U.S. and the EU.

A-6-3 THE REGULATORY ENVIRONMENT IN THE UNITED STATES

The U.S. FDA is responsible for interpreting Congressional statutes provided for in Title 21 of the Code of Federal Regulations (CFR). Title 21 regulates food, drugs and medical devices within the U.S., and defines the regulatory authority of the U.S. Food and Drug Administration (FDA), the Drug Enforcement Administration (DEA), and the Office of National Drug Control Policy. The regulations that apply strictly to the FDA are contained in 21 CFR Parts 1 to 1499 [7]. The Center for Devices and Radiological Health (CDRH), a branch of the FDA, is responsible for the premarket approval of all medical devices, and oversees the manufacturing, performance and safety of these devices.

Either the 510(k) or the Pre-market Approval (PMA) process governs FDA/CDRH compliant devices, depending on their classification. Determining which application process to use is not complex, but it does seem to be somewhat arbitrary. Therefore, it is recommended that prior to making any assumptions about the device type, class or application process that the following determinations are made for a medical device:

- The degree of development rigor placed on the manufacturer is dependent on a number of factors including the intended use of the device and predicate device classification play a large role in establishing the class of the device. The FDA allows a great deal of latitude in establishing predicated use. Attempts should be made to either reduce or eliminate the degree of regulatory controls placed on the device in question.

- Work closely with the FDA or a qualified consultant throughout the process to avoid mistakes that require restarting the process.

A-6-4 FDA 510(K)

While one often hears the term "Certification" and "FDA 510(k)/PMA" used in the same sentence, in reality the 510(k) is not really a standard. It is the section of the Federal Food, Drug and Cosmetic Act (FD&CA) that defines how medical devices requiring FDA review qualify to be sold in the US market. The FDA 510(k) process is used to obtain marketing clearance for a device that is substantially equivalent in safety and effectiveness to another lawfully marketed device, or to a standard recognized by the FDA when used for the same intended purpose [8].

A-6-5 FDA PREMARKET APPROVAL

Pre-market Approval (PMA) is the most stringent type of application required by the FDA and applies to "Class III" devices such as life-support devices, devices with the potential to do great injury or new devices, which have an unknown safety and hazard potential. To gain approval, the manufacturer must present adequate scientific evidence to assure that the device is safe and effective for its intended uses [8].

A-6-6 FDA DEVELOPMENT GUIDANCE

Once the application and device are established, the FDA provides the following documentation that provides guidance as to how the software should be developed, documented and controlled [9]:

- Guidance for the Content of Premarket Submissions for Software Contained in Medical Devices

- General Principles of Software Validation

- Guidance for Off-the-Shelf Software Use in Medical Devices

- Cybersecurity for Networked Medical Devices Containing Off-the-Shelf (OTS) Software

The IEC 62304 Standard incorporates equivalent or superior software life-cycle processes compared with those above, and it is recognized in more markets than the FDA's clearance.

A-6-7 DEVICE CLASS

The FDA defines medical devices as: Class I, Class II, or Class III. The classifications are assigned based on the level of potential hazard associated with a device. The probability that harm will manifest also influences the Class of the device.

- Class I devices represent the lowest degree of hazard and is thereby subject to the lowest amount of regulatory controls. Many Class I devices are exempt and do not have to apply for clearance. If not found exempt, then a 510(k) is required.

  Low-hazard devices are devices such as thermometers, blood pressure monitors, and certain laboratory equipment.

- Class II has a higher likelihood of hazard and is therefore subject to greater number of regulatory controls. There are also a number of exempt Class II devices. If not found exempt, then a 510(k) is required.

- Class III is associated with the greatest hazard and level of regulatory controls and is required to submit a PMA. Some Class III devices that have a manufacturer with a proven record of safety, use best practices, etc., may be allowed to use the 510(k) option.

Life-support and critical monitoring equipment are generally considered to be high-hazard devices. If they fail or are faulty, the probability for an adverse patient outcome is high. Devices that have the potential of doing significant harm to the operator also qualify as a Class III device.

Examples include anesthesia equipment that has the potential to harm more than the patient. During an operation, it can release a flammable gas and pure O_2 into an enclosed space. Another class of device that is usually considered a class III device is a therapeutic device that uses energetic energy as part of the therapy. Neutron or electron treatment devices can do large degrees of harm if they fail, or used improperly.

A-6-8 LEVEL OF CONCERN (FDA/CDRH)

Not to be confused with the Medical Device Classification (Class I, II, or III), the FDA has defined additional protocols for devices that use or contain software. In this case, the system as a whole is considered, i.e. consisting of operators, patient, environment, hardware and software (including OTS software) but the Level of Concern (LOC) protocol is a measure of the hazard contributed solely by the software.

The LOC for software falls into one of three categories:

▪ Major - The software LOC is Major if the software could contribute, either directly or indirectly result in death or serious injury to the patient or operator.

▪ Moderate - The software LOC is Moderate if the software could contribute, either directly or indirectly result in minor injury to the patient or operator.

▪ Minor - The software LOC is Minor if failures or latent design flaws are unlikely to cause any injury to the patient or operator.

The FDA provides Table 2-01 [10] to assist in determining the degree of Verification and Validation that is required in order to support the clearance of the device.

Software Documentation	Minor Concern	Moderate Concern	Major Concern
Level of Concern	A statement indicating the Level of Concern and a description of the rationale for that level.		
Software Description	A summary overview of the features and software operating environment.		
Device Hazard Analysis	Tabular description of identified hardware and software hazards, including severity assessment and mitigations.		
Software Requirements Specification (SRS)	Summary of functional requirements from SRS.	The complete Software Requirements Specification (SRS) document.	
Architectural Design Chart	No documentation is necessary in the submission.	Detailed depiction of functional units and software modules. May include state diagrams as well as flow charts.	

Software Documentation	Minor Concern	Moderate Concern	Major Concern
Software Design Specification (SDS)	No documentation is necessary in the submission.	Software Design Specification (SDS) document.	
Traceability Analysis	Traceability among requirements, specifications, identified hazards and mitigations, and verification and validation testing.		
Software Development Environment Description	No documentation is necessary in the submission.	Summary of software life cycle development plan, including a summary of the configuration management and maintenance activities.	Summary of software life cycle development plan. Annotated list of control documents generated during development process. Include the configuration management and maintenance plan documents.
Verification and Validation Document (V&V)	Software functional test plan, pass / fail criteria, and results.	Description of V&V activities at the unit, integration, and system level. System level test protocol, including pass/fail criteria, and tests results.	Description of V&V activities at the unit, integration, and system level. Unit, integration and system level test protocols, including pass/fail criteria, test report, summary, and tests results.
Revision Level History	Revision history log, including release version number and date		
Unresolved Anomalies	No documentation is necessary in the submission.	List of remaining software anomalies, annotated with an explanation of the impact on safety or effectiveness, including operator usage and human factors.	

Table A-1 **Degrees of Verification and Validation**

A-7 REGULATORY ENVIRONMENT IN THE EUROPEAN UNION

Medical devices in the European Union and the standards that govern them have been harmonized and codified under a set of comprehensive Medical Device Directives. The primary directives are:

- Directive 90/385/EEC for implantable medical devices

- Directive 2007/47/EEC medical devices

- Directive 98/79/EC in vitro diagnostic medical devices

2007/47/EC is a set of regulations comparable to the ones discussed in the Regulatory Environment in the U.S.

A-7-1 EU DEVICE CLASSES

The EU uses a ranking system similar to the FDA's except it allows for four categories, ranging from low risk to high risk.

- Class I (including Is & Im)

- Class IIa

- Class IIb

- Class III

The difference between a Class IIa, and Class IIb device are beyond the scope of this book.

A-8 MEDICAL STANDARDS

A-8-1 IEC 62304

IEC 62304 Medical device software - Software life-cycle processes, was created by a joint working group of the ISO and IEC team members and released in 2006. As of March 2010, it is mandatory for medical products carrying the CE mark and sold in the EU. With recognition by the FDA as a consensus standard, IEC 62304 is the de facto standard for manufacturers selling to the international market.

IEC 62304 recognizes that the software life cycle involves not just development, but that software is also released and used in the field. It requires up front planning and addresses real-life product issues such as software maintenance, problem resolution, and change management. IEC 62304 makes the assumption that the software life cycle exists within a quality and risk management system. With regard to the risk management process, ISO 14971 is assumed and is a normative standard. ISO 14971 is dominant in the risk management category, while ISO 13485 is the quality management system of choice.

IEC 62304 defines the software lifecycle as a framework of essential processes, including:

- Software development process

- Software maintenance process

- Software hazard management process

- Software configuration management process

- Software problem resolution process

- Risk management process - ISO 14971

- Quality management system (Suggested ISO 13485)

IEC 62304 divides each process into a set of activities, and each set is subdivided into a set of tasks. In addition to identifying the set of processes, activities and tasks that are necessary and sufficient to undertake the project, IEC 62304 also provides a scale, which manufacturers are to use to evaluate the hazard associated with the software as implemented within the device.

Similar to the "Level of Concern" used by the FDA, these software safety classes are assigned based on severity as follows:

- Class A: No injury or damage to health is possible

- Class B: Non-serious injury is possible

- Class C: Death or serious injury is possible

Once the Class of the software is established, IEC 62304 provides a list of the processes, activities and tasks that must be performed in order to develop software that will meet the needs of the application. Table A-2 below is a sample of the direction provided by the standard. As expected, Process 5, Activity 5.1 requires that the planning task is performed for all classes of software. But for activity 5.1.5, "Software development standards, methods and tools planning" this level of planning is only required for Class C.

Clauses and Sub-clauses	Class A	Class B	Class C
4.0 General Requirements			
Clause 4 All Requirements	X	X	X
5.0 Software Development Process			
5.1 Software development Planning (activity)	X	X	X
5.1.1 Software Development Plan (task)	X	X	X
5.1.2 Keep Software Development plan ...	X	X	X
5.1.3 Software Development plan reference ...	X	X	X
5.1.4 Software Development standards, ...			X
5.1.5 Software integration and ...		X	X
...	...	...	...
Clause 8 All requirements	X	X	X
Clause 9 All requirements	X	X	X

Table A-2 **Software safety classes**

949

IEC is not perfect and there is room for improvement. Observations consistently find that IEC 62304 is easier to understand and has less ambiguity, it is provided as a single document and incorporates mechanisms for handling off the shelf software as an integral part of the process, and it provides a process for partitioning software into separate classes to reduce validation costs without sacrificing the integrity of the device.

A-8-2 ISO 14971

The latest release, formally known as ISO 14971:2007 "Medical Devices — Risk Management — Application of Risk Management to Medical Devices," is recognized by the FDA and specified by the EU's Medical Device Directive (MDD) and is the normative risk management process used by IEC 62304. Unless otherwise stated, the assumption is that manufacturers use ISO 14971 as their defined and documented process that satisfies risk analysis, evaluation, and control. Similar to IEC 62304, ISO 14971 applies to the device life cycle, not just development [10], [11]. It is best treated as an absolute requirement.

A-8-3 ISO 13485

ISO 13485 "Medical devices -- Quality management systems -- Requirements for regulatory purposes," is seen as required infrastructure for medical device manufacturers. While other standards such as ISO 9001 are also acceptable, ISO 13495 is tailored to meet the specific regulatory and quality requirements of broad needs of the medical device industry and certain sectors such as implantable devices, and sterile medical devices [10], [11]. It is best treated as an absolute requirement.

A-9 MEDICAL SOFTWARE IN THE FUTURE

The working group tasked with predicting the future had a much easier job than either the FDA or the industry as a whole will in the years to come. While the medical industry is not missing ethics, it is optimistic rather than pragmatic. That optimism is exhibited by the "Tell me it is Safe" FDA process compared with a "Prove it" process used in avionics.

While the institutional goals of the FDA are worthy, it is clear that the process to approve device for market represents a clash of two cultures. What other organization in the world drives a safety critical process by detailing the documents that must be submitted rather than the steps needed to ensure that the device is safe?

Why is that important? It is not the paperwork that is critical. The paperwork is a by-product of doing the right thing at the right time. If documentation alone drives the process, safety will never truly catch up.

The convergence of technologies similar to in cell phones and other consumer electronics such as wireless connectivity, 2D and 3D graphics, multimedia, etc will increase convenience, expand capabilities, and drive portability. Many of these technologies will in turn drive the need for even more software such as security and privacy software that is needed because of the wireless and other connectivity. All of this will result in device software code bases that will grow by a magnitude or more, and for many companies most of this software will have to come from outside.

The problem for manufacturers will not be the availability of software, but the availability of software that is qualified or able to be qualified for use in medical devices. Companies such as Micrium, and Validated Software provide software and the evidence of compliance with both FDA and IEC 62304 standards.

A-10 COMMON SAFETY-CRITICAL DEVELOPMENT STANDARDS

Globally, there are many regional, and industry specific standards. Two robust standards specifically involved in software development are IEC 61508 and DO-178B. Given that standards apply to not only software, but all aspect of design, each industry and its related equipment poses dramatically different hazards. Therefore the methods used to evaluate and mitigate these hazards promote the use of diverse standards governing device creation. Specific standards that address not only the medical industry are:

- IEC 61508 Functional safety of electrical/electronic/programmable electronic safety-related systems. IEC-61508-3 specifically addresses software.

- UK Defense Standard 00-56 Issue 2, Safety Management Requirements for Defense Systems

- US Requirements and Technical Concepts for Aviation (RTCA) DO-178B Software Considerations in Airborne Systems and Equipment Certification

- US RTCA DO-278B Guidelines for Communications, Navigation, Surveillance, and Air Traffic Management (CNS/ATM) Systems Software Integrity Assurance

■ US RTCA DO-254 North American Avionics Hardware

■ EUROCAE ED-12B European Airborne Flight Safety Systems. Technically equivalent to DO- 178B

■ IEC 62304 - Medical Device Software - Software Life Cycle Processes

■ IEC 61513, Nuclear power plants – Instrumentation and control for systems important to safety General requirements for systems, based on EN 61508

■ IEC 61511 Functional safety - safety instrumented systems for the process industry sector

■ IEC 62061, Safety of machinery - Functional safety of safety- related electrical, electronic and programmable electronic control systems, based on EN 61508

■ EN 50128, Railway applications - Communications, signaling and processing systems. Software for railway control and protection systems

■ EN 50129, Railway Industry Specific

■ NASA Safety Critical Guidelines

A-11 STANDARDS BODIES AND WORLDWIDE STANDARDS ORGANIZATIONS

■ American National Standards Institute (ANSI) - www.ansi.org

■ American Society for Testing and Materials (ASTM) - www.astm.org

■ Association for the Advancement of Medical Instrumentation (AAMI) - www.aami.org

■ Australian Therapeutic Goods Administration - www.tga.gov.au

■ British Standards Institution (BSI) - www.bsi-global.com

■ Canadian Standards Association (CSA) - www.csa.ca

- European Committee for Electrotechnical Standardization (CENLELEC) - www.cenelec.eu

- European Committee for Standardization (CEN) - www.cen.eu

- European Telecommunications Standards Institute (ETSI) - www.etsi.org

- Finnish Standards Association - www.sfs.fi

- French Association for Standardization (AFNOR) - www.afnor.fr

- German Standards Institute (DIN) - www.din.de

- Global Harmonization Task Force (GHTF) - www.ghtf.org

- IEEE-SA Standards Association (IEEE-SA) – www.standards.ieee.org

- International Electrotechnical Commission (IEC) – www.iec.org

- International Standards Organization (ISO) - www.iso.org

- Medicines and Healthcare Products Regulatory Agency (UK) - www.mhra.gov.uk

- National Institute for Standards and Technology (NIST) - www.nist.gov

- Radio Technical Commission for Aeronautics (RTCA) - http://www.rtca.org

- Standards Association of Australia - www.standards.org.au

- Standards Council Canada (SCC) - www.scc.ca

- Swedish Standards Institute (SIS) - www.sis.se

- Swiss Association for Standardization (SNV) - www.snv.ch

A-12 FDA GUIDANCE AND DOCUMENTS

The FDA/CDRH website contains an easily searchable wealth of information. Although access to some specifications such as IEC 62304 is fee-based, it is possible to meet FDA requirements by using strictly public material. A worthwhile place to begin the process is at: How to Market Your Device:

http://www.fda.gov/MedicalDevices/DeviceRegulationandGuidance/HowtoMarketYourDevice

Additional helpful documents to download include:

- Design Control Guidance for Medical Device Manufacturers, CDRH, FDA, March 1997

  http://www.fda.gov/MedicalDevices/DeviceRegulationandGuidance/
  GuidanceDocuments/ucm070627.htm

- Do It by Design, An Introduction to Human Factors in Medical Devices, CDRH, FDA, March 1997

  http://www.fda.gov/downloads/MedicalDevices/DeviceRegulationandGuidance/
  GuidanceDocuments/ucm095061.pdf

- Electronic Records; Electronic Signatures Final Rule, 62, Federal Register 13430, March, 1997

  http://www.fda.gov/downloads/RegulatoryInformation/Guidances/ucm125125.pdf

- General Principles of Software Validation; Final Guidance for Industry and FDA Staff Document, Center for Devices and Radiological Health, FDA, January 2002

  http://www.fda.gov/downloads/MedicalDevices/DeviceRegulationandGuidance/
  GuidanceDocuments/ucm085371.pdf

- Glossary of Computerized System and Software Development Terminology, Division of Field Investigations, Office of Regional Operations, Office of Regulatory Affairs, FDA, August 1995

  http://www.fda.gov/iceci/inspections/inspectionguides/ucm074875.htm

■ Guidance for the Content of Pre-market Submissions for Software Contained in Medical Devices, Office of Device Evaluation, CDRH, Food and Drug Administration, May 11, 2005

http://www.fda.gov/downloads/MedicalDevices/DeviceRegulationandGuidance/
GuidanceDocuments/ucm089593.pdf

■ Guidance for Industry, FDA Reviewers and Compliance on Off-the-Shelf Software Use in Medical Devices, Office of Device Evaluation, Center for Devices and Radiological Health, Food and Drug Administration, September 1999

http://www.fda.gov/downloads/MedicalDevices/DeviceRegulationandGuidance/
GuidanceDocuments/ucm073779.pdf

■ Guidance for Industry Process Validation: General Principles and Practices, Center for Biologics Evaluation and Research (CBER), Food and Drug Administration January 2011

http://www.fda.gov/downloads/Drugs/GuidanceComplianceRegulatoryInformation/
Guidances/UCM070336.pdf

■ Medical Devices; Current Good Manufacturing Practice (CGMP) Final Rule; Quality System Regulation, 61 Federal Register 52602, October 7 1996

http://www.fda.gov/downloads/MedicalDevices/DeviceRegulationandGuidance/
PostmarketRequirements/QualitySystemsRegulations/
MedicalDeviceQualitySystemsManual/UCM122806.pdf

■ Reviewer Guidance for a Pre-Market Notification Submission for Blood Establishment Computer Software, Center for Biologics Evaluation and Research, Food and Drug Administration, January 1997

http://www.fda.gov/downloads/BiologicsBloodVaccines/
GuidanceComplianceRegulatoryInformation/OtherRecommendationsforManufacturers/
MemorandumtoBloodEstablishments/UCM062208.pdf

■ Blood Establishment Computer Software: Understanding What to Include in a 510 (K) Submission, Transcript J Murray, Nov 2009, pg. 180

http://www.fda.gov/downloads/BiologicsBloodVaccines/NewsEvents/ WorkshopsMeetingsConferences/UCM198711.pdf

■ Guidance for Industry - Cybersecurity for Networked Medical Devices Containing Off-the-Shelf (OTS) Software, January 2005

http://www.fda.gov/downloads/MedicalDevices/DeviceRegulationandGuidance/ GuidanceDocuments/ucm077823.pdf

■ Implementation of Risk Management Principles and Activities within a Quality System, Management, July 2005

http://www.ghtf.org/documents/sg3/sg3n15r82005.pdf

■ Quality Management Systems - Process Validation Guidance, FDA Draft Guidance, January 2004

http://www.ghtf.org/documents/sg3/sg3_fd_n99-10_edition2.pdf

A-13 REFERENCES

[1]   W. Herman, G. Devey, "Future Trends in Medical Device Technologies", 2008.

[2]   U.S. Food and Drug Administration (FDA), "General Principles of Software Validation; Final Guidance for Industry and FDA Staff", 2002.

[3]   J. Murray Jr., "CDRH Software Update", 2008.

[4]   U.S. Food and Drug Administration (FDA), "Glossary of Computerized System and Software Development Terminology", 2005.

[5]   RTI - Health, Social, and Economic Research, G. Tassey , Ph.D. (NIST), "The Economic Impacts of Inadequate Infrastructure for Software Testing - Final Report", 2002.

[6]   B. Dolan, Interview: "The iPhone medical app denied 510(k)", Mobile Health News, 2010.

[7]   U.S. Food and Drug Administration (FDA), "Guidance for Industry, FDA Reviewers and Compliance on: Off-The- Shelf Software Use in Medical Devices", 1999.

[8]   U.S. Food and Drug Administration (FDA), "How to market your device", 2011

[9]   U.S. Food and Drug Administration (FDA), "Device classification", 2011

[10]   Swiss International Electrotechnical Commission, "International standard 62304: Medical device software – Software life cycle processes", 2006.

[11]   European Commission, Health & Consumers Directorate-General, "Implementation of Directive 2007/47/EC Amending Directives 90/385/EEC, 93/42/EEC AND 98/8/EC", 2009.

Appendix A

μC/OS-III Port for the Cortex-M4

This appendix describes the adaptation of μC/OS-III to the Cortex-M4 which is called a *Port*.

The port files are found in the following directory:

`\Micrium\Software\uCOS-III\Ports\ARM-Cortex-M4\Generic\IAR`

The port consists of three files:

`os_cpu.h`
`os_cpu_c.c`
`os_cpu_a.asm`

They are described in the following sections.

B-1 OS_CPU.H

os_cpu.h contains processor- and implementation-specific **#defines** constants, macros, and typedefs. **os_cpu.h** is shown in Listing B-1.

```
#ifndef  OS_CPU_H                                              (1)
#define  OS_CPU_H
#ifdef   OS_CPU_GLOBALS                                        (2)
#define  OS_CPU_EXT
#else
#define  OS_CPU_EXT  extern
#endif
/*
*********************************************************************************************
*                                         MACROS
*********************************************************************************************
*/
#define  OS_TASK_SW()              OSCtxSw()                   (3)
#define  OS_TS_GET()               CPU_TS_TmrRd()              (4)
/*
*********************************************************************************************
*                                       PROTOTYPES
*********************************************************************************************
*/
void  OSCtxSw               (void);                            (5)
void  OSIntCtxSw            (void);
void  OSStartHighRdy        (void);
void  OS_CPU_PendSVHandler  (void);                            (6)
void  OS_CPU_SysTickHandler (void);                            (7)
void  OS_CPU_SysTickInit    (CPU_INT32U  cnts);
#endif
```

Listing B-1 **os_cpu.h**

LB-1(1)   Typical multiple header file inclusion protection.

LB-1(2)   **OS_CPU_GLOBALS** and **OS_CPU_EXT** allow us to declare global variables that are specific to this port. However, the port doesn't contain any global variables and thus these statements are just included for completeness and consistency.

LB-1(3)   The task level context switch code is performed by **OSCtxSw()**. This function is actually implemented in **os_cpu_a.asm**.

LB-1(4)   Timestamps are obtained by calling **CPU_TS_TmrRd()**. On the Cortex-M4, **CPU_TS_TmrRd()** reads the **DWT_CYCCNT** register which is a 32-bit free-running up counter.

LB-1(5)   The prototypes of mandatory µC/OS-III functions.

LB-1(6)   The Cortex-M4 processor provides a special interrupt handler specifically designed for use by context switch code. This is called the PendSV Handler and is implemented by **OS_CPU_PendSVHandler()**. The function is found in **os_cpu_a.asm**

LB-1(7)   The Cortex-M4 has a timer dedicated for RTOS use called the SysTick. The code to initialize and handle the SysTick interrupt is found in **os_cpu_c.c**. Note that this code is part of the µC/OS-III port file and not the Board Support Package (BSP), because the SysTick is available to all Cortex-M4 implementations and is always handled the same by µC/OS-III.

B-2 OS_CPU_C.C

A µC/OS-III port requires that the following functions be declared:

```
OSIdleTaskHook()
OSInitHook()
OSStatTaskHook()
OSTaskCreateHook()
OSTaslDelHook()
OSTaskReturnHook()
OSTaskStkInit()
OSTaskSwHook()
OSTimeTickHook()
```

The Cortex-M4 port implements two additional functions as described in the previous sections:

```
OS_CPU_SysTickHandler()
OS_CPU_SysTickInit()
```

B-2-1 OS_CPU_C.C – OSIdleTaskHook()

The idle task hook allows the port developer to extend the functionality of the idle task. For example, you can place the processor in low power mode when no other higher-priority tasks are running. This is especially useful in battery-powered applications. Listing B-2 shows the typical code for **OSIdleTaskHook()**.

```
void   OSIdleTaskHook (void)
{
#if OS_CFG_APP_HOOKS_EN > 0u                                     (1)
    if (OS_AppIdleTaskHookPtr != (OS_APP_HOOK_VOID)0) {          (2)
        (*OS_AppIdleTaskHookPtr)();                              (3)
    }
#endif
}
```

Listing B-2 **os_cpu_c.c – OSIdleTaskHook()**

LB-2(1)   Application level hook functions are enabled by **OS_CFG_APP_HOOKS_EN**.

LB-2(2)   If the application developer wants his/her own function to be called on every iteration of the idle task, the developer needs to initialize the value of **OS_AppIdleTaskHookPtr** to point to the desired function to call.

Note that µC/OS-III initializes **OS_AppIdleTaskHookPtr** to **NULL** when **OSInit()** is called and therefore, the code must set this pointer only after calling **OSInit()**.

The application hook function *must not* make any blocking calls because the idle task must never block. In other words, it cannot call **OSTimeDly()**, **OSTimeDlyHMSM()**, or **OSTaskSuspend()** (to suspend 'self'), and any of the **OS???Pend()** functions.

Examples of application hooks are found in **os_app_hooks.c**.

LB-2(3)   The application level idle task hook is called without any argument.

B-2-2 OS_CPU_C.C – OSInitHook()

Listing B-3 shows the typical code for OSInitHook().

```
void   OSInitHook (void);
```

Listing B-3 **os_cpu_c.c – OSInitHook()**

OSInitHook() does not call any application-level hook functions because it can't, and thus there is no application hook function pointer. The reason for this is that OSInit() initializes all the application hook pointers to NULL and because of that, it would not be possible to redefine the application init hook pointer before OSInit() returns.

B-2-3 OS_CPU_C.C – OSStatTaskHook()

OSTaskStatHook() allows the port developer to extend the functionality of the statistic task by allowing him/her to add additional statistics. OSStatTaskHook() is called after computing the total CPU usage (see OS_StatTask() in os_stat.c). Listing B-4 shows the typical code for OSStatTaskHook().

```
void   OSStatTaskHook (void)
{
#if OS_CFG_APP_HOOKS_EN > 0u
    if (OS_AppStatTaskHookPtr != (OS_APP_HOOK_VOID)0) {     (1)
        (*OS_AppStatTaskHookPtr)();                          (2)
    }
#endif
}
```

Listing B-4 **os_cpu_c.c – OSStatTaskHook()**

LB-4(1)   If the application developer wants his/her own function to be called by µC/OS-III's statistic task (i.e., OS_StatTask()) then he/she needs to initialize the value of OS_AppStatTaskHookPtr to point to the desired function to call.

Note that µC/OS-III initializes OS_AppStatTaskHookPtr to NULL when OSInit() is called and therefore, the code must set this pointer only after calling OSInit().

The application hook function *must not* make any blocking calls because it would affect the behavior of the statistic task. Examples of application hooks are found in **os_app_hooks.c**.

LB-4(2)   The application level statistic task hook is called without any argument.

B-2-4 OS_CPU_C.C – OSTaskCreateHook()

OSTaskCreateHook() gives the port developer the opportunity to add code specific to the port when a task is created. **OSTaskCreateHook()** is called once the **OS_TCB** fields are initialized, but prior to making the task ready to run. Listing B-5 shows the typical code for **OSTaskCreateHook()**.

```
void  OSTaskCreateHook (OS_TCB *p_tcb)
{
#if OS_CFG_APP_HOOKS_EN > 0u
    if (OS_AppTaskCreateHookPtr != (OS_APP_HOOK_TCB)0) {          (1)
        (*OS_AppTaskCreateHookPtr)(p_tcb);                       (2)
    }
#else
    (void)&p_tcb;          /* Prevent compiler warning */
#endif
}
```

Listing B-5 **os_cpu_c.c – OSTaskCreateHook()**

LB-5(1)   If the application developer wants his/her own function to be called when a task is created, the developer needs to initialize the value of **OS_AppTaskCreateHookPtr** to point to the desired function to call. The application hook function *must not* make any blocking calls and should perform its function as quickly as possible.

Note that μC/OS-III initializes **OS_AppTaskCreateHookPtr** to **NULL** when **OSInit()** is called. The code must set this pointer only after calling **OSInit()**.

Examples of application hooks are found in **os_app_hooks.c**.

LB-5(2)   The application level task create hook is passed the address of the **OS_TCB** of the task being created.

B-2-5 OS_CPU_C.C – OSTaskDelHook()

OSTaskDelHook() gives the port developer the opportunity to add code specific to the port when a task is deleted. OSTaskDelHook() is called once the task has been removed from all lists (the ready list, the tick list or a pend list). Listing B-6 shows the typical code for OSTaskDelHook().

```
void  OSTaskDelHook (OS_TCB *p_tcb)
{
#if OS_CFG_APP_HOOKS_EN > 0u
    if (OS_AppTaskDelHookPtr != (OS_APP_HOOK_TCB)0) {        (1)
        (*OS_AppTaskDelHookPtr)(p_tcb);                      (2)
    }
#else
    (void)&p_tcb;           /* Prevent compiler warning */
#endif
}
```

Listing B-6 **os_cpu_c.c – OSTaskDelHook()**

LB-6(1)   If the application developer wants his/her own function to be called when a task is deleted, the developer needs to initialize the value of **OS_AppTaskDelHookPtr** to point to the desired function to call.

The application hook function *must not* make any blocking calls, and should perform its function as quickly as possible.

Note that μC/OS-III initializes **OS_AppTaskDelHookPtr** to **NULL** when **OSInit()** is called and the code must set this pointer only after calling **OSInit()**.

Examples of application hooks are found in **os_app_hooks.c**.

LB-6(2)   The application level task delete hook is passed the address of the **OS_TCB** of the task being created.

B-2-6 OS_CPU_C.C – OSTaskReturnHook()

With µC/OS-III, a task is never allowed to return. However, if this happens accidentally, µC/OS-III will catch this and delete the offending task. However, **OSTaskDelHook()** will be called before the task is deleted. Listing B-7 shows the typical code for **OSTaskReturnHook()**.

```
void  OSTaskReturnHook (OS_TCB *p_tcb)
{
#if OS_CFG_APP_HOOKS_EN > 0u
    if (OS_AppTaskReturnHookPtr != (OS_APP_HOOK_TCB)0) {         (1)
        (*OS_AppTaskReturnHookPtr)(p_tcb);                      (2)
    }
#else
    (void)&p_tcb;            /* Prevent compiler warning */
#endif
}
```

Listing B-7 **os_cpu_c.c – OSTaskReturnHook()**

LB-7(1)   If the application developer wants his/her own function to be called when a task returns, the developer needs to initialize the value of **OS_AppTaskReturnHookPtr** to point to the desired function to call.

The application hook function *must not* make any blocking calls and should perform its function as quickly as possible.

Note that µC/OS-III initializes **OS_AppTaskReturnHookPtr** to **NULL** when **OSInit()** is called and the code must set this pointer only after calling **OSInit()**.

Examples of application hooks are found in **os_app_hooks.c**.

LB-7(2)   The application level task return hook is passed the address of the **OS_TCB** of the task being created.

B-2-7 OS_CPU_C.C – OSTaskStkInit()

This function initializes the stack frame of a task being created. When μC/OS-III creates a task it makes its stack look as if an interrupt just occurred and simulates pushing the context of the task onto the task stack. **OSTaskStkInit()** is called by **OSTaskCreate()**.

Listing B-8 shows the Cortex-M4 code for **OSTaskStkInit()**.

```
CPU_STK *OSTaskStkInit (OS_TASK_PTR   p_task,              (1)
                        void         *p_arg,
                        CPU_STK      *p_stk_base,
                        CPU_STK      *p_stk_limit,
                        CPU_STK_SIZE  stk_size,
                        OS_OPT        opt)
{
    CPU_STK  *p_stk;


    (void)&opt;
    (void)&p_stk_limit;
     p_stk    = &p_stk_base[stk_size - 1u];                (2)
    *p_stk-- = (CPU_INT32U)0x01000000L;                    (3)
    *p_stk-- = (CPU_INT32U)p_task;                         (4)
    *p_stk-- = (CPU_INT32U)OS_TaskReturn;                  (5)
    *p_stk-- = (CPU_INT32U)0x12121212L;                    (6)
    *p_stk-- = (CPU_INT32U)0x03030303L;
    *p_stk-- = (CPU_INT32U)0x02020202L;
    *p_stk-- = (CPU_INT32U)0x01010101L;
    *p_stk-- = (CPU_INT32U)p_arg;                          (7)
    *p_stk-- = (CPU_INT32U)0x11111111L;                    (8)
    *p_stk-- = (CPU_INT32U)0x10101010L;
    *p_stk-- = (CPU_INT32U)0x09090909L;
    *p_stk-- = (CPU_INT32U)0x08080808L;
    *p_stk-- = (CPU_INT32U)0x07070707L;
    *p_stk-- = (CPU_INT32U)0x06060606L;
    *p_stk-- = (CPU_INT32U)0x05050505L;
    *p_stk    = (CPU_INT32U)0x04040404L;
    return (p_stk);                                        (9)
}
```

Listing B-8 **os_cpu_c.c – OSTaskStkInit()**

LB-8(1)   **OSTaskStkInit()** is called by **OSTaskCreate()** and is passed six arguments:

1   The task's entry point (i.e., the address of the task).

2   A pointer to an argument that will be passed to the task when the task starts, i.e., **p_arg**.

3   The base address of the storage area in RAM of the stack. Typically a stack is declared as an array of **CPU_STKs** as shown below.

    CPU_STK MyTaskStk[stk_size];

In this case, the base address is simply **&MyTaskStk[0]**.

4   The address of where the stack limit is to point to. This assumes that the CPU supports stack limit checking. If not then this pointer is not used.

5   The size of the stack is also passed to **OSTaskStkInit()**.

6   Finally, the '**opt**' argument of **OSTaskCreate()** is passed to **OSTaskStkInit()** in case any of these are needed by **OSTaskStkInit()** for special options.

LB-8(2)   A local pointer is initialized to the top-of-stack to initialize. In the case of the Cortex-M4, the stack grows from high memory to low memory and therefore, the top-of-stack is at the highest address of the stack storage area.

LB-8(3)   The Cortex-M4's PSR register is initialized. The initial value sets the 'T' bit in the PSR, which causes the Cortex-M4 to use Thumb instructions (this should always be the case).

LB-8(4)   This register corresponds to R15 which is the program counter. We initialize this register to point to the task entry point.

LB-8(5)   This register corresponds to R14 (the link register), which contains the return address of the task. As previously mentioned, a task is not supposed to return. This pointer allows us, therefore, to catch this fault and properly terminate the task. µC/OS-III provides a function just for that purpose, **OS_TaskReturn()**.

LB-8(6)   Registers R12, R3, R2 and R1 are initialized to a value that makes it easy for them to be identified when a debugger performs a memory dump.

LB-8(7)   R0 is the register used by the C compiler to pass the first argument to a function. Recall that the prototype for a task looks as shown below.

```
void  MyTask (void *p_arg);
```

In this case, 'p_arg' is simply passed in R0 so that when the task starts, it will think it was called as with any other function.

LB-8(8)   Registers R11, R10, R9 and R8, R7, R6, R5 and R4 are initialized to a value that makes it easy for them to be identified when a debugger performs a memory dump.

LB-8(9)   Notice that the stack pointer is not decremented after the last register is placed onto the stack. This is because the Cortex-M4 assumes that the stack pointer points to the last element pushed onto the stack.

OSTaskStkInit() returns the new top-of-stack pointer to OSTaskCreate(), which will save this value in the task's OS_TCB in the .StkPtr field.

The stack frame of the task being created is shown in Figure B-1.

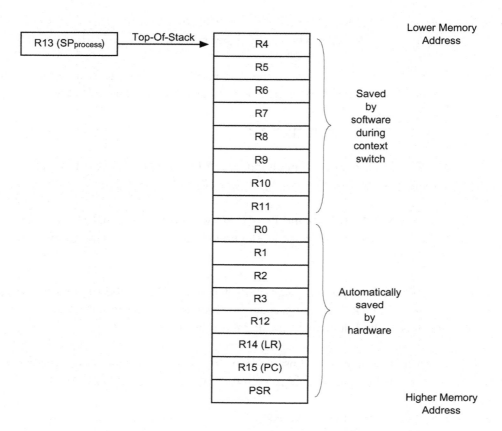

Figure B-1 **Stack frame of task being created**

B-2-8 OS_CPU_C.C – OSTaskSwHook()

OSTaskSwHook() is called when µC/OS-III performs a context switch. If fact, OSTaskSwHook() is called after saving the context of the task being suspended. Also, OSTaskSwHook() is called with interrupts disabled.

Listing B-9 shows the code for OSTaskSwHook(). This function is fairly complex and contains a lot of conditional compilation.

```c
void  OSTaskSwHook (void)
{
#if OS_CFG_TASK_PROFILE_EN > 0u
    CPU_TS      ts;
#ifdef  CPU_CFG_INT_DIS_MEAS_EN
    CPU_TS      int_dis_time;
#endif
#endif
#if OS_CFG_APP_HOOKS_EN > 0u
    if (OS_AppTaskSwHookPtr != (OS_APP_HOOK_VOID)0) {           (1)
        (*OS_AppTaskSwHookPtr)();                               (2)
    }
#endif
#if OS_CFG_TASK_PROFILE_EN > 0u
    ts = OS_TS_GET();                                           (3)
    if (OSTCBCurPtr != OSTCBHighRdyPtr) {
        OSTCBCurPtr->CyclesDelta  = ts - OSTCBCurPtr->CyclesStart;
        OSTCBCurPtr->CyclesTotal += (OS_CYCLES)OSTCBCurPtr->CyclesDelta;
    }
    OSTCBHighRdyPtr->CyclesStart  = ts;                         (4)
#ifdef  CPU_CFG_INT_DIS_MEAS_EN
    int_dis_time = CPU_IntDisMeasMaxCurReset();                 (5)
    if (int_dis_time > OSTCBCurPtr->IntDisTimeMax) {
        OSTCBCurPtr->IntDisTimeMax = int_dis_time;
    }
#if OS_CFG_SCHED_LOCK_TIME_MEAS_EN > 0u
    if (OSSchedLockTimeMaxCur > OSTCBCurPtr->SchedLockTimeMax) {   (6)
        OSTCBCurPtr->SchedLockTimeMax = OSSchedLockTimeMaxCur;
        OSSchedLockTimeMaxCur         = (CPU_TS)0;
    }
#endif
#endif
#endif
}
```

Listing B-9 **os_cpu_c.c – OSTaskSwHook()**

LB-9(1) If the application developer wants his/her own function to be called when a context switch occurs, the developer needs to initialize the value of **OS_AppTaskSwHookPtr** to point to the desired function to call.

The application hook function *must not* make any blocking calls and should perform its function as quickly as possible.

Note that µC/OS-III initializes **OS_AppTaskSwHookPtr** to **NULL** when **OSInit( )** is called and your code must set this pointer only after calling **OSInit( )**.

Examples of application hooks are found in **os_app_hooks.c**.

LB-9(2) The application level task switch hook is not passed any arguments. However, the global µC/OS-III variables **OSTCBCurPtr** and **OSTCBHighRdyPtr** will point to the **OS_TCB** of the task being switched out and the **OS_TCB** of the task being switched in, respectively.

LB-9(3) This code measures the execution time of each task. This will be used by the statistic task to compute the relative CPU usage (in percentage) that each task uses.

If task profiling is enabled (i.e., **OS_CFG_TASK_PROFILE_EN** is set to 1) then we obtain the current timestamp. If we are switching to a new task, we simply compute how long the task that is being switched out ran for. We then accumulate this in the **.CyclesTotal** field (64 bits) of the **OS_TCB** for that task.

LB-9(4) **OSTaskSwHook( )** stores the timestamp read as the beginning time of the new task being switched in.

Note is that the execution time of each task also includes the execution time of any interrupt that occurred while the task was executing. It would be possible to exclude this, but it would require more overhead on the CPU.

LB-9(5) If **CPU_CFG_INT_DIS_MEAS_EN** is set to 1, µC/CPU measures the interrupt disable time on a per-task basis. The code simply detects the maximum amount of interrupt disable time for each task and stores it in the **.IntDisTimeMax** field of the **OS_TCB** for the task being switched out.

LB-9(6)   If OS_CFG_SCHED_LOCK_TIME_MEAS_EN is set to 1, µC/OS-III keeps track of the maximum amount of time a task will have the scheduler locked for critical sections. This value is saved in the .SchedLockTimeMax field of the OS_TCB of the task being switched out.

B-2-9 OS_CPU_C.C – OSTimeTickHook()

OSTimeTickHook() gives the port developer the opportunity to add code that will be called by OSTimeTick(). OSTimeTickHook() is called from the tick ISR and must not make any blocking calls (it would be allowed to anyway) and must execute as quickly as possible.

Listing B-10 shows the typical code for OSTimeTickHook().

```
void  OSTimeTickHook (void)
{
#if OS_CFG_APP_HOOKS_EN > 0u
    if (OS_AppTimeTickHookPtr != (OS_APP_HOOK_VOID)0) {        (1)
        (*OS_AppTimeTickHookPtr)();                            (2)
    }
#else
    (void)&p_tcb;          /* Prevent compiler warning */
#endif
}
```

Listing B-10 **os_cpu_c.c – OSTimeTickHook()**

LB-10(1)   If the application developer wants his/her own function to be called when a tick interrupt occurs, the developer needs to initialize the value of OS_AppTimeTickHookPtr to point to the desired function to call.

Note that µC/OS-III initializes OS_AppTimeTickHookPtr to NULL when OSInit() is called and the code must set this pointer only after calling OSInit().

Examples of application hooks are found in os_app_hooks.c.

LB-10(2)   The application level time tick hook is not passed any arguments.

B-2-10 OS_CPU_C.C – OS_CPU_SysTickHandler()

`OS_CPU_SysTickHandler()` is automatically invoked by the Cortex-M4 when a SysTick interrupt occurs and interrupts are enabled. For this to happen, however, the address of `OS_CPU_SysTickHandler()` must be placed in the interrupt vector table at the SysTick entry (the 15th entry in the vector table of the Cortex-M4).

Listing B-11 shows the Cortex-M4 code for `OS_CPU_SysTickHandler()`.

```
void  OS_CPU_SysTickHandler (void)                    (1)
{
    CPU_SR_ALLOC();


    CPU_CRITICAL_ENTER();
    OSIntNestingCtr++;                                (2)
    CPU_CRITICAL_EXIT();
    OSTimeTick();                                     (3)
    OSIntExit();                                      (4)
}
```

Listing B-11 **os_cpu_c.c – OS_CPU_SysTickHandler()**

LB-11(1) When the Cortex-M4 enters an interrupt, the CPU automatically saves critical registers (R0, R1, R2, R3, R12, PC, LR and XPSR) onto the current task's stack and switches to the Main Stack (MSP) to handle the interrupt.

This means that R4 through R11 are not saved when the interrupt starts and the ARM Architecture Procedure Call Standard (AAPCS) requires that all interrupt handlers preserve the values of the other registers, if they are required during the ISR.

LB-11(2) The interrupt nesting counter is incremented in a critical section because the **SysTick** interrupt handler could be interrupted by a higher priority interrupt.

LB-11(3) The µC/OS-III tick interrupt needs to call **OSTimeTick()**.

LB-11(4) Every interrupt handler must call **OSIntExit()** at the end of the handler.

B-2-11 OS_CPU_C.C – OS_CPU_SysTickInit()

OS_CPU_SysTickInit( ) is called by your application code to initialize the SysTick interrupt.

Listing B-12 shows the Cortex-M4 code for OS_CPU_SysTickInit( ).

```
void  OS_CPU_SysTickInit (CPU_INT32U  cnts)                      (1)
{
    CPU_REG_NVIC_ST_RELOAD = cnts - 1u;                         (1)
    CPU_REG_NVIC_SHPRI3    |= 0xFF000000u;                      (2)
    CPU_REG_NVIC_ST_CTRL   |= CPU_REG_NVIC_ST_CTRL_CLKSOURCE
                            | CPU_REG_NVIC_ST_CTRL_ENABLE;
    CPU_REG_NVIC_ST_CTRL   |= CPU_REG_NVIC_ST_CTRL_TICKINT;
}
```

Listing B-12 **os_cpu_c.c – OS_CPU_SysTickInit()**

LB-12(1)   OS_CPU_SysTickInit( ) must be informed about the counts to reload into the SysTick timer. The counts to reload depend on the CPU clock frequency and the configured tick rate (i.e., OS_CFG_TICK_RATE_HZ in os_cfg_app.h).

The reload value is typically computed by the first application task to run as follows:

```
cpu_clk_freq = BSP_CPU_ClkFreq();
cnts         = cpu_clk_freq / (CPU_INT32U)OS_CFG_TICK_RATE_HZ;
```

BSP_CPU_ClkFreq( ) is a BSP function that returns the CPU clock frequency. We then compute reload counts from the tick rate.

LB-12(2)   The SysTick interrupt is set to the lowest priority because ticks are mostly used for coarse time delays and timeouts, and we want application interrupts to be handled first.

B-3 OS_CPU_A.ASM

os_cpu_a.asm contains processor-specific code for three functions that must be written in assembly language:

```
OSStartHighRdy()
OSCtxSw()
OSIntCtxSw()
```

In addition, the Cortex-M4 requires the definition of a function to handle the PendSV exception.

```
OS_CPU_PendSVHandler()
```

B-3-1 OS_CPU_A.ASM – OSStartHighRdy()

OSStartHighRdy() is called by OSStart() to start the process of multitasking. µC/OS-III will switch to the highest priority task that is ready to run.

Listing B-13 shows the Cortex-M4 code for OSStartHighRdy().

```
OSStartHighRdy
        LDR     R0, =NVIC_SYSPRI14                    (1)
        LDR     R1, =NVIC_PENDSV_PRI
        STRB    R1, [R0]
        MOVS    R0, #0
        MSR     PSP, R0
        LDR     R0, =NVIC_INT_CTRL                    (2)
        LDR     R1, =NVIC_PENDSVSET
        STR     R1, [R0]
        CPSIE   I                                     (3)
OSStartHang
        B       OSStartHang                           (4)
```

Listing B-13 **os_cpu_a.asm – OSStartHighRdy()**

LB-13(1)   OSStartHighRdy() starts by setting the priority level of the PendSV handler. The PendSV handler is used to perform all context switches and is always set at the lowest priority so that it executes after the last nested ISR.

LB-13(2)   The PendSV handler is invoked by 'triggering' it. However, the PendSV will not execute immediately because it is assumed that interrupts are disabled.

LB-13(3)   Interrupts are enabled and this should cause the Cortex-M4 processor to vector to the PendSV handler (described later).

LB-13(4)   The PendSV handler should pass control to the highest-priority task that was created and the code should never come back to OSStartHighRdy().

B-3-2 OS_CPU_A.ASM – OSCtxSw() and OSIntCtxSw()

OSCtxSw() is called by OSSched() and OS_Sched0() to perform a context switch from a task.

OSIntCtxSw() is called by OSIntExit() to perform a context switch after an ISR has completed.

Both of these functions simply 'trigger' the PendSV exception handler, which does the actual context switching.

Listing B-14 shows the Cortex-M4 code for OSCtxSw() and OSIntCtxSw().

```
OSCtxSw
    LDR     R0, =NVIC_INT_CTRL
    LDR     R1, =NVIC_PENDSVSET
    STR     R1, [R0]
    BX      LR
OSIntCtxSw
    LDR     R0, =NVIC_INT_CTRL
    LDR     R1, =NVIC_PENDSVSET
    STR     R1, [R0]
    BX      LR
```

Listing B-14 **os_cpu_a.asm – OSCtxSw() and OSIntCtxSw()**

B-3-3 OS_CPU_A.ASM – OS_CPU_PendSVHandler()

OS_CPU_PendSVHandler() is the code that performs a context switch initiated by a task, or at the completion of an ISR. OS_CPU_PendSVHandler() is invoked by OSStartHighRdy(), OSCtxSw() and OSIntCtxSw().

Listing B-15 shows the Cortex-M4 code for OS_CPU_PendSVHandler().

```
OS_CPU_PendSVHandler
      CPSID   I                                         (1)
      MRS     R0, PSP                                   (2)
      CBZ     R0, OS_CPU_PendSVHandler_nosave
      SUBS    R0, R0, #0x20                             (3)
      STM     R0, {R4-R11}
      LDR     R1, =OSTCBCurPtr                          (4)
      LDR     R1, [R1]
      STR     R0, [R1]


OS_CPU_PendSVHandler_nosave
      PUSH    {R14}                                     (5)
      LDR     R0, =OSTaskSwHook
      BLX     R0
      POP     {R14}
      LDR     R0, =OSPrioCur                            (6)
      LDR     R1, =OSPrioHighRdy
      LDRB    R2, [R1]
      STRB    R2, [R0]
      LDR     R0, =OSTCBCurPtr                          (7)
      LDR     R1, =OSTCBHighRdyPtr
      LDR     R2, [R1]
      STR     R2, [R0]
      LDR     R0, [R2]                                  (8)
      LDM     R0, {R4-R11}                              (9)
      ADDS    R0, R0, #0x20
      MSR     PSP, R0                                   (10)
      ORR     LR, LR, #0x04
      CPSIE   I                                         (11)
      BX      LR                                        (12)
```

Listing B-15 **os_cpu_a.asm – OS_CPU_PendSVHandler()**

LB-15(1)   **OS_CPU_PendSVHandler()** starts by disabling all interrupts because interrupt should not occur during a context switch.

LB-15(2)   This code skips saving the remaining eight registers if this is the first time the PendSV is called. In other words, when **OSStartHighRdy()** triggers the PendSV handler, there is nothing to save from the 'previous task' as there is no previous task.

LB-15(3)   If **OS_CPU_PendSVHandler()** is invoked from either **OSCtxSw()** or **OSIntCtxSw()**, the PendSV handler saves the remaining eight CPU registers (R4 through R11) onto the stack of the task switched out.

LB-15(4)   **OS_CPU_PendSVHandler()** saves the stack pointer of the task switched out into that task's **OS_TCB**. Note that the first field of an **OS_TCB** is **.StkPtr** (the task's stack pointer), which makes it convenient for assembly language code since there are no offsets to determine.

LB-15(5)   The task switch hook (**OSTaskSwHook()**) is then called.

LB-15(6)   **OS_CPU_PendSVHandler()** copies the priority of the new task into the priority of the current task, i.e.:

              OSPrioCur = OSPrioHighRdy;

LB-15(7)   **OS_CPU_PendSVHandler()** copies the pointer to the new task's **OS_TCB** into the pointer to the current task's **OS_TCB**, i.e.,:

              OSTCBCurPtr = OSTCBHighRdyPtr;

LB-15(8)   **OS_CPU_PendSVHandler()** retrieves the stack pointer from the new task's **OS_TCB**.

LB-15(9)   CPU registers R4 through R11 from the new task are loaded into the CPU.

LB-15(10)   The task stack pointer is updated with the new top-of-stack pointer.

LB-15(11)   Interrupts are re-enabled since we are finished performing the critical portion of the context switch. If another interrupt occurs before we return from the PendSV handler, the Cortex-M4 knows that there are eight registers still saved on the stack, and there would be no need for it to save them. This is called Tail Chaining and it makes servicing back-to-back interrupts quite efficient on the Cortex-M4.

LB-15(12)   By performing a return from the PendSV handler, the Cortex-M4 processors knows that it is returning from interrupt and will thus restore the remaining registers.

µC/CPU Port for the Cortex-M4

µC/CPU consists of files that encapsulate common CPU-specific functionality and CPU compiler-specific data types. Appendix B describes the adaptation of µC/CPU to the Cortex-M4 as it relates to µC/OS-III.

Notice how each variable, function, **#define** constant, or macro is prefixed with **CPU_**. This makes it easier to identify them as belonging to the µC/CPU module when invoked by other modules, or application code.

The µC/CPU files are found in the following three directories:

```
\Micrium\Software\uC-CPU\cpu_core.c
\Micrium\Software\uC-CPU\cpu_core.h
\Micrium\Software\uC-CPU\cpu_def.h
\Micrium\Software\uC-CPU\Cfg\Template\cpu_cfg.h
\Micrium\Software\uC-CPU\ARM-Cortex-M4\IAR\cpu.h
\Micrium\Software\uC-CPU\ARM-Cortex-M4\IAR\cpu_a.asm
\Micrium\Software\uC-CPU\ARM-Cortex-M4\IAR\cpu_c.c
```

C

C-1 CPU_CORE.C

cpu_core.c contains C code that is common to all CPU architectures and this file must not be changed. Specifically, **cpu_core.c** contains functions to allow µC/OS-III and your application to obtain time stamps, measure the interrupt disable time of the **CPU_CRITICAL_ENTER()** and **CPU_CRITICAL_EXIT()** macros, a function that emulates a count leading zeros instruction (if the processor does not have that instruction built-in), and a few other functions.

The application code must call **CPU_Init()** before it calls any other µC/CPU function. This call can be placed in **main()** before calling µC/OS-III's **OSInit()**.

C-2 CPU_CORE.H

cpu_core.h contains function prototypes for the functions provided in **cpu_core.c** and allocation of the variables used by the module to measure interrupt disable time. This file must not be modified.

C-3 CPU_DEF.H

cpu_def.h contains miscellaneous **#define** constants used by the µC/CPU module. This file must not be modified.

C-4 CPU_CFG.H

cpu_cfg.h contains a template to configure µC/CPU for an actual project. **cpu_cfg.h** determines whether to enable measurement of the interrupt disable time, whether the CPU implements a count leading zeros instruction in assembly language, or whether it will be emulated in C, and more.

You should copy **cpu_cfg.h** to the application directory for a project and modify this file as necessary.

Listing C-1 shows the recommended values for the Cortex-M4.

```
#define   CPU_CFG_NAME_EN                    DEF_ENABLED        (1)
#define   CPU_CFG_NAME_SIZE                          16u        (2)
#define   CPU_CFG_TS_EN                      DEF_ENABLED        (3)
#define   CPU_CFG_INT_DIS_MEAS_EN           DEF_ENABLED        (4)
#define   CPU_CFG_INT_DIS_MEAS_OVRHD_NBR             1u        (5)
#define   CPU_CFG_LEAD_ZEROS_ASM_PRESENT    DEF_ENABLED        (6)
```

Listing C-1 **cpu_cfg.h recommended values**

LC-1(1)   Assign an ASCII name to the CPU by calling **CPU_NameSet()**. This is useful for debugging purposes.

LC-1(2)   The name of the CPU should be limited to 15 characters plus a NUL, unless this value is changed.

LC-1(3)   This **#define** enables the code to measure timestamps. It is a feature required by µC/OS-III, and should always be set to **DEF_ENABLED**.

LC-1(4)   This **#define** determines whether to measure interrupt disable time. This is a useful feature during development but it may be turned off when deploying a system as measuring interrupt disable time adds measurement artifacts (i.e., overhead).

LC-1(5)   This **#define** determines how many iterations will be performed when determining the overhead involved in measuring interrupt disable time. For the Cortex-M4, the recommended value is 1.

LC-1(6)   The ARMv7 instruction set of the Cortex-M4 contains a Count Leading Zeros (CLZ) instruction, which significantly improves the performance of the µC/OS-III scheduler and, therefore, this option always needs to be enabled.

C-5 µC/CPU FUNCTIONS IN BSP.C

µC/CPU also requires two Board Support Package (BSP) specific functions:

```
CPU_TS_TmrInit()
CPU_TS_TmrRd()
```

These functions are typically implemented in **bsp.c** of the evaluation or target board.

The Cortex-M4's Debug Watch Trace (DWT) contains a 32-bit CPU cycle counter (CYCCNT) that is used by µC/CPU for time stamping. The 32-bit counter is incremented at the CPU clock rate which provides excellent time measurement accuracy. The CYCCNT will overflow and reset from 0 after counting 4,294,967,296 CPU clock cycles. This is not a problem since µC/CPU maintains a 64-bit timestamp using two 32-bit values. The overflows are therefore accounted for. However, for µC/OS-III, we only need the lower 32 bits because that offers sufficient resolution for what µC/OS-III needs to do with it.

A 64-bit timestamp is unlikely to ever overflow for the life of a product. For example, if the Cortex-M4 is clocked at 1 GHz (this is not possible at this time), the 64-bit timestamp would overflow after approximately 585 years!

C-5-1 µC/CPU FUNCTIONS IN BSP.C, CPU_TS_TmrInit()

Listing C-2 shows how to initialize the DWT's cycle counter.

```
#if (CPU_CFG_TS_TMR_EN == DEF_ENABLED)
CPU_INT16U  CPU_TS_TmrInit (void)
{
    DEM_CR      |= (CPU_INT32U)DEM_CR_TRCENA;                    (1)
    DWT_CYCCNT  = (CPU_INT32U)0;
    DWT_CR      |= (CPU_INT32U)0x00000001;                      (2)
    return ((CPU_INT16U)0);                                     (3)
}
#endif
```

Listing C-2 **bsp.c, CPU_TS_TmrInit()**

LC-2(1)   We need to enable the trace module.

LC-2(2)   To initialize the DWT's CYCCNT set bit 0 in the DWT's Control Register
             (DWT_CR). A read-modify-write avoids altering the other bits in the DWT_CR.

LC-2(3)   **CPU_TS_TmrInit()** requires that the function returns the number of left shifts
             needed to make **CPU_TS_TmrRd()** (described below) return a 32-bit value. Since
             CYCCNT is already a 32-bit counter, no shifts are needed, and this value is 0.

C-5-2 µC/CPU FUNCTIONS IN BSP.C, CPU_TS_TmrRd()

The DWT's CYCCNT register is read by calling **CPU_TS_TmrRd()**. This function is
implemented as shown in Listing C-3.

```
#if (CPU_CFG_TS_TMR_EN == DEF_ENABLED)
CPU_TS  CPU_TS_TmrRd (void)
{
    return ((CPU_TS)DWT_CYCCNT);
}
#endif
```

Listing C-3 **bsp.c, CPU_TS_TmrRd()**

C-6 CPU.H

`cpu.h` contains processor- and implementation-specific **#defines** constants, macros and typedefs.

C-6-1 CPU.H – #DEFINES

`cpu.h` declares a number of processor specific **#define** constants and macros. The most important ones related to µC/OS-III are shown in Listing C-4.

```
#define  CPU_CFG_STK_GROWTH            CPU_STK_GROWTH_HI_TO_LO          (1)
#define  CPU_CFG_LEAD_ZEROS_ASM_PRESENT                                 (2)
#define  CPU_SR_ALLOC()                CPU_SR  cpu_sr = (CPU_SR)0;      (3)
#define  CPU_CRITICAL_ENTER()          { cpu_sr = CPU_SR_Save(); }      (4)
#define  CPU_CRITICAL_EXIT()           { CPU_SR_Restore(cpu_sr);}       (5)
```

Listing C-4 **cpu.h, #defines**

LC-4(1)   This **#define** specifies that the Cortex-M4 stack grows from high memory to lower-memory addresses.

LC-4(2)   This **#define** indicates that the Cortex-M4 has an assembly language instruction that counts leading zeros in a data word. This feature significantly speeds up µC/OS-III's scheduling algorithm.

LC-4(3)   The macro is used to allocate a local variable in a function that needs to protect a critical section by disabling interrupts. µC/OS-III uses **CPU_SR_ALLOC()** as follows:

```
void  OSFunction (void)
{
    CPU_SR_ALLOC();
    CPU_CRITICAL_ENTER();
    /* Code protected by critical section */
    CPU_CRITICAL_EXIT();
    :
}
```

The macro might not appear necessary if we are only declaring a single variable, but the actual code in **cpu.h** is slightly more complex. Therefore the macro hides this complexity from the user.

LC-4(4)   **CPU_CRITICAL_ENTER()** is invoked by µC/OS-III to disable interrupts. As shown, the macro calls **CPU_SR_Save()**, which is declared in **cpu_a.asm** (described later). **CPU_SR_Save()** saves the current state of the Cortex-M4's PSR and then disables interrupts. The saved value of the PSR is returned to the function that invokes **CPU_CRITICAL_ENTER()**. The PSR is saved in the local variable allocated by **CPU_SR_ALLOC()**. **CPU_SR_Save()** is implemented in assembly language because C cannot access CPU registers.

LC-4(5)   **CPU_CRITICAL_EXIT()** calls the function **CPU_SR_Restore()** (see **cpu_a.asm**) to restore the previously saved state of the PSR. The reason the PSR was saved in the first place is because interrupts might already be disabled before invoking **CPU_CRITICAL_ENTER()** and we want to keep them disabled when we exit the critical section. If interrupts were enabled before calling **CPU_CRITICAL_ENTER()**, they will be re-enabled by **CPU_CRITICAL_EXIT()**.

C-6-2 CPU.H – DATA TYPES

Micrium does not make use of the standard C data types. Instead, data types are declared that are highly portable and intuitive. In addition, all data types are always declared in upper case, which follows Micrium's coding standard.

Listing C-5 shows the data types used by Micrium specific to the Cortex-M4 (assuming the IAR C compiler).

```
typedef           void      CPU_VOID;
typedef           char      CPU_CHAR;              /*  8-bit character           */  (1)
typedef  unsigned char      CPU_BOOLEAN;          /*  8-bit boolean or logical  */  (2)
typedef  unsigned char      CPU_INT08U;           /*  8-bit unsigned integer    */  (3)
typedef    signed char      CPU_INT08S;           /*  8-bit   signed integer    */
typedef  unsigned short     CPU_INT16U;           /* 16-bit unsigned integer    */
typedef    signed short     CPU_INT16S;           /* 16-bit   signed integer    */
typedef  unsigned int       CPU_INT32U;           /* 32-bit unsigned integer    */
typedef    signed int       CPU_INT32S;           /* 32-bit   signed integer    */
typedef  unsigned long long CPU_INT64U;           /* 64-bit unsigned integer    */  (4)
typedef    signed long long CPU_INT64S;           /* 64-bit   signed integer    */
typedef           float     CPU_FP32;             /* 32-bit floating point      */  (5)
typedef           double    CPU_FP64;             /* 64-bit floating point      */
typedef  volatile CPU_INT08U CPU_REG08;           /*  8-bit register            */
typedef  volatile CPU_INT16U CPU_REG16;           /* 16-bit register            */
typedef  volatile CPU_INT32U CPU_REG32;           /* 32-bit register            */
typedef  volatile CPU_INT64U CPU_REG64;           /* 64-bit register            */
typedef           void      (*CPU_FNCT_VOID)(void);
typedef           void      (*CPU_FNCT_PTR )(void *);
```

Listing C-5 **cpu.h, Data Types**

LC-5(1)   Characters are assumed to be 8-bit quantities on the Cortex-M4.

LC-5(2)   It is often convenient to declare Boolean variables. However, even though a Boolean represents either 1 or 0, a whole byte is used. This is done because ANSI C does not define single bit variables.

LC-5(3)   The signed and unsigned integer data types are declared for 8, 16 and 32-bit quantities.

LC-5(4)   µC/OS-III requires that the compiler defines 64-bit data types. These are used when computing CPU usage on a per-task basis. The 64-bit data types are used when declaring **OS_CYCLES** in **os_type.h**.

LC-5(5)   Most of Micriµm's software components do not use floating-point values. These data types are declared for consistency and to provide portable data types to the application developer.

```
#define   CPU_CFG_ADDR_SIZE       CPU_WORD_SIZE_32                    (6)
#define   CPU_CFG_DATA_SIZE       CPU_WORD_SIZE_32
#if       (CPU_CFG_ADDR_SIZE == CPU_WORD_SIZE_32)
typedef   CPU_INT32U              CPU_ADDR;
#elif     (CPU_CFG_ADDR_SIZE == CPU_WORD_SIZE_16)
typedef   CPU_INT16U              CPU_ADDR;
#else
typedef   CPU_INT08U              CPU_ADDR;
#endif
#if       (CPU_CFG_DATA_SIZE == CPU_WORD_SIZE_32)
typedef   CPU_INT32U              CPU_DATA;
#elif     (CPU_CFG_DATA_SIZE == CPU_WORD_SIZE_16)
typedef   CPU_INT16U              CPU_DATA;
#else
typedef   CPU_INT08U              CPU_DATA;
#endif
typedef   CPU_DATA               CPU_ALIGN;
typedef   CPU_ADDR               CPU_SIZE_T;
typedef   CPU_INT16U             CPU_ERR;
typedef   CPU_INT32U             CPU_STK;                             (7)
typedef   CPU_ADDR               CPU_STK_SIZE;
typedef   CPU_INT32U             CPU_SR;                              (8)
```

Listing C-6 **cpu.h, Data Type (Continued)**

LC-6(6)   Miscellaneous types are declared.

LC-6(7)   **CPU_STK** declares the width of a CPU stack entry and they are 32-bits wide on the Cortex-M4. All µC/OS-III stacks must be declared using **CPU_STK**.

LC-6(8)   µC/CPU provides code to protect critical sections by disabling interrupts. This is implemented by **CPU_CRITICAL_ENTER()** and **CPU_CRITICAL_EXIT()**. When **CPU_CRITICAL_ENTER()** is invoked, the current state of the Cortex-M4's Program Status Register (PSR) is saved in a local variable so that it can be restored when **CPU_CRITICAL_EXIT()** is invoked. The local variable that holds the saved PSR is declared as a **CPU_SR**.

C-6-3 CPU.H – FUNCTION PROTOTYPES

cpu.h also contains a number of data types. The most significant prototypes related to μC/OS-III are shown in Listing C-6.

```
CPU_SR      CPU_SR_Save      (void);
void        CPU_SR_Restore   (CPU_SR      cpu_sr);
CPU_DATA    CPU_CntLeadZeros (CPU_DATA    val);
```

Listing C-7 **cpu.h, Data Type**

C-7 CPU_A.ASM

cpu_a.asm contains assembly language functions provided by μC/CPU. Three functions of particular importance to μC/OS-III are shown in Listing C-7.

CPU_SR_Save() obtains the current value of the Cortex-M4 PSR and then disables all CPU interrupts. The value of the saved PSR is returned to the caller.

CPU_SR_Restore() reverses the process and restores the PSR to the value passed to

CPU_SR_Restored() as an argument.

CPU_CntLeadZeros() counts the number of zero bits starting from the most significant bit position. This function is implemented in assembly language because the ARMv7 instruction incorporates this functionality.

In all of the functions below, R0 contains the value passed to the function, as well as the returned value.

```
CPU_SR_Save
        MRS     R0, PRIMASK
        CPSID   I
        BX      LR


CPU_SR_Restore
        MSR     PRIMASK, R0
        BX      LR


CPU_CntLeadZeros
        CLZ     R0, R0
        BX      LR
```

Listing C-8 **cpu_a.asm**

Micriµm's µC/Probe

µC/Probe is an award-winning Microsoft Windows™-based application that allows a user to display or change the value (at run time) of virtually any variable or memory location on a connected embedded target. The user simply populates µC/Probe's graphical environment with gauges, numeric indicators, tables, graphs, virtual LEDs, bar graphs, sliders, switches, push buttons, and other components, and associates each of these to a variable or memory location.

With µC/Probe, it is not necessary to instrument the target code in order to display or change variables at run time. In fact, there is no need to add `printf()` statements, hardware such as Light Emitting Diodes (LEDs), Liquid Crystal Displays (LCDs), or use any other means to get visibility inside an embedded target at run time.

Two versions of µC/Probe are available from Micriµm (See section D-1 "Downloading µC/Probe" on page 995).

µC/OS-III licensees will receive one free license of the full version of µC/Probe. This full version supports J-Link, RS-232C, TCP/IP, USB, and other interfaces, and allows you to display or change an unlimited number of variables. The trial version only allows you to display or change up to eight application variables. However, it allows you to monitor any µC/OS-III variables since µC/Probe is µC/OS-III aware.

The examples provided with this book assume that you have downloaded and installed one of these two versions of µC/Probe.

This appendix provides a brief introduction to µC/Probe.

Figure D-1 shows a block diagram of a typical development environment with the addition of µC/Probe as used with the TWR-K53N512, available from Freescale.

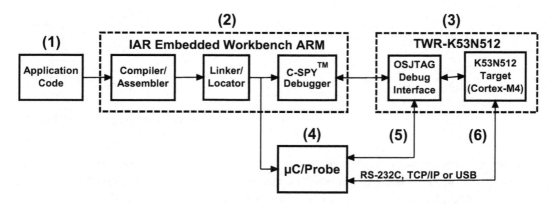

Figure D-1 **Development environment using the TWR-K53N512**

FD-1(1)   This is the application code you are developing. It is assumed that you are using µC/OS-III provided with this book. However, µC/Probe does not require an RTOS, and can work with or without an RTOS.

FD-1(2)   The examples provided with this book assumes the IAR Embedded Workbench for ARM, but µC/Probe works with any toolchain as long as the linker/locator is able to produce an .ELF or .IEEE695 output file.

FD-1(3)   The TWR-K53N512 evaluation board available from Freescale is able to interface to a J-Link SWD provided by Segger. The J-Link allows the C-SPY™ debugger to download Flash code onto the on-board Cortex-M4-based Micro Controller Unit (MCU). C-SPY also allows you to debug application code.

FD-1(4)   µC/Probe reads the exact same .ELF or .IEEE695 output file produced by the linker/locator. From this file, µC/Probe is able to extract names, data types and addresses of all the global variables of the application code. This information allows µC/Probe to display any of the values of the variables using the display objects available in µC/Probe (gauges, meters, virtual LEDs, bar graphs, numeric indicators, graphs, and more.

FD-1(5)   µC/Probe is able to interface to the Cortex-M4 processor via the SWD interface of the J-Link. In fact, both the C-SPY debugger and µC/Probe can access the target through the J-Link at the same time. This allows µC/Probe to monitor or change any target variable while you are stepping through the code using the

C-SPY debugger. Interfacing through the J-Link also has the advantage of not requiring any target resident code to interface to µC/Probe.

FD-1(6)   µC/Probe can also interface to the TWR-K53N512 evaluation board using RS-232C, Ethernet (using TCP/IP) or USB.

Target resident code must be added when using RS-232C. This code is however provided by Micrium, and the user needs only to add it to the application code as part of the build. Also, unlike when using the J-Link, target data can only be displayed or changed by µC/Probe when the target is running. However, the RS-232C interface allows data to be collected faster than through the onboard J-Link.

Target resident code is also required if using the Ethernet port on the TWR-K53N512 evaluation board. In fact, you'll need a full TCP/IP stack such as Micrium's µC/TCP-IP. Again, data can only be displayed and changed when the target is running. However, the Ethernet interface provides the best throughput and data update rates for µC/Probe.

Finally, µC/Probe also works over the onboard USB-Device connector and requires a USB-Device (HID) stack such as Micrium's µC/USB-Device with HID option. As with the RS-232C and TCP/IP, data can only be displayed or changed when the target is running when using this interface.

D-1 DOWNLOADING µC/PROBE

The Full Version of µC/Probe is included with all µC/OS-III licenses. The full version supports J-Link, RS-232C, TCP/IP, USB, and other interfaces, and allows users to display or change an unlimited number of variables. The Trial Version is not time limited, but only allows users to display or change up to eight application variables. Both versions are available from Micrium's website. Simply point your favorite browser to:

`www.Micrium.com/Books/Micrium-uCOS-III`

Follow the links to download the desired version (or both). If not already registered on the Micrium website, you will be asked to do so. Once downloaded, execute the appropriate µC/Probe setup file:

`Micrium-uC-Probe-Setup-Full.exe Micrium-uC-Probe-Setup-Trial.exe`

D-2 µC/PROBE IS A WINDOWS™-BASED APPLICATION

As previously mentioned, µC/Probe is a Microsoft Windows-based application. When opening µC/Probe you will see the environment shown in Figure D-2.

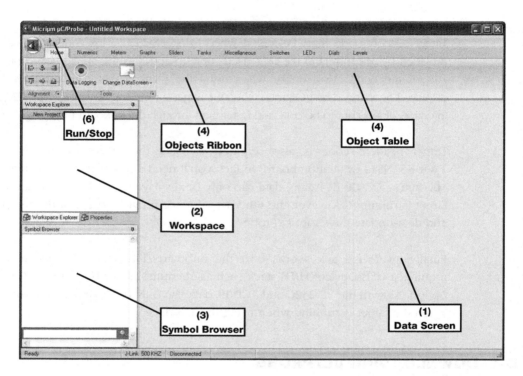

Figure D-2 **Empty µC/Probe project**

FD-2(1)   µC/Probe's main focus is the *Data Screen*. This is where you drag and drop such *Objects* as gauges, meters, graphs, virtual LEDs, sliders, switches, and more, which are used to display or change the value of target variables at run time. µC/Probe allows you to define any number of Data Screens and each Data Screen can be assigned a name. Each data screen is selected by using a *Tab* at the top of the data screen area.

FD-2(2)   When data screens are created, their names also appear in the *Workspace* area. The Workspace defines the structure of the µC/Probe project. Data screens can be imported from other projects, and can be exported.

FD-2(3)   The *Symbol Browser* contains a list of all the variables that can be displayed or changed in the target by µC/Probe. The variables are organized alphabetically by compile modules (i.e., source files). You can expand each of those files and view all the variables defined in that module, and search symbols by using the search box.

FD-2(4)   The *Object Ribbon* is where to find the objects (gauges, meters, numeric indicators, sliders, graphs, etc.) to drag and drop onto the data screen.

FD-2(5)   Similar objects are grouped together. Each group is selected by clicking on the appropriate tab. Drag and drop any object onto a data screen of your choice, and associate a variable to the instantiated object. Some objects even allow you to associate multiple variables.

Figure D-3 shows a group of *Meter* objects and Figure D-4 shows a group of *Level* objects.

Figure D-3 **µC/Probe meter objects**

Figure D-4 **µC/Probe level objects**

Figure D-5 shows a group of Slider objects, which can be used to modify target variables.

Figure D-5 **µC/Probe slider objects**

997

D

D-3 ASSIGNING A VARIABLE TO AN OBJECT

Assigning a variable to an object is quite simple as illustrated in Figure D-6. It is assumed that the code has been downloaded to the target and the target is running.

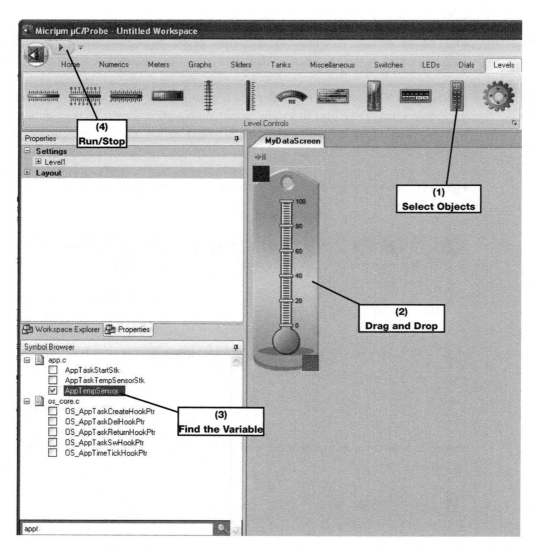

Figure D-6 **Assigning a variable to an object**

FD-6(1)   Select the object that will allow you to better visualize the variable (a meter, a thermometer, an LED, etc.).

FD-6(2)   Drag and drop the object onto the data screen.

FD-6(3)   Find the variable in the symbol browser. Simply type the first few letters of the variable and µC/Probe will narrow down the search. Click on the small box to the left of the variable.

FD-6(4)   When you want to see the value of the variable, simply click on the 'Run/Stop' button on the upper left corner.

Add as many objects as you want to each data screen and use as many data screens as you want. However, remember that the trial-version of µC/Probe only allows you to have a total of eight application variables, but enables the display of any µC/OS-III variable.

IAR Systems IAR Embedded Workbench for ARM

IAR Embedded Workbench is a set of highly sophisticated and easy-to-use development tools for embedded applications. It integrates the IAR C/C++ Compiler™, assembler, linker, librarian, text editor, project manager and C-SPY® Debugger in an integrated development environment (IDE).

With its built-in chip-specific code optimizer, IAR Embedded Workbench generates very efficient and reliable FLASH/ROMable code for ARM devices. In addition to this solid technology, the IAR Systems also provides professional world-wide technical support.

The KickStart™ edition of IAR Embedded Workbench is free of charge and you may use it for as long as you want. KickStart tools are ideal for creating small applications, or for getting started fast on a new project. The only requirement is that you register to obtain a license key.

The KickStart edition is code-size limited, but a fully functional integrated development environment that includes a project manager, editor, compiler, assembler, linker, librarian, and debugger tools. A complete set of user guides is included in PDF format.

The KickStart edition corresponds to the latest release of the full edition of IAR Embedded Workbench, with the following exceptions:

- It has a code size limitation (32 Kbytes).

- It does not include source code for runtime libraries.

- It does not include support for MISRA C.

- There is limited technical support.

The KickStart edition of IAR Embedded Workbench allows you to run all of the examples provided in this book.

E

E-1 IAR EMBEDDED WORKBENCH FOR ARM – HIGHLIGHTS

The full version of the IAR Embedded Workbench for ARM offers the following features.

- Support for:

    - ARM7™ (ARM7TDMI, ARM7TDMI-S and ARM720T)

    - ARM7E™ (ARM7EJ-S)

    - ARM9™ (ARM9TDMI, ARM920T, ARM922T and ARM940T)

    - ARM9E™ (ARM926EJ-S, ARM946E-S and ARM966E-S, ARM968E-S)

    - ARM10E™ (ARM1020E and ARM1022E)

    - ARM11™

    - SecurCore™ (SC000, SC100, SC110, SC200, SC210, SC300)

    - Cortex-A5™

    - Cortex-A8™

    - Cortex-R4(F)

    - Cortex-M0™

    - Cortex-M1™

    - Cortex-M3™

    - Cortex-M4™

    - XScale™

- Most compact and efficient code

- ARM Embedded Application Binary Interface (EABI)

- Extensive support for hardware and RTOS-aware debugging

- Total solutions for ARM

- New Cortex-M4 debug features

- Function profiler

- Interrupt graph window

- Data log window

- MISRA C:2004 support

- Extensive device support

- Over 1400 example projects

- µC/OS-II Kernel Awareness built-into the C-Spy debugger

Figure E-1 shows a block diagram of the major EWARM components.

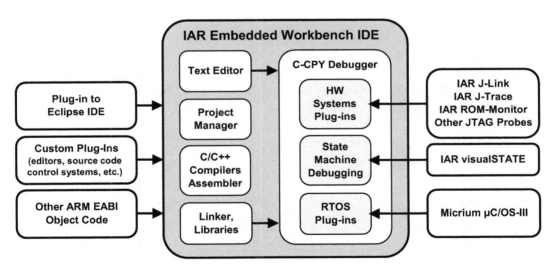

Figure E-1 **IAR Embedded Workbench**

E

E-2 MODULAR AND EXTENSIBLE IDE

■ A seamlessly Integrated Development Environment (IDE) for building and debugging embedded applications

■ Powerful project management allowing multiple projects in one workspace

■ Build integration with IAR visualSTATE

■ Hierarchical project representation

■ Dockable and floating windows management

■ Smart source browser

■ Tool options configurable on global, group of source files, or individual source files level

■ Multi-file compilation support for even better code optimization

■ Flexible project building via batch build, pre/post-build or custom build with access to external tools in the build process.

■ Integration with source code control systems

Hierarchical Project Representation

Source code control system integration

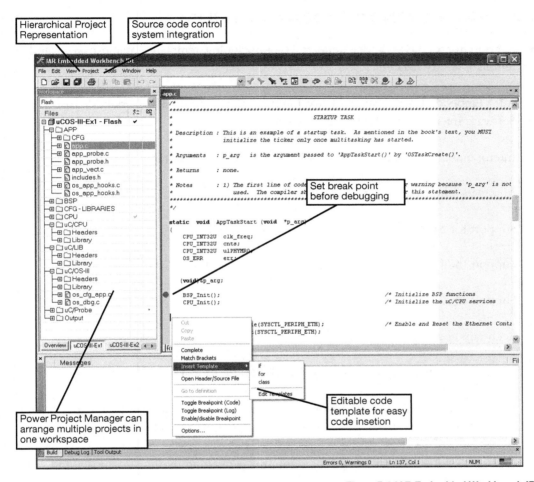

Set break point before debugging

Editable code template for easy code insetion

Power Project Manager can arrange multiple projects in one workspace

Figure E-2 **IAR Embedded Workbench IDE**

E

E-3 HIGHLY OPTIMIZING C/C++ COMPILER

■ Support for C, EC++ and extended EC++ including templates, namespace, standard template library (STL) etc.

■ ARM Embedded Application Binary Interface (EABI) and ARM Cortex Microcontroller Software Interface Standard (CMSIS) compliant

■ Interoperability and binary compatibility with other EABI compliant tools

■ Automatic checking of MISRA C rules

■ Support for ARM, Thumb1 and Thumb2 processor modes

■ Support for 4 Gbyte applications in all processor modes

■ Support for 64-bit long

■ Reentrant code

■ 32- and 64-bit floating-point types in standard IEEE format

■ Multiple levels of optimizations on code size and execution speed allowing different transformations enabled, such as function inlining, loop unrolling etc.

■ Advanced global and target-specific optimizer generating the most compact and stable code

■ Compressed initializers

■ Support for ARM7, ARM7E, ARM9, ARM9E, ARM10E, ARM11, Cortex-M0, Cortex-M1, Cortex-M3, Cortex-M4, Cortex-R4 and Intel XScale

■ Support for ARM, Thumb1 and Thumb2 processor modes

■ Generates code for ARM VFP series of floating-point coprocessors

■ Little/big endian mode

E-4 DEVICE SUPPORT

Device support on five levels:

■ Core support - instruction set, debugger interface (for all supported devices)

■ Header/DDF files - peripheral register names in C/asm source and debugger (for all supported devices)

■ Flash loader for on-chip flash or off-chip EVB flash (for most of our supported devices)

■ Project examples - varies from simple to fairly complex applications (for most of our supported devices)

■ Detailed device support list at www.iar.com/ewarm

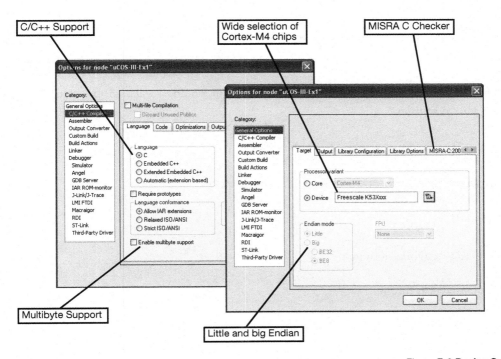

Figure E-3 **Device Support**

E-5 STATE-OF-THE-ART C-SPY® DEBUGGER

- Cortex-M4 SWV/SWO debugger support

- Complex code and data breakpoints

- User selectable breakpoint types (hardware/software)

- Unlimited number of breakpoints in flash via optional license for J-Link

- Runtime stack analysis - stack window to monitor the memory consumption and integrity of the stack

- Complete support for stack unwinding even at high optimization levels

- Profiling and code coverage performance analysis tools

- Trace utility with expressions, such as variables and register values, to examine execution history

- Versatile monitoring of registers, structures, call chain, locals, global variables and peripheral registers

- Smart STL container display in Watch window

- Symbolic memory window and static watch window

- I/O and interrupt simulation

- True editing-while-debugging

- Drag and drop model

- Target access to host file system via file I/O

- Built-in µC/OS-II Kernel Awareness

E

E-6 C-SPY DEBUGGER AND TARGET SYSTEM SUPPORT

The C-SPY Debugger for the ARM core is available with drivers for the following target systems:

■ Simulator

■ Emulator (JTAG/SWD)

  ■ IAR J-Link probe, JTAG and SWD support, connection via USB or TCP/IP server

  ■ RDI (Remote Debug Interface), such as Abatron BDI1000 & BDI2000, EPI Majic, Ashling Opella, Aiji OpenICE, Signum JTAGjet, ARM Multi-ICE

  ■ Macraigor JTAG interfaces: Macraigor Raven, Wiggler, mpDemon, usbDemon, usb2Demon and usb2Sprite

  ■ ST ST-LINK JTAG debug probe

E-7 IAR ASSEMBLER

■ A powerful relocating macro assembler with a versatile set of directives and operators

■ Built-in C language preprocessor, accepting all C macro definitions

E-8 IAR J-LINK LINKER

■ Complete linking, relocation and format generation to produce FLASH/PROMable code

■ Flexible commands allowing detailed control of code and data placement

■ Optimized linking removing unused code and data

■ Direct linking of raw binary images, for instance multimedia files

■ Comprehensive cross-reference and dependency memory maps

■ Link compatibility with object files and libraries generated by other EABI compliant tools

E-9 IAR LIBRARY AND LIBRARY TOOLS

- All required ISO/ANSI C and C++ libraries and source included

- All low-level routines such as **writechar()** and **readchar()** provided in full source code

- Lightweight runtime library, user-configurable to match the needs of the application; full source included

- Library tools for creating and maintaining library projects, libraries and library modules

- Listings of entry points and symbolic information

E-10 COMPREHENSIVE DOCUMENTATION

- Efficient coding hints for embedded application

- Extensive step-by-step tutorials

- Context sensitive help and hypertext versions of the user documentation available online

E-11 FIRST CLASS TECHNICAL SUPPORT

IAR Systems has a global organization with local presence through branch offices and a worldwide distributor network. Extended, customized technical services are available.

Freescale Semiconductor's CodeWarrior for MCUs

The four medical application projects presented in this book are also available as CodeWarrior IDE projects. You can download CodeWarrior for Microcontrollers v 10.1 from the Freescale website at:

http://www.freescale.com/CodeWarrior

Look for the big Download button. That URL also points to all the information on CodeWarrior Suites, pricing, and other information.

This appendix serves as a very brief introduction to the CodeWarrior tools, and not as training. You can find training materials, such as Eclipse-style "cheat sheets" built into the product. Additional training is available on the Freescale website.

When you download the CodeWarrior tools you have a choice:

- a full-featured and unlimited evaluation version good for 30 days (renewable for up to 90 days)

- a free Special Edition version of the tools with a permanent license

The Special Edition tools have a code-size limit for the compiler and debugger. The size varies per target processor:

- HCS08/RS08: 32KB

- V1 ColdFire: 64KB

- V2-V4 ColdFire: 128KB

- Kinetis: 128KB

- MPC56xx: 512KB

There is no limit to assembler code.

CodeWarrior Development Studio for Microcontrollers v10.1 integrates the development tools for RS08, HCS08, ColdFire, Kinetis and Qorivva MPC56xx products into a single software development environment based on the Eclipse platform. The CodeWarrior tools also include Processor Expert, which has full support for the Kinetis platform used in this book. Processor Expert builds drivers and embedded software components for Freescale silicon. It combines easy-to-use component-based application/driver creation with an expert knowledge system that enables you to find errors at design time, rather than at runtime. More information about ProcessorExpert can be found at their website at http://www.freescale.com/ProcessorExpert

You will not need to use Processor Expert for the examples in this book. All of the drivers and firmware required will be provided as part of the projects.

However, in the real world you don't get examples, and you don't want to build everything from scratch every time. If you use Processor Expert, migrating between Freescale microcontrollers is a breeze. Just define the functionality you need for your application and Processor Expert generates tested, optimized C-code tuned for your application and the selected processor. For the critical and unique interrupt service routines, you get function stubs with clear indicators of where you need to put your code. When you change the processor with the Change Wizard, Processor Expert automatically maps the software and peripheral components that describe your application's functionality to the resources available on the new processor. The only issue arises when your use of system resources causes a conflict on the new processor. Even then, Processor Expert flags all the issues so you know precisely what you need to resolve.

That previous sentence is the real value of Processor Expert, for either initial design or migration to new hardware. Processor Expert contains a comprehensive knowledge base of every subsystem on the chip and how it uses available resources like pins and registers. If you attempt to do something that will cause problems, the issue is immediately flagged for your attention. It is a genuine expert-system partner in your development effort. You can even encapsulate, reuse, and deliver your own platform-independent software modules across your company to your development teams.

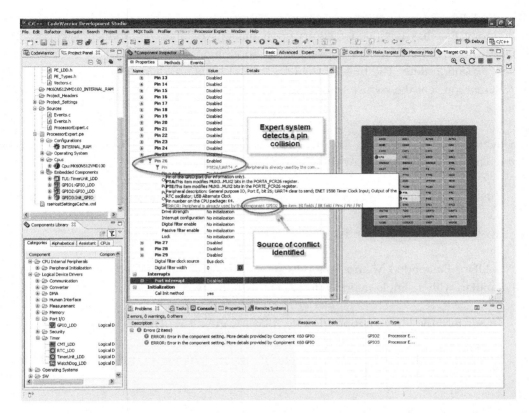

Figure F-1 **The ProcessorExpert perspective within the CodeWarrior IDE**

Processor Expert is a tool to assist your first and most critical task in any development project, getting your software to use the hardware without error. After that - and in fact even while doing that - you will need to write code. You need a development environment, build tools, and a debugger.

Because the CodeWarrior IDE is based on the Eclipse environment, it has all the features you expect: project management, ability to handle multiple projects simultaneously, excellent code comparison, perspective management, and much more. With the increasing use of the Eclipse environment by multiple tools vendors (including Freescale), IDE functionality is becoming common. While the details vary, the general look, feel, and approach is becoming consistent across vendors. This is a good thing.

Unique value comes from the tools that fit within the IDE's umbrella, such as Processor Expert, build tools, and debugger technology.

The CodeWarrior compilers are capable of producing highly optimized code, with technology that has compiled millions upon millions of lines of production code. The CodeWarrior build system helps you develop applications with the smallest code size and fastest execution time. The build system for RS08, HCS08, ColdFire, ColdFire+, Kinetis and MPC56xx represent the robust, reliable tools you can trust from Freescale. Primary features include:

Optimizing ANSI C compilers for HCS08, RS08, ColdFire, ColdFire+, Kinetis and MPC56xx that: Generate standard ELF/DWARF files for execution and debugging

■ ANSI C compatible standard libraries and compact runtime libraries

■ HCS08 C++ compiler includes support for EC++ guidelines

■ ColdFire Embedded Warrior Libraries provide scalable C/C++ standard libraries and a librarian with a simple interface to select functionality

■ Kinetis intrinsic library support for the ARM® Cortex™-M4 DSP instructions

■ Macro assemblers for HCS08, RS08, ColdFire, ColdFire+, Kinetis and MPC56xx processors

■ Linkers that dead-strip unused code for the optimal code size

On the debugger front, the graphical source-level debugger adds significant extensions to the Eclipse C/C++ Development Tools platform specifically focused at the needs of embedded developers. The debugger gives you consistent debug tools for the Controller Continuum, but some features will vary based on target capabilities. For example, Segger J-Link hardware is supported for Kinetis microcontrollers, but irrelevant for other architectures. Key capabilities include:

■ C and assembly source code windows

■ Precise breakpoints and watch points help solve sophisticated problems

■ Complex, emulator-like debug capability using HCS08, V1 ColdFire and Kinetis on-chip trace features

■ Display of data values, complex data structures and expressions to speed run-time analysis, without stopping or single stepping the processor

■ Detailed information on every aspect of your project: break points, watch points, stack, symbol table

■ Full-chip simulation for most HCS08 and RS08 microcontrollers, including CPU instruction set, peripherals, interrupts and I/O

■ Support for kernel-aware debugging with several real-time operating systems

■ Fast flash programming support

■ Ability to preserve a memory range during programming

■ Support for open source BDM and open source JTAG connection interfaces

■ Ability to program user-selectable TRIM values with P&E Microcomputer Systems' Multilink and Cyclone Pro hardware interfaces

■ Support for P&E Microcomputer Systems' Cyclone Pro/Max stand-alone programmers and multilink universal hardware interfaces

■ Support for Segger J-Link hardware interface with Kinetis microcontrollers

In the end, the goal is to enable you to produce code quickly, reliably, effectively, and get to market as fast as possible. To achieve that goal, Freescale provides a comprehensive platform enablement solution: Processor Expert, the CodeWarrior development environment, build tools, debug technology, and various software stacks, components and runtime software. In almost every case however, you have choices beyond Freescale.

Freescale builds its tools to enable partners as well as customers. For example, customers can use any standards-based debugger because the CodeWarrior compiler and linker generate standard debug information. The kernel-awareness capability of the debugger is openly available to partners who wish to enable this inside the CodeWarrior debugger. Anyone can easily build Processor Expert components to deliver to their customers, or internally for their own development teams. These are just a few examples of the Freescale philosophy toward enablement.

F

Appendix

G

Bibliography

■ Webster John G. *Medical Instrumentation: Application and Design*. Wiley, 4th. edition, 2009.

■ Rangayyan Rangaraj M. *Biomedical Signal Analysis*. Wiley-IEEE Press, 1st. edition, 2001.

■ Freescale Semiconductor. *K53 Sub-Family Reference Manual: K53P144M100SF2RM*. Rev. 4, 2011.

G

Licensing Policy

This book contains μC/OS-III in source form for free short-term evaluation, for educational use or for peaceful research. If you plan or intend to use μC/OS-III in a commercial application/product then, you need to contact Micriμm to properly license μC/OS-III for its use in your application/product.

We provide all the source code for your convenience and to help you experience μC/OS-III. The fact that the source is provided does not mean that you can use it commercially without paying a licensing fee. Knowledge of the source code may not be used to develop a similar product.

The reader can purchase the TWR-K53N512 controller along with the AFE medical modules (MED-EKG, MED-GLU, MED-SPO2 and MED-BPM) separately from Freescale. The user may use μC/OS-III with the TWR-K53N512 controller and it is not necessary to purchase anything else as long as the initial purchase is used for short-term evaluation or educational purposes. It is necessary to purchase the license when the decision to use μC/OS-III in a design is made, not when the design is ready to go to production.

If you are unsure about whether you need to obtain a license for your application, please contact Micriμm and discuss the intended use with a sales representative.

Micriμm
1290 Weston Road, Suite 306
Weston, FL 33326

+1 954 217 2036
+1 954 217 2037 (FAX)

E-Mail : sales@micrium.com
Website : www.micrium.com

H

Index

A

ADC 772
adding tasks to the ready list 149
adipose 830
adrenal glands 901
air pump controller
  MED-BPM 910
aldosterone 901
alpha cells 829
alveoli 861
analog comparators 772
analog modules 772
analog to digital converter 772
angiotensin I 899
angiotensin II 900
angiotensin-converting enzyme 900
angiotensinogen 899
ANSI C 35, 51, 343, 355, 725
aorta 792
aortic arch 896
API 36, 689
API changes 702
app.c 821, 823–825, 848, 851, 853–855, 877, 880, 882–884, 919, 922, 924–926
APP_BASELINE_UPPER_LIMIT_MAX_VOLTS 889–890
APP_BASELINE_UPPER_LIMIT_MIN_VOLTS 889–890
APP_BLOOD_DETECT_THR_MVOLTS 856
AppCalcResults() 825, 855, 884, 891, 926, 931
AppCalibrateLED_IR() 889
AppCalibrateLED_Red() 889
AppCardiacCycleState 821, 825, 880, 884
app_cfg.h 68, 398
AppCuffCtrl() 930–931
AppLeakTest.Pressure.Init 930
application code 52
application programming interface 36, 689
APP_MAX_BLOOD_PRESSURE_DIA_MMHG 931
APP_MAX_BLOOD_PRESSURE_SYS_MMHG 931
APP_MAX_CUFF_HOLDING_TIME 931
APP_MAX_CUFF_PRESSURE_MMHG 930
APP_MAX_GLUCOSE_LEVEL_MGDL 856
APP_MAX_HEARTRATE_BPM 891, 931

APP_MAX_OXYGEN_SATURATION 891
APP_MIN_BLOOD_PRESSURE_DIA_MMHG 931
APP_MIN_BLOOD_PRESSURE_SYS_MMHG 931
APP_MIN_CUFF_PRESSURE_MMHG 930–931
APP_MIN_GLUCOSE_LEVEL_MGDL 856
APP_MIN_HEARTBEATS_PER_CALC 886
APP_MIN_HEARTRATE_BPM 891, 931
APP_MIN_OXYGEN_SATURATION 891
APP_MIN_PULSE_SLOPE 826
AppPeakRingBufferClr() 889
AppPulsesAtRampDown 931
AppPulsesAtRampUp 930–931
AppPulsesIR 890–891
AppPulsesRed 891
AppResults 891, 931
AppSamplesCtr 889–891, 930
AppSignal1stSpl 825–826
AppSignal2ndSpl 825–826
AppSignal3rdSpl 825–826
AppSignalCuffPressure.Result 930
AppSignalWorking.Result 856
APP_SMA_WIN_SIZE 856
AppSplsBtwPulsesCtr 825–826
AppTaskDAQ() .821, 823–824, 851, 853–854, 880, 882–883, 922, 924–925
AppTaskDAQ_DetectBlood() 856
AppTaskDAQ_DetectQRS() 825
AppTaskDAQ_ExecCmd() 824, 854, 883, 925
AppTaskDAQ_Init() 856, 930
AppTaskDAQ_ProcessCmd() .823–824, 853–854, 882–883, 924–925
AppTaskDAQ_ProcessData() . 823, 825, 853, 855, 882, 884, 887, 924, 926, 929
AppTaskHeartbeat() 821, 825, 880, 884
AppTaskSim() ..821, 823–824, 851, 853–854, 880, 882–883, 922, 924–925
AppTaskStart() 72–74, 81, 135–137
AppTaskUserIF() 821, 823, 851, 853, 880, 882, 922, 924
ARM real-time trace interface 767
assigning a variable to an object 998
asynchronous wake-up interrupt controller 767
atrioventricular (AV) node 797
atriums 791

autonomic nervous system 896
aVF 803
aVL 803
aVR 802
AWIC 767

B

background 32, 35
baroreceptor 896
    reflex 896
Beer-Lambert law 867
beta cells 829
bilateral rendezvous 292, 313–314
binary semaphores 239
biological electrical potentials 798
biomedical signal analysis 825, 926
blood glucose meter 749, 774, 788, 829, 836–837, 842, 844–846, 849–851, 857
    block diagram 844
    communication via JTAG 845
    dashboard 850
    design 842
blood glucose sensor 837
blood pressure 894–895
    arterial 895
    arterial, measurement 904
blood pressure monitor . 749, 776, 788, 893, 906–907, 914–915, 917, 921–922, 926, 932
    block diagram 906
    dashboard 921
    design 906
    setup 915
board support package 51, 54, 68, 358, 391–392, 411, 724, 783, 961, 984
bounded 255–256
broadcast 281, 307, 311, 331
    on post calls 89, 193
    to a semaphore 306
bronchi 861
BSP 782–783, 984–985
bsp.c 392, 823, 825, 853, 882, 884, 924, 984
    CPU_TS_TmrInit() 984
    CPU_TS_TmrRd() 985
    μC/CPU functions 984–985
bsp.h 68, 392
bsp_adc.c 823–825, 853–855, 882–884, 924–926
BSP_ADC0_ISR 824, 854, 883, 925
BSP_ADC0_ISR() 824, 854, 884, 926
BSP_ADC1_ISR 823–824, 853–854, 882–883, 924–925
BSP_ADC1_ISR() 824–825, 854–855, 883–884, 925–926
BSP_Init() 68, 74, 80, 136, 392
bsp_int.c 393
bsp_int.h 393
BSP_LED_Off() 392, 823, 825, 853, 882, 884, 924
BSP_LED_On() 68, 75, 392, 825, 884
BSP_LED_Toggle() 392
BSP_MUX_Select() 889–890

BSP_PB_Rd() 393
BSP_POX_LED_On() 889–890
BSP_STATUS_CHECK_INTERVAL 823, 853, 882, 924
BSP_StatusRd() 823, 853, 882, 924
bundle of His 797

C

callback function 137, 213, 215–216, 228–229
CAN 776
capacitive touch sense input 777
capillaries 861
carbaminohemoglobin 863
cardiovascular diseases 806
carotid sinuses 896
carrier modulator timer 775
CAU 771
certification 740, 933, 935, 937, 943, 951
Clark-type electrode 837
clock tick 193
clocks 770
CLZ 39, 142, 145, 694, 983
CMT 775
CodeWarrior 1011
communication interfaces 776
compile-time, configurable 41, 97, 690
configurable 696
    compile-time 41, 97, 690
    message queue 311
    OS_StatTask() 680
    OS_TickTask() 127
    OS_TmrTask() 137, 221
    run-time 37, 41, 690
conjunctive 294
consumer 314–315
context switch ..39, 46, 86, 88, 96, 104, 115, 122, 127, 165, 167, 169, 171, 173, 236, 239, 416, 419, 435
controller area network 776
conventions 43
Cortex-M4 766, 784, 961, 967–969, 974–978, 980, 983–984, 986, 989–990, 994
    debug watch trace 984
    μC/CPU port 981
    μC/OS-III port 959
count leading zeros 982–983
countdown 38, 137, 214–217
counter electrode 841, 854
counting semaphores 246
CPU usage 963, 972, 988
cpu.h 61, 69, 358, 364, 367, 986–987, 989
    #defines 986
    data types 987–988
    function prototypes 990
cpu_a.asm 62, 358, 363, 367–368, 987, 990–991
cpu_bsp.h 361
cpu_c.c 62, 367–368

cpu_cfg.h 61, 86, 90, 124, 361, 419, 982
   recommended values 983
CPU_CFG_ADDR_SIZE 366
CPU_CFG_CRITICAL_METHOD 367
CPU_CFG_DATA_SIZE 366
CPU_CFG_ENDIAN_TYPE 366
CPU_CFG_INT_DIS_MEAS_EN 362, 972
CPU_CFG_INT_DIS_MEAS_OVRHD_NBR 362
CPU_CFG_LEAD_ZEROS_ASM_PRESENT 362
CPU_CFG_NAME_EN 361
CPU_CFG_NAME_SIZE 361
CPU_CFG_STK_GROWTH 367
CPU_CFG_TRAIL_ZEROS_ASM_PRESENT 362
CPU_CFG_TS_32_EN 361
CPU_CFG_TS_64_EN 362
CPU_CFG_TS_TMR_SIZE 362
CPU_CntLeadZeros 363
CPU_CntLeadZeros() 990
cpu_core.c 61, 358, 363–364, 982
cpu_core.h 61, 69, 364, 982
CPU_CRITICAL_ENTER() 61, 86, 88, 234–236, 366, 368,
618, 702, 982, 987, 989
CPU_CRITICAL_EXIT() .61, 86, 88, 234–236, 366, 368, 702,
982, 987, 989
CPU_DATA 142–145, 365
CPU_DATA_SIZE_MAX 367
cpu_def.h 61, 361, 982
CPU_Init() 74, 80, 363
CPU_SR_Restore() 368
CPU_SR_Save() 368
CPU_STK 69, 968, 989
CPU_TS_Get32 363
CPU_TS_TmrFreqSet 363
CPU_TS_TmrInit() 393, 984–985
   µC/CPU functions 984
CPU_TS_TmrRd() 393, 961, 984–985
   µC/CPU functions 985
CRC 771
creating a memory partition 344
credit tracking 279, 308
critical region 85, 425, 438
cryptographic acceleration unit 771
C-SPY Debugger 1009
CVD 806
cyclic redundancy check 771

D

DAC 772
DAQ task 821, 823–825, 827, 851, 853–855, 857, 880, 882–
886, 892, 922, 924–926, 932
data processing state machine 887, 929
data screen 996–997, 999
data types (os_type.h) 683
deadlock 39–40, 252, 267–270, 690
   prevention 39–40, 690

deadly embrace 267
deferred post 152–153, 161, 186, 189, 191–195
deoxyhemoglobin 863
device class 944, 947
device support 1007
dextrose 829
diabetes 835–836
diabetes mellitus 835
diaphragm 860
diastole 894
diastolic pressure 893
digital to analog converter 772
direct post 152, 186–188, 190, 192–193, 195
direct vs. deferred post method 192
disjunctive 294
DO-178B 951
DO-254 952
DO-278B 951
downloading
   IAR Embedded Workbench for ARM 787
   µC/OS-III projects 780
   µC/Probe 786
DWT 961, 984–985
DWT_CYCCNT 961

E

ECG design 808
ECG leads 801
ED-12B 952
Einthoven's law 802
Einthoven's triangle 801
electrical potentials 798
electrocardiogram 791
electrocardiograph 749
electrode ..777, 799–801, 803–804, 808–809, 814–816, 841
   anode 839–840
   biopotential 798–799, 804
   cathode 839
   Clark-type 837
   counter 841, 854
   ECG 801
   illustration 815
   reference 839, 841–842
   signals 845, 851
   skin 808
   test strip 841–842
   test strip signal conditioning schematics 843
   working 839, 841, 854, 856
electroenzymatic 837
electrolyte 837
ELF/DWARF 43
embedded systems . 19, 31, 37, 91, 93, 102, 184, 350, 354,
725, 731
EN 50128 952
EN 50129 952
endocrine system 829
error checking 38

Ethernet 34, 43, 49, 55, 94, 176, 289, 310, 312
Ethernet MAC 776
EUROCAE 952
EvalBoards 782
event flags 40, 46–47, 89, 193, 197, 273, 281, 294–296, 298–300, 305–308, 423–424, 448, 690, 703
    internals 300
    synchronization 448
    using 296
EWARM 740, 787, 816, 847, 875–876, 917–918
    block diagram 1003
extinction coefficient 866

F

FDA 510(k) 943
FDA development guidance 943
FDA guidance 954
FDA premarket approval 943
FIFO 81, 311, 318, 322, 326, 451–452
fixed-size memory partitions 455
flash memory 770
FlexBus 770
flexible timer modules 775
FlexMemory 770
floating-point 988
flow control 314
footprint 40, 438–439, 441, 690
foreground 32, 35
foreground/background systems 32
FPU 102, 178
fragmentation 98, 343–344, 354
free() 343, 354
Freescale 758, 782
FTM 775

G

gauges 993–994, 996–997
general purpose input/output 777
general statistics – run-time 414
getting a memory block from a partition 348
ghrelin 835
glucagon 829
glucono delta-lactone 840
glucose 749, 774, 788, 829–842, 844–846, 849–851, 853, 855–857
    measuring concentration 839
    oxidase enzyme 837
    oxidation 837
    regulation 830, 833
    stock solution 841
glycogen 834
GPIO 777
granularity 213, 685
graphs 993–994, 996–997
GUI 35

H

heart 791
heart rate monitor ...788, 791, 808–810, 812, 814, 819–821, 823, 827–828
    block diagram 809–810
    dashboard 820
heartbeat 798
heartbeat task 821, 825, 827, 880, 884, 892
hemoglobin 861
HID 995
hooks and port 723
hormones 829
human-machine interfaces 777
hydroxides 840
hyperglycaemia 835
hypertension 902
hypoxia 904

I

I2C 776
I2S 776
IAR 782
IAR assembler 1009
IAR Embedded Workbench for ARM 1002
    downloading 787
IAR J-LINK Linker 1009
IAR Library 1010
idle task (OS_IdleTask()) 125
IEC 61508 951
IEC 61511 952
IEC 61513 952
IEC 62061 952
IEC 62304 ....948, 952
IEEE 1149.1 JTAG 767
IEEE 1149.7 JTAG (cJTAG) 767
IEEE 1588 timers 775
industry and standards bodies 941
infinite loop 71, 75, 91, 93, 97, 125, 139, 417–418, 724
insulin 829, 833
integrated interchip sound 776
inter-integrated circuit 776
internal tasks 125
interrupt ..85–87, 89–90, 138, 160, 175–181, 183–187, 189–193, 195, 233–236, 271, 273, 309, 393–394, 676, 684, 702
    controller 177–177, 183–185, 368, 393–395
    disable 86
    disable time 61, 87, 90, 138, 175, 187–188, 191–192, 233, 271, 413–414, 419
    disable time, measuring 86
    disable/enable 234
    handler task 138
    latency ..74, 175, 188, 190–191, 193, 233, 235, 271, 419, 676, 694
    management 175
    periodic 203
    recovery 176, 188, 190–191

response 175, 188, 190–191
    vector to a common location 183
interrupt service routine 273, 350
Introduction 739
intuitive 36, 44, 100
ISO 13485 950
ISO 14971 950
ISR 273, 350
    epilogue 180, 183–184, 188, 191
    handler task 138–139, 147, 154, 671, 678, 684
    handler task (OS_IntQTask()) 138
    prologue 180, 183–185, 188, 191
    typical µC/OS-III ISR 177

J

J-Link 786, 993–995, 1009
J-Link Ultra 788, 812, 816, 845–846, 873, 875, 914, 917
J-Link-Lite for ARM Processors 741
JTAG 1009
jumper settings
    MED-EKG 815
    TWR-K53N512 755–757
juxtaglomerular cells 898

K

kernel awareness debuggers 39
kernel object 422

L

lancing device 836, 840
larynx 861
LCD 777
lead 800
LED 42, 51, 75, 392
LED driver
    MED-PULSE 871
level of concern 945
lib_ascii.c 63
lib_ascii.h 63
lib_cfg.h 64
lib_def.h 63, 69, 784
lib_math.c 63
lib_mem.c 63–64
lib_mem.h 63
lib_mem_a.asm 64
lib_str.c 63
lib_str.h 63
licensing 43, 47, 733, 1011, 1019
LIFO 311, 451–452
lipids 829
liver 830
lock/unlock 236
locking 36, 87–90, 138, 156, 233, 236, 271, 309, 416
locking the scheduler 87

low power 126, 195
low-power timer 775
LPT 775
lungs 861

M

MAC 776
main() 818, 848, 877, 919
malloc() 69, 98, 343, 345–347, 349, 354
manometer 904
MCG 770
MCU 51–52, 54, 358
mean arterial pressure 895
MED-BGM 740, 749, 788, 843, 845–846
    block diagram 844
    signal conditioning circuit 843
    with TWR-K53N512 846
MED-BPM 740, 749, 788, 909–911, 913–915, 917
    air pump controller 910
    pin-out 916
    sensor signal conditioning 912
    solenoid valve controller 911
    with TWR-K53N512 909
MED-EKG 740, 749, 788, 809, 811–814
    jumper settings 815
    signal conditioning circuit 812
    with TWR-K53N512 813
MEDICAL CONNECTOR 755
Medical Connector 754
medical connector . 741, 811, 814, 843, 845–846, 871, 873, 875, 909, 913–914, 917
medical device software
    recalls 935
medical standards 948
MED-PULSE 740, 749, 788, 871, 873–875, 883
    LED driver 871
    signal conditioning 870
    with TWR-K53N512 874
memory management 707
memory management unit 103
memory partitions .. 317, 344, 346, 350, 354, 415, 424, 455, 676
    using 350
memory protection unit 103
message mailboxes 705
message passing 47, 309, 451–452
message queue .47, 198, 309–317, 319, 321, 323–325, 331, 333, 341, 705, 710–711, 717
    configurable 311
    internals 328
    message passing 451
    task 312, 452
    using 319
messages 310
meters 994, 996–997
migrating 47, 689
miscellaneous 721

MISRA-C
    2004, Rule 14.7 (Required) 728
    2004, Rule 15.2 (Required) 729
    2004, Rule 17.4 (Required) 730
    2004, Rule 8.12 (Required) 727
    2004, Rule 8.5 (Required) 726
mitral 797
MMU 62, 103
mode 886
modular and extensible IDE 1004
monosaccharides 833
MPU 103
multiple tasks
    application with kernel objects 76
    waiting on a semaphore 281
multipurpose clock generator 770
multitasking 33, 36, 40, 91, 96, 139, 690
mutual exclusion semaphore . 256, 260–264, 271, 422–423, 677, 708–709
    internals 261
    resource management 447

N

nasal passage 860
nested task suspension 38
nested vector interrupt controller 766
numeric indicators 993–994, 997
NVIC 766

O

object names 39
object ribbon 997
objects 996–999
one-shot timers 215
oral cavity 860
os.h 58, 69, 71, 73, 113
os_app_hooks.c 56, 962, 964–966, 972–973
OS_AppIdleTaskHookPtr 962
OS_AppStatTaskHookPtr 963
OS_AppTaskDelHookPtr 965
OS_AppTaskReturnHookPtr 966
OS_AppTaskSwHookPtr 972
OS_AppTimeTickHookPtr 973
os_cfg.h 56–57, 69, 124, 419, 671–672
os_cfg_app.c 57, 438, 818, 848, 877, 919
os_cfg_app.h 56–57, 671, 683, 975
OS_CFG_APP_HOOKS_EN 672, 962
OS_CFG_ARG_CHK_EN 674
OS_CFG_CALLED_FROM_ISR_CHK_EN 674
OS_CFG_DBG_EN 675
OS_CFG_FLAG_DEL_EN 675
OS_CFG_FLAG_EN 675
OS_CFG_FLAG_MODE_CLR_EN 675
OS_CFG_FLAG_PEND_ABORT_EN 675
OS_CFG_IDLE_TASK_STK_SIZE 684

OS_CFG_INT_Q_SIZE 684
OS_CFG_INT_Q_TASK_STK_SIZE 684
OS_CFG_ISR_POST_DEFERRED_EN 676
OS_CFG_ISR_STK_SIZE 684
OS_CFG_MEM_EN 676
OS_CFG_MSG_POOL_SIZE 684
OS_CFG_MUTEX_DEL_EN 677
OS_CFG_MUTEX_EN 677
OS_CFG_MUTEX_PEND_ABORT_EN 677
OS_CFG_OBJ_TYPE_CHK_EN 677
OS_CFG_PEND_MULTI_EN 677
OS_CFG_PRIO_MAX 677
OS_CFG_Q_DEL_EN 678
OS_CFG_Q_EN 678
OS_CFG_Q_FLUSH_EN 679
OS_CFG_Q_PEND_ABORT_EN 679
OS_CFG_SCHED_LOCK_TIME_MEAS_EN 679, 973
OS_CFG_SCHED_ROUND_ROBIN_EN 679
OS_CFG_SEM_DEL_EN 679
OS_CFG_SEM_EN 679
OS_CFG_SEM_PEND_ABORT_EN 679
OS_CFG_SEM_SET_EN 679
OS_CFG_STAT_TASK_EN 680
OS_CFG_STAT_TASK_PRIO 685
OS_CFG_STAT_TASK_RATE_HZ 685
OS_CFG_STAT_TASK_STK_CHK_EN 680
OS_CFG_STAT_TASK_STK_SIZE 685
OS_CFG_STK_SIZE_MIN 680
OS_CFG_TASK_CHANGE_PRIO_EN 681
OS_CFG_TASK_DEL_EN 681
OS_CFG_TASK_PROFILE_EN 681, 972
OS_CFG_TASK_Q_EN 681
OS_CFG_TASK_Q_PEND_ABORT_EN 681
OS_CFG_TASK_REG_TBL_SIZE 681
OS_CFG_TASK_SEM_PEND_ABORT_EN 682
OS_CFG_TASK_STK_LIMIT_PCT_EMPTY 683
OS_CFG_TASK_SUSPEND_EN 682
OS_CFG_TICK_RATE_HZ 685, 975
OS_CFG_TICK_TASK_PRIO 685
OS_CFG_TICK_TASK_STK_SIZE 685
OS_CFG_TICK_WHEEL_SIZE 686
OS_CFG_TIME_DLY_HMSM_EN 682
OS_CFG_TIME_DLY_RESUME_EN 682
OS_CFG_TMR_DEL_EN 682
OS_CFG_TMR_EN 682
OS_CFG_TMR_TASK_PRIO 686
OS_CFG_TMR_TASK_RATE_HZ 687
OS_CFG_TMR_TASK_STK_SIZE 687
OS_CFG_TMR_WHEEL_SIZE 687
oscillator 770
oscillometric method 904
os_core.c 57
os_cpu.h 60, 69, 371, 960
os_cpu_a.asm 60, 381, 960–961, 976

OS_CPU_PendSVHandler() 978
OSCtxSw() 977
OSIntCtxSw() 977
OSStartHighRdy() 976
os_cpu_a.inc 388
os_cpu_c.c 60, 372, 961
  OS_CPU_SysTickHandler() 974
  OS_CPU_SysTickInit() 975
  OSIdleTaskHook() 962
  OSInitHook() 963
  OSStatTaskHook() 963
  OSTaskCreateHook() 964
  OSTaskDelHook() 965
  OSTaskReturnHook() 966
  OSTaskStkInit() 967
  OSTaskSwHook() 971
  OSTimeTickHook() 973
OS_CPU_PendSVHandler() 978
OS_CPU_SysTickHandler() 961, 974
OS_CPU_SysTickInit() 961, 975
OS_CTX_RESTORE 389
OS_CTX_SAVE 388
OSCtxSw() 168, 371, 382, 456, 960, 976–979
os_dbg.c 57, 425
os_flag.c 57
OSFlagCreate() 458
OSFlagDel() 460
OSFlagPend() 93, 462
OSFlagPendAbort() 466
OSFlagPendGetFlagsRdy() 469
OSFlagPost() 471
OSIdleTaskHook() 372, 474, 961–962
OSInit() 147, 476
OSInitHook() 373, 479, 961, 963
os_int.c 57
OSIntCtxSw() 170, 371, 384, 480, 976–979
OSIntEnter() 482
OSIntExit() 160, 484
OS_IntQTask() 138
OS_ISR_ENTER 390
OS_ISR_EXIT 391
os_mem.c 57
OSMemCreate() 485
OSMemGet() 488
OSMemPut() 246, 490
os_msg.c 57
os_mutex.c 57
OSMutexCreate() 492
OSMutexDel() 494
OSMutexPend() 93, 259–260, 496
OSMutexPendAbort() 500
OSMutexPost() 503
os_pend_multi.c 57
OSPendMulti() 93, 506
os_prio.c 58
os_q.c 58
OSQCreate() 511

OSQDel() 514
OSQFlush() 516
OSQPend() 93, 519
OSQPendAbort() 523
OSQPost() 526
OSSafetyCriticalStart() 530
OSSched() 159, 531
OSSchedLock() 533
OS_SchedRoundRobin() 161
OSSchedRoundRobinCfg() 535
OSSchedRoundRobinYield() 537
OSSchedUnlock() 539
os_sem.c 58
OSSemCreate() 541
OSSemDel() 544
OSSemPend() 93, 547
OSSemPendAbort() 551
OSSemPost() 554
OSSemSet() 557
OSStart() 559
OSStartHighRdy() 371, 381, 561, 976–979
os_stat.c 58, 963
OSStatReset() 563
OS_StatTask() 680
OSStatTaskCPUUsageInit() 565
OSStatTaskHook() 373, 567, 961, 963
os_task.c 58
OSTaskChangePrio() 569
OSTaskCreate() 149, 571
OSTaskCreateHook() 96, 374, 581, 961, 964
OSTaskDel() 93, 583
OSTaskDelHook() 374, 586, 965
OSTaskQPend() 93, 588, 823, 853, 882, 924
OSTaskQPendAbort() 593
OSTaskQPost() .595, 823–825, 853–855, 882–884, 924–926
OSTaskRegGet() 598
OSTaskRegSet() 601
OSTaskResume() 606
OSTaskReturnHook() 374–375, 604, 961, 966
OSTaskSemPend() 93, 608
OSTaskSemPendAbort() 611
OSTaskSemPost() 613, 825, 884
OSTaskSemSet() 615
OSTaskStatHook() 617
OSTaskStkChk() 619
OSTaskStkInit() 376, 622, 961, 967–969
OSTaskSuspend() 93, 627
OS_TASK_SW() 371
OSTaskSwHook() 379, 629, 961, 971–972, 979
OSTaskTimeQuantaSet() 632
OSTaslDelHook() 961
os_tick.c 58
OSTickISR() 385, 634
os_time.c 58

OSTimeDly() 93, 132, 204–205, 207, 636
OSTimeDlyHMSM() 93, 209, 639
OSTimeDlyResume() 211, 642
OSTimeGet() 644
OSTimeSet() 646
OSTimeSet() and OSTimeGet() 212
OSTimeTick() 128, 212, 648
OSTimeTickHook() 380, 649, 961, 973
os_tmr.c 58
OSTmrCreate() 226, 651
OSTmrDel() 656
OSTmrRemainGet() 658
OSTmrStart() 660
OSTmrStateGet() 662
OSTmrStop() 664
OS_TmrTask(), configurable 137, 221
OS_TS_GET() 68, 82, 122, 188, 191, 242, 253, 266, 283, 290, 302, 324, 371
os_type.h 58, 69, 671, 683, 988
os_var.c 58
OSVersion() 667
oxygen saturation 859
oxyhemoglobin 861

P

pancreas 829–830
parasympathetic 896
partition 316–317, 343–354, 424
partition memory manager 676
PDB 775
pend
    lists 46, 138, 197, 202
    on a task semaphore 290
    on multiple objects ...38, 41, 89, 193, 333, 430, 453, 691
periodic (no initial delay) 216
periodic (with initial delay) 217
periodic interrupt 203
periodic interrupt timers 775
peripherals 31, 51, 99, 358
per-task statistics - run-time 419
pharynx 861
pin usage
    TWR-K53N512 752–754
PITinterrupt
    timers 775
polling 175
porting 47, 165, 355, 358
posting (i.e. signaling) a task semaphore 291
potassium chloride 839
precordial leads 804
preemption lock 85
preemptive scheduling 100, 152–153
Primary hypertension 903

priority   ...81, 83, 89, 100–101, 139, 155–156, 161, 163, 168, 173, 175–176, 185, 193, 221, 273, 279, 281, 306, 420, 422, 677–678, 690
    inheritance 37, 233, 257, 271
    inversion 248, 254–255
    level 37, 142, 145–146, 149–150
    OS_IdleTask() 125
    OS_StatTask() 134, 680
    OS_TmrTask() 137, 221
    pend list 197
    priority ready bitmap 158
    round-robin scheduling 36
Processors with Multiple Interrupt Priorities 181
producer 314–315
program status register 989
programmable delay block 775
protocol mechanism 237, 274
pulse oximeter 749, 859, 865, 867, 870, 872–873, 875, 879, 891
    block diagram 872
    dashboard 879
    design 870
    signal conditioning 870
pulse oximetry 865
Purkinje fibers 797

R

RAAS 898
random number generator 771
ready list 46, 109, 138, 141, 146–150, 197
    adding tasks 149
real-time clock 775
real-time kernels 33
real-time operating system 19–20, 35, 127
red blood cells 861
reentrant 92–93, 260, 355
reference electrode 839, 841–842
regulators 941
regulatory environment 941–942, 947
rendezvous 276, 292, 306–307, 313–314
renin 898
renin-angiotensin-aldosterone system 896, 898
resource sharing 233
respiration 860
response time 32, 38, 175, 299
retriggering 216
returning a memory block to a partition 349
RMS 100–101
RNG 771
ROMable 21, 35, 37, 40, 690
round-robin scheduling 156
RTC 775
RTCA 951
run-time configurable 37, 41, 690

S

safety critical 936
safety critical software
    cost 939
safety-critical development standards 951
scalable 21, 35–36, 40, 690
scheduling algorithm 194–195
scheduling internals 158
scheduling points 154, 163
SDHC 776
secondary hypertension 903
secure digital host controller 776
semaphore ..77, 96, 119, 123, 200, 233, 237–256, 260–264, 267, 269, 271, 274–292, 294, 306–309, 315–316, 333, 337, 339, 352–353, 420–423, 558, 677, 679, 690, 708–709, 712–713, 717
    internals (for resource sharing) 249
    internals (for synchronization) 282
    synchronization 449
sensor signal conditioning
    MED-BPM 912
serial peripheral interface 776
serial wire debug 767
servers 327
setting up 788
short interrupt service routine 180
sim task ... 821, 823–824, 851, 853–854, 880, 882–883, 922, 924–925
single task application 68
sinoatrial (SA) 797
sliders 993, 996–997
small intestine 830
software timers 37–38, 40, 46, 58, 690
solenoid valve controller
    MED-BPM 911
source files 692
sphygmomanometer 904
SPI 776
SRAM 770
stack .94–96, 98–99, 102–106, 110, 115, 117–118, 123–124, 134, 137, 139, 165–167, 178–179, 199, 202, 356, 360, 369–370, 421, 671, 680–681, 683–685, 687, 693, 695, 718, 724
    pointer 165, 167, 369
    size 102
stack overflows 102–103, 105–106
statistic task (OS_StatTask()) 134
statistics 44, 47, 134–135, 137, 139, 413–414, 419, 680, 694
status 114
stethoscope 904
stock glucose solutions 841
superloops 32
SWD 767, 994, 1009
switched in 104, 109
symbol browser 996–997, 999
sympathetic 896
synchronization 294

synchronizing multiple tasks 306
system tick 127, 193, 195
SysTick 961, 974–975
systole 894
systolic pressure 893

T

tail chaining 980
task
    adding to the readylist 149
    latency 176, 188, 190–191, 420, 679
    management 444, 714
    message 38
    message queue 312, 452
    priorities, assigning 100
    registers 38, 41, 121, 691
    semaphore 289–292, 308, 315–316
    semaphores, synchronization 450
    signals 38, 44, 151, 154, 287, 291, 341
    stack overflows 103
    states 108
task control block 69, 94, 113, 330
task management
    internals 108
    services 107
task message queues 827, 857, 892, 932
task semaphores 827, 892
test strip 836, 841–843, 846, 850, 854, 856
thread 33, 91
tick task (OS_TickTask()) 127
tick wheel 47, 116, 131, 414, 440, 671, 683
time management 37, 42, 46, 203, 446, 718–719
time slicing 120, 156
time stamps 41, 74, 691
timeouts 39, 127, 194–195, 203, 212, 685
timer management 719
    internals 217
    internals - OS_TMR 219
    internals - Timer List 223
    internals - Timer Task 221
    internals - Timers States 217
timer modules 775
timer task (OS_TmrTask()) 137
timer wheel 224, 226, 440, 671, 683, 686
timers 137, 195, 213, 215–217, 223–224, 229, 454
timestamp 87–88, 194, 200, 242, 250–251, 253, 262, 264, 266, 283, 290, 299, 302–303, 310, 324, 328, 337, 352, 393, 422–424, 706, 711, 713
tower system ...737, 740–742, 749, 758–759, 762–763, 788, 811–813, 828, 845, 857, 873–874, 892, 914, 932
traceability 938
trachea 861
transient events 299–300
transimpedance amplifier 842
tricuspid 797
TSI 777
TWR-ELEV 758

TWR-K53N512 740–742, 749, 751, 758, 762, 782–783, 788, 809, 811–814, 816, 820–821, 843, 845–846, 850–851, 871, 873–875, 879–880, 909, 913, 917, 921
    block diagram 750
    connecting 789
    documentation 790
    jumper settings 755–757
    pin usage 752–754
    pinout 761
    with MED-BGM 846
    with MED-BPM 909
    with MED-EKG 813
    with MED-PULSE 874
TWR-K53N512.eww 782
TWR-K53N512-KIT 758, 788
TWR-LCD 763
TWR-PROTO 762
TWR-SER 758

U

UART 776
UARTs 49
uC-CPU 784
uC-LIB 784
uCOS-III 785
uCOS-III-Ex1-HRM 783
uCOS-III-Ex1-HRM-Probe.wsp 819
uCOS-III-Ex2-BGM 783
uCOS-III-Ex2-BGM-Probe.wsp 849
uCOS-III-Ex3-POX 783
uCOS-III-Ex3-POX-Probe.wsp 878
uCOS-III-Ex4-BPM 783
uCOS-III-Ex4-BPM-Probe.wsp 920
UK Defense Standard 00-56 Issue 2 951
unbounded priority inversion ...37, 233, 254–256, 262, 267, 271
unilateral rendezvous 276, 292
universal asynchronous receiver/transmitters 49, 776
unlock 236
unlocking 138, 233, 271
USB 43
USB device charger detect 776
USB OTG 776
USB voltage regulator 776
USBDCD 776
user definable hooks 39
user IF task 821, 823, 851, 853, 880, 882, 922, 924
using event flags 296
using memory partitions 350

V

variable name changes 701
vasoconstriction 897
vector 92, 176–177, 183, 185, 195
vector address 176, 183

venae cavae 792
ventricles 791

W

wait lists 42, 46, 138, 197
walks the stack 105
watermark 72, 95, 115
Wilson's central terminal 803
working electrode 839, 841, 854, 856
workspace 782, 996

Y

yielding 156

Micrium

µC/CPU 784, 972, 981–982, 984–985, 989–990
µC/CPU functions
    in bsp.c 984–985
    in CPU_TS_TmrInit() 984
    in CPU_TS_TmrRd() 985
µC/FS 35
µC/GUI 35
µC/LIB 51, 62–64, 784
    portable library functions 62
µC/OS-III 35
    features 40
    features (os_cfg.h) 672
    features with longer critical sections 89
    porting 369
    stacks, pools and other (os_cfg_app.h) 683
µC/OS-III convention changes 695
µC/Probe 39, 42–44, 57, 120, 123, 220, 240, 249, 261, 263, 283–284, 301, 303, 413, 426, 441, 993–994
µC/Probe 995
µC/Probe 996–997
    downloading 786
µC/Probe
    downloading 995
µC/TCP-IP 35, 995
µC/USB 35, 995

It's embedded design made easy.

At Freescale, we work hard to make the entire design process easier. That's why our MCU solutions offer you one consistent development environment across S08, ColdFire and ARM® architectures. It's why our comprehensive smart mobile device solutions include i.MX processors, sensors and power management components. And it's why our networking multicore designs come to you as production-ready solutions complete with an array of enablement tools and reference designs for quick development. From silicon to software to third-party support, it's easier to design with Freescale. Learn more at freescale.com/discover

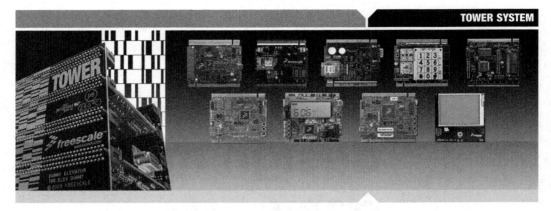

8-, 16- and 32-bit Microcontrollers/Microprocessors

Freescale Tower System
Modular development platform

Overview

The Freescale Tower System is a modular development platform for 8-, 16- and 32-bit microcontrollers and microprocessors that enables advanced development through rapid prototyping. Featuring multiple development boards or modules, the Tower System provides designers with building blocks for entry-level to advanced microcontroller development.

Modular and Expandable

- Controller modules provide easy-to-use, reconfigurable hardware
- Interchangeable peripheral modules (including serial, memory and graphical LCD) make customization easy
- Open-source hardware and standardized specifications promote the development of additional modules for added functionality and customization

Speeds Development Time

- Open source hardware and software allows quick development with proven designs
- Integrated debugging interface allows for easy programming and run-control via standard USB cable

Cost Effective

- Peripheral modules can be re-used with all Tower System controller modules, eliminating the need to purchase redundant hardware for future designs
- Enabling technologies like LCD, serial and memory interfacing are offered off-the-shelf at a low cost to provide a customized enablement solution

Software Enablement and Support

The increasing complexity of industrial applications and expanding functionality of semiconductors are driving embedded developers toward solutions that require the integration of proven hardware and software platforms. Freescale, along with a strong alliance network, offers comprehensive solutions, including development tools, debuggers, programmers and software.

Complimentary Software and Tools

- Ethernet, FileSystem, USB stacks and more*
- CodeWarrior Development Studio
- Processor Expert software: A rapid application development tool in the CodeWarrior tool suite
- Digital signal processing library: Provides algorithms optimized for the ColdFire architecture

  * Visit freescale.com/software for a list of supported devices

Take Your Design to the Next Level

For a complete list of development kits and modules offered as part of the Freescale Tower System, please visit **freescale.com/Tower**.

Tower System Modules

Features	Benefits
Controller Modules (8-, 16-, 32-bit)	
• Works stand-alone or as part of Tower System	• Allows rapid prototyping
• Features open source debugging interface	• Provides easy programming and run-control via standard USB cable
Peripheral Modules	
• Can be re-used with all Tower System controller modules	• Eliminates the need to buy/develop redundant hardware
• Interchangeable peripheral modules—serial, memory, graphical LCD, prototyping, sensor	• Enables advanced development and broad functionality
Elevator Boards	
• Two 2x80 connectors	• Provides easy signal access and side-mounting board (i.e. LCD module)
• Power regulation circuitry	• Provides power to all boards
• Standardized signal assignments	• Allows for customized peripheral module development
• Four card-edge connectors available	• Allows easy expansion using PCI Express connectors (x16, 90 mm/3.5" long, 164 pins)

Build Your System in Three Steps or Less

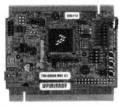

1. Choose a controller module

2. Choose peripheral modules
(up to three standard modules plus side-mounting module(s))

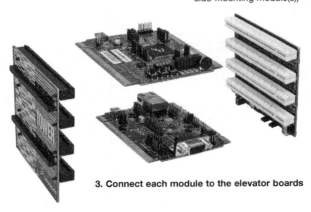

3. Connect each module to the elevator boards

Available Tower System Modules

Controller Modules	Features
• TWR-MCF51CN	MCF51CN ColdFire V1 Ethernet module
• TWR-MCF5225X	MCF5225X ColdFire V2 connectivity module
• TWR-S08LL64	MC9S08LL64 8-bit segment LCD module
• TWR-S08LH64	MC9S08LH64 8-bit segment LCD module with integrated 16-bit ADC
• TWR-MPC5125	MPC5125 e300c4 module built on Power Architecture® technology
• TWR-MCF51MM	MCF51MM ColdFire V1 microcontroller module designed for medical applications
• TWR-S08MM128	MC9S08MM128 8-bit microcontroller module designed for medical applications
• TWR-MCF51JE	MCF51JE ColdFire V1 USB microcontroller module
• TWR-MCF5441X	MCF5441X ColdFire V4 connectivity module with dual Ethernet
• TWR-56F8257	MC56F8257 DSC module
• TWR-K40X256	K40X256 Kinetis module (based on ARM® Cortex™-M4 core) with full-speed USB 2.0 On-The-Go and segment LCD controller
• TWR-K60N512	K60N512 Kinetis module (based on ARM Cortex-M4 core) with IEEE® 1588 Ethernet, full- and High-Speed USB 2.0 On-the-Go, hardware encryption and tamper detection
Peripheral Modules	**Features**
• TWR-ELEV	Elevator modules: Primary and secondary
• TWR-SER	Serial module with RS232/RS485, Ethernet, CAN, USB
• TWR-SER2	Enhanced serial module featuring dual Ethernet and High-Speed USB
• TWR-PROTO	Prototyping module
• TWR-LCD	Graphical LCD module with 3.2" QVGA display
• TWR-MEM	Memory module with serial flash, MRAM, SD card and compact flash interfaces
• TWR-SENSOR-PAK	Swappable sensor module with accelerometer, barometer and touch-sensing controller
• TWR-WIFI-RS2101	802.11n Wi-Fi® board featuring Redpine Signals' RS9110-N-11-21 Connect-io-n™ Wi-Fi module on board
• TWR-WIFI-G1011MI	802.11b Wi-Fi board featuring GainSpan's GS1011MIP Wi-Fi module on board
• TWR-WIFI-AR4100	802.11n Wi-Fi module featuring the Atheros AR4100 ultra-low power Wi-Fi solution
• TWR-RF-SNAP	Wireless Mesh Networking module featuring SNAP Technology from Synapse Wireless (based on the Freescale MC13224 802.15.4 platform)
• MED-EKG	Sold as part of a complete kit, electrocardiograph sensor for medical applications
• TWR-ADCDAC-LTC	Linear Technology analog module featuring high-precision ADCs and DACs
Complete Kits	**Includes**
• TWR-MCF51CN-KIT	TWR-MCF51CN, TWR-SER and TWR-ELEV modules
• TWR-MCF5225X-KIT	TWR-MCF5225X, TWR-SER and TWR-ELEV modules
• TWR-S08LL64-KIT	TWR-S08LL64, TWR-PROTO and TWR-ELEV modules
• TWR-S08LH64-KIT	TWR-S08LH64, TWR-PROTO and TWR-ELEV modules
• TWR-MPC5125-KIT	TWR-MPC5125, TWR-SER and TWR-ELEV modules
• TWR-MCF51MM-KIT	TWR-MCF51MM, TWR-SER, TWR-ELEV and MED-EKG modules
• TWR-S08MM128-KIT	TWR-S08MM128, TWR-SER, TWR-ELEV and MED-EKG modules
• TWR-MCF51JE-KIT	TWR-MCF51JE-KIT, TWR-SER and TWR-ELEV modules
• TWR-MCF5441X-KIT	TWR-MCF5441X, TWR-SER2 and TWR-ELEV modules
• TWR-K40X256-KIT	TWR-K40X256, TWR-SER and TWR-ELEV modules
• TWR-K60N512-KIT	TWR-K60N512, TWR-SER and TWR-ELEV modules
• TWR-K60N512-IAR	TWR-K60N512-KIT, TWR-PROTO, IAR J-Link (Lite) Debug Probe

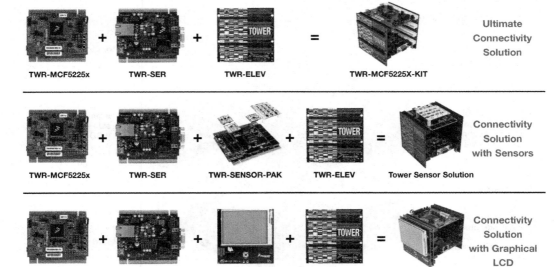

TWR-MCF5225x + TWR-SER + TWR-ELEV = TWR-MCF5225X-KIT — Ultimate Connectivity Solution

TWR-MCF5225x + TWR-SER + TWR-SENSOR-PAK + TWR-ELEV = Tower Sensor Solution — Connectivity Solution with Sensors

TWR-MCF5225x + TWR-SER + TWR-LCD + TWR-ELEV = Tower LCD Solution — Connectivity Solution with Graphical LCD

Example Configurations Partner Modules

Tap into a powerful ecosystem of Freescale technology alliances for building smarter, better connected solutions. Designed to help you shorten your design cycle and get your products to market faster, these technology alliances provide you with access to rich design tools, peripherals and world-class support and training.

A number of partners have developed modules for the Tower System. Some examples include the i.MX515 ARM® Cortex™-A8 Tower Computer Module and StackableUSB™ I/O Device Carrier module from Micro/sys, as well as the Rapid Prototyping System (RPS) AM1 and FM1 modules from iMN MicroControl.

A complete list of partner-developed modules is available at freescale.com/Tower.

Multiple Power Options

The Freescale Tower System can be powered entirely over a USB cable via a host PC or USB wall power adaptor. Alternatively, power can be supplied to the Tower via a screw terminal on the Primary Elevator.

Protection circuitry is built into all Tower System modules to avoid contention on the power rails. Although power can be supplied through any module, power supplied through the elevator modules takes precedence.

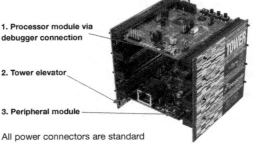

1. Processor module via debugger connection

2. Tower elevator

3. Peripheral module

All power connectors are standard USB connectors that can be powered by a USB host/hub or an AC-to-DC adapter with a USB cable.

Tower Geeks Online Community

TowerGeeks.org is an online design engineer community that allows members to interact, develop designs and share ideas. Offering a direct path to explore and interact with other engineers designing with the Tower System, TowerGeeks.org is a great way to discuss your projects, post videos of your progress, ask questions through the forum and upload software. With updates through Twitter and Facebook, it's easy to get involved.

freescale™ semiconductor

The Freescale Tower System

Controller Module

- Tower MCU/MPU board

- Works stand-alone or in Tower System

- Features integrated debugging interface for easy programming and run control via standard USB cable

Secondary Elevator

- Additional and secondary serial and expansion bus signals

- Standardized signal assignments

- Mounting holes and expansion connectors for side-mounting peripheral boards

Primary Elevator

- Common serial and expansion bus signals

- Two 2x80 connectors on backside for easy signal access and side-mounting board (LCD module)

- Power regulation circuitry

- Standardized signal assignments

- Mounting holes

Board Connectors

- Four card-edge connectors

- Uses PCI Express® connectors (x16, 90 mm/ 3.5" long, 164 pins)

Size

- Tower is approx. 3.5" H x 3.5" W x 3.5" D when fully assembled

Peripheral Module

- Examples include serial interface module, memory expansion module and Wi-Fi®

Tower Geeks Online Community

TowerGeeks.org is an online design engineer community that allows members to interact, develop designs and share ideas. Offering a direct path to explore and interact with other engineers designing with the Tower System, **TowerGeeks. org** is a great way to discuss your projects, post videos of your progress, ask questions through the forum and upload software. With updates through **Twitter** and **Facebook**, it's easy to get involved.

Follow Tower Geeks on Twitter
twitter.com/towergeeks

Visit Freescale on Facebook
facebook.com/freescale

Learn More: For more information about the Freescale Tower System, please visit **freescale.com/Tower**.

It's design potential realized.

Freescale introduces the industry's most scalable 32-bit MCU portfolio—Kinetis MCUs based on ARM® Cortex™-M4 technology. This portfolio expands your 32-bit choices with over 200 pin- and software-compatible MCUs. Kinetis MCUs are also supported by a market-leading enablement bundle, including the CodeWarrior IDE, Tower development systems and a huge community of ARM third-party ecosystem partners. Get started today with a complete package that is key to your design success and a faster time to market. Learn more at freescale.com/realize

freescale™
semiconductor

Linear Technology Analog Playground Module
for the Freescale Tower System

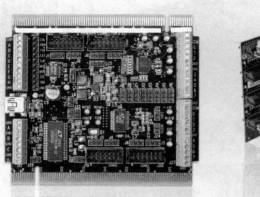 

Quickly evaluate Linear Technology data converters and other mixed signal solutions with the Freescale Tower System. The easy-to-use plug-in analog module (TWR-ADCDAC-LTC) expands the capabilities of the Freescale Tower System. It's a complete solution with a high precision analog peripheral module controllable by any Freescale Tower processor module with an SPI interface. The QuikEval™ interface on the analog module allows connection of more than 130 Linear Technology evaluation boards with the Freescale Tower processor for a broad range of applications.

TWR-ADCDAC-LTC Features

- Digital-to-Analog Converters (DACs)
    - LTC®2704-16: Quad 16-Bit V_{OUT} SoftSpan™ DAC with Readback
    - LTC2600: Octal 16-Bit Rail-to-Rail DACs
- Analog-to-Digital Converters (ADCs)
    - LTC1859: 8-Channel, 16-Bit, 100ksps SoftSpan ADC with Shutdown
    - LTC2498: 24-Bit 8-/16-Channel ΔΣ ADC with Easy Drive™ Input Current Cancellation
- Voltage Regulator
    - LTC3471: Dual 1.3A, 1.2MHz Boost/Inverter
- Voltage Reference
    - LTC6655-5: 0.25ppm Noise, Low Drift Precision Buffered 5V Reference
- Four 14-Pin Headers for Connecting to any Linear Technology QuikEval Demonstration Boards
- Demos/Applications Include:

     ADC Data Logger/DAC Waveform Generator

     Thermocouple Reader

Applications

- Data Acquisition
- Instrumentation
- Temperature Measurement
- Industrial Process
- Medical
- Weight Scales

ARROW

 freescale
semiconductor

LTC2498: 24-Bit, 16-Channel Easy Drive ΔΣ ADC

Features

- 8 Differential/16 Single-Ended Input Channels
- Easy Drive Technology Enables Rail-to-Rail Inputs with Zero Differential Current
- Directly Digitizes High Impedance Sensors with Full Accuracy
- 600nV$_{RMS}$ Noise
- Internal Temperature Sensor (2°C Maximum), Internal Oscillator
- Selectable 50Hz, 60Hz Rejection, Up to 15Hz Output Rate

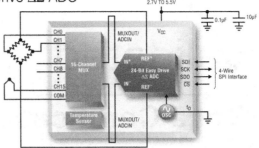

LTC1859: 8-Channel, 16-Bit, 100ksps SoftSpan A/D Converter with Shutdown

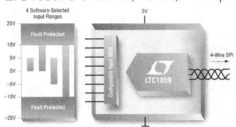

Features

- 8-Channel Multiplexer with ±25V Protection
- Software-Programmable Input Ranges: 0V to 5V, 0V to 10V, ±5V or ±10V, Single-Ended or Differential
- Power Dissipation: 40mW (Typ)
- SPI/MICROWIRE Compatible Serial I/O
- Signal-to-Noise Ratio: 87dB (Typ)

LTC2600: Octal 16-Bit Rail-to-Rail DACs

Features

- Guaranteed 16-Bit Monotonic Over Temperature
- Low Power Operation: 250µA per DAC at 3V
- Individual Channel Power-Down to 1µA, Max
- Ultralow Crosstalk Between DACs (<10µV)
- High Rail-to-Rail Output Drive (±15mA, Min)
- Double-Buffered Digital Inputs

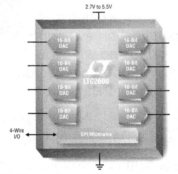

Quad 12-, 14- and 16-Bit Voltage Output SoftSpan DACs with Readback

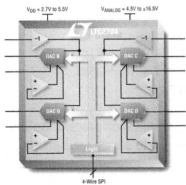

Features

- Six Programmable Output Ranges
- Unipolar: 0V to 5V, 0V to 10V
- Bipolar: ±5V, ±10V, ±2.5V, –2.5V to 7.5V
- Serial Readback of All On-Chip Registers
- 1LSB INL and DNL Over the Industrial Temperature Range (LTC2704-14/LTC2704-12)
- Force/Sense Outputs Enable Remote Sensing
- Glitch Impulse: < 2nV per Second
- Outputs Drive ±5mA

CPSIA information can be obtained
at www.ICGtesting.com
Printed in the USA
LVOW03*1529210616

493514LV00024B/238/P